THE DOUGLAS OPINIONS

THE DOUGLAS OPINIONS

Edited by Vern Countryman

A BERKLEY WINDHOVER BOOK
published by
BERKLEY PUBLISHING CORPORATION

CONTENTS

5 ⮑ Freedom of Speech and Press

6 ⮑ Obscenity

7 ⮑ Privacy

8 ⮑ Military Service

9 ⮑ Equal Treatment

10   Due Process of Law

11   More Specific Guarantees

INTRODUCTION

On April 17, 1939, at age forty, William O. Douglas took his seat on the Supreme Court, appointed by President Franklin D. Roosevelt to succeed Justice Louis D. Brandeis.

Justice Douglas came to the bench with a remarkable background. The self-supporting son of an impoverished West Coast family had a scholastic record at the Yakima, Washington, high school that won him a tuition scholarship at Whitman College in Walla Walla, Washington. He arrived there in the fall of 1916 with little else than the clothes on his back and the bicycle that he rode. Varying jobs as store clerk, waiter, and janitor provided food and a tent provided shelter during the school terms. During summer vacations there was employment in the wheat fields and an opportunity to debate with other laborers the revolutionary doctrine of the Industrial Workers of the World. This experience may have built up some immunity against alarm over extravagant political discussion, but it did not produce a revolutionary. When young Douglas graduated with honors in economics in 1920, his heroes in public life were Gifford Pinchot, Hiram Johnson and William E. Borah—doughty exponents of the democratic-capitalist system whom he admired as honest, strong, free, and independent.

After competing unsuccessfully for a Rhodes scholarship, Douglas returned to Yakima as a high school teacher of English and Latin. When his $1,300 salary proved insufficient to enable him in two years to save money to attend law school, he decided to go anyway. Traveling to Minnesota as custodian of a trainload of sheep and to New York City by hopping freights, he enrolled at Columbia Law School in the fall of 1922. A variety of odd jobs, including tutoring and writing a correspondence school course in commercial law, kept him there.

Also instrumental in keeping him there after an unsatisfying first year was Professor Underhill Moore, whose work on the relationship of law to business inspired Douglas to his own first specialty and provided him with a new and lasting idol—Louis D. Brandeis, Justice of the Supreme Court and, before that, distinguished lawyer, student of business and finance, and ardent advocate of the view that those entrusted with the management of other people's money occupy positions of trust and must be held to the highest standards of fiduciary responsibility.

After graduating second in his class in 1925, Douglas continued his education in the area of business and finance with the Wall Street law firm of Cravath, de Gersdorff, Swain and Wood. Following a two-year apprenticeship in the Cravath firm, during which he taught law at Columbia on the side, Douglas returned to Yakima to practice law. In less than a year, however, he was back in New York to accept a full-time teaching job at Columbia. One year later he resigned because Columbia President Nicholas Murry Butler appointed a new dean of the law school without consulting the faculty. A return to Yakima was in prospect when Douglas met Dean Robert Maynard Hutchins of Yale Law School at a party, had a brief discussion with him about plans for a new approach to the teaching of courses in business organization, and ended up the following day with an appointment to the Yale faculty.

In the next five years Douglas did pioneering work in recasting the teaching of the law of business and finance along functional lines, broadened his work during the depression years to encompass the subject of bankruptcy, and directed government-sponsored clinical studies of the causes of financial failure.

When the newly created Securities and Exchange Commission in 1934 undertook a study of the manner in which financially distressed corporations were reorganized under the limited supervision of equity receivership courts and the active direction of investment bankers and Wall Street lawyers, Professor Douglas, because of his outstanding work in the field, was a natural selection as director of the project. He took it on as a part-time diversion from his teaching duties and produced a monumental eight-volume study which documented the manner in which equity receiverships were operated for the profit of the bankers and lawyers and at the expense of investors. This work laid the basis for new laws which brought corporate reorganizations under the comprehensive administration of the bankruptcy courts and the SEC and prescribed new standards of conduct for bondholders' trustees, investment trusts, and investment advisers, to be enforced by the SEC.

Before this work was completed, however, Douglas was, on January 21, 1936, appointed a member of the SEC, and on September 21, 1937, at the age of thirty-eight, he became the chairman. He brought to the commission the tremendous energy and incisive grasp of financial affairs which had characterized his earlier work, but he also demonstrated extraordinary administrative ability and a toughness of character rare in academicians. The SEC, which, prior to his chairmanship, had been primarily concerned with perfecting its own organization and procedures, moved into action.

To the members of the Bond Club of New York, including nearly every important investment banker in that city, Douglas delivered a speech in 1937 reviewing the practices by which the bankers, when

retained by a business to aid in the issuance of new securities, tended
to end up with a "continuity of relationship" in the form of director-
ships, voting trusteeships, or strategic investments enabling them to
control the business. "The economic utility of continuity of banking
relationships," he told his shocked audience, "is of unestablished value
to anyone except the banker."

Members of the New York Stock Exchange were equally shocked to
hear the Exchange described as "a cross between a casino and a private
club" whose function of maintaining a free market for securities was
subverted by the predatory practices of "financial termites."

But what most infuriated the financial community was the impregnable position Douglas took in calling for reform. The investment
banker and the stock exchange, he said, had legitimate functions to
perform in maintaining a free and stable money market. The concern
of government was only that they perform those functions honestly
and with full recognition of their responsibilities as *servants* rather
than *masters* of investors and business." The SEC's supervisory role
was a residual one, to be performed "only to the extent that business
itself fails to perform its function and make its profits in a decent way."

In this vein he called on the New York Stock Exchange, late in 1937,
to initiate its own reform program as an alternative to SEC regulation. Some members of the Exchange favored this proposal, but others
were opposed, and by March 1938, no progress had been made. Then
an SEC investigation of the brokerage firm of Richard Whitney &
Company, a member of the Exchange, revealed that senior partner
Richard Whitney (a past president of the Exchange and a member of
its governing committee) had been misappropriating customers' securities for the past twelve years and that the firm had been insolvent
for the past three. The New York Stock Exchange was reorganized in
May, 1938, and reorganization of other large exchanges followed. In-
stallation of a similar system of self-regulation for the over-the-counter
securities markets was nearly completed when Chairman Douglas resigned to become Associate Justice Douglas of the Supreme Court.[1]

That Court, since the turn of the century, had been busily engaged
in developing certain constitutional tests which much social legislation
failed to meet.

One basis for the Court's review of legislation was the constitutional
prohibition against deprivation of "life, liberty, or property, without due
process of law"—a prohibition imposed on the federal government by
the Fifth Amendment to the Constitution and on the states by the

[1] This period in Douglas' life is covered by the first volume of his autobiography,
Go East, Young Man (1974).

Fourteenth Amendment. Originally, the due process clause was regarded only as imposing a requirement of procedural fairness, but in 1905 the Court shifted its approach and struck down, as "unreasonable" under a "substantive due process" test, a state statute forbidding bakeries to work their employees more than ten hours a day. Such a statute, the Court said, interfered with "freedom to contract" which was included in the "liberty" protected by the due process clause.[2] In a later case,[3] the Court explained that freedom of contract was "as essential to the laborer as to the capitalist, to the poor as to the rich"—despite their patently unequal bargaining power.

The due process clause did not provide the only serious limitation on state and federal economic legislation. The Constitution authorizes Congress to "regulate Commerce . . . among the several States,"[4] and this congressional power, even where unexercised, was found by the Court to preclude a variety of state laws which, though not discriminating against interstate commerce, either regulated aspects of it which the Court labeled "national" so as to be subject only to "uniform" regulation by Congress,[5] or constituted a "direct," as distinguished from an "indirect," burden on interstate commerce.[6] On the other hand, the commerce clause had its limitations so far as Congress was concerned. Interstate commerce was one thing and the manufacture of goods for such commerce was another. Hence, in 1895 the Court held that the Sherman Antitrust Act would not reach a virtually complete monopoly in the refining of sugar because refining was manufacture and "[c]ommerce succeeds to manufacture and is not a part of it."[7]

Much of President Roosevelt's recovery program ran afoul of the Supreme Court's constitutional interpretation in the first years of his administration, which doubtless inspired his disingenuous "Court-packing" plan, presented to Congress in February, 1937, and buried in Senate Committee the following July.

But that plan was not without effectiveness. The Supreme Court suddenly began to find the Constitution less restrictive. In March, 1937, the Court upheld a Washington State minimum-wage law for women indistinguishable from a New York law held unconstitutional under the due process clause a year before.[8] Two weeks later the National Labor

---

[2] *Lochner v. New York*, 198 U.S. 45 (1905).

[3] *Adkins v. Children's Hospital*, 261 U.S. 525 (1923).

[4] U.S. Const., Art. I, § 8, Cl. 3.

[5] *Missouri v. Kansas Natural Gas Co.*, 265 U.S. 298 (1924).

[6] *Real Silk Hosiery Mills v. Portland*, 268 U.S. 325 (1925).

[7] *United States v. E. C. Knight Co.*, 156 U.S. 1 (1895).

[8] *West Coast Hotel Co. v. Parrish*, 300 U.S. 379 (1937).

Relations Act was upheld in its application to that hitherto "purely local activity," production.[9]

The shift in constitutional interpretation was intensified as Justice Black replaced Justice Van Devanter in 1937, Justice Reed replaced Justice Sutherland six months later, and Justice Murphy replaced Justice Butler in 1940. Shortly after his own appointment in 1939, Douglas wrote for the Court to uphold federal power to fix the prices for bituminous coal sold in interstate commerce[10] and state power to regulate the fees of private employment agencies,[11] explaining in the latter case that "the wisdom, need, or appropriateness of . . . legislation" were questions for the legislature, not for the Courts. By 1942, when a unanimous Court upheld federal regulation of wheat production, which reached to the fixing of quotas on wheat produced for the farmers' own consumption, as a proper part of a congressional effort to increase the price for wheat in the interstate market,[12] the power of government to govern was well established.

The Court during Douglas' years on it was primarily concerned with other matters. The strains of World War II, the ensuing Cold War, and the undeclared wars in Korea and Vietnam have produced a host of new problems concerning primarily the relation of man to his government.

To these problems, largely unrelated to his former concerns with business and finance, Douglas has brought the same remarkable ability and industry that characterized his earlier career. As many of the opinions in this volume show, he has also retained the same salty vocabulary he formerly employed on the membership of the New York Stock Exchange and the Bond Club. His opinions lay bare the issues, come quickly to the point, and dispose of the case in language that is frequently blunt and bold. As his former clerk, Professor Charles Ares, has said, "he doesn't write for the law professors." Those who favor the elaborate formulation and the elegant phrase were offended when Douglas wrote that the purpose of the Bill of Rights is to "keep the government off the backs of the people." At an earlier time, some of those critics were inclined to the view that Justice Douglas' approach led him frequently into error. Today, many of them would complain only that he has reached the right conclusion by the wrong route.

It is now a commonplace that most of the dissents of Justices Holmes

9 *National Labor Relations Board v. Jones & Laughlin Steel Corp.*, 301 U.S. 1 (1937).

10 *Sunshine Anthracite Coal Co. v. Adkins*, 310 U.S. 381 (1940).

11 *Olsen v. Nebraska*, 313 U.S. 236 (1941).

12 *Wickard v. Filburn*, 317 U.S. 111 (1942).

and Brandeis became the law during the period of Douglas' tenure on the Court. What is less well appreciated is that during the same period of time even more of the dissents of Douglas became the law. All of the reversals of position did not come from other members of the Court. As Douglas grew on the job, as experience and reflection persuaded him that he himself had been in error, he did not hesitate to take a new position.

When Justice Douglas retired because of ill health on November 12, 1975, he had served for more than thirty-six years on the Court, surpassing by more than two years the record previously established by Justice Stephen Field. Because of his long service, and because he consistently did more than his share of the Court's work, the opinions that follow represent only a small sampling of his more than 1,200 majority, concurring, and dissenting opinions.

THE DOUGLAS OPINIONS

1

THOSE WHO GOVERN

The powers of the federal government are allocated by the Constitution among the legislative, executive, and judicial branches. Under the theory of separation of powers, an allocation to one branch may be viewed as a limitation on the others. In addition, the Constitution imposes some express limitations on both the federal and state governments and Congress, in the exercise of its constitutional power to legislate, may impose other limitations. The Constitution also confers some protections on those who occupy public office and exercise the powers of government.

The Legislature

TENNEY v. BRANDHOVE
341 U.S. 367 (1951)

One protection for members of Congress is the constitutional provision that "for any Speech or Debate in either House, they shall not be questioned in any other Place."[1] The "Speech or Debate Clause" was long ago held to protect members of a congressional committee, although not the sergeant-at-arms of the House, from a damage action for false imprisonment by a witness whom the House had held in contempt for refusal to answer questions of the committee, even though the Court held the questions to be invalid because not for a proper legislative purpose. The Speech or Debate Clause, said the Court, was designed to secure to every member of Congress an exemption for everything done by him as a congressman, in exercising the functions of that office. Hence, it should not be confined narrowly to debates on the floor of the House or to speeches addressed to the chair, but should extend also to the report of the committee to the House on the wit-

---

[1] U.S. Const., Art. I, §6, Cl. 1.

ness's delinquency, to the introduction of a resolution to hold him in contempt, and to the vote on the resolution.[2]

The Speech or Debate Clause of the federal Constitution does not reach to members of state legislatures. Most, but not all, states have similar clauses in their state constitutions which do protect state legislators, although those provisions would not limit the federal government should it seek to impose sanctions on state legislators.

Brandhove sought to invoke a federal sanction against members of the California Senate Committee on Un-American Activities. Brandhove had recanted earlier testimony he had given before that committee and publicly alleged that the committee had used him in a deliberate campaign to smear a candidate for California public office as a "Red." He was then summoned back before the committee, refused to testify, and was tried for contempt in a state proceeding which ended with a hung jury. Thereafter he brought this action for damages against members of the committee, alleging that they had conspired to violate a federal Civil Rights Act which prescribes liability for those who "under color of [law]" intentionally and knowingly deprive others "of any rights, privileges, or immunities secured by the Constitution." Specifically, Brandhove alleged that the purpose of the committee was to intimidate him and prevent him from exercising his right of free speech under the First Amendment to the federal Constitution.

The Court, assuming without deciding that Congress had the power to impose liability on state legislators in such circumstances, concluded that it had not intended to do so by the Civil Rights Act. "We cannot believe that Congress—itself a staunch advocate of legislative freedom— would impinge on a tradition [of similar freedom for members of the English Parliament, and for state legislators under speech or debate clauses in forty-one of the then forty-eight state constitutions, not including California's] so well grounded in history and reason by covert inclusion in the general language" of the Civil Rights Act. Accordingly, it held that the action must be dismissed without giving Brandhove an opportunity to try to prove his allegations.

MR. JUSTICE DOUGLAS, dissenting.

I agree with the opinion of the Court as a statement of general principles governing the liability of legislative committees and members of the legislatures. But I do not agree that all abuses of legislative committees are solely for the legislative body to police.

We are dealing here with a right protected by the Constitution—the

---

[2] *Kilbourn v. Thompson,* 103 U.S. 168 (1880).

right of free speech. The charge seems strained and difficult to sustain; but it is that a legislative committee brought the weight of its authority down on respondent for exercising his right of free speech. Reprisal for speaking is as much an abridgment as a prior restraint. If a committee departs so far from its domain to deprive a citizen of a right protected by the Constitution, I can think of no reason why it should be immune. Yet that is the extent of the liability sought to be imposed on [the legislators] under [the Civil Rights Act].

It is speech and debate in the legislative department which our constitutional scheme makes privileged. Included, of course, are the actions of legislative committees that are authorized to conduct hearings or make investigations so as to lay the foundation for legislative action. But we are apparently holding today that the actions of those committees have no limits in the eyes of the law. May they depart with impunity from their legislative functions, sit as kangaroo courts, and try men for their loyalty and their political beliefs? May they substitute trial before committees for trial before juries? May they sit as a board of censors over industry, prepare their blacklists of citizens, and issue pronouncements as devastating as any bill of attainder?

No other public official has complete immunity for his actions. Even a policeman who exacts a confession by force and violence can be held criminally liable under the Civil Rights Act, as we ruled only the other day in *Williams* v. *United States*, 341 U.S. 97. Yet now we hold that no matter the extremes to which a legislative committee may go it is not answerable to an injured party under the civil rights legislation. That result is the necessary consequence of our ruling since the test of the statute, so far as material here, is whether a constitutional right has been impaired, not whether the domain of the committee was traditional. It is one thing to give great leeway to the legislative right of speech, debate, and investigation. But when a committee perverts its power, brings down on an individual the whole weight of government for an illegal or corrupt purpose, the reason for the immunity ends. It was indeed the purpose of this civil rights legislation to secure federal rights against invasion by officers and agents of the states. I see no reason why any officer of government should be higher than the Constitution from which all rights and privileges of an office obtain.

GRAVEL v. UNITED STATES
408 U.S. 606 (1972)

After the Brandhove *decision, Douglas concurred in a decision reversing the conviction of a former congressman for conspiracy to defraud the United States on the ground that part of the evidence on which the* iction was based consisted of a speech he had made, while in Congress, on the floor of the House. In this decision it was explained that the legislative privilege was designed to protect legislative independence "against possible prosecution by an unfriendly executive and conviction by a hostile judiciary."[3] But Douglas dissented from a later holding that the Speech or Debate Clause would not bar conviction of a senator for accepting bribes to influence his votes on pending legislation[4]—he thought that the only remedy authorized for such behavior was the one to be found in another constitutional provision: "Each House may determine the Rules of its Proceedings, punish its Members for disorderly Behavior, and with the Concurrence of two thirds, expel a Member."[5] He has also agreed with the Court that the Speech or Debate Clause protects members of Congress, though not congressional employees, from suits for damages based on their allegedly illegal seizure of evidence in connection with a committee hearing[6] and from declaratory judgment actions as to the legality of their conduct in excluding an elected member of the House.[7]

This case arose in quite a different context. In mid-June 1971, various newspapers around the country began publishing extracts from the "Pentagon Papers," a forty-seven-volume "Top Secret" government document covering the history of our involvement in Vietnam from 1945 to 1967. The government countered with an effort to enjoin publication which ultimately failed. (See pp. 215–219, infra). Meanwhile, Senator Mike Gravel, chairman of the Subcommittee on Buildings and Grounds of the Senate Public Works Committee, convened a meeting of his subcommittee on the night of June 29, 1971, read extensively from a copy of the Pentagon Papers and placed the entire forty-seven volumes in the public record of the subcommittee. Thereafter he supplied a copy of the papers to the Beacon Press for publication without profit to him.

Sometime thereafter a federal grand jury investigating possible crimes involved in the release of the papers subpoenaed Leonard Rodberg, an assistant to Senator Gravel. The senator intervened in the proceeding and moved to quash the subpoena on Rodberg, under the Speech or Debate Clause. The Court, recognizing that the clause would give little protection to congressmen if their aides could be compelled to testify, agreed that it should be interpreted to prohibit "inquiry into things done by Dr. Rodberg as the Senator's agent or assistant which

[3] United States v. Johnson, 383 U.S. 169 (1966).
[4] United States v. Brewster, 408 U.S. 501 (1972).
[5] U.S. Const., Art. I, §5, Cl. 2.
[6] Dombrowski v. Eastland, 387 U.S. 82 (1967).
[7] Powell v. McCormack, 395 U.S. 486 (1969).

would have been legislative acts, and therefore privileged, if performed by the Senator personally." Prior cases denying protection to congressional employees were distinguished as cases in which the employees were charged with criminal activity. Hence, the Court seemed to be saying that, while members of Congress are "shielded by the Speech or Debate Clause both from liability for their illegal legislative act and from having to defend themselves with respect to it," their aides were protected only with respect to legal legislative acts. In any event, that clause was held not to "immunize Senator or aide from testifying at trials or grand jury proceedings involving third-party crimes where the questions do not require testimony about or impugn a legislative act" nor to protect them from inquiry about the Senator's arrangement for publication by Beacon Press, since such private republication of the Pentagon Papers would not be a "legislative act."

MR. JUSTICE DOUGLAS, dissenting.

I would construe the Speech or Debate Clause to insulate Senator Gravel and his aides from inquiry concerning the Pentagon Papers, and Beacon Press from inquiry concerning publication of them, for that publication was but another way of informing the public as to what had gone on in the privacy of the Executive Branch concerning the conception and pursuit of the so-called "war" in Vietnam. . . .

Both the introduction of the Pentagon Papers by Senator Gravel into the record before his Subcommittee and his efforts to publish them were clearly covered by the Speech or Debate Clause, as construed in *Kilbourn* v. *Thompson* [note 2, *supra*]:

> "It would be a narrow view of the constitutional provision to limit it to words spoken in debate. The reason of the rule is as forcible in its application to written reports presented in that body by its committees, to resolutions offered, which, though in writing, must be reproduced in speech, and to the act of voting, whether it is done vocally or by passing between the tellers. In short, to things generally done in a session of the House by one of its members in relation to the business before it."

One of the things normally done by a Member "in relation to the business before it" is the introduction of documents or other exhibits in the record the committee or subcommittee is making. The introduction of a document into a record of the Committee or subcommittee by its Chairman certainly puts it in the public domain. Whether a particular document is relevant to the inquiry of the committee may be questioned by the Senate in the exercise of its power to prescribe rules for the governance and discipline of wayward members. But there is only one instance, as I see it, where supervisory power over that issue is vested in the courts, and that is where a witness before a committee is prosecuted for contempt and he makes the defense that the question he refused to answer was not germane to the legislative inquiry or within its permissible range. . . .

In all other situations, however, the judiciary's view of the motives or germaneness of a Senator's conduct before a committee is irrelevant. For, "[t]he claim of an unworthy purpose does not destroy the privilege." *Tenney* v. *Brandhove*, 341 U.S. 367. If there is an abuse, there is a remedy; but it is legislative, not judicial.

As to Senator Gravel's efforts to publish the Subcommittee record's contents, wide dissemination of this material as an educational service is as much a part of the Speech or Debate Clause philosophy as mailing under a frank a Senator's or a Congressman's speech across the Nation. As mentioned earlier, "[i]t is the proper duty of a representative body to look diligently into every affair of government and to talk much about what it sees. . . . The informing function of Congress should be preferred even to its legislative function." W. Wilson, Congressional Government 303 (1885). "From the earliest times in its history, the Congress has assiduously performed an 'informing function,' " *Watkins* v. *United States*, 354 U.S. 178. "Legislators have an obligation to take positions on controversial political questions so that their constituents can be fully informed by them." *Bond* v. *Floyd*, 385 U.S. 116.

We said in *United States* v. *Johnson* [note 3, *supra*] that the Speech or Debate Clause established a "legislative privilege" that protected a member of Congress against prosecution "by an unfriendly executive and conviction by a hostile judiciary" in order, as Mr. Justice Harlan put it, to ensure "the independence of the legislature." That hostility emanates from every stage of the present proceedings. It emphasizes the need to construe the Speech or Debate Clause generously, not niggardly. If republication of a Senator's speech in a newspaper carries the privilege, as it doubtless does, then republication of the exhibits introduced at a hearing before Congress must also do so. That means that republication by Beacon Press is within the ambit of the Speech or Debate Clause and that the confidences of the Senator in arranging it are not subject to inquiry "in any other Place" than the Congress.

It is said that though the Senator is immune from questioning as to what he said and did in preparation for the committee hearing and in conducting it, his aides may be questioned in his stead. Such easy circumvention of the Speech or Debate Clause would indeed make it a mockery. The aides and agents such as Beacon Press must be taken as surrogates for the Senator and the confidences of the job that they enjoy are his confidences that the Speech or Debate Clause embraces.

***

ROUDEBUSH V. HARTKE
405 U.S. 15 (1972)

The Constitution provides in Article I, §4, that "The Times, Places and Manner of holding Elections for Senators and Representatives, shall be prescribed in each State by the Legislature thereof; but the Congress may at any time by Law make or alter such Regulations, except as to the Places of chusing Senators." It also provides in Article I, §5, that "Each House shall be the Judge of the Elections, Returns and Qualifications of its own Members."

In the 1970 senatorial election in Indiana, incumbent United States Senator R. Vance Hartke was, on the first ballot count, declared the winner by slightly more than 4,000 votes—a margin of approximately one vote per state voting precinct. The governor of Indiana gave Hartke a certificate of election which he filed with the Senate. But Hartke's opponent, Richard L. Roudebush, initiated proceedings under state statutes for a recount. Hartke then brought this action to enjoin the recount, contending that under Article I, §5, the Senate had the exclusive authority to settle a recount contest.

The Court held that the Indiana statutory recount procedure was within the power to regulate senatorial elections given to the Indiana legislature by Article I, §4, and that the state recount "does not prevent the Senate from independently evaluating the election any more than the initial count does. The Senate is free to accept or reject the apparent winner in either count, and, if it chooses, to conduct its own recount."

MR. JUSTICE DOUGLAS, dissenting.

By virtue of Art. I, §5, Senate custom, and this Court's prior holdings, the Senate has exclusive authority to settle a recount contest once the contestee has been certified and seated, albeit conditionally.

Article I, §5, provides: "Each House shall be the Judge of the Elections, Returns and Qualifications of its own Members." To implement this authority, the Senate has established a custom of resolving disagreements over which of two or more candidates in a senatorial race attracted more ballots. The apparent loser may initiate the process by filing with the Senate a petition stating (a) what voting irregularities he suspects, and (b) how many votes were affected. Upon receipt of such a petition, a special committee may be authorized to investigate the charges alleged. If the allegations are not frivolous and would be sufficient, if true, to alter the apparent outcome of the election, actual ballots may be and have been subpoenaed to Washington for recounting by the committee. Also, witnesses may be required to testify. The committee performs the function of deciding both the factual issues and what allegations would be sufficient to warrant favorable action on a petition.

Thus, in the Iowa senatorial campaign of 1924, Smith Brookhart was the apparent winner over Daniel Steck, who filed with the Senate the complaint that illegal votes had been cast for his opponent. The petition was referred to the Subcommittee on Privileges and Elections which was authorized to make a full investigation. It heard testimony and recounted the ballots in Washington. The committee and eventually the Senate agreed that, contrary to earlier assumptions, Steck had won. Accordingly, Brookhart was replaced by Steck as a Senator from Iowa. See *Steck* v. *Brookhart*, Senate Election, Expulsion and Censure Cases from 1789 to 1960, S. Doc. No. 71, 87th Cong., 2d Sess., 116–117 (1962). See also *Hurley* v. *Chavez*, *id.*, at 151 (upon recounting, the subcommittee and the Senate found that neither candidate had won and the seat was declared vacant).

The Senate's procedure is flexible:

"The Senate has never perfected specific rules for challenging the right of a claimant to serve, inasmuch as each case presents different facts. The practice has been to consider and act upon each case on its own merits, although some general principles have been evolved from the precedents established.

"This practice of viewing each case affecting claims to membership on its individual merits has resulted in a variety of means by which the cases are originated. The Senator-elect to a seat in the Senate generally appears with his credentials. On some occasions, when these credentials are presented, some Senators will submit a motion that the credentials be referred to the Committee on Rules and Administration, and that, pending report, he be denied the privilege of taking the oath of office. Upon adoption of such a motion, the Senator-elect steps aside and the Senate seat is vacant for the time being. Any question or motion arising or made upon the presentation of such credentials is privileged and would be governed by a majority vote.

"On other occasions, the Senator-elect is permitted to take the oath of office, and this is now regarded and followed as the proper procedure, but thereafter inquiry as to his election is undertaken by the Senate. Resolutions calling for such investigations may be offered by any Senator. In an instance where a newspaper charged a Senator had obtained his office by illegal means, the Senator himself offered a resolution calling for an investigation of the charges.

"The usual origin of such cases, however, is by petition. The contestant may file such a petition, protesting the seating of the contestee, and asserting his own right to the seat in question. It is not required to be filed prior to the swearing-in of the contestee, and no rights are lost if filed afterwards. In some cases, petitions have been signed and filed by others than the contestant, simply protesting against the seating of the contestee, without asserting any claim in behalf of the defeated candidate. Any number of citizens may submit such a petition; and it might make charges of illegal practices in the election, or of the improper use of money, or even of the unfitness of the claimant to serve in the United States Senate.

"A petition of contest is addressed to the U.S. Senate, and may be laid before the Senate by the presiding officer or formally presented by some Senator. There is no prescribed form for such a petition. It is somewhat analogous to a complaint filed in a lawsuit. It customarily sets forth the grounds or charges upon which the contest is based, and in support of which proof is expected to be adduced. The petition is usually referred to the Committee on Rules and Administration, which has jurisdiction over '. . . matters relating to the election of the President, Vice President, or Members of Congress; corrupt practices; contested elections; credentials and qualifications; [and] Federal elections generally. . . .'" S. Doc. No. 71, 87th Cong., 2d Sess., vii–viii (1962).

Once certification by the Governor has been presented to the Senate, a State may not by conducting a recount alter the outcome of the election—a principle that has been widely recognized by state courts. See *Laxalt* v. *Cannon*, 80 Nev. 588, 397 P. 2d 466, and cases cited therein.

Thus, although the Houses of Congress may not engraft qualifications for membership beyond those already contained in Art. I, *Powell* v. *McCormack* [p. 13, *infra*], where all that is at stake is a determination of which candidates attracted the greater number of lawful ballots, each has supreme authority to resolve such controversies.

Although all agree that in the end the Senate will be the final judge of this seating contest, the nub of the instant case comes down to opposing positions on how important it may be to preserve for the Senate the opportunity to ground its choice in unimpeachable evidence. It is with regard to this phase of the cases that I disagree with the majority.

The Senate may conclude that only a recomputation supervised by it under laboratory conditions could serve as an acceptable guide for decision. Such a recomputation, however, will not be possible once local investigators have exposed these presently sealed ballots to human judgment.

Obviously, state officials might desire to preview these presently sealed ballots in order to influence the Senate's deliberations.

Charges or suspicions of inadvertent or intentional alteration, however baseless, will infect the case. No longer will the constitutionally designated tribunal be able to bottom its result on unassailed evidence. Since even a slight adjustment in the tally could dramatically reverse the outcome, the federal interest in preserving the integrity of the evidence is manifest.

What the Senate should do in the merits is not a justiciable controversy. The role of the courts is to protect the Senate's exclusive jurisdiction over the subject matter, as did this Court in *Barry* v. *Cunningham* [279 U.S. 597]. The Senate's Subcommittee on Privileges and Elections, for example, might subpoena these ballots, thereby precluding, as a practical matter, any local recount. Or the Senate might ask for a local recount. Either course is within the control and discretion of the Senate and is unreviewable by the courts.

Under either the Court's or Douglas' interpretation, the constitutional method for resolving contested congressional elections may not be the best way. In the 1974 senatorial election in New Hampshire, Republican Louis Wyman was declared the winner by 355 votes on the first ballot count. His opponent, Democrat John Durkin, asked for a recount which showed him the winner by 10 votes. Under New Hampshire law the matter then went to a state Ballot Law Commission, which pronounced Wyman the winner by 2 votes. When the 94th Congress convened in January, 1975, Durkin petitioned the Senate for a determination. After the Committee on Rules and Administration deadlocked on 35 contested ballots and a number of procedural issues, it asked the full Senate to resolve the matter. That body wrangled intermittently for a total of nearly one hundred hours, with the Republican minority filibustering to prevent a vote, until, on July 30, at the request of both candidates, it voted to declare the contested seat vacant and send the matter back to New Hampshire for another election. Until then, New Hampshire had been represented by only one senator in the 94th Congress, but its governor then appointed former

Senator Norris Cotton to fill the vacancy pending a special election, which Durkin won easily in September, 1975.

POWELL v. McCORMACK

395 U.S. 486 (1969)

The Constitution provides that no person shall be a representative who is not twenty-five years old, seven years a citizen of the United States, and an inhabitant of the state in which he is elected.[8] *It also provides that each House "shall be the Judge of the Elections, Returns and Qualifications of its own Members"*[9] *and that each House may, "with the concurrence of two thirds, expel a member."*[10]

In 1967 the House, by a more than two-thirds vote, refused to seat re-elected Congressman Adam Clayton Powell of New York. Although he admittedly met the age, citizenship, and residency requirements, the House acted on the ground that he had wrongfully used House funds and made false reports thereon and had acted improperly in some state court litigation.

The Court declared the House's action invalid. This was not an instance of expelling a member, the Court held. Powell had not yet been seated and the resolution adopted by the House had been framed as one of "exclusion" rather than "expulsion." Moreover, the Speaker had ruled in advance of the vote in the House that a majority vote would be sufficient. In addition, the conduct of Powell on which the resolution was based occurred prior to the convening of the House for the 90th Congress which took the action, and the House had previously expressed doubt about its power to expel for conduct which did not occur during the term of the House which took the expulsion action. Hence, although the vote on the exclusion was more than two-thirds, there could be no assurance that there would have been a two-thirds vote in favor of an expulsion resolution.

Since there was no expulsion, this was simply a case of the House judging the qualifications of its own members, and it was confined to those qualifications of age, citizenship, and residence specified in the Constitution.

MR. JUSTICE DOUGLAS.

While I join the opinion of the Court, I add a few words. As the Court says, the important constitutional question is whether the

---

[8] U.S. Const., Art. I, §2, Cl. 2.
[9] *Id.*, Art. I, §5, Cl. 1.
[10] *Id.*, Art. I, §5, Cl. 2.

Congress has the power to deviate from or alter the qualifications for membership as a Representative contained in Art. I, §2, cl. 2, of the Constitution. Up to now the understanding has been quite clear to the effect that such authority does not exist.[11] To be sure, Art. I, §5, provides that: "Each House shall be the Judge of the Elections, Returns and Qualifications of its own Members . . . ." Contests may arise over whether an elected official meets the "qualifications" of the Constitution, in which event the House is the sole judge. But the House is not the sole judge when "qualifications" are added which are not specified in the Constitution.

A man is not seated because he is a Socialist or a Communist.[12]

[11] The Constitutional Convention had the occasion to consider several proposals for giving Congress discretion to shape its own qualifications for office and explicitly rejected them. James Madison led the opposition by arguing that such discretion would be

"an improper & dangerous power in the Legislature. The qualifications of electors and elected were fundamental articles in a Republican Govt. and ought to be fixed by the Constitution. If the Legislature could regulate those of either, it can by degrees subvert the Constitution." 2 M. Farrand, Records of the Federal Convention of 1787, pp. 249–250 (1911).

Alexander Hamilton echoed that same conclusion:

"The qualifications of the persons who may choose or be chosen, as has been remarked upon other occasions, are defined and fixed in the Constitution, and are unalterable by the legislature." The Federalist Papers, No. 60, p. 371 (Mentor ed. 1961).

And so, too, the early Congress of 1807 decided to seat Representative-elect William McCreery on the ground that its power to "judge" was limited by the enumerated qualifications.

"The Committee of Elections considered the qualifications of members to have been unalterably determined by the Federal Convention, unless changed by an authority equal to that which framed the Constitution. . . .   Congress, by the Federal Constitution, are not authorized to prescribe the qualifications of their own members, but they are authorized to judge of their qualifications; in doing so, however, they must be governed by the rules prescribed by the Federal Constitution, and by them only." 17 Annals of Cong. 872 (1807) (remarks of Rep. Findley, Chairman of House Committee of Elections).

Constitutional scholars of two centuries have reaffirmed the principle that congressional power to "judge" the qualifications of its members is limited to those enumerated in the Constitution. 1 J. Story, Commentaries on the Constitution 462 (5th ed. 1891); C. Warren, The Making of the Constitution 420–426 (1928). See also remarks by Emmanuel Celler, Chairman of the House Select Committee which inquired into the qualifications of Adam Clayton Powell, Jr., and which recommended seating him:

"The Constitution lays down three qualifications for one to enter Congress—age, inhabitancy, citizenship. Mr. Powell satisfies all three. The House cannot add to these qualifications." 113 Cong. Rec. 4998.

[12] Case of Victor Berger, 6 C. Cannon, Precedents of the House of Representatives of the United States §56 (1935).

Another is not seated because in his district members of a minority are systematically excluded from voting.[13]

Another is not seated because he has spoken out in opposition to the war in Vietnam.[14]

The possible list is long. Some cases will have the racist overtones of the present one.

Others may reflect religious or ideological clashes.[15]

At the root of all these cases, however, is the basic integrity of the electoral process. Today we proclaim the constitutional principle of "one man, one vote." When that principle is followed and the electors choose a person who is repulsive to the Establishment in Congress, by what constitutional authority can that group of electors be disenfranchised?

By Art. I, §5, the House may "expel a Member" by a vote of two-thirds. And if this were an expulsion case I would think that no justiciable controversy would be presented, the vote of the House being two-thirds or more. But it is not an expulsion case. Whether it could have been won as an expulsion case, no one knows. Expulsion for "misconduct" may well raise different questions, different considerations. Policing the conduct of members, a recurring problem in the Senate and House as well, is quite different from the initial decision whether an elected official should be seated. It well might be easier to bar admission than to expel one already seated.

The House excluded Representative-elect Powell from the 90th Congress allegedly for misappropriating public funds and for incurring the contempt of New York courts. Twenty-six years earlier, members of the upper chamber attempted to exclude Senator-elect William Langer of North Dakota for like reasons. Langer first became State's Attorney for Morton County, North Dakota, from 1914 to 1916, and then served as State Attorney General from 1916 to 1920. He became Governor of the State in 1932 and took office in January 1933. In 1934 he was indicted for conspiring to interfere with the enforcement of federal law by illegally soliciting political contributions from federal employees, and suit was filed in the State Supreme Court to remove him from office. While that suit was pending, he called the State Legislature into special session. When it became clear that the court would order his

[13] *Id.*, at §122.

[14] See, e.g., *Bond* v. *Floyd*, 385 U.S. 116 [where the Court held that the action of the Georgia House of Representatives in excluding newly elected member Julian Bond because of statements critical of federal policy in Vietnam violated his right of free speech under the First Amendment].

[15] 1 A. Hinds, Precedents of the House of Representatives of the United States §481 (1907).

ouster, he signed a Declaration of Independence, invoked martial law, and called out the National Guard. Nonetheless, when his own officers refused to recognize him as the legal head of state, he left office in July 1934. As with Adam Clayton Powell, however, the people of the State still wanted him. In 1937 they re-elected him Governor and, in 1940, they sent him to the United States Senate.

During the swearing-in ceremonies, Senator Barkley drew attention to certain complaints filed against Langer by citizens of North Dakota, yet asked that he be allowed to take the oath of office

> "without prejudice, which is a two-sided proposition—without prejudice to the Senator and without prejudice to the Senate in the exercise of its right [to exclude him]."

The matter of Langer's qualifications to serve in the Senate was referred to committee which held confidential hearings on January 9 and 16, 1941, and open hearings on November 3 and 18, 1941. By a vote of 14 to 2, the committee reported that a majority of the Senate had jurisdiction under Art. I, §5, cl. 1, of the Constitution to exclude Langer; and, by a vote of 13 to 3, it reported its recommendation that Langer not be seated.

The charges against Langer were various. As with Powell, they included claims that he had misappropriated public funds and that he had interfered with the judicial process in a way that beclouded the dignity of Congress. Reference was also made to his professional ethics as a lawyer.

Langer enjoyed the powerful advocacy of Senator Murdock from Utah. The Senate debate itself raged for over a year. Much of it related to purely factual allegations of "moral turpitude." Some of it, however, was addressed to the power of the Senate under Art. I, §5, cl. 1, to exclude a member-elect for lacking qualifications not enumerated in Art. I, §3.

> "MR. MURDOCK. . . . [U]nder the Senator's theory that the Senate has the right to add qualifications which are not specified in the Constitution, does the Senator believe the Senate could adopt a rule specifying intellectual and moral qualifications?
>
> "MR. LUCAS. The Senate can do anything it wants to do . . . . Yes; the Senate can deny a person his seat simply because it does not like the cut of his jaw, if it wishes to."

Senator Murdock argued that the only qualifications for service in the Senate were those enumerated in the Constitution; that Congress had the power to review those enumerated qualifications; but that it could

not—while purporting to "judge" those qualifications—in reality add to
them.

> "Mr. Lucas. The Senator referred to article I, section 5. What
> does he think the framers of the Constitution meant when they
> gave to each House the power to determine or to judge the
> qualifications, and so forth, of its own Members?
>
> "Mr. Murdock. I construe the term 'judge' to mean what it is
> held to mean in its common, ordinary usage. My understanding of
> the definition of the word 'judge' as a verb is this: When we judge
> of a thing it is supposed that the rules are laid out; the law is
> there for us to look at and to apply to the facts.
>
> "But whoever heard the word 'judge' used as meaning the power
> to add to what already is the law?"

It was also suggested from the floor that the enumerated qualifications
in §3 were only a *minimum* which the Senate could supplement; and
that the Founding Fathers so intended by using words of the negative.[16]
To which Senater Murdock replied—

> "Mr. President, I think it is the very distinguished and able
> Senator from Georgia who makes the contention that the con-
> stitutional provisions relating to qualifications, because they are
> stated in the negative—that is, 'no person shall be a Senator'—are
> merely restrictions or prohibitions on the State; but—and I shall
> read it later on—when we read what Madison said, when we read
> what Hamilton said, when we read what the other framers of the
> Constitution said on that question, there cannot be a doubt as to
> what they intended and what they meant.
>
> .   .   .   .   .
>
> "Madison knew that the qualifications should be contained in the
> Constitution and not left to the whim and caprice of the legislature.
>
> .   .   .   .   .
>
> "Bear that in mind, that the positive or affirmative phraseology
> was not changed to the negative by debate or by amendment in
> the convention, but it was changed by the committee of which
> Madison was a member, the committee on style."

The Senate was nonetheless troubled by the suggestion that the Constitution compelled it to accept anyone whom the people might elect,
no matter how egregious and even criminal his behavior. No need to

---

[16] [U.S. Const., Art. I, §3, Cl. 3: "No Person shall be a Senator who shall not
have attained to the Age of thirty Years, and been nine Years a Citizen of the United
States, and who shall not, when elected, be an Inhabitant of that State for which
he shall be chosen."]

worry, said Murdock. It is true that the Senate cannot invoke its majority power to "judge" under Art. I, §5, cl. 1, as a device for excluding men elected by the people who possess the qualifications enumerated by the Constitution. But it does have the power under Art. I, §5, cl. 2, to expel anyone it designates by a two-thirds vote. Nonetheless, he urged the Senate not to bypass the two-thirds requirement for expulsion by wrongfully invoking its power to exclude.

> "MR. LUCAS. . . . The position the Senator from Utah takes is that it does not make any difference what a Senator does in the way of crime, that whenever he is elected by the people of his State, comes here with bona fide credentials, and there is no fraud in the election, the Senate cannot refuse to give him the oath. That is the position the Senator takes?
> "MR. MURDOCK. That is my position; yes.

>   .   .   .   .   .

> "My position is that we do not have the right to exclude anyone who comes here clothed with the proper credentials and possessing the constitutional qualifications. My position is that we do not have the right under the provision of the Constitution to which the Senator from Florida referred, to add to the qualifications. My position is that the State is the sole judge of the intellectual and the moral qualifications of the representatives it sends to Congress."
> "MR. MURDOCK [quoting Senator Philander Knox]. 'I know of no defect in the plain rule of the Constitution for which I am contending. . . . I cannot see that any danger to the Senate lies in the fact that an improper character cannot be excluded without a two-thirds vote. It requires the unanimous vote of a jury to convict a man accused of crime; it should require, and I believe that it does require, a two-thirds vote to eject a Senator from his position of honor and power, to which he has been elected by a sovereign State.' "

Thus, after a year of debate, on March 27, 1942, the Senate overruled the recommendation of its committee and voted 52 to 30 to seat Langer.

I believe that Senator Murdock stated the correct constitutional principle governing the present case.

SCHLESINGER v. RESERVISTS COMMITTEE TO STOP THE WAR
418 U.S. 208 (1974)

The Constitution provides that "No Senator or Representative shall, during the Time for which he was elected, be appointed to any civil

Office under the Authority of the United States, which shall have been created, or the Emoluments whereof shall have been encreased during such time; and no Person holding any Office under the United States, shall be a Member of either House during his Continuance in Office."[17] The first clause of this provision is known as the Ineligibility Clause, the second as the Incompatibility Clause.

The Reservists Committee to Stop the War, a national organization of present and former officers and enlisted men of the military Reserves, and five of its members sought to invoke the Incompatibility Clause by bringing a class action on behalf of all citizens and taxpayers against the Secretary of Defense. The complaint alleged that, at the time it was filed, some 117 senators and representatives held Reserve commissions. Plaintiffs sought and obtained from the lower courts a declaratory judgment that the Incompatibility Clause forbade members of Congress from holding Reserve commissions.

The Court reversed, holding that plaintiffs, whether viewed as citizens or as taxpayers, had no standing to maintain the action. As citizens, their complaint that service by congressmen in the Reserves "deprives . . . citizens . . . of the faithful discharge by members of Congress . . . of their [legislative] duties" was "nothing more than a matter of speculation," a "generalized grievance," and an "abstract injury" common to all citizens. But the doctrine of standing to sue requires that the plaintiff have a "personal stake in the outcome of the controversy" which "enables a complainant authoritatively to present to a court a complete perspective upon the adverse consequences flowing from the specific set of facts undergirding his grievance" because the court "must rely on the parties' treatment of the facts and claims before it to develop its rules of law." Moreover, the requirement of concrete injury further serves the function of ensuring that the courts do not decide constitutional questions unnecessarily. As taxpayers, plaintiffs had no standing because they were contending not that Congress was violating any constitutional limitation on its taxing or spending power, but that the executive branch was violating the Constitution in permitting members of Congress to maintain their Reserve status.

MR. JUSTICE DOUGLAS, dissenting.

The requirement of "standing" to sue is a judicially created instrument serving several ends: (1) It protects the status quo by reducing the challenges that may be made to it and to its institutions. It greatly restricts the classes of persons who may challenge administrative action. Its application in this case serves to make the bureaucracy of the

---

[17] U.S. Const., Art. I, §6, Cl. 2.

Pentagon more and more immune from the protests of citizens. (2) It sometimes is used to bar from the courts questions which by the Constitution are left to the other two coordinate branches to resolve, *viz.*, the so-called political question. (3) It is at times a way of ridding court dockets whether of abstract questions or questions involving no concrete controversial issue.

Our leading case is *Frothingham* v. *Mellon*, 262 U.S. 447, decided in 1923, where a taxpayer challenged the constitutionality of an Act of Congress that gave grants to States which agreed to a plan to reduce maternal and infant mortality. The Court said:

> "The administration of any statute, likely to produce additional taxation to be imposed upon a vast number of taxpayers, the extent of whose several liability is indefinite and constantly changing, is essentially a matter of public and not of individual concern. If one taxpayer may champion and litigate such a cause, then every other taxpayer may do the same, not only in respect of the statute here under review but also in respect of every other appropriation act and statute whose administration requires the outlay of public money, and whose validity may be questioned. The bare suggestion of such a result, with its attendant inconveniences, goes far to sustain the conclusion which we have reached, that a suit of this character cannot be maintained. It is of much significance that no precedent sustaining the right to maintain suits like this has been called to our attention, although, since the formation of the government, as an examination of the acts of Congress will disclose, a large number of statutes appropriating or involving the expenditure of moneys for non-federal purposes have been enacted and carried into effect."

That ruling had in it an admixture of the "political question" because, said the Court, the only occasion when the federal court may act is when a federal law results in "some direct injury suffered or threatened, presenting a justiciable issue." When that element is lacking, judicial intrusion would trespass on powers granted another department of Government. "To do so would be not to decide a judicial controversy, but to assume a position of authority over the governmental acts of another and co-equal department, an authority which plainly we do not possess."

In 1968—45 years after *Frothingham*—that case was revisited in *Flast* v. *Cohen*, 392 U.S. 83, where federal taxpayers sued to enjoin the expenditure of federal funds under an Act of Congress granting financial aid to religious schools. The Court held that those taxpayers did have "standing" to sue for two reasons. *First*, because they challenged the exercise of congressional power under the taxing and spending clause of Art. I, §8, of the Constitution,[18] not the incidental expenditure of tax funds in the administration of an essentially regulatory statute. *Second,* because the challenged enactment exceeded the limitations imposed upon the exercise of the congressional taxing and spending power. Therefore, the Court concluded that the taxpayer had "the requisite personal stake" in the litigation to have "standing" to sue and the Court went on to hold that the Establishment Clause of the First Amendment[19] "operates as a specific constitutional limitation upon the exercise by Congress of the taxing and spending power conferred by Art. I, §8."

The present case implicates two provisions of the Constitution. Article I, §8, cl. 1, provides: "The Congress shall have Power To lay and collect Taxes, Duties, Imposts and Excises, to pay the Debts and provide for the common Defence and general Welfare of the United States . . . ." Article I, §6, cl. 2, of the Constitution says that "no Person holding any Office[20] under the United States, shall be a Member of either House during his Continuance in Office."

The present suit is not one to oust Members from Congress. Rather it is brought against the Secretary of Defense challenging his keeping in the Armed Services of the United States Members of Congress who hold commissions as Reservists.

Various Acts of Congress make various appropriations for the services of Reservists.

Article I, §6, cl. 2, is often referred to as the Incompatibility Clause. At the 1787 convention some proposed that Members of Congress be allowed to serve in the Executive Branch,[21] others were opposed; Mason apparently represented the majority view when he insisted that "ineligibility will keep out corruption, by excluding office-hunters." Article I, §6, cl. 2, like the Establishment Clause of the First Amendment, "was designed as a specific bulwark against such potential abuses . . . and . . . operates as a specific constitutional limitation upon" such expenditures. *Flast* v. *Cohen, supra.*

---

[18] [U.S. Const., Art. I, §8, Cl. 1: "The Congress shall have Power To lay and collect Taxes, . . . to pay the Debts and provide for the common Defence and general Welfare of the United States. . . ."]

[19] [*Id.,* First Amendment: "Congress shall make no law respecting an establishment of religion. . . ."]

[20] I agree with the conclusion of the House Judiciary Committee, H.R. Rep. No. 885, 64th Cong., 1st Sess. (1916), that a commission in the National Guard is an "office" in the constitutional sense. A commission in the Reserves is not distinguishable. See *United States* v. *Hartwell,* 6 Wall. 385.

[21] See 2 M. Farrand, The Records of the Federal Convention of 1787, pp. 283–290, 491 (1911).

As stated by Hamilton in The Federalist No. 76, p. 476 (H. Lodge ed. 1888), the Incompatibility Clause had a specific purpose: to avoid "the danger of executive influence upon the legislative body."

While respondents have standing as taxpayers, their citizenship also gives them standing to challenge the appropriation acts financing activities of the Reservists.

We tend to overlook the basic political and legal reality that the people, not the bureaucracy, are the sovereign. Our Federal Government was created for the security and happiness of the people. Executives, lawmakers, and members of the Judiciary are inferior in the sense that they are in office only to carry out and execute the constitutional regime.

The Preamble of the Constitution states that "We the People" ordained and established the Constitution.

The Declaration of Independence stated that to insure "certain unalienable Rights," "Governments are instituted among Men, deriving their just powers from the consent of the governed" and "That whenever any Form of Government becomes destructive of these ends, it is the Right of the People to alter or to abolish it."

The present case does not involve a restructuring of society—a procedure left to legislative action in part but mostly to constitutional conventions. All that the citizens in this case seek is to have the Constitution enforced as it is written.

The interest of citizens is obvious. The complaint alleges injuries to the ability of the average citizen to make his political advocacy effective whenever it touches on the vast interests of the Pentagon. It is said that all who oppose the expansion of military influence in our national affairs find they are met with a powerful lobby—the Reserve Officers Association—which has strong congressional allies.

Whether that is true or not we do not know. So far as the Incompatibility Clause of the Constitution is concerned that contention is immaterial. It is as immaterial to the function of Art. I, §6, cl. 2, of the Constitution as would be a suggestion that the establishment of a religion under the First Amendment is benign in a given case. What the Framers did in each case was to set up constitutional fences barring certain affiliations, certain kinds of appropriations. Their judgment was that the potential for evil was so great that no appropriations of that character should be made.

The interest of citizens in guarantees written in the Constitution seems obvious. Who other than citizens has a better right to have the Incompatibility Clause enforced? It is their interests that the Incompatibility Clause was designed to protect. The Executive Branch under our regime is not a fiefdom or principality competing with the Legislative as another center of power. It operates within a constitutional framework, and it is that constitutional framework that these citizens want to keep intact. That is, in my view, their rightful concern. We have insisted that more than generalized grievances of a citizen be shown, that he must have a "personal stake in the outcome," *Baker v. Carr*, 369 U.S. 186, 204. But that "personal stake" need not be a monetary one. In *Baker v. Carr* it was the right to vote, an important badge of citizenship. The "personal stake" in the present case is keeping the Incompatibility Clause an operative force in the Government by freeing the entanglement of the federal bureaucracy with the Legislative Branch.

The Executive

UNITED STATES V. RICHARDSON
418 U.S. 166 (1974)

This action was brought by plaintiff Richardson, as a federal taxpayer, seeking to invoke a constitutional provision[22] that "No Money shall be drawn from the Treasury, but in Consequence of Appropriations made by Law; and a regular Statement and Account of the Receipts and Expenditures of all public Money shall be published from time to time."

Plaintiff alleged that he had obtained from the Treasury Department several copies of daily and monthly reports of "Combined Statements of Receipts, Expenditures and Balances of the United States Government," and that they contained no accounting of receipts and expenditures of the Central Intelligence Agency. The reason for this is to be found in the federal statute creating the CIA. While all other federal executive agencies receive specific appropriations which the Treasury Department includes in its accounting of receipts, the CIA was authorized to receive transfers of funds from other agencies. All other agencies are also required by statute to report their expenditures to the Treasury Department, except that the CIA's founding statute authorizes it to account for its expenditures "solely on the certificate of the Director." There are similar statutory dispensations on reporting of expenditures for the FBI and the Atomic Energy Commission and for executive expenditures in the field of foreign affairs. These certificates are not made public. Hence, the CIA's expenditures either are reflected

[22] U.S. Const., Art. I, §9, Cl. 7.

*in the Treasury's published accounts as the expenditures of other
agencies which transferred funds to it or are not reflected in those
accounts at all.*

Contending that the accounts published by the Treasury were in
either event false and hence did not comply with constitutional requirements, plaintiff sought to enjoin the Treasury from publishing
future accounts until they were brought into compliance.

The Court held that plaintiff lacked standing to maintain a taxpayer's suit, reversing the Court of Appeals below on this point. Plaintiff's challenge was not addressed to the taxing or spending power but
to the different accounting and reporting requirements prescribed by
Congress for the CIA, and he had no standing as a taxpayer to raise
that issue. Recognizing that if plaintiff could not litigate this issue
probably no one could, the Court said that fact "gives support to the
argument that the subject matter is committed to the surveillance of
Congress, and ultimately to the political process."

MR. JUSTICE DOUGLAS, dissenting.

I would affirm the judgment of the Court of Appeals on the "standing" issue. My views are expressed in the *Schlesinger case* [p. 18,
supra], decided this day.

The present action involves Art. I, §9, cl. 7, of the Constitution
which provides:

> "No Money shall be drawn from the Treasury, but in Conse-
> quence of Appropriations made by Law; and a regular Statement
> and Account of the Receipts and Expenditures of all public
> Money shall be published from time to time."

We held in *Flast v. Cohen*, 392 U.S. 83, that a taxpayer had "standing" to challenge the constitutionality of taxes raised to finance the
establishment of a religion contrary to the command of the First and
Fourteenth Amendments. A taxpayer making such outlays, we held,
had sufficient "personal stake" in the controversy to give the case the
"concrete adverseness" necessary for the resolution of constitutional
issues.

Respondent in the present case claims that he has a right to "a
regular statement and account" of receipts and expenditures of public
moneys for the Central Intelligence Agency. As the Court of Appeals
noted, *Flast* recognizes "standing" of a taxpayer to challenge appropriations made in the face of a constitutional prohibition, and it logi-
cally asks, "how can a taxpayer make that challenge unless he knows
how the money is being spent?"

History shows that the curse of government is not always venality; secrecy is one of the most tempting coverups to save regimes from criticism. As the Court of Appeals said:

> "The Framers of the Constitution deemed fiscal information essential if the electorate was to exercise any control over its representatives and meet their new responsibilities as citizens of the Republic; and they mandated publication, although stated in general terms, of the Government's receipts and expenditures. Whatever the ultimate scope and extent of that obligation, its elimination generates a sufficient, adverse interest in a taxpayer."

Whatever may be the merits of the underlying claim, it seems clear that the taxpayer in the present case is not making a generalized complaint about the operation of Government. He does not even challenge the constitutionality of the Central Intelligence Agency Act. He only wants to know the amount of tax money exacted from him that goes into CIA activities. Secrecy of the Government acquires new sanctity when his claim is denied. Secrecy has, of course, some constitutional sanction. Article I, §5, cl. 3, provides that "Each House shall keep a Journal of its Proceedings, and from time to time publish the same, excepting such Parts as may in their Judgment require Secrecy...."

But the difference was great when it came to an accounting of public money. Secrecy was the evil at which Art. I, §9, cl. 7, was aimed. At the Convention, Mason took the initiative in moving for an annual account of public expenditures. 2 M. Farrand, The Records of the Federal Convention of 1787, p. 618 (1911). Madison suggested it be "from time to time," because it was thought that requiring publication at fixed intervals might lead to no publication at all. Indeed under the Articles of Confederation "[a] punctual compliance being often impossible, the practice ha[d] ceased altogether."

During the Maryland debates on the Constitution, James McHenry said, "[T]he People who give their Money ought to know in what manner it is expended," 3 Farrand, supra, at 150. In the Virginia debates Mason expressed his belief that while some matters might require secrecy (e.g., ongoing diplomatic negotiations and military operations) "he did not conceive that the receipts and expenditures of the public money ought ever to be concealed. The people, he affirmed, had a right to know the expenditures of their money." 3 J. Elliot, Debates on the Federal Constitution 459 (1836). Lee said that the clause "must be supposed to mean, in the common acceptation of language, short, convenient periods" and that those "who would neglect this provision would disobey the most pointed directions." Madison added that an accounting from "time to time" insured that the accounts would be "more full and satisfactory to the public, and would be sufficiently frequent." Madison thought "this provision went farther than the constitution of any state in the Union, or perhaps in the world." In New York, Livingston said, "Will not the representatives . . . consider it as essential to their popularity, to gratify their constituents with full and frequent statements of the public accounts? There can be no doubt of it," 2 Elliot, *supra*, at 347.

From the history of the clause it is apparent that the Framers inserted it in the Constitution to give the public knowledge of the way public funds are expended. No one has a greater "personal stake" in policing this protective measure than a taxpayer. Indeed, if a taxpayer may not raise the question, who may do so? The Court states that discretion to release information is in the first instance "committed to the surveillance of Congress," and that the right of the citizenry to information under Art. I, §9, cl. 7, cannot be enforced directly, but only through the "[s]low, cumbersome, and unresponsive" electoral process. One has only to read constitutional history to realize that statement would shock Mason and Madison. Congress of course has discretion; but to say that it has the power to read the clause out of the Constitution when it comes to one or two or three agencies is astounding. That is the bare-bones issue in the present case. Does Art. I, §9, cl. 7, of the Constitution permit Congress to withhold "a regular Statement and Account" respecting any agency it chooses? Respecting all federal agencies? What purpose, what function is the clause to perform under the Court's construction? The electoral process already permits the removal of legislators for any reason. Allowing their removal at the polls for failure to comply with Art. I, §9, cl. 7, effectively reduces that clause to a nullity, giving it no purpose at all.

The sovereign in this Nation is the people, not the bureaucracy. The statement of accounts of public expenditures goes to the heart of the problem of sovereignty. If taxpayers may not ask that rudimentary question, their sovereignty becomes an empty symbol and a secret bureaucracy is allowed to run our affairs.

The resolution of that issue has not been entrusted to one of the other coordinate branches of government—the test of the "political question" under *Baker* v. *Carr*, 369 U.S., at 217. The question is "political" if there is "a textually demonstrable constitutional commitment of the issue to a coordinate political department," *ibid*. The mandate runs to the Congress and to the agencies it creates to make "a regular Statement and Account of the Receipts and Expenditures of all public Money." The beneficiary—as is abundantly clear from the constitutional history—is the public. The public cannot intelligently know how to exercise the franchise unless it has a basic knowledge concerning at least the generality of the accounts under every head of government. No greater crisis in confidence can be generated than today's decision. Its consequences are grave because it relegates to secrecy vast operations of government and keeps the public from knowing what secret plans concerning this Nation or other nations are afoot. The fact that the result is serious does not, of course, make the issue "justiciable." But resolutions of any doubts or ambiguities should be toward protecting an individual's stake in the integrity of constitutional guarantees rather than turning him away without even a chance to be heard.

ENVIRONMENTAL PROTECTION AGENCY v. MINK
410 U.S. 73 (1973)

The Constitution makes no provision for officers of the executive branch similar to the Speech or Debate Clause for congressmen. It is silent as to any executive privilege. But the Court long ago found an executive privilege available at common law. One attorney had represented thousands of postmasters in persuading Congress to enact salary increases for them and in thereafter presenting their claims for the increases to the Post Office Department. He later sued the Postmaster General for libel because the latter had caused to be enclosed with each check mailed to a postmaster a letter stating (correctly) that the new law required the check to be mailed directly to the postmaster, stating also that no attorney's services were necessary for presenting claims to the department, and calling attention to another law under which any assignment of the postmasters' claims to anyone else and any power of attorney given to anyone else to receive payment was void. Even if the Postmaster General acted maliciously, the Court said, since his action was not "palpably beyond his authority" as the head of an executive department, it was absolutely privileged and could not be made the subject of a libel action. This was so not because malicious conduct by Cabinet officers should be condoned but because "it would seriously cripple the proper and effective administration of public affairs" if cabinet officers had to perform under an apprehension that their official conduct may, at any time, be subjected to the hazards of a civil suit for damages.[23]

When, many years later, the Court applied the same absolute privilege to an acting director of the federal Office of Rent Stabilization, who was sued for libel by two subordinates because of what he said about them in a press release, Douglas joined in a dissent. He thought

---

[23] *Spalding v. Vilas,* 161 U.S. 483 (1896).

that the Court had overlooked the public interest in protecting government employees who criticize their superiors from retaliatory defamation and would have limited the absolute privilege to Cabinet officers and other executive officials appointed by the President and directly responsible to him and to lesser officials only when making required reports to their superiors. For public statements of lesser officials he would have recognized only a qualified privilege which would not survive proof of malice.[24]

The Court next considered the question of executive privilege not as a defense to a libel action for statements released but as a justification for information withheld.

In 1966 Congress enacted the Freedom of Information Act, which was designed to make available to the public much information in the files of governmental agencies, although the act contained nine exceptions. After an article appeared in a Washington, D.C., newspaper in late July, 1971, indicating that President Nixon had received conflicting recommendations on the advisability of an underground nuclear test at Amchitka Island, Alaska, scheduled for the coming fall, Representative Patsy Mink of Hawaii and thirty-two of her colleagues in the House requested release of the recommendations, and when that request was denied, brought an action under the Freedom of Information Act. It was established that the recommendations consisted of a covering letter to the President from the chairman of a committee of the National Security Council enclosing the report of the committee and eight other reports or letters from the AEC, the Defense Program Review Committee, the Council on Environmental Quality, the Environmental Protection Agency, and the Office of Science and Technology. An affidavit submitted by the chairman of the committee also asserted that nine (later reduced to six) of the ten documents were, pursuant to Executive Order 10501, classified "secret" or "top secret" because vital to national defense and foreign policy.

The agencies involved invoked exceptions in the Freedom of Information Act for matters (1) that are "specifically required by Executive order to be kept secret in the interest of national defense or foreign policy" or (2) that are "inter-agency or intra-agency memorandums or letters which would not be available by law to a party other than an agency in litigation with an agency." The district court agreed that at least one of the exceptions was applicable to each document and gave judgment for the agencies. On appeal, the Court of Appeals reversed, holding that the first exception applied only to the secret portions of the classified documents and that the second exception corresponded to

24 *Barr v. Matteo*, 360 U.S. 564 (1959).

the executive privilege recognized by lower federal courts in civil litigation between the government and private parties. But that privilege applied only to "decisional processes" and not to "factual information" unless that information is "inextricably intertwined with policymaking process." Accordingly, it remanded the case to the district judge with instructions to examine the documents in camera and to separate out those parts of the documents not covered by exceptions which could be disclosed.

The Court reversed the decision of the Court of Appeals, concluding the executive classification of six of the documents as Secret or Top Secret was conclusive and that the propriety of the classifications could not be reviewed by the courts and that there could be no in camera inspection by the court to separate the secret from the nonsecret portions. The language of the second exception "clearly contemplates that the public is entitled to all such memoranda or letters that a private party could discover in litigation with the agency," and the Court of Appeals had correctly stated the test for such litigation. But in camera inspection by the court would not be necessary and appropriate in every case if the agency could, by affidavits or oral testimony, otherwise satisfy the court that the test could be met without inspection of the documents by the court.

Mr. Justice Douglas, dissenting.

The starting point of a decision usually indicates the result. My starting point is what I believe to be the philosophy of Congress expressed in the Freedomn of Information Act.

Henry Steele Commager, our noted historian, recently wrote:

> "The generation that made the nation thought secrecy in government one of the instruments of Old World tyranny and committed itself to the principle that a democracy cannot function unless the people are permitted to know what their government is up to. Now almost everything that the Pentagon and the CIA do is shrouded in secrecy. Not only are the American people not permitted to know what they are up to but even the Congress and, one suspects, the President [witness the 'unauthorized' bombing of the North last fall and winter] are kept in darkness." The New York Review of Books, Oct. 5, 1972, p. 7.

Two days after we granted certiorari in the case on March 6, 1972, the President revoked the old Executive Order 10501 and substituted a new one, Executive Order 11652, dated March 8, 1972, and effective June 1, 1972. The new Order states in its first paragraph that: "The interests of the United States and its citizens are best served by making information regarding the affairs of Government readily available to the public. This concept of an informed citizenry is reflected in the Freedom of Information Act and in the current public information policies of the Executive branch."

While "classified information or material" as used in the Order is exempted from public disclosure, §4 of the Order states that each classified document shall "to the extent practicable, be so marked as to indicate which portions are classified, at what level, and which portions are not classified in order to facilitate excerpting and other use." And it goes on to say: "Material containing references to classified materials, which references do not reveal classified information, shall not be classified."

The Freedom of Information Act does not clash with the Executive Order. Indeed, the new Executive Order precisely meshes with the Act and with the construction given it by the Court of Appeals. The Act gives the District Court "jurisdiction to enjoin the agency from withholding agency records and to order the production of any agency records improperly withheld from the complainant." [It] goes on to prescribe the procedure to be employed by the District Court. It says "the court shall determine the matter de novo and the burden is on the agency to sustain its action."

The Act and the Executive Order read together mean at the very minimum that the District Court has power to direct the agency in question to go through the suppressed document and make the portion-by-portion classification to facilitate the excerpting as required by the Executive Order. [The Act] means also that the District Court may in its discretion collaborate with the agency to make certain that the congressional policy of disclosure is effectuated.

The Court of Appeals, in an exceedingly responsible opinion, directed the District Court to proceed as follows:

Where material is separately *unclassified* but nonetheless under the umbrella of a "secret" file, the District Court should make sure that it is disclosed under the Act. This seems clear from [the first exception] which states: "This section does not apply to matters that are—(1) specifically required by Executive order to be kept secret in the interest of the national defense or foreign policy." Unless the *unclassified* appendage to a "secret" file falls under some other exception it seems clear that it must be disclosed. The only other exception under which refuge is now sought [provides] that the section does not apply to "inter-agency or intra-agency memorandums or letters which would not be available by law to a party other than an agency in litigation with the agency."

This exemption was described in the House Report as covering "any internal memorandums which would routinely be disclosed to a private party through the discovery process in litigation with the agency." H. R. Rep. No. 1497, 89th Cong., 2d Sess., 10. It is clear from the legislative history that while opinions and staff advice are exempt, factual matters are not. *Ibid.*; S. Rep. No. 813, 89th Cong., 1st Sess., 9. And the courts have uniformly agreed on that construction of the Act. See *Soucie v. David*, 145 U.S. App. D.C. 144, 448 F. 2d 1067; *Grumman Aircraft Eng. Corp.* v. *Renegotiation Bd.*, 138 U.S. App. D.C. 147, 425 F. 2d 578; *Long Island R. Co.* v. *United States*, 318 F. Supp. 490; *Consumers Union* v. *Veterans Admin.*, 301 F. Supp. 796.

Facts and opinions may, as the Court of Appeals noted, be "inextricably intertwined with policymaking processes" in some cases. In such an event, secrecy prevails. Yet, where facts and opinions can be separated, the Act allows the full light of publicity to be placed on the facts.

[The Act] seems to seal the case against the Government when it says: "This section does not authorize withholding of information or limit the availability of records to the public, except as specifically stated in this section." Disclosure, rather than secrecy, is the rule, save for the specific exceptions.

The Government seeks to escape from the Act by making the Government stamp of "Top Secret" or "Secret" a barrier to the performance of the District Court's functions under the Act. The majority makes the stamp sacrosanct, thereby immunizing stamped documents from judicial scrutiny, whether or not factual information contained in the document is in fact colorably related to interests of the national defense or foreign policy. Yet, anyone who has ever been in the Executive Branch knows how convenient the "Top Secret" or "Secret" stamp is, how easy it is to use, and how it covers perhaps for decades the footprints of a nervous bureaucrat or a wary executive.

The Government is aghast at a federal judge's even looking at the secret files and views with disdain the prospect of responsible judicial action in the area. It suggests that judges have no business declassifying "secrets," that judges are not familiar with the stuff with which these "Top Secret" or "Secret" documents deal.

That is to misconceive and distort the judicial function under the Act. The Court of Appeals never dreamed that the trial judge would declassify documents. His first task would be to determine whether nonsecret material was a mere appendage to a "Secret" or "Top Secret" file. His second task would be to determine whether under normal discovery procedures factual material in these "Secret" or "Top Secret" materials is detached from the "Secret" and would, therefore, be available to litigants confronting the agency in ordinary lawsuits.

Unless the District Court can do those things, the much-advertised Freedom of Information Act is on its way to becoming a shambles. Unless federal courts can be trusted, the Executive will hold complete sway and by *ipse dixit* make even the time of day "Top Secret." Certainly, the decision today will upset the "workable formula," at the heart of the legislative scheme, "which encompasses, balances, and protects all interests, yet places emphasis on the fullest responsible disclosure." S. Rep. No. 813, p. 3. The Executive Branch now has *carte blanche* to insulate information from public scrutiny whether or not that information bears any discernible relation to the interests sought to be protected by [the first exception in] the Act. We should remember the words of Madison:

> "A popular Government, without popular information, or the means of acquiring it, is but a Prologue to a Farce or a Tragedy; or, perhaps both. Knowledge will forever govern ignorance: And a people who mean to be their own Governors, must arm themselves with the power which knowledge gives."

I would affirm the judgment below.

By 1974 amendments to the Freedom of Information Act, Congress substantially adopted Douglas' views on the first exception. It amended the exception to cover information "specifically authorized under criteria established by an Executive order to be kept secret in the interest of national defense or foreign policy" and authorized the courts to review the propriety of executive classification of documents under the prescribed criteria. The amendment specifically authorized the courts to make in camera inspection of information to determine whether it comes under any exception, and also provided that "Any reasonably segregable portion of a record shall be provided to any person requesting such record after deletion of the portions which [come under any exception]."

YOUNGSTOWN SHEET & TUBE CO. v. SAWYER
343 U.S. 579 (1952)

The Constitution provides in Article I that "All legislative Powers herein granted shall be vested in . . . Congress,"[25] that Congress shall have the power to "declare War,"[26] to "raise and support Armies"[27] to

[25] U.S. Const., Art. I, § 1.
[26] *Id.,* §8, Cl. 11
[27] *Id.,* Cl 12

"provide and maintain a Navy,"[28] to *"make Rules for the Government and Regulation of the land and naval Forces,"*[29] *and to levy taxes and "provide for the common Defence and general Welfare."*[30] *It also provides in Article II that the "executive Power shall be vested in" the President,*[31] *that he shall "take Care that the Laws be faithfully executed," shall inform Congress "of the State of the Union" and recommend legislative measures, shall "receive Ambassadors and other public Ministers,"*[32] *shall negotiate treaties and appoint ambassadors, Judges of the Supreme Court and other public officers with the advice and consent of the Senate,*[33] *and shall be "Commander in Chief of the Army and Navy."*[34]

During World War II, Congress enacted the War Labor Disputes Act, authorizing the President to seize production facilities necessary for the war effort whenever operation was threatened by labor disputes. But that act was a temporary measure and was no longer in force when, during the Korean War, collective bargaining negotiations between the United Steelworkers of America and the major steel companies reached a stalemate and the union threatened to strike. President Truman referred the dispute to the Wage Stabilization Board, which recommended wage increases and fringe benefits totaling about twenty-six cents an hour. This was acceptable to the union but not to the employers unless price-control regulations were relaxed to allow a $12 per ton increase in steel prices. When the union set a date for a nationwide strike, President Truman ordered Secretary of Commerce Sawyer to take possession of the steel mills and keep them in operation, and Sawyer did so. The President had also indicated that, if the parties did not settle their labor dispute promptly, the United States as the substituted "employer" would grant the employees a wage increase.

When the companies brought proceedings against Sawyer to enjoin him from enforcing the seizure order, the government did not rely on any specific statutory authority for the seizure. Rather, it argued that seizure was a proper exercise of executive power and that no legislative authority was necessary.

The Court held the seizure invalid as not within any of the constitutional executive powers of the President.

[28] *Id.,* Cl. 13.
[29] *Id.,* Cl. 14.
[30] *Id.,* Cl. 1.
[31] *Id.,* Art. II, § 1.
[32] *Id.,* § 3.
[33] *Id.,* § 2, Cl. 2.
[34] *Id.,* Cl. 1.

MR. JUSTICE DOUGLAS, concurring.

There can be no doubt that the emergency which caused the President to seize these steel plants was one that bore heavily on the country. But the emergency did not create power; it merely marked an occasion when power should be exercised. And the fact that it was necessary that measures be taken to keep steel in production does not mean that the President, rather than the Congress, had the constitutional authority to act. The Congress, as well as the President, is trustee of the national welfare. The President can act more quickly than the Congress. The President with the armed services at his disposal can move with force as well as with speed. All executive power—from the reign of ancient kings to the rule of modern dictators—has the outward appearance of efficiency.

Legislative power, by contrast, is slower to exercise. There must be delay while the ponderous machinery of committees, hearings, and debates is put into motion. That takes time; and while the Congress slowly moves into action, the emergency may take its toll in wages, consumer goods, war production, the standard of living of the people, and perhaps even lives. Legislative action may indeed often be cumbersome, time-consuming, and apparently inefficient. But as Mr. Justice Brandeis stated in his dissent in *Myers* v. *United States*, 272 U.S. 52:

> "The doctrine of the separation of powers was adopted by the Convention of 1787, not to promote efficiency but to preclude the exercise of arbitrary power. The purpose was, not to avoid friction, but, by means of the inevitable friction incident to the distribution of the governmental powers among three departments, to save the people from autocracy."

We therefore cannot decide this case by determining which branch of government can deal most expeditiously with the present crisis. The answer must depend on the allocation of powers under the Constitution. That in turn requires an analysis of the conditions giving rise to the seizure and of the seizure itself.

The relations between labor and industry are one of the crucial problems of the era. Their solution will doubtless entail many methods —education of labor leaders and business executives; the encouragement of mediation and conciliation by the President and the use of his great office in the cause of industrial peace; and the passage of laws. Laws entail sanctions—penalties for their violation. One type of sanction is fine and imprisonment. Another is seizure of property. An industry may become so lawless, so irresponsible as to endanger the whole economy. Seizure of the industry may be the only wise and practical solution.

The method by which industrial peace is achieved is of vital importance not only to the parties but to society as well. A determination that sanctions should be applied, that the hand of the law should be placed upon the parties, and that the force of the courts should be directed against them, is an exercise of legislative power. In some nations that power is entrusted to the executive branch as a matter of course or in case of emergencies. We chose another course. We chose to place the legislative power of the Federal Government in the Congress. The language of the Constitution is not ambiguous or qualified. It places not *some* legislative power in the Congress; Article I, Section 1 says "All legislative Powers herein granted shall be vested in a Congress of the United States, which shall consist of a Senate and House of Representatives."

The legislative nature of the action taken by the President seems to me to be clear. When the United States takes over an industrial plant to settle a labor controversy, it is condemning property. The seizure of the plant is a taking in the constitutional sense. *United States* v. *Pewee Coal Co.*, 341 U.S. 114.[35] A permanent taking would amount to the nationalization of the industry. A temporary taking falls short of that goal. But though the seizure is only for a week or a month, the condemnation is complete and the United States must pay compensation for the temporary possession. *United States* v. *General Motors Corp.*, 323 U.S. 373; *United States* v. *Pewee Coal Co., Inc., supra.*

The power of the Federal Government to condemn property is well established. *Kohl* v. *United States*, 91 U.S. 367. It can condemn for any public purpose; and I have no doubt but that condemnation of a plant, factory, or industry in order to promote industrial peace would be constitutional. But there is a duty to pay for all property taken by the Government. The command of the Fifth Amendment is that no "private property be taken for public use, without just compensation." That constitutional requirement has an important bearing on the present case.

The President has no power to raise revenues. That power is in the Congress by Article I, Section 8 of the Constitution. The President might seize and the Congress by subsequent action might ratify the seizure.[36] But until and unless Congress acted, no condemnation would

[35] [Where the Court held that seizure of a coal mine under the War Labor Disputes Act during World War II constituted a taking of property under Fifth Amendment which required compensation of the mineowners.]

[36] What a President may do as a matter of expediency or extremity may never reach a definitive constitutional decision. For example, President Lincoln suspended the writ of habeas corpus, claiming the constitutional right to do so. See *Ex parte Merryman*, 17 Fed. Cas. No. 9,487. Congress ratified his action by the Act of March 3, 1863.

be lawful. The branch of government that has the power to pay compensation for a seizure is the only one able to authorize a seizure or make lawful one that the President has effected. That seems to me to be the necessary result of the condemnation provision in the Fifth Amendment. It squares with the theory of checks and balances expounded by MR. JUSTICE BLACK in the opinion of the Court in which I join.

If we sanctioned the present exercise of power by the President, we would be expanding Article II of the Constitution and rewriting it to suit the political conveniences of the present emergency. Article II which vests the "executive Power" in the President defines that power with particularity. Article II, Section 2 makes the Chief Executive the Commander in Chief of the Army and Navy. But our history and tradition rebel at the thought that the grant of military power carries with it authority over civilian affairs. Article II, Section 3 provides that the President shall "from time to time give to the Congress Information of the State of the Union, and recommend to their Consideration such Measures as he shall judge necessary and expedient." The power to recommend legislation, granted to the President, serves only to emphasize that it is his function to recommend and that it is the function of the Congress to legislate. Article II, Section 3 also provides that the President "shall take Care that the Laws be faithfully executed." But, as MR. JUSTICE BLACK and MR. JUSTICE FRANKFURTER point out, the power to execute the laws starts and ends with the laws Congress has enacted.

The great office of President is not a weak and powerless one. The President represents the people and is their spokesman in domestic and foreign affairs. The office is respected more than any other in the land. It gives a position of leadership that is unique. The power to formulate policies and mould opinion inheres in the Presidency and conditions our national life. The impact of the man and the philosophy he represents may at times be thwarted by the Congress. Stalemates may occur when emergencies mount and the Nation suffers for lack of harmonious, reciprocal action between the White House and Capitol Hill. That is a risk inherent in our system of separation of powers. The tragedy of such stalemates might be avoided by allowing the President the use of some legislative authority. The Framers with memories of the tyrannies produced by a blending of executive and legislative power rejected that political arrangement. Some future generation may, however, deem it so urgent that the President have legislative authority that the Constitution will be amended. We could not sanction the seizures and condemnations of the steel plants in this case without reading Article II as giving the President not only the power to execute the laws but to make some. Such a step would most assuredly alter the pattern of the Constitution.

We pay a price for our system of checks and balances, for the distribution of power among the three branches of government. It is a price that today may seem exorbitant to many. Today a kindly President uses the seizure power to effect a wage increase and to keep the steel furnaces in production. Yet tomorrow another President might use the same power to prevent a wage increase, to curb trade-unionists, to regiment labor as oppressively as industry.thinks it has been regimented by this seizure.

Immediately following this decision, the employees went out on strike. The President then requested Congress to enact legislation authorizing seizure. Instead, Congress adopted a statute which, in effect, requested the President to seek an injunction against the strikers under the Taft-Hartley Act. No such action was taken and, two and one-half months after the Youngstown decision, the strike was settled under an arrangement whereby the employees got wage increases and fringe benefits of about twenty-one cents an hour and the steel producers were allowed to increase their prices by about $5.65 per ton.

Ex Parte Endo
323 U.S. 283 (1944)

In what many regard as a grave error in constitutional interpretation, the Court unanimously held that the President and Congress, acting jointly, could constitutionally prescribe a West Coast nighttime curfew for persons of Japanese ancestry—most of whom were American citizens by birth. The action was taken three months after Japan had invaded Pearl Harbor and Congress had declared war against Japan. It was initiated by an Executive Order pursuant to which the Army issued the curfew order, but the Court found that Congress had later ratified the executive action by enacting a statute prescribing criminal penalties for those who violated the curfew. This joint action was said to be a valid exercise of "the power to wage war conferred on Congress and on the President as Commander in Chief," because they had reasonable ground to apprehend sabotage and espionage.[37] The curfew order was followed by Army exclusion orders requiring all persons of Japanese ancestry to leave the West Coast, and, with only Justices Roberts, Murphy and Jackson dissenting, the Court likewise sustained that order as a valid exercise of the war power.[38]

[37] *Hirabayshi v. United States,* 320 U.S. 81 (1943).
[38] *Korematsu v. United States,* 323 U.S. 214 (1944).

This case involved the last stage of the relocation program under which persons of Japanese descent were evacuated to "relocation centers" in the interior of the United States and detained unless and until they received permission to leave. That permission was obtained through a two-step process: (1) Leave clearance could be obtained if the applicant satisfied the authorities that he or she was not disloyal (by showing, among other things, that he or she had never requested repatriation or expatriation, had never undergone military training in a Japanese naval vessel, had not made as many as three trips to Japan after the age of six, and was not a member of organizations considered "subversive") and if he or she took an oath of unqualified allegiance to the United States and foreswore allegiance to Japan. (2) After obtaining clearance, an applicant could obtain leave to go to an area approved by the authorities by obtaining employment approved by the authorities, or by showing other adequate resources for support, unless the authorities determined that the proposed place of residence was within a locality where "community sentiment is unfavorable."

Mitsuye Endo, who had been so detained since June, 1942, filed a petition for a writ of habeas corpus in a federal district court in July, 1942, seeking to have the second part of the leave process held unconstitutional. The district court denied relief, she appealed to the circuit court of appeals, and that court certified certain questions of law to the Supreme Court, which unanimously ruled in December, 1944, that she must be set free.

MR. JUSTICE DOUGLAS delivered the opinion of the Court.

It is conceded by the Department of Justice and by the War Relocation Authority that appellant is a loyal and law-abiding citizen. They make no claim that she is detained on any charge or that she is even suspected of disloyalty. Moreover, they do not contend that she may be held any longer in the Relocation Center. They concede that it is beyond the power of the War Relocation Authority to detain citizens against whom no charges of disloyalty or subversiveness have been made for a period longer than that necessary to separate the loyal from the disloyal and to provide the necessary guidance for relocation. But they maintain that detention for an additional period after leave clearance has been granted is an essential step in the evacuation program. Reliance for that conclusion is placed on the following circumstances.

When compulsory evacuation from the West Coast was decided upon, plans for taking care of the evacuees after their detention in the Assembly Centers, to which they were initially removed, remained to be determined. On April 7, 1942, the Director of the Authority held a conference in Salt Lake City with various state and federal officials including the Governors of the intermountain states. "Strong opposition was expressed to any type of unsupervised relocation and some of the Governors refused to be responsible for maintenance of law and order unless evacuees brought into their States were kept under constant military surveillance." The Authority thereupon abandoned plans for assisting groups of evacuees in private colonization and temporarily put to one side plans for aiding the evacuees in obtaining private employment. As an alternative the Authority "concentrated on establishment of Government-operated centers with sufficient capacity and facilities to accommodate the entire evacuee population." Accordingly, it undertook to care for the basic needs of these people in the Relocation Centers, to promote as rapidly as possible the permanent resettlement of as many as possible in normal communities, and to provide indefinitely for those left at the Relocation Centers. An effort was made to segregate the loyal evacuees from the others. The leave program was put into operation and the resettlement program commenced.

It is argued that such a planned and orderly relocation was essential to the success of the evacuation program; that but for such supervision there might have been a dangerously disorderly migration of unwanted people to unprepared communities; that unsupervised evacuation might have resulted in hardship and disorder; that the success of the evacuation program was thought to require the knowledge that the federal government was maintaining control over the evacuated population except as the release of individuals could be effected consistently with their own peace and well-being and that of the nation; that although community hostility towards the evacuees has diminished, it has not disappeared and the continuing control of the Authority over the relocation process is essential to the success of the evacuation program. It is argued that supervised relocation, as the chosen method of terminating the evacuation, is the final step in the entire process and is a consequence of the first step taken. It is conceded that appellant's detention pending compliance with the leave regulations is not directly connected with the prevention of espionage and sabotage at the present time. But it is argued that [the] Executive Order confers power to make regulations necessary and proper for controlling situations created by the exercise of the powers expressly conferred for protection against espionage and sabotage. The leave regulations are said to fall within that category.

First. We are of the view that Mitsuye Endo should be given her liberty. In reaching that conclusion we do not come to the underlying constitutional issues which have been argued. For we conclude that, whatever power the War Relocation Authority may have to detain other classes of citizens, it has no authority to subject citizens who are concededly loyal to its leave procedure.

Such power of detention as the Authority has stems from Executive Order No. 9066. We approach the construction of Executive Order No. 9066 as we would approach the construction of legislation in this field. That Executive Order must indeed be considered along with the Act of March 21, 1942, which ratified and confirmed it as the Order and the statute together laid such basis as there is for participation by civil agencies of the federal governments in the evacuation program. Broad powers frequently granted to the President or other executive officers by Congress so that they may deal with the exigencies of wartime problems have been sustained. And the Constitution when it committed to the Executive and to Congress the exercise of the war power necessarily gave them wide scope for the exercise of judgment and discretion so that war might be waged effectively and successfully. At the same time, however, the Constitution is as specific in its enumeration of many of the civil rights of the individual as it is in its enumeration of the powers of his government. Thus it has prescribed procedural safeguards surrounding the arrest, detention and conviction of individuals. Some of these are contained in the Sixth Amendment, compliance with which is essential if convictions are to be sustained.[39] And the Fifth Amendment provides that no person shall be deprived of liberty (as well as life or property) without due process of law. Moreover, as a further safeguard against invasion of the basic civil rights of the individual it is provided in Art. I, §9 of the Constitution that "The Privilege of the Writ of Habeas Corpus shall not be suspended, unless when in Cases of Rebellion or Invasion the public Safety may require it."

We mention these constitutional provisions not to stir the constitutional issues which have been argued at the bar but to indicate the approach which we think should be made to an Act of Congress or an order of the Chief Executive that touches the sensitive area of rights specifically guaranteed by the Constitution. This Court has quite consistently given a narrower scope for the operation of the presumption of constitutionality when legislation appeared on its face to violate a specific prohibition of the Constitution. We have likewise favored that

[39] [U.S. Const., Sixth Amendment: "In all criminal prosecutions, the accused shall enjoy the right to a speedy and public trial, by an impartial jury of the State and district wherein the crime shall have been committed, which district shall have been previously ascertained by law, and be informed of the nature and cause of the accusation; to be confronted with the witnesses against him; to have compulsory process for obtaining witnesses in his favor, and to have the Assistance of Counsel for his defence."]

interpretation of legislation which gives it the greater chance of surviving the test of constitutionality. Those analogies are suggestive here. We must assume that the Chief Executive and members of Congress, as well as the courts, are sensitive to and respectful of the liberties of the citizen. In interpreting a wartime measure we must assume that their purpose was to allow for the greatest possible accommodation between those liberties and the exigencies of war. We must assume, when asked to find implied powers in a grant of legislative or executive authority, that the law makers intended to place no greater restraint on the citizen than was clearly and unmistakably indicated by the language they used.

The Act of March 21, 1942, was a war measure. The House Report stated, "The necessity for this legislation arose from the fact that the safe conduct of the war requires the fullest possible protection against either espionage or sabotage to national defense material, national defense premises, and national defense utilities." That was the precise purpose of Executive Order No. 9066, for, as we have seen, it gave as the reason for the exclusion of persons from prescribed military areas the protection of such property "against espionage and against sabotage." And Executive Order No. 9102 which established the War Relocation Authority did so "in order to provide for the removal from designated areas of persons whose removal is necessary in the interests of national security." The purpose and objective of the Act and of these orders are plain. Their single aim was the protection of the war effort against espionage and sabotage. It is in light of that one objective that the powers conferred by the orders must be construed.

Neither the Act nor the orders use the language of detention. The Act says that no one shall "enter, remain in, leave, or commit any act" in the prescribed military areas contrary to the applicable restrictions. Executive Order No. 9066 subjects the right of any person "to enter, remain in, or leave" those prescribed areas to such restrictions as the military may impose. And apart from those restrictions the Secretary of War is only given authority to afford the evacuees "transportation, food, shelter, and other accommodations." Executive Order No. 9102 authorizes and directs the War Relocation Authority "to formulate and effectuate a program for the removal" of the persons covered by Executive Order No. 9066 from the prescribed military areas and "for their relocation, maintenance, and supervision." And power is given the Authority to make regulations "necessary or desirable to promote effective execution of such program." Moreover, unlike the case of curfew regulations, the legislative history of the Act of March 21, 1942, is silent on detention. And that silence may have special significance in view of the fact that detention in Relocation Centers was no part of the original program of evacuation but developed later to meet what seemed to the officials in charge to be mounting hostility to the evacuees on the part of the communities where they sought to go.

A citizen who is concededly loyal presents no problem of espionage or sabotage. Loyalty is a matter of the heart and mind, not of race, creed, or color. He who is loyal is by definition not a spy or a saboteur. When the power to detain is derived from the power to protect the war effort against espionage and sabotage, detention which has no relationship to that objective is unauthorized.

Nor may the power to detain an admittedly loyal citizen be implied as a useful or convenient step in the evacuation program, whatever authority might be implied in case of those whose loyalty was not conceded or established. If we assume (as we do) that the original evacuation was justified, its lawful character was derived from the fact that it was an espionage and sabotage measure, not that there was community hostility to this group of American citizens. The evacuation program rested explicitly on the former ground not on the latter as the underlying legislation shows. The authority to detain a citizen as protection against espionage or sabotage is exhausted at least when his loyalty is conceded. If we held that the authority to detain continued thereafter, we would transform an espionage or sabotage measure into something else. That was not done by Executive Order No. 9066 or by the Act of March 21, 1942, which ratified it. What they did not do we cannot do. Detention which furthered the campaign against espionage and sabotage would be one thing. But detention which has no relationship to that campaign is of a distinct character. Community hostility even to loyal evacuees may have been (and perhaps still is) a serious problem. But if authority for their custody and supervision is to be sought on that ground, the Act of March 21, 1942, Executive Order No. 9066, and Executive Order No. 9102, offer no support. And none other is advanced. To read them that broadly would be to assume that the Congress and the President intended that this discriminatory action should be taken against these people wholly on account of their ancestry even though the government conceded their loyalty to this country. We cannot make such an assumption.

Mitsuye Endo is entitled to an unconditional release by the War Relocation Authority.

The day before this decision was announced, the War Department revoked the exclusion orders which barred Japanese from the West Coast. By that time about 35,000 of the approximately 115,000 persons detained in relocation centers had been released through the War Relocation Authority procedures. Release of another 60,000 who, like Endo, had cleared the loyalty tests, was not completed until March

1946, four years after they were excluded from their homes and more than a year after the Endo *decision. There remained 20,000 who failed, or a member of whose family failed, to meet the loyalty tests which had gone unchallenged in* Endo—*many of them only because they refused to take the loyalty oath. They remained in detention for substantially longer periods until deported or released. When the entire operation was completed, not a single case had been discovered involving espionage or sabotage by a detainee, including those who failed to pass the loyalty tests.*

In the confusion and hysteria of their forced evacuation, many of these people were put to a choice of making inadequate arrangements for the protection and management of their property or selling it at sacrifice prices. In 1948 Congress authorized the payment of compensation for any uninsured losses and more than $26 million was paid for this purpose.

Having taken that commendable step, Congress proceeded to build upon that part of the program not declared unconstitutional. The Emergency Detention Act of 1950 provided that in the event of an invasion, insurrection, or war and the declaration by the President of an "internal security emergency," the Department of Justice was to apprehend every person "as to whom there is reasonable ground to believe that such person probably will engage in . . . acts of espionage or of sabotage." Apprehended persons were to be "confined in such places of detention as may be prescribed by the Attorney General" until termination of the emergency or until they persuaded a Detention Review Board that there was no reasonable ground to believe that they would engage in espionage or sabotage. After a long campaign by numerous persons and organizations, including the Japanese American Citizens League, Congress was persuaded in 1971 to repeal this Act.

HOLTZMAN v. SCHLESINGER

414 U.S. 1304, 1316, 1321 (1973)

Although the Constitution gives to Congress the power to "declare War,"[40] the Supreme Court has approached a consideration of this power only once. In the Prize Cases[41] *the Court upheld President Lincoln's blockade at Southern ports during the Civil War and the capture of Confederate and foreign vessels which attempted to run the blockade. As a matter of international law, the Court held, belligerents in a war were entitled to resort to blockade and capture, and*

---

[40] U.S. Const., Art. I, §8, Cl. 11.
[41] 2 Black 635 (1863).

this principle of international law was applicable to a civil war as well as to a foreign war. To the argument that Congress had not declared a war, the Court replied that the constitutional provision authorizing Congress to declare war was not applicable to a civil war:

> *By the Constitution, Congress alone has the power to declare a national or foreign war. It cannot declare war against a State, or any number of States, by virtue of any clause in the Constitution. . . . [The President] has no power to initiate or declare a war either against a foreign nation or a domestic state. But by [federal statute] he is authorized to call out the militia and use the military forces of the United States ·in cases of invasion by foreign nations, and to suppress insurrection against the government of a state or the United States.*

Alternatively, the Court held that Congress had by a subsequent enactment ratified and thus validated the President's blockade.

During the period of our military involvement in Vietnam, numerous actions were brought in the lower federal courts to challenge the legality of executive action there both because Congress had not declared war and because the manner in which we were waging war in Vietnam was alleged to violate treaties to which the United States was a party, the United Nations charter, and international law. None of these actions was successful in the lower courts; usually they were lost on the ground that the plaintiffs had no standing to raise the issues or that the issues raised were "political" rather than "justiciable." In every instance where Supreme Court review of these cases was sought, the Court declined to grant it, and in each instance Douglas dissented.

While we were still engaged in hostilities in Vietnam, President Nixon publicly revealed on April 30, 1970, what had been going on covertly for some time—we were carrying the war against the North Vietnamese into Cambodia in support of the existing regime there. Shortly thereafter Congress enacted the so-called Fulbright Proviso to a military appropriation act forbidding the use of any of the appropriated funds to provide military support to the government of Cambodia. As later qualified to permit "support of actions required to insure the safe and orderly withdrawal" of our military forces in Southeast Asia and "to aid in the release of Americans held as prisoners of war," this same proviso was attached to every subsequent military appropriation act.

After the withdrawal of American ground troops from Vietnam and the return of American prisoners of war, Congress passed a statute prohibiting the use of any funds "to support directly or indirectly combat activities in, over or from off the shores of Cambodia." President

Nixon vetoed this measure, but on June 29, 1973, he did sign another, adopted by Congress, which forbade the use of any funds after August 15, 1973, "to finance directly or indirectly combat activities by United States military forces in or over or from off the shores of North Vietnam, South Vietnam, Laos or Cambodia."

Meanwhile, on April 17, 1973, Representative Elizabeth Holtzman of New York and several Air Force officers serving in Asia brought this action to enjoin continued United States air operations over Cambodia on the ground that Congress had not declared war. The district court agreed and on July 25, 1973, enjoined the Secretary of Defense from continuing the bombing operation. The Secretary appealed to the United States Court of Appeals for the Second Circuit, and on July 27 that court stayed the operation of the district court's injunction pending its decision on the appeal. The Supreme Court not being in session, the plaintiffs then applied to Justice Marshall to vacate the stay of the Circuit Court and thus reinstate the injunction while the appeal was pending. Justice Marshall denied their application on August 1. Plaintiffs then located Justice Douglas in the state of Washington and applied to him for the relief Marshall had denied. On August 3, Douglas vacated the Circuit Court's stay.

MR. JUSTICE DOUGLAS, Circuit Justice.

My Brother MARSHALL, after a hearing, denied this application which in effect means that the decision of the District Court holding that the bombing of Cambodia is unconstitutional is stayed pending hearing on the merits before the Court of Appeals.

An application for stay denied by one Justice may be made to another. We do not, however, encourage the practice; and when the Term starts, the Justices all being in Washington, D.C., the practice is to refer the second application to the entire Court. That is the desirable practice to discourage "shopping around."

When the Court is in recess that practice cannot be followed, for the Justices are scattered. Yakima, Washington, where I have scheduled the hearing, is nearly 3,000 miles from Washington, D.C. Group action by all Members is therefore impossible.

I approached this decision, however, with deliberation, realizing that, while the judgment of my Brother MARSHALL is not binding on me, it is one to which I pay the greatest deference.

My Brother MARSHALL accurately points out that if the foreign policy goals of this Government are to be weighed the Judiciary is probably the least qualified branch to weigh them. He also states that if stays by judicial officers in cases of this kind are to be vacated the circumstances must be "exceptional." I agree with those premises, and I respect the views of those who share my Brother MARSHALL's predilections.

But this case in its stark realities involves the grim consequences of a capital case. The classic capital case is whether Mr. Lew, Mr. Low, or Mr. Lucas should die. The present case involves whether Mr. X (an unknown person or persons) should die. No one knows who they are. They may be Cambodian farmers whose only "sin" is a desire for socialized medicine to alleviate the suffering of their families and neighbors. Or Mr. X may be the American pilot or navigator who drops a ton of bombs on a Cambodian village. The upshot is that we know that someone is about to die.

Since that is true I see no reason to balance the equities and consider the harm to our foreign policy if one or a thousand more bombs do not drop. The reason is that we live under the Constitution and in Art. I, §8, cl. 11, it gives to Congress the power to "declare War." The basic question on the merits is whether Congress, within the meaning of Art. I, §8, cl. 11, has "declared war" in Cambodia.

It has become popular to think the President has that power to declare war. But there is not a word in the Constitution that grants that power to him. It runs only to Congress.

The Court in the *Prize Cases* said:

> "By the Constitution, Congress alone has the power to declare a national or foreign war. . . . The Constitution confers on the President the whole Executive power. . . . He has no power to initiate or declare a war either against a foreign nation or a domestic State. . . .
>
> "If a war be made by invasion of a foreign nation, the President is not only authorized but bound to resist force by force. He does not initiate the war, but is bound to accept the challenge without waiting for any special legislative authority."

The question of justiciability does not seem substantial. In the *Prize Cases*, decided in 1863, the Court entertained a complaint involving the constitutionality of the Civil War. In my time we held that President Truman in the undeclared Korean war had no power to seize the steel mills in order to increase war production. *Youngstown Sheet & Tube Co. v. Sawyer* [p. 32, *supra*]. The *Prize Cases* and the *Youngstown* case involved the seizure of property. But the Government conceded on oral argument that property is no more important than life under our Constitution. Our Fifth Amendment which curtails federal power under the Due Process Clause protects "life, liberty, or property" in that order. Property is important, but if President Truman could not seize it in violation of the Constitution I do not see how any President can take "life" in violation of the Constitution.

As to "standing," which my Brother MARSHALL correctly states is an issue, there seems to be no substantial question that a taxpayer at one time had no standing to complain of the lawless actions of his Government. But that rule has been modified. In *Flast* v. *Cohen*, 392 U.S. 83, the Court held that a taxpayer could invoke "federal judicial power when he alleges that congressional action under the taxing and spending clause is in derogation of those constitutional provisions which operate to restrict the exercise of the taxing and spending power." That case involved alleged violations of the Establishment [of Religion] Clause of the First Amendment. The present case involves Art. I, §8, cl. 11, which gives Congress and not the President the power to "declare War."

If applicants are correct on the merits they have standing as taxpayers. The case in that posture is in the class of those where standing and the merits are inextricably intertwined. I see no difference, constitutionally speaking, between the standing in *Flast* and the standing in the present case for our Cambodian caper contested as an unconstitutional exercise of presidential power.

When a stay in a capital case is before us, we do not rule on guilt or innocence. A decision on the merits follows and does not precede the stay. If there is doubt whether due process has been followed in the procedures, the stay is granted because death is irrevocable. By the same token I do not sit today to determine whether the bombing of Cambodia is constitutional. Some say it is merely an extension of the "war" in Vietnam, a "war" which the Second Circuit has held in *Berk* v. *Laird*, 429 F. 2d 302, to raise a "political" question, not a justiciable one. I have had serious doubts about the correctness of that decision, but our Court has never passed on the question authoritatively. I have expressed my doubts on the merits in various opinions dissenting from denial of certiorari.[42] But even if the "war" in Vietnam were assumed to be a constitutional one, the Cambodian bombing is quite a different affair. Certainly Congress did not in terms declare war against Cambodia and there is no one so reckless to say that the Cambodian forces are an imminent and perilous threat to our shores. The briefs are replete with references to recent Acts of Congress which, to avoid a presidential veto, were passed to make clear—as I read them—that no bombing of Cambodia was to be financed by appropriated funds after August 15,

[42] *Sarnoff* v. *Schultz*, 409 U.S. 929; *DaCosta* v. *Laird*, 405 U.S. 979; *Massachusetts* v. *Laird*, 400 U.S. 886; *McArthur* v. *Clifford*, 393 U.S. 1002; *Hart* v. *United States*, 391 U.S. 956; *Holmes* v. *United States*, 391 U.S. 936; *Mora* v. *McNamara*, 389 U.S. 934, 935; *Mitchell* v. *United States*, 386 U.S. 972.

1973. Arguably, that is quite different from saying that Congress has declared war in Cambodia for a limited purpose and only up to and not beyond August 15, 1973. If the acts in question are so construed the result would be, as the District Court said, that the number of votes needed to sustain a presidential veto—one-third plus one—would be all that was needed to bring into operation the new and awesome power of a President to declare war. The merits of the present controversy are therefore, to say the least, substantial, since denial of the application before me would catapult our airmen as well as Cambodian peasants into the death zone. I do what I think any judge would do in a capital case—vacate the stay entered by the Court of Appeals.

On the day after the entry of Douglas' order vacating the order of the court of appeals, the government applied to Justice Marshall for an order staying the injunction order of the district court. Marshall granted the order on the same day, stating as he did so that he had been in communication with the other members of the Court and that all but Douglas agreed with his action. Douglas filed a dissenting opinion.

MR. JUSTICE DOUGLAS, dissenting.

The order I entered August 3, 1973, in *Holtzman* v. *Schlesinger* not only vacated the stay of the Court of Appeals but also reinstated the judgment of the District Court. I mailed it on August 3, 1973, and reported its contents to the Clerk's office.

My Brother MARSHALL in his opinion of August 4, 1973, misstates the facts when he says that "the only order extant in this case is the order of the District Court." A correct statement would be that the most recent order in this case was my order of August 3, 1973, reinstating the order of the District Court, which would thus leave the Court of Appeals free to act on the merits and give full relief or, alternatively, permit this Court to reverse me.

The Court has unquestioned power to reverse me; and although I disagree with the Court's action on the merits, that is not the point of this dissent. If we who impose law and order are ourselves to be bound by law and order, we can act as a Court only when at least six of us are present. That is the requirement of the Act of Congress,[43] and heretofore it has been the practice to summon the Court to Special Term. Seriatim telephone calls cannot, with all respect, be a lawful substitute. A Conference brings us all together; views are exchanged; briefs are studied; oral argument by counsel for each side is customarily

[43] "The Supreme Court of the United States shall consist of a Chief Justice of the United States and eight associate justices, any six of whom shall constitute a quorum."

required. But even without participation the Court always acts in Conference and therefore responsibly.

Those of the Brethren out of Washington, D.C., on August 4, 1973, could not possibly have studied my opinion in this case. For, although I wrote it late on August 3, it was not released until 9:30 a.m. on August 4; and before 3 p. m., August 4, I was advised by telephone that eight Members of the Court disagreed with me. The issue tendered in the case was not frivolous; the Government on oral argument conceded as much. It involved a new point of law never yet resolved by the Court. I have participated for enough years in Conferences to realize that profound changes are made among the Brethren once their minds are allowed to explore a problem in depth. Yet there were only a few of the Brethren who saw my opinion before they took contrary action.

Whatever may be said on the merits, I am firmly convinced that the telephone disposition of this grave and crucial constitutional issue is not permissible. I do not speak of social propriety. It is a matter of law and order involving high principles. The principles are that the Court is a deliberative body that acts only on reasoned bases after full consideration, and that it is as much bound by the law of the land as is he who lives in the ghetto or in the big white house on the hill. With all respect, I think the Court has slighted that law. The shortcut it has taken today surely flouts an Act of Congress providing for a necessary quorum. A Gallup Poll type of inquiry of widely scattered Justices is, I think, a subversion of the regime under which I thought we lived.

One Justice who grants bail, issues a stay of a mandate, or issues a certificate of probable cause cannot under the statutory regime designed by Congress vacate, modify, or reverse what another Justice does.[44] The Court, of course, can do so—and only the Court[45]—but when the Court acts it must have six Members present.

---

[44] The statutes authorizing individual Justices of this Court to affirmatively grant applications for such actions do not authorize them to rescind affirmative action taken by another Justice. See, e.g., 28 U.S.C. § 2101 (f) (stays of mandate); 28 U.S.C. § 2241 (a) (writs of habeas corpus); 18 U.S.C. § 3141 and Fed. Rule Crim. Proc. 46 (a)(2) (granting of bail).

[45] This requirement of collegial action is confirmed by the Rules of this Court and by this Court's prior decisions and practices.

Rules 50 and 51 govern the in-chambers practices of the Court. Rule 50(5) provides that, when one Justice denies an application made to him, the party who has made the unsuccessful application may renew it to any other Justice. It was pursuant to this Rule that application for the stay in this case was made to me. But neither Rule 50 nor Rule 51 authorizes a party, once a stay has been granted, to contest that action before another individual Justice.

Under the law as it is written, the order of MR. JUSTICE MARSHALL of August 4, 1973, will in time be reversed by that Higher Court which invariably sits in judgment on the decisions of this Court. The order of August 4, 1973, in this case would be valid only if we had the power to agree by telephone that the rules framed by Congress to govern our procedures should be altered. We have no such power. What Members of the Court told Brother MARSHALL to do on August 4, 1973, does not, with all respect, conform with our ground rules. It may have been done inadvertently, but it is nonetheless not a lawful order. Therefore, I respectfully dissent.

Four days later, on August 8, the court of appeals ruled on the merits of the pending appeal. It held that the issues raised by the case presented a political question on which the district court should not have ruled and reversed its decision. In April of 1974, eight months after the congressionally imposed limitation on the use of funds for any military operations in Cambodia had become effective, the Supreme Court declined to review the case on the merits.[46]

LAIRD V. TATUM
408 U.S. 1 (1972)

The Constitution authorizes Congress to "raise and support Armies,"[47] *to "provide and maintain a Navy,"*[48] *and to "make Rules for the Government and Regulation of the land and naval Forces."*[49] *It also authorizes Congress to "provide for organizing, arming, and disciplining, the Militia [National Guard], and for governing such Part of them as may be employed in the Service of the United States, reserving to the States respectively, the Appointment of the Officers, and the Authority of training the Militia according to the discipline prescribed by Congress,"*[50] *and to "provide for calling forth the Militia to execute the Laws of the Union, suppress Insurrections and repel Invasions."*[51]
Other provisions make the President "Commander in Chief of the

---

The Court has previously deemed it necessary and proper to meet together in Special Term before stays granted by an individual Justice out of Term could be overturned. In *Rosenberg* v. *United States* [p. 311, *infra*], the full Court felt constrained to consider its power to vacate a stay issued by an individual Justice, finally resting that power on the Court's position—as a body—as final interpreter of the law.

[46] *Holtzman* v. *Schlesinger*, 416 U.S. 936 (1974).

[47] U.S. Const., Art. I, §8, Cl. 12.

[48] *Id.*, Cl. 13.

[49] *Id.*, Cl. 14.

[50] *Id.*, Cl. 16.

[51] *Id.*, Cl. 15.

Army and Navy of the United States, and of the Militia of the several States, when called into the actual Service of the United States"[52] and require the United States to protect the States "against Invasion; and on application of the Legislature, or the Executive (when the Legislature cannot be convened) against domestic Violence."[53]

In January, 1970, a former captain of Army intelligence published a magazine article charging that the Army had since 1965 been maintaining surveillance of lawful civilian political activity and storing the data collected on private citizens and organizations in its computerized data bank at Fort Holabird in Baltimore. In hearings before Senator Sam Ervin's Subcommittee on Constitutional Rights more than a year later, Defense Department spokesmen admitted that their department had since 1968 maintained an index of 25 million names of persons who had taken part in civil rights or antiwar activities; but the Army assured Congress that its share of the index—about 8 million—was accessible only to 688 authorized officials.

One month after the original disclosure, plaintiffs—private citizens, most of whom were able to show that they or organizations of which they were members had been the subject of Army surveillance reports and that their names appeared in the Army's index (which they characterized as a "blacklist")—brought this action against Secretary of Defense Melvin Laird as a class action on behalf of all citizens similarly situated to enjoin the surveillance and to require the destruction of the records. The very existence of such a system of surveillance and data collection, plaintiffs contended, exercised an inhibiting or "chilling" effect on the exercise of First Amendment freedoms of speech, press, and association and violated their right of privacy.

The Army answered that the purpose of its activity was for preparatory planning in order for it to be ready to respond whenever it was called out to aid in quelling civil disorders, as it had been four times, and the National Guard had been eighty-three times, during 1967–68. The Army also reported that it had reviewed its system and ordered a significant reduction in its scope, including destruction of the name index and the records in the computer data bank.

The Court held that plaintiffs had no standing to maintain the action since they could not show that the Army had taken any other action against them and hence could show no "direct injury." It was not enough that "the chilling effect arise[s] merely from the individual's knowledge that a governmental agency was engaged in certain activities or from the individual's concomitant fear that, armed with the fruits of these activities the agency might in the future take some other and

[52] *Id.*, Art. II, §2, Cl. 1.
[53] *Id.*, Art. IV, §4.

additional action detrimental to that individual." Moreover, it was
doubtful that the particular plaintiffs were "in fact suffering from any
such chill' and thus had a "personal stake" in the controversy since
they had the courage to bring the action.

MR. JUSTICE DOUGLAS, dissenting.

I

If Congress had passed a law authorizing the armed services to
establish surveillance over the civilian population, a most serious constitutional problem would be presented. There is, however, no law
authorizing surveillance over civilians, which in this case the Pentagon
concededly had undertaken. The question is whether such authority
may be implied. One can search the Constitution in vain for any such
authority.

The start of the problem is the constitutional distinction between
the "militia" and the Armed Forces. By Art. I, § 8, of the Constitution
the militia is specifically confined to precise duties: "to execute the
Laws of the Union, suppress Insurrections and repel Invasions."

This obviously means that the "militia" cannot be sent overseas to
fight wars. It is purely a domestic arm of the governors of the several
States, save as it may be called under Art. I, §8, of the Constitution
into the federal service. Whether the "militia" could be given powers
comparable to those granted the FBI is a question not now raised, for
we deal here not with the "militia" but with "armies." The Army,
Navy, and Air Force are comprehended in the constitutional term
"armies." Article I, §8, provides that Congress may "raise and support
Armies," and "provide and maintain a Navy," and make "Rules for
the Government and Regulation of the land and naval Forces." And the
Fifth Amendment excepts from the requirement of a presentment or
indictment of a grand jury "cases arising in the land or naval forces,
or in the Militia, when in actual service in time of War or public
danger."

Acting under that authority, Congress has provided a code governing
the Armed Services. That code sets the procedural standards for the
Government and regulation of the land and naval forces. It is difficult
to imagine how those powers can be extended to military surveillance
over civilian affairs.

The most pointed and relevant decisions of the Court on the limitation of military authority concern the attempt of the military to try
civilians. The first leading case was *Ex parte Milligan*, 4 Wall. 2,
where the Court noted that the conflict between "civil liberty" and
"martial law" is "irreconcilable." The Court which made that announce-

ment would have been horrified at the prospect of the military—absent a regime of martial law—establishing a regime of surveillance over civilians. The power of the military to establish such a system is obviously less than the power of Congress to authorize such surveillance. For the authority of Congress is restricted by its power to "raise" armies, Art. I, §8; and, to repeat, its authority over the Armed Forces is stated in these terms, "To make Rules for the Government and Regulation of the land and naval Forces."

The Constitution contains many provisions guaranteeing rights to persons. Those include the right to indictment by a grand jury and the right to trial by a jury of one's peers. They include the procedural safeguards of the Sixth Amendment in criminal prosecutions;[54] the protection against double jeopardy, cruel and unusual punishments—and, of course, the First Amendment. The alarm was sounded in the Constitutional Convention about the dangers of the armed services. Luther Martin of Maryland said, "when a government wishes to deprive its citizens of freedom, and reduce them to slavery, it generally makes use of a standing army." That danger, we have held, exists not only in bold acts of usurpation of power, but also in gradual encroachments. We held that court-martial jurisdiction cannot be extended to reach any person not a member of the Armed Forces at the times both of the offense and of the trial, which eliminates discharged soldiers. *Toth* v. *Quarles*, 350 U.S. 11. Neither civilian employees of the Armed Forces overseas, *McElroy* v. *Guagliardo*, 361 U.S. 281; *Grisham* v. *Hagan*, 361 U.S. 278, nor civilian dependents of military personnel accompanying them overseas, *Kinsella* v. *Singleton*, 361 U.S. 234; *Reid* v. *Covert*, 354 U.S. 1, may be tried by court-martial. And even as respects those in the Armed Forces we have held that an offense must be "service connected" to be tried by court-martial rather than by a civilian tribunal. *O'Callahan* v. *Parker*, 395 U.S. 258 [p. 259, *infra.*]

The upshot is that the Armed Services—as distinguished from the "militia"—are not regulatory agencies or bureaus that may be created as Congress desires and granted such powers as seem necessary and proper. The authority to provide rules "governing" the Armed Services means the grant of authority to the Armed Services to govern themselves, not the authority to govern civilians. Even when "martial law" is declared, as it often has been, its appropriateness is subject to judicial review, *Sterling* v. *Constantin*, 287 U.S. 378, 401.

Our tradition reflects a desire for civilian supremacy and subordination of military power. The tradition goes back to the Declaration of Independence, in which it was recited that the King "has affected to

[54] [See fn. 39, *supra.*]

render the Military independent of and superior to the Civil power."
Thus, we have the "militia" restricted to domestic use, the restriction
of appropriations to the "armies" to two years, Art. I, §8, and the
grant of command over the armies and the militia when called into
actual service of the United States to the President, our chief civilian
officer. The tradition of civilian control over the Armed Forces was
stated by Chief Justice Warren:[55]

> "The military establishment is, of course, a necessary organ of
> government; but the reach of its power must be carefully limited
> lest the delicate balance between freedom and order be upset. The
> maintenance of the balance is made more difficult by the fact that
> while the military serves the vital function of preserving the exist-
> ence of the nation, it is, at the same time, the one element of
> government that exercises a type of authority not easily assimilated
> in a free society. . . .

> "In times of peace, the factors leading to an extraordinary def-
> erence to claims of military necessity have naturally not been as
> weighty. This has been true even in the all too imperfect peace
> that has been our lot for the past fifteen years—and quite rightly
> so, in my judgment. It is instructive to recall that our Nation at
> the time of the Constitutional Convention was also faced with
> formidable problems. The English, the French, the Spanish, and
> various tribes of hostile Indians were all ready and eager to subvert
> or occupy the fledgling Republic. Nevertheless, in that environ-
> ment, our Founding Fathers conceived a Constitution and Bill of
> Rights replete with provisions indicating their determination to
> protect human rights. There was no call for a garrison state in
> those times of precarious peace. We should heed no such call now.
> If we were to fail in these days to enforce the freedom that until
> now has been the American citizen's birthright, we would be aban-
> doning for the foreseeable future the constitutional balance of
> powers and rights in whose name we arm."

Thus, we have until today consistently adhered to the belief that

> "[i]t is an unbending rule of law, that the exercise of military
> power, where the rights of the citizen are concerned, shall never
> be pushed beyond what the exigency requires." *Raymond* v.
> *Thomas*, 91 U.S. 712.

It was in that tradition that *Youngstown Sheet & Tube Co.* v.
Sawyer [p. 32, *supra*] was decided, in which President Truman's

[55] The Bill of Rights and the Military, 37 N.Y.U. L. Rev. 181 (1962).

seizure of the steel mills in the so-called Korean War was held unconstitutional. As stated by Justice Black:

> "The order cannot properly be sustained as an exercise of the
> President's military power as Commander in Chief of the Armed
> Forces. The Government attempts to do so by citing a number of
> cases upholding broad powers in military commanders engaged in
> day-to-day fighting in a theater of war. Such cases need not con-
> cern us here. Even though 'theater of war' be an expanding con-
> cept, we cannot with faithfulness to our constitutional system hold
> that the Commander in Chief of the Armed Forces has the ulti-
> mate power as such to take possession of private property in order
> to keep labor disputes from stopping production. This is a job
> for the Nation's lawmakers, not for its military authorities."

The action in turning the "armies" loose on surveillance of civilians
was a gross repudiation of our traditions. The military, though important to us, is subservient and restricted purely to military missions.
It even took an Act of Congress to allow a member of the Joint Chiefs
of Staff to address the Congress;[56] and that small step did not go un-
noticed but was in fact viewed with alarm by those respectful of the
civilian tradition. Walter Lippmann has written that during World
War II, he was asked to convey a message to Winston Churchill, while
the latter was in Washington together with his chiefs of staff. It was
desired that Churchill should permit his chiefs of staff to testify before
Congress as to the proper strategy for waging the war. Lippmann ex-
plains, however, that he "never finished the message. For the old lion
let out a roar demanding to know why I was so ignorant of the British
way of doing things that I could dare to suggest that a British general
should address a parliamentary body.

> "As I remember it, what he said was 'I am the Minister of
> Defense and I, not the generals, will state the policy of His
> Majesty's government.'" The Intervention of the General, Wash-
> ington Post, Apr. 27, 1967.

The act of turning the military loose on civilians even if sanctioned
by an Act of Congress, which it has not been, would raise serious and

---

[56] The National Security Act of 1947, amended by the Act of Aug. 10, 1949,
provided:

"No provision of this Act shall be so construed as to prevent a Secretary of a
military department or a member of the Joint Chiefs of Staff from presenting to
the Congress, on his own initiative, after first so informing the Secretary of Defense,
any recommendation relating to the Department of Defense that he may deem
proper."

profound constitutional questions. Standing as it does only on brute power and Pentagon policy, it must be repudiated as a usurpation dangerous to the civil liberties on which free men are dependent. For, as Senator Sam Ervin has said, "this claim of an inherent executive branch power of investigation and surveillance on the basis of people's beliefs and attitudes may be more of a threat to our internal security than any enemies beyond our borders." Privacy and Government Investigations, 1971 U. Ill. L. F. 137.

II

The claim that respondents have no standing to challenge the Army's surveillance of them and the other members of the class they seek to represent is too transparent for serious argument. The surveillance of the Army over the civilian sector—a part of society hitherto immune from its control—is a serious charge. It is alleged that the Army maintains files on the membership, ideology, programs, and practices of virtually every activist political group in the country, including groups such as the Southern Christian Leadership Conference, Clergy and Laymen United Against the War in Vietnam, the American Civil Liberties Union, Women's Strike for Peace, and the National Association for the Advancement of Colored People. The Army uses undercover agents to infiltrate these civilian groups and to reach into confidential files of students and other groups. The Army moves as a secret group among civilian audiences, using cameras and electronic cars for surveillance. The data it collects are distributed to civilian officials in state, federal, and local governments and to each military intelligence unit and troop command under the Army's jurisdiction (both here and abroad); and these data are stored in one or more data banks.

Those are the allegations; and the charge is that the purpose and effect of the system of surveillance is to harass and intimidate the respondents and to deter them from exercising their rights of political expression, protest, and dissent "by invading their privacy, damaging their reputations, adversely affecting their employment and their opportunities for employment, and in other ways." Their fear is that "permanent reports of their activities will be maintained in the Army's data bank, and their 'profiles' will appear in the so-called 'Blacklist' and that all of this information will be released to numerous federal and state agencies upon request."

Judge Wilkey, speaking for the Court of Appeals, properly inferred that this Army surveillance "exercises a *present inhibiting effect* on their full expression and utilization of their First Amendment rights." That is the test. The "deterrent effect" on First Amendment rights by government oversight marks an unconstitutional intrusion, *Lamont* v. *Postmaster General*, 381 U.S. 301. Or, as stated by MR. JUSTICE BRENNAN, "inhibition as well as prohibition against the exercise of precious First Amendment rights is a power denied to government." When refusal of the Court to pass on the constitutionality of an Act under the normal consideration of forbearance "would itself have an inhibitory effect on freedom of speech" then the Court will act. *United States* v. *Raines*, 362 U.S. 17.

As stated by the Supreme Court of New Jersey, "there is good reason to permit the strong to speak for the weak or the timid in First Amendment matters." *Anderson* v. *Sills*, 56 N.J. 210, 265 A. 2d 678, (1970).

One need not wait to sue until he loses his job or until his reputation is defamed. To withhold standing to sue until that time arrives would in practical effect immunize from judicial scrutiny all surveillance activities, regardless of their misuse and their deterrent effect.

The present controversy is not a remote, imaginary conflict. Respondents were targets of the Army's surveillance. First, the surveillance was not casual but massive and comprehensive. Second, the intelligence reports were regularly and widely circulated and were exchanged with reports of the FBI, state and municipal police departments, and the CIA. Third, the Army's surveillance was not collecting material in public records but staking out teams of agents, infiltrating undercover agents, creating command posts inside meetings, posing as press photographers and newsmen, posing as TV newsmen, posing as students, and shadowing public figures.

Finally, we know from the hearings conducted by Senator Ervin that the Army has misused or abused its reporting functions. Thus, Senator Ervin concluded that reports of the Army have been "taken from the Intelligence Command's highly inaccurate civil disturbance teletype and filed in Army dossiers on persons who have held, or were being considered for, security clearances, thus contaminating what are supposed to be investigative reports with unverified gossip and rumor. This practice directly jeopardized the employment and employment opportunities of persons seeking sensitive positions with the federal government or defense industry."

Surveillance of civilians is none of the Army's constitutional business and Congress has not undertaken to entrust it with any such function. The fact that since this litigation started the Army's surveillance may have been cut back is not an end of the matter. Whether there has been an actual cutback or whether the announcements are merely a ruse can be determined only after a hearing in the District Court. We are advised by an *amicus curiae* brief field by a group of former Army

Intelligence Agents that Army surveillance of civilians is rooted in secret programs of long standing:

> "Army intelligence has been maintaining an unauthorized watch over civilian political activity for nearly 30 years. Nor is this the first time that Army intelligence has, without notice to its civilian superiors, overstepped its mission. From 1917 to 1924, the Corps of Intelligence Police maintained a massive surveillance of civilian political activity which involved the use of hundreds of civilian informants, the infiltration of civilian organizations and the seizure of dissenters and unionists, sometimes without charges. That activity was opposed—then as now—by civilian officials on those occasions when they found out about it, but it continued unabated until post-war disarmament and economies finally eliminated the bureaucracy that conducted it."

This case involves a cancer in our body politic. It is a measure of the disease which afflicts us. Army surveillance, like Army regimentation, is at war with the principles of the First Amendment. Those who already walk submissively will say there is no cause for alarm. But submissiveness is not our heritage. The First Amendment was designed to allow rebellion to remain as our heritage. The Constitution was designed to keep government off the backs of the people. The Bill of Rights was added to keep the precincts of belief and expression, of the press, of political and social activities free from surveillance. The Bill of Rights was designed to keep agents of government and official eavesdroppers away from assemblies of people. The aim was to allow men to be free and independent and to assert their rights against government. There can be no influence more paralyzing of that objective than Army surveillance. When an intelligence officer looks over every nonconformist's shoulder in the library, or walks invisibly by his side in a picket line, or infiltrates his club, the America once extolled as the voice of liberty heard around the world no longer is cast in the image which Jefferson and Madison designed, but more in the Russian image.

The Judiciary

Chandler v. Judicial Council
398 U.S. 74 (1970)

The Constitution clearly contemplates independent federal judges to exercise the "judicial Power of the United States" vested by Article III in "one supreme Court, and in such inferior Courts as the Congress may from time to time ordain and establish."[57] *It provides that those judges "shall hold their Offices during good Behaviour, and shall . . . receive for their Services, a Compensation, which shall not be diminished during their Continuance in Office."*[58] *It also provides that they are subject, like other civil officers, to removal from office by "Impeachment for, and Conviction of, Treason, Bribery, or other high Crimes and Misdemeanors"*[59] *on charges filed by the House*[60] *and tried by the Senate.*[61]

In the exercise of its power to create inferior federal courts, Congress has created a basic system of federal district courts, consisting of one or more district judges, subject to review by federal courts of appeals sitting in eleven federal judicial circuits, whose decisions, in turn, are subject to review by the Supreme Court. Other federal statutes provide that the business of federal district courts having more than one judge shall be divided among the judges as provided by rules and orders of the judges, that if they are unable to agree upon the adoption of such rules and orders the necessary orders shall be made by the Judicial Council consisting of all circuit judges on regular active service in the circuit, and that each Judicial Council shall make all necessary orders for the administration of business of all courts within the circuit, which orders shall be promptly carried into effect by the district judges.

On December 13, 1965, the Judicial Council of the tenth circuit, after a long history of controversy with Chief Judge Stephen Chandler of the district court for the western district of Oklahoma, a multi-judge court, issued an order withdrawing all cases currently assigned to him for decision and directing that no new cases be so assigned "until the further order of the Judicial Council." When the Court denied Chandler's application to review this action on the ground that it was only a temporary order pending further inquiry by the Judicial Council, Douglas joined in a dissent on the ground that, whether temporary or final, the order was clearly unconstitutional since federal district judges could not be made "to account to superior court judges or to anyone else except the Senate sitting as a court of impeachment."[62] *Thereafter, the Judicial Council modified its order to permit Chandler to dispose of pending cases but to forbid assignment of new cases to him until further order of the council. The Supreme Court again rejected Chandler's application for review of this action,*

---

[57] U.S. Const., Art. III, §1.
[58] *Id.*
[59] *Id.*, Art. II, §4.
[60] *Id.*, Art. I, §2, Cl. 5.
[61] *Id.*, §3, Cl. 6.
[62] *Chandler v. Judicial Council*, 382 U.S. 1003 (1966).

this time because he had not yet sought relief from it before the Judicial Council.

MR. JUSTICE DOUGLAS, dissenting.

Some functions performed by a Judicial Council may be "administrative." But where, as here, it moves to disqualify a judge from sitting, removing him *pro tanto* from office, it moves against the individual with all of the sting and much of the stigma that impeachment carries.

The order of December 13, 1965, may have been qualified but it has not been erased. Petitioner still is disqualified to sit on incoming cases. He still carries the stigma of the brand put on him by the Council.

An independent judiciary is one of this Nation's outstanding characteristics. Once a federal judge is confirmed by the Senate and takes his oath, he is independent of every other judge. He commonly works with other federal judges who are likewise sovereign. But neither one alone nor any number banded together can act as censor and place sanctions on him. Under the Constitution the only leverage that can be asserted against him is impeachment, where pursuant to a resolution passed by the House, he is tried by the Senate, sitting as a jury. Our tradition even bars political impeachments as evidenced by the highly partisan, but unsuccessful, effort to oust Justice Samuel Chase of this Court in 1805.[63] The Impeachment Provision of the Constitution indeed provides for the removal of "Officers of the United States," which includes judges, on "Impeachment for, and Conviction of, Treason, Bribery, or other high Crimes and Misdemeanors."

What the Judicial Council did when it ordered petitioner to "take no action whatsoever in any case or proceeding now or hereafter pending" in his court was to do what only the Court of Impeachment can do. If the business of the federal courts needs administrative oversight, the flow of cases can be regulated. Some judges work more slowly than others; some cases may take months while others take hours or days. Matters of this kind may be regulated by the assignment procedure. But there is no power under our Constitution for one group of federal judges to censor or discipline any federal judge and no power to declare him inefficient and strip him of his power to act as a judge.

The mood of some federal judges is opposed to this view and they are active in attempting to make all federal judges walk in some uniform step. What has happened to petitioner is not a rare instance; it has happened to other federal judges who have had perhaps a more

[63] See Trial of Samuel Chase, vols. 1 and 2 (1805, taken in shorthand by Samuel H. Smith and Thomas Lloyd).

libertarian approach to the Bill of Rights than their brethren. The result is that the nonconformist has suffered greatly at the hands of his fellow judges.

The problem is not resolved by saying that only judicial administrative matters are involved. The power to keep a particular judge from sitting on a racial case, a church-and-state case, a free-press case, a search-and-seizure case, a railroad case, an antitrust case, or a union case may have profound consequences. Judges are not fungible; they cover the constitutional spectrum; and a particular judge's emphasis may make a world of difference when it comes to rulings on evidence, the temper of the courtroom, the tolerance for a proffered defense, and the like. Lawyers recognize this when they talk about "shopping" for a judge; Senators recognize this when they are asked to give their "advice and consent" to judicial appointments; laymen recognize this when they appraise the quality and image of the judiciary in their own community.

These are subtle, imponderable factors which other judges should not be allowed to manipulate to further their own concept of the public good. That is the crucial issue at the heart of the present controversy.

All power is a heady thing as evidenced by the increasing efforts of groups of federal judges to act as referees over other federal judges.

On June 10, 1969, the Judicial Conference[64] adopted resolutions for the governance of many activities of circuit judges and districts judges. Resolution I provided:[65]

---

[64] [The Judicial Conference of the United States is made up of the Chief Justice of the United States, the Chief Judge of each judicial circuit, the Chief Judge of the special Court of Customs and Patent Appeals, and one district judge from each judicial circuit chosen by the circuit and district judges of the circuit. Its statutory mandate is "to make a comprehensive survey of the condition of business in the courts of the United States and prepare plans for the assignment of judges to or from circuits or districts where necessary," and "[to] submit suggestions to the various courts, in the interest of uniformity and the expedition of business."]

[65] Resolution I was suspended on November 1, 1969, by the Judicial Conference pending further study, the only residue presently in force being a requirement that a judge who in any quarterly period "receives compensation for non-judicial services in a total amount exceeding $100" shall report the same to a "receiving officer" named by the Chief Justice and acting for the federal judges. In March 1970, the Judicial Conference approved procedures and forms for judges to report outside income pursuant to the Conference Resolution of November 1, 1969. The approved form requires listing of outside income received by the judge, gifts received by the judge or his immediate family in excess of $100, any knowing participation in cases in which the judge or a member of his immediate family had a financial interest in any of the named parties, and all "fiduciary positions" held by the judge, "such as trustee or executor."

"A judge in regular active service shall not accept compensation of any kind, whether in the form of loans, gifts, gratuities, honoraria or otherwise, for services hereafter performed or to be performed by him except that provided by law for the performance of his judicial duties.

"Provided however, the judicial council of the circuit (or in the case of courts not part of a circuit, the judges of the court in active service) *may upon application of a judge* approve the acceptance of compensation for the performance of services other than his judicial duties *upon a determination that the services are in the public interest or are justified by exceptional circumstances and that the services will not interfere with his judicial duties.* Both the services to be performed and the compensation to be paid shall be made a matter of public record and reported to the Judicial Conference of the United States." (Italics added.)

In the Ninth Circuit, of which I am Circuit Justice, this resolution was assumed to bar a federal judge from even being an executor of his own mother's estate, unless of course he got a permit from the other judges. Resolution I apparently required permits for federal judges to teach in a law school—a practice which has paid enormous professional dividends and implicates nothing but the interest and energy of the judge. Justice Joseph Story (who sat here from 1811 to 1845) would, I imagine, have been appalled if he had been told that he could not write any of his many books[66] without getting permission from a group of other federal judges. And I imagine that Justice Cardozo, Judge Jerome Frank, and Judge Learned Hand would have felt the same.[67]

To obtain a permit the other judges must determine if the services are "in the public interest." Pray, how could they determine that unless they saw the lecture, or the lecture notes, or the manuscript? And

[66] Commentaries on Equity Jurisprudence (2 vols., 1836); Commentaries on Equity Pleadings (1838); Commentaries on the Conflict of Laws (1834); Commentaries on the Constitution of the United States (3 vols., 1833); Commentaries on the Law of Agency (1839); Commentaries on the Law of Bailments (1832); Commentaries on the Law of Bills of Exchange (1843); Commentaries on the Law of Partnership (1841); Commentaries on the Law of Promissory Notes (1845); A Familiar Exposition of the Constitution of the United States (1840); A Selection of Pleadings in Civil Actions (1805).

[67] Justice Cardozo: The Growth of the Law (1931); Law and Literature and Other Essays and Addresses (1931); The Nature of the Judicial Process (1921).

Judge Learned Hand: The Bill of Rights (1958).

Judge Jerome Frank: Courts on Trial—Myth and Reality in American Justice (1949); Not Guilty (1957); If Men Were Angels (1942); Fate and Freedom (1945).

whose "public interest" would control? Judges who have not been educated to the needs of ecology and of conservation? Judges who still have a "plantation" state of mind and relegate many minorities to second-class citizenship? Judges who have a narrow view of freedom of expression or a broad view of due process? Public issues deal with a vast contrariety of views; and judges, like other people, are to be found in all parts of the spectrum. How under the Constitution can one judge's lips be sealed because of the predestined view of other judges? An easy reply is that Resolution I covered only services for "compensation." But books entail royalties; and tax-wise it is not always easy to disassociate an author from royalties. Even though they go ultimately to charity, they pass through his income tax returns.

It is time that an end be put to these efforts of federal judges to ride herd on other federal judges. This is a form of "hazing" having no place under the Constitution. Federal judges are entitled, like other people, to the full freedom of the First Amendment. If they break a law, they can be prosecuted. If they become corrupt or sit in cases in which they have a personal or family stake, they can be impeached by Congress. But I search the Constitution in vain for any power of surveillance that other federal judges have over those aberrations. Some of the idiosyncrasies may be displeasing to those who walk in more measured, conservative steps. But those idiosyncrasies can be of no possible constitutional concern to other federal judges.

It is time we put an end to the monstrous practices that seem about to overtake us, by vacating the orders of the Judicial Council that brand Judge Chandler as unfit to sit in oncoming cases. Only Congress can take action, unless the Constitution is amended to allow judges to censor, police, or impeach their fellow judges.

In April 1970, two months before the second Chandler *case was decided, a resolution was introduced in the House of Representatives to impeach Justice Douglas. Its principal sponsors were Gerald Ford, then House minority leader and later President by double default, and Congressman Louis Wyman, otherwise then renowned only as a one-man Un-American Activities Committee in the state of New Hampshire while serving as its Attorney General, and later only as a participant in a closely contested race for the United States Senate (p. 12, supra).*

Their action was not unexpected. In November, 1969, while President Nixon's nomination of Clement Haynsworth, Jr., for appointment to the Supreme Court was encountering heavy opposition, and shortly before it was rejected by the Senate, Ford had publicly stated that if Haynsworth were not confirmed Douglas should be impeached. The impeachment resolution was introduced just one week after the Senate had rejected Nixon's second nominee to the Court, G. Harrold Carswell.

The list of charges tendered by Ford and Wyman against Douglas ranged from the February 1970 publication of his book Points of Rebellion, in which he allegedly incited "violence, anarchy and civil unrest," to his service as president and a director of the Parvin Foundation from 1960 to 1969 at a salary of $12,000 per year, the foundation allegedly receiving "substantial income from gambling interests" in Nevada.

A special subcommittee of the House Judiciary Committee investigated the charges and filed its report in December 1970. It found Points of Rebellion "not a call to violence but . . . a warning of rebellion . . . if divergent forces in society are not successfully assimilated under established order of law." It also found that Douglas had been associated in the Parvin Foundation with such noncriminal types as Robert Maynard Hutchins, former chancellor of the University of Chicago, Robert Goheen, president of Princeton University, and newspaperman Harry Ashmore; that the only link between Douglas and gambling elements was that the foundation was originally founded and, for a period, funded from the proceeds of the sale of a Nevada hotel by the Parvin-Dohrman Company; that the motivation for the foundation's creation was the stimulation received by Mr. Albert Parvin of that company from Douglas' 1960 book, America Challenged; that the foundation's principal functions were to provide financial aid for study in the United States by citizens from underdeveloped countries and to send lecturers and educational films to those countries; and that Douglas paid his own travel and other expenses incurred in behalf of the foundation out of the $1,000-a-month salary he received.

The subcommittee concluded that neither these nor any other charges would support endorsement by the House as impeachable offenses, and the House took no further action. Such disparate observers as editorial writers for the Washington Post, the New York Times and the Wall Street Journal concluded that the charges stated by Ford and Wyman were not the real charges—that their real objection to Justice Douglas was his judicial record.

PIERSON V. RAY
386 U.S. 547 (1967)

The Constitution is silent as to judicial immunity as it is as to executive immunity. But at common law, judges enjoyed absolute immunity for their judicial acts. In an early case[68] the Supreme Court adopted

[68] Bradley v. Fisher, 13 Wall. 335 (1872).

the common law immunity as applicable to protect a judge of a District of Columbia court from a damage action for erroneously disbarring an attorney, explaining that it "is not for the protection or benefit of a malicious or corrupt judge, but for the benefit of the public, whose interest it is that the judges should be at liberty to exercise their functions with independence, and without fear of consequences."

In this case a group of black and white clergymen had attempted to use segregated facilities of an interstate bus terminal in Jackson, Mississippi, and had been convicted in a municipal court of violating a state statute making it a crime to congregate in a public place under circumstances which might cause a breach of the peace and to refuse to disperse when ordered to do so by a police officer. On appeal, a new trial was ordered for one of them in a county court, and, when that trial resulted in a directed verdict of acquittal, the cases against the other defendants were dropped.

They then brought this action for damages against the municipal court judge and the police officers who arrested them under the federal Civil Rights Act involved in the Tenney *case [p. 3, supra] prescribing liability for "every person" who under color of law intentionally and knowingly deprives another of his rights under the federal Constitution and laws. Meanwhile, the state statute involved had been held invalid as applied in similar cases because it conflicted with a prohibition in the federal Interstate Commerce Act against discrimination in interstate bus facilities.[69] The Court held that the Civil Rights Act had in no way impaired the common law's absolute immunity for judges in their judicial acts and that the police officers had a qualified common law immunity which would protect them from liability if it was found, on retrial, that they acted in the good faith belief that the statute they were enforcing was constitutional and that the arrests were necessary to avoid violence from bystanders in the bus terminal.*

MR. JUSTICE DOUGLAS, dissenting.

I do not think that all judges, under all circumstances, no matter how outrageous their conduct are immune from suit under [the Civil Rights Act]. The Court's ruling is not justified by the admitted need for a vigorous and independent judiciary, is not commanded by the common-law doctrine of judicial immunity, and does not follow inexorably from our prior decisions.

The statute, which came on the books as §1 of the Ku Klux Klan Act of April 20, 1871, provides that "every person" who under color of state law or custom "subjects, or causes to be subjected, any citizen

[69] *Thomas* v. *Mississippi,* 380 U.S. 524 (1965).

. . . to the deprivation of any rights, privileges, or immunities secured by the Constitution and laws, shall be liable to the party injured in an action at law, suit in equity, or other proper proceeding for redress." To most, "every person" would mean *every person*, not every person *except* judges. Despite the plain import of those words, the Court decided in *Tenney v. Brandhove* [p. 3, *supra*] that state legislators are immune from suit as long as the deprivation of civil rights which they caused a person occurred while the legislators "were acting in a field where legislators traditionally have power to act." I dissented from the creation of that judicial exception as I do from the creation of the present one.

The congressional purpose seems to me to be clear. A condition of lawlessness existed in certain of the States, under which people were being denied their civil rights. Congress intended to provide a remedy for the wrongs being perpetrated. And its members were not unaware that certain members of the judiciary were implicated in the state of affairs which the statute was intended to rectify. It was often noted that "[i]mmunity is given to crime, and the records of the public tribunals are searched in vain for any evidence of effective redress."

Mr. Rainey of South Carolina noted that "[T]he courts are in many instances under the control of those who are wholly inimical to the impartial administration of law and equity." Congressman Beatty of Ohio claimed that it was the duty of Congress to listen to the appeals of those who "by reason of popular sentiment or secret organizations or prejudiced juries or bribed judges, [cannot] obtain the rights and privileges due an American citizen. . . ." The members supporting the proposed measure were apprehensive that there had been a complete breakdown in the administration of justice in certain States and that laws nondiscriminatory on their face were being applied in a discriminatory manner, that the newly won civil rights of the Negro were being ignored, and that the Constitution was being defied. It was against this background that the section was passed, and it is against this background that it should be interpreted.

It is said that, at the time of the statute's enactment, the doctrine of judicial immunity was well settled and that Congress cannot be presumed to have intended to abrogate the doctrine since it did not clearly evince such a purpose. This view is beset by many difficulties. It assumes that Congress could and should specify in advance all the possible circumstances to which a remedial statute might apply and state which cases are within the scope of a statute.

"Underlying [this] view is an atomistic conception of intention, coupled with what may be called a pointer theory of meaning.

This view conceives the mind to be directed toward individual things, rather than toward general ideas, toward distinct situations of fact rather than toward some significance in human affairs that these situations may share. If this view were taken seriously, then we would have to regard the intention of the draftsman of a statute directed against 'dangerous weapons' as being directed toward an endless series of individual objects: revolvers, automatic pistols, daggers, Bowie knives, etc. If a court applies the statute to a weapon its draftsman had not thought of, then it would be 'legislating,' not 'interpreting,' as even more obviously it would be if it were to apply the statute to a weapon not yet invented when the statute was passed." Fuller, The Morality of Law 84 (1964).

Congress of course acts in the context of existing common-law rules, and in construing a statute a court considers the "common law before the making of the Act." *Heydon's Case,* 3 Co. Rep. 7a, 76 Eng. Rep. 637 (Ex. 1584). But Congress enacts a statute to remedy the inadequacies of the pre-existing law, including the common law. It cannot be presumed that the common law is the perfection of reason, is superior to statutory law, and that the legislature always changes law for the worse. Nor should the canon of construction "statutes in derogation of the common law are to be strictly construed" be applied so as to weaken a remedial statute whose purpose is to remedy the defects of the pre-existing law.

The position that Congress did not intend to change the common-law rule of judicial immunity ignores the fact that every member of Congress who spoke to the issue assumed that the words of the statute meant what they said and that judges would be liable. Many members of Congress objected to the statute because it imposed liability on members of the judiciary. Mr. Arthur of Kentucky opposed the measure because:

"Hitherto . . . no judge or court has been held liable, civilly or criminally, for judicial acts . . . . Under the provisions of [section 1] every judge in the State court . . . will enter upon and pursue the call of official duty with the sword of Damocles suspended over him . . . ."

And Senator Thurman noted that:

"There have been two or three instances already under the civil rights bill of State judges being taken into the United States district court, sometimes upon indictment for the offense . . . of honestly and conscientiously deciding the law to be as they understood it to be. . . .

"Is [section 1] intended to perpetuate that? Is it intended to enlarge it? Is it intended to extend it so that no longer a judge sitting on the bench to decide causes can decide them free from any fear except that of impeachment, which never lies in the absence of corrupt motive? Is that to be extended, so that every judge of a State may be liable to be dragged before some Federal judge to vindicate his opinion and to be mulcted in damages if that Federal judge shall think the opinion was erroneous? That is the language of this bill."

Mr. Lewis of Kentucky expressed the fear that:

"By the first section, in certain cases, the judge of a State court, though acting under oath of office, is made liable to a suit in the Federal court and subject to damages for his decision against a suitor. . . ."

Yet despite the repeated fears of its opponents, and the explicit recognition that the section would subject judges to suit, the section remained as it was proposed: it applied to "any person."[70] There was no exception for members of the judiciary. In light of the sharply contested nature of the issue of judicial immunity it would be reasonable to assume that the judiciary would have been expressly exempted from the wide sweep of the section, if Congress had intended such a result.

The section's purpose was to provide redress for the deprivation of civil rights. It was recognized that certain members of the judiciary were instruments of oppression and were partially responsible for the wrongs to be remedied. The parade of cases coming to this Court shows that a similar condition now obtains in some of the States. Some state courts have been instruments of suppression of civil rights. The methods may have changed; the means may have become more subtle; but the wrong to be remedied still exists.

Today's decision is not dictated by our prior decisions. In Ex parte Virginia, 100 U.S. 339, the Court held that a judge who excluded Negroes from juries could be held liable under the Act of March 1, 1875, one of the Civil Rights Acts. The Court assumed that the judge was merely performing a ministerial function. But it went on to state that the judge would be liable under the statute even if his actions were judicial.[71] It is one thing to say that the common-law doctrine of

---

[70] As altered by the reviser who prepared the Revised Statutes of 1878, the statute refers to "every person" rather than to "any person."

[71] The opinion in Ex parte Virginia, supra, did not mention Bradley v. Fisher [note 68, supra], which held that a judge could not be held liable for causing the name of an attorney to be struck from the court rolls. But in Bradley, the action was not brought under any of the Civil Rights Acts.

judicial immunity is a defense to a common-law cause of action. But it is quite another to say that the common-law immunity rule is a defense to liability which Congress has imposed upon "any officer or other person," as in *Ex parte Virginia*, or upon "every person" as in these cases.

The immunity which the Court today grants the judiciary is not necessary to preserve an independent judiciary. If the threat of civil action lies in the background of litigation, so the argument goes, judges will be reluctant to exercise the discretion and judgment inherent in their position and vital to the effective operation of the judiciary. We should, of course, not protect a member of the judiciary "who is in fact guilty of using his powers to vent his spleen upon others, or for any other personal motive not connected with the public good." *Gregoire* v. *Biddle*, 177 F.2d 579. To deny recovery to a person injured by the ruling of a judge acting for personal gain or out of personal motives would be "monstrous." But, it is argued that absolute immunity is necessary to prevent the chilling effects of a judicial inquiry, or the threat of such inquiry, into whether, in fact, a judge has been unfaithful to his oath of office. Thus, it is necessary to protect the guilty as well as the innocent.[72]

The doctrine of separation of powers is, of course, applicable only to the relations of coordinate branches of the same government, not to the relations between the branches of the Federal Government and those of the States. See *Baker* v. *Carr*, 369 U.S. 186. Any argument that Congress could not impose liability on state judges for the deprivation of civil rights would thus have to be based upon the claim that doing so would violate the theory of division of powers between the Federal and State Governments. This claim has been foreclosed by the cases recognizing "that Congress has the power to enforce provisions of the Fourteenth Amendment against those who carry a badge of authority of a State . . . ." *Monroe* v. *Pape*, 365 U.S. 167. In terms of the power of Congress, I can see no difference between imposing liability on a state police officer (*Monroe* v. *Pape*, *supra*) and on a state judge. The question presented is not of constitutional dimension; it is solely a question of statutory interpretation.

The argument that the actions of public officials must not be sub-

---

[72] Other justifications for the doctrine of absolute immunity have been advanced: (1) preventing threat of suit from influencing decision; (2) protecting judges from liability for honest mistakes; (3) relieving judges of the time and expense of defending suits; (4) removing an impediment to responsible men entering the judiciary; (5) necessity of finality; (6) appellate review is satisfactory remedy; (7) the judge's duty is to the public and not to the individual; (8) judicial self-protection; (9) separation of powers. See generally Jennings, Tort Liability of Administrative Officers, 21 Minn. L. Rev. 263 (1937).

jected to judicial scrutiny because to do so would have an inhibiting effect on their work, is but a more sophisticated manner of saying "The King can do no wrong."[73] Chief Justice Cockburn long ago disposed of the argument that liability would deter judges:

> "I cannot believe that judges . . . would fail to discharge their duty faithfully and fearlessly according to their oaths and consciences . . . from any fear of exposing themselves to actions at law. I am persuaded that the number of such actions would be infinitely small and would be easily disposed of. While, on the other hand, I can easily conceive cases in which judicial opportunity might be so perverted and abused for the purpose of injustice as that, on sound principles, the authors of such wrong ought to be responsible to the parties wronged." *Dawkins* v. *Lord Paulet*, L. R. 5 Q. B. 94. (C. J. Cockburn, dissenting).

This is not to say that a judge who makes an honest mistake should be subjected to civil liability. It is necessary to exempt judges from liability for the consequences of their honest mistakes. The judicial function involves an informed exercise of judgment. It is often necessary to choose between differing versions of fact, to reconcile opposing interests, and to decide closely contested issues. Decisions must often be made in the heat of trial. A vigorous and independent mind is needed to perform such delicate tasks. It would be unfair to require a judge to exercise his independent judgment and then to punish him for having exercised it in a manner which, in retrospect, was erroneous. Imposing liability for mistaken, though honest judicial acts, would curb the independent mind and spirit needed to perform judicial functions. Thus, a judge who sustains a conviction on what he forthrightly considers adequate evidence should not be subjected to liability when an appellate court decides that the evidence was not adequate. Nor should a judge who allows a conviction under what is later held an unconstitutional statute.

But that is far different from saying that a judge shall be immune from the consequences of any of his judicial actions, and that he shall not be liable for the knowing and intentional deprivation of a person's civil rights. What about the judge who conspires with local law enforcement officers to "railroad" a dissenter? What about the judge who knowingly turns a trial into a "kangaroo" court? Or one who in-

---

[73] Historically judicial immunity was a corollary to that theory. Since the King could do no wrong, the judges, his delegates for dispensing justice, "ought not to be drawn into question for any supposed corruption [for this tends] to the slander of the justice of the King." *Floyd & Barker*, 12 Co. Rep. 23, 77 Eng. Rep. 1305 (Star Chamber 1607). Because the judges were the personal delegates of the King they should be answerable to him alone. *Randall* v. *Brigham*, 7 Wall. 523, 539.

tentionally flouts the Constitution in order to obtain a conviction? Congress, I think, concluded that the evils of allowing intentional, knowing deprivations of civil rights to go unredressed far outweighed the speculative inhibiting effects which might attend an inquiry into a judicial deprivation of civil rights.

NYE V. UNITED STATES
313 U.S. 33 (1941)

Included in the judicial power that the Constitution vests in the federal courts,[74] and that state constitutions vest in state courts, is the power to punish for contempt of court. That power may be exercised through a civil contempt proceeding for continuing contempts, which puts the contemnor under continuing incarceration, or increasing fines, or both until the contempt ceases. Or it may be exercised through a criminal contempt proceeding, which punishes the contemnor with a fixed sentence, or fine, or both, for past contempts.

Originally, the constitutional guarantees of indictment by grand jury[75] and trial by petit jury[76] in all criminal prosecutions were not viewed as applying to criminal contempt proceedings, which were considered not to be criminal prosecutions but rather the exercise by judges of an "inherent" power to vindicate their authority. Hence, the first Judiciary Act of 1789 provided that the federal courts should have power "to punish by fine or imprisonment, at the discretion of said courts, all contempts of authority in any cause or hearing," before them, and this power was exercised summarily by the judges, without a jury. But dissatisfaction with the manner in which some judges exercised this summary power led in 1831 to a statute which restricted the summary contempt power to cases of disobedience of court orders, misbehavior of court officials, and misbehavior of other persons "in the presence of said courts, or so near thereto as to obstruct the administration of justice." The same statute required that, for other forms of criminal contempt, prosecution should be on indictment as for other federal criminal offenses.

In an 1918 case in which Justices Holmes and Brandeis dissented,[77] the Court upheld an exercise of summary contempt power to punish newspaper publication of articles found to be intended to intimidate or unduly influence a federal judge's disposition of a pending case, although the defendants had neither published nor distributed the articles

---

[74] See p. 58, *supra*.
[75] U.S. Const., Fifth Amendment.
[76] *Id.*, Art. III, §2, Cl. 3; *Id.*, Sixth Amendment.
[77] *Toledo Newspaper Co.* v. *United States*, 247 U.S. 402 (1918).

in close proximity to the courtroom. The 1831 statute, said the Court, covered acts which had a "reasonable tendency" to obstruct the administration of justice. The connection between the act and the obstruction must be causal, not geographical.

This case arose out of a suit brought in a federal district court in North Carolina by one Elmore, who was "illiterate and feeble in mind and body," to recover from the manufacturers of a medicine which allegedly caused the death of his son. Nye, who was the father-in-law of one of the defendants in that action, and Mayers, who was Nye's tenant and acquainted with Elmore, induced Elmore, "through the use of liquor and persuasion," to attempt to dismiss his suit. To that end, Nye had his lawyer prepare for Elmore letters to the federal district court and to Elmore's attorney stating that he desired to have the case dismissed. Nye then took Elmore to the post office where the letters were mailed after he registered and paid the postage on them. Nye also had his lawyer prepare the necessary papers to have Elmore discharged as administrator of his son's estate, took Elmore to the state probate court and secured his discharge, and paid the clerk of that court a one-dollar fee. All of the acts of Nye and Mayers took place more than one hundred miles from Durham, North Carolina, where the federal district court sat.

When these matters later come to that court's attention, it held, after a hearing without indictment or jury, that Nye and Mayers were guilty of criminal contempt and fined Nye $500 and Mayers $250.

MR. JUSTICE DOUGLAS delivered the opinion of the Court.

The question is whether the conduct of petitioners constituted "misbehavior . . . so near" the presence of the court "as to obstruct the administration of justice" within the meaning of [the Act of 1831]. The Act of 1789 provided that courts of the United States "shall have power . . . to punish by fine or imprisonment, at the discretion of said courts, all contempts of authority in any cause or hearing before the same." Abuses arose, culminating in impeachment proceedings against James H. Peck, a federal district judge, who had imprisoned and disbarred one Lawless for publishing a criticism of one of his opinions in a case which was on appeal. Judge Peck was acquitted. But the history of that episode makes abundantly clear that it served as the occasion for a drastic delimitation by Congress of the broad undefined power of the inferior federal courts under the Act of 1789.

The day after Judge Peck's acquittal Congress took steps to change the Act of 1789. The House directed its Committee on the Judiciary "to inquire into the expediency of defining by statute all offences which may be punished as contempts of the courts of the United States, and also to limit the punishment for the same." Nine days later James Buchanan brought in a bill which became the Act of 1831. He had charge of the prosecution of Judge Peck and during the trial had told the Senate: "I will venture to predict, that whatever may be the decision of the Senate upon this impeachment, Judge Peck has been the last man in the United States to exercise this power, and Mr. Lawless has been its last victim."

In 1918 this Court in *Toledo Newspaper Co.* v. *United States,* 247 U.S. 402, stated that "there can be no doubt" that the Act of 1831 "conferred no power not already granted and imposed no limitations not already existing"; and that it was "intended to prevent the danger by reminiscence of what had gone before, of attempts to exercise a power not possessed which . . . had been sometimes done in the exercise of legislative power." The inaccuracy of that historic observation has been plainly demonstrated. Frankfurter & Landis, *Power of Congress Over Procedure in Criminal Contempts in "Inferior" Federal Courts—A Study in Separation of Powers,* 37 Harv. L. Rev. 1010. Congress was responding to grievances arising out of the exercise of judicial power as dramatized by the Peck impeachment proceedings. Congress was intent on curtailing that power. The Act of 1831 clearly indicates that the category of criminal cases which could be tried without a jury was narrowly confined. That the previously undefined power of the courts was substantially curtailed by that Act was early recognized by lower federal courts. And when the Act came before this Court in *Ex parte Robinson,* 19 Wall. 505, Mr. Justice Field, speaking for the Court, acknowledged that it had limited the power of those courts. So far as the decisions of this Court are concerned, that view persisted to the time when *Toledo Newspaper Co.* v. *United States, supra,* was decided.

Mindful of that history, we come to the construction of [the Act of 1831] in light of the specific facts of this case. The question is whether the words "so near thereto" have a geographical or a causal connotation. Read in their context and in the light of their ordinary meaning, we conclude that they are to be construed as geographical terms. In *Ex parte Robinson, supra,* it was said that as a result of those provisions the power to punish for contempts "can only be exercised to insure order and decorum" in court. "Misbehavior of any person in their presence" plainly falls in that category. And in *Savin, Petitioner,* [131 U.S. 267], it was also held to include attempted bribes of a witness, one in the jury room and within a few feet of the court room and one in the hallway immediately adjoining the court room. The phrase "so near thereto as to obstruct the administration of justice" likewise connotes that the misbehavior must be in the vicinity of the court. It is not sufficient that the misbehavior charged has some direct relation to the work of the court. "Near" in this context, juxtaposed to "presence," suggests physical proximity not relevancy. In fact, if the words "so near thereto" are not read in the geographical sense, they come close, as the government admits, to being surplusage. There may, of course, be many types of "misbehavior" which will "obstruct the administration of justice" but which may not be "in" or "near" to the "presence" of the court. Broad categories of such acts, however, were expressly recognized in the Act of 1831 [in the provision making other contempts punishable by ordinary criminal proceedings]. It has been held that an act of misbehavior though covered by the latter provisions may also be a contempt if committed in the "presence" of the Court. *Savin, Petitioner, supra.* Yet in view of this history of those provisions, meticulous regard for those separate categories of offenses must be had, so that the instances where there is no right to jury trial will be narrowly restricted. If "so near thereto" be given a causal meaning, then [the Act] by the process of judicial construction will have regained much of the generality which Congress in 1831 emphatically intended to remove.

.   .   .   .   .

The conduct of petitioners (if the facts found are taken to be true) was highly reprehensible. It is of a kind which corrupts the judicial process and impedes the administration of justice. But the fact that it is not reachable through the summary procedure of contempt does not mean that such conduct can proceed with impunity. The Act of 1831 embraces a broad category of offenses [punishable by ordinary criminal proceedings]. And certainly it cannot be denied that the conduct here in question comes far closer to the family of offenses there described than it does to the more limited classes of contempts [subjected to summary punishment by that Act]. The acts complained of took place miles from the District Court. The evil influence which affected Elmore was in no possible sense in the "presence" of the court or "near thereto." So far as the crime of contempt is concerned, the fact that the judge received Elmore's letter is inconsequential.

We may concede that there was an obstruction in the administration of justice, as evidenced by the long delay and large expense which the reprehensible conduct of petitioners entailed. And it would follow that under the "reasonable tendency" rule of *Toledo Newspaper Co. v. United States, supra,* the court below did not err in affirming the judgment of conviction. But for the reasons stated that decision must be overruled. . . . If petitioners can be punished for their misconduct, it must be under the Criminal Code where they will be afforded the normal safeguards surrounding cirminal prosecutions.

HARRIS v. UNITED STATES
382 U.S. 162 (1965)

The provisions of the 1831 statute limiting the summary power of federal judges to punish for criminal contempt have been carried over into the Federal Criminal Code, which also contains provisions guaranteeing jury trial for any other contempts which also constitute federal crimes. In addition, Federal Rules of Criminal Procedure promulgated by the Supreme Court in 1946 contain a Rule 42 governing the procedure for the federal punishment for all criminal contempts. Rule 42(a) provides that a criminal contempt "may be punished summarily if the judge certifies that he saw or heard the conduct constituting the contempt and that it was committed in the actual presence of the court." For all other criminal contempts, Rule 42(b) requires prior notice to the alleged contemnor stating the essential facts of the contempt charged and a hearing (before a jury where required by the Criminal Code) after allowing a reasonable time for the preparation of a defense. Rule 42(b) also provides that if the contempt charged "involves disrespect to or criticism of a judge," that judge is disqualified from presiding at the hearing except with the defendant's consent.

In a 1959 decision in which Douglas was among the dissenters,[78] Rule 42(a) was held to permit the judge to punish without prior notice and hearing a witness who had refused to answer some questions of a grand jury on the ground of self-incrimination, who was then brought before the judge and ordered to answer the questions because a federal immunity statute protected him from prosecution, and who then returned to the grand jury room and again refused to answer the questions. He was then again hailed before the judge and persisted in his refusal, whereupon the judge summarily held him in criminal contempt and ordered him to jail for 15 months.

This case, which reached the Court six years later, presented indistinguishable facts.

MR. JUSTICE DOUGLAS delivered the opinion of the Court.

This case brings back to us a question resolved by a closely divided Court in *Brown* v. *United States* [note 78, *supra*] concerning the respective scope of Rule 42(a) and of Rule 42(b) of the Federal Rules of Criminal Procedure. Petitioner was a witness before a grand jury and refused to answer certain questions on the ground of self-incrimination. He and the grand jury were brought before the District Court which

---

[78] *Brown* v. *United States,* 359 U.S. 41 (1959).

directed him to answer the questions propounded before the grand jury, stating that petitioner would receive immunity from prosecution. He refused again to give any answers to the grand jury. He was thereupon brought before the District Court and sworn. The District Court repeated the questions and directed petitioner to answer, but he refused on the ground of privilege. The prosecution at once requested that petitioner be found in contempt of court "under Rule 42(a)." Counsel for petitioner protested and requested an adjournment and a public hearing where he would be permitted to call witnesses. The District Court denied the motion and thereupon adjudged petitioner guilty of criminal contempt, imposing a sentence of one year's imprisonment.

Rule 42(a) was reserved "for exceptional circumstances," *Brown* v. *United States* [note 78, *supra*] (dissenting opinion), such as acts threatening the judge or disrupting a hearing or obstructing court proceedings.

We reach that conclusion in light of "the concern long demonstrated by both Congress and this Court over the possible abuse of the contempt power," and in light of the wording of the Rule. Summary contempt is for "misbehavior" (*Ex parte Terry*, 128 U.S. 289) in the "actual presence of the court." Then speedy punishment may be necessary in order to achieve "summary vindication of the court's dignity and authority." *Cooke* v. *United States*, 267 U.S. 517. But swiftness was not a prerequisite of justice here. Delay necessary for a hearing would not imperil the grand jury proceedings.

Cases of the kind involved here are foreign to Rule 42(a). The real contempt, if such there was, was contempt before the grand jury—the refusal to answer to it when directed by the court. Swearing the witness and repeating the questions before the judge was an effort to have the refusal to testify "committed in the actual presence of the court" for the purposes of Rule 42(a). It served no other purpose, for the witness had been adamant and had made his position known. The appearance before the District Court was not a new and different proceeding, unrelated to the other. It was ancillary to the grand jury hearing and designed as an aid to it. Even though we assume *arguendo* that Rule 42(a) may at times reach testimonial episodes, nothing in this case indicates that petitioner's refusal was such an open, serious threat to orderly procedure that instant and summary punishment, as distinguished from due and deliberate procedures, was necessary. Summary procedure, to use the words of Chief Justice Taft, was designed to fill "the need for immediate penal vindication of the dignity of the court." *Cooke* v. *United States, supra*. We start from the premise long ago stated in *Anderson* v. *Dunn*, 6 Wheat. 204, that the limits of the power to punish for contempt are "[t]he least possible power adequate to the end proposed." In the instant case, the dignity of the court was not being affronted: no disturbance had to be quelled; no insolent tactics had to be stopped. The contempt here committed was far outside the narrow category envisioned by Rule 42(a).

Rule 42(b) provides the normal procedure. It reads:

> "A criminal contempt except as provided in subdivision (a) of this rule shall be prosecuted on notice. The notice shall state the time and place of hearing, allowing a reasonable time for the preparation of the defense, and shall state the essential facts constituting the criminal contempt charged and describe it as such. The notice shall be given orally by the judge in open court in the presence of the defendant or, on application of the United States attorney or of an attorney appointed by the court for that purpose, by an order to show cause or an order of arrest. The defendant is entitled to a trial by jury in any case in which an act of Congress so provides. He is entitled to admission to bail as provided in these rules. If the contempt charged involves disrespect to or criticism of a judge, that judge is disqualified from presiding at the trial or hearing except with the defendant's consent. Upon a verdict or finding of guilt the court shall enter an order fixing the punishment."

Such notice and hearing serve important ends. What appears to be a brazen refusal to cooperate with the grand jury may indeed be a case of frightened silence. Refusal to answer may be due to fear—fear of reprisals on the witness or his family. Other extenuating circumstances may be present.[79] We do not suggest that there were circumstances of that nature here. We are wholly ignorant of the episode except for what the record shows and it reveals only the barebones of demand and refusal. If justice is to be done, a sentencing judge should know all the facts. We can imagine situations where the questions are so inconsequential to the grand jury but the fear of reprisal so great that only nominal punishment, if any, is indicated. Our point is that a hearing and only a hearing will elucidate all the facts and assure a fair administration of justice. Then courts will not act on surmise or suspicion but will come to the sentencing stage of the proceeding with insight and understanding.

[79] Chief Justice Taft said in *Cooke v. United States, supra:*
"Due process of law, therefore, in the prosecution of contempt, except of that committed in open court, requires that the accused should be advised of the charges and have a reasonable opportunity to meet them by way of defense or explanation. We think this includes the assistance of counsel, if requested, and the right to call witnesses to give testimony, relevant either to the issue of complete exculpation or in extenuation of the offense and in mitigation of the penalty to be imposed."

We are concerned solely with "procedural regularity" which, as Mr. Justice Brandeis said in *Burdeau* v. *McDowell*, 256 U.S. 465 (dissenting), has been "a large factor" in the development of our liberty. Rule 42(b) prescribes the "procedural regularity" for all contempts in the federal regime except those unusual situations envisioned by Rule 42(a) where instant action is necessary to protect the judicial institution itself.

We overrule *Brown* v. *United States, supra*.

Although the federal Criminal Code gives a statutory right to jury trial for any contempt which also constitutes a federal crime, many contempts, including some covered by Rule 42(a), do not also constitute criminal offenses. And the federal statutory jury guarantee is not applicable to state courts. Beginning in 1952, Douglas joined with a minority to assert that defendants in criminal contempt proceedings were entitled to the jury trial guaranteed by the Sixth Amendment for "all criminal prosecutions."[80] The Court finally adopted that view sixteen years later[81] for cases in state and federal courts, including those covered by Rule 42(a), where the punishment exceeds six months imprisonment, a line which it drew by reference to a federal statute declaring all federal misdemeanors for which the penalty does not exceed six months imprisonment or a fine of $500 to constitute "petty offenses." Douglas rejected this "mechanical" definition and insisted that, if an exception is to be made, it should be based on the nature and gravity of the offense and not on the length of the sentence imposed.[82]

CRAIG V. HARNEY
331 U.S. 367 (1947)

Douglas has invariably agreed with the Court when it has struck down state criminal contempt convictions based on newspaper comments or other out-of-court statements about pending litigation. Finding in each

---

[80] *Sacher* v. *United States*, 343 U.S. 1 (1952); *Isserman* v. *Ethics Committee*, 345 U.S. 927 (1953); *Offutt* v. *United States*, 348 U.S. 11 (1954); *Green* v. *United States*, 356 U.S. 165 (1958); *Piemonte* v. *United States*, 367 U.S. 556 (1961); *United States* v. *Barnett*, 376 U.S. 681 (1964).

[81] *Bloom* v. *Illinois*, 391 U.S. 194 (1968); See also *Taylor* v. *Hayes*, 418 U.S. 488 (1974); *Codispoti* v. *Pennsylvania*, 418 U.S. 506 (1974). Jury trials are not required for civil contempt proceedings. *Shillitani* v. *United States*, 384 U.S. 364 (1966).

[82] *Cheff* v. *Schnackenberg*, 384 U.S. 373 (1966); *Dyke* v. *Taylor Implement Manufacturing Co.*, 391 U.S. 216 (1968); *Frank* v. *United States*, 395 U.S. 147 (1969). The concept of the "petty offense" as an exception from the guarantee of jury trial in other criminal prosecutions is discussed at p. 392, *infra*.

*case that the comments created no "clear and present danger" of an
obstruction of justice, the Court concluded that the convictions violated
the First Amendment guarantee of free speech and press.*[83] *In this
case he also wrote for the Court to reach the same result.*

Opinion of the Court by MR. JUSTICE DOUGLAS, announced by MR.
JUSTICE REED.

Petitioners are a publisher, an editorial writer, and a news reporter
of newspapers published in Corpus Christi, Texas. The County Court
had before it a forcible detainer case, *Jackson* v. *Mayes*, whereby Jackson
sought to regain possession from Mayes of a business building in Corpus
Christi which Mayes (who was at the time in the armed services and
whose affairs were being handled by an agent, one Burchard) claimed
under a lease. That case turned on whether Mayes' lease was forfeited
because of non-payment of rent. At the close of the testimony each side
moved for an instructed verdict. The judge instructed the jury to return a verdict for Jackson. That was on May 26, 1945. The jury returned
with a verdict for Mayes. The judge refused to accept it and again
instructed the jury to return a verdict for Jackson. The jury returned
a second time with a verdict for Mayes. Once more the judge refused
to accept it and repeated his prior instruction. It being the evening of
May 26th and the jury not having complied, the judge recessed the
court until the morning of May 27th. Again the jury balked at returning
the instructed verdict. But finally it complied, stating that it acted under
coercion of the court and against its conscience.

On May 29th Mayes moved for a new trial. That motion was denied
on June 6th. On June 4th an officer of the County Court filed with that
court a complaint charging petitioners with contempt by publication.
The publications referred to were an editorial and news stories published
on May 26, 27, 28, 30, and 31 in the newspapers with which petitioners
are connected. Browning, the judge, who is a layman and who holds
an elective office, was criticised for taking the case from the jury. That
ruling was called "arbitrary action" and a "travesty on justice." It was
deplored that a layman, rather than a lawyer, sat as judge. Groups of
local citizens were reported as petitioning the judge to grant Mayes a
new trial and it was said that one group had labeled the judge's ruling
as a "gross miscarriage of justice." It was also said that the judge's
behavior had properly brought down "the wrath of public opinion upon
his head," that the people were aroused because a service man "seems
to be getting a raw deal," and that there was "no way of knowing

[83] *Bridges* v. *California,* 314 U.S. 252 (1941); *Pennekamp* v. *Florida,* 328 U.S.
331 (1946).

whether justice was done, because the first rule of justice, giving both sides an opportunity to be heard, was repudiated." And the fact that there could be no appeal from the judge's ruling to a court "familiar with proper procedure and able to interpret and weigh motions and arguments by opposing counsel" was deplored.

The trial judge concluded that the reports and editorial were designed falsely to represent to the public the nature of the proceedings and to prejudice and influence the court in its ruling on the motion for a new trial then pending. [He held petitioners in contempt and sentenced them to jail for three days. The Texas Court of Criminal Appeal denied their application for a writ of *habeas corpus*.] Petitioners contended at the hearing that all that was reported did no more than to create the same impression that would have been created upon the mind of an average intelligent layman who sat through the trial. They disclaimed any purpose to impute unworthy motives to the judge or to advise him how the case should be decided or to bring the court into disrepute. The purpose was to "quicken the conscience of the judge" and to "make him more careful in discharging his duty."

The Court of Criminal Appeals, in denying the writ of *habeas corpus*, stated that the "issue before us" is "whether the publications . . . were reasonably calculated to interfere with the due administration of justice" in the pending case. It held that "there is no escape from the conclusion that it was the purpose and intent of the publishers . . . to force, compel, and coerce Judge Browning to grant Mayes a new trial. The only reason or motive for so doing was because the publishers did not agree with Judge Browning's decision or conduct of the case. According to their viewpoint, Judge Browning was wrong and they took it upon themselves to make him change his decision." The court went on to say that "It is hard to conceive how the public press could have been more forcibly or substantially used or applied to make, force, and compel a judge to change a ruling or decision in a case pending before him than was here done." The court distinguished the *Bridges* case [note 83, *supra*], noting that there the published statements carried threats of future adverse criticism and action on the part of the publisher if the pending matter was not disposed of in accordance with the views of the publisher, that the views of the publisher in the matter were already well-known, and that the *Bridges* case was not private litigation but a suit in the outcome of which the public had an interest. It concluded that the facts of this case satisfied the "clear and present danger" rule of the *Bridges* case. That test was, in the view of the court, satisfied "because the publications and their purpose were to impress upon Judge Browning (a) that unless he granted the motion for a new trial he would be subjected to suspicion as to his integrity and fairness and to odium and hatred in the public mind; (b) that the safe and secure course to avoid the criticism of the press and public opinion would be to grant the motion and disqualify himself from again presiding at the trial of the case; and (c) that if he overruled the motion for a new trial, there would be produced in the public mind such a disregard for the court over which he presided as to give rise to a purpose in practice to refuse to respect and obey any order, judgment, or decree which ·he might render in conflict with the views of the public press."

The court's statement of the issue before it and the reasons it gave for holding that the "clear and present danger" test was satisfied have a striking resemblance to the findings which the Court in *Toledo Newspaper Co.* v. *United States* [page 71, *supra*] held adequate to sustain an adjudication of contempt by publication. That case held that comment on a pending case in a federal court was punishable by contempt if it had a "reasonable tendency" to obstruct the administration of justice. We revisited that case in *Nye* v. *United States* [p. 71, *supra*] and disapproved it. And in *Bridges* v. *California* [note 83, *supra*], we held that the compulsion of the First Amendment, made applicable to the States by the Fourteenth, forbade the punishment by contempt for comment on pending cases in absence of a showing that the utterances created a "clear and present danger" to the administration of justice. We reaffirmed and reapplied that standard in *Pennekamp* v. *Florida* [note 83, *supra*], which also involved comment on matters pending before the court. We stated:

> "Courts must have power to protect the interests of prisoners and litigants before them from unseemly efforts to pervert judicial action. In the borderline instances where it is difficult to say upon which side the alleged offense falls, we think the specific freedom of public comment should weigh heavily against a possible tendency to influence pending cases. Freedom of discussion should be given the widest range compatible with the essential requirement of the fair and orderly administration of justice."

The history of the power to punish for contempt and the unequivocal command of the First Amendment serve as constant reminders that freedom of speech and of the press should not be impaired through the exercise of that power, unless there is no doubt that the utterances in question are a serious and imminent threat to the administration of justice.

In a case where it is asserted that a person has been deprived by a state court of a fundamental right secured by the Constitution, an independent examination of the facts by this Court is often required to be made.

We start with the news articles. A trial is a public event. What transpires in the court room is public property. If a transcript of the court proceedings had been published, we suppose none would claim that the judge could punish the publisher for contempt. And we can see no difference though the conduct of the attorneys, of the jury, or even of the judge himself, may have reflected on the court. Those who see and hear what transpired can report it with impunity. There is no special perquisite of the judiciary which enables it, as distinguished from other institutions of democratic government, to suppress, edit, or censor events which transpire in proceedings before it.

The articles of May 26, 27, and 28 were partial reports of what transpired at the trial. They did not reflect good reporting, for they failed to reveal the precise issue before the judge. They said that Mayes, the tenant, had tendered a rental check. They did not disclose that the rental check was post-dated and hence, in the opinion of the judge, not a valid tender. In that sense the news articles were by any standard an unfair report of what transpired. But inaccuracies in reporting are commonplace. Certainly a reporter could not be laid by the heels for contempt because he missed the essential point in a trial or failed to summarize the issues to accord with the views of the judge who sat on the case. Conceivably, a plan of reporting on a case could be so designed and executed as to poison the public mind, to cause a march on the court house, or otherwise so disturb the delicate balance in a highly wrought situation as to imperil the fair and orderly functioning of the judicial process. But it takes more imagination than we possess to find in this rather sketchy and one-sided report of a case any imminent or serious threat to a judge of reasonable fortitude.

The accounts of May 30 and 31 dealt with the news of what certain groups of citizens proposed to do about the judge's ruling in the case. So far as we are advised, it was a fact that they planned to take the proposed action. The episodes were community events of legitimate interest. Whatever might be the responsibility of the group which took the action, those who reported it stand in a different position. Even if the former were guilty of contempt, freedom of the press may not be denied a newspaper which brings their conduct to the public eye.

The only substantial question raised pertains to the editorial. It called the judge's refusal to hear both sides "high handed," a "travesty on justice," and the reason that public opinion was "outraged." It said that his ruling properly "brought down the wrath of public opinion upon his head" since a service man "seems to be getting a raw deal." The fact that there was no appeal from his decision to a "judge who is familiar with proper procedure and able to interpret and weigh motions and arguments by opposing counsel and to make his decisions accordingly" was a "tragedy." It deplored the fact that the judge was a "layman" and not a "competent attorney." It concluded that the "first rule of justice" was to give both sides an opportunity to be heard and when that rule was "repudiated," there was "no way of knowing whether justice was done."

This was strong language, intemperate language, and, we assume, an unfair criticism. But a judge may not hold in contempt one "who ventures to publish anything that tends to make him unpopular or to belittle him. . . ." See *Craig* v. *Hecht*, 263 U.S. 255, Mr. Justice Holmes dissenting. The vehemence of the language used is not alone the measure of the power to punish for contempt. The fires which it kindles must constitute an imminent, not merely a likely, threat to the administration of justice. The danger must not be remote or even probable; it must immediately imperil.

We agree with the court below that the editorial must be appraised in the setting of the news articles which both preceded and followed it. It must also be appraised in light of the community environment which prevailed at that time. The fact that the jury was recalcitrant and balked, the fact that it acted under coercion and contrary to its conscience and said so were some index of popular opinion. A judge who is part of such a dramatic episode can hardly help but know that his decision is apt to be unpopular. But the law of contempt is not made for the protection of judges who may be sensitive to the winds of public opinion. Judges are supposed to be men of fortitude, able to thrive in a hardy climate. Conceivably a campaign could be so managed and so aimed at the sensibilities of a particular judge and the matter pending before him as to cross the forbidden line. But the episodes we have here do not fall in that category. Nor can we assume that the trial judge was not a man of fortitude.

The editorial's complaint was two-fold. One objection or criticism was that a layman rather than a lawyer sat on the bench. That is legitimate comment; and its relevancy could hardly be denied at least where judges are elected. In the circumstances of the present case, it amounts at the very most to an intimation that come the next election the newspaper in question will not support the incumbent. But it contained no threat to oppose him in the campaign if the decision on the merits was not overruled, nor any implied reward if it was changed. Judges who stand for reelection run on their records. That may be a rugged environment. Criticism is expected. Discussion of their conduct is appropriate, if not necessary. The fact that the discussion at this particular point of time was not in good taste falls far short of meeting the clear and present danger test.

The other complaint of the editorial was directed at the court's procedure—its failure to hear both sides before the case was decided. There was no attempt to pass on the merits of the case. The editorial, indeed, stated that there was no way of knowing whether justice was done. That criticism of the court's procedure—that it decided the case without giving both sides a chance to be heard—reduces the salient point of the case to a narrow issue. If the point had been made in a petition for rehearing, and reduced to lawyer's language, it would be of trifling consequence. The fact that it was put in layman's language, colorfully phrased for popular consumption, and printed in a newspaper does not seem to us to elevate it to the criminal level. It might well have a tendency to lower the standing of the judge in the public eye. But it is hard to see on these facts how it could obstruct the course of justice in the case before the court. The only demand was for a hearing. There was no demand that the judge reverse his position— or else.

"Legal trials are not like elections, to be won through the use of the meeting-hall, the radio, and the newspaper." *Bridges* v. *California, supra.* But there was here no threat or menace to the integrity of the trial. The editorial challenged the propriety of the court's procedure, not the merits of its ruling. Any such challenge, whether made prior or subsequent to the final disposition of a case, would likely reflect on the competence of the judge in handling cases. But as we have said, the power to punish for contempt depends on a more substantial showing. Giving the editorial all of the vehemence which the court below found in it we fail to see how it could in any realistic sense create an imminent and serious threat to the ability of the court to give fair consideration to the motion for rehearing.

There is a suggestion that the case is different from *Bridges* v. *California, supra,* in that we have here only private litigation, while in the *Bridges* case labor controversies were involved, some of them being criminal cases. The thought apparently is that the range of permissible comment is greater where the pending case generates a public concern. The nature of the case may, of course, be relevant in determining whether the clear and present danger test is satisfied.[84] But, the rule of the *Bridges* and *Pennekamp* cases is fashioned to serve the needs of all litigation, not merely select types of pending cases.

[84] [For Douglas' later views on the "clear and present danger" test, see pp. 199–205, *infra.*]

2

THE RIGHT TO VOTE

The Constitution provides that members of Congress shall be elected and that the qualifications of voters for representatives and senators shall be those "requisite for Electors of the most numerous Branch of the State Legislature."[1] It also provides that each state shall appoint "in such Manner as the Legislature thereof may direct," a number of electors equal to the number in its congressional delegation, which electors shall elect the President and the Vice-President of the United States.[2] While the state legislatures may themselves appoint the presidential electors, the Court long ago held that they may also by statute provide for the popular election of such electors,[3] and that is the system of selection universally in use today. The method of selection of electors is not of great consequence in any event. While the electors originally exercised an independent judgment in casting their electoral ballots, the custom early developed for them mechanically to register the choice of the party by which they had been elected. The result has been that the President and Vice-President are elected, somewhat more indirectly than members of Congress, by the voters.

There soon evolved a convention system by which members of a political party selected delegates to nominating conventions who would in turn select the party candidates and adopt the party platform. That system still survives for the selection of presidential and vice-presidential candidates, although the delegates to the national convention are themselves selected by primary election in thirty states. But beginning at the turn of the century, states now began to provide by law for a direct primary by which party members themselves select their own

[1] U.S. Const., Art. I, §2, Cl. 1; Id., Seventeenth Amendment. Article I, §3, Cl. 1 originally provided that senators should be selected by the state legislatures. That was changed in 1913 by the Seventeenth Amendment.

[2] Id., Art. II, §1, Cl. 2; Id., Twelfth Amendment.

[3] McPherson v. Blacker, 146 U.S. 1 (1892). Since 1961, the Twenty-third Amendment has empowered Congress to authorize the selection of presidential electors by the District of Columbia in a number equal to the size of the congressional delegation to which the District would be entitled if it were a state. Congress has authorized the selection of the electors at a primary election.

candidates for congressional office. Nearly all the states have now so provided.

The Constitution provides also, in the Fifteenth and Nineteenth Amendments, that neither the United States nor any state shall deny or abridge the right to vote on account of race, color, previous condition of servitude, or sex. Finally, it forbids, in the Fourteenth Amendment, any state to deny any person within its jurisdiction the equal protection of the laws or to abridge the privileges and immunities of citizens of the United States.

The Fourteenth, Fifteenth, and Nineteenth Amendments are limitations on governmental, not private, action. Before Douglas came to the Court, it had held that a state denies equal protection of law by enacting a statute forbidding blacks to vote in a party primary for the nomination of candidates for state and federal offices,[4] or by giving the authority to determine party membership to a party committee which then excludes blacks from the primaries.[5] But no state action, and hence no denial of equal protection, was found where the racial discrimination in membership was mandated by the state convention of the party, since the state convention was held not to be an organ of the state.[6] Douglas voted with the Court nine years later to overrule this last decision on the ground that the state had so far embodied the state primary into its electoral machinery as to render the action of the party convention state action which violated the Fifteenth Amendment.[7]

UNITED STATES v. CLASSIC
313 U.S. 299 (1941)

The Constitution provides that members of the House of Representatives shall be "chosen every second Year by the People of the several States"[8] and that the "Times, Places and Manner of holding Elections for . . . Representatives, shall be prescribed in each State by the Legislature thereof; but the Congress may at any time by Law make or alter such Regulations."[9]

This case was a federal criminal prosecution of Louisiana commissioners of elections for violation of provisions of a Civil Rights Act forbidding conspiracies to injure a citizen in the exercise "of any right or privilege secured to him by the Constitution or laws of the

---

[4] *Nixon v. Herndon,* 273 U.S. 536 (1927).
[5] *Nixon v. Condon,* 286 U.S. 73 (1932).
[6] *Grovey v. Townsend,* 295 U.S. 45 (1935).
[7] *Smith v. Allwright,* 321 U.S. 649 (1944).
[8] U.S. Const., Art. I, §2, Cl. 1.
[9] *Id.,* Art. I, §4, Cl. 1.

United States" and forbidding anyone "acting under color of any law" to subject any inhabitant of a state to the "deprivation of any rights, privileges, and immunities secured and protected by the Constitution and laws of the United States." The charges against the defendants were that they had conspired to, and had, altered and miscounted ballots cast in the Democratic primary to nominate a candidate for the House of Representatives—a nomination that had, as a matter of unbroken practice since 1900 (when the primary election was established in Louisiana), resulted in the nominee's victory in the general election.

The Court held that the prosecution was proper. The Constitution secured the right of the people to choose representatives, and this included the right of qualified voters to cast their ballots and have them counted, not only in the general election, but also in the primary election "when a state, exercising its privilege [to regulate the manner of choice] in the absence of Congressional action, changes the mode of choice from a single step . . . to two" and when the first step, the primary, was either (1) by state law "made . . . an integral part of the procedure of choice" or (2) "in fact . . . effectively controls the choice." And both tests were met by the Louisiana primary. It made no difference that the framers of the Constitution could not have had primaries in mind because they were unknown in 1787. The Constitution was not to be read "as we read legislative codes which are subject to continuous revision" but "as the revelation of the great purposes which were intended to be achieved by the Constitution," and one of those purposes was the free choice by the people of representatives in Congress. Moreover, the Civil Rights Act on which the prosecution was based was a proper exercise of the residual power of Congress to regulate the manner of holding elections, and that power extended also to primary elections.

Mr. Justice Douglas, dissenting.

Free and honest elections are the very foundation of our republican form of government. Hence any attempt to defile the sanctity of the ballot cannot be viewed with equanimity. As stated by Mr. Justice Miller in *Ex parte Yarbrough*, 110 U.S. 651, "the temptations to control these elections by violence and corruption" have been a constant source of danger in the history of all republics. The acts here charged, if proven, are of a kind which carries that threat and are highly offensive. Since they corrupt the process of Congressional elections, they transcend mere local concern and extend a contaminating influence into the national domain.

I think Congress has ample power to deal with them. Art. I, §2 of the Constitution provides that "The House of Representatives shall be composed of Members chosen every second Year by the People of the several States." Art. I, §4 provides that "The Times, Places and Manner of holding Elections for Senators and Representatives, shall be prescribed in each State by the Legislature thereof; but the Congress may at any time by Law make or alter such Regulations, except as to the Places of chusing Senators." And Art. I, §8, clause 18 gives Congress the power "To make all Laws which shall be necessary and proper for carrying into Execution the foregoing Powers, and all other Powers vested by this Constitution in the Government of the United States, or in any Department or Officer thereof." Those sections are an arsenal of power ample to protect Congressional elections from any and all forms of pollution. The fact that a particular form of pollution has only an indirect effect on the final election is immaterial. The fact that it occurs in a primary election or nominating convention is likewise irrelevant. The important consideration is that the Constitution should be interpreted broadly so as to give to the representatives of a free people abundant power to deal with all the exigencies of the electoral process. It means that the Constitution should be read so as to give Congress an expansive implied power to place beyond the pale acts which, in their direct or indirect effect, impair the integrity of Congressional elections. For when corruption enters, the election is no longer free, the choice of the people is affected. To hold that Congress is powerless to control these primaries would indeed be a narrow construction of the Constitution, inconsistent with the view that that instrument of government was designed not only for contemporary needs but for the vicissitudes of time.

So I agree with most of the views expressed in the opinion of the Court. And it is with diffidence that I dissent from the result there reached.

The disagreement centers on the meaning of [the Civil Rights Act], which protects every right secured by the Constitution. The right to vote at a final Congressional election and the right to have one's vote counted in such an election have been held to be protected by [that Act]. *Ex parte Yarbrough, supra; United States* v. *Mosley,* 238 U.S. 383. Yet I do not think that the principles of those cases should be, or properly can be, extended to primary elections. To sustain this indictment we must so extend them. But when we do, we enter perilous territory.

We enter perilous territory because, as stated in *United States* v. *Gradwell,* 243 U.S. 476, there is no common law offense against the United States; "the legislative authority of the Union must make an act a crime, affix a punishment to it, and declare the Court that shall have jurisdiction of the offence." *United States* v. *Hudson*, 7 Cranch 32. If a person is to be convicted of a crime, the offense must be clearly and plainly embraced within the statute. As stated by Chief Justice Marshall in *United States* v. *Wiltberger*, 5 Wheat. 76, "probability is not a guide which a court, in construing a penal statute, can safely take." It is one thing to allow wide and generous scope to the express and implied powers of Congress; it is distinctly another to read into the vague and general language of an act of Congress specifications of crimes. We should ever be mindful that "before a man can be punished, his case must be plainly and unmistakably within the statute." *United States* v. *Lacher*, 134 U.S. 624. That admonition is reëmphasized here by the fact that [the Civil Rights Act] imposes not only a fine of $5,000 and ten years in prison, but also makes him who is convicted "ineligible to any office, or place of honor, profit, or trust created by the Constitution or laws of the United States." It is not enough for us to find in the vague penumbra of a statute some offense about which Congress could have legislated, and then to particularize it as a crime because it is highly offensive. Civil liberties are too dear to permit conviction for crimes which are only implied and which can be spelled out only by adding inference to inference.

[The Civil Rights Act] does not purport to be an exercise by Congress of its power to regulate primaries. It merely penalizes conspiracies "to injure, oppress, threaten, or intimidate any citizen in the free exercise or enjoyment of any right or privilege secured to him by the Constitution or laws of the United States." Thus, it does no more than refer us to the Constitution for the purpose of determining whether or not the right to vote in a primary is there secured. Hence we must do more than find in the Constitution the power of Congress to afford that protection. We must find that protection on the face of the Constitution itself. That is to say, we must in view of the wording of [the Act] read the relevant provisions of the Constitution for the purposes of this case through the window of a criminal statute.

There can be put to one side cases where state election officials deprive negro citizens of their right to vote at a general election (*Guinn* v. *United States*, 238 U.S. 347), or at a primary. *Nixon* v. *Herndon*, 273 U.S. 536; *Nixon* v. *Condon*, 286 U.S. 73. Discrimination on the basis of race or color is plainly outlawed by the Fourteenth Amendment. Since the constitutional mandate is plain, there is no reason why [the Civil Rights Act] should not be applicable. But the situation here is quite different. When we turn to the constitutional provisions relevant to this case we find no such unambiguous mandate.

Art. I, §4 specifies the machinery whereby the times, places and manner of holding elections shall be established and controlled. Art. I,

§2 provides that representatives shall be "chosen" by the people. But for purposes of the criminal law as contrasted to the interpretation of the Constitution as the source of the implied power of Congress, I do not think that those provisions in absence of specific legislation by Congress protect the primary election or the nominating convention. While they protect the right to vote, and the right to have one's vote counted, at the final election, as held in the *Yarbrough* and *Mosley* cases, they certainly do not *per se* extend to all acts which in their indirect or incidental effect restrain, restrict, or interfere with that choice. Bribery of voters at a general election certainly is an interference with that freedom of choice. It is a corruptive influence which for its impact on the election process is as intimate and direct as the acts charged in this indictment. And Congress has ample power to deal with it. But this Court in *United States* v. *Bathgate*, 246 U.S. 220, by a unanimous vote, held that conspiracies to bribe voters at a general election were not covered by [the Civil Rights Act]. While the conclusion in that case may be reconciled with the results in the *Yarbrough* and *Mosley* cases on the ground that the right to vote at a general election is personal while the bribery of voters only indirectly affects that personal right, that distinction is not of aid here. For the failure to count votes cast at a primary has by the same token only an indirect effect on the voting at the general election. In terms of causal effect, tampering with the primary vote may be as important on the outcome of the general election as bribery of voters at the general election itself. Certainly from the viewpoint of the individual voter there is as much a dilution of his vote in the one case as in the other. So, in light of the *Mosley* and *Bathgate* cases, the test under [the Act] is not whether the acts in question constitute an interference with the effective choice of the voters. It is whether the voters are deprived of their votes in the general election. Such a test comports with the standards for construction of a criminal law, since it restricts [the Act] to protection of the rights plainly and directly guaranteed by the Constitution. Any other test entails an inquiry into the indirect or incidental effect on the general election of the acts done. But in view of the generality of the words employed, such a test would be incompatible with the criteria appropriate for a criminal case.

The *Mosley* case, in my view, went to the verge when it held that [the Act] and the relevant constitutional provisions made it a crime to fail to count votes cast at a general election. That Congress intended [the Act] to have that effect was none too clear. The dissenting opinion of Mr. Justice Lamar in that case points out that [the Act] was originally part of the Enforcement Act of 1870. Under another section of that act, which was repealed by the Act of February 8, 1894, the crime charged in the *Mosley* case would have been punishable by a fine of not less than $500 and imprisonment for 12 months. [The Act here involved imposes] a penalty of $5,000 and ten years in prison. The Committee Report (H. Rep. No. 18, 53d Cong., 1st Sess.), which recommended the repeal of other sections, clearly indicated an intent to remove the hand of the Federal Government from such elections and to restore their conduct and policing to the states. As the Report stated: "Let every trace of the reconstruction measures be wiped from the statute books; let the States of this great Union understand that the elections are in their own hands, and if there be fraud, coercion, or force used they will be the first to feel it. Responding to a universal sentiment throughout the country for greater purity in elections many of our States have enacted laws to protect the voter and to purify the ballot. These, under the guidance of State officers, have worked efficiently, satisfactorily, and beneficently; and if these Federal statutes are repealed that sentiment will receive an impetus which, if the cause still exists, will carry such enactments in every State in the Union." In view of this broad, comprehensive program of repeal, it is not easy to conclude that the general language of [the Act], which was not repealed, not only continued in effect much which had been repealed but also upped the penalties for certain offenses which had been explicitly covered by one of the repealed sections. Mr. Justice Holmes, writing for the majority in the *Mosley* case, found in the legislative and historical setting of [the Act] and in its revised form a Congressional interpretation which, if [the Act] were taken at its face value, was thought to afford voters in final Congressional elections general protection. And that view is a tenable one, since [the Act] originally was part of an Act regulating general elections, and since the acts charged had a direct rather than an indirect effect on the right to vote at a general election.

But as stated by a unanimous court in *United States* v. *Gradwell, supra,* the *Mosley* case "falls far short" of making [the Act] "applicable to the conduct of a state nominating primary." Indeed, Mr. Justice Holmes, the author of the *Mosley* opinion, joined with Mr. Justice McReynolds in [*Newberry* v. *United States*, 256 U.S. 232] in his view that Congress had no authority under Art. I, §4 of the Constitution to legislate on primaries. When [the Act] was part of the Act of 1870, it certainly would never have been contended that it embraced primaries, for they were hardly known at that time. It is true that "even a criminal statute embraces everything which subsequently falls within its scope." *Browder* v. *United States*, 312 U.S. 335. Yet the attempt to bring under [the Act] offenses "committed in the conduct of primary elections or nominating caucuses or conventions" was rejected in the *Gradwell* case, where this Court said that in absence of legislation by Congress on the subject of primaries it is not for the courts "to attempt to supply it by stretching old statutes to new uses, to which they are not adapted and for which they were not intended. . . . the section of the Criminal Code relied upon, originally enacted for the protection of the civil rights of the then lately enfranchised negro, cannot be extended so as to make it an agency for enforcing a state primary law." The fact that primaries were hardly known when [the Act] was enacted, the fact that it was part of a legislative program governing general elections, not primary elections, the fact that it has been in nowise implemented by legislation directed at primaries, give credence to the unanimous view in the *Gradwell* case that [the Act] has not by the mere passage of time taken on a new and broadened meaning. At least it seems plain that the difficulties of applying the historical reason adduced by Mr. Justice Holmes in the *Mosley* case to bring general elections within [the Act] are so great in case of primaries that we have left the safety zone of interpretation of criminal statutes when we sustain this indictment. It is one thing to say, as in the *Mosley* case, that Congress was legislating as respects general elections when it passed [the Act]. That was the fact. It is quite another thing to say that Congress by leaving [the Act] un-molested for some seventy years has legislated unwittingly on primaries. [The Act] was never part of an act of Congress directed towards primaries. That was not its original frame of reference. Therefore, unlike the *Mosley* case, it cannot be said here that [the Act] still covers primaries because it was once an integral part of primary legislation.

Furthermore, the fact that Congress has legislated only sparingly and at infrequent intervals even on the subject of general elections should make us hesitate to conclude that by mere inaction Congress has taken the greater step, entered the field of primaries, and gone further than any announced legislative program has indicated.. The acts here charged constitute crimes under the Louisiana statute. In absence of specific Congressional action we should assume that Congress has left the control of primaries and nominating conventions to the states—an assumption plainly in line with the Committee Report, quoted above, recommend-ing the repeal of portions of the Enforcement Act of 1870 so as to place the details of elections in state hands. There is no ground for inference in subsequent legislative history that Congress has departed from that policy by superimposing its own primary penal law on the primary penal laws of the states. Rather, Congress has been fairly consistent in recognizing state autonomy in the field of elections. To be sure, it has occasionally legislated on primaries. But even when dealing specifically with the nominating process, it has never made acts of the kind here in question a crime. In this connection it should be noted that the bill which became the Hatch Act contained a section which made it unlawful "for any person to intimidate, threaten, or coerce, or to attempt to intimidate, threaten, or coerce, any other person for the purpose of interfering with the right of such other person to vote or to vote as he may choose, or of causing such other person to vote for, or not to vote for, any candidate for the nomination of any party as its candidate" for various federal offices, including representatives, "*at any primary or nominating convention* held solely or in part" for that purpose. This was stricken in the Senate. That section would have extended the same protection to the primary and nominating convention as §1 of the Hatch Act extends to the general election. The Senate, however, refused to do so. Yet this Court now holds that [the Civil Rights Act] has protected the primary vote all along and that it covers conspiracies to do the precise thing on which Congress refused to legislate in 1939. The hesitation on the part of Congress through the years to enter the primary field, its refusal to do so[10] in 1939, and the restricted scope of such primary laws as it has passed, should be ample evidence that this Court is legislating when it takes the initiative in extending [the Act] to primaries.

That [the Act] lacks the requisite specificity necessary for inclusion of acts which interfere with the nomination of party candidates is reëmphasized by the test here employed. The opinion of the Court stresses, as does the indictment, that the winner of the Democratic primary in Louisiana invariably carries the general election. It is also emphasized that a candidate defeated in the Louisiana primaries cannot be a candidate at the general election. Hence, it is argued that interference with the right to vote in such a primary is "as a matter of law and in fact an interference with the effective choice of the voters at the only stage of the election procedure when their choice is of significance," and that the "primary in Louisiana is an integral part of the procedure for the popular choice" of representatives. By that means, the *Gradwell* case is apparently distinguished. But I do not think it is a valid distinction for the purposes of this case.

One of the indictments in the *Gradwell* case charged that the defendants conspired to procure one thousand unqualified persons to vote in a West Virginia primary for the nomination of a United States Senator. This Court, by a unanimous vote, affirmed the judgment which sustained a demurrer to that indictment. The Court specifically reserved the question as to whether a "primary should be treated as an election within the meaning of the Constitution." But it went on to say that, even assuming it were, certain "strikingly unusual features" of the

[10] Sec. 2 of the Hatch Act, however, does make unlawful certain acts of administrative employees even in connection with the nominations for certain federal offices.

the particular primary precluded such a holding in that case. It noted that candidates of certain parties were excluded from the primary, and that even candidates who were defeated at the primary could on certain conditions be nominated for the general election. It therefore concluded that whatever power Congress might have to control such primaries, it had not done so by [the Act].

If the *Gradwell* case is to survive, as I think it should, we have therefore this rather curious situation. Primaries in states where the winner invariably carries the general election are protected by [the Act] and the Constitution, even though such primaries are not by law an integral part of the election process. Primaries in states where the successful candidate never wins, seldom wins, or may not win in the general election are not so protected, unless perchance state law makes such primaries an integral part of the election process. Congress, having a broad control over primaries, might conceivably draw such distinctions in a penal code. But for us to draw them under [the Act] is quite another matter. For we must go outside the statute, examine local law and local customs, and then, on the basis of the legal or practical importance of a particular primary, interpret the vague language of [the Act] in the light of the significance of the acts done. The result is to make refined and nice distinctions which Congress certainly has not made, to create unevenness in the application of [the Act] among the various states, and to make the existence of a crime depend, not on the plain meaning of words employed interpreted in light of the legislative history of the statute, but on the result of research into local law or local practices. Unless Congress has explicitly made a crime dependent on such facts, we should not undertake to do so. Such procedure does not comport with the strict standards essential for the interpretation of a criminal law. The necessity of resorting to such a circuitous route is sufficient evidence to me that we are performing a legislative function in finding here a definition of a crime which will sustain this indictment. A crime, no matter how offensive, should not be spelled out from such vague inferences.

FORTSON V. MORRIS
385 U.S. 231 (1966)

The Constitution has always provided that there shall be two senators from each state, and since the adoption of the Seventeenth Amendment in 1913, it has provided also that they shall be elected by the people of the state.[11] *It has also always provided that representatives shall be*

---

[11] See note 1, *supra*.

elected by the people of the state and shall be apportioned among the states according to population on the basis of a decennial census.[12] For the first half-century, representatives in many states were elected at large with each voter having as many votes as the number of representatives to which the state was entitled. In the Reapportionment Act of 1842 Congress exercised its residual power to regulate the manner of electing representatives[13] to require that they should be elected separately from districts within the state "composed of a contiguous and compact territory." In 1850 Congress dropped this requirement but reinstated it in the Reapportionment Act of 1862. In the Reapportionment Act of 1872 the requirement was amended to require also that the congressional districts contain "as nearly as practicable an equal number of inhabitants." Similar requirements appeared in all succeeding Reapportionment Acts through 1911 and then were dropped again. Since the requirement only applied to the election of representatives "under this apportionment," it was held inapplicable to the election of representatives under successive reapportionments.[14]

The Court in 1946 refused to grant relief in a suit challenging the failure of the Illinois legislature to redistrict the state since 1901 despite substantial population shifts, with the consequence that the twenty-two congressional districts in that state ranged in population from some 112,000 to 914,000.[15] The question was held not to be a "justiciable" one, but a "political" question entrusted exclusively to Congress. Douglas joined in a dissent asserting that the state was diluting the votes of the inhabitants of its larger districts, that this dilution constituted a denial of equal protection of the law under the Fourteenth Amendment, and that the issue was no more political than questions of racial discrimination involving voting rights.

Sixteen years later the Court concluded that an action challenging the failure of Tennessee since 1901 to reapportion state legislators among the counties despite substantial population changes since that time did present a justiciable issue.[16] That decision was followed by a series of cases in which Douglas has joined establishing the "one man, one vote" rule for apportionment of state legislators[17] and members of

---

[12] U.S. Const., Art I, § 2, Cl. 3. In 1865 the Thirteenth Amendment abolished slavery and in 1868 the Fourteenth Amendment eliminated the original provision in Article I that only three-fifths of a state's slave population should be counted in making the apportionment.

[13] See text at note 9, *supra.*

[14] *Wood* v. *Broom,* 287 U.S. 1 (1932).

[15] *Colegrove* v. *Green,* 328 U.S. 549 (1946). See also *South* v. *Peters,* 339 U.S. 276 (1950).

[16] *Baker* v. *Carr,* 369 U.S. 186 (1962).

[17] *Reynolds* v. *Sims,* 377 U.S. 533 (1964).

the House of Representatives,[18] for state primaries for the nomination of candidates for United States senator and for statewide office where votes are weighted among counties,[19] and for elections to offices of local governmental units where voting is not at large.[20] But Douglas wrote for the Court to hold that the Constitution does not forbid the states to have county school boards which are elected, not by the voters, but by delegates of popularly elected local school boards.[21] The system was "basically appointive" and there was "no constitutional reason why state or local offices of the nonlegislative character here involved may not be chosen by the governor, by the legislature, or by some other appointive means rather than by an election."

Douglas voted with the Court again to hold that the equal protection clause forbids the appointment of county school boards by a grand jury from which blacks are systematically excluded and forbids also the limitation of eligibility for appointment to such boards to land-owners in the county.[22]

This case presented a challenge under the equal protection clause to a provision in the Georgia state constitution that, when no candidate for governor receives a majority vote in a general election, the legislature should select the governor from the two candidates with the highest number of votes. The Court held the state constitutional provision valid since the federal Constitution would not prevent Georgia from having its governor appointed by the legislature in the first instance and, therefore, would not prevent it from resorting to legislative appointment as an alternative where the voters at the general election had failed to elect a governor.

MR. JUSTICE DOUGLAS, dissenting.

The Court misstates the question we must decide. It is not whether Georgia may select a Governor through a legislative election.[23] It is whether the legislature may make the final choice when the election has been entrusted to the people and no candidate has received a majority of the votes. In other words, the legislative choice is only a part of the popular election machinery. The 1824 amendment to the 1798 Constitution of Georgia, which gave the legislature power to elect

---

18 *Wesberry v. Sanders*, 376 U.S. 1 (1964).

19 *Gray v. Sanders*, 372 U.S. 368 (1963).

20 *Avery v. Midland County*, 390 U.S. 474 (1968); *Hadley v. Junior College District*, 397 U.S. 50 (1970). Cf. *Wells v. Edwards*, 409 U.S. 1095 (1973).

21 *Sailors v. Board of Education*, 387 U.S. 105 (1967).

22 *Turner v. Fouche*, 396 U.S. 346 (1970).

23 Georgia's state auditor is chosen by the legislature.

a governor, treated that stage as only one of two in the general election.[24] The first stage, then as now, was an election open to "the persons qualified to vote for members of the general assembly."

It is said that the general election is over and that a new, and different, alternative procedure is now about to be used. But that is belied by the realities. The primary election selected the party candidates, the choices of the two parties are still in balance, and the legislative choice is restricted to those two candidates. The election, commencing with the primary, will indeed not be finally completed until the winner has taken the oath of office. Up to then the vacancy which occasioned the election has not been filled.

Our starting point is what we said in *Gray v. Sanders* [note 19, *supra*]:

> "Once the geographical unit for which a representative is to be chosen is designated, all who participate in the election are to have an equal vote—whatever their race, whatever their sex, whatever their occupation, whatever their income, and wherever their home may be in that geographical unit. This is required by the Equal Protection Clause of the Fourteenth Amendment. The concept of 'we the people' under the Constitution visualizes no preferred class of voters but equality among those who meet the basic qualifications."

It is argued with earnestness that if the electoral college can be used to select a President, a legislature can be used to select a governor. It is said that there is no more a violation of the "one person, one vote" principle in the one than in the other. But the Twelfth Amendment creates the exception in case of a President. There is no like exception in the choice of a governor.

> "The only weighting of votes sanctioned by the Constitution concerns matters of representation, such as the allocation of Senators irrespective of population and the use of the electoral college in the choice of a President. . . . But once the class of voters is chosen and their qualifications specified, we see no constitutional way by which equality of voting power may be evaded. . . .
>
> · · · · ·
>
> "The conception of political equality from the Declaration of Independence, to Lincoln's Gettysburg Address, to the Fifteenth,

[24] Originally Georgia left the selection of Governor to the legislature, the House selecting three candidates and the Senate choosing one of the three by majority vote.

Seventeenth, and Nineteenth Amendments can mean only one thing—one person, one vote." *Gray* v. *Sanders, supra.*

If the legislature is used to determine the outcome of a general election, the votes cast in that election would be weighted, contrary to the principle of "one person, one vote." All the vices we found inherent in the county unit system in *Gray* v. *Sanders* are inherent when the choice is left to the legislature. A legislator when voting for governor has only a single vote. Even if he followed the majority vote of his constituency, he would necessarily disregard the votes of those who voted for the other candidate, whether their votes almost carried the day or were way in the minority. He would not be under a mandate to follow the majority or plurality votes in his constituency, but might cast his single vote on the side of the minority in his district. Even if he voted for the candidate receiving a plurality of votes cast in his district and even if each Senator and Representative followed the same course, a candidate who received a minority of the popular vote might receive a clear majority of the votes cast in the legislature. As stated by the District Court:

> "The Georgia election system in the constitutional provision now under consideration permits unequal treatment of the voters within the class of voters selected, and it thus cannot stand. Many arguments may be made, but we need go no further than to point out, as stated, that the candidate receiving the lesser number of votes may be elected by the General Assembly. This would give greater weight to the votes of those citizens who voted for this candidate and necessarily dilute the votes of those citizens who cast their ballots for the candidate receiving the greater number of votes. The will of the greater number may be ignored."

I have said enough to indicate why the substitution of the Georgia Legislature for a runoff vote is an unconstitutional weighting of votes, having all the vices of the county unit system that we invalidated in *Gray* v. *Sanders.*

The fact that this constitutional provision allowing the legislature to choose the Governor was adopted by the people of Georgia is "without federal constitutional significance, if the scheme adopted fails to satisfy the basic requirements of the Equal Protection Clause, as delineated in our opinion in *Reynolds* v. *Sims.*" See *Lucas* v. *Colorado General Assembly,* 377 U.S. 713. We dealt there with an apportionment plan that had been adopted by a popular referendum. We repeat what we said: "A citizen's constitutional rights can hardly be infringed simply because a majority of the people choose that it be."

UNITED STATES v. ARIZONA
400 U.S. 112 (1970)

By providing that the qualifications to vote for members of Congress shall be the same as those to vote "for Electors of the most numerous Branch of the State Legislature,"[25] the Constitution consigns the question of voter eligibility for members of Congress largely to the state legislatures—as long as they prescribe the same qualifications for those who vote for their own most numerous house. But the state legislatures in prescribing voting qualifications for any elections are subject to other federal constitutional limitations. Thus state laws which disenfranchise residents on grounds of race violate the equal protection clause and the Fifteenth Amendment.[26]

Another limitation on the states' powers to prescribe voting qualifications has been found in provisions in the Fourteenth and Fifteenth Amendments authorizing Congress "to enforce this article by appropriate legislation."

By 1970 amendments to the Voting Rights Act of 1965, Congress lowered the voting age to eighteen in federal and state elections. In this case the Court held the amendment valid as applied to federal elections but invalidated it as applied to state elections. The vote was close. Four members of the Court thought Congress had no power to fix the voting age in state or federal elections. Justice Black voted to sustain the law as applied to federal elections because he viewed it as an exercise of Congress' residual power to change state laws fixing the "Times, Places and Manner of holding Elections for Senators and Representatives."[27] But he could find no authority in the Constitution for Congress to regulate the voting age in state elections. Three members of the Court found that authority in the equal protection clause of the Fourteenth Amendment. Douglas agreed with these three.

MR. JUSTICE DOUGLAS, dissenting in part and concurring in part.

The grant of the franchise to 18-year-olds by Congress is in my view valid across the board.

I suppose that in 1920, when the Nineteenth Amendment was ratified giving women the right to vote, it was assumed by most constitutional experts that there was no relief by way of the Equal Protection Clause of the Fourteenth Amendment. In *Minor* v. *Happersett*, 21

---

[25] U.S. Const., Art. I, §2, Cl. 1; *Id.*, Seventeenth Amendment.
[26] See p. 86, *supra.*
[27] See text at note 9, *supra.*

Wall. 162, the Court held in the 1874 Term that a State could constitutionally restrict the franchise to men. While the Fourteenth Amendment was relied upon [by the unsuccessful plaintiff], the thrust of the opinion was directed at the Privileges and Immunities Clause[28] with a subsidiary reference to the Due Process Clause. It was much later, indeed not until the 1961 Term—nearly a century after the Fourteenth Amendment was adopted—that discrimination against voters on grounds *other than race* was struck down.

The first case in which this Court struck down a statute under the Equal Protection Clause of the Fourteenth Amendment was *Strauder v. West Virginia*, 100 U.S. 303, decided in the 1879 Term.[29] In the 1961 Term we squarely held that the manner of apportionment of members of a state legislature raised a justiciable question under the Equal Protection Clause, *Baker v. Carr* [note 16, *supra*]. That case was followed by numerous others, *e.g.*: that one person could not be given twice or 10 times the voting power of another person in a statewide election merely because he lived in a rural area or in the smallest rural county;[30] that the principle of equality applied to both Houses of a bicameral legislature;[31] that political parties receive protection under the Equal Protection Clause just as voters do.[32]

The reapportionment cases, however, are not quite in point here. This case, so far as equal protection is concerned, is no whit different from a controversy over a state law that disqualifies women from certain

[28] [U.S. Const., Fourteenth Amendment: "No State shall make or enforce any law which shall abridge the privileges and immunities of citizens of the United States. . . ."]

[29] Strauder was tried for murder. He had sought removal to federal courts on the ground that "by virtue of the laws of the State of West Virginia no colored man was eligible to be a member of the grand jury or to serve on a petit jury in the State." He was convicted of murder and the West Virginia Supreme Court affirmed. This Court held the West Virginia statute limiting jury duty to whites only unconstitutional.

[30] *Gray v. Sanders* [note 19, *supra*]; *Davis v. Mann*, 377 U.S. 678; *Swann v. Adams*, 385 U.S. 440; *Kilgarlin v. Hill*, 386 U.S. 120; *Avery v. Midland County* [note 20, *supra*]; *Moore v. Ogilvie*, 394 U.S. 814; *Hadley v. Junior College District* [note 20, *supra*].

[31] *Reynolds v. Sims* [note 17, *supra*]; *WMCA v. Lomenzo*, 377 U.S. 633; *Roman v. Sincock*, 377 U.S. 695.

[32] *Williams v. Rhodes*, 393 U.S. 23. We also held in federal elections that the command of Art. I, §2, of the Constitution that representatives be chosen "by the People of the several States" means that "as nearly as is practicable one man's vote in a congressional election is to be worth as much as another's," *Wesberry v. Sanders* [note 18, *supra*], and that that meant "vote-diluting discrimination" could not be accomplished "through the device of districts containing widely varied numbers of inhabitants." *Lucas v. Colorado General Assembly*, 377 U.S. 713; *Kirkpatrick v. Preisler*, 394 U.S. 526; *Wells v. Rockefeller*, 394 U.S. 542.

types of employment, *Goesaert* v. *Cleary*, 335 U.S. 464, or that imposes a heavier punishment on one class of offender than on another whose crime is not intrinsically different. *Skinner* v. *Oklahoma*, 316 U.S. 535. The right to vote is, of course, different in one respect from the other rights in the economic, social, or political field which are under the Equal Protection Clause. The right to vote is a civil right deeply embedded in the Constitution. Article I, §2, provides that the House is composed of members "chosen . . . by the People" and the electors "shall have the Qualifications requisite for Electors of the most numerous Branch of the State Legislature." The Seventeenth Amendment states that Senators shall be "elected by the people." The Fifteenth Amendment speaks of the "right of citizens of the United States to vote"—not only in federal but in state elections. The Court in *Ex parte Yarbrough*, 110 U.S. 651, stated:

> "This new constitutional right was mainly designed for citizens of African descent. The principle, however, that the protection of the exercise of this right is within the power of Congress, is as necessary to the right of other citizens to vote as to the colored citizen, and to the right to vote in general as to the right to be protected against discrimination."

It was in that tradition that we said in *Reynolds* v. *Sims*, "The right to vote freely for the candidate of one's choice is of the essence of a democratic society, and any restrictions on that right strike at the heart of representative government."

This "right to choose, secured by the Constitution," *United States* v. *Classic* [p. 86, *supra*], is a civil right of the highest order. In *Harper* v. *Virginia Board of Elections*, 383 U.S. 663, we stated: "Notions of what constitutes equal treatment for purposes of the Equal Protection Clause *do* change." That statement is in harmony with my view of the Fourteenth Amendment, as expressed by my Brother BRENNAN: "We must therefore conclude that its framers understood their Amendment to be a broadly worded injunction capable of being interpreted by future generations in accordance with the vision and needs of those generations."

In *Carrington* v. *Rash*, 380 U.S. 89, we held that Texas could not bar a person, otherwise qualified, from voting merely because he was a member of the armed services. Occupation, we held, when used to bar a person from voting, was that invidious discrimination which the Equal Protection Clause condemns. In *Evans* v. *Cornman*, 398 U.S. 419, we held that a State could not deny the vote to residents of a federal enclave when it treated them as residents for many other purposes. In *Harper* v. *Virginia Board of Elections*, 383 U.S. 663, we held a State could not in harmony with the Equal Protection Clause keep a person from voting in state elections because of "the affluence of the voter or payment of any fee." In *Kramer* v. *Union School District*, 395 U.S. 621, we held that a person could not be barred from voting in school board elections merely because he was a bachelor. So far as the Equal Protection Clause was concerned, we said that the line between those qualified to vote and those not qualified turns on whether those excluded have "a distinct and direct interest in the school meeting decisions." In *Cipriano* v. *City of Houma*, 395 U.S. 701, we held that a state law which gave only "property taxpayers" the right to vote on the issuance of revenue bonds of a municipal utility system violated equal protection as "the benefits and burdens of the bond issue fall indiscriminately on property owner and nonproperty owner alike." And we held in *Phoenix* v. *Kolodziejski*, 399 U.S. 204, that it violates equal protection to restrict those who may vote on general obligation bonds to real property taxpayers. We looked to see if there was any "compelling state interest" in the voting restrictions. We held that "nonproperty owners" are not "substantially less interested in the issuance of these securities than are property owners," and that presumptively "when all citizens are affected in important ways by a governmental decision subject to a referendum, the Constitution does not permit weighted voting or the exclusion of otherwise qualified citizens from the franchise."

The powers granted Congress by §5 of the Fourteenth Amendment to "enforce" the Equal Protection Clause are "the same broad powers expressed in the Necessary and Proper Clause:[33] *Katzenbach* v. *Morgan*, 384 U.S. 641. As we stated in that case, "Correctly viewed, §5 is a positive grant of legislative power authorizing Congress to exercise its discretion in determining whether and what legislation is needed to secure the guarantees of the Fourteenth Amendment."

Congress might well conclude that a reduction in the voting age from 21 to 18 was needed in the interest of equal protection. The Act itself brands the denial of the franchise to 18-year-olds as "a particularly unfair treatment of such citizens in view of the national defense responsibilities imposed" on them. The fact that only males are drafted while the vote extends to females as well is not relevant, for the female component of these families or prospective families is also caught up in war and hit hard by it. Congress might well believe that men and women alike should share the fateful decision.

[33] [U.S. Const., Art. I, §8, Cl. 18: "The Congress shall have the Power . . . To make all Laws which shall be necessary and proper for carrying into Execution the foregoing Powers, and all other Powers vested by this Constitution in the Government of the United States, or in any Department or Officer thereof."]

It is said, why draw the line at 18? Why not 17? Congress can draw lines and I see no reason why it cannot conclude that 18-year-olds have that degree of maturity which entitles them to the franchise. They are "generally considered by American law to be mature enough to contract, to marry, to drive an automobile, to own a gun, and to be responsible for criminal behavior as an adult."[34] Moreover, we are advised that under state laws, mandatory school attendance does not, as a matter of practice, extend beyond the age of 18. On any of these items the States, of course, have leeway to raise or lower the age requirements. But voting is "a fundamental matter in a free and democratic society," *Reynolds* v. *Sims* [note 17, *supra*]. Where "fundamental rights and liberties are asserted under the Equal Protection Clause, classifications which might invade or restrain them must be closely scrutinized and carefully confined." *Harper* v. *Virginia Board of Elections*, 383 U.S. 663. There we were speaking of state restrictions on those rights. Here we are dealing with the right of Congress to "enforce" the principles of equality enshrined in the Fourteenth Amendment. The right to "enforce" granted by §5 of that Amendment is, as noted, parallel with the Necessary and Proper Clause whose reach Chief Justice Marshall described in *McCulloch* v. *Maryland*, 4 Wheat. 316: "Let the end be legitimate, let it be within the scope of the constitution, and all means which are appropriate, which are plainly adapted to that end, which are not prohibited, but consist with the letter and spirit of the constitution, are constitutional."

Equality of voting by all who are deemed mature enough to vote is certainly consistent "with the letter and spirit of the constitution." Much is made of the fact that Art. I, §4, of the Constitution gave Congress only the power to regulate the "Manner of holding Elections," not the power to fix qualifications for voting in elections. But the Civil War Amendments—the Thirteenth, Fourteenth, and Fifteenth— made vast inroads on the power of the States. Equal protection became a standard for state action and Congress was given authority to "enforce" it. See *Katzenbach* v. *Morgan*, 384 U.S. 641. The manner of enforcement involves discretion; but that discretion is largely entrusted to the Congress, not to the courts. If racial discrimination were the only concern of the Equal Protection Clause, then across-the-board voting regulations set by the States would be of no concern to Congress. But it is much too late in history to make that claim. Election inequalities created by state laws and based on factors other than race may violate the Equal Protection Clause, as we have held over and

[34] Engdahl, "Constitutionality of the Voting Age Statute," 39 Geo. Wash. L. Rev. 1, 36 (1970).

over again. The reach of §5 to "enforce" equal protection by eliminating election inequalities would seem quite broad. Certainly there is not a word of limitation in §5 which would restrict its applicability to matters of race alone. And if, as stated in *McCulloch* v. *Maryland*, the measure of the power of Congress is whether the remedy is consistent "with the letter and spirit of the constitution," we should have no difficulty here. We said in *Gray* v. *Sanders* [note 19, *supra*] "The conception of political equality from the Declaration of Independence, to Lincoln's Gettysburg Address, to the Fifteenth, Seventeenth, and Nineteenth Amendments can mean only one thing—one person, one vote."

It is a reasoned judgment that those who have such a large "stake" in modern elections as 18-year-olds, whether in times of war or peace, should have political equality. As was made plain in the dissent in *Colegrove* v. *Green* [note 15, *supra*] (whose reasoning was approved in *Gray* v. *Sanders* [note 19, *supra*]), the Equal Protection Clause does service to protect the right to vote in federal as well as in state elections.

I would sustain the choice which Congress has made.

Three months after this decision, Congress submitted to the state legislatures for ratification a proposed amendment to the Constitution lowering the voting age to eighteen for all state and federal elections. It took slightly more than another three months for the requisite three-fourths of the states to ratify the Twenty-sixth Amendment.

AMERICAN PARTY OF TEXAS V. WHITE
415 U.S. 767 (1974)

One remaining area of voting problems has long troubled the Court— the access of candidates and of new parties to the ballot. When it sustained an Illinois requirement that the new party—in this case Henry Wallace's Progressive Party—present a petition signed by 25,000 qualified voters including at least 200 from each of 50 counties, although 52 percent of the state's registered voters resided in Cook County alone, 87 percent resided in the 49 most popular counties, and only 13 percent resided in the 53 least populous counties,[35] Douglas dissented. Since the requirement meant that the 87 percent of the voters in the 49 most populous counties could not get their party on the ballot, while the 13 percent of the voters in the 53 remaining counties could, he thought it violated the equal protection clause. He later voted with the Court to invalidate under that clause—in this instance at the behest

---

[35] *MacDougall* v. *Green*, 335 U.S. 281 (1948).

of George Wallace's American Independent Party and the Socialist Labor Party—an "entangling web" of Ohio laws which effectively closed the ballot to all but the Republican and Democratic parties,[36] and then wrote for the Court to overrule its earlier decision in MacDougall sustaining the Illinois ballot requirements[37] as out of line with the "one man, one vote" rule of the more recently decided apportionment decisions[38] and to hold that the Illinois system violated the equal protection clause.

Thereafter, he voted with the Court to sustain, in view of the state's interest in excluding frivolous candidacies from the ballot, a Georgia requirement that independent candidates, or political parties which did not have a candidate for governor or presidential elector who received 20 percent of the vote in the preceding election, must within a six-month period file petitions signed by 5 percent of the eligible voters.[39]

In this case the American Party of Texas and one other minority political party seeking a ballot position for the general election in Texas challenged a state statute under which the complaining political parties, because they did not have a candidate for governor who polled 2 percent of the vote in the preceding general election, were required to nominate by state conventions preceded by county and precinct conventions. The precinct conventions were to be held on the day of primary election and to be attended by a number equal to 1 percent of the total vote cast for governor at the last general election or, if the attendance at the precinct conventions fell below that figure, the deficiency had to be made up by notarized signatures to nominating petitions (excluding all who voted in any primary election or participated in any convention of any other party during the preceding year), the petitions to be circulated within a fifty-five-day period after the primary election. Two independent candidates for the Congress and the state legislature in the general election also challenged another Texas statute requiring them to file, within thirty days after the date fixed for any runoff primary, notarized nominating signatures (excluding all who had voted in the primaries or signed another nominating petition for the same office) equaling, for the congressional candidate, 3 percent of the vote for governor in the congressional district at the last general election and, for the candidate for the state legislature, 5 percent of the same vote in his legislative district, but in any event no more than 500 votes for either candidate.

[36] *Williams v. Rhodes,* 393 U.S. 23 (1968).
[37] *Moore v. Ogilvie,* 394 U.S. 814 (1969).
[38] See p. 95, *supra.*
[39] *Jenness v. Fortson,* 403 U.S. 431 (1971).

When the trial court in September, 1972, sustained all aspects of the Texas law and vacated a temporary restraining order against its enforcement which that court had issued while the case was pending before it, the American Party, seeking to get on the ballot for the 1972 general election, sought a temporary restraining order from the Supreme Court pending the appeal of the case. The Court denied that request on October 5 without opinion. Douglas dissented from this action.[40]

This election scheme is not as severe or oppressive as the [Ohio statute] we condemned in *Williams* v. *Rhodes* [note 36, *supra*] nor is it as benign as the [Georgia statute] we approved in *Jenness* v. *Fortson* [note 39, *supra*].

While Texas requires only 1% of the voters for governor to endorse the new party, that requirement must be met by obtaining signatures of those attending precinct conventions, supplemented, if need be, by signatures obtained after the primaries. But all cross-over signing is barred and it is supported by criminal sanctions. Moreover, the supplemental signatures can be obtained only after the major parties have held their primaries. And only a 55-day period is available for obtaining the necessary signatures.

While the requirement of 1% of the total vote for governor may be less than Georgia's requirement of 5% of those eligible to vote in the last election for the filling of the office the candidate is seeking, the Texas machinery for launching a minority party is almost as cumbersome and involved as the one we struck down in *Williams* v. *Rhodes*.

The minority party must be statewide even though its appeal may be essentially to urban voters or to rural voters, as the case may be. That requirement did not appear in Georgia's scheme.

In Georgia 180 days was allowed for circulating a nominating petition; in Texas, less than 60 days.

In Georgia the minority party had to meet the same deadline as did candidates running in the primaries of the regular parties. In Texas the regular parties first have their primaries; only then can a minority party solicit signatures for its candidates. Moreover, no one who voted in a primary is eligible to sign the petition for the minority party.

The minority party therefore must draw its support from the ranks of those who were either unwilling or unable to vote in the primaries of the established parties.

The minority party therefore cannot compete with the regular parties; it must be content with the leftovers to get on the ballot.

We said in *Jenness* v. *Fortson*: "Georgia's election laws, unlike

---

[40] *American Party of Texas* v. *Bullock*, 409 U.S. 803 (1972).

Ohio's, do not operate to freeze the status quo." Texas, though not as
severe as Ohio, works in that direction. It therefore seems to me, at
least prima facie, to impose an invidious discrimination on the un-
orthodox political group.

Perhaps full argument would dispel these doubts. But they are so
strong that I would grant the requested stay so that candidates for the
American Party may get on the Texas ballot for next month's presidential election. To do so it must be certified by the Secretary of State
no later than October 6. We cannot possibly decide the merits by that
date. But if the American Party is on the ballot, the voting and associational rights which we have been alert to protect will be honored;
and if meanwhile the merits are reached and we affirm the three-judge
court, holding the Texas scheme constitutional, the ballots will not be
counted.

*The appeal was finally argued in the Supreme Court in November
1973, with the plaintiffs hoping now to eliminate obstacles to their
appearance on the Texas ballot in the general election of 1974. In
March, 1974, the Court announced its decision, sustaining all of the
ballot access requirements imposed on the minority political parties,
and also those imposed on the independent candidates in the absence
of proof by them that the pool from which they must obtain their
nominating signatures would be so reduced as to make the requirement
unduly burdensome.*

MR. JUSTICE DOUGLAS, dissenting in part.

While I agree with the Court on the absentee ballot aspect of these
cases,[41] I dissent on the main issue. The hurdles facing minority parties
such as the American Party of Texas in seeking to place nominees on
the ballot are set out and compared with those of *Jenness* v. *Fortson*
[note 39, *supra*] in my opinion dissenting from the denial of a temporary
restraining order in *American Party of Texas* v. *Bullock* [note 40, *supra*].
I there noted that:

> "We said in *Jenness* v. *Fortson, supra,* 'Georgia's election laws,
> unlike Ohio's, do not operate to freeze the status quo.' Texas,
> though not as severe as Ohio, works in that direction. It therefore
> seems to me, at least prima facie, to impose an invidious discrim-
> ination on the unorthodox political group.

[41] [At the urging of another minority party which had satisfied the access requirements, the Court did hold invalid under the equal protection clause the Texas practice
of printing on its absentee ballots only the names of the Democratic and Republican parties.]

"Perhaps full argument would dispel these doubts. But they are so strong that I would grant the requested stay . . . ."

Oral argument has failed to dispel the doubts. For the reasons stated in *American Party of Texas* v. *Bullock*, I believe that the totality of the requirements imposed upon minority parties works an invidious and unconstitutional discrimination.

An analysis of the requirements imposed on independent candidates leads me to the same conclusion. Under the [Georgia] procedures reviewed in *Jenness*, independent candidates seeking a ballot position had six months to secure the signatures of 5% of the eligible electorate for the office in question. The percentage required in Texas ranges, according to the office [to which election is sought], from 1% of the last statewide gubernatorial vote to 5% of the last local gubernatorial vote, and in any case no more than 500 signatures are required; the candidate, however, has only 30 days in which to gather them. In *Jenness* a voter could sign a candidate's petition even though he had already signed or would sign others. Here no voter may sign the application of more than one candidate. In *Jenness* a voter who signed the petition of an independent was free thereafter to participate in a party primary and a voter who previously voted in a party primary was fully eligible to sign a petition. Here independents are not even allowed to seek signatures until after the major party primaries and no voter who has participated in a party primary is allowed to sign an independent candidate's application. In *Jenness* no signature on a nominating petition had to be notarized, but that is not the case here.

In *Jenness* we were able to say that Georgia "has insulated not a single potential voter from the appeal of new political voices within its borders." In Texas, however, the independent, like the minority party, must "draw [his] support from the ranks of those who [are] either unwilling or unable to vote in the primaries of the established parties." *American Party of Texas* v. *Bullock* [note 40, *supra*]. As with minority parties, I do not believe that Texas may constitutionally leave independent candidates to "be content with the left-overs to get on the ballot."

3

CITIZENSHIP

The Constitution authorizes Congress to "establish an uniform Rule of Naturalization"[1] and the Fourteenth Amendment provides that "All persons born or naturalized in the United States, and subject to the jurisdiction thereof, are citizens of the United States and of the State wherein they reside."

Most of the cases in this area to reach the Court have involved the withholding of naturalized citizenship or the revocation of such citizenship after it was granted. In Schneiderman v. United States[2] Douglas concurred in a decision that the government could not revoke naturalized citizenship, on the theory that it was illegally procured in 1927, under a naturalization law requiring that for five years prior to naturalization the applicant must have "behaved as a man of good moral character, attached to the principles of the Constitution of the United States, and well disposed to the good order and happiness of the same." The Court held that the government did not show that the applicant was disqualified in 1927 by showing that he was then, and for five years prior thereto had been, a member of the Communist Party of the United States. A right so precious as United States citizenship should not be revoked except on "clear, unequivocal, and convincing" evidence. Proof of Communist Party membership would not overcome the naturalized citizen's testimony that he did not advocate forcible overthrow of the government during the five-year period for two reasons: (1) the government had not established with certainty that the Communist Party of the United States advocated forcible overthrow of the government at that time or, if it did, that the defendant so understood its program, and (2) the government relied on the doctrine of guilt by association, whereas "under our traditions beliefs are personal and not a matter of mere association"—"men in adhering to a political party or other organization notoriously do not subscribe unqualifiedly to all of its platforms or asserted principles."

Douglas joined in that opinion but thought there was also a third ground for ruling against the government. While a statute authorized

[1] U.S. Const., Art. I, §8, Cl. 4.
[2] 320 U.S. 118 (1943).

revocation of naturalized citizenship either for fraud or for illegal procurement, he contended that illegal procurement should be confined to express statutory conditions, such as the requirements that applicant not be an anarchist or a polygamist; and that, when the government relied on lack of attachment to the principles of the Constitution, it must prove that the defendant had been guilty of fraud in his naturalization proceeding. Since the government did not contend that there had been any fraud—it was not even shown that the naturalization court inquired about Communist Party membership—no case for revocation had been shown.

Douglas also concurred in the decision in Baumgartner v. United States[3] that the government had failed to meet its heavy burden of proof in an action to revoke the naturalized citizenship, as both fraudulently and illegally procured, of one of German ancestry, who had at the time of and before naturalization expressed sympathy for Hitler.

KNAUER V. UNITED STATES
328 U.S. 654 (1946)

This was another action initiated in 1943 to revoke the naturalized citizenship acquired by a native of Germany. Knauer had served in the German army during World War I and had been decorated. He had studied law and economics in Germany. He arrived in this country in 1925 at the age of thirty and settled in Milwaukee, Wisconsin, where he conducted an insurance business. In 1929 he filed a declaration of intention to become a citizen, which was required by statute. In 1936 he filed his petition for naturalization and he took his oath of allegiance to the United States and was admitted to citizenship on April 13, 1937.

This time the government charged that citizenship had been procured by fraud in that (1) Knauer falsely represented in his petition that he was attached to the principles of the Constitution and (2) he had taken a false oath of allegiance.

The district court in which the revocation proceeding was brought found that the government had established fraud and ordered Knauer's citizenship revoked. The court of appeals affirmed.

MR. JUSTICE DOUGLAS delivered the opinion of the Court.

I. In the oath of allegiance which Knauer took, he swore that he would "absolutely and entirely renounce and abjure all allegiance and fidelity to any foreign prince, potentate, state, or sovereignty, and

[3] 322 U.S. 665 (1944).

particularly to the German Reich," that he would "support and defend the Constitution and laws of the United States of America against all enemies, foreign and domestic"; that he would "bear true faith and allegiance to the same" and that he took "this obligation freely without any mental reservation or purpose of evasion." The first and crucial issue in the case is whether Knauer swore falsely and committed a fraud when he promised under oath to forswear allegiance to the German Reich and to transfer his allegiance to this nation. Fraud connotes perjury, falsification, concealment, misrepresentation. When denaturalization is sought on this (*Baumgartner* v. *United States* [Note 3, *supra*]) as well as on other grounds (*Schneiderman* v. *United States*, [Note 2,] *supra*), the standard of proof required is strict. We do not accept even concurrent findings of two lower courts as conclusive. *Baumgartner* v. *United States, supra*. We reexamine the facts to determine whether the United States has carried its burden of proving by "clear, unequivocal, and convincing" evidence, which does not leave "the issue in doubt," that the citizen who is sought to be restored to the status of an alien obtained his naturalization certificate illegally. *Schneiderman* v. *United States, supra*.

That strict test is necessary for several reasons. Citizenship obtained through naturalization is not a second-class citizenship. It has been said that citizenship carries with it all of the rights and prerogatives of citizenship obtained by birth in this country "save that of eligibility to the Presidency." *Luria* v. *United States*, 231 U.S. 9.[4] There are other exceptions of a limited character.[5] But it is plain that citizenship obtained through naturalization carries with it the privilege of full participation in the affairs of our society, including the right to speak freely, to criticize officials and administrators, and to promote changes in our laws including the very Charter of our Government. Great tolerance and caution are necessary lest good faith exercise of the rights of citizenship be turned against the naturalized citizen and be used to deprive him of the cherished status. Ill-tempered expressions, extreme views, even the promotion of ideas which run counter to our American ideals, are not to be given disloyal connotations in absence of solid, convincing evidence that that is their significance. Any other course would run counter to our traditions and make denaturalization proceedings the ready instrument for political persecutions. As stated in

---

[4] [U.S. Const., Art. II, §1, Cl. 4: "No Person except a natural born Citizen, or a Citizen of the United States, at the Adoption of this Constitution, shall be eligible to the Office of President. . . ."]

[5] Thus a naturalized citizen must wait seven years before he is eligible to sit in the House (Article I, §2) and nine years before he can enter the Senate. Article I, §3. . . .

Schneiderman v. *United States, supra,* "Were the law otherwise, valuable rights would rest upon a slender reed, and the security of the status of our naturalized citizens might depend in considerable degree upon the political temper of majority thought and the stresses of the times."

These are extremely serious problems. They involve not only fundamental principles of our political system designed for the protection of minorities and majorities alike. They also involve tremendously high stakes for the individual. For denaturalization, like deportation, may result in the loss "of all that makes life worth living." *Ng Fung Ho* v. *White,* 259 U.S. 276. Hence, where the fate of a human being is at stake, we must not leave the presence of his evil purpose to conjecture. Furthermore, we are dealing in cases of this kind with questions of intent. Here it is whether Knauer swore falsely on April 13, 1937. Intent is a subjective state, illusory and difficult to establish in absence of voluntary confession. What may appear objectively to be false may still fall short of establishing an intentional misrepresentation which is necessary in order to prove that the oath was perjurious. And as *Baumgartner* v. *United States, supra,* indicates, utterances made in years subsequent to the oath are not readily to be charged against the state of mind existing when the oath was administered. Troubled times and the emotions of the hour may elicit expressions of sympathy for old acquaintances and relatives across the waters. "Forswearing past political allegiance without reservation and full assumption of the obligations of American citizenship are not at all inconsistent with cultural feelings imbedded in childhood and youth." *Baumgartner* v. *United States, supra.* Human ties are not easily broken. Old social or cultural loyalties may still exist, though basic allegiance is transferred here. The fundamental question is whether the new citizen still takes his orders from, or owes his allegiance to, a foreign chancellory. Far more is required to establish that fact than a showing that social and cultural ties remain. And even political utterances, which might be some evidence of a false oath if they clustered around the date of naturalization, are more and more unreliable as evidence of the perjurious falsity of the oath the further they are removed from the date of naturalization.

We have read with care the voluminous record in this case. We have considered the evidence which antedates Knauer's naturalization (April 13, 1937), the evidence which clusters around that date, and that which follows it. We have considered Knauer's versions of the various episodes and the versions advanced by the several witnesses for the United States. We have considered the testimony and other evidence offered by each in corroboration or impeachment of the other's case. We have considered the appraisal of the veracity of the witnesses by the judge

who saw and heard them and have given it that "due regard" required
by the Rules of Civil Procedure. We conclude with the District Court
and the Circuit Court of Appeals that there is solid, convincing evidence that Knauer before the date of his naturalization, at that time,
and subsequently was a thoroughgoing Nazi and a faithful follower of
Adolph Hitler. The conclusion is irresistible, therefore, that when he
forswore allegiance to the German Reich he swore falsely. The character of the evidence, the veracity of the witnesses against Knauer as
determined by the District Court, the corroboration of challenged
evidence presented by the Government, the consistent pattern of
Knauer's conduct before and after naturalization convince us that the
two lower courts were correct in their conclusions. The standard of
proof, not satisfied in either the *Schneiderman* or *Baumgartner* cases,
is therefore plainly met here.

We will review briefly what we, as well as the two lower courts,
accept as the true version of the facts.

As early as 1931, Knauer told a newly arrived immigrant who came
from the same town in Germany that in his opinion the aim of Hitler
and the Nazi party was good, that it would progress, and that it was
necessary to have the same party in this country because of the Jews
and the Communists. During the same period, he told another friend
repeatedly that he was opposed to any republican form of government
and that Jewish capital was to blame for Germany's downfall. He
visited Germany for about six months in 1934 and while there read
Hitler's Mein Kampf. On his return he said with pride that he had
met Hitler, and that he had been offered a post with the German
government at 600 marks per month, that Hitler was the savior of
Germany, that Hitler was solving the unemployment problem while
this country was suffering from Jewish capitalism, that the Hitler
youth organization was an excellent influence on the children of
Germany. On occasions in 1936 and 1937 he was explosive in his criticism of those who protested against the practices and policies of Hitler.

The German Winter Relief Fund was an official agency of the
German government for which German consulates solicited money in
the United States. In the winter of 1934–1935 Knauer was active in obtaining contributions to the Fund and forwarded the money collected
to the German consulate in Chicago.

The German-American Bund had a branch in Milwaukee. Its leader
was George Froboese—midwestern gaulciter and later national leader.
The Bund taught and advocated the Nazi philosophy—the leadership
principle, racial superiority of the Germans, the principle of the totalitarian state, Pan-Germanism and of Lebensraum (living space). It

looked forward to the day when the Nazi form of government would supplant our form of government. It emphasized that allegiance and devotion to Hitler were superior to any obligation to the United States. Knauer denied that he was a member of the Bund. But the District Court found to the contrary on evidence which is solid and convincing.

Knauer participated in Bund meetings in 1936. In the summer of 1936 he and his family had a tent at the Bund camps. In the fall of 1936 he enrolled his young daughter in the Youth Movement of the Bund—a group organized to instill the Nazi ideology in the minds of children of German blood. They wore uniforms, used the Nazi salute, and were taught songs of allegiance to Hitler. Knauer attended meetings of this group.

The Federation of German-American Societies represented numerous affiliated organizations consisting of Americans of German descent and sought to coordinate their work. It was the policy of the Bund to infiltrate older German societies. This effort was made as respects the Federation. Knauer assisted Froboese and others between 1933 and 1936 in endeavoring to have the swastika displayed at celebrations of the Federation. In 1935 Knauer reprimanded a delegate to the Federation for passing out pamphlets opposing the Nazi government in Germany. At a meeting of the Federation in 1935, Knauer moved to have the Federation recognize the swastika as the flag of the German Reich. The motion failed to carry. In 1936 the swastika flag was raised at a German Day celebration without approval of the Federation. A commotion ensued in which Bundists in uniform participated, as a result of which the swastika flag was torn down. At the next meeting of the Federation, Knauer proposed a vote indicating approval of the showing of the swastika flag. The motion failed and a vote of censure of the chairman was passed. The chairman resigned. Thereupon Froboese and others proposed the formation of the German-American Citizens Alliance to compete with the Federation. It was organized early in 1937. The constitution and articles of incorporation of the Alliance provided that all of its assets on dissolution were to become the property of a German government agency for the dissemination of propaganda in foreign countries—the Deusches Auslands-Institut. The Alliance was a front organization for the Bund. It was designed to bring into its ranks persons who were sympathetic with the objectives of the Bund but who did not wish to be known as Bund members.

On February 22, 1937—less than two months before Knauer took his oath of naturalization—he was admitted to membership in the Alliance and became a member of its executive committee. His first action as a member was to volunteer the collection of newspaper articles that attacked the Alliance, Germany, and German-Americans. In 1937 and in the ensuing years, Knauer wrote many letters and telegrams to those who criticized the Bund or the German government. In 1938 Knauer was elected vice-president of the Alliance and subsequently presided over most of its meetings. He was the dominant figure in the Alliance. In May 1937 the German consul presented to the Alliance the swastika flag which had been torn down at the Federation celebration the year before. Not long after his naturalization Knauer urged that the Alliance sponsor a solstice ceremony, a solemn rite at which a wooden swastika is burned to symbolize the unity of German people everywhere. In August 1937 the Alliance refused to participate in an affair sponsored by a group which would not fly the swastika flag. In May 1938 Knauer at a meeting of the Alliance read a leaflet entitled "America, the Garbage Can of the World." In 1939 he arranged for public showings of films distributed by an official German propaganda agency and depicting the glories of Nazism.

There was an intimate cooperation between the Alliance and the Bund. The Bund camp was used for Alliance affairs and it was available to Alliance members. The Alliance supported various Bund programs. It supported the Youth Group of the Bund and the Bund's solstice celebration. In 1939 the Youth Group of the Bund held a benefit performance for the Alliance. In 1940 it admitted the Youth Group of the Bund at the request of Froboese. Knauer consistently defended the Bund when it was criticized, when it was denied the use of a park or a hall, when its members were arrested or charged with offenses. In spite of the fact that Knauer knew the real aims and purposes of the Bund and was aware of its connection and Froboese's connection with the German government, he consistently came to its defense. Thus when a Wisconsin judge freed disturbers of a Bund meeting, he wrote the judge saying that the judge's remarks against the Bund were a "slander of a patriotic American organization." He subscribed to the official Bund newspaper and to a propaganda magazine issued and circulated by an agency of the German government. He held shares in the holding company of the Bund camp which was started in 1939. A photograph taken at the dedication of the new Bund camp in 1939 shows Knauer among a group of prominent Bund leaders with arm upraised in the Nazi salute. He owned a cottage at the Bund camp. He used the Nazi salute at the beginning and end of his speeches and at the Bund meetings.

In May 1938 Knauer and Froboese formed the American Protective League with a secret list of members. Knauer was elected a director. A constitution and bylaws were adopted and copies mailed by Knauer and Froboese to Hitler. One Buerk was a German agent operating in this country and later indicted for failing to register as such. In 1939 the German consulate in Chicago supervised the recruiting of skilled workers in that region for return to Germany for work in German industries. The German consul, Buerk, Froboese and Knauer conducted the recruiting. Knauer participated actively in interviewing candidates. At intervals farewell parties were given by Knauer and Froboese to the returning workers and their families.

Important evidence implicating Knauer in promoting the cause of Hitler in this country was given by a Mrs. Merton. She testified that, prompted solely by patriotic motives, she entered the employ of Froboese in 1938 in order to obtain evidence against the Bund and its members. The truth of her testimony was vigorously denied by Knauer. But the District Court believed her version, as did the Circuit Court of Appeals. And we are persuaded on a close reading of the record not only that her testimony was strongly corroborated but also that Knauer's attempts to discredit her testimony do not ring true.

Her testimony may be summarized as follows: She acted as secretary to Froboese in 1938. During the period of her employ Froboese and Knauer worked closely together on Bund matters. He helped Froboese in the preparation of articles for the Bund newspaper, of speeches, and of Bund correspondence. He helped Froboese prepare resolutions to be offered at the 1938 Bund convention calling for a white-gentile-ruled America. When Froboese left the city to attend the convention, he told her to contact Knauer for advice concerning Bund matters. Letters signed by Froboese and Knauer jointly were sent to Hitler and other Nazi officials. One contained a list of 700 German nationals. One was the constitution and by-laws of the American Protective League which we have already mentioned. One to Hess said they had to lay low for awhile, that there was an investigation on. A birthday greeting to Hitler from Froboese and Knauer closed with the phrase, "In blind obedience we follow you." Knauer told her never to reveal that the Alliance and the Bund were linked together. One day she asked Knauer what the Bund was. His reply was that the Bund "was the Fuehrer's grip on American democracy." She reminded Knauer that he was an American citizen. He replied, "That is a good thing to hide behind."

We have given merely the highlights of the evidence. Much corroborative detail could be added. But what we have related presents the gist of the case against Knauer. If isolated parts of the evidence against Knauer were separately considered, they might well carry different inferences. His alertness to rise to the defense of Germans or of Americans of German descent could well reflect, if standing as isolated instances, attempts to protect a minority against what he deemed oppressive practices. Social and cultural ties might be complete and adequate explanations. Even utterances of a political nature which reflected tolerance or approval of the Nazi program in Germany might carry no sinister connotation, if they were considered by themselves. For many native-borns in this country did not awaken to the full implications of the Nazi program until war came to us. And as we stated in *Schneiderman* v. *United States, supra*: "Whatever attitude we may individually hold toward persons and organizations that believe in or advocate extensive changes in our existing order, it should be our desire and concern at all times to uphold the right of free discussion and free thinking to which we as a people claim primary attachment."

But we have here much more than political utterances, much more than a crusade for the protection of minorities. This record portrays a program of action to further Hitler's cause in this nation—a program of infiltration which conforms to the pattern adopted by the Nazis in country after country. The ties with the German Reich were too intimate, the pattern of conduct too consistent, the overt acts too plain for us to conclude that Knauer was merely exercising his right of free speech either to spread tolerance in this country or to advocate changes here.

Moreover, the case against Knauer is not constructed solely from his activities subsequent to April 13, 1937—the date of his naturalization. The evidence prior to his naturalization, that which clusters around that date, and that which follows in the next few years is completely consistent. It conforms to the same pattern. We do not have to guess whether subsequent to naturalization he had a change of heart and threw himself wholeheartedly into a new cause. We have clear, convincing, and solid evidence that at all relevant times he was a thoroughgoing Nazi bent on sponsoring Hitler's cause here. And this case, unlike the *Baumgartner* case, is not complicated by the fact that when the alien took his oath Hitler was not in power. On April 13, 1937, Hitler was in full command. The evidence is most convincing that at that time, as well as later, Knauer's loyalty ran to him, not to this country.

The District Court properly ruled that membership in the Bund was not in itself sufficient to prove fraud which would warrant revocation of a decree of naturalization. Otherwise, guilt would rest on implication, contrary to the rule of the *Schneiderman* and *Baumgartner* cases. But we have here much more than that. We have a clear course of conduct, of which membership in the Bund was a manifestation, designed to promote the Nazi cause in this country. This is not a case of an underling caught up in the enthusiasm of a movement, driven by ties of blood and old associations to extreme attitudes, and perhaps unaware of the conflict of allegiance implicit in his actions. Knauer is an astute person. He is a leader—the dominating figure in the cause he

sponsored, a leading voice in the councils of the Bund, the spokesman
in the program for systematic agitation of Nazi views. His activities
portray a shrewd, calculating, and vigilant promotion of an alien cause.
The conclusion seems to us plain that when Knauer forswore allegiance
to Hitler and the German Reich he swore falsely.

*In a series of cases decided before Douglas' appointment to the Court,
it had dealt with a statutory requirement that a naturalized citizen must
take an oath "that he will support and defend the Constitution and laws
of the United States against all enemies, foreign and domestic, and
bear true faith and allegiance to the same," and with the further
requirement that the applicant be "attached to the principles of the
Constitution of the United States, and well disposed to the good order
and happiness of the same." Although the applicants were willing to
take the oath, the Court concluded that these statutory requirements
disqualified Rosika Schwimmer,[6] a fifty-two-year-old woman pacifist
who was unwilling to bear arms, Douglas Macintosh,[7] a Yale theology
professor who had served as a chaplain in the Canadian army in World
War I, was forty-seven years of age at the time of the decision, and was
willing to bear arms if he were free to judge the necessity of the war,
and Marie Bland,[8] another woman applicant of undisclosed age who
had served as a nurse with our army in France in World War I and
who was unwilling, for religious reasons, to bear arms personally.*

*In 1945, when the Court, with considerable reliance on these cases,
held that a state could refuse a license to practice law to Clyde Summers[9] because he refused, for religious reasons, to bear arms, Douglas
joined dissenters who contended that the state's action infringed on
Summers' freedom of religion in violation of the First Amendment.*

GIROUARD V. UNITED STATES
328 U.S. 61 (1946)

MR. JUSTICE DOUGLAS delivered the opinion of the Court.

In 1943 petitioner, a native of Canada, filed his petition for naturalization in the District Court of Massachusetts. He stated in his application that he understood the principles of the government of the
United States, believed in its form of government, and was willing to
take the oath of allegiance which reads as follows:

[6] *United States* v. *Schwimmer,* 279 U.S. 644 (1929).
[7] *United States* v. *Macintosh,* 283 U.S. 605 (1931).
[8] *United States* v. *Bland,* 283 U.S. 636 (1931).
[9] *In re Summers,* 325 U.S. 561 (1945).

"I hereby declare, on oath, that I absolutely and entirely renounce and abjure all allegiance and fidelity to any foreign prince, potentate, state, or sovereignty of whom or which I have heretofore been a subject or citizen; that I will support and defend the Constitution and laws of the United States of America against all enemies, foreign and domestic; that I will bear true faith and allegiance to the same; and that I take this obligation freely without any mental reservation or purpose of evasion: So help me God."

To the question in the application "If necessary, are you willing to take up arms in defense of this country?" he replied, "No (Noncombatant) Seventh Day Adventist." He explained that answer before the examiner by saying "it is a purely religious matter with me, I have no political or personal reasons other than that." He did not claim before his Selective Service board exemption from all military service, but only from combatant military duty. At the hearing in the District Court petitioner testified that he was a member of the Seventh Day Adventist denomination, of whom approximately 10,000 were then serving in the armed forces of the United States as non-combatants, especially in the medical corps; and that he was willing to serve in the army but would not bear arms. The District Court admitted him to citizenship. The Circuit Court of Appeals reversed, one judge dissenting. It took that action on the authority of *United States* v. *Schwimmer* [note 6, *supra*]; *United States* v. *Macintosh* [note 7, *supra*] and *United States* v. *Bland* [note 8, *supra*], saying that the facts of the present case brought it squarely within the principle of those cases.

The *Schwimmer*, *Macintosh* and *Bland* cases involved, as does the present one, a question of statutory construction. At the time of those cases, Congress required an alien, before admission to citizenship, to declare on oath in open court that "he will support and defend the Constitution and laws of the United States against all enemies, foreign and domestic, and bear true faith and allegiance to the same." It also required the court to be satisfied that the alien had during the five-year period immediately preceding the date of his application "behaved as a man of good moral character, attached to the principles of the Constitution of the United States, and well disposed to the good order and happiness of the same." Those provisions were reenacted into the present law in substantially the same form.[10]

---

[10] We have already set forth in the opinion the present form of the oath which is required. It is to be found in the Nationality Act of 1940 [which also] provides that no person shall be naturalized unless he has been for stated periods and still is "a person of good moral character, attached to the principles of the Constitution of the United States, and well disposed to the good order and happiness of the United States."

While there are some factual distinctions between this case and the *Schwimmer* and *Macintosh* cases, the *Bland* case on its facts is indistinguishable. But the principle emerging from the three cases obliterates any factual distinction among them. As we recognized in *In re Summers* [note 9, *supra*] they stand for the same general rule—that an alien who refuses to bear arms will not be admitted to citizenship. As an original proposition, we could not agree with that rule. The fallacies underlying it were, we think, demonstrated in the dissents of Mr. Justice Holmes in the *Schwimmer* case and of Mr. Chief Justice Hughes in the *Macintosh* case.

The oath required of aliens does not in terms require that they promise to bear arms. Nor has Congress expressly made any such finding a prerequisite to citizenship. To hold that it is required is to read it into the Act by implication. But we could not assume that Congress intended to make such an abrupt and radical departure from our traditions unless it spoke in unequivocal terms.

The bearing of arms, important as it is, is not the only way in which our institutions may be supported and defended, even in times of great peril. Total war in its modern form dramatizes as never before the great cooperative effort necessary for victory. The nuclear physicists who developed the atomic bomb, the worker at his lathe, the seamen on cargo vessels, construction battalions, nurses, engineers, litter bearers, doctors, chaplains—these, too, made essential contributions. And many of them made the supreme sacrifice. Mr. Justice Holmes stated in the *Schwimmer* case that "the Quakers have done their share to make the country what it is." And the annals of the recent war show that many whose religious scruples prevented them from bearing arms, nevertheless were unselfish participants in the war effort. Refusal to bear arms is not necessarily a sign of disloyalty or a lack of attachment to our institutions. One may serve his country faithfully and devotedly, though his religious scruples make it impossible for him to shoulder a rifle. Devotion to one's country can be as real and as enduring among noncombatants as among combatants. One may adhere to what he deems to be his obligation to God and yet assume all military risks to secure victory. The effort of war is indivisible; and those whose religious scruples prevent them from killing are no less patriots than those whose special traits or handicaps result in their assignment to duties far behind the fighting front. Each is making the utmost contribution according to his capacity. The fact that his rôle may be limited by religious convictions rather than by physical characteristics has no necessary bearing on his attachments to his country or on his willingness to support and defend it to his utmost.

Petitioner's religious scruples would not disqualify him from becoming a member of Congress or holding other public offices. While Article VI, Clause 3 of the Constitution provides that such officials, both of the United States and the several States, "shall be bound by Oath or Affirmation, to support this Constitution," it significantly adds that "no religious Test shall ever be required as a Qualification to any Office or public Trust under the United States." The oath required is in no material respect different from that prescribed for aliens under the Nationality Act. It has long contained the provision "that I will support and defend the Constitution of the United States against all enemies, foreign and domestic; that I will bear true faith and allegiance to the same; that I take this obligation freely, without any mental reservation or purpose of evasion . . ." As Mr. Chief Justice Hughes stated in his dissent in the *Macintosh* case, "the history of the struggle for religious liberty, the large number of citizens of our country, from the very beginning, who have been unwilling to sacrifice their religious convictions, and in particular, those who have been conscientiously opposed to war and who would not yield what they sincerely believed to be their allegiance to the will of God"—these considerations make it impossible to conclude "that such persons are to be deemed disqualified for public office in this country because of the requirement of the oath which must be taken before they enter upon their duties."

There is not the slightest suggestion that Congress set a stricter standard for aliens seeking admission to citizenship that it did for officials who make and enforce the laws of the nation and administer its affairs. It is hard to believe that one need forsake his religious scruples to become a citizen but not to sit in the high councils of state.

As Mr. Chief Justice Hughes pointed out (*United States* v. *Macintosh, supra*) religious scruples against bearing arms have been recognized by Congress in the various draft laws. This is true of the Selective Training and Service Act of 1940 as it was of earlier acts. He who is inducted into the armed services takes an oath which includes the provision "that I will bear true faith and allegiance to the United States of America; that I will serve them honestly and faithfully against all their enemies whomsoever . . ." Congress has thus recognized that one may adequately discharge his obligations as a citizen by rendering non-combatant as well as combatant services. This respect by Congress over the years for the conscience of those having religious scruples against bearing arms is cogent evidence of the meaning of the oath. It is recognition by Congress that even in time of war one may truly support and defend our institutions though he stops short of using weapons of war.

That construction of the naturalization oath received new support in 1942. In the Second War Powers Act Congress relaxed certain of the requirements for aliens who served honorably in the armed forces of the United States during World War II and provided machinery to expedite their naturalization. Residence requirements were relaxed, educational tests were eliminated, and no fees were required. But no change in the oath was made; nor was any change made in the requirement that the alien be attached to the principles of the Constitution. Yet it is clear that these new provisions cover non-combatants as well as combatants. If petitioner had served as a non-combatant (as he was willing to do), he could have been admitted to citizenship by taking the identical oath which he is willing to take. Can it be that the oath means one thing to one who has served to the extent permitted by his religious scruples and another thing to one equally willing to serve but who has not had the opportunity? It is not enough to say that petitioner is not entitled to the benefits of the new Act since he did not serve in the armed forces. He is not seeking the benefits of the expedited procedure and the relaxed requirements. The oath which he must take is identical with the oath which both non-combatants and combatants must take. It would, indeed, be a strange construction to say that "support and defend the Constitution and laws of the United States of America against all enemies, foreign and domestic" demands something more from some than it does from others. That oath can hardly be adequate for one who is unwilling to bear arms because of religious scruples and yet exact from another a promise to bear arms despite religious scruples.

Mr. Justice Holmes stated in the *Schwimmer* case: "if there is any principle of the Constitution that more imperatively calls for attachment than any other it is the principle of free thought—not free thought for those who agree with us but freedom for the thought that we hate. I think that we should adhere to that principle with regard to admission into, as well as to life within this country." The struggle for religious liberty has through the centuries been an effort to accommodate the demands of the State to the conscience of the individual. The victory for freedom of thought recorded in our Bill of Rights recognizes that in the domain of conscience there is a moral power higher than the State. Throughout the ages, men have suffered death rather than subordinate their allegiance to God to the authority of the State. Freedom of religion guaranteed by the First Amendment is the product of that struggle. As we recently stated in *United States v. Ballard*, 322 U.S. 78, "Freedom of thought, which includes freedom of religious belief, is basic in a society of free men." The test oath is abhorrent to our tradition. Over the years, Congress has meticulously respected that tradition and even in time of war has sought to accommodate the military requirements to the religious scruples of the individual. We do not believe that Congress intended to reverse that policy when it came to draft the naturalization oath. Such an abrupt and radical departure from our traditions should not be implied. Cogent evidence would be necessary to convince us that Congress took that course.

We conclude that the *Schwimmer*, *Macintosh* and *Bland* cases do not state the correct rule of law.

Congress has from time to time enacted laws providing for forfeiture of United States citizenship—whether acquired by birth or by naturalization—on the commission of certain proscribed acts. Beginning in 1940, it greatly expanded these expatriation laws, and a variety of cases involving them came before the Court beginning in the late 1950s.

Prior to 1958 there were only four decisions of the Court which seemed to bear closely on the problem. One, decided at the turn of the century, held that a child born in the United States of Chinese parents residing here acquired United States citizenship at birth even though his parents were not eligible for citizenship under the then naturalization laws. Since the Fourteenth Amendment provides that "All persons born or naturalized in the United States . . . are citizens of the United States and of the State wherein they reside," the Court concluded that "citizenship by birth is established by the mere fact of birth under the circumstances defined in the Constitution." And it added that the "Fourteenth Amendment . . . has conferred no authority upon Congress to restrict the effect of birth, declared by the Constitution to constitute a sufficient and complete right to citizenship." Moreover, the "power of naturalization, vested in Congress by the Constitution, is a power to confer citizenship, not a power to take it away."[11]

A second decision in 1915 upheld a statute providing that an American woman who married a foreigner would take the nationality of her husband. Even if it be conceded "that a change of citizenship cannot be . . . imposed without the concurrence of the citizen," the Court said, this statute dealt "with a condition voluntarily entered into."[12]

The third decision concerned a child born in the United States of naturalized parents who later returned to Sweden with the child and renounced their American citizenship, so that by Swedish law the child acquired the Swedish citizenship of her parents. The child did not lose her American citizenship, the Court held, since she returned

---

[11] *United States v. Wong Kim Ark*, 169 U.S. 649 (1898).
[12] *Mackenzie v. Hare*, 239 U.S. 299 (1915).

to the United States on reaching majority and elected to retain that citizenship without voluntarily having done anything to relinquish it.[13]

In the fourth decision the Court held that a statute providing for forfeiture of citizenship by anyone who obtained citizenship by naturalization in any foreign state and established a residence abroad could be applied to terminate the citizenship of a native-born American regardless of the intent of the person involved.[14]

The first of the new cases to challenge an expatriation law was the Perez case, involving a law providing for forfeiture of citizenship by voting in an election in a foreign state. The Court upheld the statute as applied to a citizen by birth who had voted in elections in Mexico, explaining that while "Congress can attach loss of citizenship only as a consequence of conduct engaged in voluntarily," the voluntary conduct which had that consequence need not indicate an intent on the part of the citizen to renounce his citizenship. Douglas joined in a dissent which conceded that a "citizen may elect to renounce his citizenship, and under some circumstances he may be found to have abandoned his status by voluntarily performing acts that compromise his undivided allegiance to his country," such as acquiring foreign citizenship. But, Douglas contended in a separate dissent, "The Fourteenth Amendment grants citizenship to the native-born, as explained in United States v. Wong Kim Ark [note 11, supra]. That right may be waived or surrendered by the citizen. But I see no constitutional method by which it can be taken from him . . . . While Congress can prescribe conditions for voluntary expatriation, Congress cannot turn white to black and make any act an act of expatriation."[15]

At the same time this case was decided, the Court also considered another expatriation law which provided for forfeiture of citizenship for service in the armed forces of a foreign state by one who has or acquires citizenship in that foreign state. This law, the Court held, could not be invoked against one who held American citizenship by birth and at the same time, under Japanese law, also held Japanese citizenship because of the nationality of his parents, and who was inducted into Japanese military service while visiting in Japan, because the government had failed to prove that his military service in Japan was voluntary. Douglas concurred, but added that the decision should have been the same, even though the military service was voluntary,

---

[13] *Perkins v. Elg*, 307 U.S. 325 (1939). Douglas did not participate in this decision, which was argued before, but decided after, his appointment to the Court.

[14] *Savorgnan v. United States*, 338 U.S. 491 (1950). Douglas did not participate in this decision because he had suffered severe injuries in a horseback riding accident a few months earlier.

[15] *Perez v. Brownell*, 356 U.S. 44 (1958).

since otherwise "a citizen could be transferred into a stateless outcast for evading his taxes, for fraud upon the Government, for counterfeiting its currency, for violating its voting laws and on and on ad infinitum."[16]

In a third case decided at the same time, the Court held that another statutory provision for forfeiture of citizenship on conviction by a court-martial for desertion from the military forces in time of war could not validly be applied to a citizen by birth whose court-martial conviction was based on one day's absence without leave from his base. A plurality opinion concluded that, since the action here, unlike that in Perez, did not involve "those international problems that were thought to arise by reason of a citizen's having voted in a foreign election," the sole purpose of forfeiting citizenship was to punish for desertion, and punishment of such magnitude was "cruel and unusual" within the ban of the Eighth Amendment. Douglas concurred in that opinion, but added that even if citizenship could be involuntarily forfeited, guilt should not be determined by a military tribunal, but "in a civilian court of justice where all the protections of the Bill of Rights guard the fairness of the outcome."[17]

Five years later the Court also held invalid a provision for forfeiture of citizenship by one who departed from or remained outside the United States during time of war or national emergency for the purpose of evading military service. Again the Court found that the sole purpose was to impose punishment, and held that this could not be done in a civil proceeding without the procedural safeguards for criminal trials required by the Fifth and Sixth Amendments. Again Douglas concurred on the ground that Congress had no power to deprive a native-born person of the citizenship granted by the Fourteenth Amendment.[18]

SCHNEIDER v. RUSK

377 U.S. 163 (1964)

In this case the government invoked a provision of the Immigration and Nationality Act of 1952 which stated that a naturalized citizen should lose his citizenship by having a continuous residence for three years in the foreign state in which he was born. Angelika Schneider, a German by birth, had come to this country with her parents in 1939 when a small child and had acquired United States citizenship by

---

[16] Nishikawa v. Dulles, 356 U.S. 129 (1958).
[17] Trop v. Dulles, 356 U.S. 86 (1958).
[18] Kennedy v. Mendoza-Martinez, 372 U.S. 144 (1963).

naturalization in 1950. After graduating from Smith College, she went abroad for postgraduate work. While there in 1956 she met a German lawyer and, after a brief return to the United States, she went to Germany where she married him and took up residence. After her marriage, she returned to the United States on two occasions for visits. Two of her four sons, born in Germany, had both German citizenship by birth and American citizenship by virtue of another provision of the 1952 Act conferring such citizenship on a person born outside the United States of one alien parent and a parent of American citizenship who had resided in the United States for at least ten years. Whether or not her other two sons, born after she had resided in Germany more than three years, also had American citizenship turned on the outcome of this case.

MR. JUSTICE DOUGLAS delivered the opinion of the Court.

The Solicitor General makes his case along the following lines.

Over a period of many years this Government has been seriously concerned by special problems engendered when naturalized citizens return for a long period to the countries of their former nationalities. It is upon this premise that the argument derives that Congress, through its power over foreign relations, has the power to deprive such citizens of their citizenship.

Other nations, it is said, frequently attempt to treat such persons as their own citizens, thus embroiling the United States in conflicts when it attempts to afford them protection. It is argued that expatriation is an alternative to withdrawal of diplomatic protection. It is also argued that Congress reasonably can protect against the tendency of three years' residence in a naturalized citizen's former homeland to weaken his or her allegiance to this country. The argument continues that it is not invidious discrimination for Congress to treat such naturalized citizens differently from the manner in which it treats native-born citizens and that Congress has the right to legislate with respect to the general class without regard to each factual violation. It is finally argued that Congress here, unlike the situation in *Kennedy* v. *Mendoza-Martinez* [note 18, *supra*] was aiming only to regulate and not to punish, and that what Congress did had been deemed appropriate not only by this country but by many others and is in keeping with traditional American concepts of citizenship.

We start from the premise that the rights of citizenship of the native born and of the naturalized person are of the same dignity and are coextensive. The only difference drawn by the Constitution is that only the "natural born" citizen is eligible to be President. Art. II, §1.

While the rights of citizenship of the native born derive from §1 of the Fourteenth Amendment and the rights of the naturalized citizen derive from satisfying, free of fraud, the requirements set by Congress, the latter, apart from the exception noted, "becomes a member of the society, possessing all the rights of a native citizen, and standing, in the view of the constitution, on the footing of a native. The constitution does not authorize Congress to enlarge or abridge those rights. The simple power of the national Legislature, is to prescribe a uniform rule of naturalization, and the exercise of this power exhausts it, so far as respects the individual." *Osborn* v. *Bank of United States*, 9 Wheat. 738.

Views of the Justices have varied when it comes to the problem of expatriation.

There is one view that the power of Congress to take away citizenship for activities of the citizen is nonexistent absent expatriation by the voluntary renunciation of nationality and allegiance. See *Perez* v. *Brownell* [note 15, *supra*] (dissenting opinion of JUSTICES BLACK and DOUGLAS); *Trop* v. *Dulles* [note 17, *supra*] (opinion by CHIEF JUSTICE WARREN). That view has not yet commanded a majority of the entire Court. Hence we are faced with the issue presented and decided in *Perez* v. *Brownell, supra, i.e.,* whether the present Act violates due process. That in turn comes to the question put in the following words in *Perez*:

> "Is the means, withdrawal of citizenship, reasonably calculated to effect the end that is within the power of Congress to achieve, the avoidance of embarrassment in the conduct of our foreign relations . . . ?"

In that case, where an American citizen voted in a foreign election, the answer was in the affirmative. In the present case the question is whether the same answer should be given merely because the naturalized citizen lived in her former homeland continuously for three years. We think not.

Speaking of the provision in the Nationality Act of 1940, which was the predecessor of [the 1952 Act], Chairman Dickstein of the House said that the bill would "relieve this country of the responsibility of those who reside in foreign lands and only claim citizenship when it serves their purpose." And the Senate Report on the 1940 bill stated:

> "These provisions for loss of nationality by residence abroad would greatly lessen the task of the United States in protecting through the Department of State nominal citizens of this country who are abroad but whose real interests, as shown by the condi-

tions of their foreign stay, are not in this country." S. Rep. No. 2150, 76th Cong., 3d Sess., p. 4.

As stated by Judge Fahy, dissenting below, such legislation, touching as it does on the "most precious right" of citizenship, would have to be justified under the foreign relations power "by some more urgent public necessity than substituting administrative convenience for the individual right of which the citizen is deprived."

In *Kennedy* v. *Mendoza-Martinez* [note 18, *supra*], a divided Court held that it was beyond the power of Congress to deprive an American of his citizenship automatically and without any prior judicial or administrative proceedings because he left the United States in time of war to evade or avoid training or service in the Armed Forces. The Court held that it was an unconstitutional use of congressional power because it took away citizenship as punishment for the offense of remaining outside the country to avoid military service, without, at the same time, affording him the procedural safeguards granted by the Fifth and Sixth Amendments. Yet even the dissenters, who felt that flight or absence to evade the duty of helping to defend the country in time of war amounted to manifest nonallegiance, made a reservation. JUSTICE STEWART stated:

> "Previous decisions have suggested that congressional exercise of the power to expatriate may be subject to a further constitutional restriction—a limitation upon the kind of activity which may be made the basis of denationalization. Withdrawal of citizenship is a drastic measure. Moreover, the power to expatriate endows government with authority to define and to limit the society which it represents and to which it is responsible.
>
> "This Court has never held that Congress' power to expatriate may be used unsparingly in every area in which it has general power to act. Our previous decisions upholding involuntary denationalization all involved conduct inconsistent with undiluted allegiance to this country."

This statute proceeds on the impermissible assumption that naturalized citizens as a class are less reliable and bear less allegiance to this country than do the native born. This is an assumption that is impossible for us to make. Moreover, while the Fifth Amendment contains no equal protection clause, it does forbid discrimination that is "so unjustifiable as to be violative of due process." *Bolling* v. *Sharpe*, 347 U.S. 497 [note 22, p. 284, *infra*]. A native-born citizen is free to reside abroad indefinitely without suffering loss of citizenship. The discrimination aimed at naturalized citizens drastically limits their rights to live and work abroad in a way that other citizens may. It creates indeed a second-class citizenship. Living abroad, whether the citizen be naturalized or native born, is no badge of lack of allegiance and in no way evidences a voluntary renunciation of nationality and allegiance. It may indeed be compelled by family, business, or other legitimate reasons.

In 1967, in Afroyim v. Rusk,[19] the Court reconsidered Perez v. Brownell[20] and overruled it. Holding that Congress could not constitutionally take away the naturalized citizenship of one who had voted in an Israeli election, the Court now asserted, as Douglas had for the past nine years, that "the Fourteenth Amendment was designed to, and does, protect every citizen of this Nation against a congressional forcible destruction of his citizenship. . . . Our holding does no more than give to this citizen that which is his own, a constitutional right to remain a citizen in a free country unless he voluntarily relinquishes that citizenship."

Four years later in the Bellei case, the Court upheld another section of the 1952 Act which provided that persons who had acquired American citizenship, as had Mrs. Schneider's minor sons, by being born abroad of one alien and one American parent, should lose that citizenship unless they spent five continuous years in the United States between the ages of fourteen and twenty-eight. Conceding the power of Congress to grant citizenship at birth to Bellei, who was born in Italy of an Italian father and an American mother, the Court found the first sentence of the Fourteenth Amendment, on which it had relied in the Afroyim case, inapplicable to him. Since he was neither "born or naturalized in the United States," he was "simply . . . not a Fourteenth Amendment-first-sentence citizen." And, since the action of Congress was not "arbitrary," there was no other constitutional obstacle to termination of his citizenship. Douglas joined in a dissent which said in part:

. . . . Although those Americans who acquire their citizenship under statutes conferring citizenship on the foreign-born children of citizens are not popularly thought of as naturalized citizens, the use of the word "naturalize" in this way has a considerable constitutional history. . . . The first congressional exercise of [the constitutional power to enact naturalization laws], entitled "An Act to establish an uniform Rule of Naturalization," was passed in 1790 . . . It provided in part: And the children of citizens of

[19] 387 U.S. 253 (1967).
[20] Note 15, supra.

the United States, that may be born . . . out of the limits of the United States, shall be considered as natural born citizens. . . ." This provision is the earliest form of the statute under which Bellei acquired his citizenship.

The majority opinion appears at times to rely on the argument that Bellei, while he concededly might have been a naturalized citizen, was not naturalized "in the United States". . . . I cannot accept [this] narrow and extraordinarily technical reading of the Fourteenth Amendment. . . . If, for example, Congress should decide to vest the authority to naturalize aliens in American embassy officials abroad rather than having the ceremony performed in this country, I have no doubt that those so naturalized would be just as fully protected by the Fourteenth Amendment as are those who go through our present naturalizaton procedures. Rather than the technical reading adopted by the majority, it is my view that the word "in" as it appears in the phrase "in the United States" was surely meant to be understood in two somewhat different senses: one can become a citizen of this country by being born within it or by being naturalized into it.[21]

[21] Rogers v. Bellei, 401 U.S. 815 (1971).

4

RELIGIOUS FREEDOM

By exercising the right to vote, which was considered in Chapter 2, citizens in a democratic government periodically register their views as to who should exercise the powers of government. But the theory of the First Amendment, made applicable to the states by the Fourteenth, is that they should also remain free to formulate and register their views as to how they should be governed at all times and that in one area of belief—religion—they should be free from government interference. Hence, the First Amendment provides that "Congress shall make no law respecting an establishment of religion or prohibiting the free exercise thereof; or abridging the freedom of speech or of the press; or the right of the people peaceably to assemble, and to petition the Government for a redress of grievances."

Before Douglas joined the Court, Justice Stone in a famous footnote suggested that unlike legislation regulating economic activity, "legislation which restricts those political processes which can ordinarily be expected to bring about repeal of undesirable legislation" may be "subjected to more exacting judicial scrutiny."[1] Later, in a dissenting opinion in which Douglas joined, Stone reformulated the idea to say that the freedoms guaranteed by the First Amendment, being vital to the democratic process, are in a "preferred position" among the guarantees of the Bill of Rights.[2]

Apart from cases previously discussed,[3] finding protection in the First Amendment against convictions for contempt of court, most of the cases arising under that amendment in the first decade of Douglas' service on the Court involved Jehovah's Witnesses, who go about distributing literature, proselytizing, and soliciting contributions, thus exercising

---

[1] *United States v. Carolene Products Co.*, 304 U.S. 144, n. 4 (1938).
[2] *Jones v. Opelika*, 316 U.S. 584 (1942).
[3] See pp. 78–84, *supra*.

*rights of free speech, press, and religion. With Douglas concurring,
statutes requiring licenses for such activity and leaving discretion with
the licensing authority to grant or deny the license were invalidated.[4]
Even though the action of the licensing authority was subject to judicial
review, the license requirements constituted a "prior restraint" on the
exercise of First Amendment rights which the Court had much earlier
found to be impermissible in another context.[5] A fortiori, the absolute
prohibition of the distribution of the Witnesses' religious literature on
the public streets was invalid, even though that literature also solicited
contributions.[6]*

<hr>

MURDOCK v. PENNSYLVANIA
319 U.S. 105 (1943)

*When the Court originally held, in Jones v. Opelika,[7] that the sale of
religious literature by the Witnesses or the solicitation of contributions
in connection with its distribution rendered the activity sufficiently
commercial to justify a state license tax, Douglas joined in dissent. The
following year the Court reversed itself and adopted the dissenters'
view,[8] assigning as its reasons those given in this companion case.*

MR. JUSTICE DOUGLAS delivered the opinion of the Court.

The City of Jeannette, Pennsylvania, has an ordinance, some forty
years old, which provides in part:
"That all persons canvassing for or soliciting within said Borough,
orders for goods, paintings, pictures, wares, or merchandise of any kind
shall be required to procure from the Burgess a license to transact said
business and shall pay to the Treasurer of said Borough therefore the
following sums according to the time for which said license shall be
granted.
"For one day $1.50, for one week . . . $7.00, for two weeks . . . $12.00,
for three weeks . . . $20.00. . . ."
Petitioners are "Jehovah's Witnesses." They went about from door
to door in the City of Jeannette distributing literature and soliciting
people to "purchase" certain religious books and pamphlets, all pub-

<hr>

[4] *Cantwell v. Connecticut*, 310 U.S. 296 (1940); *Largent v. Texas*, 318 U.S.
418 (1943).
[5] *Near v. Minnesota*, 283 U.S. 697 (1931). See p. 215, *infra*.
[6] *Jamison v. Texas*, 318 U.S. 413 (1943). See also Douglas' dissenting opinion in
Poulos v. New Hampshire, 345 U.S. 395 (1953).
[7] Note 2, *supra*.
[8] *Jones v. Opelika*, 319 U.S. 103 (1943).

lished by the Watch Tower Bible & Tract Society.[9] The "price" of the books was twenty-five cents each, the "price" of the pamphlets five cents each.[10] In connection with these activities, petitioners used a phonograph[11] on which they played a record expounding certain of their views on religion. None of them obtained a license under the ordinance. Before they were arrested each had made "sales" of books. There was evidence that it was their practice in making these solicitations to request a "contribution" of twenty-five cents each for the books and five cents each for the pamphlets, but to accept lesser sums or even to donate the volumes in case an interested person was without funds. In the present case, some donations of pamphlets were made when books were purchased. Petitioners were convicted and fined for violation of the ordinance.

The First Amendment, which the Fourteenth makes applicable to the states, declares that "Congress shall make no law respecting an establishment of religion, or prohibiting the free exercise thereof; or abridging the freedom of speech, or of the press . . ." It could hardly be denied that a tax laid specifically on the exercise of those freedoms would be unconstitutional. Yet the license tax imposed by this ordinance is, in substance, just that.

Petitioners spread their interpretations of the Bible and their religious beliefs largely through the hand distribution of literature by full or part time workers. They claim to follow the example of Paul, teaching "publickly, and from house to house." Acts 20:20. They take literally the mandate of the Scriptures, "Go ye into all the world, and preach the gospel to every creature." Mark 16:15. In doing so they believe that they are obeying a commandment of God.

The hand distribution of religious tracts is an age-old form of missionary evangelism—as old as the history of printing presses.[12] It has been a potent force in various religious movements down through the years.[13]

---

[9] Two religious books—Salvation and Creation—were sold. Others were offered in addition to the Bible. The Watch Tower Bible & Tract Society is alleged to be a non-profit charitable corporation.

[10] Petitioners paid three cents each for the pamphlets and, if they devoted only their spare time to the work, twenty cents each for the books. Those devoting full time to the work acquired the books for five cents each. There was evidence that some of the petitioners paid the difference between the sales price and the cost of the books to their local congregations which distributed the literature.

[11] Purchased along with the record from the Watch Tower Bible and Tract Society.

[12] Palmer, The Printing Press and the Gospel (1912).

[13] White, The Colporteur Evangelist (1930); Home Evangelization (1850); Edwards, The Romance of the Book (1932) c. V; 12 Biblical Repository (1844) Art. VIII; 16 The Sunday Magazine (1887) pp. 43–47; 3 Meliora (1861) pp. 311–319; Felice, Protestants of France (1853) pp. 53, 513; 3 D'Aubigne, History of The

This form of evangelism is utilized today on a large scale by various religious sects whose colporteurs carry the Gospel to thousands upon thousands of homes and seek through personal visitations to win adherents to their faith.[14] It is more than preaching; it is more than distribution of religious literature. It is a combination of both. Its purpose is as evangelical as the revival meeting. This form of religious activity occupies the same high estate under the First Amendment as do worship in the churches and preaching from the pulpits. It has the same claim to protection as the more orthodox and conventional exercises of religion. It also has the same claim as the others to the guarantees of freedom of speech and freedom of the press.

The integrity of this conduct or behavior as a religious practice has not been challenged. Nor do we have presented any question as to the sincerity of petitioners in their religious beliefs and practices, however misguided they may be thought to be. Moreover, we do not intimate or suggest in respecting their sincerity that any conduct can be made a religious rite and by the zeal of the practitioners swept into the First Amendment. *Reynolds* v. *United States*, 98 U.S. 145, and *Davis* v. *Beason*, 133 U.S. 333 denied any such claim to the practice of polygamy and bigamy. Other claims may well arise which deserve the same fate. We only hold that spreading one's religious beliefs or preaching the Gospel through distribution of religious literature and through personal visitations is an age-old type of evangelism with as high a claim to constitutional protection as the more orthodox types. The manner in which it is practiced at times gives rise to special problems with which

---

Reformation (1849) pp. 103, 152, 436–437; Report of Colportage in Virginia, North Carolina & South Carolina, American Tract Society (1855). An early type of colporteur was depicted by John Greenleaf Whittier in his legendary poem, The Vaudois Teacher. And see, Wylie, History of the Waldenses.

[14] The General Conference of Seventh-Day Adventists, who filed a brief *amicus curiae* on the reargument of *Jones* v. *Opelika*, has given us the following data concerning their literature ministry: This denomination has 83 publishing houses throughout the world, issuing publications in over 200 languages. Some 9,256 separate publications were issued in 1941. By printed and spoken word, the Gospel is carried into 412 countries in 824 languages. 1942 Yearbook, p. 287. During December 1941, a total of 1,018 colporteurs operated in North America. They delivered during that month $97,997.19 worth of gospel literature, and for the whole year of 1941 a total of $790,610.36—an average per person of about $65 per month. Some of these were students and temporary workers. Colporteurs of this denomination receive half of their collections, from which they must pay their traveling and living expenses. Colporteurs are specially trained and their qualifications equal those of preachers. In the field, each worker is under the supervision of a field missionary secretary to whom a weekly report is made. After fifteen years of continuous service, each colporteur is entitled to the same pension as retired ministers.

the police power of the states is competent to deal. See for example *Cox* v. *New Hampshire* [note 20, *infra*] and *Chaplinsky* v. *New Hampshire* [note 22, *infra*]. But that merely illustrates that the rights with which we are dealing are not absolutes. We are concerned, however, in these cases merely with one narrow issue. There is presented for decision no question whatsoever concerning punishment for any alleged unlawful acts during the solicitation. Nor is there involved here any question as to the validity of a registration system for colporteurs and other solicitors. The cases present a single issue—the constitutionality of an ordinance which as construed and applied requires religious colporteurs to pay a license tax as a condition to the pursuit of their activities.

The alleged justification for the exaction of this license tax is the fact that the religious literature is distributed with a solicitation of funds. Thus it was stated, in *Jones* v. *Opelika* [note 2, *supra*], that when a religious sect uses "ordinary commercial methods of sales of articles to raise propaganda funds," it is proper for the state to charge "reasonable fees for the privilege of canvassing." Situations will arise where it will be difficult to determine whether a particular activity is religious or purely commercial. The distinction at times is vital. As we stated only the other day, in *Jamison* v. *Texas* [note 6, *supra*], "The states can prohibit the use of the streets for the distribution of purely commercial leaflets, even though such leaflets may have 'a civic appeal, or a moral platitude' appended. *Valentine* v. *Chrestensen*, 316 U.S. 52.[15] They may not prohibit the distribution of handbills in the pursuit of a clearly religious activity merely because the handbills invite the purchase of books for the improved understanding of the religion or because the handbills seek in a lawful fashion to promote the raising of funds for religious purposes." But the mere fact that the religious literature is "sold" by itinerant preachers rather than "donated" does not transform evangelism into a commercial enterprise. If it did, then the passing of the collection plate in church would make the church service a commercial project. The constitutional rights of those spreading their religious beliefs through the spoken and printed word are not to be gauged by standards governing retailers or wholesalers of books. The right to use the press for expressing one's views is not to be measured by the protection afforded commercial handbills. It should be remembered that the pamphlets of Thomas Paine were not distributed free of charge. It is plain that a religious organization needs funds to remain a going concern. But an itinerant evangelist, however misguided or intolerant he may be, does not become a mere book agent by selling

---

[15] [But see discussion at p. 139, *infra*.]

the Bible or religious tracts to help defray his expenses or to sustain him. Freedom of speech, freedom of the press, freedom of religion are available to all, not merely to those who can pay their own way. As we have said, the problem of drawing the line between a purely commercial activity and a religious one will at times be difficult. On this record it plainly cannot be said that petitioners were engaged in a commercial rather than a religious venture. It is a distortion of the facts of record to describe their activities as the occupation of selling books and pamphlets. And the Pennsylvania court did not rest the judgments of conviction on that basis, though it did find that petitioners "sold" the literature. The Supreme Court of Iowa in *State* v. *Mead*, 230 Iowa 1217, described the selling activities of members of this same sect as "merely incidental and collateral" to their "main object which was to preach and publicize the doctrines of their order." That accurately summarizes the present record.

We do not mean to say that religious groups and the press are free from all financial burdens of government. We have here something quite different, for example, from a tax on the income of one who engages in religious activities or a tax on property used or employed in connection with those activities. It is one thing to impose a tax on the income or property of a preacher. It is quite another thing to exact a tax from him for the privilege of delivering a sermon. The tax imposed by the City of Jeannette is a flat license tax, the payment of which is a condition of the exercise of these constitutional privileges. The power to tax the exercise of a privilege is the power to control or suppress its enjoyment. Those who can tax the exercise of this religious practice can make its exercise so costly as to deprive it of the resources necessary for its maintenance. Those who can tax the privilege of engaging in this form of missionary evangelism can close its doors to all those who do not have a full purse. Spreading religious beliefs in· this ancient and honorable manner would thus be denied the needy. Those who can deprive religious groups of their colporteurs can take from them a part of the vital power of the press which has survived from the Reformation.

It is contended, however, that the fact that the license tax can suppress or control this activity is unimportant if it does not do so. But that is to disregard the nature of this tax. It is a license tax—a flat tax imposed on the exercise of a privilege granted by the Bill of Rights. A state may not impose a charge for the enjoyment of a right granted by the Federal Constitution. Thus, it may not exact a license tax for the privilege of carrying on interstate commerce ·(*McGoldrick* v. *Berwind-White Co.*, 309 U.S. 33), although it may tax the property used in, or the income derived from, that commerce, so long as those taxes are not discriminatory. A license tax applied to activities guaranteed by the First

Amendment would have the same destructive effect. It is true that the First Amendment, like the commerce clause, draws no distinction between license taxes, fixed sum taxes, and other kinds of taxes. But that is no reason why we should shut our eyes to the nature of the tax and its destructive influence. The power to impose a license tax on the exercise of these freedoms is indeed as potent as the power of censorship which this Court has repeatedly struck down. *Cantwell* v. *Connecticut* [note 4, *supra*]; *Largent* v. *Texas* [note 4, *supra*]; *Jamison* v. *Texas* [note 6, *supra*]. It was for that reason that the dissenting opinions in *Jones* v. *Opelika* [note 2, *supra*] stressed the nature of this type of tax. In that case, as in the present ones, we have something very different from a registration system under which those going from house to house are required to give their names, addresses and other marks of identification to the authorities. In all of these cases the issuance of the permit or license is dependent on the payment of a license tax. And the license tax is fixed in amount and unrelated to the scope of the activities of petitioners or to their realized revenues. It is not a nominal fee imposed as a regulatory measure to defray the expenses of policing the activities in question. It is in no way apportioned. It is a flat license tax levied and collected as a condition to the pursuit of activities whose enjoyment is guaranteed by the First Amendment. Accordingly, it restrains in advance those constitutional liberties of press and religion and inevitably tends to suppress their exercise. That is almost uniformly recognized as the inherent vice and evil of this flat license tax. As stated by the Supreme Court of Illinois in a case involving this same sect and an ordinance similar to the present one, a person cannot be compelled "to purchase, through a license fee or a license tax, the privilege freely granted by the constitution." *Blue Island* v. *Kozul*, 379 Ill. 511. So, it may not be said that proof is lacking that these license taxes either separately or cumulatively have restricted or are likely to restrict petitioners' religious activities. On their face they are a restriction of the free exercise of those freedoms which are protected by the First Amendment.

The taxes imposed by this ordinance can hardly help but be as severe and telling in their impact on the freedom of the press and religion as the "taxes on knowledge" at which the First Amendment was partly aimed. *Grosjean* v. *American Press Co.* [297 U.S. 233]. They may indeed operate even more subtly. Itinerant evangelists moving throughout a state or from state to state would feel immediately the cumulative effect of such ordinances as they become fashionable. The way of the religious dissenter has long been hard. But if the formula of this type of ordinance is approved, a new device for the suppression of religious minorities will have been found. This method of disseminating religious beliefs can be crushed and closed out by the sheer weight of the toll or tribute which is exacted town by town, village by village. The spread of religious ideas through personal visitations by the literature ministry of numerous religious groups would be stopped.

The fact that the ordinance is "nondiscriminatory" is immaterial. The protection accorded by the First Amendment is not so restricted. A license tax certainly does not acquire constitutional validity because it classifies the privileges protected by the First Amendment along with the wares and merchandise of hucksters and peddlers and treats them all alike. Such equality in treatment does not save the ordinance. Freedom of press, freedom of speech, freedom of religion are in a preferred position.

It is claimed, however, that the ultimate question in determining the constitutionality of this license tax is whether the state has given something for which it can ask a return. That principle has wide applicability. But it is quite irrelevant here. This tax is not a charge for the enjoyment of a privilege or benefit bestowed by the state. The privilege in question exists apart from state authority. It is guaranteed the people by the Federal Constitution.

Considerable emphasis is placed on the kind of literature which petitioners were distributing—its provocative, abusive, and ill-mannered character and the assault which it makes on our established churches and the cherished faiths of many of us. But those considerations are no justification for the license tax which the ordinance imposes. Plainly a community may not suppress, or the state tax, the dissemination of views because they are unpopular, annoying or distasteful. If that device were ever sanctioned, there would have been forged a ready instrument for the suppression of the faith which any minority cherishes but which does not happen to be in favor. That would be a complete repudiation of the philosophy of the Bill of Rights.

Jehovah's Witnesses are not "above the law." But the present ordinance is not directed to the problems with which the police power of the state is free to deal. It does not cover, and petitioners are not charged with, breaches of the peace. They are pursuing their solicitations peacefully and quietly. Petitioners, moreover, are not charged with or prosecuted for the use of langauge which is obscene, abusive, or which incites retaliation. Cf. *Chaplinsky* v. *New Hampshire* [315 U.S. 568 (1942)]. Nor do we have here, as we did in *Cox* v. *New Hampshire* [note 20, *infra*] and *Chaplinsky* v. *New Hampshire, supra,* state regulation of the streets to protect and insure the safety, comfort, or convenience of the public. Furthermore, the present ordinance is not narrowly drawn to safeguard the people of the community in their homes against the evils of solicitations. As we have said, it is not merely a registration ordinance calling for an identification of the solicitors so as to give the authorities some basis for investigating strangers coming into the community. And the fee is not a nominal one, imposed as a regulatory measure and calculated to defray the expense of protecting those on the streets and at home against the abuses of solicitors. Nor can the present ordinance survive if we assume that it has been construed to apply only to solicitation from house to house.[16] The ordinance is not narrowly drawn to prevent or control abuses or evils arising from that activity. Rather, it sets aside the residential areas as a prohibited zone, entry of which is denied petitioners unless the tax is paid. That restraint and one which is city-wide in scope (*Jones* v. *Opelika*) are different only in degree. Each is an abridgment of freedom of press and a restraint on the free exercise of religion. They stand or fall together.

The judgment in *Jones* v. *Opelika* has this day been vacated. Freed from that controlling precedent, we can restore to their high, constitutional position the liberties of itinerant evangelists who disseminate their religious beliefs and the tenets of their faith through distribution of literature.

In other cases Douglas voted with the Court to invalidate, as applied to Jehovah's Witnesses, an ordinance forbidding knocking on doors or ringing doorbells for the purpose of distributing literature,[17] and to hold that, where an entire town was company-owned and the prohibition on distribution of literature was company-imposed, the state could not impose criminal sanctions for violation of the prohibition.[18] He also voted with the Court to hold that where the commander of a federal military fort left its streets open to the public, he could not prevent a Quaker from distributing leaflets on them.[19]

Jehovah's Witnesses did not always prevail, however. Douglas voted with the Court to hold that they were subject to reasonable state regulation of the use of the streets for parades,[20] and that the state could prohibit their minor children from distributing literature on the streets.[21] He voted with the Court again to hold that the state could punish a Witness for calling the town marshal, in a fact-to-face en-

---

[16] The Pennsylvania Superior Court stated that the ordinance has been "enforced" only to prevent petitioners from canvassing "from door to door and house to house" without a license and not to prevent them from distributing their literature on the streets.

[17] *Martin* v. *City of Struthers*, 319 U.S. 141 (1943).

[18] *Marsh* v. *Alabama*, 326 U.S. 501 (1946).

[19] *Flower* v. *United States*, 407 U.S. 197 (1972).

[20] *Cox* v. *New Hampshire*, 312 U.S. 569 (1941).

[21] *Prince* v. *Massachusetts*, 321 U.S. 158 (1944).

counter, "A God damned racketeer" and "a damned Fascist." Such "fighting words," which "by their very utterance . . . tend to incite an immediate breach of the peace" were thought to be "of such slight social value" as to find no protection in the First Amendment.[22]

The Witnesses suffered another setback in a 1940 decision, in which Douglas joined, holding that the state could subject their children to a compulsory flag salute in the public schools.[23] But in their dissenting opinion in Jones v. Opelika[24] in 1942 Justices Black, Douglas, and Murphy took occasion to say that they had concluded they were wrong in the flag salute case. The following year they joined with the Court to overrule that decision and to declare: "If there is any fixed star in our constitutional constellation, it is that no official, high or petty, can prescribe what shall be orthodox in politics, nationalism, religion, or other matters of opinion or force citizens to confess by word or act their faith therein."[25]

WISCONSIN V. YODER
406 U.S. 205 (1972)

Defendants in this case, Jonas Yoder, Wallace Miller, and Adin Yutzy, practitioners of the Amish religion, were prosecuted by the State of Wisconsin because they declined, on religious grounds, to send their children, Frieda Yoder and Barbara Miller, aged fifteen, and Vernon Yutzy, aged fourteen, to high school until they reached sixteen years of age as required by the state's compulsory school-attendance law. Although the Court had earlier held, in Pierce v. Society of Sisters,[26] that the state cannot require parents who are sending their children to parochial schools to send them to public schools instead, this case differed from Pierce, since the Wisconsin statute permitted attendance at private schools, but the defendants' children were not enrolled in any private school.

Finding that defendants under their sincerely held Amish beliefs rejected institutionalized churches, sought to return to the early, simple Christian life, de-emphasized material success, sought to insulate themselves from the modern world, required their members to make their

[22] Chaplinsky v. New Hampshire, 315 U.S. 568 (1942).
[23] Minersville School District v. Gobitis, 310 U.S. 586 (1940).
[24] Note 2, supra.
[25] West Virginia Board of Education v. Barnette, 319 U.S. 624 (1943). See also Torcaso v. Watkins, 367 U.S. 488 (1961), where Douglas voted with the Court to hold that a state cannot require notaries public to proclaim a belief in God as a test of office.
[26] 268 U.S. 510 (1925).

living by farming or closely related activities, and finding also that the
values taught in high school were in marked variance with these beliefs,
the Court held that the Wisconsin statute invalidly infringed on de-
fendants' free exercise of their religion. Rejecting the idea that reli-
giously grounded conduct (as distinguished from beliefs) is always out-
side the protection of the First Amendment, the Court concluded that
"secondary schooling, by exposing Amish children to worldly influences
in terms of attitudes, goals, and values contrary to [defendants'] beliefs,
and by substantially interfering with the religious development of the
Amish child and his integration into the way of life of the Amish com-
munity at the crucial adolescent stage of development, contravenes the
basic religious tenets and practice of the Amish faith, both as to the
parent and the child." (But the Court expressly disavowed any ruling
on the Constitutional rights of the Amish children, who were not
parties to this case.) And the state was held to have no such compelling
interest in equipping Amish children with a conventional high school
education, as opposed to the Amish system of vocational education, as
would justify an infringement of Amish freedom under the First
Amendment.

Chief Justice Burger's opinion for the Court also observed that the
Amish "are productive and very law-abiding members of society; they
reject public welfare in any of its usual modern forms." And he added:
"It cannot be overemphasized that we are not dealing with a way of
life and mode of education by a group claiming to have recently dis-
covered some 'progressive' or more enlightened process for rearing
children for modern life." The Amish had "a history of three centuries
as an identifiable religious sect and a long history as a successful and
self-sufficient segment of American society" and had made a "convincing
showing, one that probably few other religious groups or sects could
make" of the adequacy of their "alternative mode of continuing in-
formal vocational education."

MR. JUSTICE DOUGLAS, dissenting in part.

I

I agree with the Court that the religious scruples of the Amish are
opposed to the education of their children beyond the grade schools,
yet I disagree with the Court's conclusion that the matter is within the
dispensation of parents alone. The Court's analysis assumes that the
only interests at stake in the case are those of the Amish parents on
the one hand, and those of the State on the other. The difficulty with
this approach is that, despite the Court's claim, the parents are seek-

ing to vindicate not only their own free exercise claims, but also those of their high-school-age children.

It is argued that the right of the Amish children to religious freedom is not presented by the facts of the case, as the issue before the Court involves only the Amish parents' religious freedom to defy a state criminal statute imposing upon them an affirmative duty to cause their children to attend high school.

First, [defendants'] motion to dismiss in the trial court expressly asserts, not only the religious liberty of the adults, but also that of the children, as a defense to the prosecutions. It is, of course, beyond question that the parents have standing as defendants in a criminal prosecution to assert the religious interests of their children as a defense.[27] Although the lower courts and a majority of this Court assume an identity of interest between parent and child, it is clear that they have treated the religious interest of the child as a factor in the analysis.

Second, it is essential to reach the question to decide the case, not only because the question was squarely raised in the motion to dismiss, but also because no analysis of religious-liberty claims can take place in a vacuum. If the parents in this case are allowed a religious exemption, the inevitable effect is to impose the parents' notions of religious duty upon their children. Where the child is mature enough to express potentially conflicting desires, it would be an invasion of the child's rights to permit such an imposition without canvassing his views. As in *Prince* v. *Massachusetts* [note 21, *supra*], it is an imposition resulting from this very litigation. As the child has no other effective forum, it is in this litigation that his rights should be considered. And, if an Amish child desires to attend high school, and is mature enough to have that desire respected, the State may well be able to override the parents' religiously motivated objections.

Religion is an individual experience. It is not necessary, nor even appropriate, for every Amish child to express his views on the subject in a prosecution of a single adult. Crucial, however, are the views of

---

[27] Thus, in *Prince* v. *Massachusetts* [note 21, *supra*] a Jehovah's Witness was convicted for having violated a state child labor law by allowing her nine-year-old niece and ward to circulate religious literature on the public streets. There, as here, the narrow question was the religious liberty of the adult. There, as here, the Court analyzed the problem from the point of view of the State's conflicting interest in the welfare of the child. But, as Mr. Justice Brennan, speaking for the Court, has so recently pointed out, "The Court [in Prince] implicitly held that the custodian had standing to assert alleged freedom of religion . . . rights of the child that were threatened in the very litigation before the Court and that the child had no effective way of asserting herself." *Eisenstadt* v. *Baird*, 405 U.S. 438. Here, as in Prince, the children have no effective alternate means to vindicate their rights. The question, therefore, is squarely before us.

the child whose parent is the subject of the suit. Frieda Yoder has in fact testified that her own religious views are opposed to high-school education. I therefore join the judgment of the Court as to respondent Jonas Yoder. But Frieda Yoder's views may not be those of Vernon Yutzy or Barbara Miller. I must dissent, therefore, as to respondents Adin Yutzy and Wallace Miller as their motion to dismiss also raised the question of their children's religious liberty.

II

This issue has never been squarely presented before today. Our opinions are full of talk about the power of the parents over the child's education. See *Pierce* v. *Society of Sisters* [page 140, *supra*]; *Meyer* v. *Nebraska*, 262 U.S. 390.[28] And we have in the past analyzed similar conflicts between parent and State with little regard for the views of the child. See *Prince* v. *Massachusetts*, *supra*. Recent cases, however, have clearly held that the children themselves have constitutionally protectible interests.

These children are "persons" within the meaning of the Bill of Rights. We have so held over and over again. In *Haley* v. *Ohio*, 332 U.S. 596, we extended the protection of the Fourteenth Amendment in a state trial of a 15-year-old boy. In *In re Gault*, 387 U.S. 1, we held that "neither the Fourteenth Amendment nor the Bill of Rights is for adults alone." In *In re Winship*, 397 U.S. 358, we held that a 12-year-old boy, when charged with an act which would be a crime if committed by an adult, was entitled to procedural safeguards contained in the Sixth Amendment.

In *Tinker* v. *Des Moines School District*, 393 U.S. 503, we dealt with 13-year-old, 15-year-old, and 16-year-old students who wore armbands to public schools and were disciplined for doing so. We gave them relief, saying that their First Amendment rights had been abridged: "Students in school as well as out of school are 'persons' under our Constitution. They are possessed of fundamental rights which the State must respect, just as they themselves must respect their obligations to the State."

In *Board of Education* v. *Barnette* [note 25, *supra*], we held that schoolchildren, whose religious beliefs collided with a school rule requiring them to salute the flag, could not be required to do so. While the sanction included expulsion of the students and prosecution of the parents, the vice of the regime was its interference with the child's free

[28] [Holding, in 1923, that a state law forbidding the teaching of any modern language other than English in public or private grade schools deprived a teacher of German in a parochial school of his liberty without due process of law and thus violated the Fourteenth Amendment.]

exercise of religion. We said: "Here . . . we are dealing with a compulsion of students to declare a belief." In emphasizing the important and delicate task of boards of education we said: "That they are educating the young for citizenship is reason for scrupulous protection of Constitutional freedoms of the individual, if· we are not to strangle the free mind at its source and teach youth to discount important principles of our government as mere platitudes."

On this important and vital matter of education, I think the children should be entitled to be heard. While the parents, absent dissent, normally speak for the entire family, the education of the child is a matter on which the child will often have decided views. He may want to be a pianist or an astronaut or an oceanographer. To do so he will have to break from the Amish tradition.[29]

It is the future of the student, not the future of the parents, that is imperiled by today's decision. If a parent keeps his child out of school beyond the grade school, then the child will be forever barred from entry into the new and amazing world of diversity that we have today. The child may decide that that is the preferred course, or he may rebel. It is the student's judgment, not his parents', that is essential if we are to give full meaning to what we have said about the Bill of Rights and of the right of students to be masters of their own destiny.[30] If

[29] A significant number of Amish children do leave the Old Order. Professor Hostetler notes that "[t]he loss of members is very limited in some Amish districts and considerable in others." J. Hostetler, Amish Society 226 (1968). In one Pennsylvania church, he observed a defection rate of 30%. Rates up to 50% have been reported by others. Casad, Compulsory High School Attendance and the Old Order Amish: A Commentary on State v. Garber, 16 Kan. L. Rev. 423, 434 n. 51 (1968).

[30] The court below brushed aside the students' interests with the offhand comment that "[w]hen a child reaches the age of judgment, he can choose for himself his religion." But there is nothing in this record to indicate that the moral and intellectual judgment demanded of the student by the question in this case is beyond his capacity. Children far younger than the 14- and 15-year-olds involved here are regularly permitted to testify in custody and other proceedings. Indeed, the failure to call the affected child in a custody hearing is often reversible error. See, e.g., Callicott v. Callicott, 364 SW2d 455 (Civ. App. Tex.) (reversible error for trial judge to refuse to hear testimony of eight-year-old in custody battle). Moreover, there is substantial agreement among child psychologists and sociologists that the moral and intellectual maturity of the 14-year-old approaches that of the adult. See, e.g., J. Piaget, The Moral Judgment of the Child (1948); D. Elkind, Children and Adolescents 75–80 (1970); Kohlberg, Moral Education in the Schools: A Developmental View, in R. Muuss, Adolescent Behavior and Society 193, 199–200 (1971); W. Kay, Moral Development 172–183 (1968); A. Gesell & F. Ilg, Youth: The Years From Ten to Sixteen 175–182 (1956). The maturity of Amish youth, who identify with and assume adult roles from early childhood, see M. Goodman, The Culture of Childhood, 92–94 (1970), is certainly not less than that of children in the general population.

he is harnessed to the Amish way of life by those in authority over him and if his education in truncated, his entire life may be stunted and deformed. The child, therefore, should be given an opportunity to be heard before the State gives the exemption which we honor today.

The views of the two children in question were not canvassed by the Wisconsin courts. The matter should be explicitly reserved so that new hearings can be held on remand of the case.[31]

III

I think the emphasis of the Court on the "law and order" record of this Amish group of people is quite irrelevant. A religion is a religion irrespective of what the misdemeanor or felony records of its members might be. I am not at all sure how the Catholics, Episcopalians, the Baptists, Jehovah's Witnesses, the Unitarians, and my own Presbyterians would make out if subjected to such a test. It is, of course, true that if a group or society was organized to perpetuate crime and if that is its motive, we would have rather startling problems akin to those that were raised when some years back a particular sect was challenged here as operating on a fraudulent basis. *United States* v. *Ballard*, 322 U.S. 78.[32] But no such factors are present here, and the Amish, whether with a high or low criminal record,[33] certainly qualify by all historic standards as a religion within the meaning of the First Amendment.

The Court rightly rejects the notion that actions, even though religiously grounded, are always outside the protection of the Free Exercise Clause of the First Amendment. [But, in its] ruling, the Court departs from the teaching of *Reynolds* v. *United States*, 98 U.S. 145,[34] where

[31] Canvassing the views of all school-age Amish children in the State of Wisconsin would not present insurmountable difficulties. A 1968 survey indicated that there were at that time only 256 such children in the entire state.

[32] [Where Douglas wrote for the Court to hold that in a prosecution for using the mails to defraud by soliciting funds for a religious movement, the First Amendment precluded submission to the jury of the question of the "truth" of defendants' religious doctrines, as distinguished from their good faith belief in them.]

[33] The observation of Justice Heffernan, dissenting below, that the principal opinion in his court portrayed the Amish as leading a life of "idyllic agrarianism," is equally applicable to the majority opinion in this Court. So, too, is his observation that such a portrayal rests on a "mythological basis." Professor Hostetler has noted that "[d]rinking among the youth is common in all the large Amish settlements." *Amish Society* 283. Moreover, "[i]t would appear that among the Amish the rate of suicide is just as high, if not higher, than for the nation." He also notes an unfortunate Amish "preoccupation with filthy stories," as well as significant "rowdyism and stress." These are not traits peculiar to the Amish, of course. The point is that the Amish are not people set apart and different.

[34] [Which held, in 1878, that the Mormon practice of polygamy was not protected as a "free exercise" of religion under the First Amendment.]

it was said concerning the reach of the Free Exercise Clause of the First Amendment, "Congress was deprived of all legislative power over mere opinion, but was left free to reach actions which were in violation of social duties or subversive of good order." In that case it was conceded that polygamy was a part of the religion of the Mormons. Yet the Court said, "It matters not that his belief [in polygamy] was a part of his professed religion: it was still belief, and belief only."

Action, which the Court deemed to be antisocial, could be punished even though it was grounded on deeply held and sincere religious convictions. What we do today, at least in this respect, opens the way to give organized religion a broader base than it has ever enjoyed; and it even promises that in time *Reynolds* will be overruled.

UNITED STATES v. AMERICAN FRIENDS SERVICE COMMITTEE

419 U.S. 7 (1974)

In 1969, two Quaker employees of the American Friends Service Committee, a corporation whose principal operation is philanthropic work and many of whose employees are conscientious objectors to war, requested the Committee to cease withholding 51.6 percent of the taxes required by federal law to be withheld from their wages—51.6 percent being their estimate of the percentage of the federal budget which was military-related. They conceded that the full amount of the tax was legally due but their purpose in making this request was to "bear witness" to their beliefs by reporting the full amount of taxes owing on their annual tax returns but refusing to pay 51.6 percent of that amount, thus compelling the government to take legal action against them to collect that part.

In response to this request, the Committee did cease withholding 51.6 percent of the taxes from the employees' salaries but continued to pay the full amount of the tax required to be withheld to the government. The Committee then brought an action for refund of the amount it had paid over to the government but had not withheld from salaries. The employees joined in the suit and sought an injunction against the enforcement of the tax-withholding statute against the Committee with respect to 51.6 percent of the required withholding as a violation of their free exercise of religion.

The court below ordered a refund to the Committee since the government had also levied on assets of the employees and had received a double payment of the amount due; that court also enjoined the enforcement of the tax-withholding statute against the Committee with respect to 51.6 percent of the employees' salaries, and the government appealed only that portion of the judgment.

The Court reversed the injunction order, finding that it violated another federal statute forbidding suits "for the purpose of restraining the assessment or collection of any tax." The employees' remedy, the Court said, was the same as that pursued by the Committee—a suit for refund, which they would surely lose, since they conceded that the full taxes were legally due. "Even though the remitting of the employees to a refund action may frustrate their chosen method of bearing witness to their religious convictions, a chosen method which they insist is constitutionally protected, the ban of the Anti-Injunction Act is not removed."

MR. JUSTICE DOUGLAS, dissenting.

The sole question on the merits is whether the provision of the Internal Revenue Code which requires employers to deduct and withhold from wages federal income taxes is constitutional as applied to appellees, who on religious grounds object to the withholding taxes on their salaries which represent that portion of the federal budget allocated to military expenditures.[35] They invoke the Free Exercise Clause of the First Amendment, as they are Quakers who are opposed to participation in war in any form and who claim that this method of collection directly forecloses their ability freely to express that opposition, *i.e.*, to bear witness to their religious scruples.

There is no evidence that questions the sincerity of appellees' religious beliefs. Nor is there any issue raised as to whether that religious belief would give appellees a defense against ultimate payment of the tax. The District Court held that the withholding was unconstitutional as to appellees, a conclusion with which I agree.

The withholding process[36] forecloses appellees from bearing witness

---

[35] The District Court found that 51.6 percent was a reasonable estimate of the proportion of the federal budget expended for military and war purposes based on the appropriations made by Congress in the calendar year of 1968, according to a computation by the Friends Committee on National Legislation.

[36] Objections to withholding are not restricted to Quakers. Some federal judges have passionately opposed the withholding of taxes on their salaries, not on the basis that the tax is unconstitutional as was once held (see *O'Malley* v. *Woodrough*, 307 U.S. 277, overruling *Miles* v. *Graham*, 268 U.S. 501), but rather on the grounds that the loss of the use of the sums deducted during the year preceding the April 15th due date is a diminution of their compensation against the command of Art. III, §1, which provides in part: "The Judges, both of the supreme and inferior Courts, shall hold their Offices during good Behavior, and shall, at stated Times, receive for their Services, a Compensation, which shall not be diminished during their Continuance in Office." Whatever may be the merits of that contention, the command of the First Amendment permits of no exceptions, for it states: "Congress shall make no law . . . prohibiting the free exercise" of religion.

to the use of these monthly deductions for military purposes. Under the opinion of this Court, they are deprived of bearing witness to their opposition to war—these withheld portions of their salaries pay the entire tax and they therefore have "no alternative legal remedy."

Quakers with true religious scruples against participating in war may no more be barred from protesting the payment of taxes to support war than they can be forcibly inducted into the Armed Forces and required to carry a gun, and yet denied all opportunity to state their religious views against participation. See *United States* v. *Seeger*, 380 U.S. 163. The Court misses the entire point of the present controversy. Appellees are barred from protesting these monthly deductions under the Court's opinion. Here appellees challenge the withholding law as depriving them of their one and only chance of contesting the constitutionality of the tax as applied to them. So there is no remedy by way of refund.[37]

The religious belief which the Government violates here is that appellees must bear active witness to their objections to their support of war efforts. Dr. Edwin Bronner, who qualified as an expert on the history of Quakerism, gave testimony which, as summarized by the District Court, stated "that most Quakers have considered it an integral part of their faith[38] to bear witness to the beliefs which they hold. It has always been the prevailing view that simple preaching of one's beliefs is not sufficient, and that one's actions must accord with and give expression to one's beliefs. Many of the employees of the AFSC, including particularly [the two employees in this case], share in this belief, and for these employees, the operation of the withholding tax, which leaves them no option as to the payment of the taxes which they conscientiously question, operates as a direct abridgment of the expression and implementation of deeply cherished religious beliefs."

If we are faithful to the command of the First Amendment, we would honor that religious belief. I have not bowed to the view of the majority that "some compelling state interest" will warrant an infringement of

---

[37] In the present case, since the taxpayers do not claim that they are entitled to a refund (conceding that the Government could legitimately collect the tax by *some* method), a refund suit would be summarily dismissed without ever reaching the merits of their claim that the particular method of collection violated their free exercise rights.

[38] "Friends will ever be concerned to relate their religious insights to the realities of international life. Opportunities for courageous action and for the expression of invincible good will remain under any political system. Whatever the system and whatever the situation that calls for decision, Friends are called upon to make their witness." Faith and Practice, the Book of Discipline of the New York Yearly Meeting of the Religious Society of Friends 42 (1968).

the Free Exercise Clause. *Sherbert* v. *Verner*, 374 U.S. 398; *Braunfeld* v. *Brown*, 368 U.S. 599. I have previously dissented from that position and opposed amending by judicial construction the plain command of the Free Exercise Clause.

The Anti-Injunction Act is no barrier. No "assessment or collection of any tax" is restrained, only one method of collection is barred, the Government being left free to use all other means at its disposal. Moreover, to construe the Act as the Court construes it does not avoid a constitutional question but directly raises one. The Act, read as literally as the Court reads it, plainly violates the First Amendment as applied to the facts of this case, for "no law" prohibiting the free exercise of religion includes every kind of law, including a law staying the hand of a judge who enjoins a law for the collection of taxes that trespasses on the First Amendment.

The power of Congress to ordain and establish inferior courts has not to this date been assumed or held to mean that Congress could require a federal court to take action in violation of the Constitution. Thus suspension of the writ of habeas corpus is restricted to "Cases of Rebellion or Invasion" where "the public Safety may require it." Art I, §9, cl. 2. And when it comes to the First Amendment and the free exercise of religion, the mandate is that "Congress shall make no law ... prohibiting" it. The Anti-Injunction Act is a "law"; and the Constitution gives no such preference to tax laws as to permit them to override religious scruples. May Congress enact a law that prohibits a minister from preaching if he is in arrears with his taxes? Or that disallows the making of a protest to a tax assessment even though the assessment and payment violate one's religious scruples? Until today, I would have thought not. The First Amendment, as applied to the States by the Fourteenth, bars a tax on the conduct of a religious exercise by a minority even though that religious exercise is obnoxious to the majority. *Murdock* v. *Pennsylvania* [page 132, *supra*]. Dicta to the effect that an allegation of unconstitutionality is irrelevant under the Anti-Injunction Act (*Bailey* v. *George*, 259 U.S. 16)—which the Court today elevates to a holding—were based on the premise that there was an alternative remedy to the unconstitutional actions. Here, as demonstrated, there is no other remedy. A refund suit is of no value, since the religious scruples which these taxpayers invoke relate to their inability to protest the payment, not to the use of the taxes themselves for military purposes.

All of the above cases involved that clause of the First Amendment protecting the "free exercise" of religion. The meaning of the First Amendment's prohibition of any law "respecting an establishment of religion" was involved in the decision in the Everson case,[39] in which Douglas joined, holding that provision not infringed where a state provided bus transportation for parochial school students as part of a general program of providing such transportation also for students in the public schools. While the Court conceded that the establishment clause forbade the use of state funds "to support any religious activities or institutions" and that the clause was intended to erect "a wall of separation between church and State," it concluded that the free exercise clause would forbid the denial of public benefits to some persons "because of their faith, or lack of it." And here it thought the state was merely "extending its general state law benefits to all its citizens without regard to their religious belief" just as it did when it provided traffic policemen at both public and parochial schools. The First Amendment "requires the state to be a neutral in its relations with groups of religious believers and non-believers; it does not require the state to be their adversary."

ZORACH V. CLAUSON
343 U.S. 306 (1952)

In McCollum v. Board of Education[40] Douglas voted with the Court to invalidate a system of religious instruction, by religious teachers employed by private Catholic, Jewish, and Protestant religious groups, in the public schools during school hours, with students who did not wish such instruction being required to leave their classrooms and go elsewhere in the building to pursue their secular studies. This was held to be "beyond a question a utilization of the tax-established and tax-supported public school system to aid religious groups" in violation of the establishment clause. This case involved a program which the Court found to be constitutionally different.

MR. JUSTICE DOUGLAS delivered the opinion of the Court.

New York City has a program which permits its public schools to release students during the school day so that they may leave the school buildings and school grounds and go to religious centers for religious instruction or devotional exercises. A student is released on written request of his parents. Those not released stay in the classrooms. The churches make weekly reports to the schools, sending a list of children

[39] Everson v. Board of Education, 330 U.S. 1 (1947).
[40] 333 U.S. 203 (1948).

who have been released from public school but who have not reported for religious instruction.

This "released time" program involves neither religious instruction in public school classrooms nor the expenditure of public funds. All costs, including the application blanks, are paid by the religious organizations. The case is therefore unlike *McCollum* v. *Board of Education*, which involved a "released time" program from Illinois. In that case the classrooms were turned over to religious instructors. We accordingly held that the program violated the First Amendment which (by reason of the Fourteenth Amendment) prohibits the states from establishing religion or prohibiting its free exercise.

Appellants, who are taxpayers and residents of New York City and whose children attend its public schools, challenge the present law, contending it is in essence not different from the one involved in the *McCollum* case. Their argument, stated elaborately in various ways, reduces itself to this: the weight and influence of the school is put behind a program for religious instruction; public school teachers police it, keeping tab on students who are released; the classroom activities come to a halt while the students who are released for religious instruction are on leave; the school is a crutch on which the churches are leaning for support in their religious training; without the cooperation of the schools this "released time" program, like the one in the *McCollum* case, would be futile and ineffective.

The briefs and arguments are replete with data bearing on the merits of this type of "released time" program. Views *pro* and *con* are expressed, based on practical experience with these programs and with their implications. We do not stop to summarize these materials nor to burden the opinion with an analysis of them. For they involve considerations not germane to the narrow constitutional issue presented. They largely concern the wisdom of the system, its efficiency from an educational point of view, and the political considerations which have motivated its adoption or rejection in some communities. Those matters are of no concern here, since our problem reduces itself to whether New York by this system has either prohibited the "free exercise" of religion or has made a law "respecting an establishment of religion" within the meaning of the First Amendment.

It takes obtuse reasoning to inject any issue of the "free exercise" of religion into the present case. No one is forced to go to the religious classroom and no religious exercise or instruction is brought to the classrooms of the public schools. A student need not take religious instruction. He is left to his own desires as to the manner or time of his religious devotions, if any.

There is a suggestion that the system involves the use of coercion to get public school students into religious classrooms. There is no evidence in the record before us that supports that conclusion.[41] The present record indeed tells us that the school authorities are neutral in this regard and do no more than release students whose parents so request. If in fact coercion were used, if it were established that any one or more teachers were using their office to persuade or force students to take the religious instruction, a wholly different case would be presented. Hence we put aside that claim of coercion both as respects the "free exercise" of religion and "an establishment of religion" within the meaning of the First Amendment.

Moreover, apart from that claim of coercion, we do not see how New York by this type of "released time" program has made a law respecting an establishment of religion within the meaning of the First Amendment. There is much talk of the separation of Church and State in the history of the Bill of Rights and in the decisions clustering around the First Amendment. There cannot be the slightest doubt that the First Amendment reflects the philosophy that Church and State should be separated. And so far as interference with the "free exercise" of religion and an "establishment" of religion are concerned, the separation must be complete and unequivocal. The First Amendment within the scope of its coverage permits no exception; the prohibition is absolute. The First Amendment, however, does not say that in every and all respects there shall be a separation of Church and State. Rather, it studiously defines the manner, the specific ways, in which there shall be no concert or union or dependency one on the other. That is the common sense of the matter. Otherwise the state and religion would be aliens to each other—hostile, suspicious, and even unfriendly. Churches could not be required to pay even property taxes. Municipalities would not be permitted to render police or fire protection to religious groups. Policemen who helped parishioners into their places of worship would violate the Constitution. Prayers in our legislative halls; the appeals to the Almighty in the messages of the Chief Executive; the proclamations making Thanksgiving Day a holiday; "so help me God" in our courtroom oaths —these and all other references to the Almighty that run through our laws, our public rituals, our ceremonies would be flouting the First Amendment. A fastidious atheist or agnostic could even object to the supplication with which the Court opens each session: "God save the United States and this Honorable Court."

We would have to press the concept of separation of Church and

---

[41] Nor is there any indication that the public schools enforce attendance at religious schools by punishing absentees from the released time programs for truancy.

State to these extremes to condemn the present law on constitutional grounds. The nullification of this law would have wide and profound effects. A Catholic student applies to his teacher for permission to leave the school during hours on a Holy Day of Obligation to attend a mass. A Jewish student asks his teacher for permission to be excused for Yom Kippur. A Protestant wants the afternoon off for a family baptismal ceremony. In each case the teacher requires parental consent in writing. In each case the teacher, in order to make sure the student is not a truant, goes further and requires a report from the priest, the rabbi, or the minister. The teacher in other words cooperates in a religious program to the extent of making it possible for her students to participate in it. Whether she does it occasionally for a few students, regularly for one, or pursuant to a systematized program designed to further the religious needs of all the students does not alter the character of the act.

We are a religious people whose institutions presuppose a Supreme Being. We guarantee the freedom to worship as one chooses. We make room for as wide a variety of beliefs and creeds as the spiritual needs of man deem necessary. We sponsor an attitude on the part of government that shows no partiality to any one group and that lets each flourish according to the zeal of its adherents and the appeal of its dogma. When the state encourages religious instruction or cooperates with religious authorities by adjusting the schedule of public events to sectarian needs, it follows the best of our traditions. For it then respects the religious nature of our people and accommodates the public service to their spiritual needs. To hold that it may not would be to find in the Constitution a requirement that the government show a callous indifference to religious groups. That would be preferring those who believe in no religion over those who do believe. Government may not finance religious groups nor undertake religious instruction nor blend secular and sectarian education nor use secular institutions to force one or some religion on any person. But we find no constitutional requirement which makes it necessary for government to be hostile to religion and to throw its weight against efforts to widen the effective scope of religious influence. The government must be neutral when it comes to competition between sects. It may not thrust any sect on any person. It may not make a religious observance compulsory. It may not coerce anyone to attend church, to observe a religious holiday, or to take religious instruction. But it can close its doors or suspend its operations as to those who want to repair to their religious sanctuary for worship or instruction. No more than that is undertaken here.

This program may be unwise and improvident from an educational or a community viewpoint. That appeal is made to us on a theory, previously advanced, that each case must be decided on the basis of "our own prepossessions." Our individual preferences, however, are not the constitutional standard. The constitutional standard is the separation of Church and State. The problem, like many problems in constitutional law, is one of degree.

In the *McCollum* case the classrooms were used for religious instruction and the force of the public school was used to promote that instruction. Here, as we have said, the public schools do no more than accommodate their schedules to a program of outside religious instruction. We follow the *McCollum* case. But we cannot expand it to cover the present released time program unless separation of Church and State means that public institutions can make no adjustments of their schedules to accommodate the religious needs of the people. We cannot read into the Bill of Rights such a philosophy of hostility to religion.

Douglas concurred in the decision in Engel v. Vitale,[42] holding that the use in New York of a state-prescribed prayer in the public schools violates the First Amendment even though no student was required to participate in the recitation of the prayer. But he also took the occasion to say that he had been wrong to accept state-supported school busing for parochial schools as constitutional in the Everson case[43] and that he was now persuaded that the state "oversteps the bounds when it finances a religious exercise" even though there was no coercion, "no effort at indoctrination and no attempt at exposition." When the Court subsequently invalidated, due to the protest of Unitarians and atheists, a state practice of reading passages from the Bible in the public schools, Douglas again concurred, not only because the establishment clause forbids the state from conducting religious exercises but because it also forbids the state "to employ its facilities or funds in a way that gives any church, or all churches, greater strength in our society than it would have by relying on its members alone. . . . Through the mechanism of the State, all of the people are being required to finance a religious exercise that only some of the people want and that violates the sensibilities of others. . . ."[44]

---

[42] 370 U.S. 421 (1962).

[43] Note 39, *supra*. Later, in *Luetkeymeyer v. Kaufmann*, 419 U.S. 888 (1975), he concurred when the Court affirmed without opinion a lower court decision finding no constitutional violation where a state provided bus transportation for public schools but none for parochial schools.

[44] *Abington School District v. Schempp*, 374 U.S. 203 (1963). Douglas agreed with the Court in another case that prior decisions "inevitably determine" that a state law prohibiting the teaching of the theory of evolution in the public schools violated the First Amendment's requirement of state neutrality, when it was "clear that fundamentalist sectarian conviction was and is the law's reason for existence." *Epperson v. Arkansas*, 393 U.S. 97 (1968).

BOARD OF EDUCATION v. ALLEN
392 U.S. 236 (1968)

In 1965 the New York legislature amended its education law to authorize public school boards to supply textbooks not only to public school students, as they had been doing, but also to private school students for "non-sectarian subjects." Following its Everson decision approving busing for parochial schools, the Court held that the supplying of textbooks, like the supplying of buses, was for a secular purpose and had a secular primary effect—the furtherance of educational opportunities available to the young. Hence, it affirmed the decision of the New York Court of Appeals that the textbook program did not violate the establishment clause.

MR. JUSTICE DOUGLAS, dissenting.

We have for review a statute which authorizes New York State to supply textbooks to students in parochial as well as in public schools. The New York Court of Appeals sustained the law on the grounds that it involves only "secular textbooks" and that that type of aid falls within *Everson* v. *Board of Education,*[45] where a divided Court upheld a state law which made bus service available to students in parochial schools as well as to students in public schools.

The statute on its face empowers each parochial school to determine for itself which textbooks will be eligible for loans to its students, for the Act provides that the only text which the State may provide is "a book which a pupil is required to use as a text for a semester or more in a particular class in the school he legally attends." This initial and crucial selection is undoubtedly made by the parochial school's principal or its individual instructors, who are, in the case of Roman Catholic schools, normally priests or nuns. . . .

The role of the local public school board is to decide whether to veto the selection made by the parochial school. This is done by determining first whether the text has been or should be "approved" for use in public schools and second whether the text is "secular," "non-religious," or "non-sectarian."[46] The local boards apparently have broad discretion in exercising this veto power.

[45] *Everson*, relied on by the Court of Appeals of New York, did not involve textbooks and did not present the serious problems raised by a form of aid to parochial students which injects religious issues into the choice of curriculum.

[46] The State Court of Appeals used the phrases "secular textbooks" and "non-religious textbooks" without any elaboration as to what was meant. The legislature, in its "statement of policy" to the Act, speaks of aiding instruction in "non-sectarian subjects," and gives as examples "science, mathematics, [and] foreign languages."

Thus the statutory system provides that the parochial school will ask for the books that it wants. Can there be the slightest doubt that the head of the parochial school will select the book or books that best promote its sectarian creed?

If the board of education supinely submits by approving and supplying the sectarian or sectarian-oriented textbooks, the struggle to keep church and state separate has been lost. If the board resists, then the battle line between church and state will have been drawn and the contest will be on to keep the school board independent or to put it under church domination and control.

Whatever may be said of *Everson*, there is nothing ideological about a bus. There is nothing ideological about a school lunch, or a public nurse, or a scholarship. The constitutionality of such public aid to students in parochial schools turns on considerations not present in this textbook case. The textbook goes to the very heart of education in a parochial school. It is the chief, although not solitary, instrumentality for propagating a particular religious creed or faith. How can we possibly approve such state aid to a religion? A parochial school textbook may contain many, many more seeds of creed and dogma than a prayer. Yet we struck down in *Engel v. Vitale* [note 42, *supra*] an official New York prayer for its public schools, even though it was not plainly denominational. For we emphasized the violence done the Establishment Clause when the power was given religious-political groups "to write their own prayers into law." That risk is compounded here by giving parochial schools the initiative in selecting the textbooks they desire to be furnished at public expense.

Judge Van Voorhis, joined by Chief Judge Fuld and Judge Breitel, dissenting below, said that the difficulty with the textbook loan program "is that there is no reliable standard by which secular and religious textbooks can be distinguished from each other." The New York Legislature felt that science was a non-sectarian subject [note 46, *supra*]. Does this mean that any general science textbook intended for use in grades 7–12 may be provided by the State to parochial school students? May John M. Scott's Adventures in Science (1963) be supplied under the textbook loan program? This book teaches embryology in the following manner:

> "To you an animal usually means a mammal, such as a cat, dog, squirrel, or guinea pig. The new animal or embryo develops inside

---

The State Department of Education has stated that "it is necessary that . . . [t]he textbooks be non-sectarian (this eliminates denominational editions and those carrying the 'imprimatur' or 'nihil obstat' of a religious authority). . . ." Opinion of Counsel No. 181. There are no other definitions to be found. . . .

the body of the mother until birth. The fertilized egg becomes an embryo or developing animal. Many cell divisions take place. In time some cells become muscle cells, others nerve cells or blood cells, and organs such as eyes, stomach, and intestine are formed.

"The body of a human being grows in the same way, but it is much more remarkable than that of any animal, for the embryo has a human soul infused into the body by God. Human parents are partners with God in creation. They have very great powers and great responsibilities, for through their cooperation with God souls are born for heaven."[47]

Comparative economics would seem to be a non-sectarian subject. Will New York, then, provide Arthur J. Hughes' general history text, Man in Time (1964), to parochial school students? It treats that topic in this manner:

"Capitalism is an economic system based on man's right to private property and on his freedom to use that property in producing goods which will earn him a just profit on his investment. Man's right to private property stems from the Natural Law implanted in him by God. It is as much a part of man's nature as the will to self-preservation."

"The broadest definition of socialism is government ownership of all the means of production and distribution in a country. . . . Many, but by no means all, Socialists in the nineteenth century believed that crime and vice existed because poverty existed, and if poverty were eliminated, then crime and vice would disappear. While it is true that poor surroundings are usually unhealthy climates for high moral training, still, man has the free will to check himself. Many Socialists, however, denied free will and said that man was a creation of his environment. . . . If Socialists do not deny Christ's message, they often ignore it. Christ showed us by His life that this earth is a testing ground to prepare man for eternal happiness. Man's interests should be in this direction at least part of the time and not always directed toward a futile quest for material goods."[48]

[47] Although the author of this textbook is a priest, the text contains no imprimatur and no nihil obstat. Although published by a Catholic press, the Loyola University Press, Chicago, it is not marked in any manner as a "denominational edition," but is simply the general edition of the book. Accordingly, under Opinion of Counsel No. 181, the only document approaching a "regulation" on the issue involved here, Adventures in Science would qualify as "non-sectarian." See [note 46], supra.

[48] Man In Time contains a nihil obstat and an imprimatur. Thus, if Opinion of Counsel No. 181 (see [note 46, supra]), is applicable, this book may not be provided

Mr. Justice Jackson said, ". . . I should suppose it is a proper, if not an indispensable, part of preparation for a worldly life to know the roles that religion and religions have played in the tragic story of mankind." *McCollum* v. *Board of Education* [note 40, *supra*] (concurring opinion). Yet, as he inquired, what emphasis should one give who teaches the Reformation, the Inquisition, or the early effort in New England to establish " 'a Church without a Bishop and a State without a King?' " What books should be chosen for those subjects?

Even where the treatment given to a particular topic in a school textbook is not blatantly sectarian, it will necessarily have certain shadings that will lead a parochial school to prefer one text over another.[49]

The Crusades, for example, may be taught as a Christian undertaking to "save the Holy Land" from the Moslem Turks who "became a threat to Christianity and its holy places," which "they did not treat . . . with respect" (H. Wilson, F. Wilson, B. Erb & E. Clucas, Out of the Past 284 (1954)), or as essentially a series of wars born out of political and materialistic motives (see G. Leinwand, The Pageant of World History 136–137 (1965)).

Is the dawn of man to be explained in the words, "God created man and made man master of the earth" (P. Furlong, The Old World and America 5 (1937)), or in the language of evolution (see T. Wallbank, Man's Story 32–35 (1961))?

Is the slaughter of the Aztecs by Cortes and his entourage to be lamented for its destruction of a New World culture (see J. Caughey, J. Franklin, & E. May, Land of the Free 27–28 (1965)), or forgiven

---

by the State. The Opinion of Counsel, however, is only "advisory," we are told; moreover, the religious endorsements could easily be removed by the author and publisher at the next printing.

[49] Some parochial schools may prefer those texts which are liberally sprinkled with religious vignettes. This creeping sectarianism avoids the direct teaching of religious doctrine but keeps the student continually reminded of the sectarian orientation of his education. In P. Furlong, Sr. Margaret, & D. Sharkey's American history text, America Yesterday (1963), for example, the student is informed that the first mass to be said in what is now the United States was in 1526 near Chesapeake Bay, that eight French missionaries to Canada in the early 1600's were canonized in 1930, that one of the men who signed the Declaration of Independence and two who attended the Constitutional Convention were Catholic, and that the superintendent of the Hudson Bay Company's outpost in the Oregon country converted to Catholicism in 1842. And J. Scott's Adventures in Science (1963), in teaching the atmospheric conditions prevailing at the top of Mount Everest, informs the student that when Sir Edmund Hillary first scaled this peak he placed there a "tiny crucifix" which a Benedictine monk had supplied.

America Yesterday, *supra*, is another example of a text written by the clergy (here a priest and nun together with one layman) that contains no imprimatur and no nihil obstat and is not a denominational edition.

because the Spaniards "carried the true Faith" to a barbaric people who practiced human sacrifice (see P. Furlong, Sr. Margaret, & D. Sharkey, America Yesterday 17, 34 (1963))?

Is Franco's revolution in Spain to be taught as a crusade against anti-Catholic forces (see R. Hoffman, G. Vincitorio, & M. Swift, Man and His History 666–667 (1958)) or as an effort by reactionary elements to regain control of that country (see G. Leinwand, The Pageant of World History, *supra*, at 512)? Is the expansion of communism in select areas of the world a manifestation of the forces of Evil campaigning against the forces of Good? See A. Hughes, Man in Time, *supra*.

It will be often difficult, as Mr. Justice Jackson said, to say "where the secular ends and the sectarian begins in education." *McCollum* v. *Board of Education* [note 40, *supra*]. But certain it is that once the so-called "secular" textbook is the prize to be won by that religious faith which selects the book, the battle will be on for those positions of control. Judge Van Voorhis expressed the fear that in the end the state might dominate the church. Others fear that one sectarian group, gaining control of the state agencies which approve the "secular" textbooks, will use their control to disseminate ideas most congenial to their faith. It must be remembered that the very existence of the religious school—whether Catholic or Mormon, Presbyterian or Episcopalian—is to provide an education oriented to the dogma of the particular faith. . . .

The initiative to select and requisition "the books desired" is with the parochial school. Powerful religious-political pressures will therefore be on the state agencies to provide the books that are desired.

These then are the battlegrounds where control of textbook distribution will be won or lost. Now that "secular" textbooks will pour into religious schools, we can rest assured that a contest will be on to provide those books for religious schools which the dominant religious group concludes best reflect the theocentric or other philosophy of the particular church.

The stakes are now extremely high—just as they were in the school prayer cases (see *Engel* v. *Vitale* [note 42, *supra*])—to obtain approval of what is "proper." For the "proper" books will radiate the "correct" religious view not only in the parochial school but in the public school as well.

Even if I am wrong in that basic premise, we still should not affirm the judgment below. Judge Van Voorhis, dissenting in the New York Court of Appeals, thought that the result of tying parochial school textbooks to public funds would be to put nonsectarian books into religious schools, which in the long view would tend towards state domination of the church. That would, indeed, be the result if the school boards did not succumb to "sectarian" pressure or control. So, however the case be viewed—whether sectarian groups win control of school boards or do not gain such control—the principle of separation of church and state, inherent in the Establishment Clause of the First Amendment, is violated by what we today approve.

Douglas dissented again when, in 1970, the Court held that a state's granting of property tax exemptions for property used solely for religious purposes was a sufficiently neutral act to satisfy the First Amendment.[50] "There is a line between what a State may do in encouraging 'religious' activities, Zorach v. Clauson [p. 150, supra] and what a State may not do by using its resources to promote 'religious' activities, McCollum v. Board of Education [note 40, supra]. . . . Closing public schools on Sunday is in the former category; subsidizing churches, in my view, is in the latter. Indeed I would suppose that in common understanding one of the best ways to 'establish' one or more religions is to subsidize them, which a tax exemption does." And the "two centuries of uninterrupted freedom from taxation" for church properties in this country, which had influenced the Court, was irrelevant in view of the fact that the Court first held in 1931[51] that the Fourteenth Amendment, adopted in 1868, made the First Amendment applicable to the states.

TILTON V. RICHARDSON
403 U.S. 672 (1971)

Douglas concurred when the Court, in Lemon v. Kurtzman,[52] invalidated a Rhode Island plan under which the state would supplement by fifteen percent the annual salaries of teachers of secular subjects in private schools, and a Pennsylvania plan under which the state would reimburse private schools for teachers' salaries and textbooks for secular subjects. All of the schools receiving the Rhode Island supplement were Catholic schools and nearly all of the schools receiving reimbursement from Pennsylvania were Catholic. The Court concluded that the establishment clause was violated because of "excessive entanglement between government and religion. . . . [T]eachers have a substantially different ideological character from books." Douglas concurred and pointed out that policing the state grants "to detect sectarian instruction would be insufferable to religious partisans and would breed division between church and state."

At the same time, in this case, the Court upheld federal grants to

---

[50] *Walz v. Tax Commission*, 397 U.S. 664 (1970).
[51] *Stromberg v. California*, 283 U.S. 359 (1931).
[52] 403 U.S. 602 (1971). See also *Lemon v. Kurtzman*, 411 U.S. 192 (1973).

church-sponsored colleges and universities to aid in the construction of buildings. The federal law under which the grants were made provided that the buildings could not be used "for sectarian instruction or as a place for religious worship" for a period of twenty years after completion and that if they were so used within that time, a proportion of the federal grant must be returned to the United States. The Court invalidated so much of the law as would permit sectarian use of the buildings after twenty years without liability to the United States, but in other respects found no violation of the free exercise clause or of the establishment clause.

MR. JUSTICE DOUGLAS, dissenting in part.

The correct constitutional principle for this case was stated by President Kennedy in 1961 when questioned as to his policy respecting aid to private and parochial schools:

> "[T]he Constitution clearly prohibits aid to the school, to parochial schools. I don't think there is any doubt of that.
> "The Everson case, which is probably the most celebrated case, provided only by a 5 to 4 decision was it possible for a local community to provide bus rides to nonpublic school children. But all through the majority and minority statements on that particular question there was a very clear prohibition against aid to the school direct. The Supreme Court made its decision in the Everson case by determining that the aid was to the child, not to the school. Aid to the school is—there isn't any room for debate on that subject. It is prohibited by the Constitution, and the Supreme Court has made that very clear. And therefore there would be no possibility of our recommending it."

Taxpayer appellants brought this suit challenging the validity of certain expenditures, made by the Department of Health, Education, and Welfare, for the construction of (1) a library at Sacred Heart University, (2) a music, drama, and arts building at Annhurst College, (3) a library and a science building at Fairfield University, and (4) a laboratory at Albertus Magnus College. The complaint alleged that all of these institutions were controlled by religious orders and the Roman Catholic Diocese of Bridgeport, Conn., and that if the funds for construction were authorized by Title I of the Higher Education Facilities Act of 1963, then that statute was unconstitutional because it violated the Establishment Clause.

Title I of the Higher Education Facilities Act of 1963 authorizes grants and loans up to 50% of the cost for the construction of undergraduate academic facilities in both public and private colleges and universities. A project is eligible if construction will result "in an urgently needed substantial expansion of the institution's student enrollment capacity, capacity to provide needed health care to students or personnel of the institution, or capacity to carry out extention and continuing education programs on the campus of such institution." The Commissioner of Education is authorized to prescribe basic criteria and is instructed to "give special consideration to expansion of undergraduate enrollment capacity."

Academic facilities are "structures suitable for use as classrooms, laboratories, libraries, and related facilities necessary or appropriate for instruction of students, or for research . . . programs." Specifically excluded are facilities "used or to be used for sectarian instruction or as a place for religious worship" or any facilities used "primarily in connection with any part of the program of a school or department of divinity." The United States retains a 20-year interest in the facilities and should a facility be used other than as an academic facility then the United States is entitled to recover an amount equal to the proportion of present value which the federal grant bore to the original cost of the facility. According to a stipulation entered below, during the 20 years the Office of Education attempts to insure that facilities are used in the manner required by the Act primarily by on-site inspections. At the end of the 20-year period the federal interest in the facility ceases and the college may use it as it pleases.

The public purpose in secular education is, to be sure, furthered by the program. Yet the sectarian purpose is aided by making the parochial school system viable. The purpose is to increase "student enrollment" and the students obviously aimed at are those of the particular faith now financed by taxpayers' money. Parochial schools are not beamed at agnostics, atheists, or those of a competing sect. The more sophisticated institutions may admit minorities; but the dominant religious character is not changed.

The reversion of the facility to the parochial school[53] at the end of

[53] "It should be clear to all that a Roman Catholic parochial school is an integral part of that church, as definitely so as is the service of worship. A parochial school is usually developed in connection with a church. In many cases the church and school monies are not even separated. Such a school is in no sense a public school, even though some children from other groups may be admitted to it. The buildings are not owned and controlled by a community of American people, not even by a community of American Roman Catholic *people*. The title of ownership in a public school is vested in the local community, in the elected officers of the school board or the city council. But the title of ownership in a parochial school is vested in the bishop as an individual, who is appointed by, who is under the direct control of, and who reports to the pope in Rome." L. Boettner, Roman Catholicism 375 (1962).

20 years is an outright grant, measurable by the present discounted worth of the facility. A gift of taxpayers' funds in that amount would plainly be unconstitutional. The Court properly bars it even though disguised in the form of a reversionary interest.

But the invalidation of this one clause cannot cure the constitutional infirmities of the statute as a whole. The Federal Government is giving religious schools a block grant to build certain facilities. The fact that money is given once at the beginning of a program rather than apportioned annually as in *Lemon* is without constitutional significance. The First Amendment bars establishment of a religion. And as I noted today in *Lemon*, this bar has been consistently interpreted from *Everson* v. *Board of Education* [note 39, *supra*] through *Torcaso* v. *Watkins* [note 25, *supra*] as meaning: "No tax in any amount, large or small, can be levied to support any religious activities or institutions, whatever they may be called, or whatever form they may adopt to teach or practice religion." Thus it is hardly impressive that rather than giving a smaller amount of money annually over a long period of years, Congress instead gives a large amount all at once. The plurality [opinion's] distinction is in effect that small violations of the First Amendment over a period of years are unconstitutional (see *Lemon*) while a huge violation occurring only once is *de minimis*. I cannot agree with such sophistry.

What I have said in *Lemon* is relevant here. The facilities financed by taxpayers' funds are not to be used for "sectarian" purposes. Religious teaching and secular teaching are so enmeshed in parochial schools that only the strictest supervision and surveillance would insure compliance with the condition. Parochial schools may require religious exercises, even in the classroom. A parochial school operates on one budget. Money not spent for one purpose becomes available for other purposes. Thus the fact that there are no religious observances in federally financed facilities is not controlling because required religious observances will take place in other buildings. Our decision in *Engel* v. *Vitale* [note 42, *supra*] held that a requirement of a prayer in public schools violated the Establishment Clause. Once these schools become federally funded they become bound by federal standards and accordingly adherence to *Engel* would require an end to required religious exercises. That kind of surveillance and control will certainly be obnoxious to the church authorities and if done will radically change the character of the parochial school. Yet if that surveillance is not searching and continuous, this federal financing is obnoxious under the Establishment and Free Exercise Clauses.

In other words, surveillance creates an entanglement of government and religion which the First Amendment was designed to avoid. Yet after today's decision there will be a requirement of surveillance which

will last for the useful life of the building and as we have previously
noted, "[it] is hardly lack of due process for the Government to regulate
that which it subsidizes." *Wickard* v. *Filburn*, 317 U.S. 111. The price
of the subsidy under the Act is violation of the Free Exercise Clause.
Could a course in the History of Methodism be taught in a federally
financed building? Would a religiously slanted version of the Reformation or Quebec politics under Duplessis be permissible? How can the
Government know what is taught in the federally financed building
without a continuous auditing of classroom instruction? Yet both the
Free Exercise Clause and academic freedom are violated when the
Government agent must be present to determine whether the course
content is satisfactory.

As I said in *Lemon*, a parochial school is a unitary institution with
subtle blending of sectarian and secular instruction. Thus the practices
of religious schools are in no way affected by the minimal requirement
that the government financed facility may not "be used for sectarian
instruction or as a place for religious worship." Money saved from one
item in the budget is free to be used elsewhere. By conducting religious
services in another building, the school has—rent free—a building for
nonsectarian use. This is not called Establishment simply because the
government retains a continuing interest in the building for its useful
life, even though the religious schools need never pay a cent for the
use of the building.

Much is made of the need for public aid to church schools in light
of their pressing fiscal problems. Dr. Eugene C. Blake of the Presbyterian
Church, however, wrote in 1959:[54]

"When one remembers that churches pay no inheritance tax
(churches do not die), that churches may own and operate business
and be exempt from the 52 percent corporate income tax, and that
real property used for church purposes (which in some states are
most generously construed) is tax exempt, it is not unreasonable
to prophesy that with reasonably prudent management, the
churches ought to be able to control the whole economy of the
nation within the predictable future. That the growing wealth
and property of the churches was partially responsible for revolutionary expropriations of church property in England in the sixteenth century, in France in the eighteenth century, in Italy in the
nineteenth century, and in Mexico, Russia, Czechoslovakia and
Hungary (to name a few examples) in the twentieth century, seems
self-evident. A government with mounting tax problems cannot be

[54] Tax Exemption and the Churches, 3 Christianity Today, No. 22, Aug. 3,
1959, pp. 6, 7.

expected to keep its hands off the wealth of a rich church forever. That such a revolution is always accompanied by anticlericalism and atheism should not be surprising."

The mounting wealth of the churches makes ironic their incessant demands on the public treasury. I said in my dissent in *Walz* v. *Tax Comm'n* [note 50, *supra*]:

> "The religiously used real estate of the churches today constitutes a vast domain. See M. Larson & C. Lowell, The Churches: Their Riches, Revenues, and Immunities (1969). Their assets total over $141 billion and their annual income at least $22 billion. And the extent to which they are feeding from the public trough in a variety of forms is alarming.

I dissent not because of any lack of respect for parochial schools but out of a feeling of despair that the respect which through history has been accorded the First Amendment is this day lost.

Douglas concurred in a later decision in Levitt v. *Committee for Public Education*[55] *that a program of state aid to religious schools to reimburse them for the costs of administering tests required by the state violated the establishment clause because testing is "an integral part of the teaching process" and the state program provided no means to assure that the tests were "free of religious instruction."*

In subsequent cases, as the Court has scrutinized state aid to religious schools for building construction, maintenance and repair, tuition, teacher salaries, textbooks and other instructional materials, it has found violations of the establishment clause only where the purpose or primary effect of the program is to advance sectarian ends or where there is too much entanglement of church and state. In each case, Douglas concurred when the program was invalidated[56] *and dissented when it was not.*[57]

WHEELER v. BARRERA
417 U.S. 402 (1974)

This case involved a challenge to a federal statute of 1965 providing for federal funding of special programs for educationally deprived

---

[55] 413 U.S. 472 (1973).

[56] *Committee for Public Education* v. *Nyquist,* 413 U.S. 756 (1973) (building maintenance and repair and tuition); *Sloan* v. *Lemon,* 413 U.S. 825 (1973) (tuition grants); *Meek* v. *Pittinger,* 421 U.S. 349 (1975) (instructional materials).

[57] *Hunt* v. *McNair,* 413 U.S. 734 (1973) (building construction); *Meek* v. *Pittinger,* 421 U.S. 349 (textbooks).

children in both public and private schools, principally in the form of
payments of salaries of teachers providing remedial instruction. The
Court held that any First Amendment challenge to such aid to parochial
schools was premature since no plan for providing the aid to such schools
had yet been worked out by federal and state authorities and, until a
detailed plan was presented, it would be impossible to apply the Court's
purpose-primary effect-entanglement test. Douglas filed his last dis-
senting opinion on this subject.

MR. JUSTICE DOUGLAS, dissenting.

The case comes to us in an attractive posture, as the Act of Congress
is in terms aimed to help "educationally deprived" children, whether
they are in public or parochial schools, and I fear the judiciary has been
seduced. But we must remember that "the propriety of a legislature's
purposes may not immunize from further scrutiny a law which either
has a primary effect that advances religion, or which fosters excessive
entanglements between Church and State." *Committee for Public
Education* v. *Nyquist* [note 56, *supra*].

All education in essence is aimed to help children, whether bright or
retarded. Schools do not exist—whether public or parochial—to keep
teachers employed. Education is a skein with many threads—from
classical Greek to Latin, to grammar, to philosophy, to science, to
athletics, to religion. There might well be political motivation to use
federal funds to make up deficits in any part of a school's budget or
to strengthen it by financing all or a part of any sector of educational
activity.

There are some who think it constitutionally wise to do so; and
others who think it is constitutionally permissible. But the First Amendment says "Congress shall make no law respecting an establishment of
religion." In common understanding there is no surer way of "establishing" an institution than by financing it. That was true at the time of
the adoption of the First Amendment. Madison, one of its foremost
authors, fought the battle in Virginia where the *per capita* minimal
levy on each person was no more than three pence. Yet if the State
could finance a church at three pence *per capita*, the principle of
"establishment" would be approved and there would be no limit to the
amount of money the Government could add to church coffers. That
was the teaching of his Remonstrance.[58] As Mr. Justice Black stated it,
"[n]o tax in any amount, large or small, can be levied to support any

---

[58] [Madison's Memorial and Remonstrance Against Religious Assessment was
addressed to the colonial Virginia legislature in 1775 in opposition to a proposed
tax for the support of religion.]

religious activities or institutions, whatever they may be called, or whatever form they may adopt to teach or practice religion." *Everson* v. *Board of Education* [note 39, *supra*].[59]

Parochial schools are adjuncts of the church established at a time when state governments were highly discriminatory against some sects by introducing religious training in the public schools. The tale has been told often;[60] and there is no need to repeat it here. Parochial schools are tied to the proclamation and inculcation of a particular religious faith—sometimes Catholic, sometimes Presbyterian, sometimes Angelican, sometimes Lutheran, and so on.

The emanations from the Court's opinion are at war with our prior decisions. Federal financing of an apparently nonsectarian aspect of parochial school activities, if allowed, is not even a subtle evasion of First Amendment prohibitions. The parochial school is a unit; its budget is a unit; pouring in federal funds for what seems to be a nonsectarian phase of parochial school activities "establishes" the school so that in effect, if not in purpose, it becomes stronger financially and better able to proselytize its particular faith by having more funds left over for that objective. Allowing the State to finance the secular part of a sectarian school's program "makes a grave constitutional decision turn merely on cost accounting and bookkeeping entries." *Lemon* v. *Kurtzman* [note 52, *supra*] (DOUGLAS, J., concurring).

Nor could the program here be immunized from scrutiny under the Establishment Clause by portraying this aid as going to the children rather than to the sectarian schools. That argument deserves no more weight in the Establishment Clause context than it received under the Equal Protection Clause of the Fourteenth Amendment, with respect to which we summarily affirmed decisions striking down state schemes to circumvent the constitutional requirement of racial integration in public schools granting tuition aid to parents who sent their children to segregated private schools.[61]

[59] *Everson* was a 5–4 decision sustaining a state law which provided reimbursement to parents of children in sectarian schools for the cost of public bus transportation used by the students in traveling to school, but even the majority recognized that the law went to the "verge" of forbidden territory under the Religion Clauses of the First Amendment. Although I was with the majority in that case, I have since expressed my doubts about the correctness of that decision, *e.g., Engel* v. *Vitale* [note 42, *supra*]; *Walz* v. *Tax Comm'n* [note 50, *supra*].

[60] [In his concurring opinion in *Lemon* v. *Kurtzman*, note 52, *supra*, Douglas recognized that parochial schools came into existence in this country "because Protestant groups were perverting the public schools by using them to propagate their faith."]

[61] [*Poindexter* v. *Louisiana Financial Assistance Comm'n*, 275 F. Supp. 833, *aff'd* 389 U.S. 571, and 296 F. Supp. 833, *aff'd*, 393 U.S. 17; *Griffin* v. *County School Board*, 377 U.S. 218 (1964). Court found unconstitutional the closing of

It is clear that if the traditional First Amendment barriers are to be maintained, no program serving students in parochial schools could be designed under this Act—whether regular school hours are used, or after-school hours, or weekend hours. The plain truth is that under the First Amendment, as construed to this day, the Act is unconstitutional to the extent it supports sectarian schools, whether directly or through its students.

We should say so now, and save the endless hours and efforts which hopeful people will expend in an effort to constitutionalize what is impossible without a constitutional amendment.[62]

---

public schools, in one of the counties involved in the first group of school deseg-regation cases decided together with *Brown* v. *Board of Education*, where the closing was accompanied by grants of public funds to white children to attend private schools.]

[62] [Douglas' views on the treatment of conscientious objectors under the Selective Service Act are discussed at pages 245–256, *infra*.]

FREEDOM OF
SPEECH AND PRESS

Numerous other First Amendment problems have come to the Court without the involvement of religious issues. They arose in a variety of contexts. Some were provoked by legislative efforts to purge the political process of coercion and corruption.

One such effort, to protect at least some government employees from political pressure, was the Civil Service Act of 1883, which authorized the Civil Service Commission to promulgate rules to prevent civil service employees from using their "official authority or influence to coerce the political action of any person" and under which the commission in 1907 had promulgated a rule forbidding civil servants to take any "active part in political management or political campaigns," which the commission enforced by a variety of sanctions. By the Hatch Act of 1940 Congress extended the prohibition to all employees in the federal executive branch, except the President and his staff, the Vice-President and officers appointed by the President and confirmed by the Senate. It was soon amended to extend the prohibition to all state employees whose principal employment is in connection with an activity financed in whole or in part by federal funds. The Hatch Act also provided that an "active part in political management or political campaigns" meant such Acts as were forbidden to civil service employees by rules of the commission prior to 1940. The Court in United Public Workers v. Mitchell[1] upheld the Hatch Act, as applied to a roller in the federal mint who had violated it by working during his off-duty hours as a ward executive committeeman for his party. The Act was, the Court held, a "reasonable" restriction of First Amendment rights, confined to activities on behalf of a political party, and imposed in the interest of "efficiency of the public service." Douglas dissented. He thought that, at least as to an industrial worker "as remote from contact with the public or from policy making or from the functioning of the administrative process as a charwoman," the statute went too far by its "partial political sterilization," particularly since a statute could

---

[1] 330 U.S. 75 (1947).

be drafted which would focus on the real source of the evil—those who would use coercion on government employees for political purposes.[2]

UNITED STATES CIVIL SERVICE COMMISSION V. NATIONAL ASSOCIATION OF LETTER CARRIERS
413 U.S. 548 (1973)

In this case a union representing federal mail carriers launched a new attack on the Hatch Act, arguing that the Mitchell *case should be overruled and that, in any event, the* Mitchell *decision had not addressed itself to the argument now made that the Act's prohibition was so overly broad and vague that it must necessarily have a "chilling effect" on federal employees' exercise of First Amendment rights, which all would concede that Congress could not prohibit. The Court reaffirmed its decision in* Mitchell *and concluded that the Act's prohibition, as defined by pre-1940 Civil Service Commission rules, "as refined by further adjudications" of the commission in disciplinary cases since 1940, covered a range of "easily identifiable and constitutionally proscribable partisan conduct."*

MR. JUSTICE DOUGLAS, dissenting.

The Hatch Act by § 9 (a) prohibits federal employees from taking "an active part in political management or in political campaigns." Some of the employees, whose union is speaking for them, want

> "to run in state and local elections for the school board, for city council, for mayor";
> "to write letters on political subjects to newspapers";
> "to be a delegate in a political convention";
> "to run for an office and hold office in a political party or political club";
> "to campaign for candidates for political office";
> "to work at polling places in behalf of a political party."

There is no definition of what "an active part . . . in political campaigns" means. The Act incorporates over 3,000 rulings of the Civil Service Commission between 1886 and 1940 and many hundreds of rulings since 1940. But even with that gloss on the Act, the critical phrases lack precision. In 1971 the Commission published a three-volume work entitled Political Activities Reporter which contains over 800 of its decisions since the enactment of the Hatch Act. One can

---

[2] At the same time Douglas concurred when the Court upheld the Act as applied to a member of a state Highway Commission, which administered federal loans and grants, who violated the Act by serving as chairman on the Democratic State Central Committee. *Oklahoma* v. *Civil Service Commission*, 330 U.S. 127 (1947).

learn from studying those volumes that it is not "political activity" to march in a band during a political parade or to wear political badges or to "participate fully in public affairs, except as prohibited by law, in a manner which does not materially compromise his efficiency or integrity as an employee or the neutrality, efficiency, or integrity of his agency."

That is to say, some things, like marching in a band, are clear. Others are pregnant with ambiguity as "participate fully in public affairs, except as prohibited by law, in a manner which does not materially compromise," etc. Permission to "[t]ake an active part . . . in a nonpartisan election" also raises large questions of uncertainty because one may be partisan for a person, an issue, a candidate without feeling an identification with one political party or the other.

The District Court felt that the prohibitions in the Act are "worded in generalities that lack precision," with the result that it is hazardous for an employee "if he ventures to speak on a political matter since he will not know when his words or acts relating to political subjects will offend."

The chilling effect of these vague and generalized prohibitions is so obvious as not to need elaboration. That effect would not be material to the issue of constitutionality if only the normal contours of the police power were involved. On the run of social and economic matters the "rational basis" standard which *United Public Workers* v. *Mitchell* applied would suffice.[3] But what may have been unclear to some in *Mitchell* should by now be abundantly clear to all. We deal here with a First Amendment right to speak, to propose, to publish, to petition Government, to assemble. Time and place are obvious limitations. Thus no one could object if employees were barred from using office time to engage in outside activities whether political or otherwise. But it is of no concern of Government what an employee does in his spare time, whether religion, recreation, social work, or politics is his lobby— unless what he does impairs efficiency or other facets of the merits of his job. Some things, some activities do affect or may be thought to affect the employee's job performance. But his political creed, like his religion, is irrelevant. In the areas of speech, like religion, it is of no concern what the employee says in private to his wife or to the public in Constitution Hall. If Government employment were only a "privilege," then all sorts of conditions might be attached. But it is now settled that Government employment may not be denied or penalized "on a basis that infringes [the employee's] constitutionally protected interests—especially, his interest in freedom of speech." See *Perry* v.

---

[3] "For regulation of employees it is not necessary that the act regulated be anything more than an act reasonably deemed by Congress to interfere with the efficiency of the public service." *United Public Workers* v. *Mitchell*.

Sindermann, 408 U.S. 593. If Government, as the majority stated in *Mitchell*, may not condition public employment on the basis that the employee will not "take any active part in missionary work," it is difficult to see why it may condition employment on the basis that the employee not take "an active part . . . in political campaigns." For speech, assembly, and petition are as deeply embedded in the First Amendment as proselytizing a religious cause.

Free discussion of governmental affairs is basic in our constitutional system. Laws that trench on that area must be narrowly and precisely drawn to deal with precise ends. Overbreadth in the area of the First Amendment has a peculiar evil, the evil of creating chilling effects which deter the exercise of those freedoms. *Dombrowski* v. *Pfister*, 380 U.S. 479. As we stated in *NAACP* v. *Button*, 371 U.S. 415, in speaking of First Amendment freedoms and the unconstitutionality of over-broad statutes: "These freedoms are delicate and vulnerable, as well as supremely precious in our society. The threat of sanctions may deter their exercise almost as potently as the actual application of sanctions."

Mitchell is of a different vintage from the present case. Since its date, a host of decisions have illustrated the need for narrowly drawn statutes that touch First Amendment rights. A teacher was held to be unconstitutionally discharged for sending a letter to a newspaper that criticized the school authorities. *Pickering* v. *Board of Education*, 391 U.S. 563. "In these circumstances we conclude that the interest of the school administration in limiting teachers' opportunities to contribute to public debate is not significantly greater than its interest in limiting a similar contribution by any member of the general public." We followed the same course in *Wood* v. *Georgia*, 370 U.S. 375, when we relieved a sheriff from a contempt conviction for making a public statement in connection with a current political controversy. As in the present case, the sheriff spoke as a private citizen and what he said did not interfere with his duties as sheriff.

The present Act cannot be appropriately narrowed to meet the need for narrowly drawn language not embracing First Amendment speech or writing without substantial revision. . . .

The Commission, on a case-by-case approach, has listed 13 categories of prohibited activities, starting with the catch-all "include but are not limited to." So the Commission ends up with open-end discretion to penalize X or not to penalize him. For example, a "permissible" activity is the employee's right to "[e]xpress his opinion as an individual privately and publicly on political subjects and candidates." Yet "soliciting votes" is prohibited. Is an employee safe from punishment if he expresses his opinion that candidate X is the best and candidate Y the worst? Is that crossing the forbidden line of soliciting votes?

A nursing assistant at a veterans' hospital put an ad in a newspaper reading:

> "To All My Many Friends of Poplar Bluff and Butler County I want to take this opportunity to ask your vote and support in the election, TUESDAY, AUGUST 7th. A very special person is seeking the Democratic nomination for Sheriff. I do not have to tell you of his qualifications, his past records stand.
> "This person is my dad, Lester (Less) Massingham.
> "THANK YOU
> "WALLACE (WALLY) MASSINGHAM"

He was held to have violated the Act. *Massingham*, 1 Political Activity Reporter 792 (1959).

Is a letter a permissible "expression" of views or a prohibited "solicitation?" The Solicitor General says it is a "permissible" expression; but the Commission ruled otherwise. For an employee who does not have the Solicitor General as counsel great consequences flow from an innocent decision. He may lose his job. Therefore the most prudent thing is to do nothing. Thus is self-imposed censorship imposed on many nervous people who live on narrow economic margins.

I would strike this provision of the law down as unconstitutional so that a new start may be made on this old problem that confuses and restricts nearly five million federal, state, and local public employees today that live under the present Act.

In a companion case[4] the Court also upheld an Oklahoma statute similar to the Hatch Act and applicable to all state civil service employees. Douglas again dissented and said in part:

> *First Amendment rights are indeed fundamental, for "we the people" are the sovereigns, not those who sit in the seat of the mighty. It is the voice of the people who ultimately have the say; once we fence off a group and bar them from public dialogue, the public interest is the loser. . . .*
> *A bureaucracy that is alert, vigilant, and alive is more efficient than one that is quiet and submissive. It is the First Amendment that makes them alert, vigilant, and alive. It is the suppression of First Amendment rights that creates faceless, nameless bureaucrats who are inert in their localities and submissive to some master's voice. High values ride on today's decision in this case and in Letter Carriers. I would not allow the bureaucracy in the State or Federal Government to be deprived of First Amendment rights.*

[4] *Broderick* v. *Oklahoma*, 413 U.S. 601 (1973).

Their exercise certainly is as important in the public sector as it is in the private sector. Those who work for government have no watered-down constitutional rights. So far as the First Amendment goes, I would keep them on the same plane with all other people.

Other instances of legislative efforts to protect the political process from undue influence and corruption are provided by corrupt practices acts. Douglas concurred in the reversal of a conviction of a newspaper publisher, under a state statute, for publishing an editorial on election day urging electors to vote for a mayor-council form of government, saying that the statute was "a blatant violation of freedom of the press."[5] When the Court in United States v. CIO,[6] in order to avoid constitutional questions, construed the federal Corrupt Practices Act forbidding corporations and labor unions to make "contributions" or "expenditures" in federal elections as not applying to the cost of ᵤ union newspaper distributed to union members, he did not agree that the Act could be so construed. But he concurred in dismissal of prosecution on the ground that the Act violated the First Amendment's guarantees of freedom of speech, press, and assembly. Assuming that valid limitations might be placed on expenditures to protect against corruption, or against undue influence by unions and corporations in the electoral process, he thought that outright prohibition of all expenditures went too far.

UNITED STATES V. UNITED AUTO WORKERS
352 U.S. 567 (1957)

In this case the Court construed the federal Corrupt Practices Act to apply to the expenditure of union funds to pay for television time for broadcasts indorsing certain candidates for Congress. But, since it was ruling on a motion to dismiss an indictment, it declined to rule on the constitutionality of the Act as here applied. Instead it remanded the case for trial so that, in the event of conviction, a ruling on the constitutional issues could be made in a "concrete factual setting."

MR. JUSTICE DOUGLAS, dissenting.

We deal here with a problem that is fundamental to the electoral process and to the operation of our democratic society. It is whether a union can express its views on the issues of an election and on the merits of the candidates, unrestrained and unfettered by the Congress.

---

[5] *Mills v. Alabama*, 384 U.S. 214 (1966).
[6] 335 U.S. 106 (1948).

The principle at stake is not peculiar to unions. It is applicable as well to associations of manufacturers, retail and wholesale trade groups, consumers' leagues, farmers' unions, religious groups and every other association representing a segment of American life and taking an active part in our political campaigns and discussions. It is as important an issue as has come before the Court, for it reaches the very vitals of our system of government.

Under our Constitution it is We The People who are sovereign. The people have the final say. The legislators are their spokesmen. The people determine through their votes the destiny of the nation. It is therefore important—vitally important—that all channels of communication be open to them during every election, that no point of view be restrained or barred, and that the people have access to the views of every group in the community.

In *United States* v. *C.I.O.* [note 6, *supra*] Mr. Justice Rutledge spoke of the importance of the First Amendment rights—freedom of expression and freedom of assembly—to the integrity of our elections. "The most complete exercise of those rights," he said, "is essential to the full, fair and untrammeled operation of the electoral process. To the extent they are curtailed the electorate is deprived of information, knowledge and opinion vital to its function."

What the Court does today greatly impairs those rights. It sustains an indictment charging no more than the use of union funds for broadcasting television programs that urge and endorse the selection of certain candidates for the Congress of the United States. The opinion of the Court places that advocacy in the setting of corrupt practices. The opinion generates an environment of evil-doing and points to the oppressions and misdeeds that have haunted elections in this country.

Making a speech endorsing a candidate for office does not, however, deserve to be identified with antisocial conduct. Until today political speech has never been considered a crime. The making of a political speech up to now has always been one of the preferred rights protected by the First Amendment. It usually costs money to communicate an idea to a large audience. But no one would seriously contend that the expenditure of money to print a newspaper deprives the publisher of freedom of the press. Nor can the fact that it costs money to make a speech—whether it be hiring a hall or purchasing time on the air— make the speech any the less an exercise of First Amendment rights. Yet this statute, as construed and applied in this indictment, makes criminal any "expenditure" by a union for the purpose of expressing its views on the issues of an election and the candidates. It would make no difference under this construction of the Act whether the union spokesman made his address from the platform of a hall, used a sound truck in the streets, or bought time on radio or television. In each case the mere "expenditure" of money to make the speech is an indictable offense. The principle applied today would make equally criminal the use by a union of its funds to print pamphlets for general distribution or to distribute political literature at large.

Can an Act so construed be constitutional in view of the command of the First Amendment that Congress shall make no law that abridges free speech or freedom of assembly?

The Court says that the answer on the constitutional issue must await the development of the facts at the trial.

It asks, "Did the broadcast reach the public at large or only those affiliated with appellee?" But the size of the audience has heretofore been deemed wholly irrelevant to First Amendment issues. One has a right to freedom of speech whether he talks to one person or to one thousand. One has a right to freedom of speech not only when he talks to his friends but also when he talks to the public. It is startling to learn that a union spokesman or the spokesman for a corporate interest has fewer constitutional rights when he talks to the public than when he talks to members of his group.

The Court asks whether the broadcast constituted "active electioneering" or simply stated "the record of particular candidates on economic issues." What possible difference can it make under the First Amendment whether it was one or the other? The First Amendment covers the entire spectrum. It protects the impassioned plea of the orator as much as the quiet publication of the tabulations of the statistician or economist. If there is an innuendo that "active electioneering" by union spokesmen is not covered by the First Amendment, the opinion makes a sharp break with our political and constitutional heritage.

The Court asks, "Did the union sponsor the broadcast with the intent to affect the results of the election?" The purpose of speech is not only to inform but to incite to action. As Mr. Justice Holmes said in his dissent in *Gitlow* v. *New York*, 268 U.S. 652, "Every idea is an incitement. It offers itself for belief and if believed it is acted on unless some other belief outweighs it or some failure of energy stifles the movement at its birth." To draw a constitutional line between informing the people and inciting or persuading them and to suggest that one is protected and the other not by the First Amendment is to give constitutional dignity to an irrelevance. Any political speaker worth his salt intends to sway voters. His purpose to do so cannot possibly rob him of his First Amendment rights, unless we are to reduce that great guarantee of freedom to the protection of meaningless mouthings of ineffective speakers.

Finally, the Court asks whether the broadcast was "paid for out of the general dues of the union membership or may the funds be fairly said to have been obtained on a voluntary basis." Behind this question is the idea that there may be a minority of union members who are of a different political school than their leaders and who object to the use of their union dues to espouse one political view. This is a question that concerns the internal management of union affairs. To date, unions have operated under a rule of the majority. Perhaps minority rights need protection. But this way of doing it is, indeed, burning down the house to roast the pig. All union expenditures for political discourse are banned because a minority might object.

When the exercise of First Amendment rights is tangled with conduct which government may regulate, we refuse to allow the First Amendment rights to be sacrificed merely because some evil may result. Our insistence is that the regulatory measure be "narrowly drawn" to meet the evil that the government can control. *Cantwell* v. *Connecticut* [note 4, p. 132, *supra*]. Or as the Court said in *De Jonge* v. *Oregon*, 299 U.S. 353, when speaking of First Amendment rights, ". . . the legislative intervention can find constitutional justification only by dealing with the abuse. The rights themselves must not be curtailed."

If minorities need protection against the use of union funds for political speech-making, there are ways of reaching that end without denying the majority their First Amendment rights.[7]

First Amendment rights are not merely curtailed by the construction of the Act which the Court adopts. Today's ruling abolishes First Amendment rights on a wholesale basis. Protection of minority groups, if any, can be no excuse. The Act is not "narrowly drawn" to meet that abuse.[8]

---

[7] There are alternative measures appropriate to cure this evil which Congress has seen in the expenditure of union funds for political purposes. The protection of union members from the use of their funds in supporting a cause with which they do not sympathize may be cured by permitting the minority to withdraw their funds from that activity. The English have long required labor unions to permit a dissenting union member to refuse to contribute funds for political purposes.

[8] [The Railway Labor Act makes a union selected by a majority of the employees the exclusive bargaining agent for all employees and permits the railway unions and carriers to enter into "union shop" contracts whereby all employees must join the union. In *International Association of Machinists* v. *Street*, 367 U.S. 740 (1961), where minority members under such a union shop agreement were complaining that the union dues which they were required to pay were used to finance campaigns for federal and state offices and to propagate political and economic views with which they did not agree, the Court construed the Railway Labor Act not to permit such expenditure of funds collected under a union shop agreement. Douglas did not agree that the Act could be so construed, but concurred in the decision on the ground that the Act violated the First Amendment.]

Some may think that one group or another should not express its views in an election because it is too powerful, because it advocates unpopular ideas, or because it has a record of lawless action. But these are not justifications for withholding First Amendment rights from any group—labor or corporate. First Amendment rights are part of the heritage of all persons and groups in this country. They are not to be dispensed or withheld merely because we or the Congress thinks the person or group is worthy or unworthy.

These constitutional questions are so grave that the least we should do is to construe this Act, as we have in comparable situations (*United States v. C.I.O.* [note 6, *supra*]; *United States v. Rumely*, 345 U.S. 41; *United States v. Harriss*, 347 U.S. 612, to limit the word "expenditure" to activity that does not involve First Amendment rights.[9]

The Act, as construed and applied, is a broadside assault on the freedom of political expression guaranteed by the First Amendment. It cannot possibly be saved by any of the facts conjured up by the Court. The answers to the questions reserved are quite irrelevant to the constitutional questions tendered under the First Amendment.

In Pipefitters Local Union No. 562 *v.* United States,[10] *a decision in which Douglas joined, the Court construed the Corrupt Practices Act to apply only to contributions and expenditures from the union treasury and not to prohibit the union from making contributions or expenditures from a separate fund made up of voluntary contributions from its members and others so long as such a fund was strictly segregated from union funds and solicitations were conducted "under circumstances plainly indicating that donations are for a political purpose and that those solicited may decline to contribute without loss of job, union membership, or any other reprisal within the union's institutional power."*

Shortly after Douglas retired, the Court decided, in Buckley *v.* Valeo,[11] *a number of questions about the constitutionality of a new approach to federal elections as embodied in 1974 amendments to the*

---

[9] If Congress is of the opinion that large contributions by labor unions to candidates for office and to political parties have had an undue influence upon the conduct of elections, it can prohibit such contributions. And, in expressing their views on the issues and candidates, labor unions can be required to acknowledge their authorship and support of those expressions. Undue influence, however, cannot constitutionally form the basis for making it unlawful for any segment of our society to express its views on the issues of a political campaign.

[10] 407 U.S. 385 (1972).

[11] 424 U.S. 1 (1976).

Federal Election Campaign Act of 1971 It upheld limitations. of $1,000 per candidate by persons, corporations and groups of persons, $5,000 per candidate by political committees, and an overall $25,000 limitation on total contributions by an individual during any calendar year. But it invalidated, as infringements on freedom of speech and association,[12] *a limitation of $1,000 on expenditures by persons, corporations and groups of persons on behalf of any one candidate, limitations on expenditures by candidates of their own or their family's funds, and overall limitations on all expenditures in any one candidate's campaign. It also upheld requirements that candidates and political committees disclose the identity of everyone contributing as much as $10 and, if the contribution exceeds $100, disclose the contributor's occupation and principal place of business also. Finally it upheld the establishment of a Presidential Election Campaign Fund, financed by individual taxpayers who authorize payment to the fund of one dollar of their tax liability.*

Other laws raising First Amendment problems are designed to protect some persons from annoyance, offense, or more serious injury from the conduct of others. Some of these laws are aimed directly at speech and press. Others would also cover activity not protected by the First Amendment.

TERMINIELLO V. CHICAGO

337 U.S. 1 (1949)

Terminiello, an unfrocked Catholic priest, was convicted of disorderly conduct because of a speech he made in a Chicago auditorium under the auspices of the Christian Veterans of America. The speech was violent and vulgar. He referred to Jews as "scum," to Eleanor Roosevelt as "one of the world's Communists," and to Franco as "the savior of what was left of Europe." He also made predictions of "violence." These remarks were received with expressions of hostility by some members of the audience of over eight hundred persons. In addition, about a thousand more had gathered outside of the auditorium to protest the meeting, and members of this "angry and turbulent crowd" threw stones, ice picks, and bottles through the doors and windows of the auditorium. A cordon of policemen assigned to the meeting was unable to prevent these disturbances.

---

[12] In *NAACP v. Alabama*, 357 U.S. 449 (1958), a decision in which Douglas joined, the Court recognized that there was a right under the First Amendment to "engage in association for the advancement of beliefs and ideas," since effective advocacy "is undeniably enhanced by group association."

MR. JUSTICE DOUGLAS delivered the opinion of the Court.

Petitioner after jury trial was found guilty of disorderly conduct in violation of a city ordinance of Chicago[13] and fined.

The trial court charged that "breach of the peace" consists of any "misbehavior which violates the public peace and decorum"; and that the "misbehavior may constitute a breach of the peace if it stirs the public to anger, invites dispute, brings about a condition of unrest, or creates a disturbance, or if it molests the inhabitants in the enjoyment of peace and quiet by arousing alarm." Petitioner did not take exception to that instruction. But he maintained at all times that the ordinance as applied to his conduct violated his right of free speech under the Federal Constitution.

The argument here has been focused on the issue of whether the content of petitioner's speech was composed of derisive, fighting words, which carried it outside the scope of the constitutional guarantees. See *Chaplinsky* v. *New Hampshire*, 315 U.S. 568. We do not reach that question, for there is a preliminary question that is dispositive of the case.

As we have noted, the statutory words "breach of the peace" were defined in instructions to the jury to include speech which "stirs the public to anger, invites dispute, brings about a condition of unrest, or creates a disturbance. . . ." That construction of the ordinance is a ruling on a question of state law that is as binding on us as though the precise words had been written into the ordinance.

The vitality of civil and political institutions in our society depends on free discussion. As Chief Justice Hughes wrote in *De Jonge* v. *Oregon*, 299 U.S. 353, it is only through free debate and free exchange of ideas that government remains responsive to the will of the people and peaceful change is effected. The right to speak freely and to promote diversity of ideas and programs is therefore one of the chief distinctions that sets us apart from totalitarian regimes.

Accordingly a function of free speech under our system of government is to invite dispute. It may indeed best serve its high purpose when it induces a condition of unrest, creates dissatisfaction with conditions as they are, or even stirs people to anger. Speech is often provocative and challenging. It may strike at prejudices and preconceptions and have profound unsettling effects as it presses for acceptance of an idea. That is why freedom of speech, though not absolute, *Chaplinsky* v.

[13] "All persons who shall make, aid, countenance, or assist in making any improper noise, riot, disturbance, breach of the peace, or diversion tending to a breach of the peace, within the limits of the city . . . shall be deemed guilty of disorderly conduct, and upon conviction thereof, shall be severally fined not less than one dollar nor more than two hundred dollars for each offense."

New Hampshire, supra, is nevertheless protected against censorship or punishment, unless shown likely to produce a clear and present danger of a serious substantive evil that rises far above public inconvenience, annoyance, or unrest. There is no room under our Constitution for a more restrictive view. For the alternative would lead to standardization of ideas either by legislatures, courts, or dominant political or community groups.

The ordinance as construed by the trial court seriously invaded this province. It permitted conviction of petitioner if his speech stirred people to anger, invited public dispute, or brought about a condition of unrest. A conviction resting on any of those grounds may not stand. . . .

The statute as construed in the charge to the jury was passed on by the Illinois courts and sustained by them over the objection that as so read it violated the Fourteenth Amendment. The fact that the parties did not dispute its construction makes the adjudication no less ripe for our review. We can only take the statute as the state courts read it. From our point of view it is immaterial whether the state law question as to its meaning was controverted or accepted. The pinch of the statute is in its application. It is that question which the petitioner has brought here. To say therefore that the question on this phase of the case is whether the trial judge gave a wrong charge is wholly to misconceive the issue.

But it is said that throughout the appellate proceedings the Illinois courts assumed that the only conduct punishable and punished under the ordinance was conduct constituting "fighting words." [But] petitioner was not convicted under a statute so narrowly construed. For all anyone knows he was convicted under the parts of the ordinance (as construed) which, for example, make it an offense merely to invite dispute or to bring about a condition of unrest. We cannot avoid that issue by saying that all Illinois did was to measure petitioner's conduct, not the ordinance, against the Constitution. Petitioner raised both points—that his speech was protected by the Constitution; that the inclusion of his speech within the ordinance was a violation of the Constitution. We would, therefore, strain at technicalities to conclude that the constitutionality of the ordinance as construed and applied to petitioner was not before the Illinois courts. The record makes clear that petitioner at all times challenged the constitutionality of the ordinance as construed and applied to him.

When, in a later case, the Court sustained the disorderly conduct conviction of a speaker who had characterized the mayors of New York and Syracuse and President Truman as "bums" and the American Legion as "a Nazi Gestapo," and who had ignored a police officer's order to stop speaking (after one man in the audience told the officer he would remove the speaker from the platform if the officer did not), Douglas dissented. He thought that the "fighting words" doctrine was not applicable to mere "exaggeration, . . . vilification of ideas and men, [and] the making of false charges," and that the police should have directed their efforts to protecting the speaker rather than throwing their weight on the side of those who would break up the meeting.[14]

BEAUHARNAIS V. ILLINOIS
343 U.S. 250 (1952)

Libel laws, providing for damages to persons injured by untrue defamatory statements, are older than the Constitution. But some states in relatively recent times have added to their traditional libel laws, which protected only individuals specifically defamed, "group" libel laws. One such law came before the Court in this case. It provided criminal penalties for anyone who falsely portrayed "depravity, criminality, unchastity, or lack of virtue of a class of citizens, of any race, color, creed or religion," and it had been employed to convict one who had defamed blacks in petitions which he had circulated in order to persuade the city council and mayor to pass segregation laws.

The Court concluded that the state law did not violate the First Amendment. Although no clear and present danger of disorder was shown, certain classes of speech—"the lewd and obscene, the profane, the libelous, and the insulting or 'fighting' words"—were considered to be "of such slight social value as a step toward truth that any benefit that may be derived from them is clearly outweighed by the social interest in order and morality."[15]

MR. JUSTICE DOUGLAS, dissenting.

Hitler and his Nazis showed how evil a conspiracy could be which was aimed at destroying a race by exposing it to contempt, derision, and obloquy. I would be willing to concede that such conduct directed at a race or group in this country could be made an indictable offense. For such a project would be more than the exercise of free speech. Like picketing, it would be free speech plus.

---

[14] *Feiner v. New York*, 340 U.S. 315 (1951).

[15] The majority opinion's assumption that the First Amendment makes an exception for profane speech remains to be tested. A state statute authorizing censorship of "sacrilegious" films was invalidated because the term "sacrilegious" was too vague in *Joseph Burstyn, Inc. v. Wilson*, 343 U.S. 495 (1952), a decision in which Douglas joined. The exception for obscenity is considered at pp. 220–230, *infra*.

I would also be willing to concede that even without the element of conspiracy there might be times and occasions when the legislative or executive branch might call a halt to inflammatory talk, such as the shouting of "fire" in a school or a theatre.

My view is that if in any case other public interests are to override the plain command of the First Amendment, the peril of speech must be clear and present, leaving no room for argument, raising no doubts as to the necessity of curbing speech in order to prevent disaster.

The First Amendment is couched in absolute terms— freedom of speech shall not be abridged. Speech has therefore a preferred position as contrasted to some other civil rights. For example, privacy, equally sacred to some, is protected by the Fourth Amendment only against unreasonable searches and seizures. There is room for regulation of the ways and means of invading privacy. No such leeway is granted the invasion of the right of free speech guaranteed by the First Amendment. Until recent years that had been the course and direction of constitutional law. Yet recently the Court in this and in other cases[16] has engrafted the right of regulation onto the First Amendment by placing in the hands of the legislative branch the right to regulate "within reasonable limits" the right of free speech. This to me is an ominous and alarming trend. The free trade in ideas which the Framers of the Constitution visualized disappears. In its place there is substituted a new orthodoxy—an orthodoxy that changes with the whims of the age or the day, an orthodoxy which the majority by solemn judgment proclaims to be essential to the safety, welfare, security, morality, or health of society. Free speech in the constitutional sense disappears. Limits are drawn—limits dictated by expediency, political opinion, prejudices or some other desideratum of legislative action.

An historic aspect of the issue of judicial supremacy was the extent to which legislative judgment would be supreme in the field of social legislation. The vague contours of the Due Process Clause were used to strike down laws deemed by the Court to be unwise and improvident.[17] That trend has been reversed. In matters relating to business, finance, industrial and labor conditions, health and the public welfare, great leeway is now granted the legislature,[18] for there is no guarantee in the Constitution that the *status quo* will be preserved against regula-

[16] *Dennis v. United States* [p. 199, *infra*]; *Feiner v. New York* [note 14, *supra*]. Cf. *Breard v. Alexandria*, 341 U.S. 622; *American Communications Assn. v. Douds*, 339 U.S. 382; *Osman v. Douds*, 339 U.S. 846.

[17] *Lochner v. New York*, 198 U.S. 45; *Coppage v. Kansas*, 236 U.S. 1; *Ribnik v. McBride*, 277 U.S. 350.

[18] *Nebbia v. New York*, 291 U.S. 502; *West Coast Hotel Co. v. Parrish*, 300 U.S. 379; *Lincoln Union v. Northwestern Co.*, 335 U.S. 525; *Day-Brite Lighting, Inc. v. Missouri*, 342 U.S. 421.

tion by government. Freedom of speech, however, rests on a different constitutional basis. The First Amendment says that freedom of speech, freedom of press, and the free exercise of religion shall not be abridged. That is a negation of power on the part of each and every department of government. Free speech, free press, free exercise of religion are placed separate and apart; they are above and beyond the police power; they are not subject to regulation in the manner of factories, slums, apartment houses, production of oil, and the like.

The Court in this and in other cases places speech under an expanding legislative control. Today a white man stands convicted for protesting in unseemly language against our decisions invalidating restrictive covenants. Tomorrow a Negro will be haled before a court for denouncing lynch law in heated terms. Farm laborers in the West who compete with field hands drifting up from Mexico; whites who feel the pressure of orientals; a minority which finds employment going to members of the dominant religious group—all of these are caught in the mesh of today's decision. Debate and argument even in the courtroom are not always calm and dispassionate. Emotions sway speakers and audiences alike. Intemperate speech is a distinctive characteristic of man. Hotheads blow off and release destructive energy in the process. They shout and rave, exaggerating weaknesses, magnifying error, viewing with alarm. So it has been from the beginning; and so it will be throughout time. The Framers of the Constitution knew human nature as well as we do. They too had lived in dangerous days; they too knew the suffocating influence of orthodoxy and standardized thought. They weighed the compulsions for restrained speech and thought against the abuses of liberty. They chose liberty. That should be our choice today no matter how distasteful to us the pamphlet of Beauharnais may be. It is true that this is only one decision which may later be distinguished or confined to narrow limits. But it represents a philosophy at war with the First Amendment—a constitutional interpretation which puts free speech under the legislative thumb. It reflects an influence moving ever deeper into our society. It is notice to the legislatures that they have the power to control unpopular blocs. It is a warning to every minority that when the Constitution guarantees free speech it does not mean what it says.

Other cases in recent years have involved the permissible reach of the traditional libel laws. In 1964, in New York Times Co. v. Sullivan,[19] *the Court read the First Amendment to mean that the state could not award damages for libel because of the publication of defamatory criti-*

[19] 376 U.S. 254 (1964).

cism of a "public official" (a county commissioner) unless the criticism were made with "actual malice—that is, with knowledge that it was false or with reckless disregard of whether it was false or not." Such a reading was necessary, the Court thought, because otherwise "would-be critics of official conduct may be deterred from voicing their criticism, even though it is believed to be true and even though it is in fact true, because of doubt whether it can be proved in court or fear of the expense of having to do so," and the result would be to "dampen the vigor and limit the variety of public debate." Douglas concurred, but thought that there should be absolute immunity for such criticism and that the Court's rule would still leave the would-be critic subject to the dampening effect of possible libel actions. He has persisted in that view, as the Court has extended its rule from "public officials" to "public figures," such as a private citizen seeking nomination in a primary election to become a candidate for the United States Senate,[20] former state university football coaches, and retired generals who inject themselves into public affairs.[21] He has persisted too as the Court has extended the doctrine to limit the power of a school board to discharge a public teacher for criticism of the board,[22] and to limit the power of the states to award damages for invasion of privacy to private citizens whose private lives had been brought into the news by events over which they had no control.[23]

GERTZ V. ROBERT WELCH, INC.
418 U.S. 323 (1974)

In 1968 a Chicago policeman shot and killed a youth named Nelson, and the policeman was convicted of second-degree murder. Attorney Elmer Gertz, neither a public official nor a public figure, was retained by Nelson's family to represent them in a civil action to recover damages from the policeman.

Although Gertz had nothing to do with the criminal prosecution of the policeman, the case fit into a campaign being waged by American Opinion, a monthly published by Welsh to air the views of the John Birch Society. Its campaign was to warn of a nationwide Communist conspiracy to discredit local law enforcement agencies. Welsh published an article announcing that the policeman's conviction was a "frame-up," that testimony against him at the criminal trial was false,

[20] *Monitor Patriot Co.* v. *Roy*, 401 U.S. 265 (1971).
[21] *Curtis Publishing Co.* v. *Butts*, 388 U.S. 130 (1967).
[22] *Pickering* v. *Board of Education*, 391 U.S. 563 (1968).
[23] *Cox Broadcasting Corp* v. *Cohn*, 420 U.S. 469 (1975); *Cantrell* v. *Forest City Publishing Co.*, 419 U.S. 245 (1974); *Time, Inc.* v. *Hill*, 385 U.S. 374 (1967).

and that his prosecution was part of the Communist campaign against the police. Gertz was portrayed as an architect of this frame-up, as a "Leninist", a "Communist-fronter," and an official of the Marxist League for Industrial Democracy. None of these statements was true. Neither was the statement that Gertz had been an officer of the National Lawyers Guild which "probably did more than any other outfit to plan the Communist attack on the Chicago police during the 1968 Democratic Convention." Gertz had been an officer of the Guild some 15 years earlier, but neither he nor the Guild had taken any part in planning the Chicago demonstrations.

Welsh sought to defend by extending the rule of New York Times v. Sullivan to "public issues." The Court refused so to extend the rule, thus allowing Gertz to recover without proving either that Welsh knew the published statements were false or that Welsh acted with reckless disregard of whether they were false or not. But in an effort at "accommodation of the competing values" of free speech and press and the individual's claim to compensation for wrongful injury, it imposed a limitation. Where a private individual, such as Gertz, proves that he has been defamed but does not prove that the defamer acted with knowledge or with reckless disregard, his recovery must be limited to compensation for his actual injury. The past practice in many states of allowing presumed or punitive damages in such cases would no longer be allowed.

Mr. Justice Douglas, dissenting.

The Court describes this case as a return to the struggle of "defin[ing] the proper accommodation between the law of defamation and the freedoms of speech and press protected by the First Amendment." It is indeed a struggle, once described by Mr. Justice Black as "the same quagmire" in which the Court "is now helplessly struggling in the field of obscenity." *Curtis Publishing Co. v. Butts,* 388 U.S. 130 (concurring opinion). I would suggest that the struggle is a quite hopeless one, for, in light of the command of the First Amendment, no "accommodation" of its freedoms can be "proper" except those made by the Framers themselves.

Unlike the right of privacy which, by the terms of the Fourth Amendment, must be accommodated with reasonable searches and seizures and warrants issued by magistrates, the rights of free speech and of a free press were protected by the Framers in verbiage whose proscription seems clear. I have stated before my view that the First Amendment would bar Congress from passing any libel law.[24] This was

[24] See, e.g., *Rosenblatt v. Baer,* 383 U.S. 75 (concurring).

the view held by Thomas Jefferson[25] and it is one Congress has never challenged through enactment of a civil libel statute. The sole congressional attempt at this variety of First Amendment muzzle was in the Sedition Act of 1798—a criminal libel act never tested in this Court and one which expired by its terms three years after enactment. As President, Thomas Jefferson pardoned those who were convicted under the Act, and fines levied in its prosecution were repaid by Act of Congress.[26] The general consensus was that the Act constituted a regrettable legislative exercise plainly in violation of the First Amendment.[27]

With the First Amendment made applicable to the States through the Fourteenth,[28] I do not see how States have any more ability to "accommodate" freedoms of speech or of the press than does Congress. This is true whether the form of the accommodation is civil or criminal since "[w]hat a State may not constitutionally bring about by means of a criminal statute is likewise beyond the reach of its civil law of libel." *New York Times Co.* v. *Sullivan,* 376 U.S. 254. Like Congress, States are without power "to use a civil libel law or any other law to impose damages for merely discussing public affairs." *Id.* (Black, J., concurring).[29]

---

[25] In 1798 Jefferson stated:
"[The First Amendment] thereby guard[s] in the same sentence, and under the same words, the freedom of religion, of speech, and of the press: insomuch, that whatever violates either, throws down the sanctuary which covers the others, *and that libels, falsehood, and defamation, equally with heresy and false religion, are withheld from the cognizance of federal tribunals. . . .*" 8 The Works of Thomas Jefferson 464–465 (Ford ed. 1904) (emphasis added).

[26] See, *e.g.,* Act of July 4, 1840, c. 45, 6 Stat. 802, accompanied by H. R. Rep. No. 86, 26th Cong., 1st Sess. (1840).

[27] Senator Calhoun in reporting to Congress assumed the invalidity of the Act to be a matter "which no one now doubts." Report with Senate Bill No. 122, S. Doc. No. 118, 24th Cong., 1st Sess., 3 (1836).

[28] See *Stromberg* v. *California,* 283 U.S. 359, 368–369.

[29] Since this case involves a discussion of public affairs, I need not decide at this point whether the First Amendment prohibits all libel actions. "An unconditional right to say what one pleases about public affairs is what I consider to be the *minimum* guarantee of the First Amendment." *New York Times Co.* v. *Sullivan,* 376 U.S. 254 (Black, J., concurring) (emphasis added). But "public affairs" includes a great deal more than merely political affairs. Matters of science, economics, business, art, literature, etc., are all matters of interest to the general public. Indeed, any matter of sufficient general interest to prompt media coverage may be said to be a public affair. Certainly police killings, "Communist conspiracies," and the like qualify.

A more regressive view of free speech has surfaced but it has thus far gained no judicial acceptance. Solicitor General Bork has stated:
"Constitutional protection should be accorded only to speech that is explicitly political. There is no basis for judicial intervention to protect any other form of

Continued recognition of the possibility of state libel suits for public discussion of public issues leaves the freedom of speech honored by the Fourteenth Amendment a diluted version of First Amendment protection. This view is only possible if one accepts the position that the First Amendment is applicable to the States only through the Due Process Clause of the Fourteenth, due process freedom of speech being only that freedom which this Court might deem to be "implicit in the concept of ordered liberty."[30] But the Court frequently has rested state free speech and free press decisions on the Fourteenth Amendment generally rather than on the Due Process Clause alone. The Fourteenth Amendment speaks not only of due process but also of "privileges and immunities" of United States citizenship. I can conceive of no privilege or immunity with a higher claim to recognition against state abridgment than the freedoms of speech and of the press. In our federal system we are all subject to two governmental regimes, and freedoms of speech and of the press protected against the infringement of only one are quite illusory. The identity of the oppressor is, I would think, a matter of relative indifference to the oppressed.

There can be no doubt that a State impinges upon free and open discussion when it sanctions the imposition of damages for such discussion through its civil libel laws. Discussion of public affairs is often marked by highly charged emotions, and jurymen, not unlike us all, are subject to those emotions. It is indeed this very type of speech which is the reason for the First Amendment since speech which arouses little emotion is little in need of protection. The vehicle for publication in this case was the American Opinion, a most controversial periodical which disseminates the views of the John Birch Society, an organization which many deem to be quite offensive. The subject matter involved

---

expression, be it scientific, literary or that variety of expression we call obscene or pornographic. Moreover, within that category of speech we ordinarily call political, there should be no constitutional obstruction to laws making criminal any speech that advocates forcible overthrow of the government or the violation of any law." Bork, Neutral Principles and Some First Amendment Problems, 47 Ind. L. J. 1, 20 (1971).

According to this view, Congress, upon finding a painting aesthetically displeasing or a novel poorly written or a revolutionary new scientific theory unsound could constitutionally prohibit exhibition of the painting, distribution of the book or discussion of the theory. Congress might also proscribe the advocacy of the violation of any law, apparently without regard to the law's constitutionality. Thus, were Congress to pass a blatantly invalid law such as one prohibiting newspaper editorials critical of the Government, a publisher might be punished for advocating its violation. Similarly, the late Dr. Martin Luther King, Jr., could have been punished for advising blacks to peacefully sit in the front of buses or to ask for service in restaurants segregated by law.

[30] [See discussion at pp. 321–325, infra.]

"Communist plots," "conspiracies against law enforcement agencies," and the killing of a private citizen by the police. With any such amalgam of controversial elements pressing upon the jury, a jury determination, unpredictable in the most neutral circumstances, becomes for those who venture to discuss heated issues, a virtual roll of the dice separating them from liability for often massive claims of damage.

It is only the hardy publisher who will engage in discussion in the face of such risk, and the Court's preoccupation with proliferating standards in the area of libel increases the risks. It matters little whether the standard be articulated as "malice" or "reckless disregard of the truth" or "negligence," for jury determinations by any of those criteria are virtually unreviewable. This Court, in its continuing delineation of variegated mantles of First Amendment protection, is, like the potential publisher, left with only speculation on how jury findings were influenced by the effect the subject matter of the publication had upon the minds and viscera of the jury. The standard announced today leaves the States free to "define for themselves the appropriate standard of liability for a publisher or broadcaster" in the circumstances of this case. This of course leaves the simple negligence standard as an option, with the jury free to impose damages upon a finding that the publisher failed to act as "a reasonable man." With such continued erosion of First Amendment protection, I fear that it may well be the reasonable man who refrains from speaking.

Since in my view the First and Fourteenth Amendments prohibit the imposition of damages upon respondent for this discussion of public affairs, I would affirm the judgment below.

BRANZBURG V. HAYS

408 U.S. 665 (1972)

Branzburg, a newsman who wrote about drug traffic in Kentucky, and Pappas and Caldwell, newsmen who covered the Black Panther Party in Massachusetts and California, respectively, were each summoned before a separate grand jury to testify about the subjects covered by them. They each asserted a privilege to refuse to answer under the First Amendment, arguing that to gather news it was often necessary to agree not to identify the source of the information published or to publish only part of the facts revealed, or both, and that, if they were forced to reveal their confidences to a grand jury, the sources so identified and other confidential sources of other reporters would be deterred from furnishing publishable information.

They did not claim an absolute privilege, but only that they should not be required to testify before a grand jury or at trial unless the gov-

ernment first showed that they possessed information relevant to a crime the grand jury was investigating, that the information was unavailable from other sources, and that there was a compelling public need for the disclosure. Their cases were consolidated for argument and decision and the Court rejected their claim of privilege, finding "no basis for holding that the public interest in law enforcement and in ensuring effective grand jury proceedings is insufficient to override the consequential, but uncertain, burden on news gathering."

Justice Douglas, in his dissent, focused on Caldwell's case, but would have applied the same rule to all three cases.

MR. JUSTICE DOUGLAS, dissenting.

Caldwell, a black, is a reporter for the New York Times and was assigned to San Francisco with the hope that he could report on the activities and attitudes of the Black Panther Party. Caldwell in time gained the complete confidence of its members and wrote in-depth articles about them.

He was subpoenaed to appear and testify before a federal grand jury and to bring with him notes and tapes covering interviews with its members. A hearing on a motion to quash was held. The District Court ruled that while Caldwell had to appear before the grand jury, he did not have to reveal confidential communications unless the court was satisfied that there was a "compelling and overriding national interest."

Caldwell refused to appear and was held in contempt. On appeal, the Court of Appeals vacated the judgment of contempt. It said that the revealing of confidential sources of information jeopardized a First Amendment freedom and that Caldwell did not have to appear before the grand jury absent a showing that there was a "compelling and overriding national interest" in pursuing such an interrogation.

The District Court had found that Caldwell's knowledge of the activities of the Black Panthers "derived in substantial part" from information obtained "within the scope of a relationship of trust and confidence." It also found that confidential relationships of this sort are commonly developed and maintained by professional journalists, and are indispensable to their work of gathering, analyzing, and publishing the news.

The District Court further had found that compelled disclosure of information received by a journalist within the scope of such confidential relationships jeopardized those relationships and thereby impaired the journalist's ability to gather, analyze, and publish the news.

The District Court, finally, had found that, without a protective order delimiting the scope of interrogation of Earl Caldwell by the grand jury, his appearance and examination before the jury would severely impair and damage his confidential relationships with members of the Black Panther Party and other militants, and thereby severely impair and damage his ability to gather, analyze, and publish news concerning them; and that it would also damage and impair the abilities of all reporters to gather, analyze, and publish news concerning them.

The Court of Appeals agreed with the findings of the District Court but held that Caldwell did not have to appear at all before the grand jury absent a "compelling need" shown by the Government.

It is my view that there is no "compelling need" that can be shown which qualifies the reporter's immunity from appearing or testifying before a grand jury, unless the reporter himself is implicated in a crime. His immunity in my view is therefore quite complete, for, absent his involvement in a crime, the First Amendment protects him against an appearance before a grand jury and if he is involved in a crime, the Fifth Amendment stands as a barrier. Since in my view there is no area of inquiry not protected by a privilege, the reporter need not appear for the futile purpose of invoking one to each question. And, since in my view a newsman has an absolute right not to appear before a grand jury, it follows for me that a journalist who voluntarily appears before that body may invoke his First Amendment privilege to specific questions. The basic issue is the extent to which the First Amendment (which is applicable to investigating committees) must yield to the Government's asserted need to know a reporter's unprinted information.

The starting point for decision pretty well marks the range within which the end result lies. The New York Times, whose reporting functions are at issue here, takes the amazing position that First Amendment rights are to be balanced against other needs or conveniences of government.[31] My belief is that all of the "balancing" was done by those who wrote the Bill of Rights. By casting the First Amendment in absolute terms, they repudiated the timid, watered-down, emasculated versions of the First Amendment which both the Government and the New York Times advance in the case.

My view is close to that of the late Alexander Meiklejohn:[32]

[31] "The three minimal tests we contend must be met before testimony divulging confidences may be compelled from a reporter are these: 1. The government must clearly show that there is probable cause to believe that the reporter possesses information which is specifically relevant to a specific probable violation of law. 2. The government must clearly show that the information it seeks cannot be obtained by alternative means, which is to say, from sources other than the reporter. 3. The government must clearly demonstrate a compelling and overriding interest in the information." Brief for New York Times as *Amicus Curiae* 29.

[32] The First Amendment Is An Absolute, 1961 Sup. Ct. Rev. 245.

"For the understanding of these principles it is essential to keep clear the crucial difference between 'the rights' of the governed and 'the powers' of the governors. And at this point, the title 'Bill of Rights' is lamentably inaccurate as a designation of the first ten amendments. They are not a 'Bill of Rights' but a 'Bill of Powers and Rights.' The Second through the Ninth Amendments limit the powers of the subordinate agencies in order that due regard shall be paid to the private 'rights of the governed.' The First and Tenth Amendments protect the governing 'powers' of the people from abridgment by the agencies which are established as their servants. In the field of our 'rights,' each one of us can claim 'due process of law.' In the field of our governing 'powers,' the notion of 'due process' is irrelevant."

He also believed that "[s]elf-government can exist only insofar as the voters acquire the intelligence, integrity, sensitivity, and generous devotion to the general welfare that, in theory, casting a ballot is assumed to express," and that "[p]ublic discussions of public issues, together with the spreading of information and opinion bearing on those issues, must have a freedom unabridged by our agents. Though they govern us, we, in a deeper sense, govern them. Over our governing, they have no power. Over their governing we have sovereign power."

Two principles which follow from this understanding of the First Amendment are at stake here. One is that the people, the ultimate governors, must have absolute freedom of, and therefore privacy of, their individual opinions and beliefs regardless of how suspect or strange they may appear to others. Ancillary to that principle is the conclusion that an individual must also have absolute privacy over whatever information he may generate in the course of testing his opinions and beliefs. In this regard, Caldwell's status as a reporter is less relevant than is his status as a student who affirmatively pursued empirical research to enlarge his own intellectual viewpoint. The second principle is that effective self-government cannot succeed unless the people are immersed in a steady, robust, unimpeded, and uncensored flow of opinion and reporting which are continuously subjected to critique, rebuttal, and re-examination. In this respect, Caldwell's status as a news gatherer and an integral part of that process becomes critical.

I

Government has many interests that compete with the First Amendment. Congressional investigations determine how existing laws actually operate or whether new laws are needed. While congressional committees have broad powers, they are subject to the restraints of the First Amendment. As we said in *Watkins* v. *United States*, 354 U.S. 178: "Clearly, an investigation is subject to the command that the Congress shall make no law abridging freedom of speech or press or assembly. While it is true that there is no statute to be reviewed, and that an investigation is not a law, nevertheless an investigation is part of lawmaking. It is justified solely as an adjunct to the legislative process. The First Amendment may be invoked against infringement of the protected freedoms by law or by lawmaking."

Hence, matters of belief, ideology, religious practices, social philosophy, and the like are beyond the pale and of no rightful concern of government, unless the belief or the speech, or other expression has been translated into action.

Also at stake here is Caldwell's privacy of association. We have held that "[i]nviolability of privacy in group association may in many circumstances be indispensable to preservation of freedom of association, particularly where a group espouses dissident beliefs." *NAACP* v. *Alabama*, 357 U.S. 449.

As I said in *Gibson* v. *Florida Legislative Investigation Committee*, 372 U.S. 539: "the associational rights protected by the First Amendment . . . cover the entire spectrum in political ideology as well as in art, in journalism, in teaching, and in religion. . . . [G]overnment is . . . precluded from probing the intimacies of spiritual and intellectual relationships in the myriad of such societies and groups that exist in this country, *regardless of the legislative purpose sought to be served.* . . . If that is not true, I see no barrier to investigation of newspapers, churches, political parties, clubs, societies, unions, and any other association for their political, economic, social, philosophical, or religious views." (Concurring opinion.) (Emphasis added.)

The Court has not always been consistent in its protection of these First Amendment rights and has sometimes allowed a government interest to override the absolutes of the First Amendment. For example, under the banner of the "clear and present danger" test,[33] and later

[33] *E.g., Schenck* v. *United States*, 249 U.S. 47 (wartime anti-draft "leafleting"); *Debs* v. *United States*, 249 U.S. 211 (wartime anti-draft speech); *Abrams* v. *United States*, 250 U.S. 616 (wartime leafleting calling for general strike); *Feiner* v. *New York*, 340 U.S. 315 (arrest of radical speaker without attempt to protect him from hostile audience); *Dennis* v. *United States*, 341 U.S. 494 (reformulation of test as "not improbable" rule to sustain conviction of knowing advocacy of overthrow); *Scales* v. *United States*, 367 U.S. 203 (knowing membership in group which espouses forbidden advocacy is punishable). For a more detailed account of the infamy of the "clear and present danger" test see my concurring opinion in *Brandenburg* v. *Ohio*, 395 U.S. 444, 450.

under the influence of the "balancing" formula,[34] the Court has permitted men to be penalized not for any harmful conduct but solely for holding unpopular beliefs.

In recent years we have said over and over again that where First Amendment rights are concerned any regulation "narrowly drawn,"[35]

---

[34] E.g., *Adler v. Board of Education*, 342 U.S. 485 (protection of schools from "pollution" outweighs public teachers' freedom to advocate violent overthrow); *Uphaus v. Wyman*, 360 U.S. 72, 79, 81 (preserving security of New Hampshire from subversives outweighs privacy of list of participants in suspect summer camp); *Barenblatt v. United States*, 360 U.S. 109 (legislative inquiry more important than protecting HUAC witness' refusal to answer whether a third person had been a Communist); *Wilkinson v. United States*, 365 U.S. 399 (legislative inquiry more important than protecting HUAC witness' refusal to state whether he was currently a member of the Communist Party); *Braden v. United States*, 365 U.S. 431, 435 (legislative inquiry more important than protecting HUAC witness' refusal to state whether he had once been a member of the Communist Party); *Konigsberg v. State Bar*, 366 U.S. 36 (regulating membership of bar outweighs interest of applicants in refusing to answer question concerning Communist affiliations); *In re Anastaplo*, 366 U.S. 82 (regulating membership of bar outweighs protection of applicant's belief in Declaration of Independence that citizens should revolt against an oppressive government); *Communist Party v. Subversive Activities Control Board*, 367 U.S. 1 (national security outweighs privacy of association of leaders of suspect groups); *Law Students Research Council v. Wadmond*, 401 U.S. 154 (regulating membership of bar outweighs privacy of applicants' views on the soundness of the Constitution).

[35] Thus, we have held "overbroad" measures which unduly restricted the time, place, and manner of expression. *Schneider v. State*, 308 U.S. 147, 161 (anti-leafleting law); *Thornhill v. Alabama*, 310 U.S. 88, 102 (anti-boycott statute); *Cantwell v. Connecticut*, 310 U.S. 296 (breach-of-peace measure); *Cox v. Louisiana*, 379 U.S. 536 (breach-of-peace measure); *Edwards v. South Carolina*, 372 U.S. 229 (breach-of-peace statute); *Cohen v. California*, 403 U.S. 15, 22 (breach-of-peace statute); *Gooding v. Wilson*, 405 U.S. 518 (breach-of-peace statute). But insofar as penalizing the *content* of thought and opinion is concerned, the Court has not in recent Terms permitted any interest to override the absolute privacy of one's philosophy. To be sure, opinions have often adverted to the absence of a compelling justification for attempted intrusions into philosophical or associational privacy. E.g., *Bates v. Little Rock*, 361 U.S. 516, 523 (disclosure of NAACP membership lists to city officials); *Gibson v. Florida Legislative Investigation Committee*, 372 U.S. 539, 546 (disclosure of NAACP membership list to state legislature); *DeGregory v. Attorney General of New Hampshire*, 383 U.S. 825, 829 (witness' refusal to state whether he had been a member of the Communist Party three years earlier); *Baird v. State Bar of Arizona*, 401 U.S. 1, 6–7 (refusal of bar applicant to state whether she had been a member of the Communist Party); *In re Stolar*, 401 U.S. 23 (refusal of bar applicant to state whether he was "loyal" to the Government); see also *Street v. New York*, 394 U.S. 576 (expression of disgust for flag). Yet, while the rhetoric of these opinions did not expressly embrace an absolute privilege for the privacy of opinions and philosophy, the trend of those results was not inconsistent with and in their totality appeared to be approaching such a doctrine. Moreover, in another group of opinions invalidating for overbreadth

must be "compelling" and not merely "rational" as is the case where other activities are concerned.[36] But the "compelling" interest in regulation neither includes paring down or diluting the right, nor embraces penalizing one solely for his intellectual viewpoint; it concerns the State's interest, for example, in regulating the time and place or perhaps manner of exercising First Amendment rights. Thus, one has an undoubted right to read and proclaim the First Amendment in the classroom or in a park. But he would not have the right to blare it forth from a sound truck rolling through the village or city at 2 a.m. The distinction drawn in *Cantwell v. Connecticut*, 310 U.S. 296, should still stand: "[T]he Amendment embraces two concepts,—freedom to believe and freedom to act. The first is absolute but, in the nature of things, the second cannot be."

Under these precedents there is no doubt that Caldwell could not be brought before the grand jury for the sole purpose of exposing his political beliefs. Yet today the Court effectively permits that result under the guise of allowing an attempt to elicit from him "factual information." To be sure, the inquiry will be couched only in terms of extracting Caldwell's recollection of what was said to him during the interviews, but the fact remains that his questions to the Panthers and therefore the respective answers were guided by Caldwell's own preconceptions and views about the Black Panthers. His entire experience was

---

intrusions into the realm of belief and association, there was no specification of whether a danger test, a balancing process, an absolute doctrine, or a compelling justification inquiry had been used to detect invalid applications comprehended by the challenged measures. *E.g., Wieman v. Updegraff*, 344 U.S. 183 (loyalty test which condemned mere unknowing membership in a suspect group); *Shelton v. Tucker*, 364 U.S. 479 (requirement that public teachers disclose all affiliations); *Louisiana ex rel. Gremillion v. NAACP*, 366 U.S. 293, 296 (disclosure of NAACP membership lists); *Whitehill v. Elkins*, 389 U.S. 54, 59 (nonactive membership in a suspect group a predicate for refusing employment as a public teacher); *United States v. Robel*, 389 U.S. 258 (mere membership in Communist Party a sole ground for exclusion from employment in defense facility). Regrettably, the vitality of the overdue trend toward a complete privilege in this area has been drawn into question by quite recent decisions of the Court, *Law Students Research Council v. Wadmond*, 401 U.S. 154, holding that bar applicants may be turned away for refusing to disclose their opinions on the soundness of the Constitution; *Cole v. Richardson*, 405 U.S. 676, sustaining an oath required of public employees that they will "oppose" a violent overthrow; and, of course, by today's decision.

[36] Where no more than economic interests were affected this Court has upheld legislation only upon a showing that it was "rationally connected" to some permissible state objective. *E.g., United States v. Carolene Products Co.*, 304 U.S. 144, 152; *Goesaert v. Cleary*, 335 U.S. 464; *Williamson v. Lee Optical Co.*, 348 U.S. 483; *McGowan v. Maryland*, 366 U.S. 420; *McDonald v. Board of Election Comm'rs*, 394 U.S. 802; *United States v. Maryland Savings-Share Ins. Corp.*, 400 U.S. 4; *Richardson v. Belcher*, 404 U.S. 78; *Schilb v. Kuebel*, 404 U.S. 357.

shaped by his intellectual viewpoint. Unlike the random bystander, those who affirmatively set out to test a hypothesis, as here, have no tidy means of segregating subjective opinion from objective facts.

Sooner or later, any test which provides less than blanket protection to beliefs and associations will be twisted and relaxed so as to provide virtually no protection at all. As Justice Holmes noted in *Abrams* v. *United States*, 250 U.S. 616, such was the fate of the "clear and present danger" test which he had coined in *Schenck* v. *United States*, 249 U.S. 47. Eventually, that formula was so watered down that the danger had to be neither clear nor present but merely "not improbable." *Dennis* v. *United States*, 341 U.S. 494. See my concurring opinion in *Brandenburg* v. *Ohio* [p. 205, *infra*]. A compelling-interest test may prove as pliable as did the clear-and-present-danger test. Perceptions of the worth of state objectives will change with the composition of the Court and with the intensity of the politics of the times. For example, in *Uphaus* v. *Wyman*, 360 U.S. 72, sustaining an attempt to compel a witness to divulge the names of participants in a summer political camp, JUSTICE BRENNAN dissented on the ground that "it is patent that there is really no subordinating interest . . . demonstrated on the part of the State." The majority, however, found that "the governmental interest in self-preservation is sufficiently compelling to subordinate the interest in associational privacy. . . ." That is to enter the world of "make believe," for New Hampshire, the State involved in *Uphaus*, was never in fear of being overthrown.

II

Today's decision will impede the wide-open and robust dissemination of ideas and counterthought which a free press both fosters and protects and which is essential to the success of intelligent self-government. Forcing a reporter before a grand jury will have two retarding effects upon the ear and the pen of the press. Fear of exposure will cause dissidents to communicate less openly to trusted reporters. And, fear of accountability will cause editors and critics to write with more restrained pens.

I see no way of making mandatory the disclosure of a reporter's confidential source of the information on which he bases his news story.

The press has a preferred position in our constitutional scheme, not to enable it to make money, not to set newsmen apart as a favored class, but to bring fulfillment to the public's right to know. The right to know is crucial to the governing powers of the people, to paraphrase Alexander Meiklejohn. Knowledge is essential to informed decisions.

As Mr. Justice Black said in *New York Times Co.* v. *United States*,

403 U.S. 713 (concurring opinion), "The press was to serve the governed, not the governors. . . . The press was protected so that it could bare the secrets of government and inform the people."

Government has an interest in law and order; and history shows that the trend of rulers—the bureaucracy and the police—is to suppress the radical and his ideas and to arrest him rather than the hostile audience. See *Feiner* v. *New York* [note 14, *supra*]. Yet, as held in *Terminiello* v. *Chicago* [p. 179, *supra*], one "function of free speech under our system of government is to invite dispute." We went on to say, "It may indeed best serve its high purpose when it induces a condition of unrest, creates dissatisfaction with conditions as they are, or even stirs people to anger. Speech is often provocative and challenging. It may strike at prejudices and preconceptions and have profound unsettling effects as it presses for acceptance of an idea."

The people who govern are often far removed from the cabals that threaten the regime; the people are often remote from the sources of truth even though they live in the city where the forces that would undermine society operate. The function of the press is to explore and investigate events, inform the people what is going on, and to expose the harmful as well as the good influences at work. There is no higher function performed under our constitutional regime. Its performance means that the press is often engaged in projects that bring anxiety or even fear to the bureaucracies, departments, or officials of government. The whole weight of government is therefore often brought to bear against a paper or a reporter.

A reporter is no better than his source of information. Unless he has a privilege to withhold the identity of his source, he will be the victim of governmental intrigue or aggression. If he can be summoned to testify in secret before a grand jury, his sources will dry up and the attempted exposure, the effort to enlighten the public, will be ended. If what the Court sanctions today becomes settled law, then the reporter's main function in American society will be to pass on to the public the press releases which the various departments of government issue.

It is no answer to reply that the risk that a newsman will divulge one's secrets to the grand jury is no greater than the threat that he will in any event inform to the police. Even the most trustworthy reporter may not be able to withstand relentless badgering before a grand jury.

The record in this case is replete with weighty affidavits from responsible newsmen, telling how important is the sanctity of their sources of information. When we deny newsmen that protection, we deprive the people of the information needed to run the affairs of the Nation in an intelligent way.

Madison said:

> "A popular Government, without popular information, or the means of acquiring it, is but a Prologue to a Farce or a Tragedy; or, perhaps both. Knowledge will forever govern ignorance: And a people who mean to be their own Governors, must arm themselves with the power which knowledge gives." (To W. T. Barry, Aug. 4, 1822.) 9 Writings of James Madison 103 (G. Hunt ed. 1910).

Today's decision is more than a clog upon news gathering. It is a signal to publishers and editors that they should exercise caution in how they use whatever information they can obtain. Without immunity they may be summoned to account for their criticism. Entrenched officers have been quick to crash their powers down upon unfriendly commentators. *E.g., Gravel v. United States* [p. 5, *supra*].

The intrusion of government into this domain is symptomatic of the disease of this society. As the years pass the power of government becomes more and more pervasive. It is a power to suffocate both people and causes. Those in power, whatever their politics, want only to perpetuate it. Now that the fences of the law and the tradition that has protected the press are broken down, the people are the victims. The First Amendment, as I read it, was designed precisely to prevent that tragedy.

A great number of First Amendment issues have arisen out of federal and state efforts to purge the government and, in some instances, the body politic, of persons variously described as "disloyal," "security risks" and "subversives." These efforts to some extent seek to protect against "seditious" speech and to some extent are intended to be prophylactic—to go beyond laws defining such hostile acts as treason, sabotage, and espionage and to identify, isolate, and, in some instances, incarcerate those thought likely to commit hostile acts in the future. In the enforcement of laws directed at hostile acts, Douglas consistently voted to sustain convictions in the several treason prosecutions which reached the Court after World War II.[37] In the only other case during his tenure involving guilt or innocence of an act hostile to the government, he voted to affirm an espionage conviction.[38] But in the cases in this area involving governmental action against belief, expression, and association, he frequently found obstacles in the First Amendment, as well as in certain procedural guarantees to be mentioned later.

---

[37] *Cramer v. United States,* 325 U.S. 1 (1945); *Haupt v. United States,* 330 U.S. 631 (1947); *Kawakita v. United States,* 343 U.S. 717 (1952).
[38] *Gorin v. United States,* 312 U.S. 19 (1941).

DENNIS v. UNITED STATES
341 U.S. 494 (1951)

One method employed by government to protect against subversion is the sedition law, which forbids advocacy thought to be dangerous. It was in cases involving such laws, in prosecutions during and after World War I, that Justices Holmes and Brandeis formulated the "clear and present danger" test in an effort to give the First Amendment more effect than the Court was then disposed to give it [see note 33, supra].

Defendants in this case, national officers of the Communist Party of the United States, were convicted under the 1940 Smith Act of conspiring to advocate and to organize a group to advocate forcible overthrow of the government. The Court affirmed the convictions, holding that the "clear and present danger" test was satisfied because (1) the requisite danger was not actual forcible overthrow of the government but an attempt to do so, "even though doomed from the outset because of inadequate numbers or power of the revolutionists," and (2) the danger was clear and present enough if a group "aiming at . . . overthrow is attempting to indoctrinate its members and to commit them to a course whereby they will strike when the leaders feel the circumstances permit."

MR. JUSTICE DOUGLAS, dissenting.

If this were a case where those who claimed protection under the First Amendment were teaching the techniques of sabotage, the assassination of the President, the filching of documents from public files, the planting of bombs, the art of street warfare, and the like, I would have no doubts. The freedom to speak is not absolute; the teaching of methods of terror and other seditious conduct should be beyond the pale along with obscenity and immorality. This case was argued as if those were the facts. The argument imported much seditious conduct into the record. That is easy and it has popular appeal, for the activities of Communists in plotting and scheming against the free world are common knowledge. But the fact is that no such evidence was introduced at the trial. There is a statute which makes a seditious conspiracy unlawful. Petitioners, however, were not charged with a "conspiracy to overthrow" the Government. They were charged with a conspiracy to form a party and groups and assemblies of people who teach and advocate the overthrow of our Government by force or violence and with a conspiracy to advocate and teach its overthrow by force and violence. It may well be that indoctrination in the techniques of terror to destroy the Government would be indictable under either statute. But the teaching which is condemned here is of a different character.

So far as the present record is concerned, what petitioners did was to organize people to teach and themselves teach the Marxist-Leninist doctrine contained chiefly in four books: Stalin, Foundations of Leninism (1924); Marx and Engels, Manifesto of the Communist Party (1848); Lenin, The State and Revolution (1917); History of the Communist Party of the Soviet Union (B.) (1939).

Those books are to Soviet Communism what Mein Kampf was to Nazism. If they are understood, the ugliness of Communism is revealed, its deceit and cunning are exposed, the nature of its activities becomes apparent, and the chances of its success less likely. That is not, of course, the reason why petitioners chose these books for their classrooms. They are fervent Communists to whom these volumes are gospel. They preached the creed with the hope that some day it would be acted upon.

The opinion of the Court does not outlaw these texts nor condemn them to the fire, as the Communists do literature offensive to their creed. But if the books themselves are not outlawed, if they can lawfully remain on library shelves, by what reasoning does their use in a classroom become a crime? It would not be a crime under the Act to introduce these books to a class, though that would be teaching what the creed of violent overthrow of the Government is. The Act, as construed, requires the element of intent—that those who teach the creed believe in it. The crime then depends not on what is taught but on who the teacher is. That is to make freedom of speech turn not on *what is said*, but on the *intent* with which it is said. Once we start down that road we enter territory dangerous to the liberties of every citizen.

There was a time in England when the concept of constructive treason flourished. Men were punished not for raising a hand against the king but for thinking murderous thoughts about him. The Framers of the Constitution were alive to that abuse and took steps to see that the practice would not flourish here. Treason was defined to require overt acts—the evolution of a plot against the country into an actual project.[39] The present case is not one of treason. But the analogy is close when the illegality is made to turn on intent, not on the nature of the act. We then start probing men's minds for motive and purpose; they become entangled in the law not for what they did but *for what they thought*; they get convicted not for what they said but for the purpose with which they said it.

---

[39] [U.S. Const., Art. III, §3: "Treason against the United States, shall consist only in levying War against them, or in adhering to their Enemies, giving them Aid and Comfort. No Person shall be convicted of Treason unless on the Testimony of two Witnesses to the same overt Act, or on Confession in open Court."]

Intent, of course, often makes the difference in the law. An act otherwise excusable or carrying minor penalties may grow to an abhorrent thing if the evil intent is present. We deal here, however, not with ordinary acts but with speech, to which the Constitution has given a special sanction.

Free speech has occupied an exalted position because of the high service it has given our society. Its protection is essential to the very existence of a democracy. The airing of ideas releases pressures which otherwise might become destructive. When ideas compete in the market for acceptance, full and free discussion exposes the false and they gain few adherents. Full and free discussion even of ideas we hate encourages the testing of our own prejudices and preconceptions. Full and free discussion keeps a society from becoming stagnant and unprepared for the stresses and strains that work to tear all civilizations apart.

Full and free discussion has indeed been the first article of our faith. We have founded our political system on it. It has been the safeguard of every religious, political, philosophical, economic, and racial group amongst us. We have counted on it to keep us from embracing what is cheap and false; we have trusted the common sense of our people to choose the doctrine true to our genius and to reject the rest. This has been the one single outstanding tenet that has made our institutions the symbol of freedom and equality. We have deemed it more costly to liberty to suppress a despised minority than to let them vent their spleen. We have above all else feared the political censor. We have wanted a land where our people can be exposed to all the diverse creeds and cultures of the world.

There comes a time when even speech loses its constitutional immunity. Speech innocuous one year may at another time fan such destructive flames that it must be halted in the interests of the safety of the Republic. That is the meaning of the clear and present danger test. When conditions are so critical that there will be no time to avoid the evil that the speech threatens, it is time to call a halt. Otherwise, free speech which is the strength of the Nation will be the cause of its destruction.

Yet free speech is the rule, not the exception. The restraint to be constitutional must be based on more than fear, on more than passionate opposition against the speech, on more than a revolted dislike for its contents. There must be some immediate injury to society that is likely if speech is allowed. The classic statement of these conditions was made by Mr. Justice Brandeis in his concurring opinion in *Whitney* v. *California*, 274 U.S. 357,

"Fear of serious injury cannot alone justify suppression of free speech and assembly. Men feared witches and burnt women. It is the function of speech to free men from the bondage of irrational fears. To justify suppression of free speech there must be reasonable ground to fear that serious evil will result if free speech is practiced. There must be reasonable ground to believe that the danger apprehended is imminent. There must be reasonable ground to believe that the evil to be prevented is a serious one. Every denunciation of existing law tends in some measure to increase the probability that there will be violation of it. Advocacy of law-breaking heightens it still further. But even advocacy of violation, however reprehensible morally, is not a justification for denying free speech where the advocacy falls short of incitement and there is nothing to indicate that the advocacy would be immediately acted on.

'Those who won our independence by revolution were not cowards. They did not fear political change. They did not exalt order at the cost of liberty. To courageous, self-reliant men, with confidence in the power of free and fearless reasoning applied through the processes of popular government, no danger flowing from speech can be deemed clear and present, unless the incidence of the evil apprehended is so imminent that it may befall before there is opportunity for full discussion. *If there be time to expose through discussion the falsehood and fallacies, to avert the evil by the processes of education, the remedy to be applied is more speech, not enforced silence.*" (Italics added.)

This record contains no evidence whatsoever showing that the acts charged, *viz.*, the teaching of the Soviet theory of revolution with the hope that it will be realized, have created any clear and present danger to the Nation. The Court, however, rules to the contrary. It says, "The formation by petitioners of such a highly organized conspiracy, with rigidly disciplined members subject to call when the leaders, these petitioners, felt that the time had come for action, coupled with the inflammable nature of world conditions, similar uprisings in other countries, and the touch-and-go nature of our relations with countries with whom petitioners were in the very least ideologically attuned, convince us that their convictions were justified on this score."

That ruling is in my view not responsive to the issue in the case. We might as well say that the speech of petitioners is outlawed because Soviet Russia and her Red Army are a threat to world peace.

The nature of Communism as a force on the world scene would, of course, be relevant to the issue of clear and present danger of petitioners' advocacy within the United States. But the primary consideration is the strength and tactical position of petitioners and their converts in this country. On that there is no evidence in the record. If we are to take judicial notice of the threat of Communists within the nation, it should not be difficult to conclude that *as a political party* they are of little consequence. Communists in this country have never made a respectable or serious showing in any election. I would doubt that there is a village, let alone a city or county or state, which the Communists could carry. Communism in the world scene is no bogeyman; but Communism as a political faction or party in this country plainly is. Communism has been so thoroughly exposed in this country that it has been crippled as a political force. Free speech has destroyed it as an effective political party. It is inconceivable that those who went up and down this country preaching the doctrine of revolution which petitioners espouse would have any success. In days of trouble and confusion, when bread lines were long, when the unemployed walked the streets, when people were starving, the advocates of a short-cut by revolution might have a chance to gain adherents. But today there are no such conditions. The country is not in despair; the people know Soviet Communism; the doctrine of Soviet revolution is exposed in all of its ugliness and the American people want none of it.

How it can be said that there is a clear and present danger that this advocacy will succeed is, therefore, a mystery. Some nations less resilient than the United States, where illiteracy is high and where democratic traditions are only budding, might have to take drastic steps and jail these men for merely speaking their creed. But in America they are miserable merchants of unwanted ideas; their wares remain unsold. The fact that their ideas are abhorrent does not make them powerful.

The political impotence of the Communists in this country does not, of course, dispose of the problem. Their numbers; their positions in industry and government; the extent to which they have in fact infiltrated the police, the armed services, transportation, stevedoring, power plants, munitions works, and other critical places—these facts all bear on the likelihood that their advocacy of the Soviet theory of revolution will endanger the Republic. But the record is silent on these facts. If we are to proceed on the basis of judicial notice, it is impossible for me to say that the Communists in this country are so potent or so strategically deployed that they must be suppressed for their speech. I could not so hold unless I were willing to conclude that the activities in recent years of committees of Congress, of the Attorney General, of labor unions, of state legislatures, and of Loyalty Boards were so futile as to leave the country on the edge of grave peril. To believe that petitioners and their following are placed in such critical positions as to endanger the Nation is to believe the incredible. It is safe to say that the followers of the creed of Soviet Communism are known to the F. B. I.; that in case of war with Russia they will be picked up overnight as were all prospective saboteurs at the commencement of World War II; that the invisible army of petitioners is the best known, the most beset, and the least thriving of any fifth column in history. Only those held by fear and panic could think otherwise.

This is my view if we are to act on the basis of judicial notice. But the mere statement of the opposing views indicates how important it is that we know the facts before we act. Neither prejudice nor hate nor senseless fear should be the basis of this solemn act. Free speech—the glory of our system of government—should not be sacrificed on anything less than plain and objective proof of danger that the evil advocated is imminent. On this record no one can say that petitioners and their converts are in such a strategic position as to have even the slightest chance of achieving their aims.

The First Amendment provides that "Congress shall make no law . . . abridging the freedom of speech." The Constitution provides no exception. This does not mean, however, that the Nation need hold its hand until it is in such weakened condition that there is no time to protect itself from incitement to revolution. Seditious conduct can always be punished. But the command of the First Amendment is so clear that we should not allow Congress to call a halt to free speech except in the extreme case of peril from the speech itself. The First Amendment makes confidence in the common sense of our people and in their maturity of judgment the great postulate of our democracy. Its philosophy is that violence is rarely, if ever, stopped by denying civil liberties to those advocating resort to force. The First Amendment reflects the philosophy of Jefferson "that it is time enough for the rightful purposes of civil government, for its officers to interfere when principles break out into overt acts against peace and good order."[40] The political censor has no place in our public debates. Unless and until extreme and necessitous circumstances are shown, our aim should be to keep speech unfettered and to allow the processes of law to be invoked only when the provocateurs among us move from speech to action.

Vishinsky wrote in 1938 in The Law of the Soviet State, "In our

[40] 12 Hening's Stat. (Virginia 1823), c. 34, p. 84. Whipple, Our Ancient Liberties (1927), p. 95, states: "This idea that the limit on freedom of speech or press should be set only by an actual overt act was not new. It had been asserted by a long line of distinguished thinkers including John Locke, Montesquieu in his The Spirit of the Laws ('Words do not constitute an overt act'), the Rev. Phillip Furneaux, James Madison, and Thomas Jefferson."

state, naturally, there is and can be no place for freedom of speech, press, and so on for the foes of socialism."

Our concern should be that we accept no such standard for the United States. Our faith should be that our people will never give support to these advocates of revolution, so long as we remain loyal to the purposes for which our Nation was founded.

BRANDENBURG v. OHIO
395 U.S. 444 (1969)

In this case the Court reversed the convictions of an Ohio leader of the Ku Klux Klan under a state statute forbidding the advocacy of force because the statute did not distinguish between "mere advocacy" and "incitement to imminent lawless action."

MR. JUSTICE DOUGLAS, concurring.

While I join the opinion of the Court, I desire to enter a *caveat.*

The "clear and present danger" test was adumbrated by Mr. Justice Holmes in a case arising during World War I—a war "declared" by the Congress, not by the Chief Executive. The case was *Schenck* v. *United States,* 249 U.S. 47, where the defendant was charged with attempts to cause insubordination in the military and obstruction of enlistment. The pamphlets that were distributed urged resistance to the draft, denounced conscription, and impugned the motives of those backing the war effort. The First Amendment was tendered as a defense. Mr. Justice Holmes in rejecting that defense said:

> "The question in every case is whether the words used are used in such circumstances and are of such a nature as to create a clear and present danger that they will bring about the substantive evils that Congress has a right to prevent. It is a question of proximity and degree."

Frohwerk v. *United States,* 249 U.S. 204, also authored by Mr. Justice Holmes, involved prosecution and punishment for publication of articles very critical of the war effort in World War I. *Schenck* was referred to as a conviction for obstructing security "by words of persuasion." And the conviction in *Frohwerk* was sustained because "the circulation of the paper was in quarters where a little breath would be enough to kindle a flame."

Debs v. *United States,* 249 U.S. 211, was the third of the trilogy of the 1918 Term. Debs was convicted of speaking in opposition to the war where his "opposition was so expressed that its natural and intended effect would be to obstruct recruiting."

> "If that was intended and if, in all the circumstances, that would be its probable effect, it would not be protected by reason of its being part of a general program and expressions of a general and conscientious belief."

In the 1919 Term, the Court applied the *Schenck* doctrine to affirm the convictions of other dissidents in World War I. *Abrams* v. *United States*, 250 U.S. 616, was one instance. Mr. Justice Holmes, with whom Mr. Justice Brandeis concurred, dissented. While adhering to *Schenck*, he did not think that on the facts a case for overriding the First Amendment had been made out:

> "It is only the present danger of immediate evil or an intent to bring it about that warrants Congress in setting a limit to the expression of opinion where private rights are not concerned. Congress certainly cannot forbid all effort to change the mind of the country."

Another instance was *Schaefer* v. *United States*, 251 U.S. 466, in which Mr. Justice Brandeis, joined by Mr. Justice Holmes, dissented. A third was *Pierce* v. *United States*, 252 U.S. 239, in which again Mr. Justice Brandeis, joined by Mr. Justice Holmes, dissented.

Those, then, were the World War I cases that put the gloss of "clear and present danger" on the First Amendment. Whether the war power —the greatest leveler of them all—is adequate to sustain that doctrine is debatable. The dissents in *Abrams*, *Schaefer*, and *Pierce* show how easily "clear and present danger" is manipulated to crush what Brandeis called "[t]he fundamental right of free men to strive for better conditions through new legislation and new institutions" by argument and discourse even in time of war. Though I doubt if the "clear and present danger" test is congenial to the First Amendment in time of a declared war, I am certain it is not reconcilable with the First Amendment in days of peace.

Mr. Justice Holmes, though never formally abandoning the "clear and present danger" test, moved closer to the First Amendment ideal when he said in dissent in *Gitlow* v. *New York*, 268 U.S. 652, 673:

> "Every idea is an incitement. It offers itself for belief and if believed it is acted on unless some other belief outweighs it or some failure of energy stifles the movement at its birth. The only difference between the expression of an opinion and an incitement in the narrower sense is the speaker's enthusiasm for the result. Eloquence

may set fire to reason. But whatever may be thought of the re-
dundant discourse before us it had no chance of starting a present
conflagration. If in the long run the beliefs expressed in proletarian
dictatorship are destined to be accepted by the dominant forces of
the community, the only meaning of free speech is that they should
be given their chance and have their way."

We have never been faithful to the philosophy of that dissent.

The Court in *Herndon* v. *Lowry*, 301 U.S. 242, overturned a conviction for exercising First Amendment rights to incite insurrection because of lack of evidence of incitement. In *Bridges* v. *California*, 314
U.S. 252, we approved the "clear and present danger" test in an
elaborate dictum that tightened it and confined it to a narrow
category. But in *Dennis* v. *United States* [p. 199, *supra*] we opened wide
the door, distorting the "clear and present danger" test beyond recognition.

In that case the prosecution dubbed an agreement to teach the
Marxist creed a "conspiracy." The case was submitted to a jury on a
charge that the jury could not convict unless it found that the defendants "intended to overthrow the Government 'as speedily as circumstances would permit.'" The Court sustained convictions under that
charge, construing it to mean a determination of " 'whether the gravity
of the "evil," discounted by its improbability, justifies such invasion of
free speech as is necessary to avoid the danger.' "

When one reads the opinions closely and sees when and how the
"clear and present danger" test has been applied, great misgivings are
aroused. First, the threats were often loud but always puny and made
serious only by judges so wedded to the *status quo* that critical analysis
made them nervous. Second, the test was so twisted and perverted in
Dennis as to make the trial of those teachers of Marxism an all-out political trial which was part and parcel of the cold war that has eroded
substantial parts of the First Amendment.

---

*Another method frequently employed by the government to protect
against apprehended danger is the exaction of a loyalty oath from
government officials and employees and, for a time under a federal law
now repealed, from labor union officials. Douglas has voted with the
Court to sustain an oath requiring candidates for political office to
swear that they are not engaged in an attempt to overthrow the government by force and are not knowingly members of an organization
engaged in such an attempt.[41] He has also voted with the Court to*

[41] *Gerende* v. *Board of Supervisors*, 341 U.S. 56 (1951).

invalidate, as overly broad under the First Amendment, oaths which go further and require state employees to swear they do not belong to designated organizations without regard to their knowledge of the organizations' purposes,[42] *or require all teachers to list annually every organization to which they have belonged or regularly contributed during the past five years,*[43] *or require all state employees to swear that they have never lent their "aid, support, advice, counsel or influence to the Communist Party,"*[44] *or require all teachers to swear that they are not "subversive persons" and "will by precept and example promote respect for the flag and the institutions of the United States . . . and the [s]tate . . . , reverence for law and order and undivided allegiance to the government of the United States."*[45]

ELFBRANDT v. RUSSELL
384 U.S. 11 (1966)

Arizona required a rather conventional oath from state employees by which they swore to support the Constitution of the United States and the Constitution and laws of Arizona. But the state legislature also enacted a statute providing that anyone who took the oath and who "knowingly and wilfully becomes or remains a member of the Communist Party of the United States or its successors or any of its subordinate organizations" or any other organization having for "one of its purposes" the overthrow of the government of Arizona or any of its subdivisions, if the employee had knowledge of that purpose, would be guilty of perjury and should be discharged. The validity of that provision was challenged by Barbara Elfbrandt, a teacher and a Quaker.

MR. JUSTICE DOUGLAS delivered the opinion of the Court.

We recognized in *Scales* v. *United States*, 367 U.S. 203, that "quasi-political parties or other groups . . . may embrace both legal and illegal aims." We noted that a "blanket prohibition of association with a group having both legal and illegal aims" would pose "a real danger that legitimate political expression or association would be impaired." The statute with which we dealt in *Scales*, the so-called "membership clause" of the Smith Act, was found not to suffer from this constitutional infirmity because, as the Court construed it, the statute reached

---

[42] *Wieman* v. *Updegraff*, 344 U.S. 183 (1952).
[43] *Shelton* v. *Tucker*, 364 U.S. 479 (1960).
[44] *Cramp* v. *Board of Public Instruction*, 368 U.S. 278 (1961).
[45] *Baggett* v. *Bullitt*, 377 U.S. 360 (1964).

only "active" membership with the "specific intent" of assisting in achieving the unlawful ends of the organization. The importance of this limiting construction from a constitutional standpoint was emphasized in *Noto* v. *United States*, 367 U.S. 290, decided the same day:

> "[I]t should also be said that this element of the membership crime [the defendant's 'personal criminal purpose to bring about the overthrow of the Government by force and violence'], like its others, must be judged *strictissimi juris*, for otherwise there is a danger that one in sympathy with the legitimate aims of such an organization, but not specifically intending to accomplish them by resort to violence, might be punished for his adherence to lawful and constitutionally protected purposes, because of other and unprotected purposes which he does not necessarily share."

Any lingering doubt that proscription of mere knowing membership, without any showing of "specific intent," would run afoul of the Constitution was set at rest by our decision in *Aptheker* v. *Secretary of State*, 378 U.S. 500. We dealt there with a statute which provided that no member of a Communist organization ordered by the Subversive Activities Control Board to register shall apply for or use a passport. We concluded that the statute would not permit a narrow reading of the sort we gave [the Smith Act] in *Scales*. The statute, as we read it, covered membership which was not accompanied by a specific intent to further the unlawful aims of the organization, and we held it unconstitutional.

The oath and accompanying statutory gloss challenged here suffer from an identical constitutional infirmity. One who subscribes to this Arizona oath and who is, or thereafter becomes, a knowing member of an organization which has as "one of its purposes" the violent overthrow of the government, is subject to immediate discharge and criminal penalties. Nothing in the oath, the statutory gloss, or the construction of the oath and statutes given by the Arizona Supreme Court, purports to exclude association by one who does not subscribe to the organization's unlawful ends. Here as in *Baggett* v. *Bullitt* [note 45, *supra*] the "hazard of being prosecuted for knowing but guiltless behavior" is a reality. People often label as "communist" ideas which they oppose; and they often make up our juries. "[P]rosecutors too are human." *Cramp* v. *Board of Public Instruction*, 368 U.S. 278. Would a teacher be safe and secure in going to a Pugwash Conference? Would it be legal to join a seminar group predominantly Communist and therefore subject to control by those who are said to believe in the overthrow of the Government by force and violence? Juries might convict though the teacher did not subscribe to the wrongful aims of the organization. And there is apparently no machinery provided for getting clearance in advance.

Those who join an organization but do not share its unlawful purposes and who do not participate in its unlawful activities surely pose no threat, either as citizens or as public employees. Laws such as this which are not restricted in scope to those who join with the "specific intent" to further illegal action impose, in effect, a conclusive presumption that the member shares the unlawful aims of the organization. See *Aptheker* v. *Secretary of State, supra.* The unconstitutionality of this Act follows *a fortiori* from *Speiser* v. *Randall,* 357 U.S. 513, where we held that a State may not even place on an applicant for a tax exemption the burden of proving that he has not engaged in criminal advocacy.

This Act threatens the cherished freedom of association protected by the First Amendment, made applicable to the States through the Fourteenth Amendment. *Baggett* v. *Bullitt, supra; Cramp* v. *Board of Public Instruction, supra.* And, as a committee of the Arizona Legislature which urged adoption of this law itself recognized, public employees of character and integrity may well forgo their calling rather than risk prosecution for perjury or compromise their commitment to intellectual and political freedom:

> "The communist trained in fraud and perjury has no qualms in taking any oath; the loyal citizen, conscious of history's oppressions, may well wonder whether the medieval rack and torture wheel are next for the one who declines to take an involved negative oath as evidence that he is a True Believer."

A statute touching those protected rights must be "narrowly drawn to define and punish specific conduct as constituting a clear and present danger to a substantial interest of the State." *Cantwell* v. *Connecticut,* 310 U.S. 296. Legitimate legislative goals "cannot be pursued by means that broadly stifle fundamental personal liberties when the end can be more narrowly achieved." *Shelton* v. *Tucker,* 364 U.S. 479. As we said in N. A. A. C. P. v. *Button,* 371 U.S. 415:

> "The objectionable quality of . . . overbreadth does not depend upon absence of fair notice to a criminally accused or upon unchanneled delegation of legislative powers, but upon the danger of tolerating, in the area of First Amendment freedoms, the existence of a penal statute susceptible of sweeping and improper application. . . . These freedoms are delicate and vulnerable, as well as supremely precious in our society. The threat of sanctions

may deter their exercise almost as potently as the actual application of sanctions. . . ."

A law which applies to membership without the "specific intent" to further the illegal aims of the organization infringes unnecessarily on protected freedoms. It rests on the doctrine of "guilt by association" which has no place here. See *Schneiderman* v. *United States*, 320 U.S. 118. Such a law cannot stand.

In 1971 the Court held that a Florida oath for teachers was constitutional insofar as it required them to support the constitutions of the state and the United States, but that it violated procedural due process insofar as it would bar from employment, without hearing, any who would not swear also that they did not believe in forcible overthrow of the government. Douglas concurred in the decision, but on a different ground with respect to the latter feature of the oath: "[T]he Court has left the clear implication that its objection runs, not against Florida's determination to exclude those who 'believe in the overthrow,' but only against the State's decision to regard unwillingness to take the oath as conclusive, irrebuttable proof of the proscribed belief. . . . But in my view it simply does not matter what kind of evidence a State can muster to show that a job applicant 'believes in the overthrow.' For state action injurious to an individual cannot be justified on account of the nature of the individual's beliefs, whether he 'believe[s] in the overthrow' or has any other sort of belief. . . . I would strike down Florida's 'overthrow' oath plainly and simply on the ground that belief as such cannot be the predicate of governmental action."[46]

Another of the prophylactic programs much in vogue since World War II is the "loyalty" or "security risk" program, designed to detect and exclude or remove from the public service potential traitors, spies, and saboteurs. Typically, these programs involve probing into the beliefs, expressions, and associations of their subjects and hence raise grave questions under the First Amendment. They also involve serious questions of constitutional procedure, which will be considered later.

When questions as to the constitutionality of the federal loyalty program first reached it, the Court was evenly divided[47] and hence affirmed without opinion a decision of a lower court sustaining the program.[48] But Douglas, in a concurring opinion in a companion case

---

[46] *Connell* v. *Higginbotham*, 403 U.S. 207 (1971).

[47] Justice Tom Clark, who as Attorney General had helped set up the program, did not participate in the decision.

[48] *Bailey* v. *Richardson*, 341 U.S. 918 (1951).

involving only procedural issues, made clear that he was one of the four who would have reversed.[49]

ADLER V. BOARD OF EDUCATION
342 U.S. 485 (1952)

As authorized by the state Feinberg Law, the New York Board of Regents compiled a list of "subversive organizations" and issued regulations providing that present membership in a listed organization would constitute prima facie *evidence of disqualification for employment as a public school teacher and that past membership should be presumptive evidence of present membership. When Adler and other teachers challenged this law the Court held that there was no violation of the First Amendment. New York schoolteachers were left, the Court said, with a free choice. They could work for the school system on its terms or "retain their beliefs and associations and go elsewhere."*

MR. JUSTICE DOUGLAS, dissenting.

I have not been able to accept the recent doctrine that a citizen who enters the public service can be forced to sacrifice his civil rights.[50] I cannot for example find in our constitutional scheme the power of a state to place its employees in the category of second-class citizens by denying them freedom of thought and expression. The Constitution guarantees freedom of thought and expression to everyone in our society. All are entitled to it; and none needs it more than the teacher.

The public school is in most respects the cradle of our democracy. The increasing role of the public school is seized upon by proponents of the type of legislation represented by New York's Feinberg law as proof of the importance and need for keeping the school free of "subversive influences." But that is to misconceive the effect of this type of legislation. Indeed the impact of this kind of censorship on the public school system illustrates the high purpose of the First Amendment in freeing speech and thought from censorship.

The present law proceeds on a principle repugnant to our society—guilt by association. A teacher is disqualified because of her membership in an organization found to be "subversive." The finding as to the "subversive" character of the organization is made in a proceeding to which the teacher is not a party and in which it is not clear that she may even be heard. To be sure, she may have a hearing when charges

[49] *Joint Anti-Fascist Refugee Committee* v. *McGrath*, 341 U.S. 123 (1951).
[50] *United States Workers* v. *Mitchell* [p. 169, *supra*].

of disloyalty are leveled against her. But in that hearing the finding as to the "subversive" character of the organization apparently may not be reopened in order to allow her to show the truth of the matter. The irrebuttable charge that the organization is "subversive" therefore hangs as an ominous cloud over her own hearing. The mere fact of membership in the organization raises a prima facie case of her own guilt. She may, it is said, show her innocence. But innocence in this case turns on knowledge; and when the witch hunt is on, one who must rely on ignorance leans on a feeble reed.

The very threat of such a procedure is certain to raise havoc with academic freedom. Youthful indiscretions, mistaken causes, misguided enthusiasms—all long forgotten—become the ghosts of a harrowing present. Any organization committed to a liberal cause, any group organized to revolt against an hysterical trend, any committee launched to sponsor an unpopular program becomes suspect. These are the organizations into which Communists often infiltrate. Their presence infects the whole, even though the project was not conceived in sin. A teacher caught in that mesh is almost certain to stand condemned. Fearing condemnation, she will tend to shrink from any assôciation that stirs controversy. In that manner freedom of expression will be stifled.

But that is only part of it. Once a teacher's connection with a listed organization is shown, her views become subject to scrutiny to determine whether her membership in the organization is innocent or, if she was formerly a member, whether she has *bona fide* abandoned her membership.

The law inevitably turns the school system into a spying project. Regular loyalty reports on the teachers must be made out. The principals become detectives; the students, the parents, the community become informers. Ears are cocked for tell-tale signs of disloyalty. The prejudices of the community come into play in searching out the disloyal. This is not the usual type of supervision which checks a teacher's competency; it is a system which searches for hidden meanings in a teacher's utterances.

What was the significance of the reference of the art teacher to socialism? Why was the history teacher so openly hostile to Franco Spain? Who heard overtones of revolution in the English teacher's discussion of the Grapes of Wrath? What was behind the praise of Soviet progress in metallurgy in the chemistry class? Was it not "subversive" for the teacher to cast doubt on the wisdom of the venture in Korea?

What happens under this law is typical of what happens in a police state. Teachers are under constant surveillance; their pasts are combed for signs of disloyalty; their utterances are watched for clues to dangerous thoughts. A pall is cast over the classrooms. There can be no real academic freedom in that environment. Where suspicion fills the air and holds scholars in line for fear of their jobs, there can be no exercise of the free intellect. Supineness and dogmatism take the place of inquiry. A "party line"—as dangerous as the "party line" of the Communists—lays hold. It is the "party line" of the orthodox view, of the conventional thought, of the accepted approach. A problem can no longer be pursued with impunity to its edges. Fear stalks the classroom. The teacher is no longer a stimulant to adventurous thinking; she becomes instead a pipe line for safe and sound information. A deadening dogma takes the place of free inquiry. Instruction tends to become sterile; pursuit of knowledge is discouraged; discussion often leaves off where it should begin.

This, I think, is what happens when a censor looks over a teacher's shoulder. This system of spying and surveillance with its accompanying reports and trials cannot go hand in hand with academic freedom. It produces standardized thought, not the pursuit of truth. Yet it was the pursuit of truth which the First Amendment was designed to protect. A system which directly or inevitably has that effect is alien to our system and should be struck down. Its survival is a real threat to our way of life. We need be bold and adventuresome in our thinking to survive. A school system producing students trained as robots threatens to rob a generation of the versatility that has been perhaps our greatest distinction. The Framers knew the danger of dogmatism; they also knew the strength that comes when the mind is free, when ideas may be pursued wherever they lead. We forget these teachings of the First Amendment when we sustain this law.

Of course the school systems of the country need not become cells for Communist activities; and the classrooms need not become forums for propagandizing the Marxist creed. But the guilt of the teacher should turn on overt acts. So long as she is a law-abiding citizen, so long as her performance within the public school system meets professional standards, her private life, her political philosophy, her social creed should not be the cause of reprisals against her.

Fifteen years later the Court again considered the constitutionality of the New York program and invalidated it, both because the standards employed for disqualification of teachers were unconstitutionally vague, and because, as Douglas had written for the Court in the Elfbrandt *case [p. 208, supra], "those who join an organization but do not share its unlawful purposes and who do not participate in its unlawful ac-*

tivities surely pose no threat, either as citizens or as public employees."
Constitutional doctrine "which has emerged" since the Adler decision
was said to have "rejected its major premise."[51]

In 1931 Chief Justice Hughes wrote for the Court in Near v.
Minnesota[52] to hold that a state could not enjoin the publication of a
newspaper on the ground that it published "malicious, scandalous and
defamatory" matter about public officials, private citizens, and Jews.
The injunction, which would have subjected the owner of the paper to
contempt proceedings if he had resumed publication, was held to violate the guarantee of a free press by imposing a "previous restraint" on
publication. The fact that the state law recognized a defense for a
publisher who could convince the court that what he had published was
true and was published with good motives was held not to avoid the
constitutional problem. If such a law is valid, "it would be equally
permissible for the legislature to provide that at any time the publisher
of any newspaper could be brought before a court . . . and required
to produce proof of the truth of his publication, or of what he intended
to publish, and of his motives, or stand enjoined. If this can be done,
the legislature may provide machinery for determining in the complete
exercise of its discretion what are justifiable ends and restrain publication accordingly. And it would be but a step to a complete system
of censorship."

NEW YORK TIMES CO. v. UNITED STATES
403 U.S. 713 (1971)

On June 12–14, 1971, the New York Times published summaries and
extracts from a 47-volume "top secret" government document entitled
"History of U.S. Decision-Making Process on Vietnam Policy," covering
the period 1945 to 1967. On June 15, the United States obtained a
temporary restraining order against further publication from a federal
district court in New York but, after an in camera hearing, that court
on June 19 concluded that the government had not shown that publication of these historical documents would seriously jeopardize national security. But the stay was continued while an appeal was taken
and the federal court of appeals reversed and remanded the case to
the district court for further hearings, again continuing the stay.

Meanwhile, the Washington Post began publication of other material from these "Pentagon Papers" on June 17. The United States

---

[51] Keyishian v. Board of Regents, 385 U.S. 587 (1967).
[52] 283 U.S. 697 (1931).

sought a temporary restraining order from a federal district court in the District of Columbia which was denied. The federal court of appeals in the District reversed and remanded for a hearing, granting a stay against publication in the meantime. After an in camera *hearing the district court again denied a stay and this time the court of appeals on June 23 affirmed, agreeing that the government had not shown a sufficient risk of harm to national security to override First Amendment interests. But it granted a stay pending submission of the case to the Supreme Court.*

With further Washington Post publication stayed, the Boston Globe began publishing the material. The government obtained a stay pending hearing from a federal district court in Boston. But when newspapers in the Midwest and on the Pacific Coast began publications from the materials, the government abandoned further applications for stays and concentrated its efforts on the argument of the New York Times and Washington Post cases in the Supreme Court on June 26.

The Court had on June 25 agreed to hear the cases and had continued the stays in both cases pending decision. This action was taken over the dissents of Justices Black, Douglas, Brennan, and Marshall, who would have vacated the order of the court of appeals in New York, vacated all stays, and declined to hear arguments on the cases.

The Supreme Court decided the cases on June 30, agreeing by a 6–3 vote with both district courts and with the court of appeals for the District of Columbia that the government had not met its "heavy burden of showing justification for the imposition of such a restraint." The decision was announced in a brief per curiam *order. But each Justice filed a separate opinion and, in addition, some concurred in the opinions of others. Those in the majority expressed a variety of opinions. Justice Brennan thought all restraining orders issued in the cases had been erroneously issued on the facts shown but preserved for the future whether there might be a "narrow class of cases in which the First Amendment's ban on prior restraint may be overridden," such as news of troop movements in time of war. Justices Stewart and White agreed that the government had not met "the very heavy burden that it must meet . . . at least in the absence of express and appropriately limited congressional authorization for prior restraints in circumstances such as these." Justice Marshall thought that the executive branch had no authority to seek an injunction in these cases without express congressional authorization. Justice Black, in an opinion in which Douglas joined, took the position that the First Amendment forbade all three branches of government to restrain freedom of press in the name of "national security."*

MR. JUSTICE DOUGLAS, concurring.

While I join the opinion of the Court I believe it necessary to express my views more fully.

It should be noted at the outset that the First Amendment provides that "Congress shall make no law . . . abridging the freedom of speech, or of the press." That leaves, in my view, no room for governmental restraint on the press.[53]

There is, moreover, no statute barring the publication by the press of the material which the Times and the Post seek to use. [Section 793(e) of the federal Criminal Code] provides that "[w]hoever having unauthorized possession of, access to, or control over any document, writing . . . or information relating to the national defense which information the possessor has reason to believe could be used to the injury of the United States or to the advantage of any foreign nation, willfully communicates . . . the same to any person not entitled to receive it . . . [s]hall be fined not more than $10,000 or imprisoned not more than ten years, or both."

The Government suggests that the word "communicates" is broad enough to encompass publication.

There are eight sections in the chapter on espionage and censorship, §§792–799. In three of those eight "publish" is specifically mentioned: §794 (b) applies to "Whoever, in time of war, with intent that the same shall be communicated to the enemy, collects, records, *publishes*, or communicates . . . [the disposition of armed forces]."

Section 797 applies to whoever "reproduces, *publishes*, sells, or gives away" photographs of defense installations.

Section 798 relating to cryptography applies to whoever: "communicates, furnishes, transmits, or otherwise makes available . . . *or publishes*" the described material. (Emphasis added.)

Thus it is apparent that Congress was capable of and did distinguish between publishing and communication in the various sections of the Espionage Act.

The other evidence that §793 does not apply to the press is a rejected version of §793. That version read: "During any national emergency resulting from a war to which the United States is a party, or from threat of such a war, the President may, by proclamation,

[53] See *Beauharnais* v. *Illinois,* 343 U.S. 250, 267 (dissenting opinion of MR. JUSTICE BLACK), 284 (my dissenting opinion); *Roth* v. *United States,* 354 U.S. 476, 508 (my dissenting opinion which MR. JUSTICE BLACK joined); *Yates* v. *United States,* 354 U.S. 298, 339 (separate opinion of MR. JUSTICE BLACK which I joined); *New York Times Co.* v. *Sullivan,* 376 U.S. 254, 293 (concurring opinion of MR. JUSTICE BLACK which I joined); *Garrison* v. *Louisiana,* 379 U.S. 64, 80 (my concurring opinion which MR. JUSTICE BLACK joined).

declare the existence of such emergency and, by proclamation, prohibit the publishing or communicating of, or the attempting to publish or communicate any information relating to the national defense which, in his judgment, is of such character that it is or might be useful to the enemy." 55 Cong. Rec. 1763. During the debates in the Senate the First Amendment was specifically cited and that provision was defeated. 55 Cong. Rec. 2167.

Judge Gurfein's holding in the *Times* case that this Act does not apply to this case was therefore preeminently sound. Moreover, the Act of September 23, 1950, in amending §793 states in §1 (b) that:

> "Nothing in this Act shall be construed to authorize, require, or establish military or civilian censorship or in any way to limit or infringe upon freedom of the press or of speech as guaranteed by the Constitution of the United States and no regulation shall be promulgated hereunder having that effect." 64 Stat. 987.

Thus Congress has been faithful to the command of the First Amendment in this area.

So any power that the Government possesses must come from its "inherent power."

The power to wage war is "the power to wage war successfully." See *Hirabayshi* v. *United States*, 320 U.S. 81. But the war power stems from a declaration of war. The Constitution by Art. I, §8, gives Congress, not the President, power "[t]o declare War." Nowhere are presidential wars authorized. We need not decide therefore what leveling effect the war power of Congress might have.

These disclosures[54] may have a serious impact. But that is no basis for sanctioning a previous restraint on the press. As stated by Chief Justice Hughes in *Near* v. *Minnesota* [p. 215, *supra*]:

> "While reckless assaults upon public men, and efforts to bring obloquy upon those who are endeavoring faithfully to discharge official duties, exert a baleful influence and deserve the severest condemnation in public opinion, it cannot be said that this abuse is greater, and it is believed to be less, than that which characterized the period in which our institutions took shape. Meanwhile, the administration of government has become more complex,

---

[54] There are numerous sets of this material in existence and they apparently are not under any controlled custody. Moreover, the President has sent a set to the Congress. We start then with a case where there already is rather wide distribution of the material that is destined for publicity, not secrecy. I have gone over the material listed in the *in camera* brief of the United States. It is all history, not future events. None of it is more recent than 1968.

the opportunities for malfeasance and corruption have multiplied, crime has grown to most serious proportions, and the danger of its protection by unfaithful officials and of the impairment of the fundamental security of life and property by criminal alliances and official neglect, emphasizes the primary need of a vigilant and courageous press, especially in great cities. The fact that the liberty of the press may be abused by miscreant purveyors of scandal does not make any the less necessary the immunity of the press from previous restraint in dealing with official misconduct."

As we stated only the other day in *Organization for a Better Austin* v. *Keefe*, 402 U.S. 415, "[a]ny prior restraint on expression comes to this Court with a 'heavy presumption' against its constitutional validity."

The Government says that it has inherent powers to go into court and obtain an injunction to protect the national interest, which in this case is alleged to be national security.

Near v. *Minnesota* [*supra*] repudiated that expansive doctrine in no uncertain terms.

The dominant purpose of the First Amendment was to prohibit the widespread practice of governmental suppression of embarrassing information. It is common knowledge that the First Amendment was adopted against the widespread use of the common law of seditious libel to punish the dissemination of material that is embarrassing to the powers-that-be. See T. Emerson, The System of Freedom of Expression, c. V (1970); Z. Chafee, Free Speech in the United States, c. XIII (1941). The present cases will, I think, go down in history as the most dramatic illustration of that principle. A debate of large proportions goes on in the Nation over our posture in Vietnam. That debate antedated the disclosure of the contents of the present documents. The latter are highly relevant to the debate in progress.

Secrecy in government is fundamentally anti-democratic, perpetuating bureaucratic errors. Open debate and discussion of public issues are vital to our national health. On public questions there should be "uninhibited, robust, and wide-open" debate. *New York Times Co.* v. *Sullivan*, 376 U.S. 254.

I would affirm the judgment of the Court of Appeals in the *Post* case, vacate the stay of the Court of Appeals in the *Times* case and direct that it affirm the District Court.

The stays in these cases that have been in effect for more than a week constitute a flouting of the principles of the First Amendment as interpreted in *Near* v. *Minnesota*.

6

OBSCENITY

There is another large area of First Amendment problems which may seem to have little to do with political freedom: the problems of obscenity.

ROTH V. UNITED STATES
354 U.S. 476 (1957)

In this case the Court affirmed the conviction of Roth for sending obscene material through the mails in violation of a federal statute and the conviction of Alberts for keeping obscene material for sale in violation of a California statute. Defining obscenity as that "which deals with sex in a manner appealing to prurient interest" and which is "utterly without redeeming social importance," the Court announced that it was "not within the area of constitutionally protected speech or press."

MR. JUSTICE DOUGLAS, dissenting.

When we sustain these convictions, we make the legality of a publication turn on the purity of thought which a book or tract instills in the mind of the reader. I do not think we can approve that standard and be faithful to the command of the First Amendment, which by its terms is a restraint on Congress and which by the Fourteenth is a restraint on the States.

In the *Roth* case the trial judge charged the jury that the statutory words "obscene, lewd and lascivious" describe "that form of immorality which has relation to sexual impurity and has a tendency to excite lustful thoughts." He stated that the term "filthy" in the statute pertains "to that sort of treatment of sexual matters in such a vulgar and indecent way, so that it tends to arouse a feeling of disgust and revulsion." He went on to say that the material "must be calculated to corrupt and debauch the minds and morals" of "the average person in the community," not those of any particular class. "You judge the circulars, pictures and publications which have been put in evidence by present-day standards of the community. You may ask yourselves does it offend the common conscience of the community by present-day standards."

The trial judge who, sitting without a jury, heard the *Alberts* case and the appellate court that sustained the judgment of conviction, took California's definition of "obscenity" from *People* v. *Wepplo*, 78 Cal. App. 2d Supp. 959. That case held that a book is obscene "if it has a substantial tendency to deprave or corrupt its readers by inciting lascivious thoughts or arousing lustful desire."

By these standards punishment is inflicted for thoughts provoked, not for overt acts nor antisocial conduct. This test cannot be squared with our decisions under the First Amendment. Even the ill-starred *Dennis* case [p. 199, *supra*] conceded that speech to be punishable must have some relation to action which could be penalized by government. This issue cannot be avoided by saying that obscenity is not protected by the First Amendment. The question remains, what is thé constitutional test of obscenity?

The tests by which these convictions were obtained require only the arousing of sexual thoughts. Yet the arousing of sexual thoughts and desires happens every day in normal life in dozens of ways. Nearly 30 years ago a questionnaire sent to college and normal school women graduates asked what things were most stimulating sexually. Of 409 replies, 9 said "music"; 18 said "pictures"; 29 said "dancing"; 40 said "drama"; 95 said "books"; and 218 said "man." Alpert, Judicial Censorship of Obscene Literature, 52 Harv. L. Rev. 40, 73.

The test of obscenity the Court endorses today gives the censor free range over a vast domain. To allow the State to step in and punish mere speech or publication that the judge or the jury thinks has an *undesirable* impact on the thoughts but that is not shown to be a part of unlawful action is drastically to curtail the First Amendment. As recently stated by two of our outstanding authorities on obscenity, "The danger of influencing a change in the current moral standards of the community, or of shocking or offending readers, or of stimulating sex thoughts or desires apart from objective conduct, can never justify the losses to society that result from interference with literary freedom." Lockhart & McClure, Literature, The Law of Obscenity, and the Constitution, 38 Minn. L. Rev. 295.

If we were certain that impurity of sexual thoughts impelled to action, we would be on less dangerous ground in punishing the distributors of this sex literature. But it is by no means clear that obscene literature, as so defined, is a significant factor in influencing substantial deviations from the community standards.

"There are a number of reasons for real and substantial doubts as to the soundness of that hypothesis. (1) Scientific studies of juvenile delinquency demonstrate that those who get into trouble, and are the greatest concern of the advocates of censorship, are far less inclined to read than those who do not become delinquent. The delinquents are generally the adventurous type, who have little use for reading and other non-active entertainment. Thus, even assuming that reading sometimes has an adverse effect upon moral conduct, the effect is not likely to be substantial, for those who are susceptible seldom read. (2) Sheldon and Eleanor Glueck, who are among the country's leading authorities on the treatment and causes of juvenile delinquency, have recently published the results of a ten year study of its causes. They exhaustively studied approximately 90 factors and influences that might lead to or explain juvenile delinquency, but the Gluecks gave no consideration to the type of reading material, if any, read by the delinquents. This is, of course, consistent with their finding that delinquents read very little. When those who know so much about the problem of delinquency among youth—the very group about whom the advocates of censorship are most concerned—conclude that what delinquents read has so little effect upon their conduct that it is not worth investigating in an exhaustive study of causes, there is good reason for serious doubt concerning the basic hypothesis on which obscenity censorship is defended. (3) The many other influences in society that stimulate sexual desire are so much more frequent in their influence, and so much more potent in their effect, that the influence of reading is likely, at most, to be relatively insignificant in the composite of forces that lead an individual into conduct deviating from the community sex standards. The Kinsey studies show the minor degree to which literature serves as a potent sexual stimulant. And the studies demonstrating that sex knowledge seldom results from reading indicates [sic] the relative unimportance of literature in sex thoughts as compared with other factors in society." Lockhart & McClure, *op. cit. supra.*

The absence of dependable information on the effect of obscene literature on human conduct should make us wary. It should put us on the side of protecting society's interest in literature, except and unless it can be said that the particular publication has an impact on action that the government can control.

As noted, the trial judge in the *Roth* case charged the jury in the alternative that the federal obscenity statute outlaws literature dealing with sex which offends "the common conscience of the community."

That standard is, in my view, more inimical still to freedom of expression.

The standard of what offends "the common conscience of the community" conflicts, in my judgment, with the command of the First Amendment that "Congress shall make no law . . . abridging the freedom of speech, or of the press." Certainly that standard would not be an acceptable one if religion, economics, politics or philosophy were involved. How does it become a constitutional standard when literature treating with sex is concerned?

Any test that turns on what is offensive to the community's standards is too loose, too capricious, too destructive of freedom of expression to be squared with the First Amendment. Under that test, juries can censor, suppress, and punish what they don't like, provided the matter relates to "sexual impurity" or has a tendency "to excite lustful thoughts." This is community censorship in one of its worst forms. It creates a regime where in the battle between the literati and the Philistines, the Philistines are certain to win. If experience in this field teaches anything, it is that "censorship of obscenity has almost always been both irrational and indiscriminate." Lockhart & McClure, *op. cit. supra*, at 371. The test adopted here accentuates that trend.

I can understand (and at times even sympathize) with programs of civic groups and church groups to protect and defend the existing moral standards of the community. I can understand the motives of the Anthony Comstocks who would impose Victorian standards on the community. When speech alone is involved, I do not think that government, consistently with the First Amendment, can become the sponsor of any of these movements. I do not think that government, consistently with the First Amendment, can throw its weight behind one school or another. Government should be concerned with antisocial conduct, not with utterances. Thus, if the First Amendment guarantee of freedom of speech and press is to mean anything in this field, it must allow protests even against the moral code that the standard of the day sets for the community. In other words, literature should not be suppressed merely because it offends the moral code of the censor.

The legality of a publication in this country should never be allowed to turn either on the purity of thought which it instills in the mind of the reader or on the degree to which it offends the community conscience. By either test the role of the censor is exalted, and society's values in literary freedom are sacrificed.

The Court today suggests a third standard. It defines obscene material as that "which deals with sex in a manner appealing to prurient interest." Like the standards applied by the trial judges below, that standard does not require any nexus between the literature which is prohibited and action which the legislature can regulate or prohibit. Under the First Amendment, that standard is no more valid than those which the courts below adopted.

I do not think that the problem can be resolved by the Court's statement that "obscenity is not expression protected by the First Amendment." With the exception of *Beauharnais* v. *Illinois* [p. 182, *supra*], none of our cases has resolved problems of free speech and free press by placing any form of expression beyond the pale of the absolute prohibition of the First Amendment. Unlike the law of libel, wrongfully relied on in *Beauharnais*, there is no special historical evidence that literature dealing with sex was intended to be treated in a special manner by those who drafted the First Amendment. In fact, the first reported court decision in this country involving obscene literature was in 1821. Lockhart & McClure, *op. cit. supra.* I reject too the implication that problems of freedom of speech and of the press are to be resolved by weighing against the values of free expression, the judgment of the Court that a particular form of that expression has "no redeeming social importance." The First Amendment, its prohibition in terms absolute, was designed to preclude courts as well as legislatures from weighing the values of speech against silence. The First Amendment puts free speech in the preferred position.

I would give the broad sweep of the First Amendment full support. I have the same confidence in the ability of our people to reject noxious literature as I have in their capacity to sort out the true from the false in theology, economics, politics, or any other field.

Douglas has persisted in that view as the Court has tested literature and motion pictures against the original definition of obscenity—or as different Justices have abandoned that definition and substituted their own—to conclude, among other things: that a film version of Lady Chatterley's Lover *may not be barred because it "alluringly portrays adultery as proper behavior;"*[1] *that publishers of books may be punished if their publications appeal to the prurient interest of a "clearly defined deviant sexual group" for which they are designed, though not to the prurient interest of the "average person";*[2] *that the sale of material to children under seventeen may be prohibited on the basis of its prurient appeal to them;*[3] *and that* Fanny Hill *could not be suppressed because it is not "utterly without redeeming social value" (three justices), or*

---

[1] *Kingsley International Pictures Corp.* v. *Regents*, 360 U.S. 684 (1959).
[2] *Mishkin* v. *New York*, 383 U.S. 502 (1966).
[3] *Ginsberg* v. *New York*, 390 U.S. 629 (1968).

not "hard core pornography" (one justice) or because the First Amendment forbids suppression (two justices).[4]

And, as the Court has given its approval or disapproval to procedures for advance state screening of allegedly obscene matter, depending on the time involved and the clarity of the standards employed, he has maintained that all such advance screening systems constitute unconstitutional prior restraints on speech and press.[5] Thus, when the Court found screening procedures by which the directors of a municipal auditorium decided to bar from the premises the production of the musical Hair unconstitutional because too time-consuming, Douglas objected that no form of censorship—no matter how speedy—is permissible.[6]

BYRNE V. KARALEXIS
396 U.S. 976 (1969)

Karalexis, the owner and operator of a motion picture theater, was convicted in a Massachusetts state court of possessing with intent to exhibit an obscene film, I am Curious (Yellow). Prior to his conviction he had brought action in a federal district court to enjoin future prosecutions for showing the film. After the conviction the federal court issued a temporary injunction against the District Attorney enjoining him from interfering with exhibitions of the film pending a final decision by that court on the constitutionality of the conviction. The District Attorney then applied to the Supreme Court for a stay of that injunction pending the filing by the District Attorney, and the disposition, of an appeal from the order of the federal district court.

MR. JUSTICE DOUGLAS, dissenting.

The injunction issued by the District Court does not interfere in any way with the criminal conviction already obtained in the Massachusetts courts. That case will proceed unaffected by anything the federal court does, save for final execution of the state judgment. All that the federal court proposes is protection of respondents against repeated prosecutions, while both the state courts and the federal courts are resolving the constitutional issues.

[4] A Book Named "John Cleland's Memoirs of a Woman of Pleasure" v. Attorney General, 383 U.S. 413 (1966).
[5] See, e.g., Superior Films, Inc. v. Department of Education, 346 U.S. 587 (1954); Kingsley Books, Inc. v. Brown, 354 U.S. 436 (1957); Times Film Corp. v. Chicago, 365 U.S. 43 (1961); Freedman v. Maryland, 380 U.S. 51 (1965).
[6] Southeastern Promotions, Ltd. v. Conrad, 420 U.S. 546 (1975).

There may in time be a collision between the two systems for us to resolve. Meanwhile I would let the two orderly processes go ahead. For I can imagine no better and smoother accommodation of the needs of the two regimes than that designed by the District Court.

Underlying the state case and the federal case is an important First Amendment question. Some people think that "obscenity" is not protected by the Free Speech and Free Press Clauses of the First Amendment. They believe that both Congress and the States can set up regimes of censorship to weed out "obscenity" from literature, movies, and other publications so as to rid the press of what they, the judges, deem to be beyond the pale.

I have consistently dissented from that course but not because, as frequently charged, I relish "obscenity." I have dissented before and now because I think the First Amendment bars all kinds of censorship. To impose a regime of censors requires, in my view, a constitutional amendment. "Obscenity" is no exception. "Obscenity" certainly was not an established exception to free speech and free press when the Bill of Rights was adopted. It is a relatively new arrival on the American scene, propelled by dedicated zealots to cleanse all thought.

Prior to the Bill of Rights, state law, when it spoke of freedom of the press, meant only freedom from prior restraint. But an author or publisher could be held accountable for publishing what the statehouse thought was against "the public good." In other words, the First Amendment did not build on existing law; it broke with tradition, set a new standard, and exalted freedom of expression. There is no trace of a suggestion that "obscenity," however defined, was excepted.

That does not mean that "obscenity" is good or that it should be encouraged. It only means that we cannot be faithful to our constitutional mandate and allow any form or shadow of censorship over speech and press.

When our rewards go to people for thinking alike, it is no surprise that we become frightened at those who take exception to the current consensus. Then the hue and cry goes up for censors; and that is the start of an ominous trend. What can be done to literature under the banner of "obscenity" can be done to other parts of the spectrum of ideas when party or majoritarian demands mount and propagandists start declaiming the law.

The "obscenity" issue raises large questions. To what extent may government watch over one's shoulder as he reads?

Judge Jerome Frank said in *Roth* v. *Goldman*, 172 F. 2d 788:

> "I think that no sane man thinks socially dangerous the arousing of normal sexual desires. Consequently, if reading obscene

books has merely that consequence, Congress, it would seem, can constitutionally no more suppress such books than it can prevent the mailing of many other objects, such as perfumes, for example, which notoriously produce that result. But the constitutional power to suppress obscene publications might well exist if there were ample reason to believe that reading them conduces to socially harmful sexual conduct on the part of normal human beings. . . . Macaulay, replying to demands for suppression of obscene books, said: 'We find it difficult to believe that in a world so full of temptations as this, any gentleman, whose life would have been virtuous if he had not read Aristophanes and Juvenal, will be made vicious by reading them.' "

If "obscenity" can be carved out of the First Amendment, what other like exceptions can be created? Is "sacrilege" also beyond the pale? Are utterances or publications made with "malice" unprotected? How about "seditious" speech or articles? False, scandalous, and malicious writings or utterances against the Congress or the President "with intent to defame" or to bring them "into contempt or disrepute" or to "excite" against them "the hatred of the good people" or "to stir up sedition," or to "excite" people to "resist, oppose, or defeat" any law were once made a crime [under the Alien and Sedition Acts of 1798]. Now that the First Amendment applies to the States, *Stromberg v. California*, 283 U.S. 359, may the States embark on such totalitarian controls over thought or over the press? May Congress do so?

We forget today that under our constitutional system neither Congress nor the States have any power to pass on the value, the propriety, the Americanism, the soundness of any idea or expression. It is that insulation from party or majoritarian control provided by the First Amendment—not our gross national product or mass production or pesticides or space ships or nuclear arsenal—that distinguishes our society from the other planetary regimes.

PARIS ADULT THEATRE I V. SLATON
413 U.S. 49 (1973)

By 1973, the Court could say in a companion case to this one[7] that "[a]part from the initial formulation in the Roth case [p. 220, supra], no majority of the Court has at any given time been able to agree on a standard to determine what constitutes obscene, pornographic material." But in that case, five members of the Court were able to agree

[7] *Miller v. California,* 413 U.S. 15 (1973).

on a new test which must be satisfied before the states can suppress "works which depict or describe sexual conduct." Affirmative findings must be made with respect to three questions: "(a) whether 'the average person, applying contemporary community standards' would find that the work, taken as a whole, appeals to the prurient interest . . . ; (b) whether the work depicts or describes, in a patently offensive way, sexual conduct specifically defined by the applicable state law; and (c) whether the work, taken as a whole, lacks serious literary, artistic, political, or scientific value." And, in recognition of the fact that "[p]eople in different States vary in their tastes and attitudes" and in the belief that the First Amendment should not be read "as requiring that the people of Maine or Mississippi accept public depiction of conduct found tolerable in Las Vegas, or in New York City," it was held that what appeals to the "prurient interest" and what is "patently offensive" was to be determined by "statewide standards" and not by "national standards."

This case was an action by Georgia to enjoin the showing of two allegedly obscene movies. (In deference to the Court's prevailing views about impermissible prior restraints in such cases, exhibition of the films was not enjoined until after the trial court had found them obscene and the Georgia Supreme Court had affirmed that finding.) The Court remanded the case to the Georgia Supreme Court for reconsideration in the light of the new standards just announced, but it also expressly rejected the notion that the films would be immune from state suppression if they were shown to consenting adults only.

MR. JUSTICE DOUGLAS, dissenting.

I have expressed on numerous occasions my disagreement with the basic decision that held that "obscenity" was not protected by the First Amendment. I disagreed also with the definitions that evolved. Art and literature reflect tastes; and tastes, like musical appreciation, are hardly reducible to precise definitions. That is one reason I have always felt that "obscenity" was not an exception to the First Amendment. For matters of taste, like matters of belief, turn on the idiosyncrasies of individuals. They are too personal to define and too emotional and vague to apply, as witness the prison term for Ralph Ginzburg, *Ginzburg* v. *United States*, 383 U.S. 463, not for what he printed but for the sexy manner in which he advertised his creations.

The other reason I could not bring myself to conclude that "obscenity" was not covered by the First Amendment was that prior to the adoption of our Constitution and Bill of Rights the Colonies had no law excluding "obscenity" from the regime of freedom of expression and press that then existed. I could find no such laws; and more important, our leading colonial expert, Julius Goebel, could find none, J. Goebel, Development of Legal Institutions (1946); J. Goebel, Felony and Misdemeanor (1937). So I became convinced that the creation of the "obscenity" exception to the First Amendment was a legislative and judicial *tour de force*; that if we were to have such a regime of censorship and punishment, it should be done by constitutional amendment.

People are, of course, offended by many offerings made by merchants in this area. They are also offended by political pronouncements, sociological themes, and by stories of official misconduct. The list of activities and publications and pronouncements that offend someone is endless. Some of it goes on in private; some of it is inescapably public, as when a government official generates crime, becomes a blatant offender of the moral sensibilities of the people, engages in burglary, or breaches the privacy of the telephone, the conference room, or the home. Life in this crowded modern technological world creates many offensive statements and many offensive deeds. There is no protection against offensive ideas, only against offensive conduct.

"Obscenity" at most is the expression of offensive ideas. There are regimes in the world where ideas "offensive" to the majority (or at least to those who control the majority) are suppressed. There life proceeds at a monotonous pace. Most of us would find that world offensive. One of the most offensive experiences in my life was a visit to a nation where bookstalls were filled only with books on mathematics and books on religion.

I am sure I would find offensive most of the books and movies charged with being obscene. But in a life that has not been short, I have yet to be trapped into seeing or reading something that would offend me. I never read or see the materials coming to the Court under charges of "obscenity," because I have thought the First Amendment made it unconstitutional for me to act as a censor.

I see no constitutional basis for fashioning a rule that makes a publisher, producer, bookseller, librarian, or movie house operator criminally responsible, when he fails to take affirmative steps to protect the consumer against literature, books, or movies offensive[8] to those who temporarily occupy the seats of the mighty.

---

[8] What we do today is rather ominous as respects librarians. The net now designed by the Court is so finely meshed that, taken literally, it could result in raids on libraries. Libraries, I had always assumed, were sancrosanct, representing every part of the spectrum. If what is offensive to the most influential person or group in a community can be purged from a library, the library system would be destroyed.

When man was first in the jungle he took care of himself. When he entered a societal group, controls were necessarily imposed. But our society—unlike most in the world—presupposes that freedom and liberty are in a frame of reference that makes the individual, not government, the keeper of his tastes, beliefs, and ideas. That is the philosophy of the First Amendment; and it is the article of faith that sets us apart from most nations in the world.

The "statewide standard" approved by the Court for testing obscenity when the state moves against it left matters uncertain when the federal government moved to enforce its laws about the importation, mailing, or transportation in interstate commerce of obscenity. That question arose in another case, like Roth [p. 220, supra], where the federal government was prosecuting defendants for using the mails to disseminate obscene material. The answer, the Court said, was not a "national standard" for federal cases but the application of "contemporary community standards." Since the prosecution in that case was in a federal district court for the southern district of California, consisting of Imperial and San Diego counties, that would be the "community" from which the jury should draw its standards.[9] At the same time the Court held that a state need not use a "statewide standard" in its obscenity prosecutions; the jury could be instructed to apply "community standards" without specifying what community.[10]

[9] Hamling v. United States, 418 U.S. 87 (1974).
[10] Jenkins v. Georgia, 418 U.S. 153 (1974).

7

PRIVACY

The recently developed concept of a constitutional right of privacy is not confined to cases arising under the First Amendment.

PUBLIC UTILITIES COMMISSION V. POLLAK
343 U.S. 451 (1952)

Capital Transit Company, a privately owned public utility operating street cars and buses in the District of Columbia, sold to a radio station the right to install loudspeakers in the vehicles for the broadcasting of the station's programs. The Public Utilities Commission of the District of Columbia, which had authority to require the transit company service to conform to "public convenience, comfort, and safety," initiated an investigation of this "music-as-you-ride" system. In its hearing the commission received evidence showing that 90 percent of the programs consisted of music, 5 percent of news and weather reports, and 5 percent of commercial advertising. It considered a public-opinion poll which showed that 76 percent of the passengers favored the system, 14 percent didn't care, 4 percent didn't like it but would not object to it, 3 percent objected, and 3 percent had no opinion. The commission also heard testimony of passengers favoring and objecting to the system. It then concluded that the system had no impact on safety and that, far from impairing public comfort and convenience, "through the creation of better will among passengers, it tends to improve the conditions under which the public ride." Accordingly, it dismissed the proceeding.

Two passengers in whom the system had not created better will appealed from the commission's action, advancing two novel constitutional arguments: (1) the First Amendment guarantees a right of freedom to listen only to points of view which the listener wishes to hear, and (2) the system violated a right of privacy included in the guarantee of "liberty" contained in the due process clause of the Fifth Amendment.[1] The Court concluded that the failure of the commission to

---

[1] "No person shall . . . be deprived of life, liberty, or property, without due process of law. . . ."

prohibit the broadcasts constituted governmental action subject to con-
stitutional limitations, but held that neither the First nor the Fifth
Amendment was violated.

MR. JUSTICE DOUGLAS, dissenting.

This is a case of first impression. There are no precedents to construe; no principles previously expounded to apply. We write on a clean slate.

The case comes down to the meaning of "liberty" as used in the Fifth Amendment. Liberty in the constitutional sense must mean more than freedom from unlawful governmental restraint; it must include privacy as well, if it is to be a repository of freedom. The right to be let alone is indeed the beginning of all freedom. Part of our claim to privacy is in the prohibition of the Fourth Amendment against un-reasonable searches and seizures. It gives the guarantee that a man's home is his castle beyond invasion either by inquisitive or by officious people. A man loses that privacy of course when he goes upon the streets or enters public places. But even in his activities outside the home he has immunities from controls bearing on privacy. He may not be compelled against his will to attend a religious service; he may not be forced to make an affirmation or observe a ritual that violates his scruples; he may not be made to accept one religious, political, or philosophical creed as against another. Freedom of religion and free-dom of speech guaranteed by the First Amendment give more than the privilege to worship, to write, to speak as one chooses; they give freedom not to do nor to act as the government chooses. The First Amendment in its respect for the conscience of the individual honors the sanctity of thought and belief. To think as one chooses, to believe what one wishes are important aspects of the constitutional right to be let alone.

If we remembered this lesson taught by the First Amendment, I do not believe we would construe "liberty" within the meaning of the Fifth Amendment as narrowly as the Court does. The present case involves a form of coercion to make people listen. The listeners are of course in a public place; they are on streetcars traveling to and from home. In one sense it can be said that those who ride the street-cars do so voluntarily. Yet in a practical sense they are forced to ride, since this mode of transportation is today essential for many thousands. Compulsion which comes from circumstances can be as real as com-pulsion which comes from a command.

The streetcar audience is a captive audience. It is there as a matter of necessity, not of choice. One who is in a public vehicle may not of course complain of the noise of the crowd and the babble of tongues. One who enters any public place sacrifices some of his privacy. My protest is against the invasion of his privacy over and beyond the risks of travel.

The government may use the radio (or television) on public vehicles for many purposes. Today it may use it for a cultural end. Tomorrow it may use it for political purposes. So far as the right of privacy is concerned the purpose makes no difference. The music selected by one bureaucrat may be as offensive to some as it is soothing to others. The news commentator chosen to report on the events of the day may give overtones to the news that please the bureau head but which rile the streetcar captive audience. The political philosophy which one radio speaker exudes may be thought by the official who makes up the street-car programs to be best for the welfare of the people. But the man who listens to it on his way to work in the morning and on his way home at night may think it marks the destruction of the Republic.

One who tunes in on an offensive program at home can turn it off or tune in another station, as he wishes. One who hears disquieting or unpleasant programs in public places, such as restaurants, can get up and leave. But the man on the streetcar has no choice but to sit and listen, or perhaps to sit and to try *not* to listen.

When we force people to listen to another's ideas, we give the propagandist a powerful weapon. Today it is a business enterprise working out a radio program under the auspices of government. To-morrow it may be a dominant political or religious group. Today the purpose is benign; there is no invidious cast to the programs. But the vice is inherent in the system. Once privacy is invaded, privacy is gone. Once a man is forced to submit to one type of radio program, he can be forced to submit to another. It may be but a short step from a cultural program to a political program.

If liberty is to flourish, government should never be allowed to force people to listen to any radio program. The right of privacy should in-clude the right to pick and choose from competing entertainments, competing propaganda, competing political philosophies. If people are let alone in those choices, the right of privacy will pay dividends in character and integrity. The strength of our system is in the dignity, the resourcefulness, and the independence of our people. Our con-fidence is in their ability as individuals to make the wisest choice. That system cannot flourish if regimentation takes hold. The right of privacy, today violated, is a powerful deterrent to any one who would control men's minds.

When the Court in 1958 held that a constitutional right of free association was guaranteed by the First Amendment,[2] it held at the same time that members of the National Association for the Advancement of Colored People were "constitutionally entitled" to "privacy" in their association so that, at least in the absence of a showing of a "compelling" state interest, Alabama could not require the NAACP to reveal the names and addresses of all its Alabama members.

GRISWOLD v. CONNECTICUT
381 U.S. 479 (1965)

A Connecticut statute made it a crime to use "any drug, medicinal article or instrument" for birth-control purposes. Another general section of the Connecticut criminal code provided that anyone who abetted another in committing any crime might be punished as a principal offender. The executive director and the medical director of the Planned Parenthood League of Connecticut were convicted under these statutes of prescribing birth-control devices or material for married couples. The Court reversed the convictions.

MR. JUSTICE DOUGLAS delivered the opinion of the Court.

The association of people is not mentioned in the Constitution nor in the Bill of Rights. The right to educate a child in a school of the parents' choice—whether public or private or parochial—is also not mentioned. Nor is the right to study any particular subject or any foreign language. Yet the First Amendment has been construed to include certain of those rights.

By *Pierce v. Society of Sisters*, 268 U.S. 510, the right to educate one's children as one chooses is made applicable to the States by the force of the First and Fourteenth Amendments. By *Meyer v. Nebraska*, 262 U.S. 390, the same dignity is given the right to study the German language in a private school. In other words, the State may not, consistently with the spirit of the First Amendment, contract the spectrum of available knowledge. The right of freedom of speech and press includes not only the right to utter or to print, but the right to distribute, the right to receive, the right to read and freedom of inquiry, freedom of thought, and freedom to teach—indeed the freedom of the entire university community. *Baggett v. Bullitt* [note 45, at p. 208, *supra*]. Without those peripheral rights the specific rights would be less secure. And so we reaffirm the principle of the *Pierce* and the *Meyer* cases.

[2] *NAACP v. Alabama*, note 12, at p. 179, *supra*.

In *NAACP* v. *Alabama* [note 12, at p. 179, *supra*], we protected the "freedom to associate and privacy in one's associations," noting that freedom of association was a peripheral First Amendment right. Disclosure of membership lists of a constitutionally valid association, we held, was invalid "as entailing the likelihood of a substantial restraint upon the exercise by petitioner's members of their right to freedom of association." In other words, the First Amendment has a penumbra where privacy is protected from governmental intrusion. In like context, we have protected forms of "association" that are not political in the customary sense but pertain to the social, legal, and economic benefit of the members. *NAACP* v. *Button*, 371 U.S. 415.

Those cases involved more than the "right of assembly"—a right that extends to all irrespective of their race or ideology. *De Jonge* v. *Oregon*, 299 U.S. 353. The right of "association," like the right of belief (*Board of Education* v. *Barnette*, 319 U.S. 624), is more than the right to attend a meeting; it includes the right to express one's attitudes or philosophies by membership in a group or by affiliation with it or by other lawful means. Association in that context is a form of expression of opinion; and while it is not expressly included in the First Amendment its existence is necessary in making the express guarantees fully meaningful.

The foregoing cases suggest that specific guarantees in the Bill of Rights have penumbras, formed by emanations from those guarantees that help give them life and substance. Various guarantees create zones of privacy. The right of association contained in the penumbra of the First Amendment is one, as we have seen. The Third Amendment in its prohibition against the quartering of soldiers "in any house" in time of peace without the consent of the owner is another facet of that privacy. The Fourth Amendment explicitly affirms the "right of the people to be secure in their persons, houses, papers, and effects, against unreasonable searches and seizures." The Fifth Amendment in its Self-Incrimination Clause enables the citizen to create a zone of privacy which government may not force him to surrender to his detriment. The Ninth Amendment provides: "The enumeration in the Constitution, of certain rights, shall not be construed to deny or disparage others retained by the people."

The present case, then, concerns a relationship lying within the zone of privacy created by several fundamental constitutional guarantees. And it concerns a law which, in forbidding the *use* of contraceptives rather than regulating their manufacture or sale, seeks to achieve its goals by means having a maximum destructive impact upon that relationship. Such a law cannot stand in light of the familiar principle, so often applied by this Court, that a "governmental purpose to control or prevent activities constitutionally subject to state regulation may not be achieved by means which sweep unnecessarily broadly and thereby invade the area of protected freedoms." *NAACP* v. *Alabama,* 377 U.S. 288. Would we allow the police to search the sacred precincts of marital bedrooms for telltale signs of the use of contraceptives? The very idea is repulsive to the notions of privacy surrounding the marriage relationship.

We deal with a right of privacy older than the Bill of Rights—older than our political parties, older than our school system. Marriage is a coming together for better or for worse, hopefully enduring, and intimate to the degree of being sacred. It is an association that promotes a way of life, not causes; a harmony in living, not political faiths; a bilateral loyalty, not commercial or social projects. Yet it is an association for as noble a purpose as any involved in our prior decisions.

The Court concluded in 1969 that a state could not convict a man for the possession of an obscene film in his own home. The "fundamental" right to privacy guaranteed by the First Amendment was held to forbid it. "If the First Amendment means anything, it means that a State has no business telling a man, sitting alone in his own house, what books he may read and what films he may watch."[3] Douglas joined in that decision but consistently dissented thereafter when the Court rejected the apparently logical implications of this decision to hold that customs agents could confiscate obscene material which a traveler sought to bring into the United States for his own private use[4] and that the government may punish one who carries obscene material in interstate commerce for his own private use.[5]

EISENSTADT v. BAIRD

405 U.S. 438 (1972)

A Massachusetts statute made it a crime to supply any "article whatever for the prevention of conception." After the decision in Griswold *[p. 234, supra], it was amended to provide an exception for registered physicians prescribing contraceptives for married persons and registered pharmacists filling such prescriptions. William Baird, in the course of delivering a lecture on contraception to a group of students and faculty*

---

[3] *Stanley* v. *Georgia,* 394 U.S. 557 (1969).

[4] *United States* v. 12 200-Ft. Reels of Super 8 mm. Film, 413 U.S. 123 1(973); *United States* v. *Thirty-seven Photographs,* 402 U.S. 363 (1971).

[5] *United States* v. *Orito,* 413 U.S. 139 (1973). Apparently the government may also punish one who uses the mails to supply obscene material to those who order it for their own private use. See *United States* v. *Reidel,* 402 U.S. 351 (1971).

at Boston University, gave a package of vaginal foam to a young woman in his audience and was thereafter convicted under this statute. He sought relief in the federal courts by writ of habeas corpus on the ground that the statute was unconstitutional, and he prevailed.

The Court held that the statute violated the equal protection clauses of the Fourteenth Amendment[6] in its distinction between married and unmarried persons. While that clause does not prevent the states from making all distinctions or classifications, the classification must rest upon some difference having a rational relation to the objective of the legislation. Here, if the statute be regarded as a measure designed to protect against contraceptives dangerous to health, the distinction between married and single persons had no relation to that objective. If it be viewed as a measure to promote a moral standard by discouraging nonmarital sexual relations, the distinction was similarly defective since the statute made contraceptives available to married persons without regard to their intended use and since, as interpreted by the Supreme Judicial Court of Massachusetts, it also permitted anyone to supply to anyone devices used to prevent not pregnancy but disease. In short, the Massachusetts statute appeared to be aimed simply at prohibiting the use of contraceptives to the extent permitted by the Griswold *decision. But in attempting to accommodate to* Griswold, *Massachusetts had made an impermissable distinction. "If the right of privacy means anything, it is the right of the* individual, *married or single, to be free from unwarranted governmental intrusion into matters so fundamentally affecting a person as the decision whether to bear or beget a child."*

MR. JUSTICE DOUGLAS, concurring.

While I join the opinion of the Court, there is for me a narrow ground for affirming the Court of Appeals. This to me is a simple First Amendment case, that amendment being applicable to the States by reason of the Fourteenth.

Under no stretch of the law as presently stated could Massachusetts require a license for those who desire to lecture on planned parenthood, contraceptives, the rights of women, birth control, or any allied subject, or place a tax on that privilege. As to license taxes on First Amendment rights we said in *Murdock* v. *Pennsylvania*, 319 U.S. 105:

> "A license tax certainly does not acquire constitutional validity because it classifies the privileges protected by the First Amendment along with the wares and merchandise of hucksters and

---

[6] That clause forbids the states to "deny to any person . . . the equal protection of the laws."

peddlers and treats them all alike. Such equality in treatment does not save the ordinance. Freedom of press, freedom of speech, freedom of religion are in a preferred position."

Baird addressed an audience of students and faculty at Boston University on the subject of birth control and overpopulation. His address was approximately one hour in length and consisted of a discussion of various contraceptive devices displayed by means of diagrams on two demonstration boards, as well as a display of contraceptive devices in their original packages. In addition, Baird spoke of the respective merits of various contraceptive devices; overpopulation in the world; crises throughout the world due to overpopulation; the large number of abortions performed on unwed mothers; and quack abortionists and the potential harm to women resulting from abortions performed by quack abortionists. Baird also urged members of the audience to petition the Massachusetts Legislature to make known their feelings with regard to birth control laws in order to bring about a change in the laws. At the close of the address Baird invited members of the audience to come to the stage and help themselves to the contraceptive articles. We do not know how many accepted Baird's invitation. We only know that Baird personally handed one woman a package of Emko Vaginal Foam.

Had Baird not "given away" a sample of one of the devices whose use he advocated, there could be no question about the protection afforded him by the First Amendment. A State may not "contract the spectrum of available knowledge." *Griswold* v. *Connecticut* [p. 234, *supra*]. However noxious Baird's ideas might have been to the authorities, the freedom to learn about them, fully to comprehend their scope and portent, and to weigh them against the tenets of the "conventional wisdom," may not be abridged. *Terminiello* v. *Chicago* [p. 179, *supra*]. Our system of government requires that we have faith in the ability of the individual to decide wisely, if only he is fully apprised of the merits of a controversy.

> "Freedom of discussion, if it would fulfill its historic function in this nation, must embrace all issues about which information is needed or appropriate to enable the members of society to cope with the exigencies of their period." *Thornhill* v. *Alabama*, 310 U.S. 88.

The teachings of Baird and those of Galileo might be of a different order; but the suppression of either is equally repugnant.

As Milton said in the Areopagitica, "Give me the liberty to know, to utter, and to argue freely according to conscience, above all liberties."

It is said that only Baird's conduct is involved. The distinction between "speech" and "conduct" is a valid one, insofar as it helps to
determine in a particular case whether the purpose of the activity was
to aid in the communication of ideas, and whether the form of the
communication so interferes with the rights of others that reasonable
regulations may be imposed. See *Public Utilities Comm'n v. Pollak*
[p. 231, *supra*] (DOUGLAS, J., dissenting). Thus, excessive noise might
well be "conduct"—a form of pollution—which can be made subject to
precise, narrowly drawn regulations. But "this Court has repeatedly
stated, [First Amendment] rights are not confined to verbal expression.
They embrace appropriate types of action . . . ." *Brown v. Louisiana,*
383 U.S. 131.

Baird gave an hour's lecture on birth control and as an aid to
understanding the ideas which he was propagating he handed out one
sample of one of the devices whose use he was endorsing. A person giving a lecture on coyote-getters would certainly improve his teaching
technique if he passed one out to the audience; and he would be protected in doing so unless of course the device was loaded and ready to
explode, killing or injuring people. The same holds true in my mind for
mousetraps, spray guns, or any other article not dangerous *per se* on
which speakers give educational lectures.

It is irrelevant to the application of these principles that Baird
went beyond the giving of information about birth control and advocated the use of contraceptive articles. The First Amendment protects
the opportunity to persuade to action whether that action be unwise or
immoral or whether the speech incites to action. See, *e.g., Brandenburg
v. Ohio* [p. 205, *supra*].

In this case there was not even incitement to action. There is no
evidence or finding that Baird intended that the young lady take the
foam home with her when he handed it to her or that she would not
have examined the article and then returned it to Baird, had he not
been placed under arrest immediately upon handing the article over.

First Amendment rights are not limited to verbal expression. The
right to petition often involves the right to walk. The right of assembly
may mean pushing or jostling. Picketing involves physical activity as
well as a display of a sign. A sit-in can be a quiet, dignified protest that
has First Amendment protection even though no speech is involved, as
we held in *Brown v. Louisiana, supra*. Putting contraceptives on display
is certainly an aid to speech and discussion. Handing an article under
discussion to a member of the audience is a technique known to all
teachers and is commonly used. A handout may be on such a scale as to
smack of a vendor's marketing scheme. But passing one article to an
audience is merely a projection of the visual aid and should be a per-

missible adjunct of free speech. Baird was not making a prescription nor purporting to give medical advice. Handing out the article was not even a suggestion that the lady use it. At most it suggested that she become familiar with the product line.

I do not see how we can have a Society of the Dialogue, which the First Amendment envisages, if time-honored teaching techniques are barred to those who give educational lectures.

DOE v. BOLTON
410 U.S. 179 (1973)

In this case the Court held unconstitutional a Georgia statute prescribing criminal penalties for performing an abortion unless performed by a licensed physician when in "his best clinical judgment" it is necessary because (1) of danger to the life or serious and permanent injury to the health of the mother, or (2) the fetus would very likely be born with grave, permanent, and irremedial mental or physical defect, or (3) the pregnancy resulted from forcible or statutory rape. In the companion case of Roe v. Wade,[7] the Court also held unconstitutional a Texas statute making illegal the performance of an abortion unless procured "by medical advice for the purpose of saving the life of the mother."

The constitutional right of privacy, which a majority of the Court was now ready to base on the Fourteenth Amendment's guarantee of liberty," just as Douglas had argued in the Pollak case [p. 231, supra] was held to be "broad enough to encompass a woman's decision whether or not to terminate her pregnancy." But the right was not absolute. The state had an interest both in safeguarding the mother's health and in protecting potential life, and "[a]t some point in pregnancy those respective interests become sufficiently compelling to sustain regulation of the factors that govern the abortion decision." During the first trimester of pregnancy, while the fetus was not "viable" in the sense that it was potentially able to live outside the mother's womb, and while the risk of death to the mother is less than that risk in normal childbirth, the attending physician, in consultation with his patient, must remain free to make the abortion decision without interference from the state. During the second trimester, while the fetus is still not viable but when the mortality risk to the mother increases, the state may regulate the abortion procedure for her protection, as by imposing requirements as to the qualifications of the person performing the

---

[7] 410 U.S. 113 (1973). "Jane Roe" was a pseudonym used by a pregnant unmarried woman and "Mary Doe" a pseudonym used by a pregnant married woman in order to protect their privacy while maintaining this litigation.

abortion and the facility in which it is to be performed. Only in the last trimester, after the fetus has become viable, may the state go so far as to proscribe abortion except where it is necessary to preserve the life and health of the mother.

Douglas filed a single concurring opinion for both cases in the case involving the Georgia statute.

MR. JUSTICE DOUGLAS, concurring.

While I join the opinion of the Court, I add a few words.

I

The questions presented in the present cases involve the right of privacy, one aspect of which we considered in *Griswold* v. *Connecticut*, 381 U. S. 479, when we held that various guarantees in the Bill of Rights create zones of privacy.

The Ninth Amendment obviously does not create federally enforceable rights. It merely says, "The enumeration in the Constitution, of certain rights, shall not be construed to deny or disparage others retained by the people." But a catalogue of these rights includes customary, traditional, and time-honored rights, amenities, privileges, and immunities that come within the sweep of "the Blessings of Liberty" mentioned in the preamble to the Constitution. Many of them, in my view, come within the meaning of the term "liberty" as used in the Fourteenth Amendment.

First is the autonomous control over the development and expression of one's intellect, interests, tastes, and personality.

These are rights protected by the First Amendment and, in my view, they are absolute, permitting of no exceptions. See *Terminiello* v. *Chicago*, 337 U.S. 1; *Roth* v. *United States*, 354 U.S. 476, 508 (dissent). The Free Exercise Clause of the First Amendment is one facet of this constitutional right. The right to remain silent as respects one's own beliefs is protected by the First and the Fifth. The First Amendment grants the privacy of first-class mail, *United States* v. *Van Leeuwen*, 397 U.S. 249. All of these aspects of the right of privacy are rights "retained by the people" in the meaning of the Ninth Amendment.

Second is freedom of choice in the basic decisions of one's life respecting marriage, divorce, procreation, contraception, and the education and upbringing of children.

These rights, unlike those protected by the First Amendment, are subject to some control by the police power. Thus, the Fourth Amendment speaks only of "unreasonable searches and seizures" and of "probable cause." These rights are "fundamental," and we have held that in order to support legislative action the statute must be narrowly and precisely drawn and that a "compelling state interest" must be shown in support of the limitation. *E.g.*, *NAACP* v. *Alabama*, 357 U.S. 449.

The liberty to marry a person of one's own choosing, *Loving* v. *Virginia*, 388 U.S. 1; the right of procreation, *Skinner* v. *Oklahoma*, 316 U.S. 535; the liberty to direct the education of one's children, *Pierce* v. *Society of Sisters*, 268 U.S. 510, and the privacy of the marital relation, *Griswold* v. *Connecticut, supra*, are in this category. Only last Term in *Eisenstadt* v. *Baird* [p. 236, *supra*], another contraceptive case, we expanded the concept of *Griswold* by saying:

> "It is true that in *Griswold* the right of privacy in question inhered in the marital relationship. Yet the marital couple is not an independent entity with a mind and heart of its own, but an association of two individuals each with a separate intellectual and emotional makeup. If the right of privacy means anything, it is the right of the *individual*, married or single, to be free from unwarranted governmental intrusion into matters so fundamentally affecting a person as the decision whether to bear or beget a child."

This right of privacy was called by Mr. Justice Brandeis the right "to be let alone." *Olmstead* v. *United States*, 277 U.S. 438 (dissenting opinion). That right includes the privilege of an individual to plan his own affairs, for, " 'outside areas of plainly harmful conduct, every American is left to shape his own life as he thinks best, do what he pleases, go where he pleases.' " *Kent* v. *Dulles*, 357 U.S. 116.

Third is the freedom to care for one's health and person, freedom from bodily restraint or compulsion, freedom to walk, stroll, or loaf.

These rights, though fundamental, are likewise subject to regulation on a showing of "compelling state interest." We stated in *Papachristou* v. *City of Jacksonville*, 405 U.S. 156, that walking, strolling, and wandering "are historically part of the amenities of life as we have known them."

In *Union Pacific R. Co.* v. *Botsford*, 141 U.S. 250, 252, the Court said, "The inviolability of the person is as much invaded by a compulsory stripping and exposure as by a blow."

In *Terry* v. *Ohio*, 392 U.S. 1, 8–9, the Court, in speaking of the Fourth Amendment stated, "This inestimable right of personal security belongs as much to the citizen on the streets of our cities as to the homeowner closeted in his study to dispose of his secret affairs."

Katz v. *United States*, 389 U.S. 347, 350, emphasizes that the Fourth Amendment "protects individual privacy against certain kinds of governmental intrusion."

In *Meyer* v. *Nebraska*, 262 U.S. 390, 399, the Court said:

> "Without doubt, [liberty] denotes not merely freedom from bodily restraint but also the right of the individual to contract, to engage in any of the common occupations of life, to acquire useful knowledge, to marry, establish a home and bring up children, to worship God according to the dictates of his own conscience, and generally to enjoy those privileges long recognized at common law as essential to the orderly pursuit of happiness by free men."

The Georgia statute is at war with the clear message of these cases—that a woman is free to make the basic decision whether to bear an unwanted child. Elaborate argument is hardly necessary to demonstrate that childbirth may deprive a woman of her preferred lifestyle and force upon her a radically different and undesired future. For example, rejected applicants under the Georgia statute are required to endure the discomforts of pregnancy; to incur the pain, higher mortality rate, and aftereffects of childbirth; to abandon educational plans; to sustain loss of income; to forgo the satisfactions of careers; to tax further mental and physical health in providing child care; and, in some cases, to bear the lifelong stigma of unwed motherhood, a badge which may haunt, if not deter, later legitimate family relationships.

II

Such reasoning is, however, only the beginning of the problem. The State has interests to protect. Vaccinations to prevent epidemics are one example, as [*Jacobson* v. *Massachusetts*, 197 U.S. 11] holds. The Court held that compulsory sterilization of imbeciles afflicted with hereditary forms of insanity or imbecility is another. *Buck* v. *Bell*, 274 U.S. 200. Abortion affects another. While childbirth endangers the lives of some women, voluntary abortion at any time and place regardless of medical standards would impinge on a rightful concern of society. The woman's health is part of that concern; as is the life of the fetus after quickening. These concerns justify the State in treating the procedure as a medical one.

Georgia's enactment has a constitutional infirmity because, as stated by the District Court, it "limits the number of reasons for which an abortion may be sought." I agree with the holding of the District Court, "This the State may not do, because such action unduly restricts a decision sheltered by the Constitutional right to privacy." 319 F. Supp., at 1056.

The vicissitudes of life produce pregnancies which may be unwanted, or which may impair health, or which may imperil the life of the

mother, or which in the full setting of the case may create such suffering, dislocations, misery, or tragedy as to make an early abortion the only
civilized step to take. These hardships may be properly embraced in
the "health" factor of the mother as appraised by a person of insight.
Or they may be part of a broader medical judgment based on what is
"appropriate" in a given case, though perhaps not "necessary" in a
strict sense.

The "liberty" of the mother, though rooted as it is in the Constitution, may be qualified by the State for the reasons we have stated. But
where fundamental personal rights and liberties are involved, the correc-
tive legislation must be "narrowly drawn to prevent the supposed evil,"
Cantwell v. *Connecticut,* 310 U.S. 296, and not be dealt with in an
"unlimited and indiscriminate" manner. *Shelton* v. *Tucker,* 364 U.S.
479. Unless regulatory measures are so confined and are addressed to the
specific areas of compelling legislative concern, the police power would
become the great leveler of constitutional rights and liberties.

There is no doubt that the State may require abortions to be performed by qualified medical personnel. The legitimate objective of
preserving the mother's health clearly supports such laws. Their impact
upon the woman's privacy is minimal. But the Georgia statute outlaws
virtually all such operations—even in the earliest stages of pregnancy. In
light of modern medical evidence suggesting that an early abortion is
safer healthwise than childbirth itself, it cannot be seriously urged that
so comprehensive a ban is aimed at protecting the woman's health.
Rather, this expansive proscription of all abortions along the temporal
spectrum can rest only on a public goal of preserving both embryonic
and fetal life.

The present statute has struck the balance between the woman's and
the State's interests wholly in favor of the latter. I am not prepared to
hold that a State may equate, as Georgia has done, all phases of matura-
tion preceding birth. We held in *Griswold* that the States may not
preclude spouses from attempting to avoid the joinder of sperm and
egg. If this is true, it is difficult to perceive any overriding public
necessity which might attach precisely at the moment of conception.

In summary, the enactment is overbroad. It is not closely correlated
to the aim of preserving prenatal life. In fact, it permits its destruction
in several cases, including pregnancies resulting from sex acts in which
unmarried females are below the statutory age of consent. At the same
time, however, the measure broadly proscribes aborting other pregnancies which may cause severe mental disorders. Additionally, the
statute is overbroad because it equates the value of embryonic life immediately after conception with the worth of life immediately before
birth.

8

MILITARY SERVICE

As *previously indicated, Douglas was unable to persuade the Court to consider the validity of the use of the Selective Service Act to conscript men for military service abroad in a conflict that had not been sanctioned by a congressional declaration of war and which had been challenged as in violation of international law and of treaties to which the United States was a party.[1] But in a number of cases in recent years, the Court has considered other aspects of that Act.*

GILLETTE v. UNITED STATES

401 U.S. 437 (1971)

The Selective Service Act exempted from service one who, "by reason of religious training and belief, is conscientiously opposed to war in any form" and defined "religious training and belief" to exclude "essentially political, sociological, or philosophical views, or a merely personal moral code." In an earlier decision in which Douglas concurred, the Court held that a Jehovah's Witness could qualify for exemption, since he was opposed to participation in all secular wars, even though he conceded his willingness to engage in a "theocratic war" if Jehovah so commanded and to fight at Armageddon albeit without the use of "carnal weapons" of warfare. The Court concluded that he was opposed to "war in any form," since the war he did not oppose had "neither the bark nor the bite of war as we know it today."[2]

In this case the Court held that the exemption was not available to two men—Negre, a devout Catholic, and Gillette, a Humanist—who were "selective objectors," being opposed only to "unjust" wars, and who viewed the war in Vietnam as unjust. There was no question as to the sincerity of their beliefs, and the Court did not inquire as to whether the basis for their beliefs was religious. It was enough that they were not opposed to "participating personally in any war and all war."

Assuming both Negre's and Gillette's beliefs to be religious, the

---

[1] See pp. 44–50, *supra.*
[2] *Sicurella v. United States,* 348 U.S. 385 (1955).

Court also held that the limitation of the exemption only to those whose religious beliefs reached to all wars did not amount to an establishment of religion or interfere with the free exercise of religion. Douglas did not disagree with the interpretation of the statute, but dissented on the ground that it was unconstitutional, not only as applied to Negre, but also as applied to Gillette, whose Humanist views he apparently did not regard as religious.

MR. JUSTICE DOUGLAS, dissenting.

Gillette's objection is to combat service in the Vietnam war, not to wars in general, and the basis of his objection is his conscience. His objection does not put him into the statutory exemption which extends to one "who, by reason of religious training and belief, is conscientiously opposed to participation in war in any form."

He stated his views as follows:

> "I object to any assignment in the United States Armed Forces while this unnecessary and unjust war is being waged, on the grounds of religious belief specifically 'Humanism.' This essentially means respect and love for man, faith in his inherent goodness and perfectability, and confidence in his capability to improve some of the pains of the human condition."

This position is substantially the same as that of Sisson in *United States v. Sisson,* 297 F. Supp. 902, appeal dismissed, 399 U.S. 267, where the District Court summarized the draftee's position as follows:

> "Sisson's table of ultimate values is moral and ethical. It reflects quite as real, pervasive, durable, and commendable a marshalling of priorities as a formal religion. It is just as much a residue of culture, early training, and beliefs shared by companions and family. What another derives from the discipline of a church, Sisson derives from the discipline of conscience."

There is no doubt that the views of Gillette are sincere, genuine, and profound. The District Court in the present case faced squarely the issue presented in *Sisson* and being unable to distinguish the case on the facts, refused to follow *Sisson.*

The question, Can a conscientious objector, whether his objection be rooted in "religion" or in moral values, be required to kill? has never been answered by the Court.[3] *Hamilton v. Regents,* 293 U.S. 245, did

---

[3] It is probably a universal truth that "the one thing which authority, whether political, social, religious or economic, tends instinctively to fear is the insistence of conscience." Mehta, The Conscience of a Nation or Studies in Gandhism p. ii (Calcutta, 1933).

no more than hold that the Fourteenth Amendment did not require a State to make its university available to one who would not take military training. *United States* v. *Macintosh*, 283 U.S. 605, denied naturalization to a person who "would not promise in advance to bear arms in defense of the United States unless he believed the war to be morally justified."[4] The question of compelling a man to kill against his conscience was not squarely involved. Most of the talk in the majority opinion concerned "serving in the armed forces of the Nation in time of war." Such service can, of course, take place in noncombatant roles. The ruling was that such service is "dependent upon the will of Congress and not upon the scruples of the individual, except as Congress provides." The *dicta* of the Court in the *Macintosh* case squint towards the denial of Gillette's claim, though as I have said, the issue was not squarely presented.

Yet if dicta are to be our guide, my choice is the dicta of Chief Justice Hughes who, dissenting in *Macintosh*, spoke as well for Justices Holmes, Brandeis, and Stone:

> "Nor is there ground, in my opinion, for the exclusion of Professor Macintosh because his conscientious scruples have particular reference to wars believed to be unjust. There is nothing new in such an attitude. Among the most eminent statesmen here and abroad have been those who condemned the action of their country in entering into wars they thought to be unjustified. Agreements for the renunciation of war presuppose a preponderant public sentiment against wars of aggression. If, while recognizing the power of Congress, the mere holding of religious or conscientious scruples against all wars should not disqualify a citizen from holding office in this country, or an applicant otherwise qualified from being admitted to citizenship, there would seem to be no reason why a reservation of religious or conscientious objection to participation in wars believed to be unjust should constitute such a disqualification."

I think the Hughes view is the constitutional view. It is true that the First Amendment speaks of the free exercise of religion, not of the free exercise of conscience or belief. Yet conscience and belief are the main ingredients of First Amendment rights. They are the bedrock of free speech as well as religion. The implied First Amendment right of "conscience" is certainly as high as the "right of association" which we

---

[4] [The precise holding in *Macintosh* as to eligibility for naturalization was overruled in *Girouard* v. *United States*, p. 118, *supra*.]

recognized in *NAACP v. Alabama,* 357 U.S. 449. Some indeed have thought it higher.[5]

Conscience is often the echo of religious faith. But, as [Gillette's] case illustrates, it may also be the product of travail, meditation, or sudden revelation related to a moral comprehension of the dimensions of a problem, not to a religion in the ordinary sense.

[T]he constitutional infirmity in the present Act seems obvious once "conscience" is the guide. As Chief Justice Hughes said in the *Macintosh* case:

> "But, in the forum of conscience, duty to a moral power higher than the State has always been maintained. The reservation of that supreme obligation, as a matter of principle, would unquestionably be made by many of our conscientious and law-abiding citizens. The essence of religion is belief in a relation to God involving duties superior to those arising from any human relation." 283 U.S., at 633–634.

The law as written is a species of those which show an invidious discrimination in favor of religious persons and against others with like scruples. MR. JUSTICE BLACK once said: "The First Amendment has lost much if the religious follower and the atheist are no longer to be judicially regarded as entitled to equal justice under law." *Zorach v. Clauson,* 343 U.S. 306 (dissenting). We said as much in our recent decision in *Epperson v. Arkansas,* 393 U.S. 97, where we struck down as unconstitutional a state law prohibiting the teaching of the doctrine of evolution in the public schools:

> "Government in our democracy, state and national, must be neutral in matters of religious theory, doctrine, and practice. It may not be hostile to any religion or to the advocacy of no-religion; and it may not aid, foster, or promote one religion or religious theory against another or even against the militant opposite. The First

---

[5] See M. Konvitz, Religious Liberty and Conscience 106 (1968); Redlich & Feinberg, Individual Conscience and the Selective Service Objector: The Right Not to Kill, 44 N.Y.U.L. Rev. 875, 891 (1969): "Free expression and the right of personal conscientious belief are closely intertwined. At the core of the first amendment's protection of individual expression is the recognition that such expression represents the oral or written manifestation of conscience. The performance of certain acts, under certain circumstances, involves such a crisis of conscience as to invoke the protection which the first amendment provides for similar manifestations of conscience when expressed in verbal or written expressions of thought. The most awesome act which any society can demand of a citizen's conscience is the taking of a human life."

Amendment mandates governmental neutrality between religion and religion, and between religion and nonreligion."

While there is no Equal Protection Clause in the Fifth Amendment, our decisions are clear that invidious classifications violate due process. *Bolling v. Sharpe*, 347 U.S. 497, held that segregation by race in the public schools was an invidious discrimination, and *Schneider v. Rusk*, 377 U.S. 163, reached the same result based on penalties imposed on naturalized, not nativeborn, citizens. A classification of "conscience" based on a "religion" and a "conscience" based on more generalized, philosophical grounds is equally invidious by reason of our First Amendment standards.

I had assumed that the welfare of the single human soul was the ultimate test of the vitality of the First Amendment.

This is an appropriate occasion to give content to our dictum in *Board of Education v. Barnette* [319 U.S. 642]:

"[F]reedom to differ is not limited to things that do not matter much. . . . The test of its substance is the right to differ as to things that touch the heart of the existing order."

Negre is opposed under his religious training and beliefs to participation in any form in the war in Vietnam. His sincerity is not questioned. His application for a discharge, however, was denied because his religious training and beliefs led him to oppose only a particular war which according to his conscience was unjust.

For the reasons stated, I would reverse [both judgments].

When the Court later reversed a decision denying conscientious objector status to Cassius Clay because of procedural errors, Douglas concurred on a different ground. Clay, a Moslem, had testified that he would not take part in any war "unless declared by Allah himself, or unless it's an Islamic World War, or a Holy War." Hence, for Douglas, "[b]oth Clay and Negre [in the Gillette case] were 'by reason of religious training and belief' conscientiously opposed to participation in war of the character proscribed by their respective religions. That belief is a matter of conscience protected by the First Amendment which Congress has no power to qualify or dilute as it did . . . when it restricted the exemption to those 'conscientiously opposed to participation in war in any form.' "[6]

---

[6] *Clay v. United States*, 403 U.S. 698 (1971).

EHLERT v. UNITED STATES
402 U.S. 99 (1971)

The claim for conscientious objector status could be made at any time before an order to report for induction was mailed and would be ruled on by the registrant's local Selective Service board. The claim could also be made after induction, in which event it was ruled on by the military authorities. A Selective Service regulation provided that the classification of a registrant should not be reopened before the local board after the board had mailed an order to report for induction unless there had been a change in status "resulting from circumstances over which the registrant had no control."

In this case the Court held that a local board was justified in refusing to consider a claim to conscientious objector status filed by a registrant in the interval between his receipt of the order to report for induction and the date set for induction, despite his contention that his conscientious objection had crystallized after receipt of the induction notice. The Court agreed with the board that the regulation should be construed to permit exceptions only for "objectively identifiable" and "extraneous" circumstances relating to other exemptions from service, such as physical injury to the registrant or the death of a brother which left the registrant exempt as the only surviving son.

MR. JUSTICE DOUGLAS, dissenting.

The rather stuffy judicial notion that an inductee's realization that he has a "conscientious" objection to war is not a circumstance over which he has "no control" within the meaning of the Regulation is belied by experience. Saul of Tarsus would be a good witness:[7]

> "Now as he journeyed he approached Damascus, and suddenly a light from heaven flashed about him. And he fell to the ground and heard a voice saying to him, 'Saul, Saul, why do you persecute me?' And he said, 'Who are you, Lord?' And he said, 'I am Jesus, whom you are persecuting; but rise and enter the city, and you will be told what you are to do.'"

The stories of sudden conversion are legion in religious history; and there is no reason why the Selective Service boards should not recognize them, deal with them, and, if sincere, act on them even though they come after notice of induction has been received.

The Court holds that the proper remedy is in-service processing of

[7] 9 Acts 3–6 (rev. Standard ed. 1952).

these claims. That is to say, the claims that come so late, even though they come prior to induction, are to be processed by military rather than by civilian personnel.

This conclusion is not required by the Regulation for, as I have said, sudden conversion is a commonplace in religious experiences. And we deal here with religious, ethical, philosophical attitudes that are commonly summarized in capsule form by reference to "conscience."

It is therefore a *tour de force* for the Court to say that in-service processing by the military is required. Certainly that result is not mandated by the Act.[8] Since it is not, we have a choice in construction which really involves a choice of policy. Faced with that choice we should not hesitate to leave these matters to civilian authorities.

The mind of the military has reacted more violently to the conscientious objector than the mind of the priest or other civilian.

The story of in-service processing of these claims in World War I is an unpleasant one:

> "The phrase 'well-recognized religious sect' was given the most rigorous interpretation, and any who based conscientious objections on political rather than religious foundations got short shrift. Such objectors were either 'shot to death by musketry,' 'imprisoned for long terms by court martial,' or subjected to indignities and physical violence 'by their more patriotic fellows.' "[9]

Another account[10] is substantially the same:

> "In military camp and prison alike, objectors were often subjected to indignities and to physical cruelty. Some were beaten; others were hung by their fingers to the doors of their cells in such a way that their feet barely touched the floor. In one case, an objector who refused to don the army uniform was kept in a damp cell, where he contracted pneumonia and died. His dead body was then dressed in the uniform that in life he had spurned, and, thus attired, was sent home to his family. A number of objectors among the absolutists went on hunger strikes and had to be fed forcibly."

According to the accounts, the treatment of conscientious objectors in World War II was not as severe as in World War I. But the main disciplinary device was to give the man an order and then court-martial

[8] See §6(j): "Nothing contained in this title . . . shall be construed to require any person to be subject to combatant training and service in the armed forces of the United States who, by reason of religious training and belief, is conscientiously opposed to participation in war in any form."

[9] A. Mason, Harlan Fiske Stone: Pillar of the Law 102 (1956).

[10] M. Sibley & P. Jacob, Conscription of Conscience 15 (1952).

him for failure to obey the order. "Here punishment *varied*, but common sentences for objectors were five to ten years, although these were not infrequently reduced on review by Washington. Sentences on the whole were much lighter than those imposed by *courts-martial* during the First World War but more severe, on the average, than those meted out by *civil courts* during the Second World War. Sentences of general courts-martial were served in the several disciplinary barracks of the Army, but in some instances objectors were first sent to a 'rehabilitation center,' where the Army gave prisoners a second chance to 'reform'; if 'reformation' did not take place, they served out their sentences in the disciplinary barracks. Army regulations provided for periodic and automatic clemency reviews, the first during the initial six months of the sentence and subsequent reviews once each year."[11] (Emphasis added.)

[I]n my time[12] every conscientious objector was "fair game" to most top sergeants who considered that he had a "yellow streak" and therefore was a coward or was un-American. The conscientious objector never had an easy time asserting First Amendment rights in the Armed Services.

What might happen to him in the barracks or in the detention center is, of course, not the measure of what would transpire at the hearings. But the military mind is educated in other values; it does not reflect the humanistic, philosophical values most germane to ferreting out First Amendment claims that are genuine.

Moreover, proof of a conscientious objector's claim will usually be much more difficult after induction than before. Military exigencies may take him far from his neighborhood, the only place where he can find the friends and associates who know him. His chances of having a fair hearing are therefore lessened when the hearing on his claim is relegated to in-service procedures. For these reasons I would resolve any ambiguities in the law in favor of pre-induction review of his claim and not relegate him to the regime where military philosophy, rather than the First Amendment, is supreme.

Beyond all these arguments is a constitutional one. Induction itself may violate the privileges of conscience engrained in the First Amendment. A compelled act was the heart of the case presented by *Board of Education v. Barnette*, 319 U.S. 624, when children of Jehovah's Witnesses protested the requirement that they salute the flag.

To some conscientious objectors, taking the one step forward is an act violating the conscience, since wearing the uniform in any form is as

---

[11] *Id.*, at 108.
[12] [Douglas was an acting sergeant in the Army in World War I.]

revolting to them as saluting the flag was to the children in the *Barnette* case. To another conscientious objector the bearing of arms, not acting as orderlies, say, in military hospitals, is the act at which he rebels. The sorting and sifting of these claims and all varieties of them are best processed by civilians rather than the military. The present Regulations permit it and I would resolve any ambiguities in favor of the procedure most protective of the rights of conscience involved here.

JOHNSON v. ROBISON
415 U.S. 361 (1974)

The Veterans' Readjustment Act of 1966 provides educational benefits for those who served in the armed forces, but makes no provision for conscientious objectors who performed alternate civilian service. Robison, a conscientious objector who served two years of alternate civilian service at Peter Bent Brigham Hospital in Boston, brought this action to have the Act declared unconstitutional as infringing on his free exercise of religion under the First Amendment and as discriminatory under the due process clause of the Fifth Amendment. The court below found no violation of the First Amendment but a violation of the Fifth. The Court reversed, finding a violation of neither.

MR. JUSTICE DOUGLAS, dissenting.

In my dissent applicable to *Braunfeld* v. *Brown*, 366 U.S. 599, I expressed the view that Pennsylvania's Sunday closing law was unconstitutional as applied to Sabbatarians. The State imposed a penalty on a a Sabbatarian for keeping his shop open on the day which was the Sabbath of the Christian majority; and that seemed to me to exact an impermissible price for the free exercise of the Sabbatarian's religion. Indeed, in that case the Sabbatarian would be unable to continue in business if he could not stay open on Sunday and would lose his capital investment.

In *Girouard* v. *United States* [p. 118, *supra*] we held, in overruling *United States* v. *Schwimmer*, 279 U.S. 644, that the words of the oath prescribed by Congress for naturalization—"will support and defend the Constitution and laws of the United States of America against all enemies, foreign and domestic"—should not be read as requiring the bearing of arms, as there is room under our Constitution for the support and defense of the Nation in times of great peril by those whose religious scruples bar them from shouldering arms. We said: "The effort of war is indivisible; and those whose religious scruples prevent them from killing are no less patriots than those whose special traits or handicaps result in their assignment to duties far behind the fighting front. Each is making the utmost contribution according to his capacity. The fact that his role may be limited by religious convictions rather than by physical characteristics has no necessary bearing on his attachment to his country or on his willingness to support and defend it to his utmost."

Closer in point to the present problem is *Sherbert* v. *Verner*, 374 U.S. 398, where a Seventh Day Adventist was denied unemployment benefits by the State because she would not work on Saturday, the Sabbath day of her faith. We held that that disqualification for unemployment benefits imposed an impermissible burden on the free exercise of her religion, saying: "Here not only is it apparent that appellant's declared ineligibility for benefits derives solely from the practice of her religion, but the pressure upon her to [forgo] that practice is unmistakable. The ruling forces her to choose between following the precepts of her religion and forfeiting benefits, on the one hand, and abandoning one of the precepts of her religion in order to accept work, on the other hand. Governmental imposition of such a choice puts the same kind of burden upon the free exercise of religion as would a fine imposed against appellant for her Saturday worship."

And we found no "compelling" state interest to justify the State's infringement of one's religious liberty in that manner.

In *Wisconsin* v. *Yoder* [p. 140, *supra*] we held that Wisconsin's compulsory school attendance law as applied to Amish children would gravely impair the free exercise of their religious beliefs.

The District Court in the present case said that the penalty which the present Act places on conscientious objectors is of a lesser "order or magnitude"[13] than that which has been upheld in past cases.

That is true; yet the discrimination against a man with religious scruples seems apparent. The present Act derives from a House bill that had as its purpose solely an education program to "help a veteran to follow the educational plan that he might have adopted had he never entered the Armed Forces." H. R. Rep. No. 1258, 89th Cong., 2d Sess., 5. Full benefits are available to occupants of safe desk jobs and the thousands of veterans who performed civilian type duties at home and for whom the rigors of the "war" were far from "totally disruptive," to use

[13] "First, the denial is felt, not immediately, as in *Sherbert*, but at a point in time substantially removed from that when a prospective conscientious objector must consider whether to apply for an exemption from military service. Secondly, the denial does not produce a positive economic injury of the sort effected by a Sunday closing law or ineligibility for unemployment payments. Considering these factors, the court doubts that the denial tends to make a prospective alternate service performer choose between following and not following the dictates of his conscience."

the Government's phrase. The benefits are provided, though the draftee did not serve overseas but lived with his family in a civilian community and worked from nine until five as a file clerk on a military base or attended college courses in his off-duty hours. No condition of hazardous duty was attached to the educational assistance program. As Senator Yarborough said, the benefits would accrue even to those who never served overseas, because their "educational progress and opportunity" "[have] been impaired in just as serious and damaging a fashion as if they had served on distant shores. Their educational needs are no less than those of their comrades who served abroad."

But the line drawn in the Act is between conscientious objectors who performed alternative civilian service and all other draftees. Such conscientious objectors get no educational benefits whatsoever. It is, indeed, demeaning to those who have religious scruples against shouldering arms to suggest, as the Government does, that those religious scruples must be susceptible of compromise before they will be protected. The urge to forgo religious scruples to gain a monetary advantage would certainly be a burden on the Free Exercise Clause in cases of those who were spiritually weak. But that was not the test in *Sherbert* or *Girouard*. We deal with people whose religious scruples are unwavering. Those who would die at the stake for their religious scruples may not constitutionally be penalized by the Government by the exaction of penalties because of their free exercise of religion. Where Government places a price on the free exercise of one's religious scruples it crosses the forbidden line. The issue of "coercive effects," to use another Government phrase, is irrelevant. Government, as I read the Constitution and the Bill of Rights, may not place a penalty on anyone for asserting his religious scruples. That is the nub of the present case and the reason why the judgment below should be affirmed.

Most of the conduct of members of the armed forces is governed by the congressionally enacted Uniform Code of Military Justice, which in 1950 replaced earlier Articles of War, and which is administered in the first instance by courts-martial staffed by military personnel. The court-martial decisions are subject to review by other military personnel, by some civilian members of the executive branch, including the President, and by a three-judge Court of Military Appeals appointed by the President from civilian life for fifteen-year terms. The federal civil courts in the judicial branch enter the picture when military defendants file petitions for writs of habeas corpus raising questions which go to the jurisdiction of the military tribunals, including a contention that constitutional rights have been violated. But Douglas wrote for the Court to hold that habeas corpus review would not extend to an alleged error by a court-martial in evaluating the evidence on the question of a defendant's insanity defense in a rape case.[14] *The same decision held that there was no constitutional right to have enlisted men sitting on the court-martial—a right which Congress later conferred by statute. Douglas also wrote for the Court when it held that habeas corpus is not available until the defendant has exhausted all avenues of review within the military system.*[15]

Lee v. Madigan
358 u.s. 228 (1959)

A provision in Article 92 of the earlier Articles of War, not carried forward into the Uniform Code of Military Justice, forbade trial by court-martial "for murder or rape committed within the geographical limits of the States of the Union . . . in time of peace." Lee was convicted by a court-martial of conspiracy to commit murder in California on June 10, 1949, after the 1945 cessation of hostilities in World War II but before formal termination of the war with Germany and Japan by Congressional Resolution and Presidential Proclamations in 1951 and 1952. By a petition for habeas corpus he challenged the jurisdiction of the court which had convicted him and he prevailed.

Mr. Justice Douglas delivered the opinion of the Court.

Since June 10, 1949—the critical date involved here—preceded [the congressional and presidential actions], and since no previous action by the political branches of our Government had specifically lifted Article 92 from the "state of war" category, it is argued that we were not then "in time of peace" for the purposes of Article 92. That argument gains support from a *dictum* in *Kahn* v. *Anderson*, 255 U.S. 1, 9–10, that the term "in time of peace" as used in Article 92 "signifies peace in the complete sense, officially declared." Of like tenor are generalized statements that the termination of a "state of war" is "a political act" of the other branches of Government, not the Judiciary. See *Ludecke* v. *Watkins*, 335 U.S. 160. We do not think that either of those authorities is dispositive of the present controversy. A more particularized and discriminating analysis must be made. We deal with a term that must be construed in light of the precise facts of each case and the impact of the particular statute involved. Congress in drafting laws may decide that the Nation may be "at war" for one purpose, and "at peace" for

---

[14] *Whelchel* v. *McDonald*, 340 U.S. 122 (1950).
[15] *Gusik* v. *Schilder*, 340 U.S. 128 (1950).

another. It may use the same words broadly in one context, narrowly in another. The problem of judicial interpretation is to determine whether "in the sense of this law" peace had arrived. *United States* v. *Anderson*, 9 Wall. 56. Only mischief can result if those terms are given one meaning regardless of the statutory context.

In the *Kahn* case, the offense was committed on July 29, 1918, and the trial started November 4, 1918—both dates being before the Armistice. It is, therefore, clear that the offense was not committed "in time of peace." Moreover, a military tribunal whose jurisdiction over a case attaches in a time of actual war does not lose jurisdiction because hostilities cease. Once a military court acquires jurisdiction that jurisdiction continues until the end of the trial and the imposition of the sentence. See *Carter* v. *McClaughry*, 183 U.S. 365. The broad comments of the Court in the *Kahn* case on the meaning of the term "in time of peace" as used in Article 92 were, therefore, quite unnecessary for the decision.

Ludecke v. *Watkins*, 335 U.S. 160, belongs in a special category of cases dealing with the power of the Executive or the Congress to deal with the aftermath of problems which a state of war brings and which a cessation of hostilities does not necessarily dispel. That case concerns the power of the President to remove an alien enemy after hostilities have ended but before the political branches have declared the state of war ended.

Our problem is not controlled by those cases. We deal with the term "in time of peace" in the setting of a grant of power to military tribunals to try people for capital offenses. Did Congress design a broad or a narrow grant of authority? Is the authority of a court-martial to try a soldier for a civil crime, such as murder or rape, to be generously or strictly construed?

We do not write on a clean slate. The attitude of a free society toward the jurisdiction of military tribunals—our reluctance to give them authority to try people for nonmilitary offenses—has a long history.

We reviewed both British and American history, touching on this point, in *Reid* v. *Covert*, 354 U.S. 1. We pointed out the great alarms sounded when James II authorized the trial of soldiers for nonmilitary crimes and the American protests that mounted when British courts-martial impinged on the domain of civil courts in this country. The views of Blackstone on military jurisdiction became deeply imbedded in our thinking: "The necessity of order and discipline in an army is the only thing which can give it countenance; and therefore it ought not to be permitted in time of peace, when the king's courts are open for all persons to receive justice according to the laws of the land."

1 Blackstone's Commentaries 413. We spoke in that tradition in *Toth* v. *Quarles*, 350 U.S. 11, "Free countries of the world have tried to restrict military tribunals to the narrowest jurisdiction deemed absolutely essential to maintaining discipline among troops in active service."

The power to try soldiers for the capital crimes of murder and rape was long withheld. Not until 1863 was authority granted. And then it was restricted to times of "war, insurrection, or rebellion."[16] The theory was that the civil courts, being open, were wholly qualified to handle these cases. As Col. William Winthrop wrote in Military Law and Precedents (2d ed. 1920) 667, about this 1863 law:

> "It's main object evidently was to provide for the punishment of these crimes in localities where, in consequence of military occupation, or the prevalence of martial law, the action of the civil courts is suspended, or their authority can not be exercised with the promptitude and efficiency required by the exigencies of the period and the necessities of military government."

Civil courts were, indeed, thought to be better qualified than military tribunals to try nonmilitary offenses. They have a more deeply engrained judicial attitude, a more thorough indoctrination in the procedural safeguards necessary for a fair trial. Moreover, important constitutional guarantees come into play once the citizen—whether soldier or civilian—is charged with a capital crime such as murder or rape. The most significant of these is the right to trial by jury, one of the most important safeguards against tyranny which our law has designed.[17] We must assume that the Congress, as well as the courts, was alive to the importance of those constitutional guarantees when it gave Article 92 its particular phrasing. Statutory language is construed to conform as near as may be to traditional guarantees that protect the rights of the citizen. We will attribute to Congress a purpose to guard jealously against the dilution of the liberties of the citizen that would result if the jurisdiction of military tribunals were enlarged at the expense of civil courts. General Enoch H. Crowder, Judge Advocate General, in testifying in favor of the forerunner of the present proviso of Article 92, spoke of the protection it extended the officer and soldier by securing

[16] Prior to that time only state courts could try a soldier for murder or rape. *Coleman* v. *Tennessee*, 97 U.S. 509, 514.

[17] [Of the various constitutional guarantees, only the Fifth Amendment's provision for indictment by grand jury contains an express exception for "cases arising in the land or naval forces." But the Sixth Amendment's guarantee of jury trial in "all criminal prosecutions" is held inapplicable to trials before courts-martial. *Kahn* v. *Anderson*, 255 U.S. 1 (1921); *Ex parte Quirin*, 317 U.S. 1 (1942).]

them "a trial by their peers."[18] We think the proviso should be read generously to achieve that end.

We refused in *Duncan* v. *Kahanamoku*, 327 U.S. 304, to construe "martial law," as used in an Act of Congress, broadly so as to supplant all civilian laws and to substitute military for judicial trials of civilians not charged with violations of the law of war. We imputed to Congress an attitude that was more consonant with our tradition of civil liberties. We approach the analysis of the term "in time of peace" as used in Article 92 in the same manner. Whatever may have been the plan of a later Congress in continuing *some* controls long after hostilities ceased, we cannot readily assume that the earlier Congress used "in time of peace" in Article 92 to deny soldiers or civilians the benefit of jury trials for capital offenses four years after all hostilities had ceased. To hold otherwise would be to make substantial rights turn on a fiction. We will not presume that Congress used the words "in time of peace" in that sense. The meaning attributed to them is at war with common sense, destructive of civil rights, and unnecessary for realization of the balanced scheme promulgated by the Articles of War. We hold that June 10, 1949, was "in time of peace" as those words were used in Article 92.

O'CALLAHAN v. PARKER
395 U.S. 258 (1969)

O'Callahan, a sergeant in the United States Army, was convicted by court-martial of housebreaking, attempted rape, and assault with intent to commit rape, all committed on a single victim in a hotel in Honolulu in time of peace while O'Callahan was off his military base on an evening pass.

Mr. Justice Douglas delivered the opinion of the Court.

The Constitution gives Congress power to "make Rules for the Government and Regulation of the land and naval Forces," Art. I, §8, cl. 14, and it recognizes that the exigencies of military discipline require the existence of a special system of military courts in which not all of the specific procedural protections deemed essential in Art. III trials

[18] See S. Rep. No. 130, 64th Cong., 1st Sess., p. 88.
General Crowder was opposed to a proposal of the General Staff that capital crimes even when committed in this country be tried by court-martial as well as by civil courts. He said, "We never have had that law, and I doubt very much whether it is desirable to divorce the Army to that extent from accountability in the civil courts. . . . I think that here in the United States proper the Army should be under the same accountability as civilians for capital crimes." *Id.*, at 32.

need apply. The Fifth Amendment specifically exempts "cases arising *in the land or naval forces,* or in the Militia, when in actual service in time of War or public danger" from the requirement of prosecution by indictment and, inferentially, from the right to trial by jury. (Emphasis supplied.) See *Ex parte Quirin,* 317 U.S. 1, 40. The result has been the establishment and development of a system of military justice with fundamental differences from the practices in the civilian courts.

If the case does not arise *"in the land or naval forces,"* then the accused gets *first,* the benefit of an indictment by a grand jury and *second,* a trial by jury before a civilian court as guaranteed by the Sixth Amendment.

Those civil rights are the constitutional stakes in the present litigation. What we wrote in *Toth* v. *Quarles,* 350 U.S. 11, is worth emphasis:

> "We find nothing in the history or constitutional treatment of military tribunals which entitles them to rank along with Article III courts as adjudicators of the guilt or innocence of people charged with offenses for which they can be deprived of their life, liberty or property. Unlike courts, it is the primary business of armies and navies to fight or be ready to fight wars should the occasion arise. But trial of soldiers to maintain discipline is merely incidental to an army's primary fighting function. To the extent that those responsible for performance of this primary function are diverted from it by the necessity of trying cases, the basic fighting purpose of armies is not served. And conceding to military personnel that high degree of honesty and sense of justice which nearly all of them undoubtedly have, it still remains true that military tribunals have not been and probably never can be constituted in such way that they can have the same kind of qualifications that the Constitution has deemed essential to fair trials of civilians in federal courts. For instance, the Constitution does not provide life tenure for those performing judicial functions in military trials. They are appointed by military commanders and may be removed at will. Nor does the Constitution protect their salaries as it does judicial salaries. Strides have been made toward making courts-martial less subject to the will of the executive department which appoints, supervises and ultimately controls them. But from the very nature of things, courts have more independence in passing on the life and liberty of people than do military tribunals.
>
> "Moreover, there is a great difference between trial by jury and trial by selected members of the military forces. It is true that military personnel because of their training and experience may be

espccially competent to try soldiers for infractions of military rules. Such training is no doubt particularly important where an offense charged against a soldier is purely military, such as disobedience of an order, leaving post, etc. But whether right or wrong, the premise underlying the constitutional method for determining guilt or innocence in federal courts is that laymen are better than specialists to perform this task. This idea is inherent in the institution of trial by jury."

A court-martial is tried, not by a jury of the defendant's peers which must decide unanimously, but by a panel of officers[19] empowered to act by a two-thirds vote. The presiding officer at a court-martial is not a judge whose objectivity and independence are protected by tenure and undiminishable salary and nurtured by the judicial tradition, but is a military law officer.[20] Substantially different rules of evidence and procedure apply in military trials.[21] Apart from those differences, the suggestion of the possibility of influence on the actions of the court-martial by the officer who convenes it, selects its members and the counsel on both sides, and who usually has direct command authority over its members is a pervasive one in military law, despite strenuous efforts to eliminate the danger.

A court-martial is not yet an independent instrument of justice but remains to a significant degree a specialized part of the overall mechanism by which military discipline is preserved.

That a system of specialized military courts, proceeding by practices different from those obtaining in the regular courts and in general less favorable to defendants, is necessary to an effective national defense establishment, few would deny. But the justification for such a system rests on the special needs of the military, and history teaches that expan-

[19] Under Art. 25 of the Uniform Code of Military Justice, at least one-third of the members of the court-martial trying an enlisted man are required to be enlisted men if the accused requests that enlisted personnel be included in the court-martial. In practice usually only senior enlisted personnel, *i.e.*, noncommissioned officers, are selected.

[20] At the time petitioner was tried, a general court-martial was presided over by a "law officer," who was required to be a member of the bar and certified by the Judge Advocate General for duty as a law officer. U. C. M. J. Art. 26(a). The "law officer" could be a direct subordinate of the convening authority. Manual for Courts-Martial, United States, 1951, ¶4g (1). The Military Justice Act of 1968, 82 Stat. 1335, establishes a system of "military judges" intended to insure that where possible the presiding officer of a court-martial will be a professional military judge, not directly subordinate to the convening authority.

[21] For example, in a court-martial, the access of the defense to compulsory process for obtaining evidence and witnesses is, to a significant extent, dependent on the approval of the prosecution.

sion of military discipline beyond its proper domain carries with it a threat to liberty.

We have held in a series of decisions that court-martial jurisdiction cannot be extended to reach any person not a member of the Armed Forces at the times of both the offenses and the trial. Thus, discharged soldiers cannot be court-martialed for offenses committed while in service. *Toth* v. *Quarles*, 350 U.S. 11. Similarly, neither civilian employees of the Armed Forces overseas, *McElroy* v. *Guagliardo*, 361 U.S. 281; *Grisham* v. *Hagan*, 361 U.S. 278; nor civilian dependents of military personnel accompanying them overseas, *Kinsella* v. *Singleton*, 361 U.S. 234; *Reid* v. *Covert*, 354 U.S. 1, may be tried by court-martial.

These cases decide that courts-martial have no jurisdiction to try those who are not members of the Armed Forces, no matter how intimate the connection between their offense and the concerns of military discipline. From these cases, the Government invites us to draw the conclusion that once it is established that the accused is a member of the Armed Forces, lack of relationship between the offense and identifiable military interests is irrelevant to the jurisdiction of a court-martial.

The fact that courts-martial have no jurisdiction over nonsoldiers, whatever their offense, does not necessarily imply that they have unlimited jurisdiction over soldiers, regardless of the nature of the offenses charged. Nor do the cases of this Court suggest any such interpretation. The Government emphasizes that these decisions—especially *Kinsella* v. *Singleton*—establish that liability to trial by court-martial is a question of "status"—"whether the accused in the court-martial proceeding is a person who can be regarded as falling within the term 'land and naval Forces.'" 361 U.S., at 241. But that is merely the beginning of the inquiry, not its end. "Status" is necessary for jurisdiction; but it does not follow that ascertainment of "status" completes the inquiry, regardless of the nature, time, and place of the offense.

It was, therefore, the rule in Britain at the time of the American Revolution that a soldier could not be tried by court-martial for a civilian offense committed in Britain; instead military officers were required to use their energies and office to insure that the accused soldier would be tried before a civil court. Evasion and erosion of the principle that crimes committed by soldiers should be tried according to regular judicial procedure in civil, not military, courts, if any were available, were among the grievances protested by the American Colonists.

Early American practice followed the British model. The Continental Congress, in enacting articles of war in 1776, emphasized the importance of military authority cooperating to insure that soldiers who committed crimes were brought to justice. But it is clear from the context of the provision it enacted that it expected the trials would be in civil courts. The "general article," which punished "[a]ll crimes not capital, and all disorders and neglects, which officers and soldiers may be guilty of, to the prejudice of good order and military discipline, though not mentioned in the foregoing articles of war," was interpreted to embrace only crimes the commission of which had some direct impact on military discipline. While practice was not altogether consistent, during the 19th century court-martial convictions for ordinary civil crimes were from time to time set aside by the reviewing authority on the ground that the charges recited only a violation of the general criminal law and failed to state a military offense.

During the Civil War, Congress provided for military trial of certain civil offenses without regard to their effect on order and discipline, but the act applied only "in time of war, insurrection, or rebellion." In 1916, on the eve of World War I, the Articles of War were revised to provide for military trial, even in peacetime, of certain specific civilian crimes committed by persons "subject to military law" and the general article, Art. 96, was modified to provide for military trial of "all crimes or offenses not capital." In 1950, the Uniform Code of Military Justice extended military jurisdiction to capital crimes as well.

We have concluded that the crime to be under military jurisdiction must be service connected, lest "cases arising in the land or naval forces, or in the Militia, when in actual service in time of War or public danger," as used in the Fifth Amendment, be expanded to deprive every member of the armed services of the benefits of an indictment by a grand jury and a trial by a jury of his peers. The power of Congress to make "Rules for the Government and Regulation of the land and naval Forces," Art. I, §8, cl. 14, need not be sparingly read in order to preserve those two important constitutional guarantees. For it is assumed that an express grant of general power to Congress is to be exercised in harmony with express guarantees of the Bill of Rights. We were advised on oral argument that Art. 134 [of the Uniform Code of Military Justice] is construed by the military to give it power to try a member of the armed services for income tax evasion. This article[22] has been called "a catch-all" that "incorporates almost every Federal penal statute into the Uniform Code." R. Everett, Military Justice in the Armed Forces of the United States 68–69 (1956). The catalogue of cases put within reach of the military is indeed long; and we see no way of saving to service-

[22] ["Though not specifically mentioned in this chapter, all disorders and neglects to the prejudice of good order and discipline in the armed forces, all conduct of a nature to bring discredit upon the armed forces, and crimes and offenses not capital, of which persons subject to this chapter may be guilty, shall be taken cognizance of by a . . . court-martial . . . and shall be punished at the discretion of that court."]

men and servicewomen in any case the benefits of indictment and of trial by jury, if we conclude that this petitioner was properly tried by court-martial.

In the present case petitioner was properly absent from his military base when he committed the crimes with which he is charged. There was no connection—not even the remotest one—between his military duties and the crimes in question. The crimes were not committed on a military post or enclave; or was the person whom he attacked performing any duties relating to the military. Moreover, Hawaii, the situs of the crime, is not an armed camp under military control, as are some of our far-flung outposts.

Finally, we deal with peacetime offenses, not with authority stemming from the war power. Civil courts were open. The offenses were committed within our territorial limits, not in the occupied zone of a foreign country. The offenses did not involve any question of the flouting of military authority, the security of a military post, or the integrity of military property.

We have accordingly decided that since petitioner's crimes were not service connected, he could not be tried by court-martial but rather was entitled to trial by the civilian courts.

Douglas later joined with a unanimous Court to hold that the ruling in O'Callahan *did not apply to a serviceman charged with the rape of the sister of one fellow serviceman and the wife of another, committed on his military base in New Jersey in 1961.*[23]

BURNS v. WILSON
346 U.S. 137 (1953)

Two servicemen, Dennis and Burns, were tried by separate courts-martial on the island of Guam, found guilty of murder and rape, and sentenced to death. They filed petitions for habeas corpus *in a federal district court alleging that they had been denied due process of law in that Dennis was held incommunicado and repeatedly examined over a five-day period until he gave the confession which was introduced against him at his trial, at which time he repudiated it, and that another co-defendant who testified against Burns at his trial was beaten and forced to confess and then promised money and a light sentence if he would implicate the others. The district court dismissed the petitions without a hearing. The court of appeals affirmed after reviewing the evidence taken in the military proceedings.*

The Court also affirmed. Although the same statute confers the

---

[23] *Relford v. Commandant,* U.S. Disciplinary Barracks, 401 U.S. 355 (1971).

habeas corpus *jurisdiction over civil and military courts*,[24] *it was said that "in military habeas corpus the inquiry, the scope of matters open for review, has always been more narrow than in civil cases." The rights of those in the armed forces "must perforce be conditioned to meet certain overriding demands of discipline and duty, and the civil courts are not the agencies which must determine the precise balance to be struck in this adjustment." This meant that, had the military courts refused to consider the petitioners' constitutional claims, the district court should have done so. But where, as here, the military courts had "given fair consideration to" those claims and rejected them, the petitioners were not entitled to try to prove in the district court the same claims they failed to prove in the military courts.*

MR. JUSTICE DOUGLAS, dissenting.

I think petitioners are entitled to a judicial hearing on the circumstances surrounding their confessions.

Congress has power by Art. I, §8, cl. 14 of the Constitution "To make Rules for the Government and Regulation of the land and naval Forces." The rules which Congress has made relative to trials for offenses by military personnel are contained in the Uniform Code of Military Justice. Those rules do not provide for judicial review. But it is clear from our decisions that habeas corpus may be used to review some aspects of a military trial.

The question whether the military tribunal has exceeded the powers granted it by Congress may be tested by habeas corpus. See *Hiatt* v. *Brown*, 339 U.S. 103; *Whelchel* v. *McDonald* [note 14, *supra*]; *Gusik* v. *Schilder* [note 15, *supra*]. But it is also clear that that review is not limited to questions of "jurisdiction" in the historic sense.

Of course the military tribunals are not governed by the procedure for trials prescribed in the Fifth and Sixth Amendments. That is the meaning of *Ex parte Quirin*, 317 U.S. 1, holding that indictment by grand jury and trial by jury are not constitutional requirements for trials before military commissions. Nor do the courts sit in review of the weight of the evidence before the military tribunal. *Whelchel* v. *McDonald*, *supra*. But never have we held that all the rights covered by the Fifth and the Sixth Amendments were abrogated by Art. I, §8, cl. 14 of the Constitution, empowering Congress to make rules for the armed forces. I think it plain from the text of the Fifth Amendment that that position is untenable. The Fifth Amendment provides:

[24] "Writs of habeas corpus may be granted by the Supreme Court, any justice thereof, the district courts and any circuit judge. . . . The writ of habeas corpus shall not extend to a prisoner unless . . . [h]e is in custody in violation of the Constitution or laws or treaties of the United States. . . ."

"No person shall be held to answer for a capital, or otherwise infamous crime, unless on a presentment or indictment of a Grand Jury, except in cases arising in the land or naval forces, or in the Militia, when in actual service in time of War or public danger; nor shall any person be subject for the same offence to be twice put in jeopardy of life or limb; nor shall be compelled in any criminal case to be a witness against himself, nor be deprived of life, liberty, or property, without due process of law; nor shall private property be taken for public use, without just compensation."

What reason is there for making one specific exception for cases arising in the land or naval forces or in the militia if none of the Fifth Amendment is applicable to military trials? Since the requirement for indictment before trial is the only provision of the Fifth Amendment made inapplicable to military trials, it seems to me clear that the other relevant requirements of the Fifth Amendment (including the ban on coerced confessions) are applicable to them. And if the ban on coerced confessions is applicable, how can it mean one thing in civil trials and another in military trials?

The prohibition against double jeopardy is one of those provisions. And consistently with the construction I urge, we held in *Wade* v. *Hunter*, 336 U.S. 684, 690, that court-martial action was subject to that requirement of the Fifth Amendment. The mandates that no person be compelled to be a witness against himself or be deprived of life or liberty without due process of law are as specific and as clear. They too, as the Court of Appeals held, are constitutional requirements binding on military tribunals.

If a prisoner is coerced by torture or other methods to give the evidence against him, if he is beaten or slowly "broken" by third-degree methods, then the "trial" before the military tribunal becomes an empty ritual. The real trial takes place in secret where the accused without benefit of counsel succumbs to physical or psychological pressures. A soldier or sailor convicted in that manner has been denied due process of law; and, like the accused in criminal cases, he should have relief by way of habeas corpus.

The opinion of the Court is not necessarily opposed to this view. But the Court gives binding effect to the ruling of the military tribunal on the constitutional question, provided it has given fair consideration to it.

If the military agency has fairly and conscientiously applied the standards of due process formulated by this Court, I would agree that a rehash of the same facts by a federal court would not advance the cause of justice. But where the military reviewing agency has not done that, a court should entertain the petition for habeas corpus. In the first place, the military tribunals in question are federal agencies subject to no other judicial supervision except what is afforded by the federal courts. In the second place, the rules of due process which they apply are constitutional rules which we, not they, formulate.

The *undisputed* facts in this case make a prima facie case that our rule on coerced confessions expressed in *Watts v. Indiana*, 338 U.S. 49, was violated here.[25] No court has considered the question whether repetitious questioning over a period of 5 days while the accused was held incommunicado without benefit of counsel violated the Fifth Amendment. The highest reviewing officer, the Judge Advocate General of the Air Force, said only this:

> "After reading and re-reading the record of trial, there is no reasonable doubt in my mind that all the confessions were wholly voluntary, as the court decided, and were properly admitted. Where the evidence as to whether there was coercion is conflicting, or where different inferences may fairly be drawn from the admitted facts, the question whether a confession was voluntary is for the triers of the facts. Thus the court's decision on the voluntary nature of the testimony, arrived at from first-hand hearing and observation, is presumptively correct and will not be disturbed unless manifestly erroneous."

There has been at no time any considered appraisal of the facts surrounding these confessions in light of our opinions. Before these men go to their death, such an appraisal should be made.

PARKER v. LEVY
417 U.S. 733 (1974)

Howard Levy, a drafted doctor serving in the Army as Chief of the Dermatological Service at a hospital on an Army base, refused to obey the order of a superior officer that he help to train aid men for Special Forces. He also made public statements to enlisted men that blacks should refuse to go to Vietnam, and if sent, should refuse to fight, since blacks were given the most hazardous duty and suffered the heaviest casualties, and that "Special Forces personnel are liars and thieves and killers of peasants and murderers of women and children."

For his refusal to obey the training order he was convicted by a court-martial of a violation of Article 90 of the Uniform Code of

[25] [*Watts* upset a state murder conviction because it was based on a confession obtained by holding the accused incommunicado for six days while he was interrogated by relays of police officers.]

Military Justice, which makes it an offense willfully to disobey a lawful command of a superior officer. For his public statements he was convicted by the same court-martial of violation of Article 134, which punishes "all disorders and neglects to the prejudice of good order and discipline in the armed forces,"[26] and of Article 133, which provides punishment for "conduct unbecoming an officer and a gentleman." When he sought relief by habeas corpus, *the court of appeals below ruled that Articles 133 and 134 were void for vagueness under Supreme Court decisions invalidating under the due process clause other criminal statutes which were not drawn with sufficient clarity to provide a reasonably ascertainable standard of guilt. With respect to the conviction under Article 90, the court of appeals held that the joint consideration of that charge with the two invalid charges had given rise to a reasonable probability that his trial on the Article 90 charge was prejudiced so that a new trial was required.*

The Court reversed the action of the court of appeals. Because the military is, "by necessity, a specialized society separate from civilian society" whose "law is that of obedience," the Code of Military Justice could not be equated to a civilian criminal code; the former "essays more varied regulation of a much larger segment of the activities of the more tightly knit military community." Congress is permitted to "legislate both with greater breadth and with greater flexibility" when prescribing rules for the military. Moreover, even if Articles 133 and 134 might be too vague in other applications, Levy could have had no reasonable doubt that his statements were both "unbecoming to an officer and a gentlemen" and "to the prejudice of good order and discipline in the armed forces."

While Levy was "not excluded from the protection granted by the First Amendment, the different character of the military community and of the military mission requires a different application of those protections" since "[s]peech that is protected in the civil population may nonetheless undermine the effectiveness of response to command." And Levy, "a commissioned officer publicly urging enlisted personnel to refuse to obey orders which might send them into combat, was unprotected under the most expansive notions of the First Amendment."

MR. JUSTICE DOUGLAS, dissenting.

So far as I can discover the only express exemption of a person in the Armed Services from the protection of the Bill of Rights is that contained in the Fifth Amendment which dispenses with the need for "a presentment or indictment" of a grand jury "in cases arising in

---

[26] See note 22, *supra.*

the land or naval forces, or in the Militia, when in actual service in time of War or public danger."

By practice and by construction the words "all criminal prosecutions" in the Sixth Amendment do not necessarily cover all military trials. One result is that the guarantee of the Sixth Amendment of trial "by an impartial jury" is not applicable to military trials.[3] But Judge Ferguson in *United States* v. *Tempia*, 16 U. S. C. M. A. 629, properly said:[27]

> "[B]oth the Supreme Court and this Court itself are satisfied as to the applicability of constitutional safeguards to military trials, except insofar as they are made inapplicable either expressly or by necessary implication. The Government, therefore, is correct in conceding the point, and the Judge Advocate General, United States Navy, as *amicus curiae*, is incorrect in his contrary conclusion. Indeed, as to the latter, it would appear from the authorities on which he relies that the military courts applied what we now know as the constitutional protection against self-incrimination in trials prior to and contemporaneous with the adoption of the Constitution. Hence, we find Major Andre being extended the privilege at his court-martial in 1780. Wigmore, Evidence, 3d ed, §2251. The same reference was made in the trial of Commodore James Barron in 1808. Proceedings of the General Court Martial Convened for the Trial of Commodore James Barron (1822), page 98. And, the Articles of War of 1776, as amended May 31, 1786, provided for objection by the judge advocate to any question put to the accused, the answer to which might tend to incriminate him. See Winthrop's Military Law and Precedents, 2d ed, 1920 Reprint, pages 196, 972."

But the cases we have had so far have concerned only the nature of the tribunal which may try a person and/or the procedure to be followed. This is the first case that presents to us a question of what protection, if any, the First Amendment gives people in the Armed Services:

[27] The Court of Military Appeals has held that the "probable cause" aspect of the Fourth Amendment is applicable to military trials. See, *e.g., United States* v. *Battista*, 14 U.S.C.M.A. 70; *United States* v. *Gebhart*, 10 U.S.C.M.A. 606; *United States* v. *Brown*, 10 U.S.C.M.A. 482.

It has been held that the right to counsel under the Sixth Amendment extends to military trials, see *United States* v. *Culp*, 14 U.S.C.M.A. 199 (opinions of Quinn, C. J., Ferguson, J.).

There are rulings also that freedom of speech protects, to some extent at least, those in the Armed Services. *United States* v. *Wysong*, 9 U.S.C.M.A. 249, and see *United States* v. *Gray*, 20 U.S.C.M.A. 63.

"Congress shall make no law . . . abridging the freedom of speech, or of the press."

On its face there are no exceptions—no preferred classes for whose benefit the First Amendment extends, no exempt classes.

The military by tradition and by necessity demands discipline; and those necessities require obedience in training and in action. A command is speech brigaded with action, and permissible commands may not be disobeyed. There may be a borderland or penumbra that in time can be established by litigated cases.

I cannot imagine, however, that Congress would think it had the power to authorize the military to curtail the reading list of books, plays, poems, periodicals, papers, and the like which a person in the Armed Services may read. Nor can I believe Congress would assume authority to empower the military to suppress conversations at a bar, ban discussions of public affairs, prevent enlisted men or women or draftees from meeting in discussion groups at times and places and for such periods of time that do not interfere with the performance of military duties.

Congress has taken no such step here. By Art. 133 it has allowed punishment for "conduct unbecoming an officer and a gentleman." In our society where diversities are supposed to flourish it never could be "unbecoming" to express one's views, even on the most controversial public issue.

Article 134 covers only "all disorders and neglects to the prejudice of good order and discipline in the armed forces, all conduct of a nature to bring discredit upon the armed forces."

Captain Levy, the appellee in the present case, was not convicted under Arts. 133 and 134 for failure to give the required medical instructions. But as he walked through the facilities and did his work, or met with students, he spoke of his views of the "war" in Vietnam.

[His] ideas affronted some of his superiors. The military, of course, tends to produce homogenized individuals who think—as well as march—in unison. In *United States* v. *Blevens*, 5 U.S.C.M.A. 480, the Court of Military Appeals upheld the court-martial conviction of a serviceman who had "affiliated" himself with a Communist organization in Germany. The serviceman argued that there was no allegation that he possessed any intent to overthrow the Government by force, so that the Smith Act would not reach his conduct. The Court of Military Appeals affirmed on the theory that his affiliation, nonetheless, brought "discredit" on the Armed Forces within the meaning of Art. 134:

"Most important to the case is the Government's contention that regardless of any deficiencies under the Smith Act, the specification properly alleges, and the evidence adequately establishes, conduct to the discredit of the armed forces, in violation of Article 134.

"Membership by a school teacher in an organization advocating the violent disestablishment of the United States Government has been regarded as conduct requiring dismissal. Adler v. Board of Education [p. 212, *supra*]. It seems to us that such membership is even more profoundly evil in the case of a person in the military establishment. True, affiliation implies something less than membership but the supreme duty of the military is the protection and security of the government and of the people. Hence, aside from a specific intent on the part of the accused to overthrow the government by violence, the conduct alleged is definitely discrediting to the armed forces."

The limitations on expressions of opinion by members of the military continue to date. During the Vietnam war, a second lieutenant in the reserves, off duty, out of uniform, and off base near a local university, carried a placard in an antiwar demonstration which said "END JOHNSON'S FACIST [*sic*] AGGRESSION IN VIET NAM." He was convicted by a court-martial under Art. 88 for using "contemptuous words" against the President and under Art. 133 for "conduct unbecoming an officer." The Court of Military Appeals affirmed, theorizing that suppression of such speech was essential to prevent a military "man on a white horse" from challenging "civilian control of the military." *United States* v. *Howe*, 17 U.S.C.M.A. 165.

The power to draft an army includes, of course, the power to curtail considerably the "liberty" of the people who make it up. But Congress in these articles has not undertaken to cross the forbidden First Amendment line. Making a speech or comment on one of the most important and controversial public issues of the past two decades cannot by any stretch of dictionary meaning be included in "disorders and neglects to the prejudice of good order and discipline in the armed forces." Nor can what Captain Levy said possibly be "conduct of a nature to bring discredit upon the armed forces." He was uttering his own belief—an article of faith that he sincerely held. This was no mere ploy to perform a "subversive" act. Many others who loved their country shared his views. They were not saboteurs. Uttering one's beliefs is sacrosanct under the First Amendment. Punishing the utterances is an "abridgment" of speech in the constitutional sense.

9

EQUAL TREATMENT

The Fourteenth Amendment provides that "No State . . shall deprive any person of life, liberty, or property, without due process of law; nor deny to any person within its jurisdiction the equal protection of the laws." The Fifth Amendment, applicable to the federal government, contains a due process clause but no equal protection clause.

The Court's interpretation of the equal protection clause of the Fourteenth Amendment, along with the Fifteenth and Nineteenth Amendments, to require substantive equality in voting rights is de scribed in Chapter 2. In a variety of other contexts the Court has also dealt with constitutional requirements that the government act with an even hand.

WHEELING STEEL CORP. v. GLANDER
337 U.S. 562 (1949)

The Court has consistently read the word "person" in the Fourteenth Amendment's due process and equal protection clauses to include corporations. Before Douglas came to the Court, Justice Black challenged that interpretation, contending (1) that as a matter of history the purpose of this post–Civil War Amendment was to give citizenship to and provide fair and equal treatment for blacks, and (2) that as a matter of language the Fourteenth Amendment also used the word "person" in conferring citizenship, in apportioning representatives among the states, and in imposing limitations on who could serve as senators and representatives—uses of the term which clearly did not include corporations.[1]

In this case the Court sustained the contentions of a Delaware and a Virginia corporation, both doing business in Ohio, that Ohio had violated the equal protection clause by imposing on their notes and accounts receivable derived from shipments of goods originating in Ohio an ad valorem tax which was not imposed on the notes and accounts receivable of Ohio corporations.

---

[1] *Connecticut General Life Ins. Co. v. Johnson*, 303 U.S. 77 (1938).

MR. JUSTICE DOUGLAS, dissenting.

It has been implicit in all of our decisions since 1886 that a corporation is a "person" within the meaning of the Equal Protection Clause of the Fourteenth Amendment. *Santa Clara County* v. *Southern Pac. R. Co.,* 118 U.S. 394, so held. The Court was cryptic in its decision. It was so sure of its ground that it wrote no opinion on the point, Chief Justice Waite announcing from the bench:

> "The court does not wish to hear argument on the question whether the provision in the Fourteenth Amendment to the Constitution, which forbids a State to deny to any person within its jurisdiction the equal protection o᾿ the laws, applies to these corporations. We are all of opinion that it does᾿·

There was no history, logic, or reason given to support that view. Nor was the result so obvious that exposition was unnecessary.

The Fourteenth Amendment became a part of the Constitution in 1868. In 1871 a corporation claimed that Louisiana had imposed on it a tax that violated the Equal Protection Clause of the new Amendment. Mr. Justice Woods (then Circuit Judge) held that "person" as there used did not include a corporation and added, "This construction of the section is strengthened by the history of the submission by congress, and the adoption by the states of the 14th amendment, so fresh in all minds as to need no rehearsal." *Insurance Co.* v. *New Orleans,* 1 Woods 85.

What was obvious to Mr. Justice Woods in 1871 was still plain to the Court in 1873. Mr. Justice Miller in the *Slaughter-House Cases,* 16 Wall. 36, adverted to events "almost too recent to be called history" to show that the purpose of the Amendment was to protect human rights—primarily the rights of a race which had just won its freedom. And as respects the Equal Protection Clause he stated, "The existence of laws in the States where the newly emancipated negroes resided, which discriminated with gross injustice and hardship against them as a class, was the evil to be remedied by this clause, and by it such laws are forbidden."

Moreover what was clear to these earlier judges was apparently plain to the people who voted to make the Fourteenth Amendment a part of our Constitution. For as MR. JUSTICE BLACK pointed out in his dissent in *Connecticut General Co.* v. *Johnson* [note 1, *supra*], the submission of the Amendment to the people was on the basis that it protected human beings. There was no suggestion in its submission that it was designed to put negroes and corporations into one class and so dilute the police power of the States over corporate affairs.

Arthur Twining Hadley once wrote that "The Fourteenth Amendment was framed to protect the negroes from oppression by the whites, not to protect corporations from oppression by the legislature. It is doubtful whether a single one of the members of Congress who voted for it had any idea that it would touch the question of corporate regulation at all."[2]

Both Mr Justice Woods in *Insurance Co.* v. *New Orleans, supra,* and MR. JUSTICE BLACK in his dissent in *Connecticut General Co.* v. *Johnson, supra,* have shown how strained a construction it is of the Fourteenth Amendment so to hold. Section 1 of the Amendment provides:

> "All *persons* born or naturalized in the United States, and subject to the jurisdiction thereof, are *citizens* of the United States and of the State wherein they reside. No State shall make or enforce any law which shall abridge the privileges or immunities of *citizens* of the United States; nor shall any State deprive any *person* of life, liberty, or property, without due process of law; nor deny to any *person* within its jurisdiction the equal protection of the laws." (Italics added.)

"Persons" in the first sentence plainly includes only human beings, for corporations are not "born or naturalized."

Corporations are not "citizens" with the meaning of the first clause of the second sentence. *Western Turf Assn.* v. *Greenberg,* 204 U.S. 359, 363; *Selover, Bates & Co.* v. *Walsh,* 226 U.S. 112, 126.

It has never been held that they are persons whom a State may not deprive of "life" within the meaning of the second clause of the second sentence.

"Liberty" in that clause is "the liberty of natural, not artificial, persons." *Western Turf Assn.* v. *Greenberg, supra.*

But "property" as used in that clause has been held to include that of a corporation since 1889 when *Minneapolis & St. L. R. Co.* v. *Beckwith,* 129 U.S. 26, was decided.

It requires distortion to read "person" as meaning one thing, then another within the same clause and from clause to clause. It means,

[2] The Constitutional Position of Property in America, 64 Independent 834, 836 (1908). He went on to say that the *Dartmouth College* case (4 Wheat. 518) and the construction given the Fourteenth Amendment in the *Santa Clara* case "have had the effect of placing the modern industrial corporation in an almost impregnable constitutional position." *Id.,* p. 836.

As to whether the framers of the Amendment may have had such an undisclosed purpose, see Graham, The "Conspiracy Theory" of the Fourteenth Amendment, 47 Yale L. J. 371.

in my opinion, a substantial revision of the Fourteenth Amendment. As to the matter of construction, the sense seems to me to be with Mr. Justice Woods in *Insurance Co. v. New Orleans, supra,* where he said, "The plain and evident meaning of the section is, that the persons to whom the equal protection of the law is secured are persons born or naturalized or endowed with life and liberty, and consequently natural and not artificial persons."

History has gone the other way. Since 1886 the Court has repeatedly struck down state legislation as applied to corporations on the ground that it violated the Equal Protection Clause. Every one of our decisions upholding legislation as applied to corporations over the objection that it violated the Equal Protection Clause has assumed that they are entitled to the constitutional protection. But in those cases it was not necessary to meet the issue since the state law was not found to contain the elements of discrimination which the Equal Protection Clause condemns. But now that the question is squarely presented I can only conclude that the *Santa Clara* case was wrong and should be overruled.

One hesitates to overrule cases even in the constitutional field that are of an old vintage. But that has never been a deterrent heretofore[3] and should not be now.

We are dealing with a question of vital concern to the people of the nation. It may be most desirable to give corporations this protection from the operation of the legislative process. But that question is not for us. It is for the people. It they want corporations to be treated as humans are treated, if they want to grant corporations this large degree of emancipation from state regulation, they should say so. The Constitution provides a method by which they may do so. We should not do it for them through the guise of interpretation.

LEVY V. LOUISIANA
391 U.S. 68 (1968)

All states have some type of Wrongful Death Act under which one who wrongfully causes the death of another is liable to specified relatives or the estate of the deceased. The Louisiana statute provides for liability to "the surviving spouse and child or children." This action was

---

[3] *In re Ayers,* 123 U.S. 443, overruled in part *Osborn v. United States Bank,* 9 Wheat. 738, a decision 63 years old; *Leisy v. Hardin,* 135 U.S. 100, overruled *Peirce v. New Hampshire,* 5 How. 504, a decision 42 years old. *Erie R. Co. v. Tompkins,* 304 U.S. 64, overruled *Swift v. Tyson,* 16 Pet. 1, a decision 95 years old; *Graves v. N.Y. ex rel. O'Keefe,* 306 U.S. 466, overruled *Collector v. Day,* 11 Wall. 113, a decision 68 years old. *United States v. Underwriters Assn.,* 322 U.S. 533, overruled in part *Paul v. Virginia,* 8 Wall. 168, a decision 75 years old.

brought in a Louisiana court on behalf of five illegitimate children of Louise Levy against a doctor and his insurance company on the theory that the doctor's malpractice had caused her death. The action was dismissed because the Louisiana courts construe the word "child" in their statute to mean only a legitimate child, the exclusion of illegitimates being "based on morals and general welfare because it discourages bringing children into the world out of wedlock."

MR. JUSTICE DOUGLAS delivered the opinion of the Court.

We assume in the present state of the pleadings that the mother, Louise Levy, gave birth to these five illegitimate children and that they lived with her; that she treated them as a parent would treat any other child; that she worked as a domestic servant to support them, taking them to church every Sunday and enrolling them, at her own expense, in a parochial school.

We start from the premise that illegitimate children are not "nonpersons." They are humans, live, and have their being. They are clearly "persons" within the meaning of the Equal Protection Clause of the Fourteenth Amendment.

While a State has broad power when it comes to making classifications, it may not draw a line which constitutes an invidious discrimination against a particular class. Though the test has been variously stated, the end result is whether the line drawn is a rational one.

In applying the Equal Protection Clause to social and economic legislation, we give great latitude to the legislature in making classifications. Even so, would a corporation, which is a "person," for certain purposes, within the meaning of the Equal Protection Clause be required to forgo recovery for wrongs done its interests because its incorporators were all bastards? However that might be, we have been extremely sensitive when it comes to basic civil rights and have not hesitated to strike down an invidious classification even though it had history and tradition on its side. (*Brown* v. *Board of Education* [note 21, *infra*]). The rights asserted here involve the intimate, familial relationship between a child and his own mother. When the child's claim of damage for loss of his mother is in issue, why, in terms of "equal protection," should the tortfeasors go free merely because the child is illegitimate? Why should the illegitimate child be denied rights merely because of his birth out of wedlock? He certainly is subject to all the responsibilities of a citizen, including the payment of taxes and conscription under the Selective Service Act. How under our constitutional regime can he be denied correlative rights which other citizens enjoy?

Legitimacy or illegitimacy of birth has no relation to the nature of the wrong allegedly inflicted on the mother. These children, though illegitimate, were dependent on her; she cared for them and nurtured them; they were indeed hers in the biological and in the spiritual sense; in her death they suffered wrong in the sense that any dependent would.

We conclude that it is invidious to discriminate against them when no action, conduct, or demeanor of theirs[4] is possibly relevant to the harm that was done the mother.

In a companion case Douglas again wrote for the Court to hold that Louisiana also violated the equal-protection clause when it denied a mother recovery for the wrongful death of an illegitimate child while allowing such recovery for the wrongful death of legitimate children.[5] But the Court later found no unconstitutional infirmity in a Louisiana law which provided that an illegitimate child could not inherit property from its father where the father died without leaving a will and where other relatives survived, although, if the father during his lifetime has executed a document publicly acknowledging the child as his, he could then leave the child property by will. This law, as applied to a publicly acknowledged child whose father died without a will, did discriminate against illegitimate children, and other Louisiana statutes discriminated in a similar way against concubines. But this was held to be a constitutionally permissible discrimination because "[t]he social difference between a wife and a concubine is analogous to the difference between a legitimate and an illegitimate child," and the state was entitled to distinguish between licit and illicit relationships. Douglas joined in a dissenting opinion which protested that the Court was allowing Louisiana to punish "illegitimate children for the misdeeds of their parents" and that "only a moral prejudice, prevalent in 1825 when the . . . statutes under consideration were adopted, can support" such discrimination.[6]

ALEXANDER V. LOUISIANA
405 U.S. 625 (1972)

Since 1968 the federal Judicial Code has provided that no citizen shall be excluded from service on a grand or petit jury in the federal district court "on account of race, color, religion, sex, national origin, or

---

[4] We can say with Shakespeare: "Why bastard, wherefore base? When my dimensions are as well compact, My mind as generous, and my shape as true, As honest madam's issue? Why brand they us With base? with baseness? bastardy? base, base?" King Lear, Act I, Scene 2.

[5] *Glona* v. *American Guarantee & Liability Ins. Co.,* 391 U.S. 73 (1968).

[6] *Labine* v. *Vincent,* 401 U.S. 532 (1971).

economic status." Earlier the prohibition ran only against exclusions on account of "race, color, or previous condition of servitude," but the Code also provided that federal jurors should have the same qualifications as those prescribed by the states. In 1946 Douglas wrote for the Court to invalidate federal fraud convictions of a mother and son in California, where women were eligible for jury service, because women had been intentionally and systematically excluded from both the grand jury which indicted them and the petit jury which convicted them.[7] He also voted with the Court to invalidate the use in federal civil cases of juries from which wage earners had been intentionally and systematically excluded.[8] But he dissented when the Court sanctioned the use, in state criminal prosecutions, of "blue ribbon juries" because he read the equal protection clause to guarantee a jury "impartially drawn from a cross-section of the community."[9]

In 1961 the Court affirmed the Florida conviction of a woman for second-degree murder of her husband despite the fact that she had been convicted by an all-male jury. Florida did not bar women from jury service, but had a statute providing that women would not be called unless they voluntarily registered for jury duty. The Court concluded both (1) that the difference in treatment of men and women was reasonable because "woman is still regarded as the center of home and family" and (2) that there was no showing that the state had "arbitrarily undertaken to exclude women from jury service." Douglas concurred on the second ground only.[10] And he had dissented when the Court held that a state did not violate the equal-protection clause by denying a woman a license to work as a bartender unless she was the "wife or daughter of the male owner" of a licensed liquor establishment.[11]

Only four months before the present case was decided, a unanimous Court had invalidated a state statute providing that, as between persons equally entitled to administer the estates of decedents, males must be preferred to females. Recognizing that the statute would work to eliminate litigation between persons equally entitled (here the divorced parents of the deceased), the Court nonetheless concluded that the state could not eliminate controversy by "the very kind of arbitrary legislative choice forbidden by" the equal protection clause.[12]

[7] *Ballard* v. *United States*, 329 U.S. 187 (1946).
[8] *Thiel* v. *Southern Pacific Co.*, 328 U.S. 217 (1946).
[9] *Fay* v. *New York*, 332 U.S. 261 (1947); *Moore* v. *New York*, 333 U.S. 565 (1948).
[10] *Hoyt* v. *Florida*, 368 U.S. 57 (1961).
[11] *Goesaert* v. *Cleary*, 335 U.S. 464 (1948).
[12] *Reed* v. *Reed*, 404 U.S. 71 (1971).

In this case Alexander, a black, was convicted in Louisiana of rape and sentenced to life imprisonment. He challenged the conviction on the ground that blacks were included in only token numbers, and women were excluded entirely, from the venire from which was drawn the grand jury that indicted him.

It appeared that the all-white jury commission for the parish compiled a list of names, sent out to all on the list questionnaires which included a question as to race, received back some 7,000 questionnaires (none from women, although 52 percent of the adults in the parish were women, and 14 percent from blacks, although 21 percent of the adults were black); it then reduced the number to 2,000, ostensibly by eliminating those ineligible for or exempt from jury duty, and then selected 400 of these, purportedly at random, from which the 20-member venire was selected. When Alexander's grand jury of 12 was selected, it was composed entirely of white males. Louisiana also had a statute, like the one involved in the Hoyt *case [note 10, supra], exempting women from jury service unless they volunteered for it.*

The Court found that blacks had been deliberately and systematically discriminated against in the selection of the grand jury and reversed the conviction for that reason. It declined to rule on Alexander's further contention that women had been similarly discriminated against.

Mr. Justice Douglas, concurring.

While I join Part I of the Court's opinion, I am convinced we should also reach the constitutionality of Louisiana's exclusion of women from jury service. The issue is squarely presented, it has been thoroughly briefed and argued, and it is of recurring importance. The Court purports to follow "our usual custom" of avoiding unnecessary constitutional issues. But that cannot be the sole rationale, for both questions are of constitutional dimension. We could just as well say that deciding the constitutionality of excluding women from juries renders it unnecessary to reach the question of racial exclusion.

It can be argued that the racial exclusion admits of the "easier" analysis. But this Court does not sit to decide only "easy" questions. And even when faced with "hard" constitutional questions, we have often decided cases on alternate grounds where a decision on only one would have been dispositive. See, *e.g.,* Dunn v. *Blumstein, ante,* p. 330.

Petitioner complains of the exclusion of blacks and women from the grand jury which indicted him. Conceivably, he could have also complained of the exclusion of several other minority groups. Would he then be relegated to suffer repetitive re-indictment and re-conviction while this court considered the exclusion of each group in a separate lawsuit?

I would here reach the question we reserved in *Hoyt* v. *Florida* [note 10, *supra*] and hold that [the statute exempting women from jury duty unless they volunteer], as applied to exclude women as a class from Lafayette Parish jury rolls, violated petitioner Alexander's constitutional right to an impartial jury drawn from a group representative of a cross-section of the community.

It is irrelevant to our analysis that Alexander attacks the composition of the grand jury that indicted him, not the petit jury which convicted him, for it is clear that a State which has a grand jury procedure must administer that system consonantly with the Federal Constitution. [T]his Court has said time and again, regardless of a State's freedom to reject the federal grand jury, and to reject even the petit jury for offenses punishable by less than six months' imprisonment, *Baldwin* v. *New York*, 399 U.S. 66, "Once the State chooses to provide grand and petit juries, whether or not constitutionally required to do so, it must hew to federal constitutional criteria. . . ." *Carter* v. *Jury Commission*, 396 U.S. 320.

It is furthermore clear that just such a "federal constitutional criteri[on]" is that the grand jury, just as the petit jury, must be drawn from a representative cross-section of the community. The Court was speaking of both grand and petit juries in *Carter* v. *Jury Commission*, *supra*, when, quoting *Smith* v. *Texas*, 311 U.S. 128, it *defined* the jury as "a body truly representative of the community." The Court was speaking of grand and petit juries when it said in *Brown* v. *Allen*, 344 U.S. 443: "Our duty to protect the federal constitutional rights of all does not mean we must or should impose on states our conception of the proper source of jury lists, *so long as the source reasonably reflects a cross-section of the population* suitable in character and intelligence for that civic duty." (Emphasis supplied.) As Mr. Justice Black said, speaking for the Court in *Pierre* v. *Louisiana*, 306 U.S. 354: "Indictment by Grand Jury and trial by jury cease to harmonize with our traditional concepts of justice at the very moment particular groups, classes or races . . . are excluded as such from jury service."

This is precisely the constitutional infirmity of the Louisiana statute. For a jury list from which women have been systematically excluded is not representative of the community.

"It is said, however, that an all male panel drawn from the various groups within a community will be as truly representative as if women were included. The thought is that the factors which tend to influence the action of women are the same as those which influence the action of men—personality, background, economic status—and not sex. Yet it is not enough to say that women when sitting as jurors neither act nor tend to act as a class. Men likewise do not act as a class. But, if the shoe were on the other foot, who would claim that a jury was truly representative of the community if all men were intentionally and systematically excluded from the panel? The truth is that the two sexes are not fungible; a community made up exclusively of one is different from a community composed of both; the subtle interplay of influence one on the other is among the imponderables. To insulate the courtroom from either may not in a given case make an iota of difference. Yet a flavor, a distinct quality is lost of either sex is excluded. *The exclusion of one may indeed make the jury less representative of the community than would be true if an economic or racial group were excluded."* Ballard v. United States [note 7, supra]. (Emphasis supplied.)

The record before us, moreover, indisputably reveals that such a systematic exclusion operated with respect to the Lafayette Parish jury lists. There were no women on the grand jury that indicted petitioner, and there were no women on the venire from which the jury was chosen. While the venire was selected from returns to questionnaires sent to parish residents, not a single one of the some 11,000 questionnaires was even sent to a woman. This was done deliberately.[13]

The State relies on the fact that the automatic exemption it grants to women is the same as the one upheld in *Hoyt* v. *Florida* [note 10, supra]. In *Hoyt*, however, there were women on the jury rolls, and the jury commissioners had made good-faith efforts to include women on

[13] Mr. LeBlanc, clerk of the court in Lafayette Parish, and a member of the parish jury commission, testified as to the process by which the venire was chosen at the hearing on the motion to quash Alexander's indictment:

"A. The slips or list that are put in the general venire box are made from questionnaires that I mailed out.

"Q. Now, who is this questionnaire sent to? How is that determined?
"A. To the different people in the Parish by the registrar of voter's list and the telephone book, city directory, different lists that are submitted by school board or any list that we can find that we think we got address [sic] for the mixed race one way or the other.

"Q. Was the questionnaire mailed to any women at all?
"A. We have received some that was filled in by some ladies. I think one.
"Q. Did you mail any to any women intentionally or did you intentionally exclude women when you mailed them?
"A. We didn't mail any to the women." App. 35, 53.

the jury lists despite the fact that they had an automatic exemption unless they volunteered for service. Here, on the other hand, only the feeblest efforts were made to interest women in service,[14] and there was testimony that only a single woman had filled out a jury service questionnaire.[15] This, out of a parish population of 45,000 adults, 52% of whom were female.

The absolute exemption provided by Louisiana, and no other State,[16] betrays a view of a woman's role which cannot withstand scrutiny under modern standards. We once [in 1872] upheld the constitutionality of a state law denying to women the right to practice law, solely on grounds of sex. *Bradwell* v. *State*, 16 Wall. 130. The rationale underlying the Louisiana [statute] is the same as that which was articulated by Justice Bradley in *Bradwell*:

> "Man is, or should be, woman's protector and defender. The natural and proper timidity and delicacy which belongs to the female sex evidently unfits it for many of the occupations of civil life. The constitution of the family organization, which is founded in the divine ordinance, as well as in the nature of things, indicates the domestic sphere as that which properly belongs to the domain and functions of womanhood. The harmony, not to say identity, of interests and views which belong, or should belong, to the family institution is repugnant to the idea of a woman adopting a distinct and independent career from that of her husband. . . .
>
> ". . . The paramount destiny and mission of woman are to fulfil the noble and benign offices of wife and mother. This is the law of the Creator. And the rules of civil society must be adapted to the general constitution of things, and cannot be based upon exceptional cases."

[14] The only evidence in the record that any effort whatsoever was expended to encourage women to volunteer for jury service was a statement by Mr. LeBlanc that he had "discussed that with the Assistant District Attorney," and that he had "sent her at [sic] different women's clubs to explain to the women the possibility of being on the jury." He also averred that "we're working on the women to submit names and intention to serve."

[H]owever, these efforts produced but a single questionnaire from a woman. The 11,000 questionnaires sent to men, on the other hand, resulted in over 7,000 responses. App. 15.

[15] Testimony of Mr. LeBlanc. *See* [note 13], *supra*.

[16] No State now prohibits women from service on juries altogether, Alabama's prohibition having been found unconstitutional in *White* v. *Crook*, 251 F. Supp. 401 (MD Ala. 1966). Most States afford equal treatment to men and women, although exemptions are frequently provided for women who are pregnant or who have children under 18 at home. Five States now allow women an absolute exemption, based solely on their sex, but they must affirmatively request it.

Classifications based on sex are no longer insulated from judicial scrutiny by a legislative judgment that "woman's place is in the home," or that woman is by her "nature" ill-suited for a particular task. See, *e.g., Reed* v. *Reed* [note 12, *supra*]. But such a judgment is precisely that which underpins the absolute exemption from jury service at issue. Insofar as *Hoyt* [note 10, *supra*], embodies this discredited stereotype, it should be firmly disapproved.

Louisiana says, however, that women are not totally excluded from service; they may volunteer. The State asserts it is impractical to require women affirmatively to claim the statutory exemption because of the large numbers who would do so. This argument misses the point. Neither man nor woman can be expected to volunteer for jury service. *Hoyt, supra.* See L. Kanowitz, Women and the Law 30 (1969). Thus, the automatic exemption, coupled with the failure even to apprise parish women of their right to volunteer, results in as total an exclusion as would obtain if women were not permitted to serve at all.

A statutory procedure which has the effect of excluding all women does not produce a representative jury, and is therefore repugnant to our constitutional scheme.

In Frontiero v. Richardson,[17] *Douglas voted with the Court to invalidate federal statutes under which a woman member of the armed forces who wanted to claim her husband as a dependent for purposes of obtaining increased quarters allowances and medical benefits had to prove he was in fact dependent on her for over one-half of his support, whereas a serviceman could claim his wife as a dependent without regard to whether she was in fact dependent on him for any part of her support. This discrimination was not justifiable in terms of administrative convenience on the assumption that "the husband in our society is generally the 'breadwinner' in the family—and the wife typically the 'dependent' partner"—even though 99 percent of all members of the armed forces were male. But Douglas wrote for the Court in* Kahn v. Shevin[18] *to uphold Florida's $500 property tax exemption for widows, finding that the classification bore a reasonable relation to the purpose of the statute—to cushion the impact of spousal loss. "Whether from overt discrimination or from the socialization process of a male-dominated culture, the job market is inhospitable to the woman seeking any but the lowest paid jobs." In 1972 women working full time had a median income only 57.9 percent of the male median.*

Most of the Court's decisions under the equal protection clause in

[17] 411 U.S. 677 (1973).
[18] 416 U.S. 351 (1974).

recent years have involved racial discrimination. Douglas dissented when, in 1952, the Court declined to consider whether the concept of "separate but equal"—which it had adopted to justify state-imposed segregated seating in railroad coaches in 1896[19]—was applicable to public schools.[20] Two years later, a unanimous Court held that separate was not equal in public schools so that, in Brown v. Board of Education,[21] state-imposed segregation violated the equal protection clause, and in Bolling v. Sharpe,[22] federally imposed segregation in the District of Columbia schools violated the due process clause of the Fifth Amendment. Thereafter he voted with the Court to extend this ruling to government-imposed segregation in state universities[23] and professional schools,[24] public auditoriums,[25] public parks,[26] public golf courses,[27] public beaches,[28] courtrooms,[29] prisons,[30] city buses, and privately owned transportation systems.[31] He also wrote for the Court to hold that government could forbid segregation in privately owned restaurants.[32]

PALMER V. THOMPSON
403 U.S. 217 (1971)

In 1962 a federal district court held that the city of Jackson, Mississippi, had violated the equal protection clause by segregating its five public swimming pools, one for the blacks and four for the whites. The federal court of appeals affirmed and the Supreme Court declined to review the case. The city then closed its pools.

In this case a number of black citizens of Jackson brought an action to compel the city to reopen the pools on a desegregated basis. The Court held that they were not entitled to relief. To their argument that the decision to close the pools was motivated by a desire to avoid integration, the Court replied that "no case in this Court has held that

[19] Plessy v. Ferguson, 163 U.S. 537 (1896).
[20] Briggs v. Elliott, 342 U.S. 350 (1952).
[21] 347 U.S. 483 (1954).
[22] 347 U.S. 497 (1954).
[23] Adams v. Lucy, 351 U.S. 931 (1956).
[24] Hawkins v. Board of Control, 350 U.S. 413 (1956).
[25] Schire v. Bynum, 373 U.S. 395 (1964).
[26] Holmes v. Atlanta, 350 U.S. 879 (1955).
[27] Holmes v. Atlanta, note 26, supra.
[28] Mayor and City Council v. Dawson, 350 U.S. 877 (1955).
[29] Johnson v. Virginia, 373 U.S. 61 (1963).
[30] Lee v. Washington, 390 U.S. 333 (1968).
[31] Gayle v. Browder, 352 U.S. 903 (1956); Bailey v. Patterson, 369 U.S. 31 (1962).
[32] District of Columbia v. John R. Thompson Co., Inc., 346 U.S. 100 (1953).

a legislative act may violate equal protection solely because of the motivations of the men who voted for it."

MR. JUSTICE DOUGLAS, dissenting.

May a State in order to avoid integration of the races abolish all of its public schools? That would dedicate the State to backwardness, ignorance, and existence in a new Dark Age. Yet is there anything in the Constitution that says that a State must have a public school system? Could a federal court enjoin the dismantling of a public school system? Could a federal court order a city to levy the taxes necessary to construct a public school system? Such supervision over municipal affairs by federal courts would be a vast undertaking, conceivably encompassing schools, parks, playgrounds, civic auditoriums, tennis courts, athletic fields, as well as swimming pools.

My conclusion is that the Ninth Amendment has a bearing on the present problem. It provides:

> "The enumeration in the Constitution, of certain rights, shall not be construed to deny or disparage others retained by the people."

Rights, not explicitly mentioned in the Constitution, have at times been deemed so elementary to our way of life that they have been labeled as basic rights. Such is the right to travel from State to State. *United States* v. *Guest*, 383 U.S. 745. Such is also the right to marry. *Loving* v. *Virginia*, 388 U.S. 1.[33] The "rights" retained by the people within the meaning of the Ninth Amendment may be related to those "rights" which are enumerated in the Constitution. Thus the Fourth Amendment speaks of the "right of the people to be secure in their persons, houses, papers, and effects" and protects it by well-known procedural devices. But we have held that that enumerated "right" also has other facets commonly summarized in the concept of privacy. *Griswold* v. *Connecticut* [p. 234, *supra*].

There is, of course, not a word in the Constitution, unlike many modern constitutions, concerning the right of the people to education or to work or to recreation by swimming or otherwise. Those rights, like the right to pure air and pure water, may well be rights "retained by the people" under the Ninth Amendment. May the people vote them down as well as up?

[33] [Which invalidated, under the equal protection clause, a state antimiscegenation law forbidding marriage between "white persons" and "colored persons and Indians."]

In *Anderson v. Martin*, 375 U.S. 399, the State required designation on the ballots of every candidate's race. We said:

"In the abstract, Louisiana imposes no restriction upon anyone's candidacy nor upon an elector's choice in the casting of his ballot. But by placing a racial label on a candidate at the most crucial stage in the electoral process—the instant before the vote is cast—the State furnishes a vehicle by which racial prejudice may be so aroused as to operate against one group because of race and for another. This is true because by directing the citizen's attention to the single consideration of race or color, the State indicates that a candidate's race or color is an important—perhaps paramount—consideration in the citizen's choice, which may decisively influence the citizen to cast his ballot along racial lines."

A constitutional right cannot be so burdened. We stated in *West Virginia State Board of Education v. Barnette* [p. 140, *supra*] that: "One's right to life, liberty, and property . . . and other fundamental rights may not be submitted to vote; they depend on the outcome of no elections." And we added in *Lucas v. Colorado General Assembly*, 377 U.S. 713, "A citizen's constitutional rights can hardly be infringed simply because a majority of the people choose that [they] be." Thus the right of privacy, which we honored in *Griswold*, may not be overturned by a majority vote at the polls, short of a constitutional amendment.

Closing of the pools probably works a greater hardship on the poor than on the rich; and it may work greater hardship on poor Negroes than on poor whites, a matter on which we have no light. Closing of the pools was at least in part racially motivated. And, as stated by the dissenters in the Court of Appeals:

"The closing of the City's pools has done more than deprive a few thousand Negroes of the pleasures of swimming. It has taught Jackson's Negroes a lesson: In Jackson the price of protest is high. Negroes there now know that they risk losing even segregated public facilities if they dare to protest segregation. Negroes will now think twice before protesting segregated public parks, segregated public libraries, or other segregated facilities. They must first decide whether they wish to risk living without the facility altogether, and at the same time engendering further animosity from a white community which has lost its public facilities also through the Negroes' attempts to desegregate these facilities.

"The long-range effects are manifold and far-reaching. If the City's pools may be eliminated from the public domain, parks, athletic activities, and libraries also may be closed. No one can say how many other cities may also close their pools or other public facilities. The City's action tends to separate the races, encourage private discrimination, and raise substantial obstacles for Negroes asserting the rights of national citizenship created by the Wartime Amendments."

That view has strong footing in our decisions. "The clear and central purpose of the Fourteenth Amendment was to eliminate all official state sources of invidious racial discrimination in the States." *Loving* v. *Virginia*, 388 U.S., at 10. When the effects is "to chill the assertion of constitutional rights by penalizing those who choose to exercise them" (*United States* v. *Jackson*, 390 U.S. 570) that state action is "patently unconstitutional."

I believe that freedom from discrimination based on race, creed, or color has become by reason of the Thirteenth, Fourteenth, and Fifteenth Amendments one of the "enumerated rights" under the Ninth Amendment that may not be voted up or voted down.

Our cases condemn the creation of state laws and regulations which foster racial discrimination—segregated schools, segregated parks, and the like. The present case, to be sure, is only an analogy. The State enacts no law saying that the races may not swim together. Yet it eliminates all its swimming pools so that the races will not have the opportunity to swim together. While racially motivated state action is involved, it is of an entirely negative character. Yet it is in the penumbra of the policies of the Thirteenth, Fourteenth, and Fifteenth Amendments and as a matter of constitutional policy should be in the category of those enumerated rights protected by the Ninth Amendment. If not included, those rights become narrow legalistic concepts which turn on the formalism of laws, not on their spirit.

I conclude that though a State may discontinue any of its municipal services—such as schools, parks, pools, athletic fields, and the like—it may not do so for the purpose of perpetuating or installing *apartheid* or because it finds life in a multi-racial community difficult or unpleasant. If that is its reason, then abolition of a designated public service becomes a device for perpetuating a segregated way of life. That a State may not do.

BELL v. MARYLAND
378 U.S. 226 (1964)

The Fourteenth Amendment reaches only to state, not to private, action, although the Court has found the state sufficiently involved to

*make the Amendment applicable where it has leased space to the
private operator of a segregated restaurant in a public parking facility[34]
or a public airport.[35]*

No state lease was involved in this case, one of many of the time
involving "sit-in" demonstrations against racial discrimination. Black
students went to Hooper's restaurant in Baltimore, owned by a private
corporation, were told that they would not be served solely because of
their color, refused to leave when requested to do so, and were arrested
and convicted of criminal trespass. Their convictions were affirmed by
the Maryland Court of Appeals. By the time the case reached the
Supreme Court, their conduct no longer constituted a crime under the
law of Maryland, that state having enacted a law forbidding the denial
of public accommodations on the ground of race. The Court remanded
the case to the Maryland courts for reconsideration in the light of this
change in Maryland law.

MR. JUSTICE DOUGLAS, for reversing and directing dismissal of the
indictment.

I

I reach the merits of this controversy. The issue is ripe for decision
and petitioners, who have been convicted of asking for service in
Hooper's restaurant, are entitled to an answer to their complaint here
and now.

The whole Nation has to face the issue; Congress is conscientiously
considering it; some municipalities have had to make it their first order
of concern; law enforcement officials are deeply implicated, North as
well as South; the question is at the root of demonstrations, unrest,
riots, and violence in various areas. The issue in other words consumes
the public attention. Yet we stand mute.

The clash between Negro customers and white restaurant owners is
clear; each group claims protection by the Constitution and tenders
the Fourteenth Amendment as justification for its action. Yet we leave
resolution of the conflict to others, when, if our voice were heard, the
issues for the Congress and for the public would become clear and
precise. The Court was created to sit in troubled times as well as in
peaceful days.

We have in this case a question that is basic to our way of life and
fundamental in our constitutional scheme. No question preoccupies the
country more than this one; it is plainly justiciable; it presses for a
decision one way or another; we should resolve it. The people should

---

[34] *Burton v. Wilmington Parking Authority,* 365 U.S. 715 (1961).
[35] *Turner v. Memphis,* 369 U.S. 350 (1962).

know that when filibusters occupy other forums, when oppressions are great, when the clash of authority between the individual and the State is severe, they can still get justice in the courts. When we default, as we do today, the prestige of law in the life of the Nation is weakened.

For these reasons I reach the merits; and I vote to reverse the judgments of conviction outright.

II

The issue in this case, according to those [dissenting Justices] who would affirm, is whether a person's "personal prejudices" may dictate the way in which he uses his property and whether he can enlist the aid of the State to enforce those "personal prejudices." With all respect, that is not the real issue. The corporation that owns this restaurant did not refuse service to these Negroes because "it" did not like Negroes. The reason "it" refused service was because "it" thought "it" could make more money by running a segregated restaurant.

In the instant case, G. Carroll Hooper, president of the corporate chain owing the restaurant here involved, testified concerning the episode that gave rise to these convictions. The reasons were wholly commercial ones:

> "I set at the table with him and two other people and reasoned and talked to him why my policy was not yet one of integration and told him that I had two hundred employees and half of them were colored. I thought as much of them as I did the white employees. I invited them back in my kitchen if they'd like to go back and talk to them. *I wanted to prove to them it wasn't my policy, my personal prejudice*, we were not, that I had valuable colored employees and I thought just as much of them. I tried to reason with these leaders, told them that *as long as my customers were the deciding who they want to eat with, I'm at the mercy of my customers. I'm trying to do what they want. If they fail to come in, these people are not paying my expenses, and my bills.* They didn't want to go back and talk to my colored employees because every one of them are in sympathy with me and that is **we're** in sympathy with what their objectives are, with what they **are** trying to abolish. . . ." (Italics added.)

Here, as in most of the sit-in cases before us, the refusal of service did not reflect "personal prejudices" but business reasons. Were we today to hold that segregated restaurants, whose racial policies were enforced by a State, violated the Equal Protection Clause, all restaurants would be on an equal footing and the reasons given in this and most of the companion cases for refusing service to Negroes would evaporate. Moreover, when corporate restaurateurs are involved, whose "personal prejudices" are being protected? The stockholders'? The directors'? The officers'? The managers'? The truth is, I think, that the corporate interest is in making money, not in protecting "personal prejudices."

III

I turn to an even more basic issue.

I now assume that the issue is the one stated by those who would affirm. The case in that posture deals with a relic of slavery—an institution that has cast a long shadow across the land, resulting today in a second-class citizenship in this area of public accommodations.

The Thirteenth, Fourteenth, and Fifteenth Amendments had "one pervading purpose . . . we mean the freedom of the slave race, the security and firm establishment of that freedom, and the protection of the newly-made freeman and citizen from the oppressions of those who had formerly exercised unlimited dominion over him." *Slaughter-House Cases*, 16 Wall. 36.[36]

Prior to those Amendments, Negroes were segregated and disallowed the use of public accommodations except and unless the owners chose to serve them. To affirm these judgments would remit those Negroes to their old status and allow the States to keep them there by the force of their police and their judiciary.

The Fourteenth Amendment says "No State shall make or enforce any law which shall abridge the privileges or immunities of citizens of the United States." The Fourteenth Amendment also makes every person who is born here a citizen; and there is no second or third or fourth class of citizenship.

When one citizen because of his race, creed, or color is denied the privilege of being treated as any other citizen in places of public accommodation, we have classes of citizenship, one being more degrading than the other. That is at war with the one class of citizenship created by the Thirteenth, Fourteenth, and Fifteenth Amendments.

IV

The problem in this case is presented as though it involved the situation of "a private operator conducting his own business on his

---

[36] [The Thirteenth Amendment provides that: "Neither slavery nor involuntary servitude, except as punishment for crime whereof the party shall have been duly convicted, shall exist within the United States, or any place subject to their jurisdiction." The Fifteenth provides that the right of citizens to vote shall not be denied or abridged on account of race, color, or previous condition of servitude.]

own premises and exercising his own judgment"[37] as to whom he will admit to the premises.

The property involved is not, however, a man's home or his yard or even his fields. Private property is involved, but it is property that is serving the public. As my Brother GOLDBERG says, it is a "civil" right, not a "social" right, with which we deal. Here it is a restaurant refusing service to a Negro. But so far as principle and law are concerned it might just as well be a hospital refusing admission to a sick or injured Negro, or a drugstore refusing antibiotics to a Negro, or a bus denying transportation to a Negro, or a telephone company refusing to install a telephone in a Negro's home.

The problem with which we deal has no relation to opening or closing the door of one's home. The home of course is the essence of privacy, in no way dedicated to public use, in no way extending an invitation to the public. Some businesses, like the classical country store where the owner lives overhead or in the rear, make the store an extension, so to speak, of the home. But such is not this case. The facts of these sit-in cases have little resemblance to any institution of property which we customarily associate with privacy.

There is no specific provision in the Constitution which protects rights of privacy and enables restaurant owners to refuse service to Negroes. The word "property" is, indeed, not often used in the Constitution, though as a matter of experience and practice we are committed to free enterprise. The Fifth Amendment makes it possible to take "private property" for public use only on payment of "just compensation." The ban on quartering soldiers in any home in time of peace, laid down by the Third Amendment, is one aspect of the right of privacy. The Fourth Amendment in its restrictions on searches and seizures also sets an aura of privacy around private interests. And the Due Process Clauses of the Fifth and Fourteenth Amendments lay down the command that no person shall be deprived "of life, liberty, or *property*, without due process of law." (Italics added.) From these provisions those who would affirm find emanations that lead them to the conclusion that the private owner of a restaurant serving the public can pick and choose whom he will serve and restrict his dining room to *whites* only.

Apartheid, however, is barred by the common law as respects innkeepers and common carriers. There were, to be sure, criminal statutes that regulated the common callings. But the civil remedies were made

[37] Wright, The Sit-in Movement: Progress Report and Prognosis, 9 Wayne L. Rev. 445, 450 (1963).

by judges who had no written constitution. We, on the other hand, live under a constitution that proclaims equal protection under the law. Why then, even in the absence of a statute, should *apartheid* be given constitutional sanction in the restaurant field? Constitutionally speaking, why should Hooper Food Co., Inc., or Peoples Drug Stores— or any other establishment that dispenses food or medicines—stand on a higher, more sanctified level than Greyhound Bus when it comes to a constitutional right to pick and choose its customers?

The debates on the Fourteenth Amendment show, as my Brother GOLDBERG points out, that one of its purposes was to grant the Negro "the rights and guarantees of the good old common law." The duty of common carriers to carry all, regardless of race, creed, or color, was in part the product of the inventive genuis of judges. We should make that body of law the common law of the Thirteenth and Fourteenth Amendments so to speak. Restaurants in the modern setting are as essential to travelers as inns and carriers.

Are they not as much affected with a public interest? Is the right of a person to eat less basic than his right to travel, which we protected in *Edwards* v. *California*, 314 U.S. 160? Does not a right to travel in modern times shrink in value materially when there is no accompanying right to eat in public places?

The right of any person to travel *interstate* irrespective of race, creed, or color is protected by the Constitution. *Edwards* v. *California, supra.* Certainly his right to travel *intrastate* is as basic. Certainly his right to eat at public restaurants is as important in the modern setting as the right of mobility. In these times that right is, indeed, practically indispensable to travel either interstate or intrastate.

V

The requirement of equal protection, like the guarantee of privileges and immunities of citizenship, is a constitutional command directed to each State.

State judicial action is as clearly "state" action as state administrative action. Indeed, we held in *Shelley* v. *Kraemer*, 334 U.S. 1, that "State action, as that phrase is understood for the purposes of the Fourteenth Amendment, refers to exertions of state power in all forms."

That case involved suits in state courts to enforce restrictive covenants in deeds of residential property whereby the owner agreed that it should not be used or occupied by any person except a Caucasian. There was no state statute regulating the matter. That is, the State had not authorized by legislative enactment the use of restrictive covenants in residential property transactions; nor was there any administrative regulation of the matter. Only the courts of the State were involved.

We held without dissent in an opinion written by Chief Justice Vinson that there was nonetheless state action within the meaning of the Fourteenth Amendment:

> "The short of the matter is that from the time of the adoption of the Fourteenth Amendment until the present, it has been the consistent ruling of this Court that the action of the States to which the Amendment has reference includes action of state courts and state judicial officials. Although, in construing the terms of the Fourteenth Amendment, differences have from time to time been expressed as to whether particular types of state action may be said to offend the Amendment's prohibitory provisions, it has never been suggested that state court action is immunized from the operation of those provisions simply because the act is that of the judicial branch of the state government."

Maryland's action against these Negroes was as authoritative as any case where the State in one way or another puts its full force behind a policy. The policy here was segregation in places of public accommodation; and Maryland enforced that policy with her police, her prosecutors, and her courts.

The preferences involved in *Shelley* v. *Kraemer* and its companion cases were far more personal than the motivations of the corporate managers in the present case when they declined service to Negroes. Why should we refuse to let state courts enforce *apartheid* in residential areas of our cities but let state courts enforce *apartheid* in restaurants? If a court decree is state action in one case, it is in the other. Property rights, so heavily underscored, are equally involved in each case.

The customer in a restaurant is transitory; he comes and may never return. The colored family who buys the house next door is there for keeps—night and day. If "personal prejudices" are not to be the criterion in one case they should not be in the other. We should put these restaurant cases in line with *Shelley* v. *Kraemer*, holding that what the Fourteenth Amendment requires in restrictive covenant cases it also requires from restaurants.

Segregation of Negroes in the restaurants and lunch counters of parts of America is a relic of slavery. It is a badge of second-class citizenship. It is a denial of a privilege and immunity of national citizenship and of the equal protection guaranteed by the Fourteenth Amendment against abridgment by the States. When the state police, the state prosecutor, and the state courts unite to convict Negroes for renouncing that relic of slavery, the "State" violates the Fourteenth Amendment.

Shortly after this decision, the Court sustained provisions in the federal Civil Rights Act of 1964 forbidding private discrimination in public accommodations as a valid exercise of the congressional power to regulate interstate commerce. Douglas concurred, but preferred to base his position on a provision in the Fourteenth Amendment authorizing Congress to enforce its other provisions by "appropriate legislation."[38] Consistently with this view, he was one of six Justices who later took the position that an 1870 Civil Rights Act, penalizing conspiracies to "injure, oppress, threaten, or intimidate any citizen in the free exercise . . . of any right" guaranteed by the Constitution, would reach to a wholly private conspiracy to interfere with the right guaranteed by the Fourteenth Amendment to use of publicly owned facilities without discrimination as to race.[39]

DeFunis v. Odegaard
416 U.S. 312 (1974)

In this case a white student, Marco DeFunis, challenged the "minority admissions program" employed by the University of Washington Law School in admitting entering classes to the school. For all applicants the school calculated an index called the Predicted First Year Average on the basis of a formula combining the applicant's grades in the last two years of college and his score on the Law School Admission Test (LSAT), a test employed by virtually all of the law schools in · the country. Having made this calculation, the school did not proceed strictly "by the numbers" but examined other information in the application for indications of greater or lesser promise than suggested by the Predicted Average.

Among the large number of nonminority applicants for the fall of 1971, all with Predicted Averages above 78 were admitted, as were 93 of 105 applicants with averages between 77 and 78, and 75 of 379 applicants with averages between 75 and 77. DeFunis, with a Predicted Average of 76.23, was not admitted.

If, however, applicants indicated in response to an optional question on· the application that their "dominant" ethnic origin was black, Chicano, American Indian, or Filipino, their applications were somewhat differently treated. While they were considered competitively with one another, they were never directly compared with the other applicants, and the Admissions Committee admittedly attached less weight to the Predicted Average, and in a a publicly distributed "Guide

---

[38] *Heart of Atlanta Motel, Inc. v. United States*, 379 U.S. 241 (1964).
[39] *United States v. Guest*, 383 U.S. 745 (1966).

to Applicants," the committee explained that an applicant's "racial or
ethnic background was considered as one factor in our general attempt
to convert formal credentials into realistic predictions." Under this procedure, 37 minority applicants were admitted, 36 with averages below
DeFunis' 76.23 and 30 with averages below 74.5. There were also 48
nonminority applicants admitted who had Predicted Averages below
DeFunis. Twenty-three of them were applicants who had been accepted in earlier years but who had been unable to come or forced to
leave before graduation because of the military draft and who were admittedly given preferential treatment. The other 25 were presumably
admitted because of other factors in their applications.

The state trial court agreed with DeFunis that denial of his application violated the equal protection clause and ordered him admitted.
He was admitted in the fall of 1971. On appeal, the Washington Supreme Court reversed. By this time DeFunis was in his second year of
law school. Pending review by the Supreme Court, Douglas stayed the
judgment of the Washington Supreme Court so that DeFunis could
remain in school. By the time the case was argued in the Supreme
Court, DeFunis was in his final quarter in the law school, and the
school assured the Court that he would be allowed to finish regardless
of the outcome of the litigation. The Court for that reason concluded
that the case had become moot and remanded it to the state supreme
court.

MR. JUSTICE DOUGLAS, dissenting.

I agree with MR. JUSTICE BRENNAN that this case is not moot, and
because of the significance of the issues raised I think it is important
to reach the merits.

It is reasonable to conclude that while other factors were considered
by the Committee, and were on occasion crucial, the Average was for
most applicants a heavily weighted factor, and was at the extremes
virtually dispositive. A different balance was apparently struck, however, with regard to the minority applicants. Indeed, at oral argument,
the respondents' counsel advised us that were the minority applicants
considered under the same procedure as was generally used, none of
those who eventually enrolled at the Law School would have been
admitted.

The educational policy choices confronting a university admissions
committee are not ordinarily a subject for judicial oversight; clearly
it is not for us but for the law school to decide which tests to employ,
how heavily to weigh recommendations from professors or undergraduate grades, and what level of achievement on the chosen criteria

are sufficient to demonstrate that the candidate is qualified for admission. What places this case in a special category is the fact that the school did not choose one set of criteria but two, and then determined which to apply to a given applicant on the basis of his race. The Committee adopted this policy in order to achieve "a reasonable representation" of minority groups in the Law School. Although it may be speculated that the Committee sought to rectify what it perceived to be cultural or racial biases in the LSAT or in the candidates' undergraduate records, the record in this case is devoid of any evidence of such bias, and the school has not sought to justify its procedures on this basis.

Although testifying that "[w]e do not have a quota . . ." the Law School dean explained that "[w]e want a reasonable representation. We will go down to reach it if we can," without "taking people who are unqualified in an absolute sense. . . ." By "unqualified in an absolute sense" the dean meant candidates who "have no reasonable probable likelihood of having a chance of succeeding in the study of law . . . ." But the dean conceded that in "reaching," the school does take "some minority students who at least, viewed as a group, have a less such likelihood than the majority student group taken as a whole."

It thus appears that by the Committee's own assessment, it admitted minority students who, by the tests given, seemed less qualified than some white students who were not accepted, in order to achieve a "reasonable representation." In this regard it may be pointed out that for the year 1969–1970—two years before the class to which DeFunis was seeking admission—the Law School reported an enrollment of eight black students out of a total of 356. That percentage, approximately 2.2%, compares to a percentage of blacks in the population of Washington of approximately 2.1%.

The Equal Protection Clause did not enact a requirement that law schools employ as the sole criterion for admissions a formula based upon the LSAT and undergraduate grades, nor does it prohibit law schools from evaluating an applicant's prior achievements in light of the barriers that he had to overcome. A black applicant who pulled himself out of the ghetto into a junior college may thereby demonstrate a level of motivation, perseverance, and ability that would lead a fair-minded admissions committee to conclude that he shows more promise for law study than the son of a rich alumnus who achieved better grades at Harvard. That applicant would be offered admission not because he is black, but because as an individual he has shown he has the potential, while the Harvard man may have taken less advantage of the vastly superior opportunities offered him. Because of the weight of the prior handicaps, that black applicant may not realize his full potential in the first year of law school, or even in the full three years, but in the long pull of a legal career his achievements may far outstrip those of his classmates whose earlier records appeared superior by conventional criteria. There is currently no test available to the Admissions Committee that can predict such possibilities with assurance, but the Committee may nevertheless seek to gauge it as best it can, and weigh this factor in its decisions. Such a policy would not be limited to blacks, or Chicanos or Filipinos, or American Indians, although undoubtedly groups such as these may in practice be the principal beneficiaries of it. But a poor Appalachian white, or a second generation Chinese in San Francisco, or some other American whose lineage is so diverse as to defy ethnic labels, may demonstrate similar potential and thus be accorded favorable consideration by the Committee.

The difference between such a policy and the one presented by this case is that the Committee would be making decisions on the basis of individual attributes, rather than according a preference solely on the basis of race. To be sure, the racial preference here was not absolute—the Committee did not admit all applicants from the four favored groups. But it did accord all such applicants a preference by applying, to an extent not precisely ascertainable from the record, different standards by which to judge their applications, with the result that the Committee admitted minority applicants who, in the school's own judgment, were less promising than other applicants who were rejected. Furthermore, it is apparent that because the Admissions Committee compared minority applicants only with one another, it was necessary to reserve some proportion of the class for them, even if at the outset a precise number of places were not set aside.[40] That proportion, apparently 15% to 20%, was chosen because the school determined it to be "reasonable," although no explanation is provided as to how that number rather than some other was found appropriate. Without becoming embroiled in a semantic debate over whether this practice constitutes a "quota," it is clear that, given the limitation on the total number of applicants who could be accepted, this policy did reduce the total number of places for which DeFunis could compete—solely on account of his race. Thus, as the Washington Supreme Court concluded, whatever label one wishes to apply to it, "the minority admissions policy is certainly not benign with respect to nonminority

[40] At the outset the Committee may have chosen only a range, with the precise number to be determined later in the process as the total number of minority applicants, and some tentative assessments of their quality, could be determined.

students who are displaced by it." A finding that the state school employed a racial classification in selecting its students subjects it to the strictest scrutiny under the Equal Protection Clause.

The consideration of race as a measure of an applicant's qualification normally introduces a capricious and irrelevant factor working an invidious discrimination. Once race is a starting point educators and courts are immediately embroiled in competing claims of different racial and ethnic groups that would make difficult manageable standards consistent with the Equal Protection Clause. "The clear and central purpose of the Fourteenth Amendment was to eliminate all official state sources of invidious racial discrimination in the States." [*Loving* v. *Virginia*, note 33, *supra*]. The Law School's admissions policy cannot be reconciled with that purpose, unless cultural standards of a diverse rather than a homogeneous society are taken into account. The reason is that professional persons, particularly lawyers, are not selected for life in a computerized society. The Indian who walks to the beat of Chief Seattle of the Muckleshoot Tribe in Washington has a different culture from examiners at law schools.

The key to the problem is the consideration of each application *in a racially neutral way*. Since the LSAT reflects questions touching on cultural backgrounds, the Admissions Committee acted properly in my view in setting minority applications apart for separate processing. These minorities have cultural backgrounds that are vastly different from the dominant Caucasian. Many Eskimos, American Indians, Filipinos, Chicanos, Asian Indians, Burmese, and Africans come from such disparate backgrounds that a test sensitively tuned for most applicants would be wide of the mark for many minorities.

Insofar as LSAT's reflect the dimensions and orientation of the Organization Man they do a disservice to minorities. I personally know know that admissions tests were once used to eliminate Jews. How many other minorities they aim at I do not know. My reaction is that the presence of an LSAT is sufficient warrant for a school to put racial minorities into a separate class in order better to probe their capacities and potentials.

The merits of the present controversy cannot in my view be resolved on this record. A trial would involve the disclosure of hidden prejudices, if any, against certain minorities and the manner in which substitute measurements of one's talents and character were employed in the conventional tests. I could agree with the majority of the Washington Supreme Court only if, on the record, it could be said that the Law School's selection was racially neutral. The case, in my view, should be remanded for a new trial to consider, *inter alia*, whether the established LSAT's should be eliminated so far as racial minorities are concerned.

This does not mean that a separate LSAT must be designed for minority racial groups, although that might be a possibility. The reason for the separate treatment of minorities as a class is to make more certain that racial factors do not militate *against an applicant or on his behalf.*

The key to the problem is consideration of such applications *in a racially neutral way.* Abolition of the LSAT would be a start. The invention of substitute tests might be made to get a measure of an applicant's cultural background, perception, ability to analyze, and his or her relation to groups. They are highly subjective, but unlike the LSAT they are not concealed, but in the open. A law school is not bound by any legal principle to admit students by mechanical criteria which are insensitive to the potential of such an applicant which may be realized in a more hospitable environment. It will be necessary under such an approach to put more effort into assessing each individual than is required when LSAT scores and undergraduate grades dominate the selection process. Interviews with the applicant and others who know him is a time-honored test. Some schools currently run summer programs in which potential students who likely would be bypassed under conventional admissions criteria are given the opportunity to try their hand at law courses, and certainly their performance in such programs could be weighed heavily. There is, moreover, no bar to considering an individual's prior achievements in light of the racial discrimination that barred his way, as a factor in attempting to assess his true potential for a successful legal career. Nor is there any bar to considering on an individual basis, rather than according to racial classifications, the likelihood that a particular candidate will more likely employ his legal skills to service communities that are not now adequately represented than will competing candidates. Not every student benefited by such an expanded admissions program would fall into one of the four racial groups involved here, but it is no drawback that other deserving applicants will also get an opportunity they would otherwise have been denied. Certainly such a program would substantially fulfill the Law School's interest in giving a more diverse group access to the legal profession. Such a program might be less convenient administratively than simply sorting students by race, but we have never held administrative convenience to justify racial discrimination.

The problem tendered by this case is important and crucial to the operation of our constitutional system; and educators must be given leeway. It may well be that a whole congeries of applicants in the marginal group defy known methods of selection. Conceivably, an admissions committee might conclude that a selection by lot of, say, the last 20 seats is the only fair solution. Courts are not educators; their their expertise is limited; and our task ends with the inquiry whether, judged by the main purpose of the Equal Protection Clause—the protection against racial discrimination—there has been an "invidious" discrimination.

10

DUE PROCESS OF LAW

The due process clauses of the Fifth and Fourteenth Amendments impose requirements of procedural fairness on the federal and state governments, respectively, when they act to deprive a person of life, liberty, or property. Thus, at a minimum, due process requires notice of the basis for the proposed action and a fair opportunity to be heard, not only in criminal prosecutions,[1] but also in proceedings for the deportation of aliens,[2] for the admission of lawyers to practice[3] or for their disbarment,[4] and for the condemnation of property.[5]

JOINT ANTI-FASCIST REFUGEE COMMITTEE V. McGRATH
341 U.S. 123 (1951)

By Executive Order in 1947 President Truman set up a procedure for eliminating from federal employment persons whose loyalty was suspect. Loyalty boards, in identifying such persons, were directed by the Order to take into consideration "[m]embership in, affiliation with or sympathetic association with" any organization designated by the Attorney General as "totalitarian, fascist, communist, or subversive."

The Attorney General proceeded, without notice or hearing to the organizations involved, to compile a list which he transmitted to the loyalty boards and released to the press. Three of the listed organizations brought suit to have their listing declared invalid. The lower courts dismissed those suits but the Supreme Court reversed, four Justices, including Douglas, finding the Attorney General's procedures unconstitutional and Justice Burton concurring on a technical point of pleading.

On the same day, the Court also disposed of Bailey v. Richardson,[6] in which a woman dismissed from government employment challenged

---

[1] *Roviaro v. United States,* 353 U.S. 53 (1957).
[2] *Kwong Hai Chew v. Colding,* 344 U.S. 590 (1953).
[3] *Willner v. Committee on Character and Fitness,* 373 U.S. 96 (1963).
[4] *In re Ruffalo,* 390 U.S. 544 (1968).
[5] *Walker v. City of Hutchinson,* 352 U.S. 112 (1956).
[6] 341 U.S. 918 (1951).

the procedures employed in her case. The charges against her alleged connection with certain organizations on the Attorney General's list. Those charges were based on statements made to the FBI by informants who did not appear to testify against her in the loyalty proceeding and whose identity was not revealed to her or even to the loyalty board which decided her case. She thus had no opportunity to cross-examine or in any other way to test the veracity of those who linked her with the listed organizations. Moreover, she had no opportunity to test the correctness of the Attorney General's list—under the loyalty procedure the loyalty boards were not permitted to hear evidence or argument on that point. The lower courts also upheld this aspect of the loyalty proceedings. Justice Clark, who was Attorney General when the Loyalty Order was promulgated and who was responsible for compiling the lists in question, did not participate in the decision of either case. Bailey was affirmed by a 4-to-4 vote. No opinions were filed in the Baily case, but Justice Douglas' opinion in this case discloses his position in both.

Mr. Justice Douglas, concurring.

The resolution of the constitutional question presents one of the gravest issues of this generation. There is no doubt in my mind of the need for the Chief Executive and the Congress to take strong measures against any Fifth Column worming its way into government—a Fifth Column that has access to vital information and the purpose to paralyze and confuse. The problems of security are real. So are the problems of freedom. The paramount issue of the age is to reconcile the two.

In days of great tension when feelings run high, it is a temptation to take short-cuts by borrowing from the totalitarian techniques of our opponents. But when we do, we set in motion a subversive influence of our own design that destroys us from within. The present cases, together with *Bailey* v. *Richardson*, affirmed today by an equally divided Court, are simple illustrations of that trend.

I disagree with Mr. Justice Jackson that an organization—whether it be these petitioners, the American Red Cross, the Catholic Church, the Masonic Order, or the Boy Scouts—has no standing to object to being labeled "subversive" in these *ex parte* proceedings. The opinion of Mr. Justice Frankfurter disposes of that argument. This is not an instance of name calling by public officials. This is a determination of status—a proceeding to ascertain whether the organization is or is not "subversive." This determination has consequences that are serious to the condemned organizations. Those consequences flow in part, of course, from public opinion. But they also flow from actions of regulatory agencies that are moving in the wake of the Attorney General's determination to penalize or police these organizations.[7] An organization branded as "subversive" by the Attorney General is maimed and crippled. The injury is real, immediate, and incalculable.

The requirements for fair trials under our system of government need no elaboration. A party is entitled to know the charge against him; he is also entitled to notice and opportunity to be heard. Those principles were, in my opinion, violated here.

The charge that these organizations are "subversive" could be clearly defined. But how can anyone in the context of the Executive Order say what it means? It apparently does not necessarily mean "totalitarian," "fascist" or "communist" because they are separately listed. Does it mean an organization with socialist ideas? There are some who lump Socialists and Communists together. Does it mean an organization that thinks the lot of some peasants has been improved under Soviet auspices? Does it include an organization that is against the action of the United Nations in Korea? Does it embrace a group which on some issues of international policy aligns itself with the Soviet viewpoint? Does it mean a group which has unwittingly become the tool for Soviet propaganda? Does it mean one into whose membership some Communists have infiltrated? Or does it describe only an organization which under the guise of honorable activities serves as a front for Communist activities?

No one can tell from the Executive Order what meaning is intended. No one can tell from the records of the cases which one the Attorney General applied. The charge is flexible; it will mean one thing to one officer, another to someone else. It will be given meaning according to the predilections of the prosecutor: "subversive" to some will be synonymous with "radical"; "subversive" to others will be synonymous

---

[7] The Bureau of Internal Revenue canceled the tax-exempt status of contributions to eight "subversive" organizations shortly after the Attorney General's list was released. The Bureau's announcement of the revocation indicated that the listing provided the basis for it.

The New York Feinberg Law [see p. 212, *supra*] directed at eliminating members of subversive organizations from employment in the public schools, authorizes the Board of Regents to utilize the Attorney General's list in drawing up its own list of subversive organizations. Membership in a listed organization is *prima facie* evidence of disqualification. The New York Superintendent of Insurance recently brought an action to dissolve the International Workers Order, Inc., on the grounds that it was on the Attorney General's list.

The Maryland Ober Law requires candidates for appointive or elective office to certify whether they are members of "subversive" organizations. The Commission which drafted the Act contemplated that the Attorney General's list would be employed in policing these oaths.

with "communist." It can be expanded to include those who depart from the orthodox party line—to those whose words and actions (though completely loyal) do not conform to the orthodox view on foreign or domestic policy. These flexible standards, which vary with the mood or political philosophy of the prosecutor, are weapons which can be made as sharp or as blunt as the occasion requires. Since they are subject to grave abuse, they have no place in our system of law. When we employ them, we plant within our body politic the virus of the totalitarian ideology which we oppose.

It is not enough to know that the men applying the standard are honorable and devoted men. This is a government of *laws*, not of *men*. The powers being used are the powers of government over the reputations and fortunes of citizens. In situations far less severe or important than these a party is told the nature of the charge against him. Thus when a defendant is summoned before a federal court to answer to a claim for damages or to a demand for an injunction against him, there must be a "plain statement of the claim showing that the pleader is entitled to relief."[8] If that is necessary for even the most minor claim asserted against a defendant, we should require no less when it comes to determinations that may well destroy the group against whom the charge of being "subversive" is directed. When the Government becomes the moving party and levels its great powers against the citizen, it should be held to the same standards of fair dealing as we prescribe for other legal contests. To let the Government adopt such lesser ones as suits the convenience of its officers is to start down the totalitarian path.

The trend in that direction is only emphasized by the failure to give notice and hearing on the charges in these cases and by the procedure adopted in *Bailey* v. *Richardson*.

Notice and opportunity to be heard are fundamental to due process of law. We would reverse these cases out of hand if they were suits of a civil nature to establish a claim against petitioners. Notice and opportunity to be heard are indispensable to a fair trial whether the case be criminal or civil. The gravity of the present charges is proof enough of the need for notice and hearing before the United States officially brands these organizations as "subversive." No more critical governmental ruling can be made against an organization these days. It condemns without trial. It destroys without opportunity to be heard. The condemnation may in each case be wholly justified. But government in this country cannot by edict condemn or place beyond the pale.

---

[8] Rule 8(a), Federal Rules of Civil Procedure.

The rudiments of justice, as we know it, call for notice and hearing—an opportunity to appear and to rebut the charge.

The system used to condemn these organizations is bad enough. The evil is only compounded when a government employee is charged with being disloyal. Association with or membership in an organization found to be "subversive" weighs heavily against the accused. He is not allowed to prove that the charge against the organization is false. That case is closed; that line of defense is taken away. The technique is one of guilt by association—one of the most odious institutions of history. The fact that the technique of guilt by association was used in the prosecutions at Nuremberg[9] does not make it congenial to our constitutional scheme. Guilt under our system of government is personal. When we make guilt vicarious we borrow from systems alien to ours and ape our enemies. Those short-cuts may at times seem to serve noble aims; but we depreciate ourselves by indulging in them. When we deny even the most degraded person the rudiments of a fair trial, we endanger the liberties of everyone. We set a pattern of conduct that is dangerously expansive and is adaptable to the needs of any majority bent on suppressing opposition or dissension.

It is not without significance that most of the provisions of the Bill of Rights are procedural. It is procedure that spells much of the difference between rule by law and rule by whim or caprice. Steadfast adherence to strict procedural safeguards is our main assurance that there will be equal justice under law. The case of Dorothy Bailey is an excellent illustration of how dangerous a departure from our constitutional standards can be. She was charged with being a Communist and with being active in a Communist "front organization." The Review Board stated that the case against her was based on reports, some of which came from "informants certified to us by the Federal Bureau of Investigation as experienced and entirely reliable."

Counsel for Dorothy Bailey asked that their names be disclosed. That was refused.

[9] The International Tribunal tried Nazi organizations to determine whether they were "criminal." Art. 9, Charter of the International Military Tribunal, Nazi Conspiracy and Aggression. That procedure, unlike the present one, provided that accused organizations might defend themselves against that charge. But the finding of guilt as to an organization was binding on an individual who was later brought to trial for the crime of membership in a criminal organization. Article 10 provided: "In cases where a group or organization is declared criminal by the Tribunal, the competent national authority of any Signatory shall have the right to bring individuals to trial for membership therein before national, military or occupation courts. In any such case the criminal nature of the group or organization is considered proved and shall not be questioned."

Counsel for Dorothy Bailey asked if these informants had been active in a certain union. The chairman replied, "I haven't the slightest knowledge as to who they were or how active they have been in anything."

Counsel for Dorothy Bailey asked if those statements of the informants were under oath. The chairman answered, "I don't think so."

The Loyalty Board convicts on evidence which it cannot even appraise. The critical evidence may be the word of an unknown witness who is "a paragon of veracity, a knave, or the village idiot."[10] His name, his reputation, his prejudices, his animosities, his trustworthiness are unknown both to the judge and to the accused. The accused has no opportunity to show that the witness lied or was prejudiced or venal. Without knowing who her accusers are she has no way of defending. She has nothing to offer except her own word and the character testimony of her friends.

Dorothy Bailey was not, to be sure, faced with a criminal charge and hence not technically entitled under the Sixth Amendment to be confronted with the witnesses against her.[11] But she was on trial for her reputation, her job, her professional standing. A disloyalty trial is the most crucial event in the life of a public servant. If condemned, he is branded for life as a person unworthy of trust or confidence. To make that condemnation without meticulous regard for the decencies of a fair trial is abhorrent to fundamental justice.

I do not mean to imply that but for these irregularities the system of loyalty trials is constitutional. I do not see how the constitutionality of this dragnet system of loyalty trials which has been entrusted to the administrative agencies of government can be sustained. Every government employee must take an oath of loyalty.[12] If he swears falsely, he commits perjury and can be tried in court. In such a trial he gets the full protection of the Bill of Rights, including trial by jury and the presumption of innocence. I am inclined to the view that when a disloyalty charge is substituted for perjury and an administrative board

[10] Barth, The Loyalty of Free Men (1951), p. 109.

[11] ["In all criminal prosecutions, the accused shall enjoy the right . . . to be confronted with the witnesses against him. . . ."]

[12] [A federal statute requires that] "The oath to be taken by any person elected or appointed to any office of honor or profit either in the civil, military, or naval service, except the President of the United States shall be as follows: 'I, A B, do solemnly swear (or affirm) that I will support and defend the Constitution of the United States against all enemies, foreign and domestic; that I will bear true faith and allegiance to the same; that I take this obligation freely, without any mental reservation or purpose of evasion; and that I will well and faithfully discharge the duties of the office on which I am about to enter. So help me God.' "

substituted for the court "the spirit and the letter of the Bill of Rights" are offended.[13]

The problem of security is real; and the Government need not be paralyzed in handling it. The security problem, however, relates only to those sensitive areas where secrets are or may be available, where critical policies are being formulated, or where sabotage can be committed. The department heads must have leeway in handling their personnel problems in these sensitive areas. The question is one of the fitness or qualifications of an individual for a particular position. One can be transferred from those areas even when there is no more than a suspicion as to his loyalty. We meet constitutional difficulties when the Government undertakes to punish by proclaiming the disloyalty of an employee and making him ineligible for any government post. The British have avoided those difficulties by applying the loyalty procedure only in sensitive areas and in using it to test the qualifications of an employee for a particular post, not to condemn him for all public employment. When we go beyond that procedure and adopt the dragnet system now in force, we trench upon the civil rights of our people. We condemn by administrative edict, rather than by jury trial. Of course, no one has a constitutional right to a government job. But every citizen has a right to a fair trial when his government seeks to deprive him of the privileges of first-class citizenship.

The evil of these cases is only emphasized by the procedure employed in Dorothy Bailey's case. Together they illustrate how deprivation of our citizens of fair trials is subversion from within.

———

In a later case, the Court upheld procedures of the federal Civil Rights Commission which was investigating alleged violations of the voting rights of blacks which, if they occurred, might have violated criminal provisions of the 1866 Civil Rights Act. The commission had summoned state voting registrars to testify, without disclosing to them the identities of those who had filed complaints against them or allowing them to cross-examine others who had testified. Douglas dissented:

> "The Civil Rights Commission, it is true, returns no indictment. Yet in a real sense the hearings . . . are a trial. Moreover, these hearings . . . may be televised or broadcast on the radio. . . . This is in reality a trial in which the whole Nation sits as a jury. Their verdict does not send men to prison. But it often condemns men or

[13] See the address by Benjamin V. Cohen, 96 Cong. Rec. A785.

produces evidence to convict and even saturates the Nation with prejudice against an accused so that a fair trial may be impossible. . . . [W]hat is done is another short-cut used more and more these days to 'try' men in ways not envisaged by the Constitution. The result is as damaging as summoning before [legislative] committees men who it is known will invoke the Fifth Amendment and pillorying them for asserting their constitutional rights. This case—like the others—is a device to expose people as suspects or criminals."[14]

A decade later Douglas wrote for the Court to invalidate a state statute under which a chief of police had posted a notice in liquor establishments that a named adult woman was guilty of "excessive drinking," after the posting of which the statute made it illegal to sell or give liquor to her. This, he wrote, was "such a stigma or badge of disgrace that procedural due process requires notice and an opportunity to be heard. . . . Under the [statute, the one "posted"] is given no process at all."[15] Four months after Douglas left the bench, the Court announced that the real basis for the decision was that the "posting" deprived the one "posted" of her otherwise legal ability to purchase liquor and not the stigma resulting from the "posting." "Reputation alone," the Court now announced, was neither "liberty" nor "property" protected by the due process clause. Hence, one listed with his photograph by state police officials, without notice and hearing, on a list of "active shoplifters" which was circulated to merchants, had no due process claim.[16]

BOUTILIER v. IMMIGRATION SERVICE
387 U.S. 118 (1967)

Quite apart from the requirement that laws impinging on First Amendment rights must be narrowly and precisely drawn [p. 240, supra], the due process clause has long been interpreted to require that all criminal laws be drawn with sufficient clarity to provide an ascertainable standard of guilt.[17] And the Court once held the same requirement applicable to a statute making criminal the exaction of an "unjust or unreasonable rate or charge," not in the context of a criminal prosecution brought by the government, but in a civil context where one party to a contract,

---

[14] *Hannah* v. *Larche*, 363 U.S. 420 (1960).

[15] *Wisconsin* v. *Constantineau*, 400 U.S. 433 (1971).

[16] *Paul* v. *Davis*, 96 S. Ct. 1155 (1976).

[17] *International Harvester Co.* v. *Kentucky*, 234 U.S. 216 (1914); *Connally* v. *General Construction Co.*, 269 U.S. 385 (1926); *Lanzetta* v. *New Jersey*, 306 U.S. 451 (1939).

being sued by the other for breach of contract, sought to invoke the statute and the doctrine that the courts will not enforce illegal contracts.[18]

In this case an alien had been ordered deported on a finding that he was a homosexual and therefore subject to a statute providing for deportation of those "afflicted with [a] psychopathic personality." The Court affirmed the deportation order, explaining that the statute was not subject to the void-for-vagueness rule because Boutilier was a homosexual when he entered the United States, was "not being deported for conduct engaged in after his entry," and hence "no necessity exists for guidance so that one may avoid the applicability of the law."

MR. JUSTICE DOUGLAS, dissenting.

The term "psychopathic personality" is a treacherous one like "communist" or in an earlier day "Bolshevik." A label of this kind when freely used may mean only an unpopular person. It is much too vague by constitutional standards for the imposition of penalties or punishment.

Cleckley defines "psychopathic personality" as one who has the following characteristics:

(1) Superficial charm and good "intelligence." (2) Absence of delusions and other signs of irrational "thinking." (3) Absence of "nervousness" or psychoneurotic manifestations. (4) Unreliability. (5) Untruthfulness and insincerity. (6) Lack of remorse or shame. (7) Inadequately motivated antisocial behavior. (8) Poor judgment and failure to learn by experience. (9) Pathologic egocentricity and incapacity for love. (10) General poverty in major affective reactions. (11) Specific loss of insight. (12) Unresponsiveness in general interpersonal relations. (13) Fantastic and uninviting behavior with drink and sometimes without. (14) Suicide rarely carried out. (15) Sex life impersonal, trivial and poorly integrated. (16) Failure to follow any life plan. Cleckley, The Mask of Sanity 238–255 (1941).

The word "psychopath" according to some means "a sick mind." Many experts think that it is a meaningless designation. "Not yet is there any common agreement . . . as to classification or . . . etiology." Noyes, Modern Clinical Psychiatry 410 (3d ed. 1948). "The only conclusion that seems warrantable is that, at some time or other and by some reputable authority, the term psychopathic personality has been

---

[18] A.B. *Small Co.* v. *American Sugar Refining Co.*, 267 U.S. 233 (1925).

used to designate every conceivable type of abnormal character." Curran & Mallinson, Psychopathic Personality, 90 J. Mental Sci. 266. It is much too treacherously vague a term to allow the high penalty of deportation to turn on it.

It is common knowledge that in this century homosexuals have risen high in our own public service—both in Congress and in the Executive Branch—and have served with distinction. It is therefore not credible that Congress wanted to deport everyone and anyone who was a sexual deviate, no matter how blameless his social conduct had been nor how creative his work nor how valuable his contribution to society. I agree with Judge Moore, dissenting below, that the legislative history should not be read as imputing to Congress a purpose to classify under the heading "psychopathic personality" every person who had ever had a homosexual experience:

> "Professor Kinsey estimated that 'at least 37 per cent' of the American male population has at least one homosexual experience, defined in terms of physical contact to the point of orgasm, between the beginning of adolescence and old age. Kinsey, Pomeroy & Martin, Sexual Behavior in the Human Male 623 (1948). Earlier estimates had ranged from one per cent to 100 per cent. The sponsors of Britain's current reform bill on homosexuality have indicated that one male in 25 is a homosexual in Britain. To label a group so large 'excludable aliens' would be tantamount to saying that Sappho, Leonardo da Vinci, Michelangelo, Andre Gide, and perhaps even Shakespeare, were they to come to life again, would be deemed unfit to visit our shores. Indeed, so broad a definition might well comprise more than a few members of legislative bodies."

We held in *Jordan v. De George*, 341 U.S. 223, that the crime of a conspiracy to defraud the United States of taxes involved "moral turpitude" and made the person subject to deportation. That, however, was a term that has "deep roots in the law." But the grab-bag—"psychopathic personality"—has no "deep roots" whatsoever. Caprice of judgment is almost certain under this broad definition. Anyone can be caught who is unpopular, who is off-beat, who is nonconformist.

We deal here also with an aspect of "liberty" and the requirements of due process. They demand that the standard be sufficiently clear as to forewarn those who may otherwise be entrapped and to provide full opportunity to conform. "Psychopathic personality" is so broad and vague as to be hardly more than an epithet. The Court seeks to avoid this question by saying that the standard being applied relates only to what petitioner had done prior to his entry, not to his postentry conduct.

But at least half of the questioning of this petitioner related to his postentry conduct.

Douglas later wrote for the Court to invalidate a municipal ordinance which defined the crime of "vagrancy" to include "vagabonds," "common thieves," and "persons wandering or strolling about from place to place without any lawful purpose or object." The decision reversed the convictions of eight defendants who had been found by the state courts to fall within one or more of the above categories, two in the "common thief" category, not because theft was proved, but because they were reputed to be thieves. In his opinion, Douglas pointed out that the ordinance not only failed to give a person of ordinary intelligence fair notice that his contemplated conduct was forbidden, but it also encouraged "arbitrary and erratic arrests and convictions."[19]

In another case in which the Court upheld a statute making it a felony for a doctor to perform an abortion "unless . . . done as necessary for the preservation of the mother's life or health," he dissented. While he agreed that the doctor would be able to apply that standard, he pointed out that the judgment was necessarily highly subjective, depending on the training and insight of the particular doctor, and that it would be second-guessed, if prosecuted, by a judge or jury who might not agree with the doctor as to whether the mother's "health" would be jeopardized by such matters as the stigma of illegitimacy, anxiety about additional expense, or the physical burden of rearing an additional child.[20]

ROSENBERG v. UNITED STATES
346 U.S. 273 (1953)

This case, involving the interpretation of criminal statutes, presented no constitutional question, but came to the Court because of Douglas' concern that defendants have a full and fair hearing. Julius and Ethel Rosenberg had been convicted under the federal Espionage Act of 1917 of conspiring between 1944 and 1950 to commit espionage by transmitting military secrets, including some relating to the atom bomb, to Russia. They had been sentenced to death, their convictions and sentences had been affirmed on appeal, the Supreme Court had declined to review the case, and they were scheduled for execution on June 18, 1953. The Court had also, on June 15, 1953, denied their application for habeas corpus and a stay of execution.

---

[19] *Papachristou v. City of Jacksonville,* 405 U.S. 156 (1972).
[20] *United States v. Vuitch,* 402 U.S. 62 (1971).

On June 16, a few hours after the Court had adjourned for the summer and two days before the Rosenbergs were scheduled for execution, an application for relief was presented to Douglas which raised a new point in the case. The Atomic Energy Act of 1946 made it a crime to transmit atomic information to other nations, but unlike the older Espionage Act, it authorized the death sentence only on recommendation of the jury (which had not considered the question of penalty in the Rosenbergs' case) and only if the offense was committed with intent to injure the United States (which was not charged in the indictment or considered by the jury in the Rosenbergs' case). The question was, therefore, whether the Rosenbergs, whose offense began before but continued after the effective date of the Atomic Energy Act, were entitled to the benefit of its more lenient penalty provisions.

Douglas concluded that the question was a substantial one which should be considered by the district court and the court of appeals, since it was "important that before we allow human lives to be snuffed out we be sure—emphatically sure—that we act within the law." Accordingly, he granted a stay on June 17.

On request of the Attorney General, a Special Term of the Supreme Court was convened on June 18. The matter was argued before the full Court, which retired to deliberate, and since it did not reach a decision that day, execution was postponed. At noon on June 19, the Court announced that it had vacated the stay granted by Justice Douglas—a majority had concluded that the Atomic Energy Act did not repeal or limit the provisions of the Espionage Act. President Eisenhower denied a last-minute appeal for clemency and the Rosenbergs were executed that same day.

MR. JUSTICE DOUGLAS, dissenting.

When the motion for a stay was before me, I was deeply troubled by the legal question tendered. After twelve hours of research and study I concluded that the question was a substantial one, never presented to this Court and never decided by any court. So I issued the stay order.

Now I have had the benefit of an additional argument and additional study and reflection. Now I know that I am right on the law.

The Solicitor General says in oral argument that the Government would have been laughed out of court if the indictment in this case had been laid under the Atomic Energy Act of 1946. I agree. For a part of the crime alleged and proved antedated that Act. And obviously no criminal statute can have retroactive application. But the Solicitor General misses the legal point on which my stay order was based. It is this—whether or not the death penalty can be imposed *without the recommendation of the jury* for a crime involving the disclosure of atomic secrets where a part of that crime takes place after the effective date of the Atomic Energy Act.

The crime of the Rosenbergs was a conspiracy that started prior to the Atomic Energy Act and continued almost four years after the effective date of that Act. The overt acts *alleged* were acts which took place prior to the effective date of the new Act. But that is irrelevant for two reasons. *First*, acts in pursuance of the conspiracy were proved which took place *after* the new Act became the law. *Second*, under *Singer* v. *United States*, 323 U.S. 338, no overt acts were necessary; the crime was complete when the conspiracy was proved. And that conspiracy, as defined in the indictment itself, endured almost four years after the Atomic Energy Act became effective.

The crime therefore took place in substantial part *after* the new Act became effective, *after* Congress had written new penalties for conspiracies to disclose atomic secrets. One of the new requirements is that the death penalty for that kind of espionage can be imposed *only* if the jury recommends it. And here there was no such recommendation. To be sure, this espionage included more than atomic secrets. But there can be no doubt that the death penalty was imposed because of the Rosenbergs' disclosure of atomic secrets. The trial judge, in sentencing the Rosenbergs to death, emphasized that the heinous character of their crime was trafficking in atomic secrets. He said:

> "I believe your conduct in putting into the hands of the Russians the A-bomb years before our best scientists predicted Russia would perfect the bomb has already caused, in my opinion, the Communist aggression in Korea, with the resultant casualties exceeding 50,000 and who knows but that millions more of innocent people may pay the price of your treason. Indeed, by your betrayal you undoubtedly have altered the course of history to the disadvantage of our country."

But the Congress in 1946 adopted new criminal sanctions for such crimes. Whether Congress was wise or unwise in doing so is no question for us. The cold truth is that the death sentence may not be imposed for what the Rosenbergs did unless the jury so recommends.

Some say, however, that since *a part* of the Rosenbergs' crime was committed under the old law, the penalties of the old law apply. But it is law too elemental for citation of authority that where two penal statutes may apply—one carrying death, the other imprisonment—the court has no choice but to impose the less harsh sentence.

A suggestion is made that the question comes too late, that since the Rosenbergs did not raise this question on appeal, they are barred from raising it now. But the question of an unlawful sentence is never barred. No man or woman should go to death under an unlawful sentence merely because his lawyer failed to raise the point. It is that function among others that the Great Writ serves. I adhere to the views stated by Mr. Chief Justice Hughes for a unanimous Court in *Bowen* v. *Johnston*, 306 U.S. 19:

> "It must never be forgotten that the writ of *habeas corpus* is the precious safeguard of personal liberty and there is no higher duty than to maintain it unimpaired. The rule requiring resort to appellate procedure when the trial court has determined its own jurisdiction of an offense is not a rule denying the power to issue a writ of *habeas corpus* when it appears that nevertheless the trial court was without jurisdiction. The rule is not one defining power but one which relates to the appropriate exercise of power."

Here the trial court was without jurisdiction to impose the death penalty, since the jury had not recommended it.

Before the present argument I knew only that the question was serious and substantial. Now I am sure of the answer. I know deep in my heart that I am right on the law. Knowing that, my duty is clear.

HALEY v. OHIO
332 U.S. 596 (1948)

Bram v. *United States*[21] *long ago interpreted the Fifth Amendment's guarantee against self-incrimination to preclude the use of involuntary confessions in federal criminal trials and found that the confession was not voluntary where the accused, being suspected of murder committed aboard ship, was taken to a detective's office in a foreign country, informed that another suspect had accused him of the crime, required to remove all of his clothing, and then subjected to browbeating interrogation until he confessed.*

Brown v. *Mississippi*[22] *later placed a similar interpretation upon the due process clause of the Fourteenth Amendment to forbid the use in a state court of a confession coerced by physical brutality. Subsequent cases have held that the due process clause also forbids the use of confessions obtained by psychological coercion.*

In this case a fifteen-year-old black had been convicted in Ohio of murder committed in the course of a robbery of a confectionary. He had been arrested and taken to the police station at midnight. There-

[21] 168 U.S. 532 (1897).
[22] 297 U.S. 278 (1936).

after he was questioned for five hours by the police, acting in relays of one or two each. Around 5 A.M., after being shown the alleged confessions of two other boys also arrested for the crime (whose subsequent fates do not appear), he confessed. After the confession was signed, a newspaper photographer was allowed to see him and take his picture. Thereafter he was held incommunicado in jail for three days, and a lawyer retained by his mother was twice denied permission to see him. On the third day after his confession, he was taken before a magistrate and charged with the crime. His mother was not allowed to see him until two days after that. He testified at his trial that he was beaten by the police; his mother testified that he was bruised and skinned when she saw him and that his clothes were torn and bloodstained. The police denied that he had been beaten. His confession was admitted in evidence at the trial. The Court reversed the conviction without resolving the conflicting evidence about the use of physical force.

MR. JUSTICE DOUGLAS announced the judgment of the Court [and an opinion in which three other Justices joined. Another Justice concurred in a separate opinion.]

We do not think the methods used in obtaining this confession can be squared with that due process of law which the Fourteenth Amendment commands.

What transpired would make us pause for careful inquiry if a mature man were involved. And when, as here, a mere child—an easy victim of the law—is before us, special care in scrutinizing the record must be used. Age 15 is a tender and difficult age for a boy of any race. He cannot be judged by the more exacting standards of maturity. That which would leave a man cold and unimpressed can overawe and overwhelm a lad in his early teens. This is the period of great instability which the crisis of adolescence produces. A 15-year-old lad, questioned through the dead of night by relays of police, is a ready victim of the inquisition. Mature men possibly might stand the ordeal from midnight to 5 a.m. But we cannot believe that a lad of tender years is a match for the police in such a contest. He needs counsel and support if he is not to become the victim first of fear, then of panic. He needs someone on whom to lean lest the overpowering presence of the law, as he knows it, crush him. No friend stood at the side of this 15-year-old boy as the police, working in relays, questioned him hour after hour, from midnight until dawn. No lawyer stood guard to make sure that the police went so far and no farther, to see to it that they stopped short of the point where he became the victim of coercion. No counsel or friend was called during the critical hours of questioning. A photographer was admitted once this lad broke and confessed. But not even a gesture towards getting a lawyer for him was ever made.

This disregard of the standards of decency is underlined by the fact that he was kept incommunicado for over three days during which the lawyer retained to represent him twice tried to see him and twice was refused admission. A photographer was admitted at once; but his closest friend—his mother—was not allowed to see him for over five days after his arrest. It is said that these events are not germane to the present problem because they happened after the confession was made. But they show such a callous attitude of the police towards the safeguards which respect for ordinary standards of human relationships compels that we take with a grain of salt their present apologia that the five-hour grilling of this boy was conducted in a fair and dispassionate manner. When the police are so unmindful of these basic standards of conduct in their public dealings, their secret treatment of a 15-year-old boy behind closed doors in the dead of night becomes darkly suspicious.

The age of petitioner, the hours when he was grilled, the duration of his quizzing, the fact that he had no friend or counsel to advise him, the callous attitude of the police towards his rights combine to convince us that this was a confession wrung from a child by means which the law should not sanction. Neither man nor child can be allowed to stand condemned by methods which flout constitutional requirements of due process of law.

But we are told that this boy was advised of his constitutional rights before he signed the confession and that, knowing them, he nevertheless confessed. That assumes, however, that a boy of fifteen, without aid of counsel, would have a full appreciation of that advice and that on the facts of this record he had a freedom of choice. We cannot indulge those assumptions. Moreover, we cannot give any weight to recitals which merely formalize constitutional requirements. Formulas of respect for constitutional safeguards cannot prevail over the facts of life which contradict them. They may not become a cloak for inquisitorial practices and make an empty form of the due process of law for which free men fought and died to obtain. The Fourteenth Amendment prohibits the police from using the private, secret custody of either man or child as a device for wringing confessions from them.

RECK v. PATE
367 U.S. 433 (1961)

In reviewing federal convictions, the Supreme Court does not confine itself to constitutional requirements but exercises a general supervisory

authority over federal criminal justice. Hence, in McNabb v. United
States,[23] *a decision in which Douglas joined, it began ruling inadmissible
in federal courts a confession, even though voluntary, which was obtained during a period of time when the arresting officers were holding
the defendant in disregard of federal statutes and rules of criminal procedure requiring that, promptly after arrest, he be brought before a
committing magistrate for arraignment.*

*As the state convictions coming before the Court revealed increasingly
sophisticated methods of coercive police interrogation, Douglas began,
more than a decade before this case was decided, unsuccessfully to urge
the Court to hold unconstitutional the use by the states of any confession obtained during a period of detention by state officers which is
illegal according to applicable state arraignment law.*[24]

*In this case Emil Reck, a nineteen-year-old of subnormal intelligence,
and three others were arrested by Chicago police on a Wednesday on
suspicion of stealing bicycles. For a substantial number of hours on
Wednesday, Thursday, Friday, and Saturday, Reck was interrogated by
the police and exhibited in police lineups. Once during this time on
Friday he fainted and was taken to the Cook County Hospital. Later
the same day he became ill, vomited blood, and was again taken to the
hospital. On Friday evening two of the others who had been arrested
with Reck confessed to a murder which had occurred almost three
months before the arrest and implicated Reck. When confronted with
these facts on Saturday morning, Reck admitted that one of the con-
fessors had earlier told him of the murder but denied any participation
in it. Finally, late Saturday afternoon, he confessed to participation in
the crime. At this point he had been held incommunicado for eighty
hours without bail. On Sunday he signed another written confession.
He was not arraigned until the following Thursday, at which time he
pleaded not guilty. He had not seen any relative or any lawyer during
this entire period.*

*At his trial for murder, his confession was introduced against him
despite his testimony that it was the product of physical beatings—
testimony which the police controverted. He was convicted of murder
and sentenced to prison for 199 years.*

*On Reck's petition for habeas corpus, the Court voided his convic-
tion because of the "inherently coercive" circumstances under which his
confession was obtained.*

[23] 318 U.S. 332 (1943).
[24] *Watts* v. *Indiana,* 338 U.S. 49 (1949); *Turner* v. *Pennsylvania,* 338 U.S. 62
(1949); *Harris* v. *South Carolina,* 338 U.S. 68 (1949); *Stroble* v. *California,* 343
U.S. 181 (1952).

MR. JUSTICE DOUGLAS, concurring.

Emil Reck at the age of twelve was classified as a "high grade mental defective"[25] and placed in an institution for mental defectives. He dropped out of school when he was sixteen. Though he was retarded he had no criminal record, no record of delinquency. At the time of his arrest, confession, and conviction he was nineteen years old.

He was arrested Wednesday morning, March 25, 1936. The next day, March 26, his father went to the police asking where his son was and asking to see him. The police would give him no information. On March 27 his father came to the police station again but was not allowed to see his son. Later the father tried to see his son at the hospital but was denied admission.

The father was denied the right to see his son over and again. The son was held for at least eight full days *incommunicado*. He was arraigned before a magistrate on April 2, 1936, only after he had confessed.

The late Professor Alexander Kennedy of the University of Edinburgh has put into illuminating words the manner in which long-continued interrogation under conditions of stress can give the interrogator effective command over the prisoner.[26] The techniques—now explained in a vast literature—include (1) disorientation and disillusion; (2) synthetic conflict and tension; (3) crisis and conversion; (4) rationalization and indoctrination; (5) apologetics and exploitation.

The device of "synthetic conflict and tension" is summarized as follows:

> "Production by conditioning methods of a state of psychological tension with its concomitant physical changes in heart, respiration, skin and other organs, the feeling being unattached to any particular set of ideas. This is later caused to transfer itself to synthetic mental conflicts created out of circumstances chosen from the subject's life-history, but entirely irrelevant to the reasons for his detention. The object is to build up anxiety to the limits of tolerance so as to invoke pathological mental mechanisms of escape comparable to those of Conversion Hysteria.

[25] At an interview taking place a few weeks after his arrest in 1936, Reck knew that the Mississippi was a big river, that New York was a big city, that Washington, D.C., was our capital, and that Hoover preceded Roosevelt. But he was unable to divide 25 by 5; he did not know how many weeks were in a year, how many feet in a yard, how many quarts in a gallon, when Columbus discovered America, who the opponents were in the Civil War, or the capitals of Illinois, England, France, or Germany.

[26] Kennedy, The Scientific Lessons of Interrogation, Proc. Roy. Instn. 38, No. 170 (1960).

Whether the police used this technique on Emil Reck no one knows. We do know from this record that Emil Reck was quite ill during his detention. He was so ill that he was taken to a hospital *incommunicado*. He was so ill he passed blood. What actually transpired no one will know. The records coming before us that involve the relations between the police and a prisoner during periods of confinement are extremely unreliable. The word of the police is on the side of orderly procedure, nonoppressive conduct, meticulous regard for the sensibilities of the prisoner. There is the word of the accused against the police. But his voice has little persuasion.

We do know that long detention, while the prisoner is shut off from the outside world, is a recurring practice in this country—for those of lowly birth, for those without friends or status.[27] We also know that detention *incommunicado* was the secret of the inquisition and is the secret of successful interrogation in Communist countries. Professor Kennedy summarized the matter:

> "From the history of the Inquisition we learn that certain empirical discoveries were made and recognised as important by a thoughtful and objective minority of those concerned. The first was that if a prisoner were once induced to give a detailed history of his past and to discuss it with his interrogators in the absence of threat or persuasion or even of evidence of interest, he might after an emotional crisis recant and confess his heresies. The second discovery was that true and lasting conversion could never be produced by the threat of physical torture. Torture not infrequently had the opposite effect and induced a negative mental state in which the prisoner could no longer feel pain but could achieve an attitude of mental detachment from his circumstances and with it an immunity to inquisition. The most surprising feature was the genuine enthusiasm of those who did recant. While these results were necessarily ascribed at the time to the powers of persuasion of the Inquistadores, it is evident in retrospect that something was happening which was often beyond their control. The same facts come to light in the long history of Russian political interrogation. In the Leninist period, the success of the immensely tedious method of didactic interrogation then in use was similarly ascribed to the appeal of Marxist doctrine to reason. The fact is that in conditions of confinement, detailed history-taking without reference to incriminating topics and the forming of a personal

---

[27] "The law, in its majestic equality, forbids the rich as well as the poor to sleep under bridges, to beg in the streets, and to steal bread." Anatole France as quoted in Cournos, A Modern Plutarch (1928), p. 27.

relationship with an interrogator who subscribes to a system of political or religious explanation, there may occur an endogenous and not always predictable process of conversion to the ideas and beliefs of the interrogator."

Television teaches that confessions are the touchstone of law enforcement. Experience however teaches that confessions born of long detention under conditions of stress, confusion, and anxiety are extremely unreliable.

People arrested by the police may produce confessions that come gushing forth and carry all the earmarks of reliability. But detention *incommunicado* for days on end is so fraught with evil that we should hold it to be inconsistent with the requirements of that free society which is reflected in the Bill of Rights. It is the means whereby the commands of the Fifth Amendment (which I deem to be applicable to the States) are circumvented. It is true that the police have to interrogate to arrest; it is not true that they may arrest to interrogate. I would hold that any confession obtained by the police while the defendant is under detention is inadmissible, unless there is prompt arraignment and unless the accused is informed of his right to silence and accorded an opportunity to consult counsel. This judgment of conviction should therefore be reversed.

After later decisions had held that the Fifth Amendment's privilege against self-incrimination (p. 354, infra) and the Sixth Amendment's guarantee of the right to counsel (p. 359, infra) were applicable to the states, new constitutional standards were developed for the admissibility of confessions in both state and federal criminal trials. See pp. 361–365, infra.

11

MORE SPECIFIC GUARANTEES

The original Constitution, as submitted to the states for ratification, contained no express protection against arbitrary acts of government except provisions that neither Congress nor the states should pass any bill of attainder or ex post facto law,[1] a guarantee of jury trial in all federal criminal cases,[2] a provision that the writ of habeas corpus *should not be suspended "unless when in Cases of Rebellion or Invasion the public Safety may require it,"[3] and a definition of the crime of treason, together with the requirement that no person be convicted of that crime "unless on the Testimony of two Witnesses to the same overt Act, or on Confession in open Court."[4]*

The omission of a Bill of Rights was widely criticized, and many of the states accompanied their ratifications with proposed amendments designed to add one. The first Congress submitted twelve of these proposals to the state legislatures and ten of them were ratified. The first eight are commonly referred to today as the Bill of Rights.[5]

In 1883 the Supreme Court held that the Fifth Amendment's prohibition against the taking of private property for public use without just compensation was not applicable to the states because the first ten amendments were designed for "security against the apprehended encroachments of the general government—not against those of the local governments."[6]

After the adoption of the Fourteenth Amendment, however, its due process clause was held in 1897 to incorporate and make applicable to the states the Fifth Amendment's restrictions on the taking of private

---

[1] U.S. Const., Art. I, §9, Cl. 3; *Id.* §10, Cl. 1.

[2] *Id.*, Art. III, §2, Cl. 3.

[3] *Id.*, Art. I, §9, Cl. 2.

[4] *Id.*, Art. III, §3, Cl. 1.

[5] The Ninth Amendment provides that "The enumeration in the Constitution, of certain rights, shall not be construed to deny or disparage others retained by the people" and the Tenth that "The powers not delegated to the United States by the Constitution, nor prohibited by it to the States, are reserved to the States respectively, or to the people."

[6] *Barron v. Baltimore*, 7 Pet. 243 (1833).

property[7] *and in 1931 to incorporate the First Amendment's guarantees of freedom of speech and press.*[8] *But in 1875 it was held that the Fourteenth Amendment had not incorporated the Seventh Amendment's guarantee of jury trial in civil suits at common law*[9] *or the Second Amendment's guarantee of the right to bear arms,*[10] *in 1884 that it did not incorporate the Fifth Amendment's guarantee of indictment by grand jury,*[11] *in 1890 that it did not incorporate the Eighth Amendment's prohibition against cruel and unusual punishment,*[12] *in 1900 that it did not incorporate the Sixth Amendment's guarantee of jury trial in criminal cases,*[13] *in 1904 that it did not incorporate the Sixth Amendment's right to confront adverse witnesses in criminal prosecutions,*[14] *and in 1908 in* Twining v. New Jersey[15] *that it did not incorporate the Fifth Amendment's privilege against self-incrimination. In* Twining, *the test for incorporation was said to be, "Is it a fundamental principle of liberty and justice which inheres in the very idea of a free government and in the inalienable right of a citizen of such a government?"—a test which the privilege against self-incrimination was held not to meet.*

When, in 1937, in Palko v. Connecticut,[16] *the Court concluded also that the Fourteenth Amendment did not incorporate the Fifth Amendment's prohibition against being twice put in jeopardy for the same offense, it explained that only those guarantees of the Bill of Rights that were "implicit in the concept of ordered liberty" were made applicable to the states by the Fourteenth Amendment. There matters stood when Douglas came to the Court.*

In 1947, when the Court reaffirmed its prior decision[17] *that a defendant in a state prosecution was not denied a fair trial within the meaning of the due-process clause because the privilege against self-incrimination was not observed, Justices Black and Douglas dissented,*

---

[7] *Chicago, Burlington & Quincy Railroad Co. v. Chicago,* 166 U.S. 226 (1897).

[8] *Stromberg v. California,* 283 U.S. 359 (1931). See also *Fiske v. Kansas,* 274 U.S. 380 (1927).

[9] *Walker v. Sauvinet,* 92 U.S. 90 (1875). See also *Edwards v. Elliott,* 21 Wall. 532 (1874).

[10] *United States v. Cruikshank,* 92 U.S. 542 (1875). See also *Presser v. Illinois,* 116 U.S. 252 (1886).

[11] *Hurtado v. California,* 110 U.S. 516 (1884). See also *Gaines v. Washington,* 277 U.S. 81 (1928).

[12] *In re Kemmler,* 136 U.S. 436 (1890).

[13] *Maxwell v. Dow,* 176 U.S. 581 (1900).

[14] *West v. Louisiana,* 194 U.S. 258 (1904).

[15] 211 U.S. 78 (1908).

[16] 302 U.S. 319 (1937). See also *Brantley v. Georgia,* 217 U.S. 284 (1910).

[17] *Twining v. New Jersey,* note 15, *supra.*

arguing that the Fourteenth Amendment incorporated all of the guarantees of the Bill of Rights.[18] The Court has never accepted that view. But the application of its doctrine of "selective incorporation" in the ensuing years has resulted, as succeeding pages will show, in the overruling of many prior decisions refusing to incorporate, so that most of the specific guarantees of the Bill of Rights have now been held applicable to the states as well as to the federal government. While there has been no precise ruling on incorporation of the Sixth Amendment's guarantee of a statement of "the nature and cause of the accusation" in a criminal case, none can doubt that the due process clause requires as much. That leaves as unincorporated only the Fifth Amendment's requirement of grand jury indictment, held inapplicable to the states almost a century ago,[19] the Eighth Amendment's prohibition against excessive bail and fines, the Seventh Amendment's guarantee of jury trials in civil cases, held inapplicable to the states more than a century ago,[20] the Second Amendment's right to bear arms, also held inapplicable to the states more than a century ago,[21] and the Third Amendment's protection against the quartering of soldiers in private homes.

Unreasonable Searches and Seizures

The Fourth Amendment provides that "The right of the people to be secure in their persons, houses, papers, and effects, against unreasonable searches and seizures, shall not be violated, and no Warrants shall issue, but upon probable cause, supported by Oath or affirmation, and particularly describing the place to be searched, and the persons or things to be seized."

This provision governs both arrests and searches, but it is not construed to require that a warrant be obtained in every case. Douglas joined in a decision of the Court indicating that a federal police officer may arrest without a warrant where a misdemeanor or a felony is com-

---

[18] Adamson v. California, 332 U.S. 46 (1947).

[19] Hurtado v. California, note 11, supra.

[20] Walker v. Sauvinet, note 9, supra.

[21] United States v. Cruikshank, note 10, supra. The Second Amendment provides: "A well regulated Militia, being necessary to the security of a free State, the right of the people to keep and bear Arms, shall not be infringed." It was held in United States v. Miller, 307 U.S. 174 (1939), not to be violated by a federal statute forbidding the shipment of sawed-off shotguns in interstate commerce, since the possession and use of such a weapon was not shown to have any "reasonable relationship to the preservation or efficiency of a well regulated militia" (now known as the National Guard).

mitted in his presence or where he has probable cause to believe—as distinguished from a good faith suspicion—that a felony has been or is about to be committed,[22] although he later indicated he would limit warrantless arrests in the latter situation to cases where there is no time to obtain a warrant.[23] Some warrantless searching is also allowed where it is incident to a valid arrest whether that arrest is being made on a warrant or on probable cause without a warrant.

This rule on warrantless searches is justified "by the need to seize weapons and other things which might be used to assault an officer or effect an escape, as well as by the need to prevent the destruction of evidence of the crime—things which might easily happen where the weapon or evidence is on the accused person or under his immediate control."[24] This rationale suggests more limits on the scope of the search than the Court has always imposed. Early in his tenure on the Court, Douglas voted with the Court in the Harris case[25] to sustain a five-hour search of a suspect's four-room apartment incident to his valid arrest there, since the entire premises were "under his immediate control." In 1967 he expressly repudiated that decision,[26] and four years later so did the Court.[27]

Where a warrant for arrest was used, Douglas voted with the Court to hold that it was not properly issued on the sworn complaint of an officer that the named suspect "did receive, conceal, etc., narcotic drugs . . . with knowledge of unlawful importation." The purpose of the complaint is to enable the magistrate issuing the warrant to judge whether probable cause for arrest exists, and the magistrate "must judge for himself the persuasiveness of the facts relied on by a complaining officer to show probable cause." But a complaint which "contains no affirmative allegation that the [officer] spoke with personal knowledge" and which "does not indicate any sources for the [officer's] belief" gives the magistrate no basis for making a finding of probable cause.[28] He also voted with the Court to hold that a search warrant authorizing the seizure of "books, records, pamphlets, cards, receipts, lists, memoranda, pictures, recordings and other written instruments concerning the Communist Party of Texas" did not satisfy the constitutional re-

---

[22] United States v. Di Re, 332 U.S. 581 (1948).

[23] Wong Sun v. United States, 371 U.S. 471 (1963).

[24] Preston v. United States, 376 U.S. 364 (1964).

[25] Harris v. United States, 331 U.S. 145 (1947).

[26] Gilbert v. California, 388 U.S. 263 (1967).

[27] Coolidge v. New Hampshire, 403 U.S. 443 (1971).

[28] Giordenello v. United States, 357 U.S. 480 (1958). This case also said that a warrant of arrest could be issued on the basis of an indictment because the grand jury had already determined that probable cause for arrest existed—a procedure now specifically authorized by the Federal Rules of Criminal Procedure.

*quirement that the warrant be one "particularly describing the . . .
things to be seized."*[29]

Before the Fourth Amendment was held applicable to the states, it
had been held in federal prosecutions that, where a search was illegal,
both the evidence seized[30] and the "fruits of the poisonous tree"[31]—
other evidence obtained as a consequence of the illegal seizure—were
inadmissible at trial.

In 1949 in Wolf v. Colorado,[32] the Court concluded that the Fourth
Amendment's prohibition of unreasonable searches and seizures was
implicit in "the concept of ordered liberty" within the meaning of
Palko v. Connecticut[33] and hence applicable to the states. But the
further rule applied in federal courts—that illegally seized evidence
should be excluded at trial—was held not applicable to the states. They
were left free to select "the means by which the right should be made
effective," either by adopting their own exclusionary rules, by allowing
the person whose rights were violated to recover damages from the
police, or by disciplining the police. Hence, the Court affirmed a state
conviction in which illegally seized evidence had been admitted at trial.
Douglas dissented on the ground that this decision left the Fourth
Amendment with "no effective sanction." Twelve years later, in Mapp
v. Ohio,[34] the Court reconsidered the matter, found that only about
half of the states had adopted the exclusionary rule and that other
remedies provided by the states for illegal searches "have been worth-
less and futile," and concluded that the exclusionary rule was required
by the Fourth Amendment in state as well as federal prosecutions.

McCRAY v. ILLINOIS
386 U.S. 300 (1967)

McCray was arrested in an alley in Chicago, and the arresting officers,
who had no warrant, found a package of heroin in his possession. At his
trial in an Illinois court for unlawful possession, the arresting officers
testified that an informant who had previously been reliable in many
other instances had told them shortly before the arrest that McCray
was selling narcotics, had some in his possession, and could be found in
the vicinity of the place where he was arrested. They were not required

[29] *Stanford v. Texas*, 379 U.S. 476 (1965).
[30] *Weeks v. United States*, 232 U.S. 383 (1914).
[31] *Silverthorne Lumber Co., Inc. v. United States*, 251 U.S. 385 (1920). The
phrase itself was first used in *Nardone v. United States*, 308 U.S. 338 (1939).
[32] 338 U.S. 25 (1949).
[33] Note 16, *supra*.
[34] 367 U.S. 643 (1961).

to reveal the informant's name when asked by the defense on cross-examination. The heroin was admitted in evidence, McCray was convicted, and his conviction was affirmed by the Supreme Court, which found that there was probable cause to sustain the warrantless arrest and the search incident to that arrest.

MR. JUSTICE DOUGLAS, dissenting.

We have here a Fourth Amendment question concerning the validity of an arrest. If the police see a crime being committed they can of course seize the culprit. If a person is fleeing the scene of a crime, the police can stop him. And there are the cases of "hot pursuit" and other instances of probable cause when the police can make an arrest. But normally an arrest should be made only on a warrant issued by a magistrate on a showing of "probable cause, supported by oath or affirmation," as required by the Fourth Amendment. At least since *Mapp* v. *Ohio* [note 34, *supra*], the States are as much bound by those provisions as is the Federal Government. But for the Fourth Amendment they could fashion the rule for arrests that the Court now approves. With all deference, the requirements of the Fourth Amendment now make that conclusion unconstitutional.

No warrant for the arrest of petitioner was obtained in this case. The police, instead of going to a magistrate and making a showing of "probable cause" based on their informant's tip-off, acted on their own. They, rather than the magistrate, became the arbiters of "probable cause." The Court's approval of that process effectively rewrites the Fourth Amendment.

In *Roviaro* v. *United States*, 353 U.S. 53, we held that where a search *without a warrant* is made on the basis of communications of an informer and the Government claims the police had "probable cause," disclosure of the identity of the informant is normally required. In no other way can the defense show an absence of "probable cause." By reason of *Mapp* v. *Ohio, supra,* that rule is now applicable to the States.

In *Beck* v. *Ohio*, 379 U.S. 89, we said:

> "An arrest without a warrant bypasses the safeguards provided by an objective predetermination of probable cause, and substitutes instead the far less reliable procedure of an after-the-event justification for the arrest or search, too likely to be subtly influenced by the familiar shortcomings of hindsight judgment."

For that reason we have weighted arrests with warrants more heavily than arrests without warrants. Only through the informer's testimony can anyone other than the arresting officers determine "the persuasiveness of the facts relied on . . . to show probable cause." *Aguilar* v. *Texas,* 378 U.S. 108. Without that disclosure neither we nor the lower courts can ever know whether there was "probable cause" for the arrest. Under the present decision we leave the Fourth Amendment exclusively in the custody of the police. As stated by Mr. Justice Schaefer dissenting in *People* v. *Durr,* 28 Ill. 2d 308, unless the identity of the informer is disclosed "the policeman himself conclusively determines the validity of his own arrest." That was the view of the Supreme Court of California in *Priestly* v. *Superior Court,* 50 Cal. 2d 812:

> "Only by requiring disclosure and giving the defendant an opportunity to present contrary or impeaching evidence as to the truth of the officer's testimony and the reasonableness of his reliance on the informer can the court make a fair determination of the issue. Such a requirement does not unreasonably discourage the free flow of information to law enforcement officers or otherwise impede law enforcement. Actually its effect is to compel independent investigations to verify information given by an informer or to uncover other facts that establish reasonable cause to make an arrest or search."

There is no way to determine the reliability of Old Reliable, the informer, unless he is produced at the trial and cross-examined. Unless he is produced, the Fourth Amendment is entrusted to the tender mercies of the police.[35] What we do today is to encourage arrests and searches without warrants. The whole momentum of criminal law administration should be in precisely the opposite direction, if the Fourth Amendment is to remain a vital force. Except in rare and emergency cases, it requires magistrates to make the findings of "probable cause." We should be mindful of its command that a judicial mind should be interposed between the police and the citizen. We should also be mindful that "disclosure, rather than suppression, of relevant materials ordinarily promotes the proper administration of criminal justice." *Dennis* v. *United States,* 384 U.S. 855.

Questions as to the validity of arrests and searches usually arise only where they produce some solid, incriminating evidence which leads to a criminal charge. Where they produce nothing, and the person searched is released, that is usually the end of the matter. Hence, in the cases which reach the courts it frequently proves difficult to divorce the in-

---

[35] It is not unknown for the arresting officer to misrepresent his connection with the informer, his knowledge of the informer's reliability, or the information allegedly obtained from the informer. See, *e.g., United States* v. *Pearce,* 275 F. 2d 318.

quiry into probable cause for the search from the results of the search. Yet the rules which are fashioned in such cases apply to the conduct of the police in their nonproductive arrests and searches also. In another case very similar to McCray, save that it was a federal conviction which the Court affirmed, Douglas said in dissent:

> *Decisions under the Fourth Amendment, taken in the long view, have not given the protection to the citizen which the letter and spirit of the Amendment would seem to require. One reason, I think, is that wherever a culprit is caught red-handed, as in leading Fourth Amendment cases, it is difficult to adopt and enforce a rule that would turn him loose. A rule protective of law-abiding citizens is not apt to flourish where its advocates are usually criminals.[36]*

WYMAN v. JAMES
400 U.S. 309 (1971)

When, in 1959, the Court held that a city could authorize its health inspectors to inspect private homes without warrants because "no evidence for criminal prosecution is sought to be seized," Douglas dissented on the ground that the invasion of privacy was as great, regardless of the purpose.[37] In cases decided in 1967 involving health inspection of a private home[38] and fire inspection of a commercial warehouse,[39] the Court adopted the dissenting view: "It is surely anomalous to say that the individual and his private property are fully protected by the Fourth Amendment only when the individual is suspected of criminal behavior."

In this case the Court held that a state could deny welfare aid to a mother for her dependent child when the mother refused to permit a caseworker to visit her home without a warrant, even though she offered to supply all "reasonable and relevant" information elsewhere. The visit was not a "search" within the meaning of the Fourth Amendment, the Court said, even though the caseworker's purposes were "investigative" as well as "rehabilitative." The visit was "not forced or compelled," and where the welfare recipient refused to consent to it, there was no visit and the aid merely cease[d]." Alternatively, if the visit was viewed as a search, it was a reasonable one within the meaning of the Fourth

---

[36] *Draper v. United States,* 358 U.S. 307 (1959).
[37] *Frank v. Maryland,* 359 U.S. 360 (1959).
[38] *Camara v. Municipal Court,* 387 U.S. 523 (1967).
[39] *See v. Seattle,* 387 U.S. 541 (1967).

Amendment. "One who dispenses purely private charity naturally has an interest in and expects to know how his charitable funds are . . . put to work. The public, when it is the provider, rightly expects the same." And the proposed visit was no midnight raid. The recipient received written notice several days in advance.

MR. JUSTICE DOUGLAS, dissenting.

We are living in a society where one of the most important forms of property is government largesse which some call the "new property."[40] The payrolls of government are but one aspect of that "new property." Defense contracts, highway contracts, and the other multifarious forms of contracts are another part. So are subsidies to air, rail, and other carriers. So are disbursements by government for scientific research. So are TV and radio licenses to use the air space which of course is part of the public domain. Our concern here is not with those subsidies but with grants that directly or indirectly implicate the *home life* of the recipients.

In 1969 roughly 127 billion dollars were spent by the federal, state, and local governments on "social welfare." To farmers alone almost four billion dollars were paid, in part for not growing certain crops. Almost 129,000 farmers received $5,000 or more, their total benefits exceeding $1,450,000,000. Those payments were in some instances very large, a few running a million or more a year. But the majority were payments under $5,000 each.

Yet almost every beneficiary whether rich or poor, rural or urban, has a "house"—one of the places protected by the Fourth Amendment against "unreasonable searches and seizures." The question in this case is whether receipt of largesse from the government makes the *home* of the beneficiary subject to access by an inspector of the agency of oversight, even though the beneficiary objects to the intrusion and even though the Fourth Amendment's procedure for access to one's *house* or *home* is not followed. The penalty here is not, of course, invasion of the privacy of Barbara James, only her loss of federal or state largesse. That, however, is merely rephrasing the problem. Whatever the semantics, the central question is whether the government by force of its largesse has the power to "buy up" rights guaranteed by the Constitution. But for the assertion of her constitutional right, Barbara James in this case would have received the welfare benefit.

We spoke in *Speiser v. Randall,* 357 U.S. 513, of the denial of tax exemptions by a State because of exercise of First Amendment rights.

[40] See Reich, The New Property, 73 Yale L. J. 733, 737–739.

"It cannot be gainsaid that a discriminatory denial of a tax exemption for engaging in speech is a limitation on free speech. . . . To deny an exemption to claimants who engage in certain forms of speech is in effect to penalize them for such speech. Its deterrent effect is the same as if the State were to fine them for this speech."

Likewise, while second-class mail rates may be granted or withheld by the Government, we would not allow them to be granted "on condition that certain economic or political ideas not be disseminated." *Hannegan v. Esquire, Inc.*, 327 U.S. 146.

What we said in those cases is as applicable to Fourth Amendment rights as to those of the First. The Fourth, of course, speaks of "unreasonable" searches and seizures, while the First is written in absolute terms. But the right of privacy which the Fourth protects is perhaps as vivid in our lives as the right of expression sponsored by the First. *Griswold v. Connecticut* [p. 234, *supra*]. If the regime under which Barbara James lives were enterprise capitalism as, for example, if she ran a small factory geared into the Pentagon's procurement program, she certainly would have a right to deny inspectors access to her *home* unless they came with a warrant.

That is the teaching of *Camara v. Municipal Court* [note 38, *supra*] and *See v. City of Seattle* [note 39, *supra*]. In those cases we overruled *Frank v. Maryland* [note 37, *supra*] and held the Fourth Amendment applicable to administrative searches of both the *home* and a business. The applicable principle, as stated in *Camara* as "justified by history and by current experience" is that "except in certain carefully defined classes of cases, a search of private property without proper consent is 'unreasonable' unless it has been authorized by a valid search warrant." In *See* we added that the "businessman, like the occupant of a residence, has a constitutional right to go about his business free from unreasonable official entries upon his private commercial property." There is not the slightest hint in *See* that the Government could condition a business license on the "consent" of the licensee to the administrative searches we held violated the Fourth Amendment. It is a strange jurisprudence indeed which safeguards the businessman at his place of work from warrantless searches but will not do the same for a mother in her *home*.

Is a search of her home without a warrant made "reasonable" merely because she is dependent on government largesse?

Judge Skelly Wright has stated the problem succinctly:

"Welfare has long been considered the equivalent of charity and its recipients have been subjected to all kinds of dehumanizing experiences in the government's effort to police its welfare payments. In fact, over half a billion dollars are expended annually for administration and policing in connection with the Aid to Families with Dependent Children program. Why such large sums are necessary for administration and policing has never been adequately explained. No such sums are spent policing the government subsidies granted to farmers, airlines, steamship companies, and junk mail dealers, to name but a few. The truth is that in this subsidy area society has simply adopted a double standard, one for aid to business and the farmer and a different one for welfare." Poverty, Minorities, and Respect For Law, 1970 Duke L. J. 425.

If the welfare recipient was not Barbara James but a prominent, affluent cotton or wheat farmer receiving benefit payments for not growing crops, would not the approach be different? Welfare in aid of dependent children, like social security and unemployment benefits, has an aura of suspicion.[41] There doubtless are frauds in every sector of public welfare whether the recipient be a Barbara James or someone who is prominent or influential. But constitutional rights—here the privacy of the *home*—are obviously not dependent on the poverty or on the affluence of the beneficiary. It is the precincts of the *home* that the Fourth Amendment protects; and their privacy is as important to the lowly as to the mighty.

I would place the same restrictions on inspectors entering the *homes* of welfare beneficiaries as are on inspectors entering the *homes* of those on the payroll of government, or the *homes* of those who contract with the government, or the *homes* of those who work for those having government contracts. The values of the *home* protected by the Fourth Amendment are not peculiar to capitalism as we have known it; they are equally relevant to the new form of socialism which we are entering. Moreover, as the numbers of functionaries and inspectors multiply, the need for protection of the individual becomes indeed more essential if the values of a free society are to remain.

The bureaucracy of modern government is not only slow, lumbering,

---

[41] Juvenal wrote: "Poverty's greatest curse, much worse than the fact of it, is that it makes men objects of mirth, ridiculed, humbled, embarrassed." Satires 39 (Indiana Univ. Press 1958).

In 1837 the Court held in *City of New York* v. *Miln,* 11 Pet. 102, that New York could require ships coming in from abroad to report the names, ages, etc., of every person brought to these shores. The Court said: "We think it as competent and as necessary for a state to provide precautionary measures against the moral pestilence of paupers, vagabonds, and possibly convicts; as it is to guard against the physical pestilence, which may arise from unsound and infectious articles imported, or from a ship, the crew of which may be labouring under an infectious disease."

I regretfully conclude that today's decision is ideologically of the same vintage.

and oppressive; it is omnipresent. It touches everyone's life at numerous points. It pries more and more into private affairs, breaking down the barriers that individuals erect to give them some insulation from the intrigues and harassments of modern life. Isolation is not a constitutional guarantee; but the sanctity of the sanctuary of the *home* is such —as marked and defined by the Fourth Amendment. What we do today is to depreciate it.

ON LEE v. UNITED STATES
343 U.S. 747 (1952)

In Olmstead v. United States,[42] decided in 1928 over the dissents of Justices Holmes, Brandeis, Butler, and Stone, the Court held that government wiretapping did not violate the Fourth Amendment and that evidence so obtained could be used in a federal criminal trial. Thereafter Congress enacted the Communications Act of 1934, which contained a provision that "no person not being authorized by the sender shall intercept any communication [by wire or radio] and divulge or publish the . . . contents . . . of such intercepted communication to any person." As a result of that enactment, the Court held that evidence obtained by a federal officer by tapping telephone wires was not admissible in a federal prosecution. "No person" was held to include federal agents, and to allow the federal agent to testify in court about the contents of the intercepted message would be to "divulge" those contents to "any person."[43] In later decisions in which Douglas joined, the statutory provision and the exclusionary rule were held to apply to intrastate as well as interstate communications[44] and not merely to require the exclusion of the contents of the intercepted message, but also the "fruit of the poisonous tree"—other evidence obtained as a consequence of the illegal tap.[45]

Thereafter, at a time when he was dissenting from the Court's refusal to apply the exclusionary rule to the states so as to forbid their use of evidence obtained by searches which violated the Fourth Amendment (see p. 326, supra), Douglas also dissented when the Court held, in Schwartz v. Texas,[46] that the states might use evidence obtained by wiretaps illegal under the Communications Act. Douglas based his dissent on the ground that the wiretapping violated the Fourth Amendment. In 1968 the Court overruled Schwartz v. Texas to hold that the states

---

[42] 277 U.S. 438 (1928).
[43] *Nardone v. United States,* 302 U.S. 379 (1937).
[44] *Weiss v. United States,* 308 U.S. 321 (1939).
[45] *Nardone v. United States,* 308 U.S. 338 (1939).
[46] 344 U.S. 199 (1952).

could not use evidence obtained in violation of the Communications Act.[47]

Meanwhile, more sophisticated methods of eavesdropping were being developed which were not covered by the Communications Act. Early in his service on the Court, Douglas voted with a majority in Goldman v. United States[48] *to hold, following the* Olmstead *decision,*[49] *that neither that Act nor the Fourth Amendment was violated where eavesdropping was done by means of a detectaphone applied, without "trespass," to the partition wall of defendant's office by federal agents in an adjoining office.*

In this case, On Lee, convicted of narcotics offenses through the use of his own incriminating statements made to an old acquaintance and former employee, who was wired for sound by federal agents and sent into On Lee's laundry to visit with him, challenged his conviction under the Fourth Amendment. He failed. The Court adhered to its Goldman *decision and found no "trespass," since the informer entered the laundry "with the consent, if not the implied invitation" of On Lee.*

MR. JUSTICE DOUGLAS, dissenting.

The Court held in *Olmstead* v. *United States* over powerful dissents by Mr. Justice Holmes, Mr. Justice Brandeis, Mr. Justice Butler, and Chief Justice Stone that wire tapping by federal officials was not a violation of the Fourth and Fifth Amendments. Since that time the issue has been constantly stirred by those dissents and by an increasing use of wire tapping by the police. Fourteen years later in *Goldman* v. *United States* the issue was again presented to the Court. I joined in an opinion of the Court written by Mr. Justice Roberts, which adhered to the *Olmstead* case, refusing to overrule it. Since that time various aspects of the problem have appeared again and again in the cases coming before us. I now more fully appreciate the vice of the practices spawned by *Olmstead* and *Goldman*. Reflection on them has brought new insight to me. I now feel that I was wrong in the *Goldman* case. Mr. Justice Brandeis in his dissent in *Olmstead* espoused the cause of privacy—the right to be let alone. What he wrote is an historic statement of that point of view. I cannot improve on it.

> "When the Fourth and Fifth Amendments were adopted, 'the form that evil had theretofore taken,' had been necessarily simple. Force and violence were then the only means known to man by

[47] *Lee v. Florida*, 392 U.S. 378 (1968).
[48] 316 U.S. 129 (1942).
[49] Note 42, *supra*.

which a Government could directly effect self-incrimination. It could compel the individual to testify—a compulsion effected, if need be, by torture. It could secure possession of his papers and other articles incident to his private life—a seizure effected, if need be, by breaking and entry. Protection against such invasion of 'the sanctities of a man's home and the privacies of life' was provided in the Fourth and Fifth Amendments by specific language. *Boyd v. United States,* 116 U.S. 616. But 'time works changes, brings into existence new conditions and purposes.' Subtler and more far-reaching means of invading privacy have become available to the Government. Discovery and invention have made it possible for the Government, by means far more effective than stretching upon the rack, to obtain disclosure in court of what is whispered in the closet.

"Moreover, 'in the application of a constitution, our contemplation cannot be only of what has been but of what may be.' The progress of science in furnishing the Government with means of espionage is not likely to stop with wire-tapping. Ways may some day be developed by which the Government, without removing papers from secret drawers, can reproduce them in court, and by which it will be enabled to expose to a jury the most intimate occurrences of the home. Advances in the psychic and related sciences may bring means of exploring unexpressed beliefs, thoughts and emotions. 'That places the liberty of every man in the hands of every petty officer' was said by James Otis of much lesser intrusions than these. To Lord Camden, a far slighter intrusion seemed 'subversive of all the comforts of society.' Can it be that the Constitution affords no protection against such invasions of individual security?

.   .   .   .   .

"The makers of our Constitution undertook to secure conditions favorable to the pursuit of happiness. They recognized the significance of man's spiritual nature, of his feelings and of his intellect. They knew that only a part of the pain, pleasure and satisfactions of life are to be found in material things. They sought to protect Americans in their beliefs, their thoughts, their emotions and their sensations. They conferred, as against the Government, the right to be let alone—the most comprehensive of rights and the right most valued by civilized men. To protect that right, every unjustifiable intrusion by the Government upon the privacy of the individual, whatever the means employed, must be deemed a violation of the Fourth Amendment. And the use, as evidence in a criminal proceeding, of facts ascertained by such intrusion must be deemed a violation of the Fifth.

.   .   .   .   .

"Experience should teach us to be most on our guard to protect liberty when the Government's purposes are beneficent. Men born to freedom are naturally alert to repel invasion of their liberty by evil-minded rulers. The greatest dangers to liberty lurk in insidious encroachment by men of zeal, well-meaning but without understanding."

That philosophy is applicable not only to a detectaphone placed against the wall or a mechanical device designed to record the sounds from telephone wires but also to the "walky-talky" radio used in the present case. The nature of the instrument that science or engineering develops is not important. The controlling, the decisive factor is the invasion of privacy against the command of the Fourth and Fifth Amendments.

I would reverse this judgment. It is important to civil liberties that we pay more than lip service to the view that this manner of obtaining evidence against people is "dirty business" (see Mr. Justice Holmes, dissenting, *Olmstead* v. *United States, supra*).

———————————

In 1967, in Katz v. United States,[50] *the Court rejected its earlier notion that the Fourth Amendment's prohibition was confined to a "trespass," or a "physical intrusion," into any given area: "[t]he Fourth Amendment protects people, not places." It expressly overruled Olmstead* and *Goldman* and *held unconstitutional the interception of defendant's telephone conversations by means of an electronic device attached to the outside of a public telephone booth. Justice White, in a concurring opinion, suggested that the decision did not mean that a warrant was required if the President or the Attorney General found "national security" to be involved. Douglas wrote a separate concurrence to reply to that suggestion:*

I feel compelled to reply to the separate concurring opinion of my Brother White, which I view as a wholly unwarranted green light for the Executive Branch to resort to electronic eavesdropping without a warrant in cases which the Executive Branch itself labels "national security" matters.

Neither the President nor the Attorney General is a magistrate. In matters where they believe national security may be involved

[50] 389 U.S. 347 (1967).

they are not detached, disinterested, and neutral as a court or magistrate must be. Under the separation of powers created by the Constitution, the Executive Branch is not supposed to be neutral and disinterested. Rather it should vigorously investigate and prevent breaches of national security and prosecute those who violate the pertinent federal laws. The President and the Attorney General are properly interested parties, cast in the role of adversary, in national security cases. They may even be the intended victims of subversive action. Since spies and saboteurs are as entitled to the protection of the Fourth Amendment as suspected gamblers like petitioner, I cannot agree that where spies and saboteurs are involved adequate protection of Fourth Amendment rights is assured when the President and Attorney General assume both the position of adversary-and-prosecutor and disinterested, neutral magistrate.

Five years later, the Court held that warrantless wiretaps of domestic organizations did violate the Fourth Amendment, even though the Attorney General, acting with the authority of the President, had determined that they were necessary to protect the national security. Questions as to the reach of the Fourth Amendment when the Executive sought to eavesdrop on foreign powers or their agents, within or without the country, were expressly reserved.[51]

After the Katz decision, the Court again refused to reverse a conviction based on conversations which defendant had with a police informer wired for sound. A majority decided only that the Katz decision would not apply retroactively to invalidate police conduct which occurred before Katz was decided. But a plurality opinion of four justices took the position that Katz did not, in any event, require the overruling of On Lee (p. 332, supra). Douglas, dissenting, expressly disagreed with the view that On Lee could survive Katz.[52] When the Court later declined to review a case presenting that question, he again dissented, contending that the Court should take the case and reverse the conviction on the ground that "Fourth Amendment protections rest upon reasonable expectations of privacy rather than upon common-law property principles" so that "the Executive Branch acts unlawfully when it invades an individual's privacy through trickery or fraud."[53]

When the Court in Katz invalidated warrantless eavesdropping even though no trespass was involved, it also noted that a judicial order "could constitutionally have authorized, with appropriate safeguards, the very limited search and seizure that the Government asserts in fact

[51] *United States v. United States District Court*, 407 U.S. 297 (1972).
[52] *United States v. White*, 401 U.S. 745 (1971).
[53] *Cioffi v. United States*, 419 U.S. 917 (1974).

took place." Congressional response was to include provisions for such a procedure in the Omnibus Crime Control and Safe Streets Act of 1968. The Attorney General, "or any Assistant Attorney General specially designated by the Attorney General," may authorize application to a federal judge for an order approving interception of wire or oral communications in connection with a long list of crimes. State prosecutors may make similar applications to state court judges. If the judge finds probable cause, he may issue an ex parte order of approval of the interception for a specified period of time, not to exceed thirty days unless extended. No later than ninety days after the termination of the surveillance, those whose communications are intercepted are to be notified of that fact. In a series of cases decided in recent years, Douglas voted with the Court to hold that intercepted evidence was inadmissible when the application for the court order permitting the interception was not authorized by an Assistant Attorney General "specially designated by the Attorney General."[54] However, he has dissented when the Court has held such evidence admissible despite the fact that an application misrepresented the identity of the Justice Department official who had authorized the application,[55] or that the authorizing order permitted interceptions of conversations over a named person's telephone line between him and "others as yet unknown" where the interceptions produced evidence of conversations between the named person and his wife, on the basis of which they were both charged with illegal gambling.[56]

CALIFORNIA BANKERS ASSOCIATION v. SHULTZ
416 U.S. 21 (1974)

The federal Bank Secrecy Act of 1970, designed to require the maintenance of records and the making of reports which have "a high degree of usefulness in criminal, tax, or regulatory investigations and proceedings," and implementing regulations thereunder, promulgated by the Secretary of the Treasury, require all federally insured banks to microfilm or otherwise copy every check or draft drawn on them and to keep a record of each one received for deposit or collection—such records to be kept for six years unless the Secretary determines that a longer period is necessary. They also require the banks to report to the Secretary transportation into or out of the country of instruments of a value exceeding $5,000 and also all transactions or relationships with "foreign

[54] *United States v. Giordano,* 416 U.S. 505 (1974).
[55] *United States v. Chavez,* 416 U.S. 562 (1974).
[56] *United States v. Kahn,* 415 U.S. 143 (1974). See also *Bynum v. United States,* 423 U.S. 952 (1975).

financial institutions." The Act also requires the Secretary to make the reported information "available for a purpose consistent with the provisions" of the Act to any other department or agency of the federal government.

This action was brought by several individual bank customers, a bank, the California Bankers Association, and the American Civil Liberties Union to have the Act declared unconstitutional under, inter alia, the Fourth Amendment. The Court rejected their arguments, largely because it found the requirements "reasonable" and "not too indefinite."

MR. JUSTICE DOUGLAS, dissenting.

The Act has as its primary goal the enforcement of the criminal law.[57] The recordkeeping requirements originated according to Congressman Patman, author of the measure, with the Department of Justice and the Internal Revenue Service in response to two problems: (1) "A trend was developing in the larger banks away from their traditional practices of microfilming all checks drawn on them." (2) As respects the identification of depositors, "[a] typical example might involve a situation where a person with a criminal reputation holds an account but does not personally make deposits or withdrawals."

The purpose of the Act was to give the Secretary of the Treasury "primary responsibility" "to see to it that criminals do not take undue advantage of international trade and go undetected and unpunished." He added: "I would be the first to admit that this legislation does not provide perfect crime prevention. However, it is felt that the legislation will substantially increase the risk of discovery of any criminal who undertakes to hide his activity behind foreign secrecy."

The same purpose was reflected in the Senate. Senator Proxmire, the

---

[57] The House Report, No. 91–975, p. 10, states: "Petty criminals, members of the underworld, those engaging in 'white collar' crime and income tax evaders use, in one way or another, financial institutions in carrying on their affairs."

That was the reason for requiring the report of large domestic cash transactions. "Criminals deal in money—cash or its equivalent. The deposit and withdrawal of large amounts of currency or its equivalent (monetary instruments) under unusual circumstances may betray a criminal activity. The money in many of these transactions may represent anything from the proceeds of a lottery racket to money for the bribery of public officials." *Id.*, at 11.

While [the bill] started with a different objective, it was changed to serve an additional purpose. [Congressman Patman, author of the bill, stated:] "We also discovered that secret foreign bank accounts were not the only criminal activities related to the banking field. The major law enforcement authority—the Justice Department—of the U.S. Government called our attention to the urgent need for regulations which would make uniform and adequate the present recordkeeping practices, or lack of recordkeeping practices, by domestic banks and other financial institutions."

author of the Senate version of the bill, stated: "[T]he purpose of the bill is to provide law enforcement authorities with greater evidence of financial transactions in order to reduce the incidence of white-collar crime."

Customers have a constitutionally justifiable expectation of privacy in the documentary details of the financial transactions reflected in their bank accounts. That wall is not impregnable. Our Constitution provides the procedures whereby the confidentiality of one's financial affairs may be disclosed.

A

First, as to the recordkeeping requirements, their announced purpose [in the Act] is that they will have "a high degree of usefulness in criminal, tax, or regulatory investigations or proceedings."

It is estimated that a minimum of 20 billion checks—and perhaps 30 billion—will have to be photocopied and that the weight of these little pieces of paper will approximate 166 million pounds a year.

It would be highly useful to governmental espionage to have like reports from all our bookstores, all our hardware and retail stores, all our drugstores. These records too might be "useful" in criminal investigations.

One's reading habits furnish telltale clues to those who are bent on bending us to one point of view. What one buys at the hardware and retail stores may furnish clues to potential uses of wires, soap powders, and the like used by criminals. A mandatory recording of all telephone conversations would be better than the recording of checks under the Bank Secrecy Act, if Big Brother is to have his way. The records of checks—now available to the investigators—are highly useful. In a sense a person is defined by the checks he writes. By examining them the agents get to know his doctors, lawyers, creditors, political allies, social connections, religious affiliation, educational interests, the papers and magazines he reads, and so on *ad infinitum.* These are all tied to one's social security number; and now that we have the data banks, these other items will enrich that storehouse and make it possible for a bureaucrat—by pushing one button—to get in an instant the names of the 190 million Americans who are subversives or potential and likely candidates.

It is, I submit, sheer nonsense to agree with the Secretary that *all bank records of every citizen* "have a high degree of usefulness in criminal, tax, or regulatory investigations or proceedings." That is unadulterated nonsense unless we are to assume that every citizen is a crook, an assumption I cannot make.

Since the banking transactions of an individual give a fairly accurate account of his religion, ideology, opinions, and interests, a regulation impounding them and making them automatically available to all federal investigative agencies is a sledge-hammer approach to a problem that only a delicate scalpel can manage. Where fundamental personal rights are involved—as is true when as here the Government gets large access to one's beliefs, ideas, politics, religion, cultural concerns, and the like—the Act should be "narrowly drawn" (*Cantwell* v. *Connecticut*, 310 U.S. 296) to meet the precise evil. Bank accounts at times harbor criminal plans. But we only rush with the crowd when we vent on our banks and their customers the devastating and leveling requirements of the present Act. I am not yet ready to agree that America is so possessed with evil that we must level all constitutional barriers to give our civil authorities the tools to catch criminals.

Heretofore this Nation has confined compulsory recordkeeping to that required to monitor either (1) the recordkeeper, or (2) his business. *Marchetti* v. *United States*, 390 U.S. 39, and *United States* v. *Darby*, 312 U.S. 100, are illustrative. Even then, as Mr. Justice Harlan writing for the Court said, they must be records that would "customarily" be kept, have a "public" rather than a private purpose, and arise out of an "'essentially noncriminal and regulatory area of inquiry.'" *Marchetti* v. *United States, supra.*

Those requirements are in no way satisfied here, and yet there is saddled upon the banks of this Nation an estimated bill of over $6 million a year to spy on their customers.

B

Second, as to the *reporting* provisions of the Act, [w]e said in *Katz* v. *United States* [note 50, *supra*]: "What a person knowingly exposes to the public, even in his own home or office, is not a subject of Fourth Amendment protection. . . . But what he seeks to preserve as private, even in an area accessible to the public, may be constitutionally protected." As stated in *United States* v. *White*, 401 U.S. 745, the question is "what expectation of privacy" will be protected by the Fourth Amendment "in the absence of a warrant." A search and seizure conducted without a warrant is *per se* unreasonable, subject to "jealously and carefully drawn" exceptions, *Jones* v. *United States*, 357 U.S. 493. One's bank accounts are within the "expectations of privacy" category. For they mirror not only one's finances but his interests, his debts, his way of life, his family, and his civic commitments. There are administrative summonses for documents, cf. *Camara* v. *Municipal Court* [note 38, *supra*]; *See* v. *City of Seattle* [note 39, *supra*]. But there is a requirement that their enforcement receive judicial scrutiny and a judicial order, *United States* v. *U.S. District Court* [note 51, *supra*]. As we said in that case, "The Fourth Amendment does not contemplate the executive officers of Government as neutral and disinterested magistrates. Their duty and responsibility are to enforce the laws, to investigate, and to prosecute. . . . But those charged with this investigative and prosecutorial duty should not be the sole judges of when to utilize constitutionally sensitive means in pursuing their tasks. The historical judgment, which the Fourth Amendment accepts, is that unreviewed executive discretion may yield too readily to pressures to obtain incriminating evidence and overlook potential invasions of privacy and protected speech."

Suppose Congress passed a law requiring telephone companies to record and retain all telephone calls and make them available to any federal agency on request. Would we hesitate even a moment before striking it down? I think not, for we condemned in *United States* v. *U.S. District Court* "the broad and unsuspected governmental incursions into conversational privacy which electronic surveillance entails."

A checking account, as I have said, may well record a citizen's activities, opinion, and beliefs as fully as transcripts of his telephone conversations.

The Fourth Amendment warrant requirements may be removed by constitutional amendment but they certainly cannot be replaced by the Secretary of the Treasury's finding that certain information will be highly useful in "criminal, tax, or regulatory investigations or proceedings."

We cannot avoid the question of the constitutionality of the reporting provisions of the Act and of the regulations by saying they have not yet been applied to a customer in any criminal case. Under the Act and regulations the reports go forward to the investigative or prosecuting agency on written request without notice to the customer. Delivery of the records without the requisite hearing of probable cause[58] breaches the Fourth Amendment.

After Douglas left the Court, it held that there was no violation of the Fourth Amendment where microfilm copies of a bank's records of defendant's checks, deposit slips, and monthly statements, kept in compliance with the Bank Secrecy Act, were subpoenaed by the United States Attorney and used to convict him of violation of the liquor laws. The subpoenaed documents were not defendant's documents, but "the business records of the banks." United States v. Miller, 424 U.S. 916 (1976).

[58] A criminal prosecution in this country for not reporting an overseas transaction is still a criminal prosecution under the Bill of Rights; and to these the Fourth Amendment has been applicable from the beginning.

Self-Incrimination

*The Fifth Amendment provides that no person "shall be compelled in
any criminal case to be a witness against himself." Before Douglas
came to the Court, it had been held that the privilege was available in
any federal proceeding, civil or criminal, whenever "the answer might
tend to subject to criminal responsibility him who gives it."*[59] *It had
also been held that, where Congress undertook to confer statutory
immunity from criminal prosecution so as to make the privilege unavailable, the statute must confer immunity not only from the use
of the witness' testimony in a later criminal proceeding against him,
but also from prosecution based on other evidence obtained by the
use of that testimony.*[60]

*Other decisions had established that a party testifying in a civil pro-
ceeding who did not expressly invoke the privilege waived it,*[61] *and that
if he had not yet made "an actual admission of guilt or incriminating
facts" he was "not deprived of the privilege of stopping short in his
testimony whenever it may fairly tend to incriminate him."*[62] *But a
different rule was applied to a defendant who took the witness stand
in a criminal prosecution. He waived the privilege against self-incrimination as to all questions on cross-examination relevant to his testimony
on direct examination,*[63] *although not as to "collateral crimes" uncon-
nected with the charge.*[64]

ULLMANN V. UNITED STATES
350 U.S. 422 (1956)

In Brown v. Walker,[65] *the Court held that the privilege against self-
incrimination was not available to a witness before the Interstate
Commerce Commission because of a federal statute which provided
that, although the privilege should not be available before the commission, the witness should not be prosecuted or subjected to any penalty
or forfeiture on account of "any transaction, matter or thing, concerning which he may testify, or produce evidence," except for perjury*

[59] McCarthy v. Arndstein, 266 U.S. 34 (1924).

[60] Counselman v. Hitchcock, 142 U.S. 547 (1892).

[61] Vajtauer v. Commissioner, 273 U.S. 103 (1927).

[62] McCarthy v. Arndstein, 262 U.S. 355 (1923).

[63] Fitzpatrick v. United States, 178 U.S. 304 (1900); Raffel v. United States,
271 U.S. 494 (1926).

[64] Boyd v. United States, 142 U.S. 450 (1892).

[65] 161 U.S. 591 (1896).

*committed while testifying. After the Court had construed the statute
to grant immunity from state as well as federal prosecution, the object
of the constitutional privilege was held to be "fully accomplished by the
statutory immunity."*

*This case involved a similar statute, enacted in 1954, and directed
to witnesses before grand juries or courts who were being interrogated
about crimes endangering national security. Ullmann, having been called
to testify before a grand jury and questioned about his and other
persons' membership in the Communist Party, invoked the privilege
and challenged the constitutionality of the immunity statute, urging the
Court to overrule the Brown case or to distinguish it because of the
impact which his answers to the questions asked might have in terms
of job loss, expulsion from labor unions, state noncriminal registration
and investigation statutes, passport eligibility, and general public appro-
brium. His arguments were rejected. The Fifth Amendment was held
satisfied where "criminality has . . . been taken away."*

MR. JUSTICE DOUGLAS, dissenting.

I would overrule the five-to-four decision of *Brown* v. *Walker* and
adopt the view of the minority in that case that the right of silence
created by the Fifth Amendment is beyond the reach of Congress. The
difficulty I have with that decision and with the majority of the Court
in the present case is that they add an important qualification to the
Fifth Amendment. The guarantee is that no person "shall be compelled
in any criminal case to be a witness against himself." The majority does
not enforce that guarantee as written but qualifies it; and the qualification apparently reads, "but only if criminal conviction might result."
Wisely or not, the Fifth Amendment protects against the compulsory
self-accusation of crime without exception or qualification. In *Counselman* v. *Hitchcock* [note 60, *supra*] Mr. Justice Blatchford said, "The
privilege is limited to criminal matters, but it is as broad as the mischief
against which it seeks to guard."

The "mischief" to be prevented falls under at least three heads.

(1) One "mischief" is not only the risk of conviction but the risk of
prosecution. Mr. Justice Shiras, one of the four dissenters in *Brown* v.
Walker, alluded to this difficulty when he declared that the immunity
statute involved in that case was unconstitutional:

> ". . . all that can be said is, that the witness is *not* protected, by the
> provision in question, from being *prosecuted*, but that he has been
> furnished with a good plea to the indictment, which will secure his
> acquittal. But is that true? Not unless the plea is sustained by
> competent evidence. His condition, then, is that he has been

prosecuted, been compelled, presumably, to furnish bail, and put
to the trouble and expense of employing counsel and furnishing the
evidence to make good his plea." 161 U.S., at 621.

The risk of prosecution is not a risk which the wise take lightly. As
experienced a judge as Learned Hand once said, "I must say that, as a
litigant, I should dread a lawsuit beyond almost anything else short of
sickness and of death." See Frank, Courts on Trial (1949), 40. A part
of the dread in a case such as this is the chain of events that may be
put in motion once disclosure is made. The truth is, I think, that there
is no control left, once the right of secrecy is broken. For the statute
protects the accused only on account of the "transaction, matter, or
thing" concerning which he is compelled to testify and bars the use as
evidence of the "testimony so compelled." The forced disclosure may
open up vast new vistas for the prosecutor with leads to numerous
accusations not within the purview of the question and answer. What
related offenses may be disclosed by leads furnished by the confession?
How remote need the offense be before the immunity ceases to protect
it? How much litigation will it take to determine it? What will be the
reaction of the highest court when the facts of the case reach it?

It is, for example, a crime for a person who is a member of a Communist organization registered under the Subversive Activities Control
Act to be employed by the United States, to be employed in any defense facility, to hold office or employment with any labor organization,
or to apply for a passport or to use a passport.[66] The crime under that
Act is the application for a passport, the use of a passport, or employment by one of the named agencies, as the case may be. Are those
crimes included within the "transaction, matter, or thing" protected by
the Immunity Act?

The Taft-Hartley Act requires officers of labor organizations to file
non-Communist affidavits as a condition to the exercise by the National
Labor Relations Board of its power to make investigations or to issue
complaints.[67] A witness before a grand jury or congressional committee
is compelled under the force of the Immunity Act to testify. He testifies
that he is not a member of the Communist Party. He then files an
affidavit under the Taft-Hartley Act to that effect. May he be prosecuted
for filing a false affidavit?

These are real and dread uncertainties that the Immunity Act does

[66] [The provision relating to passports was later held unconstitutional as a deprivation of liberty without due process of law. *Aptheker* v. *Secretary of State*, 378
U.S. 500 (1964). The provision relating to employment in defense facilities was
also held unconstitutional under the First Amendment. *United States* v. *Robel*, 389
U.S. 258 (1967).]
[67] [This provision was later repealed.]

not remove. They emphasize that one protective function of the Fifth Amendment is at once removed when the guarantee against self-incrimination is qualified in the manner it is today.

The Court leaves all those uncertainties to another day, saying that the immunity granted by Congress will extend to its constitutional limits and that those constitutional limits will be determined case by case in future litigation. That means that no one knows what the limits are. The Court will not say. Only litigation on a distant day can determine it.

The concession of the Court underlines my point. It shows that the privilege of silence is exchanged for a partial, undefined, vague immunity. It means that Congress has granted far less than it has taken away.

(2) The guarantee against self-incrimination contained in the Fifth Amendment is not only a protection against conviction and prosecution but a safeguard of conscience and human dignity and freedom of expression as well. My view is that the Framers put it beyond the power of Congress to *compel* anyone to confess his crimes. The evil to be guarded against was partly self-accusation under legal compulsion. But that was only a part of the evil. The conscience and dignity of man were also involved. So too was his right to freedom of expression guaranteed by the First Amendment.[68] The Framers, therefore, created the federally protected right of silence and decreed that the law could not be used to pry open one's lips and make him a witness against himself.

A long history and a deep sentiment lay behind this decision. Some of those who came to these shores were Puritans who had known the hated oath *ex officio* used both by the Star Chamber and the High Commission. See Maguire, Attack of the Common Lawyers on the Oath *Ex Officio* as Administered in the Ecclesiastical Courts in England, Essays in History and Political Theory (1936), c. VII. They had known the great rebellion of Lilburn, Cartwright and others against those instruments of oppression. Cartwright had refused to take the oath *ex officio* before the High Commission on the grounds that "hee thought he was not bound by the lawes of God so to doe." Pearson, Thomas Cartwright and Elizabethan Puritanism 1535–1603 (1925), 318. Lilburn marshalled many arguments against the oath *ex officio*, one

---

[68] The impact of public identification on First Amendment freedoms was acknowledged by Chief Justice Vinson in *American Communications Assn.* v. *Douds*, 339 U.S. 382, where he said: "Under some circumstances, indirect 'discouragements' undoubtedly have the same coercive effect upon the exercise of First Amendment rights as imprisonment, fines, injunctions or taxes. A requirement that adherents of particular religious faiths or political parties wear identifying arm-bands, for example, is obviously of this nature."

of them being the sanctity of conscience and the dignity of man before God.

In 1653, Lilburn published The Just Defence in which he wrote:

> "Another fundamental right I then contended for, was, that no mans conscience ought to be racked by oaths imposed, to answer to questions concerning himself in matters criminal, or pretended to be so." Haller & Davies, id., at 454.

These are important declarations, as they throw light on the meaning of "compelled" as used in the Fifth Amendment.

The amending process that brought the Fifth Amendment into the Constitution is of little aid in our problem of interpretation. But there are indications in the debates on the Constitution that the evil to be remedied was the use of torture to exact confessions. See, e.g., Virginia Debates (2d ed. 1805), 221, 320–321; 2 Elliot's Debates (2d ed. 1876), 111. It was, indeed, the condemnation of torture to exact confessions that was written into the early law of the American Colonies. Article 45 of the Massachusetts Body of Liberties of 1641 provided in part, "No man shall be forced by Torture to confesse any Crime against himselfe nor any other. . . ." Connecticut adopted a similar provision. Laws of Connecticut Colony (1865 ed.), 65. Virginia soon followed suit: ". . . noe law can compell a man to sweare against himselfe in any matter wherein he is lyable to corporall punishment." Hening, Statutes at Large, Vol. II, 422.

The compulsion outlawed was moral compulsion as well as physical compulsion. An episode in the administration of Governor William Bradford of the Plymouth Plantation illustrates the point. He sought advice from his ministers asking, "How farr a magistrate may extracte a confession from a delinquente, to acuse him selfe of a capitall crime. . . ." The three ministers—Ralph Partrich, John Reynor, and Charles Chancy—were unanimous in concluding that the oath was against both the laws of God and the laws of man. Partrich's answer is typical:

> "[The magistrate] may not extracte a confession of a capitall crime from a suspected person by any violent means, whether it be by an oath imposed, or by any punishmente inflicted or threatened to be inflicted." Bradford, History of Plymouth Plantation, Mass. Hist. Soc. Coll. Ser. 4, Vol. III, 390–391.

The Court, by forgetting that history, robs the Fifth Amendment of one of the great purposes it was designed to serve. To repeat, the Fifth Amendment was written in part to prevent any Congress, any court, and any prosecutor from prying open the lips of an accused to make incriminating statements against his will. The Fifth Amendment protects the conscience and the dignity of the individual, as well as his safety and security, against the compulsion of government.[69]

(3) This right of silence, this right of the accused to stand mute serves another high purpose. Mr. Justice Field, one of the four dissenters in *Brown* v. *Walker*, stated that it is the aim of the Fifth Amendment to protect the accused from all compulsory testimony "which would expose him to infamy and disgrace," as well as that which might lead to a criminal conviction. One of the most powerful opinions in the books maintaining that thesis is by Judge Peter S. Grosscup in *United States* v. *James*, 60 F. 257, involving the same Immunity Act as the one involved in *Brown* v. *Walker*. Judge Grosscup reviewed the history of the reign of intolerance that once ruled England, the contests between Church and State, and the cruelties of the old legal procedures. Judge Grosscup said concerning the aim of the Framers in drafting the Fifth Amendment:

"Did they originate such privilege simply to safeguard themselves against the law-inflicted penalties and forfeitures? Did they take no thought of the pains of practical outlawry? The stated penalties and forfeitures of the law might be set aside; but was there no pain in disfavor and odium among neighbors, in excommunication from church or societies that might be governed by the prevailing views, in the private liabilities that the law might authorize, or in the unfathomable disgrace, not susceptible of formulation in language, which a known violation of law brings upon the offender? Then, too, if the immunity was only against the law-inflicted pains and penalties, the government could probe the secrets of every conversation, or society, by extending compulsory pardon to one of its participants, and thus turn him into an involuntary informer. Did the framers contemplate that this privilege of silence was exchangeable always, at the will of the government, for a remission of the participant's own penalties, upon a condition of disclosure, that would bring those to whom he had plighted his faith and loyalty within the grasp of the prosecutor? I cannot think so."

[69] Dean Erwin N. Griswold of Harvard recently wrote: "Where matters of a man's belief or opinions or political views are essential elements in the charge, it may be most difficult to get evidence from sources other than the suspected or accused person himself. Hence, the significance of the privilege over the years has perhaps been greatest in connection with resistance to prosecution for such offenses as heresy or political crimes. In these areas the privilege against self-incrimination has been a protection for freedom of thought and a hindrance to any government which might wish to prosecute for thoughts and opinions alone." The Fifth Amendment Today (1955).

Mr. Justice Field and Judge Grosscup were on strong historical ground. The Fifth Amendment was designed to protect the accused against infamy as well as against prosecution. A recent analysis by Professor Mitchell Franklin of Tulane illuminates the point. See The *Encyclopédiste* Origin and Meaning of the Fifth Amendment, 15 Lawyers Guild Rev. 41. He shows how the Italian jurist, Beccaria, and his French and English followers, influenced American thought in the critical years following our Revolution. The history of infamy as a punishment was notorious. Luther had inveighed against excommunication. The Massachusetts Body of Liberties of 1641 had provided in Article 60: "No church censure shall degrad or depose any man from any Civill dignitie, office, or Authoritie he shall have in the Commonwealth." Loss of office, loss of dignity, loss of face were feudal forms of punishment. Infamy was historically considered to be punishment as effective as fine and imprisonment.[70]

The Beccarian attitude toward infamy was a part of the background of the Fifth Amendment. The concept of infamy was explicitly written into it. We need not guess as to that. For the first Clause of the Fifth Amendment contains the concept *in haec verba*: "No person shall be held to answer for a capital, or otherwise *infamous* crime,[71] unless on a presentment or indictment of a Grand Jury. . . ." (Italics added.) And the third Clause, the one we are concerned with here—"No person . . . shall be compelled in any criminal case to be a witness against himself . . ."—also reflects the revulsion of society at infamy imposed by the State. Beccaria, whose works were well known here[72] and who was particularly well known to Jefferson,[73] was the main voice against the

[70] Infamy as a sanction in Roman Law is traced in Tatarczuk, Infamy of Law, Canon Law Studies No. 357, The Catholic University of America (1954), 1–13. The penalties that Roman Law attached to infamy are familiar: exclusion from the army, from all public service, and from the exercise of certain public rights. *Id.*, at 10.

[71] The cases arising under the first Clause of the Fifth Amendment recognize that what may be considered an "infamous crime" within the meaning of that Clause may be affected by changes of public opinion from one age to another. See *Ex parte Wilson*, 114 U.S. 417, 427; *Mackin v. United States*, 117 U.S. 348, 351; *United States v. Moreland*, 258 U.S. 433, 441, 451 (dissenting opinion by Brandeis, J.).

[72] Beccaria seems to have been principally introduced to America by Voltaire. See Barr, Voltaire in America (1941), 23–24. Barr states, "Beccaria's *Essay on Crimes and Punishment* with its famous commentary by Voltaire was known in America immediately after its first appearance in France and was the first of Voltaire's works to be published in America. It was popular in lending libraries and as a quickly sold item in bookstores, because of general interest in the formation of a new social order. A separate monograph would be necessary to trace the influence of this epoch-making tract." *Id.*, at 119.

[73] See Chinard, The Commonplace Book of Thomas Jefferson (1926), 298.

use of infamy as punishment. The curse of infamy, he showed, results from public opinion. Oppression occurs when infamy is imposed on the citizen by the State. The French jurist, Brissot de Warville, wrote in support of Beccaria's position, "It is in the power of the mores rather than in the hands of the legislator that this terrible weapon of infamy rests, this type of civil excommunication, which deprives the victim of all consideration, which severs all the ties which bind him to his fellow citizens, which isolates him in the midst of society. The purer and more untouched the customs are, the greater the force of infamy." I Theorie des Loix Criminelles (1781) 188. As de Pastoret said, "Infamy, being a result of opinion, exists·independently of the legislator; but he can employ it adroitly to make of it a salutary punishment." Des Loix Pénales (1790), Pt. 2, 121.

It was in this tradition that Lord Chief Justice Treby ruled in 1696 that ". . . no man is bound to answer any questions that will subject him to a penalty, or to infamy." *Trial of Freind*, 13 How. St. Tr. 1.

There is great infamy involved in the present case, apart from the loss of rights of citizenship under federal law which I have already mentioned. The disclosure that a person is a Communist practically excommunicates him from society. School boards will not hire him. See *Adler v. Board of Education* [p. 212, *supra*]. A lawyer risks exclusion from the bar (*In re Anastaplo*, 3 Ill. 2d 471); a doctor, the revocation of his license to practice (cf. *Barsky v. Board of Regents*, 347 U.S. 442). If an actor, he is on a black list. (See Horowitz, Loyalty Test for Employment in the Motion Picture Industry, 6 Stan. L. Rev. 438.) And he will be able to find no employment in our society except at the lowest level, if at all.

It is no answer to say that a witness who exercises his Fifth Amendment right of silence and stands mute may bring himself into disrepute. If so, that is the price he pays for exercising the right of silence granted by the Fifth Amendment. The critical point is that the Constitution places the right of silence *beyond the reach of government*. The Fifth Amendment stands between the citizen and his government. When public opinion casts a person into the outer darkness, as happens today when a person is exposed as a Communist, the government brings infamy on the head of the witness when it compels disclosure. That is precisely what the Fifth Amendment prohibits.

The Subversive Activities Control Act commissioned a Subversive Activities Control Board to label organizations as "Communist action" and "Communist front" organizations. After being so labeled, the organizations were required to register with the Attorney General on forms requiring disclosure of the names of their officers and, in the case of "Communist action" organizations, the names of all members. If the organization failed to register, the Act made it the duty of any member to do so. The Communist Party of the United States of America, after being labeled a "Communist action" group, failed to register and the Attorney General brought an action against a member to compel him to do so. He failed because the Act, as applied to a member, was held to violate the Fifth Amendment. A further provision in the Act, that holding office or membership in a Communist organization should not "constitute per se" a violation of any criminal statute and that the fact of registration of a person as an officer or member of any such organization should not be received as evidence against him in any criminal prosecution, was held not broad enough to meet the requirements of Counselman v. Hitchcock (note 60, supra), for an immunity statute.[74]

The effect of statutes like those upheld in Brown v. Walker and Ullmann v. United States was to give a witness complete immunity from criminal prosecution as to the "transaction, matter or thing" concerning which he testified even though the government, with no aid from his testimony, otherwise obtained evidence to sustain a prosecution. This "transactional immunity" is no longer required. The decision in Kastigar v. United States[75] *upheld an immunity statute which went no further than to forbid use of the compelled testimony "or any information directly or indirectly derived from such testimony" in any criminal case. This narrower "use immunity" was held to give the witness protection commensurate with the constitutional privilege and hence to be sufficient. Without elaborate reargument of his position in Ullmann, Douglas dissented, pointing out that the mere ban on derivative use of compelled testimony was insufficient protection for the witness since all information as to such use or nonuse would be in possession of the prosecuting authorities.*

BEILAN v. BOARD OF EDUCATION
357 U.S. 399 (1958)

Douglas voted with the Court in Slochower v. Board of Education[76] *to hold that a city may not discharge a college professor solely because he invokes the Fifth Amendment privilege when questioned about past Communist Party membership by a congressional committee. To infer guilt from invocation of a privilege available to the innocent as well as*

---

[74] *Albertson v. Subversive Activities Control Board,* 382 U.S. 70 (1965).
[75] 406 U.S. 441 (1972).
[76] 350 U.S. 551 (1956).

the guilty is to violate the due process clause of the Fourteenth Amendment.

In this case, decided while the Fifth Amendment privilege was held inapplicable to the states,[77] the Court found no denial of due process where the state discharged a schoolteacher for "incompetence" when he declined to answer his superintendent's question about past Communist Party affiliation. His lack of "frankness, candor and cooperation" was considered relevant to his "fitness to serve . . . as a public school teacher." In a companion case, Lerner v. Casey,[78] no violation of the due process clause was found where a New York City subway conductor was dismissed when he refused to answer city officials' questions about Communist Party membership, in erroneous reliance on the Fifth Amendment. His lack of "frankness" was held to justify an inference of "unreliability."

MR. JUSTICE DOUGLAS, dissenting.

The holding of the Court that the teacher in the *Beilan* case and the subway conductor in the *Lerner* case could be discharged from their respective jobs because they stood silent when asked about their Communist affiliations cannot, with due deference, be squared with our constitutional principles.

Among the liberties of the citizens that are guaranteed by the Fourteenth Amendment are those contained in the First Amendment. *Stromberg v. California* [note 8, *supra*]. These include the right to believe what one chooses, the right to differ from his neighbor, the right to pick and choose the political philosophy that he likes best, the right to associate with whomever he chooses, the right to join the groups he prefers, the privilege of selecting his own path to salvation. The Court put the matter succinctly in *Board of Education v. Barnette* [p. 140, *supra*].

> "We can have intellectual individualism and the rich cultural diversities that we owe to exceptional minds only at the price of occasional eccentricity and abnormal attitudes. When they are so harmless to others or to the State as those we deal with here, the price is not too great. But freedom to differ is not limited to things that do not matter much. That would be a mere shadow of freedom. The test of its substance is the right to differ as to things that touch the heart of the existing order.
>
> "If there is any fixed star in our constitutional constellation, it

[77] See notes 17 and 18, *supra*.
[78] 357 U.S. 468 (1958).

is that no official, high or petty, can prescribe what shall be orthodox in politics, nationalism, religion, or other matters of opinion or force citizens to confess by word or act their faith therein."

We deal here only with a matter of belief. We have no evidence in either case that the employee in question ever committed a crime, ever moved in treasonable opposition against this country. The only mark against them—if it can be called such—is a refusal to answer questions concerning Communist Party membership. This is said to give rise to doubts concerning the competence of the teacher in the *Beilan* case and doubts as to the trustworthiness and reliability of the subway conductor in the *Lerner* case.

Our legal system is premised on the theory that every person is innocent until he is proved guilty. In this country we have, however, been moving away from that concept. We have been generating the belief that anyone who remains silent when interrogated about his unpopular beliefs or affiliations is guilty. I would allow no inference of wrongdoing to flow from the invocation of any constitutional right. I would not let that principle bow to popular passions. For all we know we are dealing here with citizens who are wholly innocent of any wrongful action. That must indeed be our premise. When we make the contrary assumption, we part radically with our tradition.

If it be said that we deal not with guilt or innocence but with frankness, the answer is the same. There are areas where government may not probe. Private citizens, private clubs, private groups may make such deductions and reach such conclusions as they choose from the failure of a citizen to disclose his beliefs, his philosophy, his associates. But government has no business penalizing a citizen merely for his beliefs or associations. It is government action that we have here. It is government action that the Fourteenth and First Amendments protect against. We emphasized in *N.A.A.C.P.* v. *Alabama*, decided this day [p. 235, *supra*], that freedom to associate is one of those liberties protected against governmental action and that freedom from "compelled disclosure of affiliation with groups engaged in advocacy" is vital to that constitutional right. We gave protection in the *N.A.A.C.P.* case against governmental probing into political activities and associations of one dissident group of people. We should do the same here.

If we break with tradition and let the government penalize these citizens for their beliefs and associations, the most we can assume from their failure to answer is that they were Communists. Yet, as we said in *Wieman* v. *Updegraff*, 344 U.S. 183, membership in the Communist Party "may be innocent." The member may have thought that the

Communist movement would develop in the parliamentary tradition here, or he may not have been aware of any unlawful aim, or knowing it, may have embraced only the socialist philosophy of the group, not any political tactics of violence and terror. Many join associations, societies, and fraternities with less than full endorsement of all their aims.

We compound error in these decisions. We not only impute wrong-doing to those who invoke their constitutional rights. We go further and impute the worst possible motives to them.

As Judge Fuld said in dissent in the *Lerner* case, "It is a delusion to think that the nation's security is advanced by the sacrifice of the individual's basic liberties. The fears and doubts of the moment may loom large, but we lose more than we gain if we counter with a resort to alien procedures or with a denial of essential constitutional guarantees."

Our initial error in all this business (see *Dennis* v. *United States* [p. 199, *supra*]) was our disregard of the basic principle that government can concern itself only with the actions of men, not with their opinions or beliefs. As Thomas Jefferson said in 1779:

> ". . . the opinions of men are not the object of civil government, nor under its jurisdiction; . . . it is time enough for the rightful purposes of civil government for its officers to interfere when principles break out into overt acts against peace and good order."[79]

The fitness of a subway conductor for his job depends on his health, his promptness, his record for reliability, not on his politics or philosophy of life. The fitness of a teacher for her job turns on her devotion to that priesthood, her education, and her performance in the library, in the laboratory, and the classroom, not on her political beliefs. Anyone who plots against the government and moves in treasonable opposition to it can be punished. Government rightly can concern itself with the actions of people. But it's time we called a halt to government's penalizing people for their beliefs. To repeat, individuals and private groups can make any judgments they want. But the realm of belief—as opposed to action—is one which the First Amendment places beyond the long arm of government.

A teacher who is organizing a Communist cell in a schoolhouse or a subway conductor who is preparing the transportation system for sabotage would plainly be unfit for his job. But we have no such evidence in the records before us. As my Brother BRENNAN points out, to jump to those conclusions on these records is to short-cut procedural due process.

[79] 2 Papers of Thomas Jefferson (Boyd ed. 1950) 546.

In sum, we have here only a bare refusal to testify; and the Court holds that sufficient to show that these employees are unfit to hold their public posts. That makes qualification for public office turn solely on a matter of belief—a notion very much at war with the Bill of Rights.

When we make the belief of the citizen the basis of government action, we move toward the concept of *total security*. Yet *total security* is possible only in a totalitarian regime—the kind of system we profess to combat.

Douglas continued to dissent as the Court held that a state did not deny due process when it discharged a social worker for "insubordination" because, contrary to the state's instructions, he invoked the Fifth Amendment privilege when questioned about his political affiliations by the House Un-American Activities Committee,[80] *and, in* Cohen v. Hurley,[81] *when it disbarred a lawyer because he invoked a privilege against self-incrimination in the state's constitution when interrogated during a state inquiry into "ambulance chasing."*

Finally, in Malloy v. Hogan,[82] *the Court overruled its two prior decisions to the contrary,*[83] *and concluded that the Fifth Amendment privilege was sufficiently "fundamental" to be applied to the states "according to the same standards that protect those personal rights against federal encroachment"—including the rule excluding the use of evidence obtained in violation of the privilege and of evidence derived from such evidence. Thereafter, the Court overruled* Cohen v. Hurley *and held that a lawyer cannot be disbarred by a state for invoking the Fifth Amendment privilege.*[84] *And Douglas wrote for the Court in a companion case holding that policemen who refrained from asserting that privilege in a state investigation because of a state statute providing for discharge of those who invoked it could not thereafter be convicted of a crime on the basis of their testimony because their testimony was coerced—the state could not put them to "a choice between the rock and the whirlpool," between loss of employment and forfeiture of constitutional rights.*[85]

---

[80] *Nelson* v. *County of Los Angeles*, 362 U.S. 1 (1960).

[81] 366 U.S. 117 (1961).

[82] 378 U.S. 1 (1964).

[83] *Twining* v. *New Jersey*, note 15, *supra*; *Adamson* v. *California*, note 18, *supra*.

[84] *Spevack* v. *Klein*, 385 U.S. 511 (1967).

[85] *Garrity* v. *New Jersey*, 385 U.S. 493 (1967). The rule of *Spevack*, note 84, *supra*, has also been extended to policemen, *Gardner* v. *Broderick*, 392 U.S. 273 (1968), sanitation employees, *Uniformed Sanitation Men Assn., Inc.* v. *Commissioner of Sanitation*, 392 U.S. 280 (1968), and to licensed architects who were barred from contracting with the city. *Lefkowitz* v. *Turley*, 414 U.S. 70 (1973).

COUCH v. UNITED STATES
409 U.S. 322 (1973)

The Internal Revenue Service, in an investigation of the tax liability of Lillian Couch, owner and operator of a restaurant, issued a summons to her accountant directing him to produce all of her business and tax records which she had given to him for the purpose of preparing her tax returns. The accountant was not her employee, but maintained his own office with numerous other clients. Instead of complying with the summons, the accountant returned the records to Ms. Couch and she intervened in the IRS proceeding against the accountant to assert her Fifth Amendment privilege. The Court held that, while the records were at all times the property of Ms. Couch, the privilege was inapplicable. It was "personal." It "adheres basically to the person, not to information that may incriminate him." The Fifth Amendment prohibits compelling an accused to bear witness "against himself" and does not proscribe "incriminating statements elicited from another." The rights of the parties "became fixed when the summons was served." And "constitutional rights obviously cannot be enlarged" by the action of the accountant in thereafter returning the records to Ms. Couch.

MR. JUSTICE DOUGLAS, dissenting.

I cannot agree with the majority that the privilege against self-incrimination was not available to the petitioner merely because she did not have possession of the documents in question and was not herself subject to compulsory process. The basic concerns which, in my opinion, underlie the privilege are more subtle and far-reaching than mere aversion to the methods of the Inquisition and the Star Chamber and their modern counterparts. The decision today sanctions yet another tool of the ever-widening governmental invasion and oversight of our private lives. As I urged in dissent in *Warden* v. *Hayden*, 387 U.S. 294,[86]

---

[86] [In *Gouled* v. *United States*, 255 U.S. 298 (1921), the Court interpreted the Fourth Amendment to mean that an otherwise legal seizure must be confined to the instrumentalities by which a crime is committed, such as burglar tools; the fruits of crime, such as stolen property; weapons by which an escape of a person arrested might be effected; and contraband—property the possession of which is a crime. If the search went beyond that and produced "merely evidentiary materials" (in that case, documents from defendant's office on the basis of which he was later charged with conspiracy to defraud the United States), such materials could not be used against the defendant. If the government should attempt to subpoena such materials, that would of course give the defendant an opportunity to assert the Fifth Amendment privilege. *Warden* v. *Hayden* rejected this distinction and allowed the use, at a trial for armed robbery, of items of clothing seized in an otherwise lawful search of defendant's house.]

without the right of privacy "the Fourth Amendment and the Fifth are ready instruments for the police state that the Framers sought to avoid."

I

By looking solely to the historical antecedents of the privilege and focusing on "the ingredient of personal compulsion," the majority largely ignores the interplay of the fundamental values protected by the Fourth and Fifth Amendments. As early as 1886, the Court recognized that issues often cannot be pigeonholed within one amendment or the other, thereby foreclosing consideration of related policies. *Boyd* v. *United States*, 116 U.S. 616. In dealing with the compulsory production of a private paper for use in a forfeiture proceeding, the Court stated:

> "The principles laid down [in *Entick* v. *Carrington*, 95 Eng. Rep. 807] affect the very presence of constitutional liberty and security. . . . [T]hey apply to all invasions on the part of the government and its employés, of the sanctity of a man's home and the privacies of life. It is not the breaking of his doors, and the rummaging of his drawers, that constitutes the essence of the offence; but it is the invasion of his indefeasible right of personal security, personal liberty and private property, where that right has never been forfeited by his conviction of some public offence. . . . Breaking into a house and opening boxes and drawers are circumstances of aggravation; but any forcible and compulsory extortion of a man's own testimony or of his private papers to be used as evidence to convict him of crime or to forfeit his goods, is within the condemnation of that judgment. In this regard the Fourth and Fifth Amendments run almost into each other."

Although the subpoena in *Boyd* was directed at the person asserting the privilege, that fact cannot be allowed to obscure the basic thrust of the Court's reasoning: the Fourth and Fifth Amendments delineate a "sphere of privacy" which must be protected against governmental intrusion. We confirmed in *Murphy* v. *Waterfront Comm'n*, 378 U.S. 52, that "our respect for the inviolability of the human personality and of the right of each individual 'to a private enclave where he may lead a private life'" is a fundamental policy underlying the Fifth Amendment.

The majority contends, however, that petitioner cannot reasonably claim "an expectation of protected privacy or confidentiality." The reasons asserted for this position overlook the nature of the accountant-client relationship. The accountant, an agent for a specified purpose—*i.e.*, completing the petitioner's tax returns—bore certain fiduciary responsibilities to petitioner. One of those responsibilities was not to use the records given him for any purpose other than completing the returns. Under these circumstances, it hardly can be said that by giving the records to the accountant, the petitioner committed them to the public domain.

I defined what I believe to be the boundaries of this right to privacy in *Warden* v. *Hayden*, 387 U.S., at 323:

> "The constitutional philosophy is, I think, clear. The personal effects and possessions of the individual (all contraband and the like excepted) are sacrosanct from prying eyes, from the long arm of the law, from any rummaging by police. Privacy involves the choice of the individual to disclose or to reveal what he believes, what he thinks, what he possesses. The article may be a nondescript work of art, a manuscript of a book, a personal account book, a diary, invoices, personal clothing, jewelry, or whatnot. Those who work of art, a manuscript of a book, a personal account book, to communicate with others and to keep his affairs to himself. That dual aspect of privacy means that the individual should have the freedom to select for himself the time and circumstances when he will share his secrets with others and decide the extent of that sharing."

The majority, by the seeming implications of its opinion, has cleared the way for investigatory authorities to compel disclosure of facets of our life we heretofore considered sacrosanct. We are told that "situations may well arise where . . . the relinquishment of possession is so temporary and insignificant as to leave the personal compulsions upon the accused substantially intact." I can see no basis in the majority opinion, however, for stopping short of condemning only those intrusions resting on compulsory process against the author of the thoughts or documents. Are we now to encourage meddling by the Government and ever more ingenious methods of obtaining access to sought-after materials? The premium now will be on subterfuge, on bypassing the master of the domain by spiriting the materials away or compelling disclosure by a trusted employee or confidant.[87] Inevitably, this will lead those of us who cherish our privacy to refrain from recording our thoughts or trusting anyone with even temporary custody of documents

[87] The majority notes that "the accountant himself worked neither in petitioner's office nor as her employee." I cannot see how that factor bears on whether the "ingredient of personal compulsion against [the] accused" is present, or whether the accountant was a confidant. The majority would seem to suggest, however, that petitioner, because her business did not call for, or because she could not afford, a full-time accountant, deserves less protection under the Fifth Amendment than a taxpayer more fortunately situated.

we want to protect from public disclosure. In short, it will stultify the exchange of ideas that we have considered crucial to our democracy.

II

The decision may have a more immediate impact which the majority does not consider. Our tax laws have become so complex that very few taxpayers can afford the luxury of completing their own returns without professional assistance. If a taxpayer now wants to insure the confidentiality and privacy of his records, however, he must forgo such assistance. To my mind, the majority thus attaches a penalty to the exercise of the privilege against self-incrimination. It calls for little more discussion than to note that we have not tolerated such penalties in the past. Cf. *Uniformed Sanitation Men* v. *Commissioner of Sanitation* [note 85, *supra*]; *Gardner* v. *Broderick* [note 85, *supra*].

III

Thus, I would reverse the decision below, finding that the subpoena violated both petitioner's Fourth and Fifth Amendment rights.[88] I offer one more observation. The majority cautions that respect for our constitutional principles is eroded "when they leap their proper bounds." We should not be swayed by the popular cry for a formalistic and narrow interpretation of those provisions which safeguard our fundamental rights.

It is a Constitution we are construing, not a legislative-judicial code of conduct that suits our private value choices or that satisfies the appetite of prosecutors for more and more shortcuts that avoid constitutional barriers. Those constitutional barriers and the judicial traditions supporting them are the sources of the privacy we value so greatly. That privacy "protects people," not places, under the Fourth Amendment, *Katz* v. *United States* [note 50, *supra*]. And, as already noted, *Boyd* v. *United States, supra,* held that when it comes to the "forcible and compulsory extortion of a man's own testimony or of his private papers to be used as evidence to convict him of crime or to forfeit his goods," that is an illustration of the manner in which "the Fourth and Fifth Amendments run almost into each other."

One's privacy embraces what the person has in his home, his desk, his files, and his safe as well as what he carries on his person. It also has a very meaningful relationship to what he tells any confidant—

---

[88] In holding that "mere evidence" is not protected from seizure under the Fourth Amendment, the Court expressly refused to consider "whether there are items of evidential value whose very nature precludes them from being the object of a reasonable search and seizure." *Warden* v. *Hayden,* 387 U.S. 294. The answer to that question was clear to me when I dissented in that case and remains clear to me now.

his wife, his minister, his lawyer, or his tax accountant. The constitutional fences of law are being broken down by an ever-increasingly powerful Government that seeks to reduce every person to a digit.

After Douglas left the Court, the rule of Couch was extended to permit the IRS to reach accountant's workpapers which the taxpayer had given to his attorney whom he had retained to represent him in connection with an IRS investigation of his tax liability. The Fifth Amendment gave no more protection against extracting incriminating evidence about the taxpayer from his attorney than from his accountant. And while the lawyer-client privilege would prevent obtaining information which the taxpayer had given his lawyer for the purpose of obtaining legal advice if the client himself had a Fifth Amendment privilege to withhold it from the government, he had no such privilege here since the workpapers, prepared by the accountant and not the taxpayer, contained no "testimonial declarations" from the taxpayer. Fisher v. United States, 96 S. Ct. 1569 (1976).

Counsel

The Sixth Amendment guarantees that "In all criminal prosecutions, the accused shall enjoy the right . . . to have the Assistance of Counsel for his defence."
Shortly before Douglas came to the Court, it read this requirement to mean that, in a federal prosecution for passing counterfeit bills, the government must provide counsel at its expense for an indigent defendant who did not knowingly and intelligently waive his right to counsel.[89] Even earlier, in the famed Scottsboro case,[90] the Court had held that young, illiterate, indigent defendants prosecuted by a state in a capital case were denied due process of law where the state failed to provide counsel for them in time to prepare their defense.
When, in Betts v. Brady,[91] the Court refused to extend this ruling to a state robbery prosecution of a farm hand with little education who was convicted and sentenced to eight years—holding that the Sixth Amendment right to counsel was not so "fundamental" as to be incorporated by the Fourteenth and that there was no denial of due process because the procedure was not offensive to "common and fundamental ideas of fairness and right"—Douglas dissented on both

---

[89] *Johnson v. Zerbst*, 304 U.S. 458 (1938).
[90] *Powell v. Alabama*, 287 U.S. 45 (1932).
[91] 316 U.S. 455 (1942).

points. Thereafter, as the Court proceeded on a case-by-case basis to determine whether the gravity of the crime, the complicated nature of the charge and of possible defenses to it, the age and education of the defendant, and the conduct of the court and prosecuting officials meant that the due process clause should be read to require counsel, Douglas voted with the Court when it concluded that counsel was required and dissented when it reached the contrary conclusion. Finally, in 1963, in Gideon v. Wainright,[92] all justices concurring, Betts v. Brady was overruled and the Sixth Amendment's right to counsel in criminal cases was made applicable to the states.

HAMILTON V. ALABAMA
368 U.S. 52 (1961)

Where counsel is required—the determination of which was made on a case-by-case application of the due process clause in pre-Gideon state cases and by the Sixth Amendment in federal and post-Gideon state cases—neither constitutional provision is specific as to how soon counsel must be provided. In 1955 the Court held that a state denied due process when, in a capital case, it did not appoint counsel until after defendant was indicted because, by state law, any challenge to the racial makeup of the grand jury was required to be made before indictment.[93]

In this case, Hamilton was convicted in an Alabama court of breaking and entering a dwelling at night with intent to ravish and was sentenced to death. The state had appointed counsel for him seven weeks before his trial, but not until three days after he was arraigned on the charge and pleaded not guilty.

MR. JUSTICE DOUGLAS delivered the opinion of the Court.

The Supreme Court of Alabama, while recognizing that petitioner had a right under state law to be represented by counsel at the time of his arraignment, denied relief because there was no showing or effort to show that petitioner was "disadvantaged in any way by the absence of counsel when he interposed his plea of not guilty."

Arraignment under Alabama law is a critical stage in a criminal proceeding. It is then that the defense of insanity must be pleaded or the opportunity is lost. *Morrell v. State,* 136 Ala. 44. Thereafter that plea may not be made except in the discretion of the trial judge, and his refusal to accept it is "not revisable" on appeal. *Rohn v. State,* 186

---

[92] 372 U.S. 335 (1963).
[93] *Reece v. Georgia,* 350 U.S. 85 (1955).

Ala. 5. Pleas in abatement must also be made at the time of arraignment. It is then that motions to quash based on systematic exclusion of one race from grand juries (*Reeves* v. *State*, 264 Ala. 476), or on the ground that the grand jury was otherwise improperly drawn (*Whitehead* v. *State*, 206 Ala. 288), must be made.

Whatever may be the function and importance of arraignment in other jurisdictions,[94] we have said enough to show that in Alabama it is a critical stage in a criminal proceeding. What happens there may affect the whole trial. Available defenses may be as irretrievably lost, if not then and there asserted, as they are when an accused represented by counsel waives a right for strategic purposes. In *Powell* v. *Alabama* [note 90. *supra*] the Court said that an accused in a capital case "requires the guiding hand of counsel at every step in the proceedings against him. Without it, though he be not guilty, he faces the danger of conviction because he does not know how to establish his innocence." The guiding hand of counsel is needed at the trial "lest the unwary concede that which only bewilderment or ignorance could justify or pay a penalty which is greater than the law of the State exacts for the offense which they in fact and in law committed." *Tomkins* v. *Missouri*, 323 U.S. 485. But the same pitfalls or like ones face an accused in Alabama who is arraigned without having counsel at his side. When one pleads to a capital charge without benefit of counsel, we do not stop to determine whether prejudice resulted. *Williams* v. *Kaiser*, 323 U.S. 471. In this case the degree of prejudice can never be known. Only the presence of counsel could have enabled this accused to know all the defenses available to him and to plead intelligently.

In a later case Douglas voted with the Court to hold that where, by state law, a defendant enters his plea to the charge at a "preliminary hearing" in advance of arraignment, that hearing is a "critical stage in a criminal proceeding" at which he must have counsel.[95] For some time, however, Douglas had been suggesting that if a confession of the

---

[94] Arraignment has differing consequences in the various jurisdictions. Under federal law an arraignment is a *sine qua non* to the trial itself—the preliminary stage where the accused is informed of the indictment and pleads to it, thereby formulating the issue to be tried. That view has led some States to hold that arraignment is the first step in a trial (at least in case of felonies) at which the accused is entitled to an attorney. *People* v. *Kurant*, 331 Ill. 470.

In other States arraignment is not "a part of the trial" but "a mere formal preliminary step to an answer or plea." *Ex parte Jeffcoat*, 109 Fla. 207.

An arraignment normally, however, affords an opportunity of the accused to plead, as a condition precedent to a trial.

[95] *White* v. *Maryland*, 373 U.S. 59 (1963).

defendant was used at trial, counsel should have been available at an even earlier time.

In Crooker v. California,[96] where the Court found no violation of the due process clause where the state arrested the defendant and denied his request for an opportunity ·to call a lawyer until some five or six hours of interrogation had produced the confession used at his trial, Douglas dissented. He protested that "what takes place in the secret confines of the police station may be more critical than what takes place at the trial" and urged that "the accused who wants a counsel should have one at any time after the moment of arrest." When, in a later case, the Court found that a confession, obtained after an indicted defendant had surrendered himself to the police, was involuntary and reversed the conviction for that reason,[97] Douglas suggested that since defendant's request to consult with his counsel had been denied during interrogation, there was "an even more important ground" for decision:

> We do not have here mere suspects who are being secretly interrogated by the police as in Croocker v. California. . . . This is the case of an [indicted] accused, who is scheduled to be tried by a judge and jury, being tried in a preliminary way by the police. This is a kangaroo court procedure whereby the police produce the vital evidence in the form of a confession which is useful or necessary to obtain a conviction. They in effect deny him effective representation by counsel. This seems to me to be a flagrant violation of the principle announced in Powell v. Alabama [note 90, supra] that the right of counsel extends to the preparation for trial, as well as to the trial itself. As Professor Chafee once said, "A person accused of crime needs a lawyer right after his arrest probably more than at any other time." . . . When he is deprived of that right after indictment and before trial, he may indeed be denied effective representation by counsel at the only stage when legal aid and advice would help him.

As indicated earlier,[98] Douglas had previously argued that confessions obtained while the accused was being held without the arraignment required by law should be held inadmissible. In 1961 he combined his arguments: "I would hold that any confession obtained by the police while the defendant is under detention is inadmissible, unless there is prompt arraignment and the accused is informed of his right to silence and accorded an opportunity to consult counsel."[99] The

[96] 357 U.S. 433 (1958).
[97] *Spano v. New York*, 360 U.S. 315 (1959).
[98] See p. 316, *supra*.
[99] *Reck v. Pate*, 367 U.S. 433 (1961).

principle should be "that any accused—whether rich or poor—has the right to consult a lawyer before talking with the police; and if he makes the request for a lawyer and it is refused," he has been denied the assistance of counsel guaranteed by the Sixth Amendment. If that were required, the lawyer could then "clearly and unequivocally" advise the defendant of his Fifth Amendment privilege against self-incrimination.[100]

The Court accepted a part of these views in 1964, after the Sixth Amendment had been held applicable to the states,[101] when it held inadmissible in a federal prosecution a conversation overheard by a narcotics agent between defendant and an erstwhile friend sitting in the friend's car, which the agent had wired for sound. Defendant was denied the "basic protections" of the right to counsel, said the Court, "when there was used against him at his trial evidence of his own incriminating words, which federal agents had deliberately elicited from him after he had been indicted and in the absence of his counsel."[102]

More of Douglas' views were adopted in the same year when the Court held inadmissible in a state trial incriminating statements elicited from defendant at the police station, after his arrest but before indictment, and after denial of his request to see his attorney.

> *[W]here, as here, the investigation is no longer a general inquiry into an unsolved crime but has begun to focus on a particular suspect, the suspect has been taken into police custody, the police carry out a process of interrogations that lends itself to eliciting incriminating statements, the suspect has requested and been denied an opportunity to consult with his lawyer, and the police have not effectively warned him of his absolute constitutional right to remain silent, the accused has been denied "the Assistance of Counsel" in violation of the Sixth Amendment.*[103]

Finally, in 1966, after the Fifth Amendment privilege against self-incrimination had also been held applicable to the states,[104] the Court adopted Douglas' views entirely in the Miranda *case.[105] In order to implement both the right to counsel and the privilege against self-incrimination, that case laid down rules for police officers, state and federal, where statements stemming from custodial interrogation are used in evidence. "[U]nless other fully effective means are adopted to notify the [accused] person of his right of silence" and unless those*

---

[100] *Culombe* v. *Connecticut*, 367 U.S. 568 (1961).
[101] See note 92, *supra.*
[102] *Massiah* v. *United States*, 377 U.S. 201 (1964).
[103] *Escobedo* v. *Illinois*, 378 U.S. 478 (1964).
[104] Note 82, *supra.*
[105] *Miranda* v. *Arizona*, 384 U.S. 436 (1966).

*alternative means afford him a "continuous opportunity to exercise it,"
law enforcement officers must observe the following rules "when an
individual is taken into custody or otherwise deprived of his freedom of
action in any significant way"*: (1) *"At the outset, if a person in custody
is to be subjected to interrogation, he must first be informed in clear
and unequivocal terms that he has the right to remain silent."* (2) *"The
warning of the right to remain silent must be accompanied by the explanation that anything said can and will be used against the individual
in court."* (3) *"[He must also] be clearly informed that he has the right
to consult with a lawyer and to have the lawyer with him during interrogation"* and *"that if he is indigent a lawyer will be appointed to
represent him."* (4) *"If the individual indicates in any manner, at any
time prior to or during questioning, that he wishes to remain silent, the
interrogation must cease."* (5) *"If the individual states that he wants an
attorney, the interrogation must cease until an attorney is present."* (6)
*While he may waive his Fifth Amendment right to remain silent and
his Sixth Amendment right to counsel, if the interrogation goes on
"without the presence of an attorney and a statement is taken, a heavy
burden rests on the government to demonstrate that the defendant
knowingly and intelligently waived" those rights.*

Miranda, *which reversed one federal ·and two state convictions because confessions were used at trial which had been obtained without
compliance with what has come to be known as the "Miranda warnings," was a 5-to-4 decision with Chief Justice Warren and Justices Black,
Douglas, Brennan, Goldberg, and Fortas in the majority, and Justices
Clark, Harlan, Stewart, and White in dissent. It has not fared well as
Justice Marshall succeeded Clark in 1967, Chief Justice Burger succeeded Warren in 1969, Justice Blackmun succeeded Justice Fortas in
1970, and Justices Powell and Rehnquist succeeded Justices Black and
Harlan in 1972.*

In 1971 *the Court held that statements taken from a defendant in
violation of the* Miranda *requirements, and hence inadmissible as part
of the prosecution's case, could nonetheless be used by the prosecutor,
if defendant took the stand to testify in his defense, to impeach his
testimony on cross-examination by asking him if he had not earlier made
statements to the police which were inconsistent with his testimony.
Douglas joined dissenters who protested that to allow this use of the
tainted statement deprived the defendant of an unfettered choice to
testify or to remain silent which the privilege against self-incrimination
was intended to give him and that the courts should not so aid and abet
the law-breaking officer.*[106]

---

[106] Harris v. New York, 401 U.S. 222 (1971).

MICHIGAN v. TUCKER
417 U.S. 433 (1974)

In this case Tucker was convicted of rape after a trial in which one of the prosecution's key witnesses was a person whose identity was learned by the police while questioning the defendant at the police station after his arrest, without having advised him that he would be furnished counsel free of charge if he could not afford counsel. Tucker was an indigent who was represented at trial and in all subsequent proceedings by court-appointed counsel. The questioning took place before the Miranda *decision, but the trial, at which the defendant's counsel sought unsuccessfully to have the testimony of the witness excluded, took place after that decision.*

In this habeas corpus *proceeding the Court held that the defendant was entitled to no relief. Since the police at the time of their questioning of defendant could not have known of the* Miranda *requirements, they had not acted willfully. There was no reason to believe that the witness' testimony was unreliable because of the police's treatment of defendant, and no statement made by the defendant was introduced at trial. In short, there was no violation of the privilege against self-incrimination but only a departure "from the prophylactic standards later laid down by this Court in* Miranda *to safeguard that privilege."*

Mr. Justice Douglas, dissenting.

In *Miranda* we said:

> "The need for counsel in order to protect the privilege [against self-incrimination] exists for the indigent as well as the affluent. . . . While authorities are not required to relieve the accused of his poverty, they have the obligation not to take advantage of indigence in the administration of justice. . . .
>
> "In order to fully apprise a person interrogated of the extent of his rights under this system then, it is necessary to warn him not only that he has the right to consult with an attorney, but also that if he is indigent a lawyer will be appointed to represent him."

I cannot agree when the Court says that the interrogation here "did not abridge respondent's constitutional privilege against compulsory self-incrimination, but departed only from the prophylactic standards later laid down by this Court in *Miranda* to safeguard that privilege." The Court is not free to prescribe preferred modes of interrogation absent a constitutional basis. We held the "requirement of warnings and waiver of rights [to be] fundamental with respect to the Fifth Amendment privilege" and without so holding we would have been powerless to reverse Miranda's conviction. While *Miranda* recognized that police need not mouth the precise words contained in the Court's opinion, such warnings were held necessary "unless other fully effective means are adopted to notify the person" of his rights. There is no contention here that other means were adopted. The respondent's statements were thus obtained "under circumstances that did not meet *constitutional* standards for protection of the privilege [against self-incrimination]."

With the premise that respondent was subjected to an unconstitutional interrogation, there remains the question whether not only the testimony elicited in the interrogation but also the fruits thereof must be suppressed. Mr. Justice Holmes first articulated the "fruits" doctrine in *Silverthorne Lumber Co.* v. *United States*, 251 U.S. 385 (1920). In that case the Government had illegally seized the petitioner's corporate books and documents. The Government photographed the items before returning them and used the photographs as a basis to subpoena the petitioner to produce the originals before the grand jury. The petitioner refused to comply and was cited for contempt. In reversing, the Court noted that "[t]he essence of a provision forbidding the acquisition of evidence in a certain way is that not merely evidence so acquired shall not be used before the Court but that it shall not be used at all."

The principle received more recent recognition in *Wong Sun* v. *United States*, 371 U.S. 471 (1963). There one Toy had made statements to federal agents and the statements were held inadmissible against him. The statements led the agents to one Yee and at Yee's home the agents found narcotics which were introduced at trial against Toy. In reversing Toy's conviction the Court held that the narcotics discovered at Yee's home must be excluded just as Toy's statements which led to that discovery.

The testimony of the witness in this case was no less a fruit of unconstitutional police action than the photographs in *Silverthorne* or the narcotics in *Wong Sun*. The [state] has stipulated that the identity and the whereabouts of the witness and his connection with the case were learned about only through the unconstitutional interrogation of the respondent. His testimony must be excluded to comply with *Miranda's* mandate that "*no* evidence obtained as a result of interrogation [not preceded by adequate warnings] can be used against" an accused.

In *Johnson* v. *New Jersey*, 384 U.S. 719 (1966), the Court held that statements obtained in violation of *Miranda* standards must be excluded from all trials occurring after the date of the *Miranda* decision. MR. JUSTICE BRENNAN [in a concurring opinion in this case] suggests that *Johnson* be limited and that the fruits derived from unlawful pre-*Miranda* interrogations be admissible in trials subsequent to the *Miranda* decision. Though respondent's trial occurred subsequent to the *Miranda* decision, his interrogation preceded it. I disagree, as I disagreed in *Johnson*, that any defendant can be deprived of the full protection of the Fifth Amendment, as the Court has construed it in *Miranda*, based upon an arbitrary reference to the date of his interrogation or his trial.

I find any such reference to the calendar in determining the beneficiaries of constitutional pronouncements to be a grossly invidious discrimination. Miranda was interrogated on March 13, 1963; Tucker was interrogated more than three years later in April 1966. I can conceive of no principled way to deprive Tucker of the constitutional guarantees afforded Miranda. The reason put forward for refusing to apply the strictures of *Miranda* to interrogations which preceded the decision is that the purpose of *Miranda*'s rules is the deterrence of unconstitutional interrogation. "The inference I gather from these repeated statements is that the rule is not a right or privilege accorded to defendants charged with crime but is a sort of punishment against officers in order to keep them from depriving people of their constitutional rights. In passing I would say that if that is the sole purpose, reason, object and effect of the rule, the Court's action in adopting it sounds more like law-making than construing the Constitution." 381 U.S., at 649 (Black, J., dissenting [in *Linkletter* v. *Walker*, 381 U.S. 618 (1965)]). *Miranda*'s purpose was not promulgation of judicially preferred standards for police interrogation, a function we are quite powerless to perform; the decision enunciated "*constitutional* standards for protection of the privilege" against self-incrimination. 384 U.S., at 491. People who are in jail because of a State's use of unconstitutionally derived evidence are entitled to a new trial, with the safeguards the Constitution provides, without regard to when the constitutional violation occurred, when the trial occurred, or when the conviction became "final."

In a later case in which Douglas did not participate because of illness, the Court extended the rule of the Harris *case*[107] *to allow the state to use, for impeachment purposes on cross-examination when defendant takes the stand, statements made by defendant during police interrogation following his request for permission to call his lawyer and before he was allowed to do so.*[108]

[107] Note 106, *supra*.
[108] *Oregon* v. *Hass*, 420 U.S. 714 (1975).

*Since Douglas left the Court, there have been further erosions of
Miranda. Its requirements were held not violated where a defendant
under arrest for suspected robbery was given his* Miranda *warnings but
was not interrogated at that time (when he said he did not want to
answer questions about robberies), but then two hours later was again
given his warnings and subjected to an interrogation, about a murder
occurring during an attempted holdup, during which he made incriminating statements later used to convict him of murder.*[109] Miranda
*was held not to apply where Internal Revenue Service agents inter-
rogated a taxpayer for three hours at his home in the evening after
their investigation of possible criminal tax fraud had focused on him,
since he was not then in custody.*[110] *But, at least where an arrested
suspect who has been given his warnings, including advice of his right
to remain silent, elects to act on that advice, he cannot be impeached
at his later trial by cross-examination about his earlier silence.*[111]

ARGERSINGER v. HAMLIN
407 U.S. 25 (1972)

*Although the Sixth Amendment guarantees a right to jury trial, as
well as a right to counsel and a number of other rights, in "all criminal
prosecutions," the Court has concluded, as will be seen in more detail
later,*[112] *that the right to jury trial does not extend to "petty offenses"—
those for which punishment does not exceed six months' imprisonment
or a fine of $500.*

*The federal Criminal Justice Act of 1964, providing for the appoint-
ment of counsel in federal criminal prosecutions, excludes "petty offenses" from its coverage. And in 1971 the Supreme Court itself, over
the dissents of Justices Black and Douglas, promulgated Rules of
Procedure for the Trial of Minor Offenses before United States Magistrates, which make no provision for appointment of counsel or jury
trial for minor offenses which are "petty."*

*In this case petitioner was tried in a state court, without jury or
counsel, and convicted of carrying a concealed weapon, an offense*

---

[109] *Michigan* v. *Mosley*, 423 U.S. 96 (1975).

[110] *Beckwith* v. *United States*, 96 S. Ct. 1612 (1976). *Orozco* v. *Texas*, 394 U.S.
324 (1969), where *Miranda* was applied to police officers who interrogated a murder
suspect in his bed in a boardinghouse room in the middle of the night and one of
whom testified at the trial that the suspect was "under arrest" and not free to
leave the room, was said in *Beckwith* to be distinguishable because of "the
custodial nature of the interrogation."

[111] *Doyle* v. *Ohio*, 96 S. Ct. 2240 (1976).

[112] See p. 391, *infra*.

punishable by imprisonment up to six months, a $1,000 fine, or both. He was sentenced to serve ninety days in jail and sought by habeas corpus *to obtain his release on the ground that he had been denied his Sixth Amendment right to counsel.*

MR. JUSTICE DOUGLAS delivered the opinion of the Court.

The Sixth Amendment, which in enumerated situations has been made applicable to the States by reason of the Fourteenth Amendment, provides specified standards for "all criminal prosecutions."

One is the requirement of a "public trial." *In re Oliver* [333 U.S. 257] held that the right to a "public trial" was applicable to a state proceeding even though only a 60-day sentence was involved.

Another guarantee is the right to be informed of the nature and cause of the accusation. Still another, the right of confrontation. *Pointer* v. *Texas* [380 U.S. 400]. And another, compulsory process for obtaining witnesses in one's favor. *Washington* v. *Texas* [388 U.S. 14]. We have never limited these rights to felonies or to lesser but serious offenses.

Respecting the right to a speedy and public trial, the right to be informed of the nature and cause of the accusation, the right to confront and cross-examine witnesses, the right to compulsory process for obtaining witnesses, it was recently stated, "It is simply not arguable, nor has any court ever held, that the trial of a petty offense may be held in secret, or without notice to the accused of the charges, or that in such cases the defendant has no right to confront his accusers or to compel the attendance of witnesses in his own behalf." Junker, The Right to Counsel in Misdemeanor Cases, 43 Wash. L. Rev. 685, 705 (1968).

The right to trial by jury, also guaranteed by the Sixth Amendment by reason of the Fourteenth, was limited by *Duncan* v. *Louisiana* [391 U.S. 145] to trials where the potential punishment was imprisonment for six months or more. But the right to trial by jury has a different genealogy and is brigaded with a system of trial to a judge alone.

While there is historical support for limiting the "deep commitment" to trial by jury to "serious criminal cases,"[113] there is no such support for a similar limitation on the right to assistance of counsel:

> "Originally, in England, a person charged with treason or felony was denied the aid of counsel, except in respect of legal questions which the accused himself might suggest. At the same time parties

[113] See Frankfurter & Corcoran, Petty Federal Offenses and the Constitutional Guaranty of Trial by Jury, 39 Harv. L. Rev. 917, 980–982 (1926); *James* v. *Headley*, 410 F. 2d 325, 331. Cf. Kaye, Petty Offenders Have No Peers!, 26 U. Chi. L. Rev. 245 (1959).

in civil cases and persons accused of misdemeanors were entitled
to the full assistance of counsel. . . .

.   .   .   .   .

   "[It] appears that in at least twelve of the thirteen colonies the
rule of the English common law, in the respect now under consideration, had been definitely rejected and the right to counsel
fully recognized in all criminal prosecutions, save that in one or
two instances the right was limited to capital offenses or to the
more serious crimes. . . ." *Powell* v. *Alabama* [note 90, *supra*].

The Sixth Amendment thus extended the right to counsel beyond
its common-law dimensions. But there is nothing in the language of the
Amendment, its history, or in the decisions of this Court, to indicate
that it was intended to embody a retraction of the right in petty
offenses wherein the common law previously did require that counsel
be provided.

We reject, therefore, the premise that since prosecutions for crimes
punishable by imprisonment for less than six months may be tried
without a jury, they may also be tried without a lawyer.

The assistance of counsel is often a requisite to the very existence
of a fair trial. The Court in *Powell* v. *Alabama, supra*—a capital case—
said:

   "The right to be heard would be, in many cases, of little avail if it
   did not comprehend the right to be heard by counsel. Even the
   intelligent and educated layman has small and sometimes no skill
   in the science of law. If charged with crime, he is incapable, generally, of determining for himself whether the indictment is good
   or bad. He is unfamiliar with the rules of evidence. Left without
   the aid of counsel he may be put on trial without a proper charge,
   and convicted upon incompetent evidence, or evidence irrelevant
   to the issue or otherwise inadmissible. He lacks both the skill and
   knowledge adequately to prepare his defense, even though he have
   a perfect one. He requires the guiding hand of counsel at every
   step in the proceedings against him. Without it, though he be
   not guilty, he faces the danger of conviction because he does not
   know how to establish his innocence. If that be true of men of intelligence, how much more true is it of the ignorant and illiterate,
   or those of feeble intellect."

In *Gideon* v. *Wainwright* [note 92, *supra*], we dealt with a felony
trial. But we did not so limit the need of the accused for a lawyer.
We said:

"[I]n our adversary system of criminal justice, any person haled into court, who is too poor to hire a lawyer, cannot be assured a fair trial unless counsel is provided for him. This seems to us to be an obvious truth. Governments, both state and federal, quite properly spend vast sums of money to establish machinery to try defendants accused of crime. Lawyers to prosecute are everywhere deemed essential to protect the public's interest in an orderly society. Similarly, there are few defendants charged with crime, few indeed, who fail to hire the best lawyers they can get to prepare and present their defenses. That government hires lawyers to prosecute and defendants who have the money hire lawyers to defend are the strongest indications of the widespread belief that lawyers in criminal courts are necessities, not luxuries. The right of one charged with crime to counsel may not be deemed fundamental and essential to fair trials in some countries, but it is in ours. From the very beginning, our state and national constitutions and laws have laid great emphasis on procedural and substantive safeguards designed to assure fair trials before impartial tribunals in which every defendant stands equal before the law. This noble ideal cannot be realized if the poor man charged with crime has to face his accusers without a lawyer to assist him."

Both *Powell* and *Gideon* involved felonies. But their rationale has relevance to any criminal trial, where an accused is deprived of his liberty.

The requirement of counsel may well be necessary for a fair trial even in a petty-offense prosecution. We are by no means convinced that legal and constitutional questions involved in a case that actually leads to imprisonment even for a brief period are any less complex than when a person can be sent off for six months or more.

The trial of vagrancy cases is illustrative. While only brief sentences of imprisonment may be imposed, the cases often bristle with thorny constitutional questions. See *Papachristou* v. *Jacksonville* [page 311, supra].

Beyond the problem of trials and appeals is that of the guilty plea, a problem which looms large in misdemeanor as well as in felony cases. Counsel is needed so that the accused may know precisely what he is doing, so that he is fully aware of the prospect of going to jail or prison, and so that he is treated fairly by the prosecution.

In addition, the volume of misdemeanor cases, far greater in number than felony prosecutions, may create an obsession for speedy dispositions, regardless of the fairness of the result. The Report by the

President's Commission on Law Enforcement and Administration of Justice, The Challenge of Crime in a Free Society 128 (1967), states:

> "For example, until legislation last year increased the number of judges, the District of Columbia Court of General Sessions had four judges to process the preliminary stages of more than 1,500 felony cases, 7,500 serious misdemeanor cases, and 38,000 petty offenses and an equal number of traffic offenses per year. An inevitable consequence of volume that large is the almost total preoccupation in such a court with the movement of cases. The calendar is long, speed often is substituted for care, and casually arranged out-of-court compromise too often is substituted for adjudication. Inadequate attention tends to be given to the individual defendant, whether in protecting his rights, sifting the facts at trial, deciding the social risk he presents, or determining how to deal with him after conviction. The frequent result is futility and failure."

That picture is seen in almost every report. "The misdemeanor trial is characterized by insufficient and frequently irresponsible preparation on the part of the defense, the prosecution, and the court. Everything is rush, rush." Hellerstein, The Importance of the Misdemeanor Case on Trial and Appeal, 28 The Legal Aid Brief Case 151, 152 (1970).

There is evidence of the prejudice which results to misdemeanor defendants from this "assembly-line justice." One study concluded that "[m]isdemeanants represented by attorneys are five times as likely to emerge from police court with all charges dismissed as are defendants who face similar charges without counsel." American Civil Liberties Union, Legal Counsel for Misdemeanants, Preliminary Report 1 (1970).

We must conclude, therefore, that the problems associated with misdemeanor and petty[114] offenses often require the presence of counsel to insure the accused a fair trial. MR. JUSTICE POWELL suggests [in a concurring opinion in this case] that these problems are raised even in situations where there is no prospect of imprisonment. We need not

---

[114] Title 18 U.S.C. §1 defines a petty offense as one in which the penalty does not exceed imprisonment for six months, or a fine of not more than $500, or both. [The Criminal Justice Act of 1964] provides for the appointment of counsel for indigents in all cases "other than a petty offense." But [that Act] contains a congressional plan for furnishing legal representation at federal expense for certain indigents and does not purport to cover the full range of constitutional rights to counsel.

Indeed, the Conference Report on the Criminal Justice Act of 1964 made clear the conferees' belief that the right to counsel extends to all offenses, petty and serious alike. H. R. Conf. Rep. No. 1709, 88th Cong., 2d Sess. (1964).

consider the requirements of the Sixth Amendment as regards the right to counsel where loss of liberty is not involved, however, for here petitioner was in fact sentenced to jail. And, as we said in *Baldwin* v. *New York*, 399 U.S., at 73, "the prospect of imprisonment for however short a time will seldom be viewed by the accused as a trivial or 'petty' matter and may well result in quite serious repercussions affecting his career and his reputation."

We hold, therefore, that absent a knowing and intelligent waiver, no person may be imprisoned for any offense, whether classified as petty, misdemeanor, or felony, unless he was represented by counsel at his trial.[115]

We do not sit as an ombudsman to direct state courts how to manage their affairs but only to make clear the federal constitutional requirement. How crimes should be classified is largely a state matter.[116] The fact that traffic charges technically fall within the category of "criminal prosecutions" does not necessarily mean that many of them will be brought into the class[117] where imprisonment actually occurs.

[115] We do not share MR. JUSTICE POWELL's doubt that the Nation's legal resources are sufficient to implement the rule we announce today. It has been estimated that between 1,575 and 2,300 full-time counsel would be required to represent *all* indigent misdemeanants, excluding traffic offenders. Note, Dollars and Sense of an Expanded Right to Counsel, 55 Iowa L. Rev. 1249, 1260–1261 (1970). These figures are relatively insignificant when compared to the estimated 355,200 attorneys in the United States (Statistical Abstract of the United States 153 (1971)), a number which is projected to double by the year 1985. See Ruud, That Burgeoning Law School Enrollment, 58 A. B. A. J. 146, 147. Indeed, there are 18,000 new admissions to the bar each year—3,500 more lawyers than are required to fill the "estimated 14,500 average annual openings."

[116] One partial solution to the problem of minor offenses may well be to remove them from the court system. The American Bar Association Special Committee on Crime Prevention and Control recently recommended, *inter alia*, that:
"Regulation of various types of conduct which harm no one other than those involved (e.g., public drunkenness, narcotics addiction, vagrancy, and deviant sexual behavior) should be taken out of the courts. The handling of these matters should be transferred to nonjudicial entities, such as detoxification centers, narcotics treatment centers and social service agencies. The handling of other nonserious offenses, such as housing code and traffic violations, should be transferred to specialized administrative bodies." ABA Report, New Perspectives on Urban Crime iv (1972). Such a solution, of course, is peculiarly within the province of state and local legislatures.

[117] "Forty thousand traffic charges (arising out of 150,000 nonparking traffic citations) were disposed of by court action in Seattle during 1964. The study showed, however, that in only about 4,500 cases was there any possibility of imprisonment as the result of a traffic conviction. In only three kinds of cases was the accused exposed to any danger of imprisonment: (1) where the offense charged was hit-and-run, reckless or drunken driving; or (2) where any additional traffic

Under the rule we announce today, every judge will know when the trial of a misdemeanor starts that no imprisonment may be imposed, even though local law permits it, unless the accused is represented by counsel. He will have a measure of the seriousness and gravity of the offense and therefore know when to name a lawyer to represent the accused before the trial starts.

The run of misdemeanors will not be affected by today's ruling. But in those that end up in the actual deprivation of a person's liberty, the accused will receive the benefit of "the guiding hand of counsel" so necessary when one's liberty is in jeopardy.

Grand Jury Indictment

The Fifth Amendment provides that "No person shall be held to answer for a capital, or otherwise infamous crime, unless on a presentment or indictment of a Grand Jury, except in cases arising in the land and naval forces."[118] The question of the application of this guarantee to the states has not been raised since it was last rejected in 1928.[119] But as previously indicated,[120] though the states are not required to use grand juries and may prosecute on the charge of a prosecuting official, where they do employ a grand jury they are forbidden by the equal protection clause systematically to exclude persons from the grand jury on the basis of race.

In a series of early cases, the Court concluded that an "infamous crime" within the meaning of the Fifth Amendment's indictment guarantee is one for which the authorized punishment includes imprisonment at hard labor or in a penitentiary—regardless of the punishment actually imposed in the particular case.[121] Under current federal law,

---

violation was charged against an individual subject to a suspended sentence for a previous violation; or (3) where, whatever the offense charged, the convicted individual was unable to pay the fine imposed." Junker, The Right to Counsel in Misdemeanor Cases, 43 Wash. L. Rev. 685, 711 (1968).

[118] The "presentment" referred to in the Fifth Amendment was formerly used when the grand jury filed a charge on its own initiative rather than acting on a bill of indictment brought before it by the prosecuting attorney. Under current federal practice, all criminal charges by a grand jury are by indictment.

[119] See note 11, *supra.*

[120] See p. 322, *supra.*

[121] *Ex parte Wilson*, 114 U.S. 417 (1885); *Mackin v. United States*, 117 U.S. 348 (1886); *Wong Wing v. United States*, 163 U.S. 228 (1896); *United States v. Moreland*, 258 U.S. 433 (1922); *Brede v. Powers*, 263 U.S. 4 (1923).

this embraces all crimes for which a term of more than one year is authorized, since anyone sentenced to more than a year may be required to serve his term in a penitentiary. Crimes neither capital nor infamous may be prosecuted on an information filed by a United States Attorney.[122]

The Court has said that "the most valuable function of the grand jury [is] not only to examine into the commission of crimes, but to stand between the prosecutor and the accused, and to determine whether the charge was founded upon credible testimony or was dictated by malice or personal ill will."[123] *But in a 1956 decision in which Douglas joined, the Court held that an indictment is valid although the grand jury heard only hearsay testimony which would not be admissible at trial. "[O]ur constitutional grand jury was intended to operate substantially like its English progenitor. The . . . English . . . grand jurors could act on their own knowledge and were free to make their presentments or indictments on such information as they deemed satisfactory."*[124] *But Douglas joined dissenters when the Court later held that a witness summoned before the grand jury could not refuse to answer questions based on evidence obtained by an unlawful search and seizure.*[125]

In another case, the Court held that persons summoned by a state fire marshal, investigating a fire on their business premises, to testify in a nonpublic hearing are not entitled to have counsel present at that hearing. In doing so, the Court endorsed lower federal court decisions holding that one called before a grand jury has no right to counsel and concluded that the same rule should apply to the fire marshal's investigation, even though that investigation could culminate in arson charges.[126] *Douglas joined in a dissent which did not challenge the assumption as to grand juries, but said in part:*

> *To support its decision that Ohio can punish a witness for refusing to submit to the Fire Marshal's secret interrogation, the majority places heavy reliance on the practice of examining witnesses before a grand jury in secret without the presence of the witness' counsel. But any surface support the grand jury practice may lend disappears upon analysis of that institution. The traditional English and American grand jury is composed of 12 to 23 members selected from the general citizenry of the locality where*

[122] *Duke v. United States,* 301 U.S. 492 (1937).
[123] *Hale v. Henkel,* 201 U.S. 43 (1906).
[124] *Costello v. United States,* 350 U.S. 359 (1956).
[125] *United States v. Calandra,* 414 U.S. 338 (1974).
[126] *In re Groban,* 352 U.S. 330 (1957).

the alleged crime was committed. They bring into the grand jury room the experience, knowledge and viewpoint of all sections of the community. They have no axes to grind and are not charged personally with the administration of the law. No one of them is a prosecuting attorney or law-enforcement officer ferreting out crime. It would be very difficult for officers of the state seriously to abuse or deceive a witness in the presence of the grand jury. Similarly the presence of the jurors offers a substantial safeguard against the officers' misrepresentation, unintentional or otherwise, of the witness' statements and conduct before the grand jury. The witness can call on the grand jurors if need be for their normally unbiased testimony as to what occurred before them.

Secret inquisitions are dangerous things justly feared by free men everywhere. They are the breeding place for arbitrary misuse of official power. They are often the beginning of tyranny as well as indispensable instruments for its survival. Modern as well as ancient history bears witness that both innocent and guilty have been seized by officers of the state and whisked away for secret interrogation or worse until the groundwork has been securely laid for their inevitable conviction. While the labels applied to this practice have frequently changed, the central idea wherever and whenever carried out remains unchanging—extraction of "statements" by one means or another from an individual by officers of the state while he is held incommunicado. I reiterate my belief that it violates the Due Process Clause to compel a person to answer questions at a secret interrogation where he is denied legal assistance and where he is subject to the uncontrolled and invisible exercise of power by government officials. Such procedures are a grave threat to the liberties of a free people.

HANNAH V. LARCHE
363 U.S. 420 (1960)

The federal Commission on Civil Rights, investigating complaints that blacks had been deprived of their voting rights in Louisiana, summoned state voting registrars to appear before it at a hearing it had scheduled in Shreveport. Those summoned sought to enjoin the hearing on the ground that the commission's rules of procedure were unconstitutional under the due process clause of the Fifth Amendment in that they provided that the identity of the persons submitting complaints to the commission need not be disclosed, and that those summoned to testify before the commission, including persons against whom complaints had been filed, might not cross-examine other wit-

nesses. The Court found the commission's rules free from constitutional infirmity since the commission was not authorized to take "any affirmative action which will affect an individual's legal rights," its only function being to investigate and "to find facts which may subsequently be used as the basis for legislative or executive action."

MR. JUSTICE DOUGLAS, dissenting.

The cause which the majority opinion serves is, on the surface, one which a person dedicated to constitutional principles could not question. At the bottom of this controversy is the right to vote protected by the Fifteenth Amendment. That Amendment withholds power from either the States or the United States to deny or abridge the right to vote "on account of race, color, or previous condition of servitude." This right stands beyond the reach of government. By democratic values this right is fundamental, for the very existence of government dedicated to the concept "of the people, by the people, for the people," to use Lincoln's words, depends on the franchise.

Yet important as these civil rights are, it will not do to sacrifice other civil rights in order to protect them. We live and work under a Constitution. The temptation of many men of goodwill is to cut corners, take short cuts, and reach the desired end regardless of the means. Worthy as I think the ends are which the Civil Rights Commission advances in these cases, I think the particular means used are unconstitutional.

The Commission, created by Congress, is a part of "the executive branch" of the Government, whose members are appointed by the President and confirmed by the Senate. It is given broad powers of investigation with the view of making a report with "findings and recommendations" to the Congress.

Complaints have been filed with the Commission charging respondents, who are registrars of voters in Louisiana, with depriving persons of their voting rights by reason of their color. If these charges are true and if the registrars acted willfully, the registrars are criminally responsible under a federal [Civil Rights] statute which subjects to fine and imprisonment anyone who willfully deprives a citizen of any right under the Constitution "by reason of his color, or race."

The investigation and hearing by the Commission are therefore necessarily aimed at determining if this criminal law has been violated.

The Civil Rights Commission is an arm of the Executive. There is, in my view, only one way the Chief Executive may move against a person accused of a crime and deny him the right of confrontation and cross-examination and that is by the grand jury.

The grand jury is the accusatory body in federal law as provided by the Fifth Amendment. The essence of the institution of the grand jury was stated by 1 Stephen, History of Criminal Law of England, 252: "The body of the country are the accusers." The grand jury brings suspects before neighbors, not strangers. Just recently in *Stirone* v. *United States*, 361 U.S. 212, 218, we said, "The very purpose of the requirement that a man be indicted by grand jury is to limit his jeopardy to offenses charged by a group of his fellow citizens acting independently of either prosecuting attorney or judge."

This Commission has no such guarantee of fairness. Its members are not drawn from the neighborhood. The members cannot be as independent as grand juries because they meet not for one occasion only; they do a continuing job for the executive and, if history is a guide, tend to acquire a vested interest in that role.

The grand jury, adopted as a safeguard against "hasty, malicious, and oppressive" action by the Federal Government, *Ex parte Bain*, 121 U.S. 1, stands as an important safeguard to the citizen against open and public accusations of crime. Today the grand jury may act on its own volition, though originally specific charges by private prosecutors were the basis of its action. It has broad investigational powers to look into what may be offensive against federal criminal law. An indictment returned by a grand jury may not be challenged because it rests wholly on hearsay. *Costello* v. *United States* [note 124, *supra*]. An accused is not entitled to a hearing before a grand jury, nor to present evidence, nor to be represented by counsel; and a grand jury may act secretly— a procedure normally abhorrent to due process. In this country as in England of old, the grand jury is convened as a body of laymen, free from technical rules, acting in secret, pledged to indict no one because of prejudice and to free no one because of special favor.

Grand juries have their defects. They do not always return a true bill, for while the prejudices of the community may radiate through them, they also have the saving quality of being familiar with the people involved. They are the only accusatory body in the Federal Government that is recognized by the Constitution. I would allow no other engine of government, either executive or legislative, to take their place—at least when the right of confrontation and cross-examination are denied the accused as is done in these cases.

The might and power of the Federal Government have no equal. When its guns are leveled at a citizen on charges that he committed a federal crime, it is for me no answer to say that the only purpose is to report his activities to the President and Congress, not to turn him over to the District Attorney for prosecution. Our Constitution was drawn on the theory that there are certain things government may not do to the citizen and that there are other things that may be done only in a specific manner. The relationship of the Federal Government to a man charged with crime is carefully defined. Its power may be marshalled against him, but only in a defined way. When we allow this substitute method, we make an innovation that does not comport with that due process which the Fifth Amendment requires of the Federal Government. When the Federal Government prepares to inquire into charges that a person has violated federal law, the Fifth Amendment tells us how it can proceed.

The Civil Rights Commission, it is true, returns no indictment. Yet in a real sense the hearings on charges that a registrar has committed a federal offense are a trial. Moreover, these hearings before the Commission may be televised or broadcast on the radio.[127] In our day we have seen Congressional Committees probing into alleged criminal conduct of witnesses appearing on the television screen. This is in reality a trial in which the whole Nation sits as a jury. Their verdict does not send men to prison. But it often condemns men or produces evidence to convict and even saturates the Nation with prejudice against an accused so that a fair trial may be impossible. As stated in 37 A. B. A. J. 392 (1951), "If several million television viewers see and hear a politician, a businessman or a movie actor subjected to searching interrogation, without ever having an opportunity to cross-examine his accusers or offer evidence in his own support, that man will stand convicted, or at least seriously compromised, in the public mind, whatever the later formal findings may be." The use of this procedure puts in jeopardy our traditional concept of the way men should be tried and replaces it with "a new concept of guilt based on inquisitorial devices." Note, 26 Temp. L. Q. 70, 73.

Respondents ask no more than the right to know the charges, to be confronted with the accuser, and to cross-examine him. Absent these rights, they ask for an injunction. If the hearings are to be without the safeguards which due process requires of all trials—civil and criminal—there is only one way I know by which the Federal Government may proceed and that is by grand jury. If these trials before the Commission are to be held on charges that these respondents are criminals, the least we can do is to allow them to know what they are being tried

[127] The Rules of the Commission by Subdivision (k) provide:

"Subject to the physical limitations of the hearing room and consideration of the physical comfort of Commission members, staff, and witnesses, equal and reasonable access for coverage of the hearings shall be provided to the various means of communications, including newspapers, magazines, radio, news reels, and television. However, no witness shall be televised, filmed or photographed during the hearings if he objects on the ground of distraction, harassment, or physical handicap."

for, and to confront their accusers and to cross-examine them.[128] This protection would be extended to them in any preliminary hearing, even in one before a United States Commissioner. Confrontation and cross-examination are so basic to our concept of due process that no proceeding by an administrative agency is a fair one that denies these rights.

I think due process is described in the Constitution and limited and circumscribed by it. The Constitution is explicit as respects the permissible accusatory process that the Executive can employ against the citizen. Men of goodwill, not evil ones only, invent, under feelings of urgency, new and different procedures that have an awful effect on the citizen. The new accusatory procedure survives if a transient majority of the Court are persuaded that the device is fair or decent. My view of the Constitution confines judges—as well as the lawmakers and the Executive—to the procedures expressed in the Constitution. We look to the Constitution—not to the personal predilections of the judges—to see what is permissible. Since summoning an accused by the Government to explain or justify his conduct, that is charged as a crime, may be done only in one way, I would require a constitutional amendment before it can be done in a different way.

Speedy and Public Trial

The Sixth Amendment provides that "In all criminal prosecutions, the accused shall enjoy the right to a speedy and public trial." In 1948 Douglas joined in a decision in the Oliver case,[129] which held that the guarantee of "public" trial was made applicable to the states by the Fourteenth Amendment and that it was violated where a state judge, operating as a "one-man grand jury" in his chambers from which the public had been excluded, held a witness in criminal contempt and sentenced him to sixty days in jail:

> Here we are concerned, not with petitioner's rights as a witness in a secret grand jury session, but with his rights as defendant in a contempt proceeding. . . .
> . . . Counsel have not cited and we have been unable to find a single instance of a secret criminal trial conducted in camera in

---

[128] Rule 5(b), Rules of Criminal Procedure, provides that the defendant shall be informed of the complaint against him and of his right to retain counsel. Rule 5(c) expressly states, "The defendant may cross-examine witnesses against him and may introduce evidence in his own behalf."

[129] *In re Oliver*, 333 U.S. 257 (1948).

any federal, state, or municipal court during the history of this country. Nor have we found any record of even one such secret criminal trial in England since abolition of the Court of Star Chamber in 1641. . . .

The traditional Anglo-American distrust for secret trials has been variously ascribed to the notorious use of this practice by the Spanish Inquisition, to the excesses of the English Court of Star Chamber, and to the French monarchy's abuse of the lettre de cachet. *All of these institutions obviously symbolized a menace to liberty . . . The knowledge that every criminal trial is subject to a contemporaneous review in the forum of public opinion is an effective restraint on possible abuse of judicial power.*

The Sixth Amendment's guarantee of a "speedy" public trial has also been held applicable to the states and violated in a case[130] where a civil rights demonstrator had been indicted for trespass, a misdemeanor; his first trial ended in a hung jury; and, seventeen months after the indictment, the state court had approved the prosecutor's motion to postpone prosecution indefinitely. Douglas joined in an opinion of the Court written nearly three years after the indictment:

The petitioner [who was not in custody] is not relieved of the limitations placed upon his liberty by this prosecution merely because its suspension permits him to go "whithersoever he will." The pendency of the indictment may subject him to public scorn and deprive him of employment, and almost certainly will force curtailment of his speech, associations and participation in unpopular causes. By indefinitely prolonging this oppression, as well as the "anxiety and concern accompanying public accusation," the criminal procedure condoned [by the state court] in this case clearly denies the petitioner his right to a speedy trial.

UNITED STATES v. MARION
404 U.S. 307 (1971)

From March, 1965, through February, 1967, Marion and another operated a home-improvement company, Allied Enterprises, Inc., in the District of Columbia metropolitan area. They were soon subjected to a spate of lawsuits alleging consumer fraud, and their business was ended by a February 6, 1967, cease-and-desist order of the Federal Trade Commission. In September and October 1967 a series of articles appeared in the Washington Post reporting the results of that newspaper's in-

---

[130] *Klopfer* v. *North Carolina,* 386 U.S. 213 (1967).

vestigation of practices employed by those in the home-improvement business and reporting also that Allied Enterprises was under investigation by the United States Attorney. A special grand jury, impaneled in October, 1967, to investigate consumer fraud, did not, however, indict Marion and his associate.

Sometime between the summer of 1968 and January, 1969, they delivered their business records to the United States Attorney, but not until April 21, 1970, was an indictment returned against them—charging fraud committed between March, 1965, and February, 1967. In May, 1970, they moved to dismiss the indictment on the ground that the delay in obtaining it deprived them of their Sixth Amendment right to a speedy trial. The United States Attorney sought to excuse the delay on the grounds that his office was understaffed and that he had given priority to other types of crimes.

The courts below held that the indictment should be dismissed but the Court reversed, reading the Sixth Amendment guarantee to have no application until after the indictment.

Mr. Justice Douglas, concurring in the result.

I assume that if the three-year delay in this case had occurred *after* the indictment had been returned, the right to a speedy trial would have been impaired and the indictment would have to be dismissed. I disagree with the Court that the guarantee does not apply if the delay was at the pre-indictment stage of a case.

The majority says "that it is either a formal indictment or information or else the actual restraints imposed by arrest and holding to answer a criminal charge that engage the particular protections of the speedy trial provision. . . ."

The Sixth Amendment, to be sure, states that "the accused shall enjoy the right to a speedy and public trial." But the words "the accused," as I understand them in their Sixth Amendment setting, mean only the person who has standing to complain of prosecutorial delay in seeking an indictment or filing an information. The right to a speedy trial is the right to be brought to trial speedily which would seem to be as relevant to pre-indictment delays as it is to post-indictment delays. Much is made of the history of the Sixth Amendment as indicating that the speedy trial guarantee had no application to pre-prosecution delays.

There are two answers to that proposition. First, British courts historically did consider delay as a condition to issuance of an information.

Lord Mansfield held in *Rex* v. *Robinson*, 96 Eng. Rep. 313 (K. B. 1765), that the issuance of an information was subject to time limitations: "If delayed, the delay must be reasonably accounted for." In *Regina* v. *Hext*, 4 Jurists 339 (Q. B. 1840), an information was refused where a whole term of court had passed since the alleged assault took place. Accord: *Rex* v. *Marshall*, 104 Eng. Rep. 394 (K. B. 1811).

Baron Alderson said in *Regina* v. *Robins*, 1 Cox's C. C. 114 (Somerset Winter Assizes 1844), where there was a two-year delay in making a charge of bestiality:

> "It is monstrous to put a man on his trial after such a lapse of time. How can he account for his conduct so far back? If you accuse a man of a crime the next day, he may be enabled to bring forward his servants and family to say where he was and what he was about at the time; but if the charge be not preferred for a year or more, how can he clear himself? No man's life would be safe if such a prosecution were permitted. It would be very unjust to put him on his trial."

Second, and more basically, the 18th century criminal prosecution at the common law was in general commenced in a completely different way from that with which we are familiar today. By the common law of England which was brought to the American colonies, the ordinary criminal prosecution was conducted by a private prosecutor, in the name of the King. In case the victim of the crime or someone interested came forward to prosecute, he retained his own counsel and had charge of the case as in the usual civil proceeding. See G. Dession, Criminal Law, Administration and Public Order 356 (1948). Procedurally, the criminal prosecution was commenced by the filing of a lawsuit, and thereafter the filing of an application for criminal prosecution or rule *nisi* or similar procedure calling for the defendant to show cause why he should not be imprisoned. The English common law, with which the Framers were familiar, conceived of a criminal prosecution as being commenced prior to indictment. Thus in that setting the individual charged as the defendant in a criminal proceeding could and would be an "accused" prior to formal indictment.[131]

The right to a speedy trial, which we have characterized "as fundamental as any of the rights secured by the Sixth Amendment," *Klopfer* v. *North Carolina* [note 130, *supra*], protects several demands of criminal justice: the prevention of undue delay and oppressive incarceration prior to trial; the reduction of anxiety and concern accompanying public

---

[131] See 1 J. Stephen, History of the Criminal Law of England 493–496 (1883):
"In England, and, so far as I know, in England and some English colonies alone, the prosecution of offences is left entirely to private persons, or to public officers who act in their capacity of private persons and who have hardly any legal powers beyond those which belong to private persons." *Id.*, at 493.

accusation; and limiting the possibilities that long delay will impair the ability of an accused to defend himself. *Smith* v. *Hooey*, 393 U.S. 374 (1969). The right also serves broader interests:

> "The Speedy Trial Clause protects societal interests, as well as those of the accused. The public is concerned with the effective prosecution of criminal cases, both to restrain those guilty of crime and to deter those contemplating it. Just as delay may impair the ability of the accused to defend himself, so it may reduce the capacity of the government to prove its case. See *Ponzi* v. *Fessenden*, 258 U.S. 254 (1922). Moreover, while awaiting trial, an accused who is at large may become a fugitive from justice or commit other criminal acts. And the greater the lapse of time between commission of an offense and the conviction of the offender, the less the deterrent value of his conviction." *Dickey* v. *Florida*, 398 U.S. 30 (1970) (BRENNAN, J., concurring).

At least some of these values served by the right to a speedy trial are not unique to any particular stage of the criminal proceeding. See Note, 43 N. Y. U. L. Rev. 722, 725–726 (1968); Note, 77 Yale L. J. 767, 780–783 (1968); Comment, 11 Ariz. L. Rev. 770, 774–776 (1969). Undue delay may be as offensive to the right to a speedy trial before as after an indictment or information. The anxiety and concern attendant on public accusation may weigh more heavily upon an individual who has not yet been formally indicted or arrested for, to him, exoneration by a jury of his peers may be only a vague possibility lurking in the distant future. Indeed, the protection underlying the right to a speedy trial may be denied when a citizen is damned by clandestine innuendo and never given the chance promptly to defend himself in a court of law. Those who are accused of crime but never tried may lose their jobs or their positions of responsibility, or become outcasts in their communities.

The impairment of the ability to defend oneself may become acute because of delays in the pre-indictment stage. Those delays may result in the loss of alibi witnesses, the destruction of material evidence, and the blurring of memories. At least when a person has been accused of a specific crime, he can devote his powers of recall to the events surrounding the alleged occurrences. When there is no formal accusation, however, the State may proceed methodically to build its case while the prospective defendant proceeds to lose his.

The duty which the Sixth Amendment places on Government officials to proceed expeditiously with criminal prosecutions would have little meaning if those officials could determine when that duty was to commence. To be sure, "[t]he right of a speedy trial is necessarily

relative. It is consistent with delays and depends upon circumstances."
Beavers v. *Haubert*, 198 U.S. 77 (1905). But it is precisely because this
right is relative that we should draw the line so as not to condone
illegitimate delays whether at the *pre-* or the *post*-indictment stage.[132]

Our decisions do not support the limitations of the right to a speedy
trial adopted in the majority's conclusion that "the [Sixth] amendment
[does not extend] to the period prior to arrest." In *Miranda* v. *Arizona*
[note 105, *supra*] we held that it was necessary for the police to advise
of the right to counsel in the pre-indictment situation where "a person
has been taken into custody or otherwise deprived of his freedom of
action in any significant way." That case, like the present one, dealt
with one of the rights enumerated in the Sixth Amendment to which
an "accused" was entitled. We were not then concerned with whether
an "arrest" or an "indictment" was necessary for a person to be an
"accused" and thus entitled to Sixth Amendment protections. We
looked instead to the nature of the event and its effect on the rights
involved. We applied the *Miranda* rule even though there was no
"arrest," but only an examination of the suspect while he was in his
bed at his boarding house, the presence of the officers making him
"in custody." *Orozco* v. *Texas* [note 110, *supra*]. We should follow
the same approach here and hold that the right to a speedy trial is
denied if there were years of unexplained and inexcusable pre-indictment delay.

Dickey v. *Florida, supra,* similarly demonstrates the wisdom of

[132] "[A] preprosecution delay can result in the loss of physical evidence, the un-
availability of potential witnesses, and the impairment of the ability of the prospective defendant and his witnesses to remember the events in question. Indeed, the
possibility of such prejudice may be greater in preprosecution-delay cases than in post
indictment-delay cases. The typical prospective defendant is probably unaware of
the fact that criminal charges will eventually be brought against him. Thus, he
will have no reason to take measures to preserve his memory or the memories of
his witnesses. 'The importance of these considerations becomes clear when measured
against the state's ability to collect and document evidence as it carries out its
criminal investigation, thereby preserving its probative firepower until the time of
eventual arrest.'

"The causal factor also can be present in a preprosecution delay. Many pre-
prosecution delays are caused by the reluctance of the government to terminate
an undercover investigation. If the knowledge obtained by an undercover agent is
used as the basis for an arrest or for the issuance of a complaint, the identity of the
agent may be exposed and his effectiveness destroyed. Consequently, the government
will often delay arresting an individual against whom its case is complete if the
agent is still obtaining evidence against other individuals. In such a situation, the
government has made a deliberate choice for a supposed advantage. While this
advantage is arguably not sought vis-à-vis the defendant asserting the speedy-trial
claim, the fact remains that the advantage arises out of a deliberate and avoidable
choice on the part of law-enforcement authorities." Note, 20 Stan. L. Rev. 476, 489.

avoiding today's mechanical approach to the application of basic constitutional guarantees. While he was in custody on an unrelated federal charge, the petitioner was identified by a witness to the robbery. Petitioner remained in federal custody, but the State did not seek to prosecute him until September 1, 1967, when he moved to dismiss the detainer warrant which had been lodged against him. An information was then filed on December 15, 1967, and petitioner was tried on February 13, 1968. Although the trial took place less than two months after the filing of the information, we held that there had been a denial of the right to a speedy trial because of the delay of more than seven years between the crime and the information.

In a concurring opinion, MR. JUSTICE BRENNAN discussed the broader questions raised by that case:

> "When is governmental delay reasonable? Clearly, a deliberate attempt by the government to use delay to harm the accused, or governmental delay that is 'purposeful or oppressive,' is unjustifiable. . . . The same may be true of any governmental delay that is unnecessary, whether intentional or negligent in origin. A negligent failure by the government to ensure speedy trial is virtually as damaging to the interests protected by the right as an intentional failure; when negligence is the cause, the only interest necessarily unaffected is our common concern to prevent deliberate misuse of the criminal process by public officials. Thus the crucial question in determining the legitimacy of governmental delay may be whether it might reasonably have been avoided—whether it was unnecessary. To determine the necessity for governmental delay, it would seem important to consider, on the one hand, the intrinsic importance of the reason for the delay, and, on the other, the length of the delay and its potential for prejudice to interests protected by the speedy-trial safeguard. For a trivial objective, almost any delay could be reasonably avoided. Similarly, lengthy delay, even in the interest of realizing an important objective, would be suspect."

In the present case, two to three years elapsed between the time the District Court found that the charges could and should have been brought and the actual return of the indictment. The justifications offered were that the United States Attorney's office was "not sufficiently staffed to proceed as expeditiously" as desirable[133] and that

---

[133] The District Judge pointed out that the then Assistant Attorney General had indicated "that he didn't need any more help" and that the United States Attorney retreated from this factual assertion.

priority had been given to other cases. Appellees say that the present indictment embraces counts such as an allegedly fraudulent telephone conversation made on December 16, 1965. They argue that there is a great likelihood that the recollection of such events will be blurred or erased by the frailties of the human memory. If this were a simpler crime, I think the British precedent which I have cited would warrant dismissal of the indictment because of the speedy trial guarantee of the Sixth Amendment. But we know from experience that the nature of the crime charged here often has vast interstate aspects, the victims are often widely scattered and hard to locate, and the reconstruction of the total scheme of the fraudulent plan takes time. If we applied the simple rule that was applied in simpler days, we would be giving extraordinary advantages to organized crime as well as others who use a farflung complicated network to perform their illegal activities. I think a three-year delay even in that kind of case goes to the edge of a permissible delay. But on the bare bones of this record I hesitate to say that the guarantee of a speedy trial has been violated. Unless appellees on remand demonstrate actual prejudice, I would agree that the prosecution might go forward. Hence I concur in the result.

Bail

The Eighth Amendment provides that "[e]xcessive bail shall not be required." This guarantee has not yet been held applicable to the states.

From the first Judiciary Act of 1789 to the Bail Reform Act of 1966 and the present Federal Rules of Criminal Procedure, provision has been made for bail for persons arrested for federal prosecution. The Bail Reform Act provides that a person arrested for a noncapital offense shall be released on his own recognizance or on bail pending trial unless it is determined "that such a release will not reasonably assure the appearance of the person as required" and that a person charged with a capital offense, or convicted of any offense but unsentenced or with an appeal pending, shall be released pursuant to the same standards "unless the court or judge has reason to believe that no one or more conditions of release will reasonably assure that the person will not flee or pose a danger to any other person or to the community," or if an appeal is pending, that it is "frivolous or taken for delay."

In 1951, in a decision in which Douglas joined, the Court held that the fixing of bail at $50,000 for each of four officials of the Communist Party of the United States of America, indicted in California for viola-

*tion of the Smith Act, was not sustained by proof that four others
previously convicted of violation of the Smith Act in New York had
forfeited bail and failed to report for imprisonment, or "by assuming,
without the introduction of evidence, that each petitioner is a pawn
in a conspiracy and will, in obedience to a superior, flee the jurisdiction.
To infer from the fact of indictment alone a need for bail in an unusually high amount is an arbitrary act." "The right to release before
trial" was said to be "conditioned on the accused's giving adequate
assurance that he will stand trial and submit to sentence if found
guilty. . . . Bail set at a figure higher than an amount reasonably
calculated to fulfill this purpose is 'excessive' under the Eighth
Amendment."[134]*

HARRIS v. UNITED STATES
404 U.S. 1232 (1971)

*Harris was convicted in a federal district court of a narcotics offense
and appealed to the United States court of appeals for the ninth
circuit. Both the district court and the court of appeals denied his
application for release on bail pending appeal. He then applied for
bail to Douglas as the Justice assigned to the Ninth Circuit.*

MR. JUSTICE DOUGLAS, Circuit Justice.

Both the District Court and the Court of Appeals have previously
denied similar applications, and their action is entitled to great deference. Nevertheless, "where the reasons for the action below clearly
appear, a Circuit Justice has a non-delegable responsibility to make an
independent determination of the merits of the application." [*Reynolds
v. United States,* 80 S.Ct. 30 (1959).] While there is no automatic right
to bail after convictions, "[t]he Command of the Eighth Amendment
that 'Excessive bail shall not be required . . .' *at the very least* obligates
judges passing upon the right to bail to deny such relief only for the
strongest of reasons." [*Sellers v. United States,* 89 S.Ct. 36 (1968).]
The Bail Reform Act of 1966 further limits the discretion of a court
or judge to deny bail, as it provides that a person *shall* be entitled to
bail pending appeal, if that appeal is not frivolous or taken for delay,
or "unless the court or judge has reason to believe that no one or more
conditions of release will reasonably assure that the person will not
flee or pose a danger to any other person or to the community."

[134] *Stack v. Boyle,* 342 U.S. 1 (1951).

Applying these principles, my examination of the papers submitted by applicant and by the Solicitor General in opposition persuade me that the Government has not met its burden of showing that bail should be denied.

The primary ground upon which the Solicitor General opposes bail is that "[t]here are no substantial questions raised" by the appeal. It is true that the questions raised relate primarily to evidentiary matters. It is settled, however, that these are within the purview of review of an application of this kind, and that they may raise nonfrivolous—indeed, even "substantial"—questions. See, *e.g.*, *Wolcher* v. *United States*, 76 S. Ct. 254 (1955).

Applicant principally argues that there was no evidence in the record from which an inference is permissible that he knew that a truck guided by him and a codefendant, in a separate vehicle, from one location in Los Angeles to another location in that city contained unlawfully imported narcotics. It is beyond question, of course, that a conviction based on a record lacking any relevant evidence as to a crucial element of the offense charged would violate due process. See *Adderley* v. *Florida*, 385 U.S. 39, 44 (1966). The quantum and nature of proof constitutionally required to support an inference of knowledge in narcotics offenses is not always an easy question. Applicant cites a case from the Ninth Circuit as a factually similar example in which a conviction for a narcotics offense was reversed for lack of proof of knowledge that another possessed that contraband. While I express no opinion on the merits of the analogy, Circuit Justices have granted bail pending appeal based in part on similar claims of failure of proof. See, *e.g.*, *Brussel* v. *United States*, 396 U.S. 1229 (1969).

Applicant also challenges the hearsay testimony of an informer as to a Tijuana phone number given to him by a reputed Mexican narcotics trafficker. Other evidence demonstrated that applicant's codefendant called this number several times prior to the importation of the contraband in July 1969. The implication, presumably, is that the prior calls were made to arrange the shipment. The hearsay declaration, however, was made over a year after the codefendant's phone calls occurred, and the common scheme sought to be proven had been terminated. Under these circumstances, the admissibility of this declaration as hearsay exception is not free from doubt. Cf. *Fiswick* v. *United States*, 329 U.S. 211 (1946).

Assuming this testimony is otherwise admissible, applicant argues it is not the "best evidence" of the registration of the phone number. While it is true that Mexican phone company records were beyond the subpoena power of the court, and that courts have held that secondary evidence may be used without further ado in such a case, see, e.g., *Hartzell* v. *United States*, 72 F. 2d 569 (CA8 1934), applicant's argument is nevertheless not without merit:

> "[T]he policy of the original document requirement, and probably the weight of reason, supports the view of those courts equally numerous who demand . . . that before secondary evidence is used, the proponent must show either that he has made reasonable efforts without avail to secure the original from its possessor, or circumstances which persuade the court that such efforts would have been fruitless."

C. McCormick, Evidence § 202, p. 415 (1954), and cases cited. It is noteworthy in this regard that the District Court rejected evidence offered by applicant tending to show that the phone number in question was not registered to the purported narcotics trafficker before December 1970.

I cannot say that these contentions are all frivolous.

Where an appeal is not frivolous or taken for delay, bail "is to be denied only in cases in which, from substantial evidence, it seems clear that the right to bail may be abused or the community may be threatened by the applicant's release." *Leigh* v. *United States*, 82 S. Ct. 994, 996 (1962). According to the Solicitor General, the District Judge denied bail in part because "there was reason to believe that defendant, who had no employment, would not respond to required future appearances and would be a danger to the community." Applicant's Bail Reform Act form indicates, however, that he is a self-employed auto mechanic making $150 per week, that he has lived in Los Angeles for the past eight years, that he has several relatives, including his mother and a sister, living there, and that he has never failed to make a required court appearance while on bail. The moving papers further indicate that applicant was at liberty after sentencing, pursuant to a stay of execution granted by the Court of Appeals, and that he voluntarily submitted to the authorities upon the expiration of the stay. There is not such "substantial evidence" in this record to justify denying bail on the ground that applicant is a flight risk.

Furthermore, a far stronger showing of danger to the community must be made than is apparent from his record to justify a denial of bail on that ground. Accordingly, bail should be granted pending disposition of the appeal in this case, pursuant to the standards set forth in the Bail Reform Act.

Jury Trial

The original Constitution provides in Article III, dealing with the federal judiciary, that "The Trial of all Crimes . . . shall be by Jury."[135] *The Sixth Amendment adds, "In all criminal prosecutions, the accused shall enjoy the right to . . . trial, by an impartial jury."*

Beginning in 1952, Douglas joined with a minority to assert that defendants in federal criminal contempt proceedings were entitled to the jury trial guaranteed by the Sixth Amendment in "all criminal prosecutions."[136] *The Court finally adopted that view sixteen years later for cases where the punishment exceeds six months' imprisonment, a line which it drew by reference to a section of the federal Criminal Code declaring all federal misdemeanors for which the penalty does not exceed six months' imprisonment or a fine of $500 to constitute "petty offenses."*[137] *When, in the same year, the Court held that the Fourteenth Amendment makes the Sixth Amendment's jury trial guarantee applicable to state criminal prosecutions, it again excepted "petty offenses."*[138] *Douglas rejected the notion that such an exception could be read into the constitutional guarantee.*[139]

> *I cannot say what is and what is not a "petty crime." I certainly believe, however, that where punishment of as much as six months can be imposed, I would not classify the offense as "petty" if that means that people tried for it are to be tried as if we had no Bill of Rights . . . I do not deny that there might possibly be some offenses charged for which the punishment is so miniscule that it might be thought of as petty. But to my way of thinking, when a man is charged by a governmental unit with conduct for which the Government can impose a penalty of imprisonment for any amount of time, I doubt if I could ever hold it petty.*

---

[135] U.S. Const., Art. III, §2, C. 3. The application of the equal protection clause's prohibition against systematic exclusion of qualified groups from jury panels is discussed at pp. 277–283, *supra*.

[136] *Sacher v. United States*, 343 U.S. 1 (1952); *Isserman v. Ethics Committee*, 345 U.S. 927 (1953); *Offutt v. United States*, 348 U.S. 11 (1954); *Green v. United States*, 356 U.S. 165 (1958); *Piemonte v. United States*, 367 U.S. 556 (1961); *United States v. Bennett*, 376 U.S. 681 (1964).

[137] *Bloom v. Illinois*, 391 U.S. 194 (1968).

[138] *Duncan v. Louisiana*, 391 U.S. 145 (1968).

[139] *Frank v. United States*, 395 U.S. 147 (1969). See also *Baldwin v. New York*, 399 U.S. 66 (1970); *Johnson v. Nebraska*, 419 U.S. 949 (1974); *Muniz v. Hoffman*, 422 U.S. 454 (1975).

JOHNSON V. LOUISIANA
406 U.S. 356 (1972)

In 1970 the Court reconsidered prior readings of the federal guarantee in jury trial to require a common-law jury of twelve,[140] and in a decision in which Douglas joined on this issue, rejected them. Finding the history of both Article III and the Sixth Amendment inconclusive on this point, the Court turned to the function which the jury performed— "the interposition between the accused and his accuser of the common-sense judgment of a group of laymen, and . . . the community participation and shared responsibility that results from that group's determination of guilt or innocence"—and concluded that that function could be as well performed by a state's jury of six as by a jury of twelve.[141]

After it held the Sixth Amendment applicable to the states in Duncan v. Louisiana[142] the Court also held that the ruling in Duncan would not apply retroactively to invalidate convictions which occurred before that decision.[143]

In this case, Johnson was convicted of robbery before the decision in Duncan, after trial before a jury of twelve, but the verdict was 9 to 3, which by Louisiana law was sufficient to convict. He contended that such a conviction violated the due process clause of the Fourteenth Amendment, particularly in view of the Court's earlier decision that that clause required proof of a criminal charge beyond a reasonable doubt.[144] The Court rejected this argument. The fact that three jurors voted to acquit did not mean that any of the other nine must have a reasonable doubt of guilt and the due process clause did not require a unanimous verdict. In a companion case, Apodaca v. Oregon,[145] the Court also affirmed convictions in Oregon, after the Duncan decision, by less than unanimous verdicts where Oregon law permitted a conviction on a 10-to-2 vote. The Sixth Amendment also was held not to incorporate the common-law requirement of a unanimous verdict.

MR. JUSTICE DOUGLAS, dissenting.

With due respect to the majority, I dissent from this radical departure from American traditions.

[140] *Thompson v. Utah,* 170 U.S. 343 (1898); *Rassmussen v. United States,* 197 U.S. 516 (1905); *Patton v. United States,* 281 U.S. 276 (1930).

[141] *Williams v. Florida,* 399 U.S. 78 (1970).

[142] Note 138, *supra.*

[143] *DeStefano v. Woods,* 392 U.S. 631 (1968).

[144] *In re Winship,* 397 U.S. 358 (1970).

[145] 406 U.S. 404 (1972).

I

The Constitution does not mention unanimous juries. Neither does it mention the presumption of innocence, nor does it say that guilt must be proved beyond a reasonable doubt in all criminal cases. Yet it is almost inconceivable that anyone would have questioned whether proof beyond a reasonable doubt was in fact the constitutional standard. And, indeed, when such a case finally arose we had little difficulty disposing of the issue. *In re Winship*, 397 U.S. 358.

The Court, speaking through MR. JUSTICE BRENNAN, stated that:

> "[The] use of the reasonable-doubt standard is indispensable to command the respect and confidence of the community in applications of the criminal law. It is critical that the moral force of the criminal law not be diluted by a standard of proof that leaves people in doubt whether innocent men are being condemned. It is also important in our free society that every individual going about his ordinary affairs have confidence that his government cannot adjudge him guilty of a criminal offense without convincing a proper factfinder of his guilt with utmost certainty.
>
> "Lest there remain any doubt about the constitutional stature of the reasonable-doubt standard, we explicitly hold that the Due Process Clause protects the accused against conviction except upon proof beyond a reasonable doubt of every fact necessary to constitute the crime with which he is charged."

I had similarly assumed that there was no dispute that the Federal Constitution required a unanimous jury in all criminal cases. After all, it has long been explicit constitutional doctrine that the Seventh Amendment civil jury must be unanimous. See *American Publishing Co.* v. *Fisher*, 166 U.S. 464, where the Court said that "unanimity was one of the peculiar and essential features of trial by jury at the common law. No authorities are needed to sustain this proposition." Like proof beyond a reasonable doubt, the issue of unanimous juries in criminal cases simply never arose. Yet in cases dealing with juries it had always been assumed that a unanimous jury was required. See *Maxwell* v. *Dow*, 176 U.S. 581; *Patton* v. *United States*, 281 U.S. 276; *Andres* v. *United States*, 333 U.S. 740. Today the bases of those cases are discarded and two centuries of American history are shunted aside.

After today's decisions, a man's property may only be taken away by a unanimous jury vote, yet he can be stripped of his liberty by a lesser standard. How can that result be squared with the law of the land as expressed in the settled and traditional requirements of procedural due process?

Rule 31 (a) of the Federal Rules of Criminal Procedure states, "The verdict shall be unanimous." That Rule was made by this Court with the concurrence of Congress. After today a unanimous verdict will be required in a federal prosecution but not in a state prosecution. Yet the source of the right in each case is the Sixth Amendment. I fail to see how with reason we can maintain those inconsistent dual positions.

The plurality approves a procedure which diminishes the reliability of a jury. First, it eliminates the circumstances in which a minority of jurors (a) could have rationally persuaded the entire jury to acquit, or (b) while unable to persuade the majority to acquit, nonetheless could have convinced them to convict only on a lesser-included offense. Second, it permits prosecutors in Oregon and Louisiana to enjoy a conviction-acquittal ratio substantially greater than that ordinarily returned by unanimous juries.

The diminution of verdict reliability flows from the fact that non-unanimous juries need not debate and deliberate as fully as must unanimous juries. As soon as the requisite majority is attained, further consideration is not required either by Oregon or by Louisiana even though the dissident jurors might, if given the chance, be able to convince the majority. Such persuasion does in fact occasionally occur in States where the unanimous requirement applies: "In roughly one case in ten, the minority eventually succeeds in reversing an initial majority, and these may be cases of special importance."[146] One explanation for this phenomenon is that because jurors are often not permitted to take notes and because they have imperfect memories, the forensic process of forcing jurors to defend their conflicting recollections and conclusions flushes out many nuances which otherwise would go overlooked. This collective effort to piece together the puzzle of historical truth, however, is cut short as soon as the requisite majority is reached in Oregon and Louisiana. Indeed, if a necessary majority is immediately obtained, then no deliberation at all is required in these States. (There is a suggestion that this may have happened in the 10–2 verdict rendered in only 41 minutes in Apodaca's case.) To be sure, in jurisdictions other than these two States, initial majorities normally prevail in the end, but about a tenth of the time the rough-and-tumble of the jury room operates to reverse completely their preliminary perception of guilt or innocence. The Court now extracts from the jury room this automatic check against hasty fact-finding by relieving jurors of the duty to hear out fully the dissenters.

[146] H. Kalven & H. Zeisel, The American Jury 490 (1966). See also The American Jury: Notes For an English Controversy, 48 Chi. B. Rec. 195 (1967).

It is said that there is no evidence that majority jurors will refuse to listen to dissenters whose votes are unneeded for conviction. Yet human experience teaches that polite and academic conversation is no substitute for the earnest and robust argument necessary to reach unanimity. As mentioned earlier, in Apocada's case, whatever courtesy dialogue transpired could not have lasted more than 41 minutes.

To be sure, in *Williams* v. *Florida* [note 141, *supra*] we held that a State could provide a jury less than 12 in number in a criminal trial. We said: "What few experiments have occurred—usually in the civil area—indicate that there is no discernible difference between the results reached by the two different-sized juries. In short, neither currently available evidence nor theory suggests that the 12-man jury is necessarily more advantageous to the defendant than a jury composed of fewer members."

That rationale of *Williams* can have no application here. *Williams* requires that the change be neither more nor less advantageous to either the State or the defendant. Experience shows that the less-than-unanimous jury overwhelmingly favors the States.

Moreover, even where an initial majority wins the dissent over to its side, the ultimate result in unanimous-jury States may nonetheless reflect the reservations of uncertain jurors. I refer to many compromise verdicts on lesser-included offenses and lesser sentences. Thus, even though a minority may not be forceful enough to carry the day, their doubts may nonetheless cause a majority to exercise caution. Obviously, however, in Oregon and Louisiana, dissident jurors will not have the opportunity through full deliberation to temper the opposing faction's degree of certainty of guilt.

The new rule also has an impact on cases in which a unanimous jury would have neither voted to acquit nor to convict, but would have deadlocked. In unanimous-jury States, this occurs about 5.6% of the time. Of these deadlocked juries, Kalven and Zeisel say that 56% contain either one, two, or three dissenters. In these latter cases, the majorities favor the prosecution 44% (of the 56%) but the defendant only 12% (of the 56%). Thus, by eliminating these deadlocks, Louisiana wins 44 cases for every 12 that it loses, obtaining in this band of outcomes a substantially more favorable conviction ratio (3.67 to 1) than the unanimous-jury ratio of slightly less than two guilty verdicts for every acquittal. H. Kalven & H. Zeisel, The American Jury 461, 488 (Table 139) (1966). By eliminating the one-and-two-dissenting-juror cases, Oregon does even better, gaining 4.25 convictions for every acquittal. While the statutes on their face deceptively appear to be neutral, the use of the nonunanimous jury stacks the truth-determining process against the accused. Thus, we take one step more away from the accusatorial system that has been our proud boast.

It is my belief that a unanimous jury is necessary if the great barricade known as proof beyond a reasonable doubt is to be maintained. This is not to equate proof beyond a reasonable doubt with the requirement of a unanimous jury. That would be analytically fallacious since a deadlocked jury does not bar, as double jeopardy, retrial for the same offense. See *Dreyer* v. *Illinois*, 187 U.S. 71. Nevertheless, one is necessary for a proper effectuation of the other.

Suppose a jury begins with a substantial minority but then in the process of deliberation a sufficient number changes to reach the required 9:3 or 10:2 for a verdict. Is not there still a lingering doubt about that verdict? Is it not clear that the safeguard of unanimity operates in this context to make it far more likely that guilt is established beyond a reasonable doubt?

The late Learned Hand said that "as a litigant I should dread a lawsuit beyond almost anything else short of sickness and death."[147] At the criminal level that dread multiplies. Any person faced with the awesome power of government is in great jeopardy, even though innocent. Facts are always elusive and often two-faced. What may appear to one to imply guilt may carry no such overtones to another. Every criminal prosecution crosses treacherous ground, for guilt is common to all men. Yet the guilt of one may be irrelevant to the charge on which he is tried or indicate that if there is to be a penalty, it should be of an extremely light character.

The risk of loss of his liberty and the certainty that if found guilty he will be "stigmatized by the conviction" were factors we emphasized in *Winship* in sustaining the requirement that no man should be condemned where there is reasonable doubt about his guilt.

We therefore have always held that in criminal cases we would err on the side of letting the guilty go free rather than sending the innocent to jail. We have required proof beyond a reasonable doubt as "concrete substance for the presumption of innocence."

That procedure has required a degree of patience on the part of the jurors, forcing them to deliberate in order to reach a unanimous verdict. Up until today the price has never seemed too high. Now a "law and order" judicial mood causes these barricades to be lowered.

The requirements of a unanimous jury verdict in criminal cases and proof beyond a reasonable doubt are so embedded in our constitutional

---

[147] 3 Lectures on Legal Topics, Association of Bar of the City of New York 105 (1926).

law and touch so directly all the citizens and are such important barricades of liberty that if they are to be changed they should be introduced
by constitutional amendment.

Today the Court approves a nine-to-three verdict. Would the Court
relax the standard of reasonable doubt still further by resorting to
eight-to-four verdicts, or even a majority rule? Moreover, in light of
today's holdings and that of *Williams* v. *Florida,* in the future would it
invalidate three-to-two or even two-to-one convictions?

The vast restructuring of American law which is entailed in today's
decisions is for political not for judicial action. Until the Constitution is
rewritten, we have the present one to support and construe. It has served
us well. We lifetime appointees, who sit here only by happenstance, are
the last who should sit as a Committee of Revision on rights as basic
as those involved in the present cases.

McGAUTHA v. CALIFORNIA
402 U.S. 183 (1971)

*Douglas voted with the Court to invalidate a provision in the federal
Kidnapping Act providing for the death penalty if a kidnap victim is
not liberated unharmed "and if the verdict of the jury shall so recommend." Since a defendant could put himself in jeopardy of the death
penalty only by asserting his right to jury trial, the statute "needlessly
penalizes the assertion of a constitutional right." Its purpose—to miti-
gate the severity of capital punishment—could be achieved without
such penalizing by letting the jury decide on the penalty in every case.[148]
The similar death-penalty provision of the federal Bank Robbery Act
was later invalidated for the same reason.[149]*

*But Douglas joined dissenters in another case which sustained a
state's procedure under a habitual criminal statute.[150] As applied to the
defendant in a murder case, that statute allowed the jury in a single
proceeding to hear evidence on the murder charge and evidence of a
prior murder conviction. The jury was then instructed that it was not
to consider the prior conviction as any evidence of guilt on the current
charge; that if it found defendant guilty on the current charge and
that if he had been previously convicted of murder, it should sentence
him to death or life imprisonment, but that if it found that he was
guilty on the current charge but that he had not been earlier convicted,*

---

[148] *United States v. Jackson,* 390 U.S. 570 (1968).
[149] *Pope v. United States,* 392 U.S. 651 (1968).
[150] *Spencer v. Texas,* 385 U.S. 554 (1967).

it should sentence him to death or for a prison term of not less than two years. The jury found him guilty and sentenced him to death. The Court held that this procedure did not violate due process, pointing out that while evidence of prior crimes was generally excluded in criminal prosecutions because of its prejudicial effect, there were widely recognized exceptions which permitted introduction of evidence of prior crimes, where relevant to the issue of intent with respect to the crime charged, or to rebut evidence of character witnesses called by the defendant, or to impeach defendant's credibility when he takes the stand. The dissenters pointed out that all of the exceptions to which the Court referred were instances in which the prior convictions had some probative value on the issue of current guilt, whereas the general exclusion of evidence of prior crimes was a recognition of the danger that, despite cautionary instructions, the jury "might punish an accused for being guilty of a previous offense, or feel the incarceration is justified because the accused is a 'bad man,' without regard to his guilt of the crime currently charged." Hence, the dissenters would have read the due process clause to require that the jury reach its conclusion on the issue of guilt before hearing evidence of prior crimes.

In this case McGautha, convicted of first-degree murder in California, and Crampton, convicted of first-degree murder in Ohio, contested the manner in which each was sentenced to death. In McGautha's case, the jury determined the penalty in a separate proceeding after it had found him guilty. In Crampton's case, the jury determined guilt and punishment in a single proceeding, in which Crampton did not take the stand. Crampton's mother did testify, and in her testimony revealed his prior brushes with the law, his drug addiction, and his undesirable discharge from the Navy. Crampton's attorney also introduced reports which revealed a substantial criminal record.

Both men contended that they were denied due process of law because the jury was given no standard to apply in determining whether to impose the death penalty. The Court rejected that contention. "To identify before the fact those characteristics of criminal homicides and their perpetrators which call for the death penalty, and to express these characteristics in language which can be fairly understood and applied by the sentencing authority, appear to be tasks which are beyond present human ability." Crampton also contended that he had been denied due process by the Ohio procedure of a single trial on guilt and punishment, since he could not testify on the matter of punishment without waiving his privilege of self-incrimination on the matter of guilt. The Court also rejected this contention, relying on its decision in the Spencer case.[151]

---

[151] Note 150, *supra.*

MR. JUSTICE DOUGLAS, dissenting [in Crampton's case[152]].

In my view the unitary trial which Ohio provides in first-degree murder cases does not satisfy the requirements of procedural Due Process under the Fourteenth Amendment.

Ohio makes first-degree murder punishable by death "unless the jury trying the accused recommends mercy, in which case the punishment shall be imprisonment for life." Petitioner was indicted and tried for murder in the first degree for the killing of his wife. His pleas were "not guilty" and "not guilty by reason of insanity."

The court, after a psychiatrict examination, concluded that petitioner was sane and set the case for trial before a jury. The issues of guilt, punishment, and insanity were simultaneously tried and submitted to the jury.

Petitioner did not testify at the trial. But a psychiatrist testified on his behalf, offering medical records of his case from two state hospitals. His mother testified concerning his childhood, education, and background.

On the issue of punishment the jury was charged:

> "You must not be influenced by any consideration *of sympathy or prejudice*. It is your duty to carefully weigh the evidence, to decide all disputed questions of fact, to apply the instructions of the court to your findings and to render your verdict accordingly. In fulfilling your duty, your efforts must be to arrive at a just verdict.
>
> "Consider all the evidence and make your finding with intelligence and impartiality, and *without bias, sympathy, or prejudice,* so that the State of Ohio and the defendant will feel that their case was fairly and impartially tried. . . ." (Emphasis added.)

He was found guilty of murder in the first degree without a recommendation of mercy and the court sentenced him to death.

On the issue of guilt the State was required to produce evidence to establish it. On the issue of insanity the burden was on petitioner to prove it by a preponderance of the evidence, *State* v. *Austin*, 71 Ohio St. 317. On the issue of mercy, *viz.*, life imprisonment rather than death,

---

152 [Douglas also joined in Justice Brennan's dissent on the other point involved in both cases. They did not believe that "the legislators of the 50 States are so devoid of wisdom and the power of rational thought that they are unable to face the problem of capital punishment directly, and to determine for themselves the criteria under which convicted capital felons should be chosen to live or die." Moreover, even if they shared the view of the Court "that the rule of law and the power of the States to kill are in irreconcilable conflict," they "would have no hesitation in concluding that the rule of law must prevail."]

petitioner under Ohio law was banned from offering any specific evidence directed only toward a claim of mercy. *Ashbrook v. State*, 49 Ohio App. 298.

If a defendant wishes to testify in support of the defense of insanity or in mitigation of what he is charged with doing, he can do so only if he surrenders his right to be free from self-incrimination. Once he takes the stand he can be cross-examined not only as respects the crime charged but also on other misdeeds. In Ohio impeachment covers a wide range of subjects: prior convictions for felonies and statutory misdemeanors, pending indictments, prior convictions in military service, and dishonorable discharges.

While the defendant in Ohio has the right of allocution,[153] that right even in first-degree murder cases occurs only after the jury's verdict has been rendered. Unless there is prejudicial error vitiating the conviction or insufficient evidence to convict, the jury's verdict stands and the judge must enter the verdict. Allocution, though mandatory, is thus a ritual only.

If the right to be heard were to be meaningful, it would have to accrue before sentencing; yet, except for allocution, any attempt on the part of the accused during the trial to say why the judgment of death should not be pronounced against him entails a surrender of his right against self-incrimination. It therefore seems plain that the single-verdict procedure is a burden on the exercise of the right to be free of compulsion as respects self-incrimination. For he can testify on the issue of insanity or on other matters in extenuation of the crime charged only at the price of surrendering the protection of the Self-Incrimination Clause of the Fifth Amendment made applicable to the States by the Fourteenth.

On the question of insanity and punishment the accused should be under no restraints when it comes to putting before the court and the jury all the relevant facts. Yet he cannot have that freedom where these issues are tied to the question of guilt. For on that issue he often dare not speak lest he in substance be tried not for this particular offense but for all the sins he ever committed.

Petitioner also had to surrender much of his right to a fair hearing on the issue of punishment to assert his defense of insanity. To support his insanity plea he had to submit his hospital records, both of which

---

[153] [An Ohio statute provides: "Before sentence is pronounced, the defendant must be informed by the court of the verdict of the jury . . . and asked whether he has anything to say as to why judgment should not be pronounced against him." This procedure was followed and defendant said: "I don't believe I received a fair and impartial trial because the jury was prejudiced by my past record and the fact I had been a drug addict."]

contained information about his convictions and imprisonment for prior crimes and about his use of drugs as well.

The greatest comfort the majority has is this Court's recent decision in *Spencer* v. *Texas* [note 150, *supra*] holding that a two-stage trial is not required when a State under a habitual-offender statute seeks to introduce on the issue of guilt in a unitary trial evidence of a defendant's prior convictions. Yet *Spencer* was a five-to-four decision which meant it barely passed muster as a constitutional procedure. The dissent of Mr. Chief Justice Warren, in which three other Justices joined, will have, I think, endurance beyond the majority view.

We should not square with due process the practice which receives impetus in Ohio where reports on a man's insanity contain references to his criminal record which most assuredly prejudice his trial on the issue of guilt.

Crampton had the constitutional right as a matter of procedural due process to be heard on the issue of punishment. We emphasized in *Townsend* v. *Burke*, 334 U.S. 736, how the right to be heard through counsel might be crucial to avoid sentencing on a foundation "extensively and materially false." But the right to be heard is broader than that; it includes the right to speak for one's self.

The truth is, as MR. JUSTICE BRENNAN points out in his dissent in these cases, that the wooden position of the Court, reflected in today's decision, cannot be reconciled with the evolving gloss of civilized standards which this Court, long before the time of those who now sit here, has been reading into the protective procedural due process safeguards of the Bill of Rights. It is as though a dam had suddenly been placed across the stream of the law on procedural due process, a stream which has grown larger with the passing years.

The Court has history on its side—but history alone. Though nations have been killing men for centuries, felony crimes increase. The vestiges of law enshrined today have roots in barbaric procedures. Barbaric procedures such as ordeal by battle that became imbedded in the law were difficult to dislodge.[154] Though torture was used to exact confessions, felonies mounted. Once it was though that "sanity" was determined by ascertaining whether a person knew the difference between "right" and "wrong." Once it was a capital offense to steal from the person something "above the value of a shilling."[155]

Insight and understanding have increased with the years, though the springs of crime remain in large part unknown. Psychiatry has

---

[154] See 4 W. Blackstone, Commentaries *347–349. Ordeal by battle was finally abolished in 1819 in England. 59 Geo. 3, c. 46.

[155] 1 J. Stephen, History of the Criminal Law of England 467 (1883).

shown that blind faith in rightness and wrongness is no reliable measure of human responsibility. The convergence of new technology for criminal investigation and of new insight into mental disorders has made many ancient legal procedures seem utterly unfair.

Who today would say it was not "cruel and unusual punishment" within the meaning of the Eighth Amendment to impose the death sentence on a man who stole a loaf of bread, or in modern parlance, a sheet of food stamps? Who today would say that trial by battle satisfies the requirements of procedural due process?

We need not read procedural due process as designed to satisfy man's deep-seated sadistic instincts. We need not in deference to those sadistic instincts say we are bound by history from defining procedural due process so as to deny men fair trials. Yet that is what the Court does today.

It is a mystery how in this day and age a unitary trial that requires an accused to give up one constitutional guarantee to save another constitutional guarantee can be brought within the rubric of procedural due process. It can be done only by a *tour de force* by a majority that stops the growth and evolution of procedural due process at a wholly arbitrary line or harkens to the passions of men. What a great regression it is when the end result is to approve a procedure that makes the killing of people charged with crime turn on the whim or caprice of one man or of 12!

The unitary trial is certainly not "mercy" oriented. That is, however, not its defect. It has a constitutional infirmity because it is not neutral on the awesome issue of capital punishment. The rules are stacked in favor of death. It is one thing if the legislature decides that the death penalty attaches to defined crimes. It is quite another to leave to judge or jury the discretion to sentence an accused to death or to show mercy under procedures that make the trial death oriented. Then the law becomes a mere pretense, lacking the procedural integrity that would likely result in a fair resolution of the issues.

Compulsory Process

The Sixth Amendment provides that "In all criminal prosecutions, the accused shall enjoy the right . . . to have compulsory process for obtaining Witnesses in his favor."

Douglas voted with the Court in 1967 to hold that guarantee applicable to the states and to construe it to guarantee "[the] right to offer the testimony of witnesses, and to compel their attendance, if necessary, . . . the right to present the defendant's version of the facts as well as the prosecution's." Hence, a state was held to have violated the Constitution, not by refusing to subpoena a defense witness, but by applying a state rule that co-participants in the same crime could not testify for one another, though they could testify for the prosecution.[156]

Douglas also voted with the Court in its only other two significant considerations of this guarantee. One decision reversed a state burglary conviction because, when defendant called a witness who was serving a prison sentence, the judge told the witness, in the absence of the jury, "If you take the witness stand and lie under oath, the Court will personally see that your case goes to the grand jury and you will be indicted for perjury . . . and that [the perjury conviction] would be stacked onto what you have already got [and] will also be held against you in the penitentiary when you're up for parole"—whereupon the witness refused to testify.[157] *The other decision reversed a federal conviction because the court told a jury that it could credit the testimony of an accomplice called by the defendant if "you are convinced it is true beyond a reasonable doubt." That instruction was held to violate both the Sixth Amendment right to present exculpatory testimony and the ruling in In re Winship*[158] *that the due process clause requires proof of guilt beyond a reasonable doubt.*[159]

Confrontation and Cross-Examination

The Sixth Amendment requires that "In all criminal prosecutions, the accused shall enjoy the right . . . to be confronted with the witnesses against him." As the Court once said, the purpose of this guarantee is to the accused an opportunity of cross-examination."[160]
by witnesses are concerned, by only such witnesses as meet him face to face at the trial, who give their testimony in his presence, and give to the accused an opportunity of cross-examination."[160]

Douglas voted with the Court when it held the confrontation guarantee applicable to the states and violated by the use at trial of testimony given at a preliminary hearing by a witness who had since left the state,

---

[156] *Washington v. Texas,* 388 U.S. 14 (1967).

[157] *Webb v. Texas,* 409 U.S. 95 (1972).

[158] Note 144, *supra.*

[159] *Cool v. United States,* 409 U.S. 100 (1972).

[160] *Dowdell v. United States,* 211 U.S. 325 (1911).

where defendant was present at the preliminary hearing but had no counsel to assist him in cross-examining the witness.[161]

ADDONIZIO v. UNITED STATES
405 U.S. 936 (1972)

Quite apart from the confrontation clause of the Sixth Amendment, federal and state rules of evidence include a hearsay rule which, like the confrontation clause, is designed to preserve for parties in civil and criminal litigation the opportunity to cross-examine those whose testimony is used against them. But to date, there are many more recognized exceptions to the hearsay rule than to the constitutional guarantee, and they vary from jurisdiction to jurisdiction. When one of these exceptions to the hearsay rule is invoked in a criminal case, it is subject to challenge under the confrontation clause.

One exception to the hearsay rule, developed in cases where no constitutional challenge was made, is for the testimony of a co-conspirator. His out-of-court statements, whether or not he is charged as a codefendant or present for cross-examination at trial, are admissible if made in furtherance of the conspiracy on the theory that he is acting as an agent for the other conspirators so that his statements may be treated as admissions by them.

In this case, Hugh Addonizio and fourteen others were charged by a federal indictment, containing one count of conspiracy to interfere with interstate commerce by means of extortion and sixty-five counts of acts of extortion pursuant to the conspiracy, while Addonizio was mayor of Newark, New Jersey. Addonizio and four others were tried together and convicted on the conspiracy count and sixty-three of the other counts. Addonizio and three others appealed, but the court of appeals affirmed the convictions. The Supreme Court declined to review the case.

MR. JUSTICE DOUGLAS, dissenting.

At the trial involved in these cases there was much evidence of corrupt practices by the administration of petitioner Addonizio during his tenure as mayor of Newark, New Jersey. But the question posed to the jury below was not whether these petitioners had engaged in corrupt practices, but the narrower issue of whether they had entered into and executed a criminal agreement to extract kickbacks from public contractors through threats of physical harm or economic ruin. Although the petitioners were charged with 65 substantive acts of coercive extrac-

---

[161] *Pointer v. Texas*, 380 U.S. 400 (1965).

tion of kickbacks, the key issue in the trial was who, if anyone, had conspired to commit these acts. Absent a finding that such a confederation had been formed, most of the evidence which damaged the petitioners could not have been introduced at all inasmuch as this evidence was hearsay admitted provisionally under the so-called co-conspirator exception. That the jury found a conspiracy to have existed, however, was under the circumstances of this trial the unsurprising and virtually inevitable result of the many disabilities imposed upon an accused by the ordeal of a multi-defendant conspiracy prosecution.

Mr. Justice Jackson catalogued many of these disabilities in his well-known concurrence in *Krulewitch* v. *United States*, 336 U.S. 440 (1949), reversing a conspiracy conviction, where he concluded that the prevailing "loose practice as to [the conspiracy] offense constitutes a serious threat to fairness in our administration of justice." He criticized the tendency of courts to dispense "with even the necessity to infer any definite agreement, although that is the gist of the offense." As to the procedural evils of this device he found that the risk to a codefendant of guilt by association was abnormally high:

> "A co-defendant in a conspiracy trial occupies an uneasy seat. There generally will be evidence of wrongdoing by somebody. It is difficult for the individual to make his own case stand on its own merits in the minds of jurors who are ready to believe that birds of a feather are flocked together. If he is silent, he is taken to admit it and if, as often happens, co-defendants can be prodded into accusing or contradicting each other, they convict each other."

Mr. Justice Jackson also regretted the wide leeway that prosecutors enjoyed in the broad scope of evidence admissible to prove conspiracy (and consequently to prove substantive acts as well). Under conspiracy law, the declarations and acts of any confederate in furtherance of the joint project are attributable to and admissible against all of its participants. This is true even if the declarant is not available for cross-examination. Moreover, such statements are admissible "subject to connection" by the prosecutor later in the trial. At the close of the Government's case, for example, the judge may believe that the Government failed to present a jury question as to a defendant's participation in a collective criminal plot. In such a case, the judge must ask the jury to disregard the provisionally admitted hearsay. Obviously, however, it will be difficult in a lengthy trial (such as this one filling 5,500 pages of transcript) for jurors to excise the stricken testimony from their memories. In the alternative case where the judge believes that a jury question has been presented as to a defendant's participation in a criminal enterprise, the jury is permitted to consider the provision-ally admitted matter in determining whether or not a defendant was a conspirator. In other words, the jury is allowed to assume its ultimate conclusion. Mr. Justice Jackson was particularly sensitive to the abuse potential in this vicious logic:

> "When the trial starts, the accused feels the full impact of the conspiracy strategy. Strictly, the prosecution should first establish *prima facie* the conspiracy and identify the conspirators, after which evidence of acts and declarations of each in the course of its execution are admissible against all. But the order of proof of so sprawling a charge is difficult for a judge to control. As a practical matter, the accused often is confronted with a hodgepodge of acts and statements by others which he may never have authorized or intended or even known about, but which help to persuade the jury of existence of the conspiracy itself. In other words, a con-spiracy often is proved by evidence that is admissible only upon assumption that conspiracy existed. The naive assumption that prejudicial effects can be overcome by instructions to the jury, all practicing lawyers know to be unmitigated fiction."

There are other disabilities. Often testimony will be receivable only against a particular codefendant, yet it may also inculpate another accused such as where (a) a codefendant "opens the door" to pre-judicial evidence by placing his reputation in issue, (b) a codefendant wants to place before the jury information which is helpful to him but is damaging to other defendants, or (c) the Government desires to offer evidence admissible against less than all of the codefendants. Cautionary instructions, of course, are routinely given where such cir-cumstances arise but we have often recognized the inability of jurors to compartmentalize information according to defendants. *Bruton* v. *United States*, 391 U.S. 123 (1968).[162] This shortcoming of the jury is compounded when, as here, the jury is also asked to digest voluminous testimony.

A victim of the multi-defendant conspiracy trial has fewer options for trial strategy than the ordinary defendant tried alone. Counsel may reluctantly give up the option of pointing the accusing finger at his client's codefendants in order to obtain similar concessions from other trial counsel. Counsel must also divert his preparation in part toward generating possible responses to evidence which may be admissible only

---

[162] [Which held that it was reversible error to admit in evidence a confession of a codefendant who did not take the witness stand where that confession impli-cated defendant, even though the jury was instructed that it was not to be used against defendant.]

against other codefendants. As for the defendant, he may be put to the choice of hiring less experienced counsel or less actively pursuing discovery or investigation because of the higher legal expenses imposed by longer joint trials. Furthermore, although an accused normally has "the right to present his own witnesses to establish a defense," *Washington* v. *Texas* [note 156, *supra*], an accused in a mass conspiracy trial may not put on his codefendants without their prior waivers of their absolute right not to testify.

All of these oppressive features were present in various degrees in this trial. But, in particular, the most onerous burden cast upon these petitioners was their inability to cross-examine each other as to comments which Government witnesses said they had heard them utter. The Court of Appeals recognized that "[t]here was much testimony as to statements made by various co-conspirators during the course, and in furtherance of the conspiracy." For example, one important prosecution witness testified that he had been a contractor hired by the city administration and that one of the accused conspirators, "Tony Boy" Boiardo, had told him: "You pay me the 10% . . . I take care of the Mayor. I take care of the Council." The lawyer for the former mayor, however, was not permitted to put Boiardo on the stand and to ask him whether Addonizio had, in fact, entered into an agreement with him to coerce kickbacks. This handicap of an accused is at war with the holdings of this Court that a defendant should be permitted to confront his accusers, especially where, as here, their declarations might have been purposely misleading or self-serving.

In addition, the petitioners were deprived of the right to cross-examine codefendant Gordon (who is not one of the petitioners). He had testified at the prior grand jury proceeding and that testimony was introduced at trial by the Government to corroborate the story of the Government's key witness, Rigo, as to various kickback transactions. The circumstances at trial were substantially similar to those involved in *Bruton* [see note 162, *supra*] except that Gordon's grand jury remarks did not directly mention his codefendants. Normally, that difference would be sufficient to support the lower court's finding that *Bruton* was inapposite but for the fact that the Government's case against all of the defendants turned upon Rigo's credibility. On cross-examination of Rigo [who was not a defendant], the codefendants had relentlessly attacked his credibility. But when the Government introduced the grand jury transcript in rebuttal, the defense challenge was completely terminated because Gordon, who was also on trial, could not be called to the stand. The judge, of course, gave instructions to the jury to consider the impact of the transcript upon Rigo's credibility only when assessing Gordon's guilt, but it is doubtful that the jurors could faithfully adhere to the delicate logic that Rigo may have told the truth as to Gordon but may have lied as to his codefendants. The contrary conclusion, to borrow from Mr. Justice Jackson, would be "unmitigated fiction." *Krulewitch* v. *United States, supra.*

In light of the claims of prejudice committed in this multi-defendant conspiracy trial, I would grant certiorari to consider whether the *extensive* reliance by the prosecutor on the coconspirator exception to the hearsay rule and the admission of the Gordon transcript deprived these petitioners of constitutional rights.

TACON v. ARIZONA
410 U.S. 351 (1973)

Tacon, while in the Army and stationed in Arizona, was arrested in February, 1969, and charged with unlawful sale of marijuana. His case was later set for trial on March 31, but in the meantime he had been discharged from the Army and left Arizona for New York. Although his attorney advised him of the trial date, he did not return for trial on that date, allegedly for lack of funds. He was convicted in absentia and sentenced to 5 to 5½ years. He returned to Arizona on April 2 and appealed his conviction to the Arizona Supreme Court without success.

The Court originally agreed to review the case, believing that it presented constitutional questions as to power of the state to try in absentia one who has voluntarily left the state and is unable for financial reasons to return. On reviewing the record of the case, however, it concluded that that issue had not been raised in the case, and that the only issue raised was whether Tacon's conduct amounted to a knowing and intelligent waiver of his right to be present at trial. Since that was primarily a "factual issue," it decided not to take the case.

MR. JUSTICE DOUGLAS, dissenting.

The attorney sent word by letter on March 3, 1970, that the trial would start March 31 and asked that he return a week early for preparation. Petitioner received that letter March 6 or 7, but had no funds to return. He apparently in good faith tried to raise the money but was not successful. He eventually did succeed and arrived in Arizona April 2. But the trial was over. Petitioner was convicted in absentia and sentenced to not less than five years nor more than five and one-half years.

Under Rule 231 of Arizona's Rules of Criminal Procedure, a trial may be conducted in the defendant's absence "if his absence is voluntary." The Arizona Supreme Court held that there had been "a knowing and intelligent waiver of his right to be present at the trial." The federal rule of a knowing and intelligent waiver of his right to confrontation and to be present at the trial of his case was the test applied by the Arizona Supreme Court.

The Sixth Amendment is applicable to the States by reason of the Fourteenth. The right "to be confronted with the witnesses against" him—the right of confrontation in the popular sense—means a "face-to-face" meeting. As stated in *Illinois* v. *Allen*, 397 U.S. 337, 338: "One of the most basic of the rights guaranteed by the Confrontation Clause is the accused's right to be present in the courtroom at every stage of his trial."

It is said by the Court that the broad issue of whether a defendant charged with a felony can ever waive his right to be present at trial is not properly before us, since petitioner neglected to plead the issue in this manner before the state courts. The issue which petitioner did raise in the state courts was whether the evidence in the record was sufficient to show that his absence from trial was voluntary, *i.e.*, that he made a knowing and intelligent waiver of his right to be present. The Court disposes of this "related issue" by holding that it is a factual issue that does not justify the exercise of our jurisdiction. But the question whether a constitutional right has been waived always involves factual matters. "When constitutional rights turn on the resolution of a factual dispute we are *duty bound to make an independent examination* of the evidence in the record." *Brookhart* v. *Janis*, 384 U.S. 1 (emphasis added).

The question of a knowing and intelligent waiver of this man's federal constitutional right to be present at his trial is far from frivolous. Petitioner was not fleeing the jurisdiction or going into hiding. He knew of the trial date and was trying to raise the necessary funds to travel west. A second letter dated March 18, sent by his attorney, suggested that a guilty plea to a reduced charge might be acceptable. But due to a mail strike petitioner did not receive that letter until April 1, when his trial was over. On March 24 petitioner's counsel sent him a telegram stating that trial would proceed March 31 whether petitioner was present or not. But that telegram was never received even by Western Union in New York. On March 30, petitioner called his lawyer, who told him the court would proceed with the trial even though the accused was absent. Petitioner replied that he would attempt to make it. But, as noted, he did not arrive until April 2.

On this record, one cannot say that petitioner had knowingly and intelligently waived his Sixth Amendment right of confrontation. Heretofore, we have never treated the question of waiver cavalierly. We indulge every presumption against the waiver of a constitutional right. We said in a rate case that we "do not presume acquiescence in the loss of fundamental rights." *Ohio Bell Tel. Co. v. Commission*, 301 U.S. 292. I would treat a hapless victim of a criminal marihuana charge equally as I would a corporate victim of an incompetent regulatory commission.

The law of waiver that governs here was stated by Mr. Justice Black in an earlier case many years ago. He ruled on waiver of counsel; but there is no difference when it comes to waiver of the right of confrontation. "A waiver is ordinarily an intentional relinquishment or abandonment of a known right or privilege. The determination of whether there has been an intelligent waiver of the right to counsel must depend, in each case, upon the particular facts and circumstances surrounding that case, including the background, experience, and conduct of the accused." *Johnson v. Zerbst*, 304 U.S. 458. This Court later held that "[w]aivers of constitutional rights not only must be voluntary but must be knowing, intelligent acts done with *sufficient awareness of the relevant circumstances and likely consequences*." *Brady v. United States*, 397 U.S. 742 (emphasis added).

No such showing has been made in the present case. I would reverse the judgment below.

Double Jeopardy

The Fifth Amendment provides that no person shall "be subject for the same offence to be twice put in jeopardy of life or limb."

Since "no legal jeopardy can attach until a jury" is impaneled and sworn,[163] the double jeopardy clause does not invalidate a statute allowing the government to appeal where the trial court dismisses an indictment before the jury is called—"before the moment of jeopardy is reached."[164]

GORI V. UNITED STATES
367 U.S. 364 (1961)

Despite the notion that jeopardy attaches when the jury is sworn, the guarantee has long been construed not to forbid a second trial where the jury at the first trial is unable to reach a verdict and is discharged.[165]

---

[163] *Kepner v. United States*, 195 U.S. 100 (1904).
[164] *Taylor v. United States*, 207 U.S. 120 (1907).
[165] *United States v. Perez*, 9 Wheat. 379 (1824).

Early cases also held that reprosecution was not banned where the trial judge properly declared a mistrial after swearing the jury because a letter published in a newspaper and read by several jurors raised doubts as to the impartiality of one juror,[166] or because the judge discovered that one juror had served on the grand jury which had indicted the defendant.[167]

Douglas wrote for the Court to hold that where the jury, after being sworn, was discharged because two of the prosecution's key witnesses were not present for trial, defendant could not be retried.[168]

In this case, the trial judge on his own motion, and not at the request or with the consent of the defense, declared a mistrial apparently because he thought the prosecution guilty of a prejudicial line of questioning on the direct examination of a government witness during Gori's trial for possession of stolen goods. When Gori was retried on the same charges, he invoked the double jeopardy guarantee, but failed. While the record in the case was too skimpy to permit the Court to rule on the propriety of the trial judge's action, it was satisfied that even if he acted out of "overeager solicitude," he acted "in the sole interest of the defendant."

MR. JUSTICE DOUGLAS, dissenting.

The place one comes out, when faced with the problem of this case, depends largely on where one starts.

Today the Court phrases the problem in terms of whether a mistrial has been granted "to help the prosecution" on the one hand or "in the sole interest of the defendant" on the other. The former is plainly in violation of the provision of the Fifth Amendment that no person shall ". . . be subject for the same offence to be twice put in jeopardy of life or limb. . . ." That was what we said in *Green v. United States*, 355 U.S. 184.[169] But not until today, I believe, have we ever intimated that a mistrial ordered "in the sole interest of the defendant" was no bar to a second trial where the mistrial was not ordered at the request of the defendant or with his consent. Yet that is the situation presented here, for the Court of Appeals found that the trial judge "was acting according to his convictions in protecting the rights of the accused."

There are occasions where a second trial may be had, although the

---

[166] *Simmons v. United States*, 142 U.S. 148 (1891).

[167] *Thompson v. United States*, 155 U.S. 271 (1894).

[168] *Downum v. United States*, 372 U.S. 734 (1963).

[169] [Which held that one charged with first-degree murder but convicted of the lesser included offense of second-degree murder could not, after his conviction was reversed on appeal, again be tried for first-degree murder, although he could again be tried for second-degree murder.]

jury which was impanelled for the first trial was discharged without reaching a verdict and without the defendant's consent. Mistrial because the jury was unable to agree is the classic example; and that was the critical circumstance in *United States* v. *Perez* [note 165, *supra*]. Tactical situations of an army in the field have been held to justify the withdrawal of a courtmartial proceeding and the institution of another one in calmer days. *Wade* v. *Hunter*, 336 U.S. 684. Discovery by the judge during the trial that "one or more members of a jury might be biased against the Government or the defendant" has been held to warrant discharge of the jury and direction of a new trial. *Id.*, 689. That is to say, "a defendant's valued right to have his trial completed by a particular tribunal must in some instances be subordinated to the public's interest in fair trials designed to end in just judgments." *Wade* v. *Hunter*, *supra*. While the matter is said to be in the sound discretion of the trial court, that discretion has some guidelines—"a trial can be discontinued when particular circumstances manifest a necessity for so doing, and when failure to discontinue would defeat the ends of justice." *Id.*, 690.

To date these exceptions have been narrowly confined. Once a jury has been impanelled and sworn, jeopardy attaches and a subsequent prosecution is barred, if a mistrial is ordered—absent a showing of imperious necessity. As stated by Mr. Justice Story in *United States* v. *Coolidge*, 25 Fed. Cas. 622, the discretion is to be exercised "only in very extraordinary and striking circumstances."

That is my starting point. I read the Double Jeopardy Clause as applying a strict standard. "The prohibition is not against being twice punished; but against being twice put in jeopardy." *United States* v. *Ball*, 163 U.S. 662. It is designed to help equalize the position of government and the individual, to discourage abusive use of the awesome power of society. Once a trial starts jeopardy attaches. The prosecution must stand or fall on its performance at the trial. I do not see how a mistrial directed because the prosecutor has no witnesses is different from a mistrial directed because the prosecutor abuses his office and is guilty of misconduct. In neither is there a breakdown in judicial machinery such as happens when the judge is stricken, or a juror has been discovered to be disqualified to sit, or when it is impossible or impractical to hold a trial at the time and place set. The question is not, as the Court of Appeals thought, whether a defendant is "to receive absolution for his crime." The policy of the Bill of Rights is to make rare indeed the occasions when the citizen can for the same offense be required to run the gantlet twice. The risk of judicial arbitrariness rests where, in my view, the Constitution puts it—on the Government.

In 1971, in a decision in which Douglas joined, the Court rejected the implication in Gori that vulnerability to reprosecution should depend on an appellate court's assessment of "the motivation underlying the trial judge's action in declaring a mistrial." Rather, the test was said to be whether the mistrial was properly entered because there was "a manifest necessity for the act, or the ends of justice would otherwise be defeated." Hence, when the trial judge concluded, after inadequate inquiry, that prosecuting witnesses had not been adequately warned by the government of the privilege against self-incrimination and their right to counsel, and then proceeded, without giving the defense a chance to object, to direct a mistrial where a continuance would in any event have been more appropriate, reprosecution was held banned.[170]

North Carolina v. Pearce
395 U.S. 711 (1969)

In a companion case to this one, Benton v. Maryland,[171] the Court overruled its prior decision to the contrary [172] and held that the due process clause incorporated the double jeopardy guarantee against the states and reversed the state larceny conviction of a defendant first acquitted of larceny but convicted of burglary, who obtained a reversal of his burglary conviction on appeal and was then reindicted for and convicted of both larceny and burglary.

This case involved two defendants. Pearce was convicted in North Carolina of assault with intent to commit rape and sentenced for a term of twelve to fifteen years. Several years later he obtained a reversal of his conviction by the state supreme court on the ground that an involuntary confession had unconstitutionally been admitted in evidence against him. He was retried, reconvicted, and given an eight-year sentence which, when added to the time he had already served, amounted to a longer total sentence than the one originally imposed.

Rice had pleaded guilty in Alabama to three counts of burglary and was sentenced to prison terms aggregating ten years. Some two years later the judgments were set aside by the state court because Rice had not been accorded his constitutional right to counsel. He was retried on all three charges, reconvicted, and given sentences aggregating twenty-five years.

The Court held that the double jeopardy guarantee "protects against multiple punishments for the same offense," so that both men must be

170 United States v. Jorn, 400 U.S. 470 (1971).
171 395 U.S. 784 (1969).
172 Palko v. Connecticut, note 16, supra.

*given credit on their sentences for time already served under the earlier
sentences, but that the double jeopardy clause would not prevent a more
severe sentence on reconviction because "the original conviction has,
at the defendant's behest, been wholly nullified and the slate wiped
clean." But, the Court added, it would be a flagrant violation of the
due process clause to impose a heavier sentence because defendant had
succeeded in having his earlier conviction reversed. To protect against
that eventuality, the judge who imposes a more severe sentence on re-
conviction must give his reasons for doing so. Since that had not been
done in either case, and Pearce and Rice had now been incarcerated
longer than the terms of their original sentences, they were entitled to
be released.*

Mr. Justice Douglas, concurring.

Although I agree with the Court as to the reach of due process, I
would go further. It is my view that if for any reason a new trial is
granted and there is a conviction a second time, the second penalty
imposed cannot exceed the first penalty, if respect is had for the
guarantee against double jeopardy.

The theory of double jeopardy is that a person need run the
gantlet only once. The gantlet is the risk of the range of punishment
which the State or Federal Government imposes for that particular
conduct. It may be a year to 25 years, or 20 years to life, or death. He
risks the maximum permissible punishment when first tried. That risk
having been faced once need not be faced again. And the fact that
he takes an appeal does not waive his constitutional defense of former
jeopardy to a second prosecution. *Green* v. *United States* [note 169,
supra].

In the *Green* case, the defendant was charged with arson on one
count and on a second count was charged with either first-degree murder
carrying a mandatory death sentence, or second-degree murder carrying
a maximum sentence of life imprisonment. The jury found him guilty
of arson and second-degree murder but the verdict was silent as to first-
degree murder. He appealed the conviction and obtained a reversal.
On a remand he was tried again. This time he was convicted of first-
degree murder and sentenced to death—hence his complaint of former
jeopardy. We held that the guarantee of double jeopardy applied and
that the defendant, having been "in direct peril of being convicted and
punished for first degree murder at his first trial" could not be "forced
to run the gantlet" twice.

It is argued that that case is different because there were two different
crimes with different punishments provided by statute for each one.

That, however, is a matter of semantics. "It is immaterial to the basic purpose of the constitutional provision against double jeopardy whether the Legislature divides a crime into different degrees carrying different punishments or allows the court or jury to fix different punishments for the same crime." *People* v. *Henderson*, 60 Cal. 2d 482.

From the point of view of the individual and his liberty, the risk here of getting from one to 15 years for specified conduct is different only in degree from the risk in *Green* of getting life imprisonment or capital punishment for specified conduct.

It was established at an early date that the Fifth Amendment was designed to prevent an accused from running the risk of "double punishment." *United States* v. *Ewell*, 383 U.S. 116. When Madison introduced to the First Congress his draft of what became the Double Jeopardy Clause, it read:

> "No person shall be subject, except in cases of impeachment, to *more than one punishment* or one trial for the same offence. . . ." (Emphasis supplied.) 1 Annals of Cong. 434.

The phrasing of that proposal was changed at the behest of those who feared that the reference to but "one trial" might prevent a convicted man from obtaining a new trial on writ of error. But that change was not intended to alter the ban against double punishment. Sigler, A History of Double Jeopardy, 7 Am. J. Legal Hist. 283 (1963).

The inquiry, then, is into the meaning of "double" or "multiple" punishment. In *Ex parte Lange*, 18 Wall. 163, the petitioner had been sentenced to one-year imprisonment *and* $200 in fines, under a federal statute providing for a maximum penalty of one-year imprisonment *or* $200 in fines. On writ of habeas corpus five days later, the trial court re-examined its own prior sentence and reset it, instead, at one-year imprisonment without credit for time already served. This Court, on certiorari, ordered petitioner discharged altogether. It reasoned that the trial court had power to impose a sentence of either imprisonment or fine. Because the petitioner had paid the fine, he had already suffered complete punishment for his crime and could not be subjected to further sanction.

Ex parte Lange left it somewhat in doubt, whether the ban on double punishment applied only to situations in which the second sentence was added to one that had been completely served; or whether it also applied to the case where the second sentence was added to one still being served. It was not until *United States* v. *Benz*, 282 U.S. 304, that the Court clarified its position. In that case, having initially set the defendant's sentence at 10 months, the trial court later reduced the sentence to six months. The Government appealed, and the question was certified to this Court, whether a reduction in sentence violated the Double Jeopardy Clause:

> "The general rule is that judgments, decrees and orders are within the control of the court during the term at which they were made. . . . The rule is not confined to civil cases, but applies in criminal cases as well, *provided the punishment be not augmented. Ex parte Lange*, 18 Wall. 163. In the present case the power of the court was exercised to mitigate the punishment, not to increase it, and is thus brought within the limitation. . . .
>
> "The distinction that the court during the same term may amend a sentence so as to mitigate the punishment, but not so as to increase it, is not based upon the ground that the court has lost control of the judgment in the latter case, but upon the ground that to increase the penalty is to subject the defendant to double punishment for the same offense in violation of the Fifth Amendment to the Constitution. . . . This is the basis of the decision in *Ex parte Lange, supra*." (Emphasis supplied.)

The governing principle has thus developed that a convicted man may be retried after a successful appeal, *Bryan* v. *United States*, 338 U.S. 552; that he may run the risk, on retrial, of receiving a sentence as severe as that previously imposed, *United States* v. *Ball*, 163 U.S. 662; and that he may run the risk of being tried for a separate offense, *Williams* v. *Oklahoma*, 358 U.S. 576. But with all deference I submit that the State does not, because of prior error, have a second chance to obtain an enlarged sentence. Where a man successfully attacks a sentence that he has already "fully served" (*Street* v. *New York*, 394 U.S. 576), the State cannot create an additional sentence and send him back to prison. *Ex parte Lange, supra*. Similarly, where a defendant successfully attacks a sentence that he has begun to serve, the State cannot impose an added sentence by sending him to prison for a greater term.

The ban on double jeopardy has its roots deep in the history of occidental jurisprudence. "Fear and abhorrence of governmental power to try people twice for the same conduct is one of the oldest ideas found in western civilization." *Bartkus* v. *Illinois*, 359 U.S. 121 (BLACK, J., dissenting). And its purposes are several. It prevents the State from using its criminal processes as an instrument of harassment to wear the accused out by a multitude of cases with accumulated trials. *Abbate* v. *United States*, 359 U.S. 187 (opinion by BRENNAN, J.).

It serves the additional purpose of precluding the State, following *acquittal*, from successively retrying the defendant in the hope of securing a conviction. "The vice of this procedure lies in relitigating the same issue on the same evidence before two different juries with a man's innocence or guilt at stake" "in the hope that they would come to a different conclusion." *Hoag* v. *New Jersey*, 356 U.S. 464 (WARREN, C. J., dissenting). "Harassment of an accused by successive prosecutions or declaration of a mistrial so as to afford the prosecution a more favorable opportunity to convict are examples when jeopardy attaches." *Downum* v. *United States* [note 168, *supra*].

And finally, it prevents the State, following *conviction*, from retrying the defendant again in the hope of securing a greater penalty.

> "This case presents an instance of the prosecution being allowed to harass the accused with repeated trials and convictions on the same evidence, until it achieves its desired result of a capital verdict." *Ciucci* v. *Illinois*, 356 U.S. 571.

It is the latter purpose which is relevant here, for in these cases the Court allows the State a second chance to retry the defendant in the hope of securing a more favorable penalty.

> "Why is it that, having once been tried and found guilty, he can never be tried again for that offence? Manifestly it is not the danger or jeopardy of being a second time found guilty. It is the punishment that would legally follow the second conviction which is the real danger guarded against by the Constitution. But if, after judgment has been rendered on the conviction, and the sentence of that judgment executed on the criminal, he can be again sentenced on that conviction to another and different punishment, or to endure the same punishment a second time, is the constitutional restriction of any value? . . .
>
> "The argument seems to us irresistible, and we do not doubt that the Constitution was designed as much to prevent the criminal from being twice punished for the same offence as from being twice tried for it." *Ex parte Lange, supra.*

The Fourteenth Amendment would now prohibit North Carolina and Alabama, after trial, from retrying or resentencing these defendants in the bald hope of securing a more favorable verdict. *Benton* v. *Maryland* [note 171, *supra*]. But here, because these defendants were successful in appealing their convictions, the Court allows those States to do just that. It is said that events subsequent to the first trial[173] may justify a new and greater sentence. Of course that is true. But it is

---

[173] To rely on information that has developed after the initial trial gives the Government "continuing criminal jurisdiction" to supplement its case against the defendant, far beyond the cut-off date set by its original prosecution. Consider the defendant whose sentence on retrial is enlarged because of antisocial acts committed in prison. To increase his sentence on that original offense because of wholly subsequent conduct is indirectly to hold him criminally responsible for that conduct.

true, too, in *every* criminal case. Does that mean that the State should be allowed to reopen every verdict and readjust every sentence by coming forward with new evidence concerning guilt and punishment? If not, then why should it be allowed to do so merely because the defendant has taken the initiative in seeking an error-free trial? It is doubtless true that the State has an interest in adjusting sentences upward when it discovers new evidence warranting that result. But the individual has an interest in remaining free of double punishment. And in weighing those interests against one another, the Constitution has decided the matter in favor of the individual. See *United States* v. *Tateo*, 377 U.S. 463 (GOLDBERG, J., dissenting).

Cruel and Unusual Punishment: Excessive Fines

The Eighth Amendment also provides that "excessive fines" shall not be imposed "nor cruel and unusual punishments inflicted." The Court has never considered the prohibition against excessive fines.[174]

In 1947, assuming without deciding that the Fifth and Eighth Amendments' prohibitions against double jeopardy and cruel and unusual punishment were applicable to the states, the Court held that neither was violated by a state's second attempt to electrocute one convicted of murder where the first attempt failed because of mechanical difficulty. There was no double jeopardy because the first failure was "an accident, with no suggestion of malevolence." And the fact that "an unforeseeable accident prevented the prompt consummation of the sentence cannot

---

[174] In 1947, the Court considered punishment inflicted in contempt proceedings where a labor union violated a federal injunction against a strike in coal mines being operated by the United States during World War II under the War Labor Disputes Act. The trial court had found both the United Mine Workers and its president, John L. Lewis, guilty of civil and criminal contempt and had fined Lewis $10,000 and the union $3,500,000. Without express reference to the Eighth Amendment, the Court held that the fine against Lewis was warranted but that an unconditional fine of $3,500,000 against the union was "excessive as punishment for the criminal contempt" and that $2,800,000 of it should be converted to a civil sanction, payable only if the union did not cease the strike. Douglas dissented on this issue, contending that the $10,000 fine on Lewis and the remaining unconditional fine of $700,000 on the union were excessive under the Eighth Amendment, since they believed in good faith, though erroneously, that the injunction was illegal, and since the War Labor Disputes Act under which the mines were seized prescribed a maximum punishment of one year and $5,000 for interference with properties taken over by the United States. *United States* v. *United Mine Workers*, 330 U.S. 258 (1947).

. . . add an element of cruelty to a subsequent execution," even though the defendant "had once gone through the difficult preparation for execution and had once received through his body a current of electricity intended to cause his death."[175] *Douglas joined in a dissent which said in part:*

> *If the state officials deliberately and intentionally had placed the [defendant] in the electric chair five times and, each time, had applied electric current to his body in a manner not sufficient, until the final time, to kill him, such a form of torture would rival that of burning at the stake. Although the failure of the first attempt, in the present case, was unintended, the reapplication of the electric current will be intentional. How many deliberate and intentional reapplications of electric current does it take to produce a cruel, unusual and unconstitutional punishment? While five applications would be more cruel and unusual than one, the uniqueness of the present case demonstrates that, today, two separated applications are sufficiently "cruel and unusual" to be prohibited. If five attempts would be "cruel and unusual," it would be difficult to draw the line between two, three, four and five. It is not difficult, however, as we here contend, to draw the line between one continuous application . . . and any other application of the current.*

SWEENEY V. WOODALL
344 U.S. 86 (1952)

Woodall was convicted of burglary in Alabama and sentenced to a state penitentiary. After six years he escaped, but was later apprehended in Ohio and held for extradition to Alabama. While being so held in Ohio, he filed a petition for habeas corpus in a federal court there, alleging that during his confinement in Alabama he had been brutally mistreated, that he would be subjected to the same or worse treatment if he were returned to Alabama, and that this mistreatment constituted a violation of the Eighth Amendment's prohibition of cruel and unusual punishment.

The Court disposed of the case on procedural grounds and hence did not reach the constitutional question. Woodall had not complied with the rule that before a person convicted in a state court could file a petition for habeas corpus in federal court, he must first seek relief in the courts of the convicting state. As applied here, that rule meant that Woodall must be returned to the custody of the Alabama prison authorities while the Alabama courts considered his contentions.

[175] *Francis v. Resweber,* 329 U.S. 459 (1947).

MR. JUSTICE DOUGLAS, dissenting.

The petition presents facts which, if true, make this a shocking case in the annals of our jurisprudence.

[Woodall] offered to prove that the Alabama jailers have a nine-pound strap with five metal prongs that they use to beat prisoners; that they used this strap against him, that the beatings frequently caused him to lose consciousness and resulted in deep wounds and permanent scars.

He offered to prove that he was stripped to his waist and forced to work in the broiling sun all day long without a rest period.

He offered to prove that on entrance to the prison he was forced to serve as a "gal-boy" or female for the homosexuals among the prisoners.

Lurid details are offered in support of these main charges. If any of them is true, respondent has been subjected to cruel and unusual punishment in the past and can be expected on his return to have the same awful treatment visited upon him.

The Court allows him to be returned to Alabama on the theory that he can apply to the Alabama courts for relief from the torture inflicted on him. That answer would suffice in the ordinary sense. For a prisoner caught in the mesh of Alabama law normally would need to rely on Alabama law to extricate him. But if the allegations of the petition are true, this Negro must suffer torture and mutilation or risk death itself to get relief in Alabama. It is contended that there is no showing that the doors of the Alabama courts are closed to petitioner or that he would have no opportunity to get relief. It is said that we should not assume that unlawful action of prison officials would prevent petitioner from obtaining relief in the Alabama courts. But we deal here not with an academic problem but with allegations which, if proved, show that petitioner has in the past been beaten by guards to the point of death and will, if returned, be subjected to the same treatment. Perhaps those allegations will prove groundless. But if they are supported in evidence, they make the return of this prisoner a return to cruel torture.

I am confident that enlightened Alabama judges would make short shrift of sadistic prison guards. But I rebel at the thought that any human being should be forced to run a gamut of blood and terror in order to get his constitutional rights. That is too great a price to pay for the legal principle that before a state prisoner can get federal relief he must exhaust his state remedies.

The Court of Appeals should be sustained in its action in giving respondent an opportunity to prove his charges. If they are established, respondent should be discharged from custody and saved the ordeal of enduring torture and risking death in order to protect his constitutional rights.

ROBINSON v. CALIFORNIA
370 u.s. 660 (1962)

In this case, the Court ignored its prior decision to the contrary[176] and held the Eighth Amendment's prohibition against cruel and unusual punishment applicable to the states. And it held that that prohibition was violated when a state convicted Robinson of being "addicted to the use of narcotics." The state might impose criminal sanctions against unauthorized manufacture, prescription, sale, purchase, possession, or use, or against disorderly or antisocial behavior resulting from use, of narcotics. And it might establish a program of compulsory treatment for addicts involving involuntary confinement. But it could not make the mere status of being an addict a criminal offense, any more than it could make it a crime to be mentally ill, a leper, or afflicted with venereal disease. Narcotic addiction is also an illness. Even though defendant had been sentenced to only ninety days, so that "in the abstract" the punishment was not cruel and unusual, "[e]ven one day in prison would be a cruel and unusual punishment for the 'crime' of having a common cold."

MR. JUSTICE DOUGLAS, concurring.

While I join the Court's opinion, I wish to make more explicit the reasons why I think it is "cruel and unusual" punishment in the sense of the Eighth Amendment to treat as a criminal a person who is a drug addict.

In Sixteenth Century England one prescription for insanity was to beat the subject "until he had regained his reason." Deutsch, The Mentally Ill in America (1937), p. 13. In America "the violently insane went to the whipping post and into prison dungeons or, as sometimes happened, were burned at the stake or hanged"; and "the pauper insane often roamed the countryside as wild men and from time to time were pilloried, whipped, and jailed." Action for Mental Health (1961), p. 26.

As stated by Dr. Isaac Ray many years ago:

> "Nothing can more strongly illustrate the popular ignorance respecting insanity than the proposition, equally objectionable in its humanity and its logic, that the insane should be punished for criminal acts, in order to deter other insane persons from doing the same thing." Treatise on the Medical Jurisprudence of Insanity (5th ed. 1871), p. 56.

---

[176] *In re Kemmler*, note 12, *supra*.

Today we have our differences over the legal definition of insanity. But however insanity is defined, it is in end effect treated as a disease. While afflicted people may be confined either for treatment or for the protection of society, they are not branded as criminals.

Yet terror and punishment linger on as means of dealing with some diseases. As recently stated:

> ". . . the idea of basing treatment for disease on purgatorial acts and ordeals is an ancient one in medicine. It may trace back to the Old Testament belief that disease of any kind, whether mental or physical, represented punishment for sin; and thus relief could take the form of a final heroic act of atonement. This superstition appears to have given support to fallacious medical rationales for such procedures as purging, bleeding, induced vomiting, and blistering, as well as an entire chamber of horrors constituting the early treatment of mental illness. The latter included a wide assortment of shock techniques, such as the 'water cures' (dousing, ducking, and near-drowning), spinning in a chair, centrifugal swinging, and an early form of electric shock. All, it would appear, were planned as means of driving from the body some evil spirit or toxic vapor." Action for Mental Health (1961), pp. 27–28.

That approach continues as respects drug addicts. Drug addiction is more prevalent in this country than in any other nation of the western world. S. Rep. No. 1440, 84th Cong., 2d Sess., p. 2. It is sometimes referred to as "a contagious disease." *Id.*, at p. 3. But those living in a world of black and white put the addict in the category of those who could, if they would, forsake their evil ways.

The first step toward addiction may be as innocent as a boy's puff on a cigarette in an alleyway. It may come from medical prescriptions. Addiction may even be present at birth [if the mother is an addict].

Some say the addict has a disease. See Hesse, Narcotics and Drug Addiction (1946), p. 40 *et seq.* Others say addiction is not a disease but "a symptom of a mental or psychiatric disorder." H. R. Rep. No. 2388, 84th Cong., 2d Sess., p. 8. And see Present Status of Narcotic Addiction, 138 A. M. A. J. 1019, 1026; Narcotic Addiction, Report to Attorney General Brown by Citizens Advisory Committee to the Attorney General on Crime Prevention (1954), p. 12; Finestone, Narcotics and Criminality, 22 Law & Contemp. Prob. 69, 83–85 (1957).

Some States punish addiction, though most do not. See S. Doc. No. 120, 84th Cong., 2d Sess., pp. 41, 42. Nor does the Uniform Narcotic Drug Act, first approved in 1932 and now in effect in most of the States. Great Britain, beginning in 1920 placed "addiction and the treatment of addicts squarely and exclusively into the hands of the medical profession." Lindesmith, The British System of Narcotics Control, 22 Law & Contemp. Prob. 138 (1957). In England the doctor "has almost complete professional autonomy in reaching decisions about the treatment of addicts." Schur, British Narcotics Policies, 51 J. Crim. L. & Criminology 619, 621 (1961). Under British law "addicts are patients, not criminals." *Ibid.* Addicts have not disappeared in England but they have decreased in number and there is now little "addict-crime" there. *Id.*, at 623.

The fact that England treats the addict as a sick person, while a few of our States, including California, treat him as a criminal, does not, of course, establish the unconstitutionality of California's penal law. But we do know that there is "a hard core" of "chronic and incurable drug addicts who, in reality, have lost their power of self-control." S. Rep. No. 2033, 84th Cong., 2d Sess., p. 8. There has been a controversy over the type of treatment—whether enforced hospitalization or ambulatory care is better. H. R. Rep. No. 2388, 84th Cong., 2d Sess., pp. 66–68. But there is little disagreement with the statement of Charles Winick: "The hold of drugs on persons addicted to them is so great that it would be almost appropriate to reverse the old adage and say that opium derivatives represent the religion of the people who use them." Narcotics Addiction and its Treatment, 22 Law & Contemp. Prob. 9 (1957). The abstinence symptoms and their treatment are well known. *Id.*, at 10–11. Cure is difficult because of the complex of forces that make for addiction. *Id.*, at 18–23. "After the withdrawal period, vocational activities, recreation, and some kind of psychotherapy have a major role in the treatment program, which ideally lasts from four to six months." *Id.*, at 23–24. Dr. Marie Nyswander tells us that normally a drug addict must be hospitalized in order to be cured. The Drug Addict as a Patient (1956), p. 138.

The impact that an addict has on a community causes alarm and often leads to punitive measures. Those measures are justified when they relate to acts of transgression. But I do not see how under our system *being an addict* can be punished as a crime. If addicts can be punished for their addiction, then the insane can also be punished for their insanity. Each has a disease and each must be treated as a sick person. As Charles Winick has said:

> "There can be no single program for the elimination of an illness as complex as drug addiction, which carries so much emotional freight in the community. Cooperative interdisciplinary research and action, more local community participation, training the various healing professions in the techniques of dealing with addicts, regional treatment facilities, demonstration centers, and

a thorough and vigorous post-treatment rehabilitation program would certainly appear to be among the minimum requirements for any attempt to come to terms with this problem. The addict should be viewed as a sick person, with a chronic disease which requires almost emergency action." 22 Law & Contemp. Prob. 9, 33 (1957).

The Council on Mental Health reports that criminal sentences for addicts interferes "with the possible treatment and rehabilitation of addicts and therefore should be abolished." 165 A.M.A.J. 1968, 1972.

The command of the Eighth Amendment, banning "cruel and unusual punishments," stems from the Bill of Rights of 1688. See *Francis v. Resweber* [note 175, *supra*]. And it is applicable to the States by reason of the Due Process Clause of the Fourteenth Amendment. *Ibid.*

The historic punishments that were cruel and unusual included "burning at the stake, crucifixion, breaking on the wheel" (*In re Kemmler* [note 12, *supra*]), quartering, the rack and thumbscrew (see *Chambers* v. *Florida*, 309 U.S. 227), and in some circumstances even solitary confinement (see *Medley*, 134 U.S. 160).

The question presented in the earlier cases concerned the degree of severity with which a particular offense was punished or the element of cruelty present. A punishment out of all proportion to the offense may bring it within the ban against "cruel and unusual punishments." See *O'Neil* v. *Vermont*, 144 U.S. 323. So may the cruelty of the method of punishment, as, for example, disemboweling a person alive. See *Wilkerson* v. *Utah*, 99 U.S. 130. But the principle that would deny power to exact capital punishment for a petty crime would also deny power to punish a person by fine or imprisonment for being sick.

The Eighth Amendment expresses the revulsion of civilized man against barbarous acts—the "cry of horror" against man's inhumanity to his fellow man. See *O'Neil* v. *Vermont*, *supra* (dissenting opinion); *Francis* v. *Resweber*, *supra* (dissenting opinion).

By the time of Coke, enlightenment was coming as respects the insane. Coke said that the execution of a madman "should be a miserable spectacle, both against law, and of extreame inhumanity and cruelty, and can be no example to others." 6 Coke's Third Inst. (4th ed. 1797), p. 6. Blackstone endorsed this view of Coke. 4 Commentaries (Lewis ed. 1897), p. 25.

We should show the same discernment respecting drug addiction. The addict is a sick person. He may, of course, be confined for treatment or for the protection of society. Cruel and unusual punishment results not from confinement, but from convicting the addict of a crime. The purpose of [the California statute under which Robinson was convicted] is not to cure, but to penalize.

The Court later refused to hold similarly unconstitutional a Texas conviction of a defendant for being "found in a state of intoxication in [a] public place." Although defendant had suffered approximately one hundred convictions for the same offense in the past seventeen years, and there was psychiatric testimony that he was a "chronic alcoholic," the Court concluded that on "the comparatively primitive state of our knowledge" about alcoholism, it could not be said that imprisonment "as a means of dealing with the public aspects of problem drinking can never be defended as rational."[177] Douglas dissented, contending that Robinson stood for the principle that "[c]riminal penalties may not be inflicted upon a person for being in a condition he is powerless to change" and that that principle should be applied to the chronic alcoholic who was powerless to avoid intoxication and, once intoxicated, "could not prevent himself from appearing in public places."

He dissented again when the Court declined to review a District of Columbia vagrancy conviction, protesting that "I do not see how economic or social status can be made a crime any more than being a drug addict can be."[178]

Douglas also joined dissenters in 1963 when the Court declined to review a case in which a convicted rapist was sentenced to death, contending that the Court should face the question whether "the taking of human life to protect a value other than human life" was "consistent with" the Eighth Amendment.[179]

FURMAN V. GEORGIA
408 U.S. 238 (1972)

By a vote of 5 to 4, the Court in this case held that the carrying out of the death penalty, in one case of a Georgia murder conviction, one of a Georgia rape conviction, and one of a Texas rape conviction, would constitute cruel and unusual punishment in violation of the Eighth Amendment. Each of the five Justices in the majority (Douglas, Brennan, Stewart, White, and Marshall) filed separate opinions, as did each of those in dissent (Chief Justice Burger and Justices Blackmun, Powell and Rehnquist).

[177] Powell v. Texas, 392 U.S. 514 (1968).
[178] Hicks v. District of Columbia, 383 U.S. 252 (1966).
[179] Rudolph v. Alabama, 375 U.S. 889 (1963).

Justice Brennan declined to limit the Eighth Amendment to punishments which would have been considered cruel and unusual at the time the Bill of Rights was adopted or to those which would be virtually unanimously condemned today (since the Bill of Rights operates as a check on the majority for the protection of the minority), but invoked "evolving standards of decency that mark the progress of a maturing society" as indicating (1) that a punishment so severe as to be "degrading to the dignity of human beings" would now be forbidden, (2) that government "must not arbitrarily inflict a severe punishment," (3) that the punishment inflicted "must not be unacceptable to contemporary society," and (4) that it must not be "unnecessary"—a "pointless infliction of suffering." Finding the death penalty inconsistent with all four principles, he concluded that the death penalty was no longer tolerable under the Eighth Amendment.

Justice Stewart did not find it necessary to decide "whether capital punishment is unconstitutional for all crimes and under all circumstances." For him it was enough to establish unconstitutionality that the Georgia legislature had not prescribed death for all guilty of murder or rape, and that the California legislature had not prescribed death for all guilty of rape. Georgia law left imposition of that penalty to the unfettered discretion of the jury, and California law left it to the unfettered discretion of the judge. Since available evidence indicated that of all people convicted of murder or rape at the time of defendants' convictions, defendants were "among a capriciously selected random handful" upon whom the death penalty was imposed, the death sentences here were "cruel and unusual in the same way that being struck by lightning is cruel and unusual."

Justice White also concluded that the death penalty was not in all cases and all circumstances unconstitutional, but concluded that as a consequence of vesting sentencing authority in juries, the death penalty was so infrequently imposed that it could no longer be justified either for its deterrent effect or as satisfying "any existing general need for retribution."

Justice Marshall agreed with Justice Brennan that the death penalty was no longer acceptable under the Eighth Amendment, but added some further reasons: (1) it is discriminatorily applied against the poor and members of minority groups and against men and not women, (2) when a mistake as to guilt has been made and the death penalty is imposed, the mistake is uncorrectable, and (3) the presence of the death penalty "wreaks havoc with our entire criminal justice system" and "is [a] stumbling block in the path of general reform and of the treatment of crime and criminals."

Mr. Justice Douglas, concurring.

It has been assumed in our decisions that punishment by death is not cruel, unless the manner of execution can be said to be inhuman and barbarous. *In re Kemmler* [note 12, *supra*]. It is also said in our opinions that the proscription of cruel and unusual punishments 'is not fastened to the obsolete but may acquire meaning as public opinion becomes enlightened by a humane justice." *Weems v. United States* [217 U.S. 349]. A like statement was made in *Trop v. Dulles*,[180] 356 U.S. 86, that the Eighth Amendment "must draw its meaning from the evolving standards of decency that mark the progress of a maturing society."

The generality of a law inflicting capital punishment is one thing. What may be said of the validity of a law on the books and what may be done with the law in its application do, or may, lead to quite different conclusions.

It would seem to be incontestable that the death penalty inflicted on one defendant is "unusual" if it discriminates against him by reason of his race, religion, wealth, social position, or class, or if it is imposed under a procedure that gives room for the play of such prejudices.

There is evidence that the provision of the English Bill of Rights of 1689, from which the language of the Eighth Amendment was taken, was concerned primarily with selective or irregular application of harsh penalties and that its aim was to forbid arbitrary and discriminatory penalties of a severe nature:[181]

> "Following the Norman conquest of England in 1066, the old system of penalties, which ensured equality between crime and punishment, suddenly disappeared. By the time systematic judicial records were kept, its demise was almost complete. With the exception of certain grave crimes for which the punishment was death or outlawry, the arbitrary fine was replaced by a discretionary amercement. Although amercement's discretionary character allowed the circumstances of each case to be taken into account and the level of cash penalties to be decreased or increased accordingly, the amercement presented an opportunity for excessive or oppressive fines.

---

[180] [Which held that a federal statute providing for forfeiture of the citizenship of one convicted by a court-martial of desertion from the armed forces imposed cruel and unusual punishment. See p. 128, *supra*.]

[181] Granucci, "Nor Cruel and Unusual Punishments Inflicted": The Original Meaning, 57 Calif. L. Rev. 839 (1969).

"The problem of excessive amercements became so prevalent that three chapters of the Magna Carta were devoted to their regulation. Maitland said of Chapter 14 that 'very likely there was no clause in the Magna Carta more grateful to the mass of the people.' Chapter 14 clearly stipulated as fundamental law a prohibition of excessiveness in punishments:

" 'A free man shall not be amerced for a trivial offense, except in accordance with the degree of the offense; and for a serious offence he shall be amerced according to its gravity, saving his livelihood; and a merchant likewise, saving his merchandise; in the same way a villein shall be amerced saving his wainage; if they fall into our mercy. And none of the aforesaid amercements shall be imposed except by the testimony of reputable men of the neighborhood.' "

The English Bill of Rights, enacted December 16, 1689, stated that "excessive bail ought not to be required, nor excessive fines imposed, nor cruel and unusual punishments inflicted." These were the words chosen for our Eighth Amendment. A like provision had been in Virginia's Constitution of 1776 and in the constitutions of seven other States. The Northwest Ordinance, enacted under the Articles of Confederation, included a prohibition of cruel and unusual punishments. But the debates of the First Congress on the Bill of Rights throw little light on its intended meaning. All that appears is the following:

"Mr. SMITH, of South Carolina, objected to the words 'nor cruel and unusual punishments;' the import of them being too indefinite.

"Mr. LIVERMORE: The clause seems to express a great deal of humanity, on which account I have no objection to it; but as it seems to have no meaning in it, I do not think it necessary. What is meant by the terms excessive bail? Who are to be the judges? What is understood by excessive fines? It lies with the court to determine. No cruel and unusual punishment is to be inflicted; it is sometimes necessary to hang a man, villains often deserve whipping, and perhaps having their ears cut off; but are we in future to be prevented from inflicting these punishments because they are cruel? If a more lenient mode of correcting vice and deterring others from the commission of it could be invented, it would be very prudent in the Legislature to adopt it; but until we have some security that this will be done, we ought not to be restrained from making necessary laws by any declaration of this kind."

The words "cruel and unusual" certainly include penalties that are barbaric. But the words, at least when read in light of the English proscription against selective and irregular use of penalties, suggest that it is "cruel and unusual" to apply the death penalty—or any other penalty—selectively to minorities whose numbers are few, who are outcasts of society, and who are unpopular, but whom society is willing to see suffer though it would not countenance general application of the same penalty across the board.

The Court in *McGautha* v. *California* [p. 397, *supra*] noted that in this country there was almost from the beginning a "rebellion against the common-law rule imposing a mandatory death sentence on all convicted murderers." The first attempted remedy was to restrict the death penalty to defined offenses such as "premeditated" murder. *Ibid.* But juries "took the law into their own hands" and refused to convict on the capital offense.

> "In order to meet the problem of jury nullification, legislatures did not try, as before, to refine further the definition of capital homicides. Instead they adopted the method of forthrightly granting juries the discretion which they had been exercising in fact." *Ibid.*

The Court concluded: "In light of history, experience, and the present limitations of human knowledge, we find it quite impossible to say that committing to the untrammeled discretion of the jury the power to pronounce life or death in capital cases is offensive to anything in the Constitution."

The Court refused to find constitutional dimensions in the argument that those who exercise their discretion to send a person to death should be given standards by which that discretion should be exercised.

A recent witness at the Hearings before the House Committee on the Judiciary, 92d Cong., 2d Sess., Ernest van den Haag, testifying on H. R. 8414 et al.,[182] stated:

[182] H. R. 3243, 92d Cong., 1st Sess., introduced by Cong. Celler, would abolish all executions by the United States or by any State.

H. R. 8414, 92nd Cong., 1st Sess., introduced by Cong. Celler, would provide an interim stay of all executions by the United States or by any State and contain the following proposed finding:

"Congress hereby finds that there exists serious question—

"(a) whether the infliction of the death penalty amounts to cruel and unusual punishment in violation of the eighth and fourteenth amendments to the Constitution; and

"(b) whether the death penalty is inflicted discriminatorily upon members of racial minorities, in violation of the fourteenth amendment to the Constitution,

"and, in either case, whether Congress should exercise its authority under section 5 of the fourteenth amendment to prohibit the use of the death penalty."

"Any penalty, a fine, imprisonment or the death penalty could be unfairly or unjustly applied. The vice in this case is not in the penalty but in the process by which it is inflicted. It is unfair to inflict unequal penalties on equally guilty parties, or on any innocent parties, *regardless of what the penalty is.*" *Id.,* at 116–117. (Emphasis supplied.)

But those who advance that argument overlook *McGautha, supra.* We are now imprisoned in the *McGautha* holding. Indeed the seeds of the present cases are in *McGautha.* Juries (or judges, as the case may be) have practically untrammeled discretion to let an accused live or insist that he die.[183]

There is increasing recognition of the fact that the basic theme of equal protection is implicit in "cruel and unusual" punishments. "A penalty... should be considered 'unusually' imposed if it is administered arbitrarily or discriminatorily."[184] The same authors add that "[t]he extreme rarity with which applicable death penalty provisions are put to use raises a strong inference of arbitrariness." The President's Commission on Law Enforcement and Administration of Justice recently concluded:

"Finally there is evidence that the imposition of the death sentence and the exercise of dispensing power by the courts and the executive follow discriminatory patterns. The death sentence is

---

There is the naive view that capital punishment as "meted out in our courts, is the antithesis of barbarism." See Henry Paolucci, New York Times, May 27, 1972, p. 29, col. 1. But the Leopolds and Loebs, the Harry Thaws, the Dr. Sheppards and the Dr. Finchs of our society are never executed, only those in the lower strata, only those who are members of an unpopular minority or the poor and despised.

[183] The tension between our decision today and *McGautha* highlights, in my view, the correctness of Mr. Justice Brennan's dissent in that case, which I joined. I should think that if the Eighth and Fourteenth Amendments prohibit the imposition of the death penalty on petitioners because they are "among a capriciously selected random handful upon whom the sentence of death has in fact been imposed," opinion of Mr. Justice Stewart [in this case], or because "there is no meaningful basis for distinguishing the few cases in which [the death penalty] is imposed from the many cases in which it is not," opinion of Mr. Justice White [in this case], statements with which I am in complete agreement—then the Due Process Clause of the Fourteenth Amendment would render unconstitutional "capital sentencing procedures that are purposely constructed to allow the maximum possible variation from one case to the next, and [that] provide no mechanism to prevent that consciously maximized variation from reflecting merely random or arbitrary choice." *McGautha v. California* [*supra*] (Brennan, J., dissenting).

[184] Goldberg & Dershowitz, Declaring the Death Penalty Unconstitutional, 83 Harv. L. Rev. 1773.

disproportionately imposed and carried out on the poor, the Negro, and the members of unpopular groups."

A study of capital cases in Texas from 1924 to 1968 reached the following conclusions:[185]

> "Application of the death penalty is unequal: most of those executed were poor, young, and ignorant.
> "Seventy-five of the 460 cases involved co-defendants, who, under Texas law, were given separate trials. In several instances where a white and a Negro were co-defendants, the white was sentenced to life imprisonment or a term of years, and the Negro was given the death penalty.
> "Another ethnic disparity is found in the type of sentence imposed for rape. The Negro convicted of rape is far more likely to get the death penalty than a term sentence, whereas whites and Latins are for more likely to get a term sentence than the death penalty."

Warden Lewis E. Lawes of Sing Sing said:[186]

> "Not only does capital punishment fail in its justification, but no punishment could be invented with so many inherent defects. It is an unequal punishment in the way it is applied to the rich and to the poor. The defendant of wealth and position never goes to the electric chair or to the gallows. Juries do not intentionally favour the rich, the law is theoretically impartial, but the defendant with ample means is able to have his case presented with every favourable aspect, while the poor defendant often has a lawyer assigned by the court. Sometimes such assignment is considered part of political patronage; usually the lawyer assigned has had no experience whatever in a capital case."

Former Attorney General Ramsey Clark has said, "It is the poor, the sick, the ignorant, the powerless and the hated who are executed."[187] One searches our chronicles in vain for the execution of any member of the affluent strata of this society. The Leopolds and Loebs are given prison terms, not sentenced to death.

Jackson, a black, convicted of the rape of a white woman, was 21 years old. A court-appointed psychiatrist said that Jackson was of average education and average intelligence, that he was not an imbecile,

---

[185] Koeninger, Capital Punishment in Texas, 1924–1968, 15 Crime & Delin. 132, 141 (1969).
[186] Life and Death in Sing Sing 155–160 (1928).
[187] Crime in America 335 (1970).

or schizophrenic, or psychotic, that his traits were the product of environmental influences, and that he was competent to stand trial. Jackson had entered the house after the husband left for work. He held scissors against the neck of the wife, demanding money. She could find none and a struggle ensued for the scissors, a battle which she lost; and she was then raped, Jackson keeping the scissors pressed against her neck. While there did not appear to be any long-term traumatic impact on the victim, she was bruised and abrased in the struggle but was not hospitalized. Jackson was a convict who had escaped from a work gang in the area, a result of a three-year sentence for auto theft. He was at large for three days and during that time had committed several other offenses—burglary, auto theft, and assault and battery.

Furman, a black, killed a householder while seeking to enter the home at night. Furman shot the deceased through a closed door. He was 26 years old and had finished the sixth grade in school. Pending trial, he was committed to the Georgia Central State Hospital for a psychiatric examination on his plea of insanity tendered by court-appointed counsel. The superintendent reported that a unanimous staff diagnostic conference had concluded "that this patient should retain his present diagnosis of Mental Deficiency, Mild to Moderate, with Psychotic Episodes associated with Convulsive Disorder." The physicians agreed that "at present the patient is not psychotic, but he is not capable of cooperating with his counsel in the preparation of his defense"; and the staff believed "that he is in need of further psychiatric hospitalization and treatment."

Later, the superintendent reported that the staff diagnosis was Mental Deficiency, Mild to Moderate, with Psychotic Episodes associated with Convulsive Disorder. He concluded, however, that Furman was "not psychotic at present, knows right from wrong and is able to cooperate with his counsel in preparing his defense."

Branch, a black, entered the rural home of a 65-year-old widow, a white, while she slept and raped her, holding his arm against her throat. Thereupon he demanded money and for 30 minutes or more the widow searched for money, finding little. As he left, Jackson said if the widow told anyone what happened, he would return and kill her. The record is barren of any medical or psychiatric evidence showing injury to her as a result of Branch's attack.

He had previously been convicted of felony theft and found to be a borderline mental deficient and well below the average IQ of Texas prison inmates. He had the equivalent of five and a half years of grade school education. He had a "dull intelligence" and was in the lowest fourth percentile of his class.

We cannot say from facts disclosed in these records that these defendants were sentenced to death because they were black. Yet our task is not restricted to an effort to divine what motives impelled these death penalties. Rather, we deal with a system of law and of justice that leaves to the uncontrolled discretion of judges or juries the determination whether defendants committing these crimes should die or be imprisoned. Under these laws no standards govern the selection of the penalty. People live or die, dependent on the whim of one man or of 12.

In a Nation committed to equal protection of the laws there is no permissible "caste" aspect of law enforcement. Yet we know that the discretion of judges and juries in imposing the death penalty enables the penalty to be selectively applied, feeding prejudices against the accused if he is poor and despised, and lacking political clout, or if he is a member of a suspect or unpopular minority, and saving those who by social position may be in a more protected position. In ancient Hindu law a Brahman was exempt from capital punishment,[188] and under that law, "[g]enerally, in the law books, punishment increased in severity as social status diminished."[189] We have, I fear, taken in practice the same position, partially as a result of making the death penalty discretionary and partially as a result of the ability of the rich to purchase the services of the most respected and most resourceful legal talent in the Nation.

The high service rendered by the "cruel and unusual" punishment clause of the Eighth Amendment is to require legislatures to write penal laws that are evenhanded, nonselective, and nonarbitrary, and to require judges to see to it that general laws are not applied sparsely, selectively, and spottily to unpopular groups.

A law that stated that anyone making more than $50,000 would be exempt from the death penalty would plainly fall, as would a law that in terms said that blacks, those who never went beyond the fifth grade in school, those who made less than $3,000 a year, or those who were unpopular or unstable should be the only people executed. A law which in the overall view reaches that result in practice has no more sanctity than a law which in terms provides the same.

Thus, these discretionary statutes are unconstitutional in their operation. They are pregnant with discrimination and discrimination is an ingredient not compatible with the idea of equal protection of the laws that is implicit in the ban on "cruel and unusual" punishments.

Any law which is nondiscriminatory on its face may be applied in such a way as to violate the Equal Protection Clause of the Fourteenth Amendment. *Yick Wo* v. *Hopkins*, 118 U.S. 356. Such conceivably

[188] See P. Spellman, Political Theory of Ancient India 112 (1964).
[189] C. Drekmeier, Kingship and Community in Early India 233 (1962).

might be the fate of a mandatory death penalty, where equal or lesser sentences were imposed on the elite, a harsher one on the minorities or members of the lower castes. Whether a mandatory death penalty would otherwise be constitutional is a question I do not reach.

After Douglas had retired and been replaced by Justice Stevens, the Court concluded, with only Justices Brennan and Marshall dissenting, that three states had done what a somewhat differently constituted majority had considered "beyond present human ability" only five years earlier in McGautha v. California (p. 397, supra). They had, after the Furman decision, formulated acceptable standards identifying aggravating and mitigating circumstances to be considered in each case by the jury or judge in determining whether to impose the death penalty in murder cases. That having been done, the Eighth Amendment did not ban imposition of that penalty.[190] At the same time the Court held, over the dissents of Chief Justice Burger, and Justices White, Blackmun, and Rehnquist, that other states which had after Furman made the death penalty mandatory for all first-degree murder convictions had violated the Eighth Amendment. Justices Brennan and Marshall adhered to their views that capital punishment is unconstitutional per se. Justices Stewart, Powell, and Stevens found the mandatory sentences defective because they precluded a consideration of mitigating factors and because there would still be unguided and unchecked jury discretion on the finding of guilt, which would frequently be exercised to find defendants not guilty of first-degree murder because of the enormity of the punishment.[191]

Private Property

The Fifth Amendment provides that "private property" shall not "be taken for public use, without just compensation"—the first provision of the Bill of Rights to be held applicable to the states.[192]

Where the government expressly resorts to condemnation proceedings against privately owned property, there is no question that the property has been "taken," though there may be questions about whether it has been taken for a "public use" and about what constitutes "just

[190] Gregg v. Georgia, 96 S. Ct. 2909 (1976); Jurek v. Texas, 96 S. Ct. 2950 (1976); Proffitt v. Florida, 96 S. Ct. 2960 (1976).

[191] Woodson v. North Carolina, 96 S. Ct. 2978 (1976); Roberts v. Louisiana, 96 S. Ct. 3001 (1976).

[192] Chicago, Burlington & Quincy R. Co. v. Chicago, note 7, supra.

compensation." The latter question was involved in United States *v.* Powelson,[193] *where the Tennessee Valley Authority had condemned 12,000 of 22,000 acres of land privately owned by Powelson, who had also been given powers of eminent domain by the state that would entitle him to condemn lands for a power site and who had plans to exercise that power to acquire another 22,000 acres and then to construct a private power system. There was no question that Powelson was entitled to compensation for the 12,000 acres taken, and he did not assert that these acres alone had any value as a power site. But he contended that in view of his powers and expectations, the award should include the water-power value of those acres when combined with acreage not yet acquired. Douglas wrote for the Court to reject that contention:*

> It is "private property" which the Fifth Amendment declares shall not be taken for public use without just compensation. The power of eminent domain can hardly be said to fall in that category. It is not a personal privilege; it is a special authority impressed with a public character and to be utilized for a public end. An award based on the value of that privilege would be an appropriation of public authority to a wholly private end. The denial of such an award to [Powelson] does no injustice. It is true that [his] possession of the power of eminent domain was in part the basis of an opportunity to unite the present lands with others into a power project. But he is not being deprived of values which result from his expenditures or activities.

Sometimes a "taking" is found where the government does not expressly assert that it is exercising its power of eminent domain or initiate a condemnation proceeding. Thus, in a decision in which Douglas joined, the Court held there was a temporary taking—entitling the owner to recover operating losses attributable to government operation—where the President, acting pursuant to the War Labor Disputes Act during World War II, took over possession and operation of coal mines to avert a nationwide strike by the mine workers.[194] And Douglas dissented when the Court found no taking where the United States Army, during the same war, destroyed privately owned oil storage tanks in Manila in order to keep them from falling into the hands of the enemy.[195] What the majority regarded as a "destruction" of property that "had become a potential weapon of great significance" to the enemy

---

[193] 319 U.S. 266 (1943).

[194] *United States* v. *Pewee Coal Co., Inc.,* 341 U.S. 114 (1951).

[195] *United States* v. *Caltex (Philippines), Inc.,* 344 U.S. 149 (1952).

*rather than an "appropriation" for "subsequent use" by the United
States, Douglas regarded as clearly "appropriated" to help with the
war "as animals, food, and supplies requisitioned for the defense effort."*

UNITED STATES v. CAUSBY
328 U.S. 256 (1946)

Mr. and Mrs. Causby owned a chicken farm near an airport outside
Greensboro, North Carolina. In 1942 the United States leased the airport for military use. Thereafter, the Causbys and their chickens were
subjected to great disturbance.

The end of one of the airport's runways was 2,275 feet from the
Causbys' house, and the path of glide for military planes taking off and
landing passed directly over their property. These planes conformed
to the safe glide angle, approved by the Civil Aeronautics Authority;
the glide angle passed over the Causbys' property at 83 feet—67 feet
above the house, 63 feet above the barn, and 18 feet above the highest
tree. But this allowed the planes to come close enough at times to blow
leaves off the trees, with considerable noise, and at night, with sufficient
glare to light up the premises. More than 150 of the Causbys' chickens
had killed themselves by flying into the walls from fright, and the production of the survivors was curtailed, so that the Causbys had to give
up their chicken business. The Causby family was also apprehensive
about accidents; although there had been none on their property, there
had been several nearby.

The Causbys brought this action in the federal Court of Claims,
contending there had been a taking of their property by the United
States which entitled them to compensation. The Court of Claims
found that the United States had taken an easement over the property
and awarded the Causbys $2,000.

MR. JUSTICE DOUGLAS delivered the opinion of the Court.

The United States relies on the Air Commerce Act of 1926, as
amended by the Civil Aeronautics Act of 1938. Under those statutes
the United States has "complete and exclusive national sovereignty in
the air space" over this country. They grant any citizen of the United
States "a public right of freedom of transit in air commerce through
the navigable air space of the United States." And "navigable air space"
is defined as "airspace above the minimum safe altitudes of flight prescribed by the Civil Aeronautics Authority." And it is provided that
"such navigable airspace shall be subject to a public right of freedom
of interstate and foreign air navigation." It is, therefore, argued that

since these flights were within the minimum safe altitudes of flight which had been prescribed, they were an exercise of the declared right of travel through the airspace. The United States concludes that when flights are made within the navigable airspace without any physical invasion of the property of the landowners, there has been no taking of property. It says that at most there was merely incidental damage occurring as a consequence of authorized air navigation. It also argues that the landowner does not own superadjacent airspace which he has not subjected to possession by the erection of structures or other occupancy. Moreover, it is argued that even if the United States took airspace owned by respondents, no compensable damage was shown. Any damages are said to be merely consequential for which no compensation may be obtained under the Fifth Amendment.

It is ancient doctrine that at common law ownership of the land extended to the periphery of the universe—*Cujus est solum ejus est usque ad coelum*.[196] But that doctrine has no place in the modern world. The air is a public highway, as Congress has declared. Were that not true, every transcontinental flight would subject the operator to countless trespass suits. Common sense revolts at the idea. To recognize such private claims to the airspace would clog these highways, seriously interfere with their control and development in the public interest, and transfer into private ownership that to which only the public has a just claim.

But that general principle does not control the present case. For the United States conceded on oral argument that if the flights over respondents' property rendered it uninhabitable, there would be a taking compensable under the Fifth Amendment. It is the owner's loss, not the taker's gain, which is the measure of the value of the property taken. *United States* v. *Miller*, 317 U.S. 369. Market value fairly determined is the normal measure of the recovery. And that value may reflect the use to which the land could readily be converted, as well as the existing use. *United States* v. *Powelson*, 319 U.S. 266. If, by reason of the frequency and altitude of the flights, respondents could not use this land for any purpose, their loss would be complete.[197] It would be as complete as if the United States had entered upon the surface of the land and taken exclusive possession of it.

We agree that in those circumstances there would be a taking. Though it would be only an easement of flight which was taken, that

---

[196] 1 Coke, Institutes (19th ed. 1832) ch 1, §1 (4a); 2 Blackstone, Commentaries (Lewis ed. 1902) p. 18; 3 Kent, Commentaries (Gould ed. 1896) p. 621.

[197] The destruction of all uses of the property by flooding has been held to constitute a taking. *Pumpelly* v. *Green Bay Co.*, 13 Wall. 166; *United States* v. *Lynah*, 188 U.S. 445; *United States* v. *Welch*, 217 U.S. 333.

easement, if permanent and not merely temporary, normally would be the equivalent of a fee interest. It would be a definite exercise of complete dominion and control over the surface of the land. The fact that the planes never touched the surface would be as irrelevant as the absence in this day of the feudal livery of seisin on the transfer of real estate. The owner's right to possess and exploit the land—that is to say, his beneficial ownership of it—would be destroyed. It would not be a case of incidental damages arising from a legalized nuisance such as was involved in *Richards* v. *Washington Terminal Co.*, 233 U.S. 546. In that case, property owners whose lands adjoined a railroad line were denied recovery for damages resulting from the noise, vibrations, smoke and the like, incidental to the operations of the trains. In the supposed case, the line of flight is over the land. And the land is appropriated as directly and completely as if it were used for the runways themselves.

There is no material difference between the supposed case and the present one, except that here enjoyment and use of the land are not completely destroyed. But that does not seem to us to be controlling. The path of glide for airplanes might reduce a valuable factory site to grazing land, an orchard to a vegetable patch, a residential section to a wheat field. Some value would remain. But the use of the airspace immediately above the land would limit the utility of the land and cause a diminution in its value. That was the philosophy of *Portsmouth Co.* v. *United States*, 260 U.S. 327. In that case the petition alleged that the United States erected a fort on nearby land, established a battery and a fire control station there, and fired guns over petitioner's land. The Court, speaking through Mr. Justice Holmes, reversed the Court of Claims, which dismissed the petition on a demurrer, holding that "the specific facts set forth would warrant a finding that a servitude has been imposed."

The fact that the path of glide taken by the planes was that approved by the Civil Aeronautics Authority does not change the result. The navigable airspace which Congress has placed in the public domain is "airspace above the minimum safe altitudes of flight prescribed by the Civil Aeronautics Authority." If that agency prescribed 83 feet as the minimum safe altitude, then we would have presented the question of the validity of the regulation. But nothing of the sort has been done. The path of glide governs the method of operating—of landing or taking off. The altitude required for that operation is not the minimum safe altitude of flight which is the downward reach of the navigable airspace. The minimum prescribed by the Authority is 500 feet during the day and 1,000 feet at night for air carriers and from 300 feet to 1,000 feet for other aircraft, depending on the type of plane and the character of the terrain. Hence, the flights in question were not within the navigable airspace which Congress placed within the public domain.

We have said that the airspace is a public highway. Yet it is obvious that if the landowner is to have full enjoyment of the land, he must have exclusive control of the immediate reaches of the developing atmosphere. Otherwise buildings could not be erected, trees could not be planted, and even fences could not be run. The principle is recognized when the law gives a remedy in case overhanging structures are erected on adjoining land. The landowner owns at least as much of the space above the ground as he can occupy or use in connection with the land. See *Hinman* v. *Pacific Air Transport*, 84 F. 2d 755. The fact that he does not occupy it in a physical sense—by the erection of buildings and the like—is not material. As we have said, the flight of airplanes, which skim the surface but do not touch it, is as much an appropriation of the use of the land as a more conventional entry upon it. We would not doubt that, if the United States erected an elevated railway over respondents' land at the precise altitude where its planes now fly, there would be a partial taking, even though none of the supports of the structure rested on the land. The reason is that there would be an intrusion so immediate and direct as to subtract from the owner's full enjoyment of the property and to limit his exploitation of it. While the owner does not in any physical manner occupy that stratum of airspace or make use of it in the conventional sense, he does use it in somewhat the same sense that space left between buildings for the purpose of light and air is used. The superadjacent airspace at this low altitude is so close to the land that continuous invasions of it affect the use of the surface of the land itself. We think that the landowner, as an incident to his ownership, has a claim to it and that invasions of it are in the same category as invasions of the surface.

The airplane is part of the modern environment of life, and the inconveniences which it causes are normally not compensable under the Fifth Amendment. The airspace, apart from the immediate reaches above the land, is part of the public domain. We need not determine at this time what those precise limits are. Flights over private land are not a taking, unless they are so low and so frequent as to be a direct and immediate interference with the enjoyment and use of the land. We need not speculate on that phase of the present case. For the findings of the Court of Claims plainly establish that there was a diminution in value of the property and that the frequent, low-level flights were the direct and immediate cause. We agree with the Court of Claims that a servitude has been imposed upon the land.

The Court of Claims held, as we have noted, that an easement was taken. But the findings of fact contain no precise description as to its nature. It is not described in terms of frequency of flight, permissible altitude, or type of airplane. Nor is there a finding as to whether the easement taken was temporary or permanent. Yet an accurate description of the property taken is essential, since that interest vests in the United States.

Since on this record it is not clear whether the easement taken is a permanent or a temporary one, it would be premature for us to consider whether the amount of the award made by the Court of Claims was proper.

Douglas wrote for the Court again in a similar case, finding a taking by a county where planes taking off and landing at its airport rendered adjoining property completely uninhabitable.[198]

BERMAN v. PARKER
348 U.S. 26 (1954)

In 1945, Congress enacted a slum-clearance law for the District of Columbia which created a Planning Commission, authorized it to adopt redevelopment plans providing housing, business, and public buildings, to condemn the land involved, and to lease or sell it to private parties for clearance and redevelopment.

The commission's first plan was for the southwestern part of the District. In the area covered by the plan lived 5,000 people, 97 percent of whom were black. Of the dwellings in the area, 58 percent had outside toilets, 60 percent had no baths, 82 percent had no washbasins or laundry tubs, 84 percent had no central heating, and 29 percent had no electricity. In addition, the commission found that 64 percent of the dwellings were beyond repair, 18 percent needed major repairs, and only 17 percent were in a satisfactory state of repair.

Included in the property to be condemned under the plan was a department store. Its owners brought this action to enjoin the condemnation.

MR. JUSTICE DOUGLAS delivered the opinion of the Court.

Appellants object to the appropriation of this property for the purposes of the project. They claim that their property may not be taken constitutionally for this project. It is commercial, not residential property; it is not slum housing; it will be put into the project under the management of a private, not a public, agency and redeveloped for

[198] *Griggs Allegheny County*, 369 U.S. 84 (1962).

private, not public, use. That is the argument; and the contention is that appellants' private property is being taken contrary to two mandates of the Fifth Amendment—(1) "No person shall . . . be deprived of . . . property, without due process of law"; (2) "nor shall private property be taken for public use, without just compensation." To take for the purpose of ridding the area of slums is one thing; it is quite another, the argument goes, to take a man's property merely to develop a better balanced, more attractive community. The District Court, while agreeing in general with that argument, saved the Act by construing it to mean that the Agency could condemn property only for the reasonable necessities of slum clearance and prevention, its concept of "slum" being the existence of conditions "injurious to the public health, safety, morals and welfare."

The power of Congress over the District of Columbia includes all the legislative powers which a state may exercise over its affairs. See *District of Columbia* v. *Thompson Co.,* 346 U.S. 100, 108. We deal, in other words, with what traditionally has been known as the police power. An attempt to define its reach or trace its outer limits is fruitless, for each case must turn on its own facts. The definition is essentially the product of legislative determinations addressed to the purposes of government, purposes neither abstractly nor historically capable of complete definition. Subject to specific constitutional limitations, when the legislature has spoken, the public interest has been declared in terms well-nigh conclusive. In such cases the legislature, not the judiciary, is the main guardian of the public needs to be served by social legislation, whether it be Congress legislating concerning the District of Columbia or the States legislating concerning local affairs. This principle admits of no exception merely because the power of eminent domain is involved. The role of the judiciary in determining whether that power is being exercised for a public purpose is an extremely narrow one.

Public safety, public health, morality, peace and quiet, law and order—these are some of the more conspicuous examples of the traditional application of the police power to municipal affairs. Yet they merely illustrate the scope of the power and do not delimit it. Miserable and disreputable housing conditions may do more than spread disease and crime and immorality. They may also suffocate the spirit by reducing the people who live there to the status of cattle. They may indeed make living an almost insufferable burden. They may also be an ugly sore, a blight on the community which robs it of charm, which makes it a place from which men turn. The misery of housing may despoil a community as an open sewer may ruin a river.

We do not sit to determine whether a particular housing project is or is not desirable. The concept of the public welfare is broad and inclusive. The values it represents are spiritual as well as physical, aesthetic as well as monetary. It is within the power of the legislature to determine that the community should be beautiful as well as healthy, spacious as well as clean, well-balanced as well as carefully patrolled. In the present case, the Congress and its authorized agencies have made determinations that take into account a wide variety of values. It is not for us to reappraise them. If those who govern the District of Columbia decide that the Nation's Capital should be beautiful as well as sanitary, there is nothing in the Fifth Amendment that stands in the way.

Once the object is within the authority of Congress, the right to realize it through the exercise of eminent domain is clear. For the power of eminent domain is merely the means to the end. Once the object is within the authority of Congress, the means by which it will be attained is also for Congress to determine. Here one of the means chosen is the use of private enterprise for redevelopment of the area. Appellants argue that this makes the project a taking from one businessman for the benefit of another businessman. But the means of executing the project are for Congress and Congress alone to determine, once the public purpose has been established. The public end may be as well or better served through an agency of private enterprise than through a department of government—or so the Congress might conclude. We cannot say that public ownership is the sole method of promoting the public purposes of community redevelopment propects. What we have said also disposes of any contention concerning the fact that certain property owners in the area may be permitted to repurchase their properties for redevelopment in harmony with the over-all plan. That, too, is a legitimate means which Congress and its agencies may adopt, if they choose.

In the present case, Congress and its authorized agencies attack the problem of the blighted parts of the community on an area rather than on a structure-by-structure basis. That, too, is opposed by appellants. They maintain that since their building does not imperil health or safety nor contribute to the making of a slum or a blighted area, it cannot be swept into a redevelopment plan by the mere dictum of the Planning Commission or the Commissioners. The particular uses to be made of the land in the project were determined with regard to the needs of the particular community. The experts concluded that if the community were to be healthy, if it were not to revert again to a blighted or slum area, as though possessed of a congenital disease, the area must be planned as a whole. It was not enough, they believed, to remove existing buildings that were insanitary or unsightly. It was important to redesign the whole area so as to eliminate the conditions that cause slums—the overcrowding of dwellings, the lack of parks, the lack of adequate streets and alleys, the absence of recreational areas, the lack of light and air, the presence of outmoded street patterns. It was believed that the piecemeal approach, the removal of individual structures that were offensive, would be only a palliative. The entire area needed redesigning so that a balanced, integrated plan could be developed for the region, including not only new homes but also schools, churches, parks, streets, and shopping centers. In this way it was hoped that the cycle of decay of the area could be controlled and the birth of future slums prevented. Such diversification in future use is plainly relevant to the maintenance of the desired housing standards and therefore within congressional power.

It is not for the courts to oversee the choice of the boundary line nor to sit in review on the size of a particular projected area. Once the question of the public purpose has been decided, the amount and character of land to be taken for the project and the need for a particular tract to complete the integrated plan rests in the discretion of the legislative branch. See *Shoemaker* v. *United States*, 147 U.S. 282, 298; *United States ex. rel. T.V.A.* v. *Welch, supra,* 554; *United States* v. *Carmack,* 329 U.S. 230, 247.

The rights of these property owners are satisfied when they receive that just compensation which the Fifth Amendment exacts as the price of the taking.

Ex Post Facto Laws

Not all limitations on arbitrary governmental action are found in the Bill of Rights or later Constitutional amendments. The original Constitution forbids both the federal government and the states to pass any "ex post facto Law."[199]

In a very early decision, the Court held that this prohibition applies only to criminal laws. In a frequently quoted passage, Justice Chase defined an ex post facto law as one "that makes an action done before the passing of the law, and which was innocent when done, criminal," or which "aggravates a crime, or makes it greater than it was, when committed," or which "inflicts a greater punishment, than the law annexed to the crime, when committed," or which "alters the legal

---

[199] U.S. Const., Art. I, §9, Cl. 3; *id.,* §10, Cl. 1.

rules of evidence, *and receives less, or different testimony, than the law required at the time of the commission of the offence.*"[200]

MARCELLO v. BONDS
349 U.S. 302 (1955)

Marcello, an alien, was convicted in 1938 of a marijuana offense. In 1952, the immigration laws were amended retroactively to make such a conviction at any time a ground for deportation. He was ordered deported pursuant to the 1952 amendment and challenged the validity of the deportation order on the ground, among others, that, as applied to pre-1952 convictions, the 1952 amendment was an ex post facto law. The Court held that it was not, since the sanction it prescribed— deportation—was civil rather than criminal.

MR. JUSTICE DOUGLAS, dissenting.

The Constitution places a ban on all *ex post facto* laws. There are no qualifications or exceptions. Article I, §9, applicable to the Federal Government, speaks in absolute terms: "No . . . ex post facto Law shall be passed." The prohibition is the same whether a citizen or an alien is the victim. So far as *ex post facto* laws are concerned, the prohibition is all-inclusive and complete.

There is a school of thought that the *Ex Post Facto* Clause includes all retroactive legislation, civil as well as criminal. See Crosskey, Politics and the Constitution, Vol. I, c. XI; Vol. II, p. 1053. Mr. Justice Johnson took that view, maintaining that a restriction of the Clause to criminal acts was unwarranted. See *Ogden v. Saunders,* 12 Wheat. 213; *Satterlee v. Matthewson,* 2 Pet. 380. The Court, however, has stated over and again since *Calder v. Bull* [note 200, *supra*] that the *Ex Post Facto* Clause applies only in criminal cases. See *Carpenter v. Commonwealth,* 17 How. 456; *Johannessen v. United States,* 225 U.S. 227; *Bugajewitz v. Adams,* 228 U.S. 585; *Mahler v. Eby,* 264 U.S. 32.

At the same time, there was a parallel development in the field of *ex post facto* legislation. Chief Justice Marshall in *Fletcher v. Peck,* 6 Cranch 87, refused to construe the *Ex Post Facto* Clause narrowly and restrict it to criminal prosecutions. The *Fletcher* case held that property rights that had vested could not be displaced by legislative fiat. That liberal view persisted. It was given dramatic application in post-Civil War days. The leading cases are *Cummings v. Missouri,* 4 Wall. 277, and *Ex parte Garland,* 4 Wall. 333, where the right to practice a person's

---

[200] *Calder* v. *Bull,* 3 Dall. 385 (1798).

profession was sought to be taken away, in the first case by a State, in the second by the Federal Government, for acts which carried no such penalty when they were committed. The essence of those proceedings was the revocation of a license. Yet the Court held them to be violative of the *Ex Post Facto* Clauses because they were "punishment" for acts carrying no such sanctions when done.

Deportation may be as severe a punishment as loss of livelihood. As Mr. Justice Brandeis stated in *Ng Fung Ho* v. *White,* 259 U.S. 276, deportation may result "in loss of both property and life; or of all that makes life worth living."

I find nothing in the Constitution exempting aliens from the operation of *ex post facto* laws. I would think, therefore, that, if Congress today passed a law making any alien who had ever violated any traffic law in this country deportable, the law would be *ex post facto.* Congress, of course, has broad powers over the deportation of aliens. But the bare fact of a traffic violation would not reasonably be regarded as demonstrating that such a person was presently an undesirable resident. It would relate solely to an historic incident that carried no such punishment when committed. The present Act has the same vice. The alien is not deported after a hearing and on a finding by the authorities that he is undesirable for continued residence here. It is the bare past violation of the narcotic laws that is sufficient and conclusive, however isolated or insignificant such violation may have been. The case is, therefore, different from the earlier deportation cases where the past acts were mere counters in weighing present fitness.

In the absence of a rational connection between the imposition of the penalty of deportation and the *present* desirability of the alien as a resident in this country, the conclusion is inescapable that the Act merely adds a new punishment for a past offense. That is the very injustice that the *Ex Post Facto* Clause was designed to prevent.[201]

Bills of Attainder

The original Constitution also forbids the federal government and the states to pass any "Bill of Attainder."[202]

In Cummings v. Missouri,[203] *the Court held that a state had passed both an ex post facto law and a bill of attainder when, after the Civil*

---

[201] [Cases finding legislation to violate both the prohibition against ex post facto laws and the prohibition against bills of attainder are discussed in the next section.]

[202] U.S. Const., Art. I, §9, Cl. 3; *id.,* §10, Cl. 1.

[203] 4 Wall. 277 (1866).

War, Missouri amended its constitution to forbid, among others, a Catholic priest to practice his profession unless he first took an oath that he had not supported the Confederate cause. At the same time, in Ex parte Garland,[204] it held both prohibitions violated also when the federal government, by statute, excluded attorneys from practice in federal courts until they took a similar oath. Deprivation of "political or civil rights" was held to constitute punishment. A bill of attainder was defined as "a legislative act which inflicts punishment without a judicial trial." While the English bills of attainder which inspired the prohibition in our Constitution usually prescribed punishment for named individuals, no difference was seen in provisions which "presume the guilt" of priests and lawyers and "adjudge the deprivation of their right" to preach or practice "unless the presumption be first removed by their expurgatory oath." "As the oath prescribed cannot be taken by these parties, the [oath requirement], as against them, operates as a legislative decree of perpetual exclusion. And exclusion from any of the professions or any of the ordinary avocations of life for past conduct can be regarded in no other light than as punishment."

The attainder prohibition was violated because "the legislative body, in addition to its legitimate functions, exercises the powers and office of judge [and] pronounces upon the guilt of the party, without any of the forms and safeguards of trial. . . ." The ex post facto prohibition was also violated because the effect of the oaths was to impose punishment for some acts which were not offenses when committed and to add new punishment for other acts which were offenses when committed.

In 1946, in United States v. Lovett,[205] Douglas joined with the Court to hold the prohibition against bills of attainder violated by a rider to a federal appropriation act which forbade the payment of the salaries of named federal employees who had incurred the displeasure of Martin Dies, chairman of the House Un-American Activities Committee. Although a subcommittee of the Appropriations Committee had held hearings on Dies's charges in secret executive sessions in which the accused employees were permitted to testify, but from which their lawyers were excluded, and had concluded that the employees were guilty of "subversive activity" as the Appropriations Committee had defined that term for the purposes of the hearing, that did not cure the attainder: "[P]ermanent proscription from any opportunity to serve the Government is punishment" which was inflicted "without the safeguards of a judicial trial and 'determined by no previous law or fixed rule.'"

---

[204] 4 Wall. 333 (1866).
[205] 328 U.S. 303 (1946).

GARNER v. LOS ANGELES BOARD OF PUBLIC WORKS OF LOS ANGELES
341 U.S. 716 (1951)

In 1948 the City of Los Angeles adopted an ordinance requiring its employees to take an oath that they did not, and for the past five years had not, advocated overthrow of the government and were not, and for the past five years had not been, members of organizations so advocating. The Court held that the ordinance was not a bill of attainder, since it merely prescribed "qualifications for office," and was not an ex post facto law because a state statute had forbidden the employment of persons with the same proscribed beliefs and affiliations for seven years before the ordinance was adopted.

MR. JUSTICE DOUGLAS, dissenting.

The case is governed by *Cummings v. Missouri* [note 203, *supra*] and *Ex parte Garland* [note 204, *supra*], which struck down test oaths adopted at the close of the Civil War.

There are, of course, differences between the present case and the *Cummings* and *Garland* cases. Those condemned by the Los Angeles ordinance are municipal employees; those condemned in the others were professional people. Here the past conduct for which punishment is exacted is single—advocacy within the past five years of the overthrow of the Government by force and violence. In the other cases the acts for which Cummings and Garland stood condemned covered a wider range and involved some conduct which might be vague and uncertain. But those differences, seized on here in hostility to the constitutional provisions, are wholly irrelevant. Deprivation of a man's means of livelihood by reason of past conduct, not subject to this penalty when committed, is punishment whether he is a professional man, a day laborer who works for private industry, or a government employee. The deprivation is nonetheless unconstitutional whether it be for one single past act or a series of past acts. The degree of particularity with which the past act is defined is not the criterion. We are not dealing here with the problem of vagueness in criminal statutes. No amount of certainty would have cured the laws in the *Cummings* and *Garland* cases. They were stricken down because of the mode in which punishment was inflicted.

Petitioners were disqualified from office not for what they are today, not because of any program they currently espouse, not because of standards related to fitness for the office, but for what they once advocated. They are deprived of their livelihood by legislative act, not by judicial processes. We put the case in the aspect most invidious to petitioners [who had refused to take the oath and were, therefore, discharged]. Whether they actually advocated the violent overthrow of Government does not appear. But here, as in the *Cummings* case, the vice is in the presumption of guilt which can only be removed by the expurgatory oath. That punishment, albeit conditional, violates here as it did in the *Cummings* case the constitutional prohibition against bills of attainder. Whether the ordinance also amounts to an *ex post facto* law is a question we do not reach.

FLEMMING V. NESTOR
363 U.S. 603 (1960)

The Social Security Act of 1935 imposed a payroll tax on employees and their employers and provided for retirement benefits for the employees. Nestor, an alien who entered this country in 1913, was employed so as to be covered by the Act from 1936 to 1955, after which he retired and became eligible for retirement benefits of $55.60 per month.

But he had also been a member of the Communist Party from 1933 to 1939. In 1950 the immigration laws had been amended to make past Party membership a ground for deportation, and Nestor was deported in 1956. Because a 1954 amendment to the Social Security Act had also provided for termination of the benefits of one deported on that ground, his retirement benefits were then terminated by the Department of Health, Education and Welfare, of which Flemming was Secretary. There was no similar provision for the termination of benefits of aliens deported on other grounds, nor of aliens who left the country voluntarily.

In this case, involving only the validity of the termination of benefits and not the validity of the deportation,[206] the Court held that the 1954 amendment to the Social Security Act was not invalid as a bill of attainder, since the Court was not satisfied that there was "unmistakable evidence of punitive intent," as there had been in the Cummings, Garland, *and* Lovett *cases.*

MR. JUSTICE DOUGLAS, dissenting.

Punishment in the sense of a bill of attainder includes the "deprivation or suspension of political or civil rights." *Cummings* v. *Missouri*. In that case it was barring a priest from practicing his profession. In *Ex parte Garland*, it was excluding a man from practicing law in the

---

[206] For the validity of the deportation, see *Marcello* v. *Bonds* (p 444, *supra*); *Galvan* v. *Press*, 347 U.S. 522 (1954).

federal courts. In *United States* v. *Lovett*, it was cutting off employees' compensation and barring them permanently from government service. Cutting off a person's livelihood by denying him accrued social benefits —part of his property interests—is no less a punishment. Here, as in the other cases cited, the penalty exacted has one of the classic purposes of punishment—"to reprimand the wrongdoer, to deter others." *Trop* v. *Dulles*, 356 U.S. 86.

Social Security payments are not gratuities. They are products of a contributory system, the funds being raised by payment from employees and employers alike, or in case of self-employed persons, by the individual alone. The funds are placed in the Federal Old-Age and Survivors Insurance Trust Fund; and only those who contribute to the fund are entitled to its benefits, the amount of benefits being related to the amount of contributions made.

Congress could provide that only people resident here could get Social Security benefits. Yet both the House and the Senate rejected any residence requirements. See H. R. Rep. No. 1698, 83d Cong., 2d Sess. 24–25; S. Rep. No. 1987, 83d Cong., 2d Sess. 23. Congress concededly might amend the program to meet new conditions. But may it take away Social Security benefits from one person or from a group of persons for vindictive reasons? Could Congress on deporting an alien for having been a Communist confiscate his home, appropriate his savings accounts, and thus send him out of the country penniless? I think not. Any such Act would be a bill of attainder. The difference, as I see it, between that case and this is one merely of degree. Social Security benefits, made up in part of this alien's own earnings, are taken from him because he once was a Communist.

The view that [the termination provision] imposes a penalty was taken by Secretary Folsom, [Flemming's] predecessor, when opposing enlargement of the category of people to be denied benefits of Social Security, *e.g.*, those convicted of treason and sedition. He said:

> "Because the deprivation of benefits as provided in the amendment is in the nature of a penalty and based on considerations foreign to the objectives and provisions of the old-age and survivors insurance program, the amendment may well serve as a precedent for extension of similar provisions to other public programs and to other crimes which, while perhaps different in degree, are difficult to distinguish in principle. . . ." Hearings, Senate Finance Committee on Social Security Amendments of 1955, 84th Cong., 2d Sess. 1319.

The Committee Reports, though meagre, support Secretary Folsom in that characterization. The House Report tersely stated that termination of the benefits would apply to those persons who were deported "because of illegal entry, conviction of a crime, or subversive activity." H. R. Rep. No. 1698, 83d Cong., 2d Sess. 25. The aim and purpose are clear—to take away from a person by legislative *fiat* property which he has accumulated because he has acted in a certain way or embraced a certain ideology. That is a modern version of the bill of attainder— as plain, as direct, as effective as those which religious passions once loosed in England and which later were employed against the Tories here.

INDEX

Ludecke v. *Watkins*,
256, 257
Luetkeymeyer v. *Kauf-
mann*, 154
Luria v. *United States*,
111
Luther, Martin, 348

McArthur v. *Clifford*, 47
McCarthy v. *Arndstein*,
342
McCollum v. *Board of
Education*, 150, 151,
154, 158, 159, 160
McCray v. *Illinois*, 325–
27; background of,
325–26; dissenting
opinion, 326–27
McCreery, William, 14
McCulloch v. *Maryland*,
103, 104
McDonald v. *Board of
Election Comm'rs*, 195
MacDougall v. *Green*,
104
McElroy v. *Guagliardo*,
53, 262
McGautha v. *California*,
397–402, 429, 430,
434; background of,
397–98; dissenting
opinion, 399–402
McGoldrick v. *Berwind-
White Co.*, 136
McGowan v. *Maryland*,
195
McHenry, James, 25
Mackenzie v. *Hare*, 123
Mackin v. *United States*,
348, 374
McNabb v. *United
States*, 317
McPherson v. *Blackner*,
85
McReynolds, James C.,
91
Madison, James, 14, 17,
25–26, 58, 144, 166,
198, 204
Maguire, 345
Mahler v. *Eby*, 444
Mallinson, 310

Mansfield, Lord, 382–83
Mapp v. *Ohio*, 325, 326
Marcello v. *Bonds*, 444–
45, 448; background
of, 444; dissenting
opinion, 444–45
Marchetti v. *United
States*, 340
Margaret, Sr., 158, 159
Marsh v. *Alabama*, 139
Marshall, John, 89, 103,
444
Marshall, Thurgood, 45–
46, 48, 50, 216, 364,
425, 426, 434
Martin, 310
Martin, Luther, 53
Martin v. *City of Struth-
ers*, 139
Marx, Karl, 200
Mason, A., 251
Massachusetts v. *Laird*,
47
Massiah v. *United States*,
363
Maxwell v. *Dow*, 322,
393
May, E., 158
Mayers, 72
Mayor and City Council
v. *Dawson*, 284
Meek v. *Pittinger*, 165
Mehta, 246
Meiklejohn, Alexander,
191, 196
Meliora, 133
Mentor, 14
Merton, 116
Meyer v. *Nebraska*, 143,
234, 243
Michelangelo, 310
Michigan v. *Mosley*, 368
Michigan v. *Tucker*, 365–
67; background of,
365; dissenting opin-
ion, 365–67
Miles v. *Graham*, 147
Military Justice Act, 261
military service, 245–71
Miller, Barbara, 140, 143
Miller, Samuel F., 273
Miller, Wallace, 140, 143

Miller v. *California*, 227
Mills v. *Alabama*, 174
Milton, John, 238
*Minersville School Dis-
trict* v. *Gobitis*, 140
*Minneapolis & St. L. R.
Co.* v. *Beckwith*, 274
Minor v. *Happersett*, 99–
100
Miranda v. *Arizona*, 363,
365–66, 367, 368, 385
Mishkin v. *New York*,
224
Missouri v. *Kansas Natu-
ral Gas Co.*, xiv
Mitchell v. *United States*,
47
Monitor Patriot Co. v.
Roy, 185
Monroe v. *Pape*, 69
Montesquieu, Baron de,
204
Moore, Judge, 310
Moore, Underhill, xi
Moore v. *New York*, 278
Moore v. *Ogilvie*, 100,
105
Mora v. *McNamara*, 47
more specific guarantees,
321–50; introduction
to, 312–23; *see also*
names of cases
Morrell v. *State*, 360
Muniz v. *Hoffman*, 391
Murdock, 16–18
Murdock v. *Pennsylvania*,
132–40, 149, 237;
background of, 132;
opinion of the Court,
132–39
Murphy, Frank, xv, 37,
140
Murphy v. *Waterfront
Comm'n*, 356
Myers v. *United States*,
34

Nardone v. *United States*,
325, 332
NAACP v. *Alabama*, 179,
193, 234, 235, 236,
242, 248, 352

About the Editor

VERN COUNTRYMAN was born in Roundup, Montana, in 1917. He attended the University of Washington and was clerk to Justice Douglas from 1942 to 1943. He was an Assistant Attorney General in the state of Washington, taught at the University of Washington School of Law and then at Yale Law School. He was in private practice in Washington, D.C., was Dean of the University of Mexico School of Law from 1959 to 1964 and has, since 1964, been Professor at the Harvard Law School. He is the author of numerous articles in legal periodicals and of eleven books, including *Un-American Activities in the State of Washington, Douglas of the Supreme Court, Debtor and Creditor,* and *The Judicial Record of Justice William O. Douglas.*

Professor Countryman lives in Cambridge, Massachusetts.